THE PLACE OF HISTORY: COMMEMORATING CANADA'S PAST

Proceedings of the National Symposium held on the Occasion of the 75th Anniversary of the Historic Sites and Monuments Board of Canada

Edited by Thomas H.B. Symons, OC, FRSC

LES LIEUX DE LA MÉMOIRE : LA COMMÉMORATION DU PASSÉ DU CANADA

Actes du symposium national tenu à l'occasion du 75ᵉ anniversaire de la Commission des lieux et monuments historiques du Canada

Sous la direction de Thomas H.B. Symons, OC, FRSC

Canadian cataloguing in publication data

Main entry under title:
        The Place of History: Commemorating Canada's Past.
Proceedings of the National Symposium held on the Occasion of the
75th Anniversary of the Historic Sites and Monuments Board of
Canada = Les lieux de la mémoire : la commémoration du passé du
Canada. Actes du symposium national tenu à l'occasion du
75ᵉ anniversaire de la Commission des lieux et monuments historiques
du Canada

Text in English and French.
Symposium held 26-28 November 1994
Includes bibliographical references and index.
ISBN 0-920064-58-2

        1. Historic preservation–Canada–Congresses.
2. Cultural property, Protection of–Canada–
Congresses. 3. Canada–Civilization–Congresses.
I. Symons, T.H.B. (Thomas Henry Bull), 1929-
II. The Royal Society of Canada III. Historic Sites and
Monuments Board of Canada IV. Title: Les lieux de la
mémoire.

FC95.P53. 1997   363.6'9'0971   C96-900660-8E
F1021.P53 1997

Données de catalogage avant publication (Canada)

Vedette principale au titre :
        The Place of History: Commemorating Canada's Past.
Proceedings of the National Symposium held on the Occasion of the
75th Anniversary of the Historic Sites and Monuments Board of
Canada = Les lieux de la mémoire : la commémoration du passé du
Canada. Actes du symposium national tenu à l'occasion du
75ᵉ anniversaire de la Commission des lieux et monuments historiques
du Canada

Texte en anglais et en français.
Symposium tenu du 26 au 28 novembre 1994.
Comprend des références bibliographiques et un index.
ISBN 0-920064-58-2

        1. Patrimoine historique–Canada–Congrès.
2. Biens culturels–Protection–Canada–Congrès.
3. Canada–Civilisation–Congrès. I. Symons, T.H.B.
(Thomas Henry Bull), 1929- II. La Société royale du Canada
III. Commission des lieux et monuments historiques du Canada
IV. titre: Les lieux de la mémoire.

FC95.P53. 1997   363.6'9'0971   C96-900660-8F
F1021.P53 1997

Preface

This volume and the National Symposium on Heritage about which it reports are the product of a collaboration between The Royal Society of Canada and the Historic Sites and Monuments Board of Canada. They reflect the shared interest of the Society and the Board in the natural and the built heritage of Canada and their wish to co-operate in the study and preservation of this heritage. I want to extend the thanks of the Board to the Society, and in particular to Professor John Meisel, for the support it has given to these joint endeavours.

Particular thanks are owed to members of the Board who served on a Working Group for the planning and operation of the Symposium and who, subsequently, assisted the Symposium Chair with the conception and arrangements for this book: Professor Margaret Conrad, Ms. Trudy Cowan, and Professors Fernand Harvey and André Lalonde.

I am further and more particularly indebted to Margaret Conrad and Fernand Harvey for their thoughtful help with the editing of this volume which will, I hope, be of continuing service to the heritage community, to teachers, and to the planners and makers of public policy for years to come.

May I thank, too, Linda Vachon, the Publications Coordinator of the Society, for her indefatigable and meticulous assistance with the preparation of this volume?

I am grateful that the Parliamentary Channel filmed and recorded most of the Symposium. By this means it will be available to a wider public. Indeed, their film has already had remarkable coverage all across Canada.

Special thanks must be given to Dr. Christina Cameron, the Director General of the National Historic Sites Directorate of the Department of Canadian Heritage, for her guidance throughout this undertaking and to Larry Friend, the Executive Secretary of the Board, to Brian Van Dusen, and to others who helped in so may ways with both the Symposium and this book. First amongst these, of course, are those who presented papers and the other participants in the Symposium.

Finally, I would like to take the occasion afforded by the 75th Anniversary of the Historic Sites and Monuments Board of Canada to express my gratitude and admiration to the members of the Board, past and present, and to the

Thomas H.B. Symons

members of the staff of the National Historic Sites Directorate of Parks Canada for their valuable service to heritage and to our country.

Préface

Le présent ouvrage et le Symposium national sur le patrimoine dont il réunit les actes sont le fruit d'une collaboration entre la Société royale du Canada et la Commission des lieux et monuments historiques du Canada. Ils traduisent l'intérêt commun de ces deux organismes pour notre patrimoine naturel et architectural et leur désir de coopérer pour étudier et protéger celui-ci. Au nom de la Commission, je remercie la Société et, en particulier, le professeur John Meisel, de leur apport à ces entreprises conjointes.

Je dois des remerciements particuliers aux membres de la Commission qui ont siégé au groupe de travail chargé de la planification et du déroulement du symposium et qui ont par la suite apporté leur concours à la conception de cet ouvrage et à la prise des dispositions nécessaires à sa réalisation, soit la professeure Margaret Conrad, madame Trudy Cowan et les professeurs Fernand Harvey et André Lalonde.

Je suis tout particulièrement obligé envers Margaret Conrad et Fernand Harvey de leur judicieuse collaboration à la mise au point de cet ouvrage qui, je l'espère, se révélera précieux pour les groupes de protection du patrimoine, les enseignants, les planificateurs et les décideurs pendant des années à venir.

Je sais gré également à Linda Vachon, coordonnatrice des publications de la Société, de son aide inlassable et méticuleuse à la préparation du présent ouvrage.

Le personnel de la Chaîne parlementaire a par ailleurs filmé et enregistré la majeure partie du symposium; je lui suis reconnaissant de l'avoir ainsi mis à la disposition d'un auditoire plus étendu. En fait, ce film a déjà reçu une attention considérable partout au Canada.

Plusieurs personnes méritent une reconnaissance particulière, notamment Christina Cameron, directeur général des Lieux historiques nationaux du ministère du Patrimoine canadien, qui a guidé toute cette entreprise; Larry Friend, secrétaire exécutif de la Commission, Brian Van Dusen, et beaucoup d'autres qui ont contribué de diverses manières tant au symposium qu'à cet ouvrage. Parmi ceux-ci figurent principalement, bien sûr, les auteurs des communications présentées au symposium et les autres participants.

Je profite enfin de l'occasion que me fournit le soixante-quinzième anniversaire de la Commission des lieux et monuments historiques du Canada pour exprimer ma gratitude et mon admiration à ses membres passés et actuels, ainsi qu'au personnel de la Direction générale des lieux historiques nationaux de Parcs Canada, pour leur précieux dévouement à la cause du patrimoine et à notre pays.

JOHN MEISEL*

Foreword

There is much concern these days about the role of the modern state and its interrelationship with the community it is intended to serve. The state is seen by many as overbearing, profligate, aloof. All of us can easily recall events documenting at least some of these accusations but there is, as always in human affairs, another side. Although nowadays most are loathe to admit it governments, acting on behalf of the state, also do much good.

Few institutions attest to this more eloquently than the Historic Sites and Monuments Board of Canada, whose 75th Anniversary is celebrated in the papers in your hands. A country which was cobbled together from quite diverse pieces, occupying an immense and highly varied territory, needs several types of powerful glue to hold it together. The programmes and projects sponsored and applied by the Board over the years have been one such bond. The Board was and is a vital force in making Canadians aware of their land and of its story.

It has done so by imaginative projects sometimes launched on its own initiative and sometimes as the result of fruitful collaboration with groups and individuals pursuing goals related to the mandate of the Department of Canadian Heritage – its administrative haven.

The Royal Society of Canada has been an eager and appreciative partner of the Board on several occasions. Most recently, it responded smartly to Professor Symons' suggestion that it join the Board in sponsoring the National Symposium on "The Place of History/Les lieux de la mémoire" which, as you can see from its Proceedings, was an enormously stimulating, provocative, and informative stock-taking of numerous issues arising from our ever more diligent efforts to preserve and heighten the awareness of Canada's patrimony.

The Society's involvement in this glittering event – and the subsequent task of publishing the results – actually represents the dropping of the metaphorical second shoe. For, twenty years ago we played a key role in launching a similar event. That conference, organized in association with Heritage Canada, was held in October 1975 and resulted in the publication of *Preserving the Canadian Heritage/La Préservation du patrimoine canadien*. This report became a classic in the heritage literature of Canada. No better guide exists to the state of the art as it prevailed at the time and to the issues confronting the heritage game in this country.

Now, as the results of the new stocktaking become available in the form of the present volume, we shall not only be able to find up-to-date descriptions and analyses of the *status quo* but we also have a base-line document to which we can turn in the search for insights into the historical evolution of a field critical to the survival of Canada as a viable national community.

Neither of these important sources illuminating and documenting the heritage scene would have been available had the Board and the Society not worked so closely and well in jointly pursuing goals dear to them. A fine example of how the agents of the state – the Board in this case – and a non-governmental organization – the Society – can collaborate in the public interest.

This Foreword, on behalf of the Royal Society of Canada, would be incomplete if it did not conclude by expressing a warmly felt tribute to Professor Tom Symons, the Chair of the Board, whose vision, dedication and hectoring are responsible for the Symposium occurring in the first place, and for the opportunity offered by this volume to revisit it, or, for those who did not attend, to share its riches. In his efforts he has benefited immeasurably from the goodwill and knowledge of Dr. Christina Cameron, the Director General of the National Historic Sites Directorate of the Department of Canadian Heritage, whose role Professor Symons acknowledges in his magisterial keynote address.

* President of the Royal Society of Canada 1992-1995; Past-President 1995-96.

Avant-propos

On s'intéresse beaucoup, de nos jours, au rôle de l'État moderne et à ses rapports avec le public qu'il a pour mission de servir. Aux yeux de plusieurs, l'État est arrogant, extrêmement prodigue et distant. Nous pouvons tous relever facilement des faits à l'appui d'au moins certaines de ces accusations, mais, comme toujours dans les affaires humaines, il faut voir l'envers des événements. Même si, de nos jours, la majorité des gens détestent l'admettre, les gouvernements, agissant au nom de l'État, font également beaucoup de bien.

Peu d'institutions attestent plus éloquemment ce fait que la Commission des lieux et monuments historiques du Canada, dont le soixante-quinzième anniversaire est souligné dans les pages qui suivent. Un pays constitué d'éléments très divers et couvrant un territoire immense et extrêmement varié a besoin d'être cimenté à l'aide de plusieurs liants puissants. Les programmes et projets parrainés et exécutés par la Commission au cours des années ont procuré un tel lien. Celle-ci a été et demeure un agent capital de conscientisation des Canadiens à leur pays et à son histoire.

Ce travail, la Commission l'a accompli par le truchement de projets imaginatifs entrepris tantôt de sa propre initiative et tantôt en collaboration avec des groupes et des personnes poursuivant des buts liés au mandat du ministère du Patrimoine canadien, auquel elle se rattache sur le plan administratif.

La Société royale du Canada a été en plusieurs circonstances un partenaire enthousiaste et attentif de la Commission. Tout dernièrement, elle a répondu promptement à la suggestion du professeur Symons de se joindre à celle-ci pour parrainer le symposium national intitulé « Les lieux de la mémoire/The Place of History ». Comme en témoignent ses actes, cette manifestation a constitué un tour d'horizon extrêmement stimulant, fécond et instructif de nombreuses questions suscitées par nos efforts de plus en plus diligents pour entretenir et accroître la conscience du patrimoine canadien.

La participation de la Société à cet événement retentissant et la tâche subséquente d'en publier les actes constituent en quelque sorte la suite logique de sa contribution essentielle à une manifestation semblable tenue il y a vingt ans, plus précisément en octobre 1975. Celle-ci, organisée en collaboration avec la Fondation canadienne pour la protection du patrimoine, avait été couronnée par la publication du rapport intitulé *La Préservation du patrimoine canadien/Preserving the Canadian Heritage*, qui est devenu un classique du genre au Canada. En effet, il n'existe pas de meilleur guide sur l'état des connaissances relatives au patrimoine à l'époque et sur les questions qui se posent dans ce domaine dans notre pays.

Le présent ouvrage met à jour l'état des connaissances sur le sujet et offre en même temps un document de base auquel on pourra désormais se référer pour mieux comprendre l'évolution historique d'un domaine crucial à la survie du Canada en tant que nation.

Ni l'un ni l'autre de ces ouvrages magistraux sur les questions de patrimoine n'aurait vu le jour sans cette concertation étroite des efforts déployés par la Commission et par la Société en vue d'atteindre des objectifs qui leur étaient chers. Voilà un bel exemple de collaboration entre des agents de l'État – en l'occurrence, la Commission – et un organisme non gouvernemental – la Société – dans l'intérêt public.

On ne saurait conclure cet avant-propos rédigé au nom de la Société royale du Canada sans rendre un témoignage chaleureux au professeur Tom Symons, président de la Commission, dont la vision, le dévouement et l'autorité ont rendu ce symposium possible et permis d'en consigner les actes dans ce volume à l'intention des participants et aussi des personnes qui n'ont pas eu la chance d'y assister. Le professeur Symons a largement bénéficié, dans cette entreprise, de la coopération et des connaissances de madame Christina Cameron, directeur général des Lieux historiques nationaux du ministère du Patrimoine canadien, dont il souligne l'apport dans sa remarquable allocution d'ouverture.

* Président de la Société royale du Canada, 1992-1995; président-sortant, 1995-1996.

Table of Contents / Table des matières

Allocution du ministre / Minister's Address[*]

Ce soir, nous célébrons soixante-quinze années de commémoration; soixante-quinze années consacrées à la reconnaissance de ces lieux, de ces monuments, de ces gares ferroviaires qui sont aujourd'hui les véritables témoins de notre passé; soixante-quinze années perpétuant le souvenir de ces personnages et de ces événements qui ont façonné l'histoire de tout un pays.

Depuis sa création en 1919, la Commission des lieux et monuments historiques du Canada met en lumière la diversité de notre patrimoine commun et la richesse de notre histoire. Elle a commémoré en tout quelque 800 lieux et monuments historiques et désigné plus de 140 gares ferroviaires d'un bout à l'autre du pays. À ce jour, la Commission a installé près de 1 100 plaques qui font revivre des pages entières de l'histoire du Canada.

Le programme de commémoration de la Commission des lieux et monuments historiques constitue le plus fidèle reflet de l'âme canadienne. Au cours de ses premières années d'existence, la Commission a mis l'accent sur des thèmes de l'histoire militaire et du commerce des fourrures, qui rappelaient un passé héroïque dont les Canadiens et les Canadiennes de cette époque tiraient une grande fierté. Après la Seconde Guerre mondiale et à la suite des recommandations de la commission Massey, elle a étendu son champ d'activité à la reconnaissance du patrimoine architectural pour répondre au mouvement de protection du patrimoine et à une prise de conscience sociale à cet égard. Elle s'est ensuite ouverte aux thèmes de l'histoire socio-économique, aux peuples autochtones, aux femmes et aux collectivités culturelles. Ainsi, la Commission a élargi son champ d'action pour inclure l'ensemble des traits distinctifs de notre pays et de ses habitants, c'est-à-dire des éléments qui constituent notre patrimoine.

L'un de ces traits particuliers est sans contredit la diversité qui a caractérisé le Canada depuis sa fondation. Cette diversité peut être observée d'abord à travers l'extraordinaire variété de lieux historiques et de paysages qui jalonnent le Canada d'ouest en est et du nord au sud. Ces paysages et ces lieux ont, non seulement exercé une grande influence sur le cours de notre histoire, mais également contribué à forger la personnalité même des Canadiens et des Canadiennes. Certes, la géographie physique de notre territoire et le caractère pluraliste de notre société ne sont pas étrangers à la diversité qui distingue le

Canada et sa population. De cette diversité, nous avons fait notre force, et c'est cela que la Commission met en relief.

Par ailleurs, plusieurs monuments historiques rappellent la présence des Premières nations et l'arrivée des diverses communautés culturelles qui ont façonné le visage du Canada et qui ont participé à son essor. Nos monuments célèbres, tels Province House, commémorée par la Reine lors de son dernier voyage en terre canadienne, le Manège militaire de la Grande-Allée, à Québec, la gare Windsor, à Montréal, l'église ukrainienne orthodoxe grecque, au Manitoba, l'église indienne de Skookumchuk, en Colombie-Britannique, sont aujourd'hui les plus beaux fleurons de notre histoire.

Mais il n'y a pas que les monuments et les lieux historiques qui ont façonné l'identité canadienne à même la diversité du pays. Nombre de grands Canadiens et Canadiennes, qui ont été honorés par la Commission, ont incarné les valeurs fondamentales de notre société et enrichi de multiples façons le patrimoine canadien.

Au début du siècle, par exemple, les membres de l'équipe féminine de basket-ball, les Grads d'Edmonton, étaient citées en exemple pour leur détermination et leur désir de donner le meilleur d'elles-mêmes. Ces qualités ont fait de ces jeunes athlètes les championnes du monde et ont démontré aux Canadiens et aux Canadiennes l'importance de l'effort dans la réussite. Elles ont été les instigatrices d'une longue tradition d'excellence en matière de sport au Canada.

La Commission a également eu l'embarras du choix en ce qui concerne la reconnaissance des personnalités de la scène culturelle qui ont marqué de leur sceau l'imaginaire canadien. Je pense, entre autres, à la Bolduc, qui chantait le folklore et les traditions du Québec rural, au célèbre compositeur Claude Champagne, à qui nous venons tout juste de rendre hommage, à Emily Carr, cette peintre talentueuse de la Colombie-Britannique, et à l'écrivain Stephen Leacock, pour n'en nommer que quelques-uns. Ces artistes ont prêté leur talent à l'expression de notre identité culturelle; ils ont mis en mots, en images, en musique et en scène l'âme et le cœur du peuple canadien.

D'autres personnages célèbres, auxquels la Commission a rendu hommage, ont participé activement à l'évolution de la science et du savoir au Canada. Il n'y a qu'à penser notamment, au frère Marie-Victorin, botaniste reconnu et père du Jardin botanique de Montréal, à lord Ernest Rutherford, l'un des plus grands physiciens expérimentaux du siècle, ou à la pathologiste Maude Elizabeth Seymour Abbott, l'une des premières femmes à s'être taillé une place enviable dans le monde médical. Tous ces scientifiques ont fait progresser la société canadienne et l'humanité vers un mieux-être aujourd'hui indéniable. Leur apport est inestimable.

Fait paradoxal : malgré l'imposant travail qu'elle a réalisé au fil des ans, la Commission des lieux et monuments historiques demeure relativement peu connue du public canadien. D'une certaine manière, on peut dire que son travail lui fait ombrage. La plupart des Canadiens et des Canadiennes ne sauraient, par exemple, identifier l'un ou l'autre des membres éminents qui se sont succédé à la Commission, tels que le brigadier-général Cruikshank, l'historien Jean Daigle, la professeure Andrée Désilets, du Québec, Irene Rogers, de l'Île-du-Prince-Édouard, ou le président actuel, l'historien Thomas H.B. Symons. Par contre, ils seraient tout à fait capables de nommer plusieurs des lieux, des monuments ou des personnalités qui ont marqué notre histoire.

Nevertheless, behind the scenes there operates an institution of far-reaching influence, an institution charged with a mission of capital importance to our country. The Board's commemorative responsibilities are intimately linked to our heritage, that is, to the heritage passed down to us by our forebears, which grows richer with each successive generation. The Board draws attention to the set of signs, symbols and characteristics that allow each of us to recognize himself or herself as an individual that is part of a nation. How could we define ourselves in relation to the world and envisage our future if we had no roots, no memories, no history with which to identify ourselves?

Imagine a person afflicted by amnesia. This person would suffer a total loss of identity and would have neither past nor future – only the present, or more precisely the immediate moment, to cling to. The same is true for a country showing no interest in its history.

Certainly the mission of the Historic Sites and Monuments Board is closely tied to the Canadian identity. And this mission is all the more critical today, as Canada faces constitutional challenges at home and the need to affirm its cultural vitality in the assembly of nations.

And so, far from being restricted to the legacy of the past, the mission of the Historic Sites and Monuments Board is wholly focused on the present and future. The plaques commemorating historic places, monuments, railway stations, people and events keep the past alive for successive generations so that they can take strength from the achievements of their predecessors and draw lessons from their experience.

The history of our country is full of examples of understanding, open-mindedness, co-operation, commitment and respect. Canada is one of the oldest constitutional democracies in the world, and its citizens have always been noted for their sense of civic responsibility and spirit of compromise. There is no disputing the facts: few other countries on this earth have managed to deal so well with the difficulties that come with diversity. Thanks to the determination and vision of our parents and grandparents, the quality of life in Canada is one of the best in the world. That is essentially what this seventy-fifth anniversary is all about. Today, we are celebrating this country we have built on hopes and dreams as a good place to live and prosper.

But Canada is more than the product of historic events; it is a young nation, a nation in the making. The Board must therefore look to the future. The heritage bequeathed to us by our forebears, which we continue to enrich for the benefit of future generations, is an integral part of the Canadian identity. As outlined in the Liberal Plan for Canada, the *Red Book*, "globalization and the information and communications revolution are erasing national borders... Canada needs to commit itself more than ever to cultural development." As the Minister of Canadian Heritage, I am convinced that the Historic Sites and Monuments Board of Canada has a key role to play in this cultural development and in the strengthening of our common identity.

This means that, in the first place, the Board must strive to make Canadians more aware of and knowledgeable about their history. Children learn at school that their country is the second largest in the world in terms of area, that it is composed of ten provinces and two territories, and so on. By commemorating our cultural and historical heritage, the Board can help these young people and the public as a whole make the connection between historical events and the sites where they took place, the monuments representing them and the figures who shaped their course.

In addition, the Board must extend its influence by educating specialists in the fields of Canadian history and heritage on its role and importance. These specialists have valuable contributions to make to the work of your institution.

The Historic Sites and Monuments Board can be proud of what it has accomplished since it came into being in 1919. As a key observer of Canada's history and growth, its efforts have made it possible to preserve the memory of the people who helped build Canada, to protect places and monuments which were the scene of important events, and to focus attention on our national heritage. Our past, our heritage, our identity, and our common pride are powerful unifying forces that will carry our country toward the twenty-first century and lay the foundations of its success.

I wish a long life to the Historic Sites and Monuments Board of Canada, and offer my thanks to all of you!

*In the Minister's absence, his speech was read by Albina Guarnieri, Parliamentary Secretary to the Minister of Canadian Heritage / En l'absence du ministre du Patrimoine canadien, son discours a été lu par sa secrétaire parlementaire, Mme Albina Guarnieri.

Frère Marie-Victorin (1885-1944), botaniste, écrivain et éducateur, « père » du Jardin botanique de Montréal ; désigné en 1987 / Botanist, author, and educator, founder of the Montréal Botanical Gardens; designated 1987. (Photo : gratieuseté du Jardin botanique de Montréal / courtesy of the Montréal Botanical Gardens)

Emily Carr (1871-1945) painter and writer; designated 1950 / peintre et écrivaine ; désignée en 1950. (Photo: BC Archives, D-06009)

Lord Ernest Rutherford (1871-1937), physicist renowned for his early discoveries in radioactivity; designated 1939 / physicien renommé pour ses premières découvertes en radioactivité ; désigné en 1939. (Photo: National Archives / Archives nationales, C-18230)

Maude E. Abbott (1869-1940), pioneer in medicine and research on heart disease; designated 1993 / pionnière en médecine et en recherche sur les maladies de cœur ; désignée en 1993. (Photo: National Archives / Archives nationales, C-9479)

Stephen Leacock (1869-1944), humorist, teacher, historian, political economist, and writer; designated 1946 / humoriste, enseignant, historien, économiste et écrivain ; désigné en 1946. (Photo: National Archives / Archives nationales, PA-110154)

Commemorating Canada's Past:
From Old Crow to New Bergthal

It would be difficult to imagine a more appropriate setting for this conference. That the meeting is in the Parliament Buildings signals the national importance of its theme. That it is in the historic West Block, built on the eve of Confederation, reminds us of the important part played by the built heritage in serving, shaping, and expressing our national life.

May I begin by expressing a few thanks? First, of course, to Father Francis Bolger for his kind – and tolerant – introduction. Then, to the Royal Society of Canada, our partners in a sense in this endeavour. It was the Society that showed the way by convening, in association with Heritage Canada, a symposium on "Preserving the Canadian Heritage" in 1975. This National Symposium on heritage, some twenty years later, is building on their work. I hope that the publication of the papers from this meeting, which is to appear under the imprimatur of the Royal Society of Canada, will, like their publication of two decades ago, be a useful source of information and ideas, and a point of reference for the heritage-minded community for years to come.

Je remercie Albina Guarnieri, secrétaire parlementaire du ministre du Patrimoine canadien, de son allocution à la réception d'ouverture. Nous avons grandement apprécié son évaluation sérieuse et généreuse du travail accompli par la Commission des lieux et monuments historiques et par le personnel de la Direction générale des lieux historiques nationaux. Nous lui savons gré, également, de son vif intérêt pour ce travail et de l'appui qu'elle apporte au mouvement de défense du patrimoine.

I want, of course, to record my own admiration and thanks for all that has been accomplished by the Board and its staff colleagues in Parks Canada over the seventy-five years since 1919. In particular, may I thank the present Board members, with whom I am lucky enough to work, and our present Director General, Dr. Christina Cameron, who is surely one of the foremost people in the field of heritage, both as a scholar and as a practitioner, in Canada and on the international stage. We owe special thanks, as well, to our indefatigable Executive Secretary, Larry Friend, and to those who worked with him, so hard and so well, to make this National Symposium a reality.

It would be possible, I suppose, to mark this 75th Anniversary of the Historic Sites and Monuments Board by recounting and re-living its achievements over the past three-quarters of a century – and these are, in fact, not inconsiderable as Albina acknowledged so graciously in her opening remarks. However, this is not a line that I care to take. Rather, I prefer to take stock of where we are and to reflect upon where we should be going. A seventy-fifth anniversary provides, I suggest, a good occasion to review our state and the state of heritage preservation and use in Canada. Certainly, such a review is timely. With this in mind, I would like to explore with you a number of themes, and to put forward a few specific propositions and questions for your consideration. I am very conscious that this is a gathering of experts and, therefore, tread this path with diffidence.

The title of my paper, "Commemorating Canada's Past", may suggest a look backwards. But this is not the case. I want, almost entirely, to look ahead. My sub-title, "From Old Crow to New Bergthal", is one that sweeps over great expanses of time and geography and culture. You will recall that Old Crow is the region in north-western Yukon which escaped the great pleistocene-era glaciers, thereby serving as a refuge for the humans and many species of plants and animals that then came over the land bridge from Asia and eventually spread out to populate the Americas. New Bergthal, in Manitoba, Canada's best surviving example of a Mennonite street village, ensures that tangible aspects of Canada's prairie agricultural heritage and settlement patterns will survive into the future.

Old Crow and New Bergthal, both have been designated national historic sites. But sweeping as is the span of time, geography, and culture which they embrace, it is still not sweeping enough. The concerns of the Board with the built heritage, and with the commemoration of persons and events significant for this country, must embrace every region, every culture, and every period of time. Please take that as read and, in the meantime, perhaps you will allow the sub-title, "From Old Crow to New Bergthal", to stand as a proxy, suggestive of the full range of the Board's concerns and of the concerns of this National Symposium.

Comme nous célébrons le soixante-quinzième anniversaire de la Commission des lieux et monuments historiques, je veux parler un peu de la Commission elle-même et soulever certaines questions relatives à sa place, à ses politiques et à sa composition à propos desquelles il serait utile d'obtenir vos opinions au cours de nos délibérations des deux prochains jours, et même après le symposium.

The placement of the Board in the new mega-ministry of Canadian Heritage deserves thought. A year ago, I had the good fortune to spend some time at Cambridge University as a Visiting Professor. I took part of my time there to study the experience of the heritage organizations with the new United Kingdom Ministry of National Heritage which had been created just a few years before. This had brought together into one big department the responsibilities for broadcasting, many cultural and citizenship programmes, the major heritage agencies, and so on – very much as our Department of Canadian Heritage has now done in this country some years later.

It was assumed by heritage-minded people in the United Kingdom that the creation of a Department of National Heritage was a break-through that signalled more attention, more support, and perhaps a higher priority for heritage in government planning. But I was told by many people, and I observed that, in practice, the new Department was almost totally pre-occupied with the bonfires in broadcasting and other, already high profile, aspects of its mandate. The actual heritage agenda, despite that strong personal interest of a good minister, received little attention – perhaps less, in fact, than it had received before the so-called Ministry of Heritage was created.

It was instructive to observe this experience and it suggests to me that we should watch with care to see that it is not repeated in Canada. It would be ironical if one of the results of the creation of the Department of Canadian Heritage were to be a downgrading of the attention given to heritage by the Canadian government.

May I touch on another question about placement, but of a different sort? In some other countries with which we have close ties and many shared traditions – the United Kingdom, the United States, France, and Australia, for example – questions about the built heritage and the natural heritage of landscape and environment are dealt with as a whole, by one body, and not in isolation from one another. As you know, this is not the case in Canada where, in the matter of designating and preserving sites of national significance, there is the Historic Sites and Monuments Board which, as its title suggests, deals only with humanity and human-made things and events, and does so in isolation from any consideration of the natural heritage with which our country is so richly endowed.

By way of contrast, matters concerning the designation and preservation of both the built and the natural heritage are dealt with together and not in isolation, by one and the same public agencies in the United States, Britain, and many other countries.

Following a different route, we have grown accustomed in Canada to separating our thinking and our public policies for the built environment, on the one hand, from our thinking and public policies about the natural environment on the other. I wonder whether this is really a very sensible or desirable way of dealing with things and whether it would be timely to consider looking at all questions concerning the nationally significant heritage, whether man-made or natural, as related parts of one larger concern? It seems to me increasingly clear that it is often unhelpful, and frequently impossible, to make meaningful distinctions between these twin aspects of our national heritage. In fact, the deep connections between the past and present are more often embodied in nature than in things made by man.

As our population grows and spreads, the resulting cultural impacts upon landscape, nature, and the environment also grow and spread. What people do has environmental consequences. Conversely, the natural environment still shapes and conditions the activities of people. Thus, it is our experience of place and our sense of place that bring together these two aspects of our heritage, the built and the natural. The experiences that places make available to people are an inheritance that has been entrusted to our care.

Akin to questions of placement and context are the questions of integrity and of arms-length relationships. It is utterly crucial that, in all its decisions, the Board both be, and be seen to be, removed from the partisan political process. There must be no iota of suspicion that political considerations or pressures have affected the Board's decision-making on questions about the people or events or sites that should receive recognition as being nationally significant.

Let me assure you on this point, though I hope that, in this company, such assurance may not be necessary. I have now served as chairman of the Historic Sites and Monuments Board of Canada for eight years and under two governments. During this time there has never been an instance in which a Minister or regime has attempted to influence the outcome of any Board decision. On the contrary, the government has always been supportive and often very patient, bearing rather stoically with the various kinds of public abuse and criticisms while enabling the Board and its staff colleagues in National Historic Sites to go about their work with due process and due diligence. If I may, I would like to express admiration for the helpful correctness with which succeeding Ministers have discharged their responsibilities towards the Board.

None the less, the maintenance of appropriate arms-length relationships is something that requires constant vigilance. I should add (perhaps in parenthesis) that I have never detected in the Board the slightest sign that it would be a quiet or passive recipient of any partisan political meddling.

While the work of the Board and the concerns of the built heritage have been well served by a series of Ministers who have shown, more often than not, a strong personal interest and commitment to the field, there are problems of discontinuity in the political arena. In the past ten years there have been nine Ministers responsible for heritage. Nine Ministers in ten years! Even of good Ministers it may be said that it is possible to have too much of a good thing.

This striking rate of change in those to whom the Board reports, and through whom it maintains its liaison with the political process, points to the profound problems of continuity and communication which can arise, even when things are going well. There may be, for this reason as well as for many others, grounds to consider the idea of creating a National Heritage Commission which would be more free-standing from government and more directly related to the public than is now the case.

Some matters more directly relating to the composition and workload of both the Board and the staff need thought. The Board is, by law, composed of seventeen members, one from each province and territory plus one more each from Ontario and Québec in recognition of their large populations, plus three *ex officio* members: the National Archivist, the Director of the Museum of Civilization, and a representative of the Department of Canadian Heritage. It works, I think, pretty well. But its restricted membership, even when the most careful consideration is given to membership selection, does mean that important fields of knowledge and experience, and of culture and geography, may not be represented.

To a considerable extent, these gaps can be offset by processes of external consultation. But I wonder if there is not a case for allowing a few more members to be added to the Board so as to give to it the benefit of a fuller range of views and knowledge and experience? Alternatively, an advisory panel could be useful.

In any case, I am pleased that the Board and staff are already making use of the device of convening special forums on such subjects, for example, as the better recognition and commemoration of the contribution of women and of the Aboriginal peoples to Canadian history. We could also possibly make fuller use of the knowledge of people learned in a given subject by inviting them to participate in the Board's processes of research and evaluation.

Something similar may be said in regard to the Board's truly admirable staff colleagues in the National Historic Sites service of Parks Canada. They have a record of research of the highest standards, much of it published, which would be a credit to the history department of any university in Canada. These researchers are already severely over-taxed and the burden of work falling upon them is steadily increasing as the country grows and as the interest in heritage grows. Yet their numbers are being reduced as the result of economic cut-backs. The first thing needed is a stronger realization of the value of their work. It may also be timely to consider calling more upon outside sources for help with the preparation of research and the drafting of reports. In addition to assisting our hard-worked staff, this would have also the benefit of bringing some different perspectives and fresh views to the Board's deliberations.

Such observations lead, inescapably, to a consideration of the financial resources available to support the work of identifying, commemorating, and maintaining our National Historic Parks and Sites. At present, some 110 million dollars is spent on this work annually. Of this, perhaps two million dollars is available to assist specific projects through cost-sharing grants.

No one in his or her right mind is going to bring on a public trauma by paraphrasing the late C.D. Howe and asking "What's 110 million?" But one can surely ask what is the right order of expenditure on conserving, presenting, and developing the built national heritage for a society of some thirty million people. Is $3.66 per citizen the right amount for a national government to spend on the preservation of the national patrimony?

I am particularly concerned that there is such a low provision to assist citizens and their organizations by means of cost-sharing. Every year, the Board has to turn away proposals that are full of merit, or to give to extraordinarily worthwhile projects only a small fraction of what they deserve or need. There are several reasons why this is wrong. The most important, of course, is that we are working against the clock. Heritage of value to Canadians is being lost or destroyed daily because of our inability to do what needs to be done. Once lost, it usually cannot be replaced and is gone forever. There is urgency in this race against time and it is a race in which heritage is too often the loser.

The urgency is not such, however, that I would wish upon you the bizarre and tragic fate of Richard Nickel who, at the age of forty-four, literally died for the love of historic buildings. He was killed by a collapsing section of the Chicago Stock Exchange Building to which he had returned to save one last piece of ornamentation before the demolition was completed. So, please be careful.

Nor should our sense of urgency blunt our discernment or our respect for historical truth. We should, for example, resist the temptation to Grimthorpe. You will recall that this term derives from the well-meant activities of Sir Edmund Beckett, fifth baronet and first Baron Grimthorpe, who in the last century restored ancient buildings with generosity and enthusiasm, but without the proper knowledge and care required to retain their original quality and character. So, please don't Grimthorpe.

None the less, another reason why I would like to see a substantial increase in our cost-sharing budget – by that I mean something like a five-fold increase – is that it would be an important step in encouraging the involvement of many more people and organizations in the business of saving and using the national built heritage.

Sometimes I sense amongst heritage professionals a hesitation or reluctance to involve the wider public, and a view that the general public lacks the judgment necessary to take part in decisions affecting the preservation of the past. Let me take issue with this view that the experts should decide what's good for us while the public stand by to be reminded that splendid efforts are being made on their behalf, which they may watch from a respectful distance – and then pay for! No wonder that a Toronto taxi driver identified cognoscenti in the arts as those willing to visit museums, galleries, and historic houses when it was not actually raining.

There is, I think, a great deal to be gained by opening the door to a fuller public participation in the business of heritage. Heritage is too important to be left in the hands of a few, no matter how expert. Nor should it be allowed to become a sort of middle-class conspiracy that promotes a cozy cream tea culture.

In the same vein, I would suggest the possibility of a much more pro-active role by the heritage community in seeking funding support from the non-governmental sector of society. Indeed, I think it is essential to escape from the psychology of dependence on government which now inhibits so much of the work of the heritage community.

On the occasion of the 75th Anniversary of the Historic Sites and Monuments Board of Canada it is appropriate to extend greetings to Heritage Canada, our sister organization concerned with the preservation of the country's built heritage. I am delighted to do so, and to pay tribute to all that Heritage Canada has done over the past twenty years to promote public awareness of and support for the conservation of our national inheritance.

It would be useful, I think, for our two organizations to look further to see what more could be done to assist one another in the service of our common interests. In particular, I think it would be timely to consider whether something more might now be done to provide for a programme in Canada, along the lines of the National Trust of Britain, designed to preserve and protect aspects of our built heritage by acquisition. This is a path not without difficulty. But some move in this direction seems needed as part of an overall approach to conserve and to make good use of the national heritage.

Il y a, bien sûr, nombre d'autres questions relatives à la Commission et à son travail que j'aimerais aborder avec vous. Mais j'en ai peut-être dit suffisamment pour indiquer combien vos idées et suggestions à ce sujet seront les bienvenues, tant au cours du symposium que par la suite.

Now, may I turn to a few broader themes and to one or two propositions that I would like to put before you?

First, let us look realistically at the place of heritage in our society today. The attention of the nation in 1994 is on many things, but I think it is safe to say that heritage is not near the top of the list. The environment, however, is. And this is because the environment has been made relevant to the average Canadian (that mythical but useful person); whereas heritage has not. The environmentalists have delivered clear, popular, well-understood messages. Heritage preservationists have not. The well-being of the environment is now an accepted and fundamental concern to a great many thoughtful citizens, while heritage conservation is still seen as a fringe activity by many of those same people.

Yet environmentalists and heritage preservationists share the common concerns, the common values, and the common goals that arise from their mutual commitment to a 'conserver society'. They have a near identity of interests. Surely, then, they should make common cause?

On doit donc se demander pourquoi le patrimoine ne constitue pas un volet du mouvement de défense de l'environnement. Ou peut-être y aurait-il lieu de reformuler cette question et de demander plutôt pourquoi le mouvement environnemental n'a pas embrassé la cause du patrimoine. Une des raisons est le fait que, pendant nombre d'années, beaucoup de nos lieux historiques et de nos commémorations ont semblé souligner l'exploitation de l'environnement, car nous célébrions le mauvais aspect de réalisations matérielles. Ou, dans une veine semblable, ces lieux ont souvent souligné l'assujettissement militaire et économique des peuples autochtones. Mais les sites et les ouvrages patrimoniaux peuvent également illustrer les bonnes pratiques de préservation des cultures et de la nature, et ils le font de plus en plus.

L'environnement n'occupe pas non plus la place prépondérante qu'on lui accordait il n'y a pas si longtemps dans nos préoccupations publiques. Chose notable, tant le patrimoine que l'environnement ont pratiquement été tenus à l'écart de notre grand débat constitutionnel.

Do these observations suggest a plan of action? I think they do. I would suggest that the arguments for environmental protection can and should be extended to include heritage conservation and historic preservation, and that this could be more readily done, to the mutual advantage both of the environment and of the historical heritage, if such arguments were cast in eco-ethical terms. Good conservation practices, whether for the natural environment or for the built environment, should have both ecological and cultural integrity.

To this end, I think it will be sensible for heritage conservationists to give more attention, and support, to the environmental dimensions and consequences of their activities than is sometimes now the case. And the heritage movement must actively work for the integration of heritage values into the environmental ethic. Just as the environmental issues have been made relevant to our everyday life in the past decade, so should heritage concerns be made part of our everyday value system in this current decade.

It may be said by some that now, in these difficult and acutely sensitive times of constitutional and cultural tension for our country, it is not wise or possible to push for greater attention to heritage and to heritage values in public policy.

I do not agree with this view for one moment!

I would argue, on the contrary, that now, more than ever before, we should be paying attention to heritage in our country. It is what we have in common. It is what we share – and if we had paid more attention to this fundamental aspect of our national life during the twentieth century, we might now be able to feel some greater confidence, and enthusiasm, about the prospects for a continuing Canadian heritage during the twenty-first century.

Threats surround us: threats to our heritage, threats to our environment, threats to our national unity, threats to our national sovereignty. By addressing the threats to our heritage – that is, threats to the elements of our culture that we value – we can address many of the threats to our national unity and sovereignty.

What we choose to save, or to destroy, reveals our values as a people. In the words of Professor Robin Winks of Yale University, "Our cultural resources ought to be inviolate, for they tell us about ourselves." What is our heritage, if not the aspirations of the people who made it, and, one might add, the aspirations of the people who have chosen to preserve it?

If we are to know ourselves, if we are to serve well both ourselves and others, then we must understand and care for our heritage in all its diversities – yes, and imperfections. We must know and use well our heritage, in order to convince policy makers that it matters, that it has significance, that heritage is not merely an isolated and marginal activity. We will have to develop the arguments and demonstrate in clear and unmistakable terms why heritage conservation is important to the health and vitality of our country. Further, we will have to convey effectively the twin message that the cultural world is part of our environment and that the natural world is part of our cultural heritage.

In this situation, there is a clear role and responsibility for our educational institutions, at all levels. If we do not know and use our heritage, if we do not respect the environment, it is in large part because we have not been taught these things.

The educational system is an iceberg that moves slowly. There is certainly now some progress being made on the teaching and study of both heritage and the environment. But the iceberg is still moving too slowly on these urgent matters. The need is now, and it is acute. In this regard, I commend to you the example and experience of Simcoe County educators who are pioneering in their presentation of heritage and its linkage to environmental issues.

Beyond curriculum reform, there is much that schools can do, of a broader nature, by the values they foster and represent. Educational institutions can have a direct role in heritage and environmental matters by the way they manage the buildings, properties, and artifacts for which they have responsibility. In this arena, universities have often a special responsibility because of their extensive property holdings, and the many buildings and sites of heritage interest that still stand on many university campuses. Think, for example, of Laval's fantastic first site in the heart of old Québec; of the famous old buildings of Dalhousie and the University of New Brunswick; of McGill's many heritage buildings in downtown Montréal; and, in this province, of Queen's campus in the heart of historic Kingston, of the University of Ottawa in the heart of the capital city, of the really immense heritage holdings still remaining on the University of Toronto campus, and so on. Many of the universities in western Canada also have on campus buildings of heritage significance.

The sorry fact is that many of the educational institutions, at all levels, which ought to be in the vanguard of an enlightened concern for heritage, have often been despoilers, insensitive to heritage values as they destroyed significant and re-usable buildings. In so doing, they provided an appalling example for others in society who might make a more believable plea of ignorance.

In this regard, I would like to pay tribute to the founding governors, faculty, staff, and students of Trent University who, from the outset, have shown a deep concern and respect for heritage values that is reflected in the many historic houses that have been preserved and incorporated into the life of the University, as well as in the respect shown for cultural landscape and the environment. Trent's is by no means a perfect record, but it is one of the best in sight.

May I point also to the example of a number of schools, both secondary and elementary, that have taken such steps as the creation of a Heritage Council to recommend policies and programmes to ensure the preservation of those things which constitute their physical and cultural inheritance?

Lastly, in regard to public education, may I point to the scope and need for serious educational programmes for the general public that will provide information and raise awareness about the value of the built heritage and its relationship to the environment? Money spent on such programmes could make a genuine contribution to Canadian affairs in these critical years. And they might free us from the pathetic, feel-good blarney about Canada that we have been spoon fed at various times in recent years in paid advertisements by more than one government.

Hand in hand with education goes research. I need not tell this audience how important research is to the proper identification and conservation of heritage. This research aspect or function of heritage needs far more recognition and support than it has been receiving. It is research, and the informed knowledge resulting from research, that will bring scholarship, and the assurance of standards and integrity, to every aspect of the work of the heritage movement.

Heritage research can take many forms. There is, for example, much to be done in research of a material nature – in how to identify materials and techniques from another time, and how best to preserve or support them.

There are all the questions arising from the welcome swing to the new three Rs: *reducing, recycling, and re-using.* What are the limits to sensible recycling? and what are the constraints on re-use? The fabric of existing buildings constitute, indeed, a great bank of stored materials. But it requires knowledge, money, time, and energy to release and re-use them. Demolition is often wasteful of all these; but not always. Researched knowledge is the key in the frequent and difficult task of weighing up the comparative merits of recycling or using new materials in heritage conservation work. How do they compare as to costs and efficiency? What are the real costs?

As this will suggest, there is need also for extensive economic research in the heritage field. Across the board, and for each project, one must ask: What are the economics of building re-use? of materials re-use? and of site dispositions? What are the economics of job creation and the development of skills? Are the appropriate economic impact studies of the impact of heritage and of heritage conservation being undertaken, as communities move further in this direction?

The economics of heritage is, or ought to be, an important emerging field of specialization. Jobs, livelihoods, marketing, and the community tax base are all going to be affected by any extensive programmes of heritage conservation.

Research is needed, as well, into the public policy aspects of heritage work. What are the most appropriate legislative and regulative arrangements for heritage identification and conservation? At the municipal level? at the provincial level? at the federal level? What are, or will be, the impacts of an increasingly conserver society on political processes, on public policies, and on the political framework? Thus, in political science, too, the impact of heritage activity suggests the emergence of a new field of specialization.

Demographic research into the scope and nature and consequences for heritage of population change and population movements requires increasing attention. So does the interplay of geography and history as they have shaped and affected heritage in the different communities and regions, across the country.

And, in the midst of the many environmental and other arguments for architectural conservation, let us not forget what is perhaps the simplest and most important: a prime reason for preserving architecture is that it is a route to the discovery and appreciation of accurate and meaningful history. Heritage conservation and historical research are each other's hand maidens.

The culture and economic impacts of tourism, as it flows to heritage sites, need study.

The cultural pluralism and many other diversities of Canada pose a particular challenge for researchers in the heritage field. A knowledge of the country's ethnic and cultural pluralism is basic to any real understanding of Canadian society, its history, and its future prospects. Much of this knowledge and understanding can best be derived from research centred on the historic sites and artifacts that mark the often distinctive experiences of the diverse Canadian peoples.

Research is not just an abstraction. It depends on people. It is done by people. Thus, the demographics of research is in itself a field for research. We need to know more about those who are involved in the work of historic preservation and, also, to know more about those who are not and why they are not. We need to know more about the concept and practice of volunteerism as applied to heritage work. What are its strengths and its limitations? Which professional groups are involved and which are not, and why not? What is needed to facilitate the closer interaction of planners, architects, contractors, public officials, and many others in the field of historic preservation? And how might a new and more productive relationship be brought about between such people and the skilled craftspersons and workers on the job?

Questions of perception also need research. One of the most powerful concepts in our society is the concept of public service. To what extent has this concept so far come into play in regard to heritage? To what extent is work in the area of historic preservation seen as a service in the public interest? In what ways is it not so perceived, and why not?

There is need, as well, for more conceptual research in regard to the nature of heritage, or reflective research as it was called by Alex Corry, the late Principal of Queen's University. What is heritage? Clearly, it is a changing and evolving concept. Only a decade or so ago, heritage was seen as being simply the older buildings and what went with them. Now, we view heritage as the total environment inherited from the past. It includes our tangible legacy of physically touchable things: buildings and structures of every sort; industrial sites; archaeological sites; archives; artifacts and material items; and, also, cemeteries, gardens, landscapes, and natural resources. Marinescapes and underwater sites, too, are of special importance to Canada with its frontage on three great oceans and its remarkably extensive freshwater in tens of thousands of lakes and rivers. So, of course, is the country's distinguished scientific and technological heritage.

Heritage includes, as well, our intangible legacy of customs, values, knowledge, and beliefs. It is the sum of all we have and are, of the total historical experience of our society to this moment. It is the context into which we have been born and in which we now live. It provides us with our sense of identity and our bearings for the next journeys into coming generations.

When one reflects upon this concept of heritage, one must be struck not merely by its great importance but by its transcendent importance. Why, then has it received so little attention from our political leaders? and, let it be said, from our educators? These are questions that cry out for researched attention. The answers will tell us a lot about ourselves and about our country.

When I speak of research in the heritage context, I am sure that you will realize that I am speaking of something more than the footnote scholarship concept of research that marks, and often inhibits, the purely academic world. The focus of academic studies often excludes critical or creative studies, so that matters of taste are out of sight and out of mind.

Heritage belongs in the field of art as well as in the field of academe. Heritage is concerned with life and life is an art. It needs to be seen, therefore, in the context in which the arts are studied and where the values of imagination and creativity are safeguarded, lest our view of life, past or present, becomes the product of exclusively logical analysis. Research needs to embrace imagination, as well as intellect, if it is to fathom the meanings of heritage.

But there is one form of heritage research in which the task is not only scholarly and reflective, but also numerical. We need to get on with counting our heritage. We need inventories and registers of heritage buildings, sites, and objects – national, regional, provincial, and local. We need to know what we have – to know what is there – in order to be able to get on with its conservation and interpretation. Despite the work done in recent years, most of Canada's countable heritage is still uninventoried and, indeed, unknown.

Much of heritage is, however, uncountable. And many of those heritage items that are countable have heritage dimensions that are uncountable. In this regard, we need to give thought to heritage *in* culture and to heritage *as* culture. It is in this area that we will find the greatest significance of heritage; and our concern for historic buildings and artifacts belongs in that context.

Il importe d'envisager nos activités patrimoniales respectives dans un contexte plus large, c'est-à-dire tant canadien qu'international. On a beaucoup à gagner des comparaisons et de la coopération transnationale et internationale. Il suffit de considérer, par exemple, l'ensemble de matrices mis au point par le Conseil international des monuments et des sites afin de systématiser la consignation des bâtiments au moyen de dessins et de photos, pour se rappeler la valeur de la coopération et de la participation internationales en matière de patrimoine.

La perspective qu'apportent les associations externes est utile et souvent essentielle. Nous tirons des enseignements des idées et expériences de chacun, et il est toujours important de garder le contact avec les personnes qui partagent nos intérêts partout au Canada de même qu'à l'étranger. Il est naturel, je suppose, d'envisager le patrimoine dans le cadre limité de sa collectivité ou de sa province. Mais ces limites ne doivent pas devenir des oeillères. Nous devons également envisager le patrimoine dans le contexte plus large d'un pays qui couvre la moitié d'un continent et d'un monde international.

Some of you may recall the Speech from the Throne in the Parliament of Canada on 1 October 1986, when Her Excellency was caused to declare that: "The preservation of historic properties is important in fostering a sense of history and national identity among Canadians", and went on to note that the Government of Canada is "the largest owner of heritage sites and properties in the country", and to pledge that it would "assume a leadership role in their restoration and preservation".

Alas, that was the high water mark in the federal government's commitment to the built heritage. Since that time, there has been an appreciable diminution in that commitment. Despite the hard work and best efforts of an immensely dedicated staff in National Historic Sites at Parks Canada, and in several other Departments concerned with material heritage, you will all be familiar with heritage buildings and structures in the federal care that are in need of attention. There are a great many such, all across Canada. And, beyond them, there are many more buildings and sites of national significance which ought to be in the federal care – or in somebody's care – but are not.

As the thinking of heritage preservationists broadens from an original concern with single historic sites and buildings to a wider concern with streetscapes, with historic districts, and with entire cultural landscapes, there is a growing realization that historical resources and environmental resources are very often inextricably intertwined, that historic preservation is a significant part of environmental conservation and vice-versa. They have a shared concern for context, for the surrounding environment, whether historical or ecological. The importance of the conservation of natural habitats and of ecosystems is parallelled by the need to preserve the context of historic sites which can lose their meaning and something of their authenticity when their adjacent environment of buildings and landscape is destroyed. Similarly, heritage tourism and eco-tourism share a common interest in ensuring that tourism does not damage the natural and historic environment.

Preservationists and environmentalists must co-operate to discover, to invent, to develop, and to improve a full array of tools, both technological and political, to preserve and protect the world's natural and historic sites. They must share, too, in the long-range planning required to assure today's heritage in future generations. In short, preservationists and environmentalists should come together for the stewardship of finite natural and cultural resources. Such a concept of heritage stewardship must become a fundamental value of our society.

Our society now finds itself engaged in a perilous balancing act. We are engulfed in the mad rush and uncertainty of technological change, of an abandonment of values, of the atomization of what was once a shared community of beliefs. In these circumstances, it is difficult to know who we are and to decide what matters. Now, more than ever, we need to draw on the accumulated folk wisdom of the generations and to benefit from past experience. In this situation our heritage has a crucial role to play. We may well lose that balancing act and fall into a rootless condition like the tumbleweed if we do not, soon, rediscover our sense of history and our sense of purpose.

May I suggest again that we need a sense of urgency as we go about our heritage work? We are involved in a race against time, and it is not a race that we are presently winning. Every day, our cultural amnesia becomes a little more pronounced. Every day, the list of heritage desecrations and of opportunities lost, sometimes forever, grows longer.

Everything about which I have spoken calls for co-operation, a great deal of co-operation, within institutions, between institutions, with the public, and with government. But for co-operation we need more than the old refrains about avoiding duplication and promoting coordination. We need a new conceptual framework, one that sees the treatment of heritage as a totality, embracing both the built and cultural heritage and the natural heritage, both the built environment and the natural environment. We need an holistic approach to heritage concerns.

We need, in fact, almost a new definition and perception of heritage, one that pries it loose from the sometimes dead hand of antiquarians and professional historians and other groups who have tended to monopolize the field, however good their intentions. Heritage must become the business of everyone.

Malgré des années de militantisme, la cause du patrimoine au Canada n'a pas encore suscité un mouvement national. Cette cause nécessite un effort national total, une opération concertée qui regroupe et mobilise les énergies de tous ceux qui s'y intéressent. Tel est le degré de coopération dont nous avons vraiment besoin et ce, sans délai.

In all your work, it is time, I think, for a less reactive and more pro-active stance. It is time for those involved with heritage to take a stronger leadership role in their communities and in the broader Canadian society.

May I conclude, as one citizen, and as Chairman of the Historic Sites and Monuments Board of Canada, by thanking each of you for your participation in the heritage preservation movement? The work on which you are engaged is of immense importance to our society if Canadians are to know and to understand themselves. You are engaged in an enterprise that is of great value to your communities, to Canada, and beyond. It is fundamental to our sense of community and identity, and to our distinctiveness and diversity. It is fundamental to our heritage. It is fundamental even to our sovereignty and independence as a people, and to our ability to contribute intelligently to our own and to world affairs.

Old Crow, Yukon, aerial view / vue aérienne (Photo: Ian Macneil, 1978)

Old Crow, Yukon, street view / vue d'une rue (Photo: Ian Macneil, 1978)

New Bergthal, Manitoba: Mennonite Village cited for its distinctive settlement pattern; designated 1989. / Village mennonite cité pour son mode de colonisation caractéristique ; désigné en 1989. (Photo: Parks Canada / Parcs Canada, Lyle Dick)

New Bergthal, Manitoba: B.J. Hamm house-barn, a traditional house circa 1910 / la maison-grange B.J. Hamm, habitation traditionnelle aux environs de 1910. (Photo: Julie Harris, 1988)

General Perspectives on Commemoration
Perspectives générales sur la commémoration

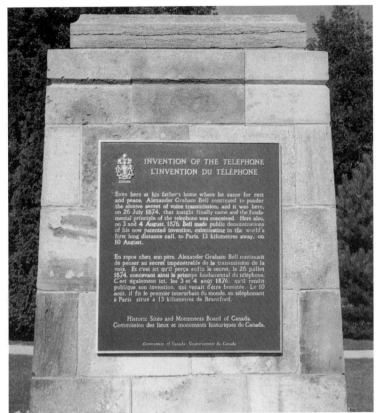

"Invention of the Telephone", Bell Homestead, Brantford, Ontario: On 26 July 1874, Alexander Graham Bell conceived of the fundamental principle of the telephone, and, on 10 August 1876, he made the world's first long distance telephone call; designated 1952. / L'invention du téléphone, propriété Bell, Brantford (Ontario) : le 26 juillet 1874, Alexander Graham Bell conçut le principe fondamental du téléphone et, le 10 août 1876, il effectua le premier appel interurbain au monde ; désigné en 1952. (Photo: Parks Canada / Parcs Canada, 1989)

CHRISTINA CAMERON

Commemoration: A Moving Target?

Abstract
This paper focuses on the first seventy-five years of partnership between the Historic Sites and Monuments Board of Canada and Parks Canada in forging a national programme of commemoration of historic places. Success in carrying out the Board's recommendations for commemoration can be measured by the degree to which the site is conserved and its national significance is communicated.

Over the years, the communication of national significance has been influenced by a number of factors: political correctness, public consultation, interpretation to meet popular demands, and living history programmes. The impact of these factors has sometimes led to a loss of focus on the national significance of historic place.

Commemorations reflect the historical values of the commemorators, as well as Canadian history. While in specific commemorations, this generation may not consider them as important as previous generations did, a failure to communicate the importance that these sites meant to an earlier generation deprives present-day Canadians of an essential part of our cultural heritage. Respect for the work of previous generations of the Historic Sites and Monuments Board of Canada means that Parks Canada must not, wittingly or unwittingly, distort or camouflage the commemorative intent of these National Historic Sites. Canada is a country big enough to accommodate an expanding target of commemoration and weave it into the national history of a living culture.

La commémoration : un objectif en devenir ? – Résumé
Depuis soixante-quinze ans, la Commission des lieux et monuments historiques du Canada et Parcs Canada travaillent de concert pour bâtir un programme national de commémoration des lieux historiques. Cette communication souligne ce long partenariat. L'état de conservation des lieux et la capacité à communiquer leur importance nationale permettent de mesurer l'ampleur du succès obtenu dans l'exécution des recommandations de commémoration formulées par la Commission.

Au fil des ans, la communication de l'importance nationale des lieux historiques a été influencée par un certain nombre de facteurs : conformisme politique, consultation publique, interprétation destinée à satisfaire les demandes de la population, programmes de reconstitution de l'histoire. Ces facteurs ont parfois fait perdre de vue l'importance nationale des lieux historiques.

Les commémorations reflètent les valeurs historiques de leurs auteurs, de même que l'histoire du Canada. Il se peut que des commémorations particulières ne revêtent pas autant d'importance pour la génération actuelle que pour les précédentes, mais le fait de ne pas communiquer l'importance de ces lieux pour une génération passée priverait nos contemporains d'une partie essentielle de leur patrimoine culturel. Pour respecter le travail accompli par les générations passées de membres de la Commission des lieux et monuments historiques du Canada, Parcs Canada doit éviter de dénaturer ou de déguiser, volontairement ou involontairement, l'intention commémorative de ces lieux historiques nationaux. Le Canada est assez vaste pour permettre l'expansion de l'objectif de commémoration et son intégration à l'histoire nationale d'une culture vivante.

The subject of my presentation, *Commemoration: A Moving Target*, grew out of discussions with Professor Tom Symons. At this moment of celebration of the Historic Sites and Monuments Board of Canada – with which I and my staff have had the privilege to work over the years – I saw an opportunity to reflect on the first seventy-five years of partnership between the Board and Parks Canada. Together we have forged a national programme of commemoration of historic places. And while some of my comments may seem rather critical, I offer them by way of stimulating discussion to help us improve this programme in the next quarter century.

The title "Commemoration: A Moving Target?" was meant to refer to the confusion and occasional frustration that we in Parks Canada experience in implementing this commemorative programme. As long as I can remember, we have been busy replacing commemorative plaques – to bring them in line with current historiography or terminology – or we have been busy updating interpretation at those National Historic Sites where we offer programming. Hence the "moving target".

Mais la question est bien plus complexe que cela, et dépasse le débat sur les changements dans les modes historiques et historiographiques. La tâche de définir l'expérience canadienne par l'intermédiaire de ces endroits d'importance nationale constitue un défi considérable. D'autres intervenants soulèveront sans aucun doute des questions sur la prise de décision comme telle à la Commission des lieux et monuments historiques du Canada, mais je voudrais faire porter ma communication sur la transmission des recommandations de la Commission au

Ministre, et sur le suivi de ces recommandations de commémoration lorsque Parcs Canada les met en œuvre.

Mais avant d'aborder ce sujet, je voudrais dire quelques mots sur l'échelle et la portée du programme des lieux historiques nationaux. Le programme couvre une série de plaques historiques et un réseau d'environ 800 endroits d'importance nationale. Depuis 1919, plus d'un millier de plaques de bronze ont été installées pour marquer l'importance nationale de personnes, de lieux et d'événements. Au sein de la famille des lieux historiques nationaux, Parcs Canada en administre 130. Les 670 autres lieux historiques nationaux sont des propriétés privées ou sont la propriété d'organismes autres que fédéraux. Au niveau du budget, les dépenses fédérales pour le programme des lieux historiques nationaux s'élèvent à environ 110 millions de dollars par année, y compris deux millions de dollars pour les ententes de partage des coûts. Les plus gros budgets de fonctionnement sont attribués au complexe de la Citadelle d'Halifax, à la Forteresse de Louisbourg, aux Fortifications de Québec, aux lieux historiques nationaux du Klondike, à Dawson City, et aux trois principaux canaux historiques, le canal de Chambly, le canal Rideau et la voie navigable Trent-Severn.

National Historic Sites, with their authenticity of place and geography, are powerful conveyors of meaning. We know from a 1991 Goldfarb poll that Canadians want to know more about their history. Over 90% of those polled said they did not know enough about their history. The specific contribution of our National Historic Sites to understanding Canada becomes clearer when we consider the findings of a 1994 poll: historic sites rate among the top five symbols of Canadian identity, in company with the flag, the anthem, National Parks, and the Charter of Rights.

Commemoration has two distinct aspects: one relates to the protection, or conservation, of the resources found at the site; the second relates to communication of the site's national significance. Success in carrying out the Board's recommendations for commemoration can be measured by the degree to which the site is conserved and its national significance is communicated. In policy terms, our goal is to achieve commemorative integrity. Parks Canada has achieved world-class standards on the conservation side. On the communications side, however, the record is uneven. This morning I intend to explore some of the forces that have influenced this commemorative programme.

Let us begin with what we now call political correctness. Parks Canada is not immune from its insidious influence. We often find ourselves in the uncomfortable situation – for a government programme – of being perceived to be the arbiter of history. On the one hand, we are charged with communicating the national significance of historic places; on the other hand, we do not wish to offend any constituencies. It is hardly surprising in this context that politically correct revisions creep into our presentation material.

In publications on Fort Chambly, beginning in the 1920s, the French colonists are described as needing "protection from the terror of the Iroquois". In 1969, there is a significant shift in the Fort Chambly brochure which acknowledges that the Iroquois were here in the beginning and that the "white man disturbed their lives in 1609 with the arrival of Samuel de Champlain". Between 1979 and 1981, the brochure for the Halifax Defence Complex was modified in a slight but revealing way. Thus, the statement that the Citadel was built "to protect settlers from the attacks of the French and Micmacs" was replaced by "to protect settlers from attacks from the interior". The brochures from Lower Fort Garry go further. The 1960 version states that "the Lower Fort was also 'raided' once by Riel and some followers"; by 1969, the text has been modified to indicate that "Riel himself, with a number of his followers, made a surprise visit to the Fort".

Another important factor is the move towards greater involvement of the public in decision-making. By the early 1970s, Parks Canada had committed itself to public consultation in the development of its parks and sites. As Daniel Tlen will show us in a few minutes in his presentation on "Skookum Jim", members of the public did not always agree with the Board's recommendations and made efforts to change them. In the course of consulting the public, Parks Canada realized that about 40% of our visitors were local residents, who as repeat visitors wanted to see periodic changes in site programming. Public consultation also made us realize that sites which had previously been experienced in relative isolation – for example, the series of War of 1812 sites scattered throughout Ontario – were now being experienced as part of a network, by visitors who travelled easily from site to site. These are sites that were designated in the 1920s, when travel was much more difficult. The net effect of experiencing these individual sites as a network of similar sites was to increase pressure for different interpretation programmes at each one.

Political correctness and public consultation have been important influences. But Parks Canada's most significant impact on Board recommendations comes from its interpretive programming. National Historic Sites are permanent vestiges of the past. When we undertake interpretation, we must always recognize the underlying spirit of the site, which is rooted in its memory, both visible and invisible, tangible and intangible. When interpretation is well done, it is capable of intensifying the profound meaning of the site and capturing the spirit of place. Over the years, there has been a tendency to drift away from the commemorative intent as defined by the Board and instead to present other elements which are deemed to have greater interest or popular appeal. Distortion or substitution of the original intent of the Board, through well-meaning but inappropriate interpretation, clearly diminishes the ability of the site to communicate national significance.

Take, for example, Province House in Charlottetown. The commemorative intent of this National Historic Site clearly focuses on its role as "the cradle of Confederation". And yet, the interpretive programme tends to concentrate on the architecture, furnishings and the guides' period costumes. The visitor ends up experiencing the site as an artifact, as something "dead" from the past, rather than as part of a continuum in the on-going saga of our constitutional evolution. I wonder how many visitors would link Province House to Meech Lake?

Prior to 1960, Board recommendations often dealt with sites that were instrumental in creating the nation. These early commemorations focused on the places themselves, and were not too specific about the reasons for commemoration. When dealing with the creative forces of nationhood, the Board at that time may well have assumed that the significance of such sites was self evident. These sites, including the Fortress of Louisbourg, Fort George, Fort Malden, Fort Wellington, and Fort Anne, have seen the greatest change in their interpretation, and have moved the farthest away from the original commemorative intent of the Board. Why? There is a belief among some Parks Canada staff that visitors prefer to see what life was like in a fort before or after a war, not during it. And so we present Louisbourg in the summer of 1744, not at the critical moment in 1758 when France lost a crucial outpost in the New World. Mind you, given the fact that the partial reconstruction of Louisbourg was a government make-work project for unemployed coal miners, it would have been rather difficult to retain the site as a battlefield.

Some sites present special interpretive challenges, particularly at sites where the physical – or rather visible – resources do not support messages of national significance, but in fact support other messages. I am thinking for example of Signal Hill in Newfoundland, where the Cabot Tower – built for the Silver Jubilee of Queen Victoria – has nothing to do with the site's national significance: its role in the defence of St. John's over 300 years and its role in the development of transatlantic wireless communication. Here again we see the influence of Parks Canada and its programming. In the 1980s, in our enthusiasm for systems planning, we concentrated on the so-called "in-situ resources" at our sites, to the detriment of the broader historical tableau. When Signal Hill was first designated, the Board and the programme comfortably dealt with the essential significance of the site itself, and would probably have felt no discomfort at the presence of the Cabot Tower.

Now let us take the example of Batoche National Historic Site. The original plaque inscription in the 1920s, which presumably reflected the commemorative intent of the Board at that time, focused on the suppression of the Métis rebellion. For many years, the local community protested against what it considered to be the anti-Métis tone of the plaque text. More recently, the Board, at the urging of Parks Canada as well as its own members (but perhaps in ignorance of the *Historic Sites and Monuments Act* that emphasizes the commemoration of historic place), has tried to "atone" for the sins of its predecessors by focusing almost exclusively on the meaning of the conflict from a Métis perspective. This putative "correction" in reality bears resemblance to substituting one version of history for another. What was once a site that celebrated maintaining the integrity of Canadian sovereignty has now become a site that celebrates the survival of the Métis. Under such circumstances, it is hardly surprising that we talk about commemoration as a moving target.

Now let us examine what might have happened if the commemoration had focused on historic place, as required by the legislation. Batoche itself would be commemorated as a place of national historic significance. But historic places are seldom, if ever, intrinsically significant (unlike natural areas, for example). Rather they derive their historical importance from some association with human history. In the case of Batoche, it is clear that its national significance derives from its association with the Battle of Batoche. But one cannot understand the significance of this battle by treating it solely as a four-day event, or as the most important event of a four-month outbreak of hostilities, which had no prologue or consequences. So good interpretation obligates Parks Canada, as custodians of this site, to interpret what for the Métis was and remains a resistance to actions and non-actions by the federal government; it obligates us to describe the conditions which led to the outbreak of hostilities; it obligates us to describe the actions undertaken by the government and why it considered it necessary to undertake such actions; it obligates us to deal with the larger consequences both to the Métis and to the nation as a whole. None of these individual components needs to be commemorated, but all must be interpreted. The fact that our interpretation has evolved means that the real moving target is interpretation, not commemoration.

In the 1970s and 1980s, the living history approach to interpretation was immensely popular. This is an interpretive approach that depicts period activities in a period setting. This has been described as an anthropological approach to the past, and it is not surprising that anthropologists and archaeologists have played a leading role at places where this type of interpretation has been done most effectively, at, for example, the Plymouth Plantation or at Williamsburg. Visitors, we are told, want to experience the past the way it really was!

There is a danger in this type of interpretation. It can become so dominant that the significance of the place becomes increasingly associated with a depiction of the past, rather than with the real reasons for the site's national significance. For Parks Canada, the living history approach sometimes worked against the commemorative intent of the Board's recommendation. In order to recreate the past, it focused on re-enacting period activities that draw the visitors' attention away from the national significance of the site and leave them with the impression that this is a "Bread-baking" or a "Barrel-making" National Historic Site.

The depiction of the life and activities of the garrison at the Halifax Citadel is interesting and, indeed, an integral part of the story. But it is not the most important part of the story, and the extent to which a visitor leaves a national historic site like the Citadel with a knowledge of military drills, parades and technology – but without a knowledge of the importance of the Citadel in Canadian and imperial history – shows that we have failed to commemorate the place.

Let us return to the commemorations themselves. It will come as no surprise to this audience that "commemoration" is as much a reflection of the historical values of the commemorators, as it is a reflection of Canadian history. While in specific commemorations, this generation may not consider them as important as previous generations did, a failure to communicate the importance that these sites meant to an earlier generation deprives present-day Canadians of an essential part of our cultural heritage. This does not mean that we should accept factual error or whitewash or endorse patriotic myth. But it does mean that we have an obligation not to trivialize the meaning of these places.

Il ne pourrait y avoir de pire condamnation des lieux historiques nationaux que de les traiter ou de les considérer, que ce soit par Parcs Canada ou par les Canadiens en général, comme des endroits morts. Les auteurs de la *Loi sur les lieux et monuments historiques* ne les voyaient sûrement pas comme les vestiges de cultures mortes. Bien au contraire. Ils croyaient que ces endroits faisaient partie intégrante d'une culture et d'un pays vivant et dynamique.

La commémoration, cette cible mouvante, ne consiste pas à refaire les lieux historiques nationaux existants selon nos points de vue actuels, ni à défroquer ou à déconsacrer les endroits qui ne cadrent pas avec les intérêts historiographiques à la mode. Il s'agit de commémorer ces choses qui concernent les intérêts de notre génération, et qui nous apportent une compréhension de l'histoire d'au moins deux façons : d'abord, en comblant des lacunes importantes dans la commémoration du passé du Canada et, ensuite, en fournissant des exemples tangibles des intérêts culturels de la génération qui procède à la commémoration.

Chaque génération commémore ce qui a de l'importance pour elle. Ainsi, le fait que nous cherchions aujourd'hui à commémorer des choses différentes signifie que nous sommes les héritiers d'une tradition bien vivante. Cela souligne la pertinence toujours actuelle d'un programme de commémoration. En ce sens, il serait plus juste de voir la commémoration comme une cible grandissante plutôt que comme une cible mouvante.

I want to conclude on a note of caution. It is sometimes difficult to accept designations with which we feel little affinity or with which we disagree. And it is often inviting to point out the shortcomings of our predecessors. However, respect for their work is essential if the commemorative programme is to be perceived as being more than a transitory exercise in scholarly ephemera. Respect for their work also means that Parks Canada must not, wittingly or unwittingly, distort or camouflage their commemorative intent. We must be mindful that if we have contempt for the work of our predecessors, we breed a climate whereby our contemporaries as well as our successors may have contempt for ours. I do not wish to see the strides we are now making on a series of fronts – women's history, Aboriginal history, the history of cultural communities, to name only three examples – dismissed by a later generation as no more than the enthusiasms of a particular time.

On the occasion of the 75th Anniversary of the Historic Sites and Monuments Board of Canada, I am struck not by how much has changed but rather by how valid the original purposes of the Board remain. The place of history is important. It merits real care and reflection to get it right. Canada is a big country, a country big enough to accommodate an expanding target of commemoration and weave it into the national history of a living culture.

Bank of Commerce and *S.S. Keno*, Dawson City, Yukon Territory. Dawson City was the site of the Gold Rush in the late 1800s and capital of the Yukon Territory until 1953. Many of Dawson's buildings were designated in 1959 and the 1922 wooden steamboat was designated in 1961. / La Banque de commerce et le *S.S. Keno*, à Dawson (Yukon). Dawson City a été le siège de la ruée vers l'or, à la fin des années 1800, et la capitale du Yukon jusqu'en 1953. La plupart de ses édifices ont été désignés en 1959; le bateau à vapeur en bois datant de 1922 l'a été en 1961. (Photo: Photothèque)

The Peterborough Lift Lock, Trent-Severn Waterway, opened in 1904, is the highest hydraulic lift lock in the world; designated 1979 / L'écluse-ascenseur de la voie navigable Trent-Severn : inaugurée en 1904, cette écluse hydraulique est la plus haute au monde ; désignée en 1979. (Photo: Brian Morin)

78th Highlanders drilling at Halifax Citadel, a restored British Masonry Fort; designated 1935. /
Exercices des 78th Highlanders à la citadelle d'Halifax, fort britannique en maçonnerie restauré ; désigné
en 1935. (Photo: Parks Canada / Parcs Canada, A. Guindon, 1985)

Batoche, Saskatchewan: A Métis village founded in 1872 was the site of the Battle of Batoche (1885);
designated 1923. / Ce village Métis fondé en 1872 fut la scène de la bataille de Batoche (1885) ;
désigné en 1923. (Photo: Photothèque)

Jim and Me

Abstract

Oral traditions are an important part of our cultural history. They not only add life to our written history, but they can serve to correct it. This was the case with the discovery of gold in the Klondike. Written history had it that George Carmack was the discoverer when, in fact, it was Kèsh or James "Skookum Jim", an Indian who had been told that he could not file a claim in his own right.

Jim et moi – Résumé

Les traditions orales forment une partie importante de notre histoire culturelle. Elles donnent de la vie à l'histoire écrite et peuvent aussi servir à la corriger. Tel fut le cas lors de la découverte de l'or au Klondike. L'histoire écrite attribuait celle-ci à George Carmack, tandis que le découvreur réel était Kèsh, ou James « Skookum Jim », un Indien qui s'était vu refuser de faire enregistrer un droit de possession de son propre chef.

Kèsh is the Tlingit name given to the boy who, much later, was to be called James "Skookum Jim" Mason. Jim was born into the Dakl'weidi Wolf Clan of the Tagish in the 1850s. He was the one who actually found the Klondike gold (not George Washington Carmack) three weeks before the "discovery" claim was staked by Carmack on 17 August 1896, and that was recorded by Charles Constantine at the Fortymile on 24 September 1896. The details about his family come from oral traditions, and the facts about the events surrounding the discovery from the written record.

Skookum Jim "spoke" to me from across the span of one hundred years. His words came to fall upon my ears from the stories passed down by people to whom Kèsh told his stories in his native languages of Tagish and Tlingit. Jim frequently recounted his stories – I would call them adventures – to his relatives and friends. These adventure stories are told all around southwest Yukon and have definitely made the circuit. When I was a small boy growing up in Burwash Landing, Yukon, I recall hearing the story, in Southern Tutchone, of Skookum Jim's discovery. I have also heard of the story told in Tlingit in Atlin, B.C. When

I worked in radio in Whitehorse I broadcasted these stories via satellite to the entire North American continent.

The southwest Yukon First Nations' stories about the gold discovery are based on an event in Skookum Jim's life when he was very ill from an injury he had received. While convalescing he managed to save the life of a frog that had fallen into a pit from which sod was taken for roofing material. This event was followed by a dream in which a wealthy Frog Chief rewarded Kèsh with great wealth, at a potlatch, for rescuing his beautiful daughter who was the frog he had saved. The Frog Spirit is a very powerful ally for Indians of southwest Yukon. In his dream, Jim said that the Chief instructed him to live properly and to be generous with his wealth. For the native people of this region, dreams help to shape the events of life.

Years later, Skookum Jim went to look for his sister who was living with George Carmack, and found the gold in a tributary of the *Tr'o Ndik* or Klondike River. Kèsh was carrying out cultural and social duties to his family, not looking for that big "paydirt in the sky", as it were, that was so much a part of the American dream for George Carmack. The record shows that Skookum Jim was indeed a good man. In 1912, he gave the largest Yukon potlatch ever held in honour of his deceased nephew Khaa Ghooxh, also called Dawson Charlie, and he left a remarkable legacy in his will to look after underprivileged natives. A potlatch is a large gathering where clans play roles of reciprocal responsibility. It is an event in which the people present are witnesses as to what occurred.

Our collective memory of Skookum Jim is preserved in the written record (in archives private and public) and in the words of the elders who take seriously the responsibility to pass down oral traditions. These traditions have evolved over thousands of years of living on the land and compel the elders to tell and retell their stories – not histories and "herstories", but our stories.

It is extremely interesting for me to observe how society is very selective about what it chooses to remember about people and events. As more factual and anecdotal information becomes available, society's understanding and tolerance can increase. As humans we tend to see what we believe rather than believe what we see. This is reflected in our view of the past by the evolving window of the present through which we view and appreciate our national experience. The discovery of gold in the Klondike is a case in point.

At the time of the gold discovery in 1896 and the Klondike Gold Rush of 1898, George Carmack was the American "superhero" of the day because he staked the discovery claim in his own name, claiming to be the original discoverer. The Canadian government desperately wanted to be part of the fame – they had already established ownership to the territory – and made a big deal about Robert Henderson because he was a Canadian who happened to be near the discovery. Henderson even got a pension from the government. At this window of the past, it was then beyond the ken of even those writers with the most fevered imaginations that an Indian could have found the gold. In 1926, a plaque commemorating the discovery mentioned that Carmack, the discoverer, had two Indian companions. In 1959, an updated plaque finally gave the names of these companions – Skookum Jim and Dawson Charlie – but no real credit. Not that these men needed recognition – they had been wealthy beyond imagination.

If anyone wanted to find the real story, all they had to do was go to the written record. William Ogilvie, the Surveyor for the Crown, interviewed all the players and satisfied himself that Skookum Jim had made the actual discovery. Skookum Jim wanted the discovery claim to be filed in his own name, but his brother-in-law, George Carmack, convinced him that they would not believe an Indian and that he would not be allowed to file the discovery claim. Nonetheless, Jim maintained a half interest in the double claim allowed to discoverers of new goldfields filing the initial claim.

One hundred years later, through our present day window on the past, Kèsh, Skookum Jim is finally recognized as the true discoverer of the Klondike gold that caused the world of the Yukon Indians to change forever after. Skookum Jim left in his legacy a trust fund that was used to create the Skookum Jim Friendship Centre.

History is for interpretation and reinterpretation, and it is written and rewritten, and the stories are told and retold. While written history has great importance, oral tradition maintains another thread of continuity about the tapestry of our past, and so needs to be recognized and incorporated into the record for what they are – living and dynamic recollections of the way we were.

Kèsh, or/ou James "Skookum Jim" Mason (ca / v. 1860-1916); designated / désigné en 1994. (Photo: Yukon Archives Project Collection, #88/58 / collection du projet des Archives du Yukon, n° 88/58)

Khaa Ghooxh, or/ou Dawson Charlie (Yukon Archives, MacBride Museum Collection #3870 / Archives du Yukon, collection du musée MacBride, n° 3870)

La langue de la commémoration

Résumé

En suivant la trame de la métaphore linguistique, cette communication explore la nature et l'évolution des rapports des collectivités à leur passé et à leur patrimoine. Elle introduit à la diversité des richesses et des valeurs que représentent les Premières Nations, les communautés culturelles et les droits de la personne. Elle balise une trajectoire historique et rend compte de la complexité de la problématique de la commémoration.

La commémoration met d'abord en évidence une trace du réel. Mais l'histoire de l'histoire montre que les préoccupations des chercheurs et des collectivités face au passé ont considérablement changé au cours du dernier demi-siècle. D'une vision linéaire axée sur les héros et les grands événements, elle s'est tournée vers le social, puis vers le culturel pluridisciplinaire. Les lieux privilégiés de la mémoire ont connu des déplacements majeurs. La lecture du passé est devenue plurielle et multiple. Tous ces nouveaux objets méritent-ils une intervention de sauvegarde, de mise en valeur, de commémoration ?

La commémoration n'est pas que trace du passé réel; elle procède d'un jugement du présent sur le passé. Elle est discours et représentation du passé. Ainsi se pose une série de questions ayant valeur d'enjeux dont les principaux se définiraient dans la gamme des rapports entre : le passé et le présent, l'identité et l'appartenance, l'oubli et la mémoire, le deuil et la célébration. L'œuvre de commémoration est ainsi confrontée au problème d'associer l'unique et l'universel, les appartenances collectives et l'image nationale.

La commémoration procède d'une médiation dans le temps et entre les composantes de la société. Elle constitue un mode culturel d'expression des collectivités, une langue de communication et une manière d'envisager l'avenir. Elle associe la mémoire dans la culture et la culture comme mémoire.

Jacques Mathieu ———————————————————

The Language of Commemoration – Abstract
In the context of linguistic metaphor, this paper explores the nature and development of the relationships of communities with their past and their heritage. It provides an introduction to the diversity of riches and values connected with the First Nations, the cultural communities and human rights. It suggests an approach to history and reflects the complexity of commemoration.

Commemoration first of all highlights a fragment of reality. However, the history of history shows that the concerns of researchers and communities with respect to the past have changed considerably over the past half century. From a linear vision focused on heroes and major events, it turned toward social dimensions, then toward multidisciplinary cultural dimensions. The special places of memory have undergone major changes. We now look at the past from many points of view. Do all these new objects of memory warrant safeguarding, development, commemoration?

Commemoration not only marks what has been real in the past; it also proceeds from a judgment made by the present on the past. It is both a discourse and a representation of the past. Thus, there are a series of issues, with the main ones falling into the area of the relationships between the past and the present, identity and belonging, oblivion and memory, mourning and celebration. In the context of commemoration, we are thus confronted with the problem of associating the unique and the universal, membership in communities and national image.

Commemoration proceeds from a mediation in time and between the components of society. It constitutes a cultural mode of expression of communities, a language of communication and a way of viewing the future. It links memory in culture and culture as memory.

SOUFFLES

Écoute plus souvent
Les choses que les êtres
La voix du feu s'entend,
Entends la voix de l'eau.
Écoute dans le vent
Le buisson en sanglot :
C'est le souffle des ancêtres

> Ceux qui sont morts ne sont jamais partis :
> Ils sont dans l'ombre qui s'éclaire
> Et dans l'ombre qui s'épaissit.
> Les morts ne sont pas sous la terre :
>
> Ils sont dans l'air qui frémit,
> Ils sont dans le bois qui gémit.
> Ils sont dans l'eau qui coule
> Ils sont dans la maison, ils sont dans la foule :
> Les morts ne sont pas morts.
> Ils sont dans la vie qui dort.
>
> *Adaptation d'un poème du Sénégalais Birago Diop*

Le titre que l'on m'a suggéré, « La langue de la commémoration », invite à poursuivre la métaphore linguistique tout au long de cette communication. Nous allons donc étudier le vocabulaire, la grammaire et les principes de communication qui font de la commémoration une langue riche et vivante.

Organe de la parole, organe du goût mais surtout système d'expression du mental, la langue allie donc les sens, les sensibilités et les sentiments communs à un groupe. À ce titre, elle introduit à la diversité des valeurs que représentent les Premières Nations, les communautés culturelles et les droits de la personne. Ainsi la place des minorités dans les évocations du passé pose clairement la question de la nature et du sens de l'entreprise de commémoration.

Cet effort de compréhension de la langue de la commémoration emprunte un parcours historique et pluridisciplinaire complexe. Même s'il prend appui sur divers exemples, il nous entraîne dans les dédales insondables des mentalités collectives. Il en ressort évidemment plus de questions que de réponses.

Le vocabulaire a changé

La commémoration met d'abord en évidence une trace du réel. Elle est document, rappel tangible du passé, par et dans l'écrit, le mobilier ou l'immobilier. On la retrouve un peu partout : dans la toponymie, sur les plaques commémoratives, dans les monuments, les bâtiments, les musées, les reconstitutions, voire dans les séries télévisées, les cartes postales et les timbres-poste, etc. Elle illustre en somme une forme de rapports des sociétés à leur passé.

Ces représentations du passé ont tout de même considérablement changé au cours du dernier demi-siècle. Que l'on s'en tienne à l'histoire au sens strict ou que l'on élargisse le regard à l'ensemble des disciplines du passé, l'on se rend compte d'une évolution similaire. D'une vision linéaire axée sur les héros et les grands événements, l'histoire s'est tournée vers le social. De même, au début, que ce soit en archivistique, en histoire de l'art, en muséologie ou en ethnologie, l'on s'est d'abord préoccupé des grands personnages ou des grands faits de notre histoire ; pour le Québec, ceux dont la vie et les actes fondateurs justifiaient la présence française en Amérique du Nord.

Quand l'histoire prend un essor considérable dans les années 1960, les disciplines voisines connaissent également une multiplication du nombre d'experts et une spécialisation des fonctions. Au moment où l'histoire adopte massivement les problématiques sociales, les chercheurs des disciplines voisines réalisent de grands inventaires et construisent des typologies de classification, souvent centrées sur les modes de vie.

Toutes ces démarches disciplinaires sont marquées en somme par un passage de l'individuel remarquable à des ensembles, de l'unicité ou de l'exemplarité à la représentativité. L'on se met à la recherche de cohérences, souvent de type sériel, fondées soit sur un environnement daté, soit dans une chaîne technologique, soit définies dans des contextes systémiques. Bientôt les typologies sont délaissées au profit des fonctionnements et des processus. On passe de l'architecture d'un bâtiment à son usage, de l'outil de l'artisan au geste qu'il commande, de l'objet à sa signification fonctionnelle et symbolique.

Puis, un nombre croissant de reconstructions du passé se tournent vers les représentations. En archéologie comme en ethnologie et en muséologie, on passe d'études *dans* la ville à des études *de* la ville. On s'attache au récit de l'intime, à la culture des apparences, à la culture de la ville. On met en évidence la ville-carrefour (Montréal), la ville-mémoire (Québec). Le moindre petit objet semble être devenu un élément de patrimoine. Par exemple, on ne saurait pas plus modifier le parcours arrondi et ondulé des avenues qui font le tour des Plaines d'Abraham, que déplacer les pierres qui constituent les vestiges du palais de l'Intendant. Cela fait partie de la conception même de l'œuvre et de son destin, est digne de mémoire et, partant, à préserver et à mettre en valeur intégralement.

De fait, il y a eu des déplacements majeurs des lieux de mémoire, de l'Église, de l'État ou de l'école vers la famille, l'Autre, l'environnement. De nouveaux sujets comme l'alimentation, l'enfance, les manuels scolaires, les récits de vie, les rapports homme-femme, la publicité sont devenus à la mode. Des champs et des approches comme l'égo-histoire et la microhistoire sont apparus et connaissent une belle vogue. Et ne nous y trompons pas, ces récits du passé qui s'inscrivent dans d'autres contextes de signification n'ont d'individuel ou de restreint que l'apparence. Dans tous les cas, l'unique rejoint ici une part d'universel. Et ces nouveaux rapports au passé bénéficient d'une très large audience sociale, comme en témoigne la multiplication des musées de civilisation, des centres d'interprétation ou des séries télévisées à fondement historique.

L'histoire, en somme, paraît avoir éclaté. Devenue plurielle, la lecture du passé a donné lieu à une multiplicité d'études qui semblent se diriger dans toutes les directions. Toutefois, des tendances se dessinent et se dégagent de cet éparpillement. En dépit des cloisonnements disciplinaires et de l'absence de concertation, des préoccupations similaires traversent l'ensemble des champs disciplinaires. De là à conclure qu'il faut y voir un ajustement constant au présent, une sorte de recherche implicite de pertinence sociale, il n'y a qu'un pas... que je n'hésiterai pas à franchir.

De fait, les tendances récentes de la recherche historique ne correspondent-elles pas aux préoccupations de notre temps ? On ne peut nier, à mon avis, l'influence d'une volonté collective, qui s'est manifestée depuis une quinzaine d'années, de reconnaître les droits des individus, des femmes, des citoyens, des consommateurs, ainsi que la protection des renseignements personnels. De même que l'on fasse entrer l'environnement au musée ou que l'on crée des parcs naturels protégés constitue une façon de les patrimonialiser, une nouvelle forme d'ancrage mémoriel.

Pratique du passé, l'entreprise de commémoration ne saurait pas plus se définir en marge de ce grand mouvement culturel qui a touché les autres champs de l'histoire, que nier l'influence du présent. L'histoire même de la Commission des lieux et monuments historiques témoigne de cette évolution; et encore plus, la composition de la table d'experts ici réunis.

J'en tire quatre constats :
- l'inévitable ajustement du passé aux préoccupations du présent ;
- le fait que les nouveaux objets d'étude du passé n'ont de petit que les apparences; en ces temps de mondialisation, ils rejoignent des universaux ;
- les objets d'études privilégiés traduisent un malaise social. Le retour au passé devient un moyen de réagir aux crises, de parer aux problèmes du présent et de concevoir l'avenir ;
- le fait que la commémoration est un mode de réinsertion du passé dans la culture.

Des mots pour des idées

La commémoration, comme les autres pratiques du passé, n'est pas seulement un rappel de ce passé, elle procède d'une volonté *actuelle* d'évoquer un fait ; que ce soit un site, une personne ou un événement. En ce sens, la commémoration est un jugement sur le passé plutôt que le passé lui-même. Et, cette trace du passé est aussi discours, représentation, symbolisation, valeur et message dans le présent. Il en découle une série de questions ayant valeur d'enjeux.

La terminologie de la commémoration met en cause trois termes principaux : le souvenir, l'histoire, la mémoire. Le souvenir se présente comme un rappel, ponctuel et immédiat, unique et exemplaire, d'une expérience vécue. L'histoire se perçoit comme une reconnaissance d'un fait passé. La mémoire se définit comme une évocation d'une représentation du passé. Leurs fonctions ne sont donc pas les mêmes. Si l'histoire procède à une reconstruction intelligible, le souvenir se présente comme un rappel sensible, la mémoire, elle, récit pris en charge par le groupe, remémore et reconstitue un contexte, afin d'ancrer le groupe dans une référence commune. Le souvenir se présente comme un temps et un espace de transition, un entrepôt où il faudra sélectionner ce que l'on juge digne de mémoire. L'histoire, sans concession envers le passé, coexiste avec la mémoire qui aménage le passé pour rendre le présent viable. Ainsi, la mémoire réunit les vainqueurs et les vaincus que l'histoire avait opposés. Le souvenir rappelle, l'histoire retrace, la mémoire évoque. Et cette évocation recrée un mouvement, fonde une interrelation dynamique entre les personnes et entre les collectivités, ainsi qu'entre le passé et le présent. Il est donc utile de tenter de préciser ce qu'est la commémoration et ce que l'on veut en faire.

Une grammaire de la commémoration

La commémoration loge au cœur de perceptions différentes, voire contradictoires, d'où une position inconfortable et une série de dilemmes à résoudre : entre passé et futur, entre oubli et mémoire, entre deuil et célébration. Elle évolue entre la bonne conscience, les silences et les dénis du passé. Elle comporte différents enjeux :

- économique par le marché en développement des industries culturelles et touristiques,
- de pouvoir par le poids qu'elle exerce sur les imaginaires collectifs,
- socio-culturel par le rapport entre les savants ou les autorités et la population,
- politique dans la relation entre l'État et le citoyen ;
- en somme, elle constitue un enjeu identitaire.

Elle se présente souvent comme un moyen que se donnent des sociétés libres pour se constituer une forme et une unité. Elle incarne un processus culturel incontournable dans les rapports des collectivités à leur passé.

Dans le rapport présent–passé, la commémoration réunit trois temps :
- le passé, constitué de faits et de pratiques, correspond au réel, au vécu, à l'authentique ;
- le présent, issu de l'imaginaire collectif, est constitué de discours, de perceptions et de préoccupations ;
- le futur est proposé dans toute une gamme de possibles et de potentialités qui visent à valoriser et à harmoniser la vie de relations en société.

Pourquoi, en somme, sauver et mettre en valeur le passé si ce n'est pour livrer un message d'avenir ? La commémoration a recours à hier pour préparer demain. La création de la Communauté européenne est éclairante à cet égard. Elle oblige à redéfinir des fondements nationaux, en particulier à régler, dans et par la mémoire, les problèmes du souvenir de ces guerres qui ont opposé les nations participantes au cours de ce siècle qui s'achève. Où se situe alors l'entreprise de commémoration ? Doit-elle fixer dans le durable le souvenir authentique ou la mémoire changeante ?

Entre l'identité et l'appartenance

Il importe de rappeler, au départ, que le patrimoine a existé avant la nation. La commémoration fait se rencontrer, et s'opposer parfois, le citoyen à portée nationale et l'humain à portée universelle. Et on voit bien que les tendances actuelles de la recherche s'orientent de plus en plus vers l'humain. Comment résoudre ce dilemme ?

Le constat que les identités et les appartenances peuvent se chevaucher, à la condition de se hiérarchiser, offre une bonne voie de solution. Le meilleur exemple que je puisse évoquer, c'est celui du Royal 22e Régiment. Une fois que l'on a reconnu à un groupe son appartenance de base, en l'occurrence son identité canadienne-française préalable, ces jeunes hommes sont allés se faire tuer pour l'Angleterre. Dans cette foulée, on peut comprendre que certains, pour des raisons qu'il faudrait mieux connaître, ont considéré comme un détournement inadmissible la transformation du site du deuil de milliers d'Irlandais à Grosse-Île en une célébration de la politique d'immigration du Canada projetant l'image d'une terre d'accueil. Les exemples liés à Grand-Pré ou aux Premières Nations ne seraient pas moins éloquents.

La commémoration doit reconnaître les appartenances préalables et plurielles pour bien fonder le processus identitaire dont elle témoigne et qu'elle met de l'avant.

Entre l'oubli et la mémoire

Mémoire et oubli entretiennent une double relation. L'oubli est une condition de construction de la mémoire ; à la limite, pourrait-on dire, un temps de la mémoire. Il permet de refouler certains souvenirs dans l'inconscient et de se donner un temps de répit avant de les affronter directement. L'histoire de toutes les personnes et de toutes les collectivités le montre bien. Il faut un certain temps avant que de pouvoir évoquer des traumatismes majeurs, comme la perte d'un être cher, l'holocauste, la déportation, la bataille des Plaines, la révolution de 1789, les grandes guerres, les génocides, la violence et les oppressions.

Mais, en même temps, la crainte de l'oubli crée un impérieux besoin de mémoire. Le constat que le souvenir s'estompe ou se banalise s'accompagne d'une volonté impérative de rappel de mémoire, de consignation de l'expérience du passé. Par peur d'oublier, on veut graver le souvenir dans le bronze ou dans la pierre. Aussi l'expérience de l'oubli va-t-elle de pair avec une nécessité de mémoire. Elle se compare à l'installation d'un monument dans un cimetière. De tous les lieux consacrés, le plus inviolable est certes celui du cimetière parce qu'on y a fixé le souvenir dans un durable qui touche l'éternel. Cette manière de faire constitue une façon d'assumer la disparition irrévocable des souvenirs. Elle est la marque du deuil.

Entre deuil et célébration

Le deuil, espace et temps entre le souvenir et la mémoire, n'équivaut en rien à un état stationnaire et figé. On en parle comme de l'opération de deuil ou du travail du deuil. Cela fait référence à un processus mental, un principe actif et agissant, une dynamique culturelle à laquelle n'échappe aucune personne, ni aucune collectivité. On le voit à l'œuvre dans les récits de vie, où, déjà, les rôles familiaux sont standardisés. On le reconnaît chez les jeunes gens qui sont entrés dans le Royal 22e Régiment. On le repère facilement dans la constitution des collections de musées, où la valeur d'un objet ne réside plus dans sa fonction en son temps, mais dans le symbole qu'il en vient à représenter. C'est ce qui explique que les objets de musées, si souvent extirpés de la cave, passent, du jour au lendemain, d'un statut de rebut à celui de trésor. Il ressort de façon encore plus visible dans les travaux consacrés aux populations migrantes ou aux communautés culturelles. Le travail de deuil du migrant est à la fois sélection, intériorisation, réappropriation et réactualisation du souvenir. Il transforme le passé en un héritage, certes immatériel, mais vivant. Non seulement définit-il ce qu'il faut retenir du passé pour lui donner sens dans le présent et pour l'avenir, mais, plus encore, il donne un sens à l'avenir ; faut-il préciser qu'il s'agit là d'un besoin vivement ressenti par les jeunes d'aujourd'hui. Par la transformation du souvenir en mémoire, il évite de répéter les erreurs d'hier et assure la survivance de valeurs positives projetées vers l'avenir. L'opération de deuil constitue en quelque sorte un acte fondateur qui permet de naître à autre chose. Ces exemples nous mènent bien près du sens de la commémoration.

Ainsi, la commémoration paraît être à la fois une *pédagogie du souvenir* et une *pédagogie de la mémoire*. Elle illustre le travail du deuil, l'espace de l'oubli, le fondement de l'appartenance, la prise en charge des malaises sociaux, la fixation du souvenir dans le durable, la construction d'un processus identitaire. Rappel sensible et compréhensif, elle constitue un moyen de ne pas laisser sombrer les souvenirs dans le néant. Mémoire, elle livre cette expérience que des collectivités se donnent du passé pour aménager l'avenir. Et voilà qu'aujourd'hui toutes les petites communautés culturelles demandent la reconnaissance et la sauvegarde de leur lieu de souvenir. Se pourrait-il qu'elles veuillent ainsi simplement compléter la nécessaire opération de deuil requise pour naître à autre chose ? Si la reconnaissance de ce souvenir et de cette appartenance préalables était le prix à payer pour développer une appartenance nationale, cela me paraîtrait bien peu coûteux; et peut-être mieux fondé. Voilà donc une conception de la nature et du sens de la commémoration !

Une langue de communication

Finalement, comment faire de la langue de la commémoration, une langue de communication ? Comment transformer cet ensemble systématique de règles en une parole qui permette de se parler et de se comprendre ?

Pratique du passé, la commémoration se présente comme un objet d'étude au carrefour de diverses disciplines dont elle a avantage à s'inspirer à la fois pour reconnaître son parcours, mais aussi sa spécificité, ses limites et sa mission principale.

Médiation, entre le savant et l'individu, entre l'État et le citoyen, elle distingue la démarche du savant qui étudie la mémoire dans la culture de celle du créateur qui part de la culture comme mémoire. Elle invite à respecter le souvenir pour s'inventer un avenir, plutôt qu'à réinventer le passé pour célébrer le présent. Elle incite à constituer des partenariats qui ne soient pas seulement de finance, mais aussi de contenu, de valeur et de recherche de sens. Car, disons-le bien franchement, si le contexte recréé par suite d'une intervention de commémoration détourne le sens du passé, il a des effets contraires à ceux recherchés. Il accentue la crainte de perte du souvenir et augmente les tensions. Il n'a pas d'avenir.

Référence commune aux membres d'un groupe, la commémoration loge dans le passé projeté dans l'avenir, dans les collectivités que l'on veut intégrer à l'État, dans le souvenir que l'on veut transformer en mémoire et donc au cœur d'enjeux diversifiés. Elle part du présent, des personnes et des sensibilités. Elle évolue entre le singulier, le collectif, le national et l'universel. Plurielle et diversifiée, elle ne saurait pas plus souffrir une image unifiée et figée que l'application de normes uniformisées et standardisées, ou encore l'assujettissement à une cause ou à une idéologie, que celle-ci soit nationale ou sociale. La commémoration n'est pas un bien de consommation, jetable après usage. Elle repose sur un besoin fondamental de mémoire pour les collectivités. Elle procède d'une responsabilité de culture qui dépasse, en l'englobant, l'enjeu politique national.

Plurielle et diversifiée, la commémoration est un processus culturel et identitaire dont il faut suivre rigoureusement les étapes. Elle repose sur le respect des souvenirs propres à chacun. Elle vise à redonner à chaque citoyen et à chaque citoyenne son passé propre. Elle reconnaît la légitimité et la primauté de leur appartenance et de leur participation à la culture de l'humanité. Bref, la commémoration, en mariant la culture comme héritage et la culture comme projet, donne sens à la parole du passé !

La citadelle de Québec est située sur les hauteurs du Cap-aux-Diamants ; désignée en 1957. / The Québec Citadel is situated on the heights of Cap-aux-Diamants; designated 1957. (Photo : Parks Canada / Parcs Canada, Pierre St-Jacques, 1995)

Loons and Landscapes:
The Place of Environmental Heritage

Abstract

This paper will attempt to explore the evolving iconography of Canadian landscapes, inquiring into the meaning of "designation". Municipal, provincial and national parks continue to reflect the priorities of the times in which they were "created". Parks are creatures of policy. They may be characterized as monuments to perceived relationships between humans and nature. They are imbued with purpose. Since 1967 issues surrounding ecology, aboriginal rights, gender, regionalism and ethnicity have forced a constant rethinking of the manner in which we "protect" the spaces surrounding and permeating our place.

Huards et paysages : la place du patrimoine environnemental – Résumé

Cette communication cherche à cerner l'iconographie mouvante des paysages canadiens en s'interrogeant sur le sens de la « désignation ». Les parcs municipaux, provinciaux et nationaux continuent de refléter les priorités des époques où ils ont été « créés ». Les parcs sont les créatures des décideurs. On peut dire qu'ils sont des monuments illustrant une façon de concevoir les rapports entre les humains et la nature. Ils sont imprégnés d'intentions. Depuis 1967, les questions relatives à l'écologie, aux droits des Autochtones, à l'égalité des sexes, au régionalisme et à l'ethnie nous ont forcés à repenser constamment la façon dont nous « protégeons » les espaces qui enveloppent et pénètrent nos lieux de vie.

Apart from the historical tonnage applauding or denying its value, a major legacy of Frederick Jackson Turner's famous 1893 essay, "The Significance of the Frontier in American History"[1], has been the durability of the imaginary landscapes to which it gave birth. There are four of them: the wilderness, the frontier, the agrarian and the urban. European-descended North Americans use them to signify cultural spaces shaped by shared assumptions about "resource" and "border", "use" and "order". These landscapes appear almost routinely in the language of environmental discourse, often without definition.

A characteristic of Canadian history has been a predisposition to examine landscapes in a context which differentiates between cultural formation in Canada and the United States. The architects of Canada's landscape history – Innis, Creighton, Lower, Careless, Morton – were to one degree or another moved by Turner's thesis to pursue variables it neglects. By 1967, the year of Canada's Centennial, they had helped to satisfy our illusion that we understood our place, our home, that collectively we had grasped our landscapes of the imagination and assigned to them their reasons.

In America, Turner's westward marching frontier required a wilderness to be transformed by labour to human purpose. Specifically, wilderness harboured the agricultural possibility. The frontier was the margin of conquest over the unknown, the edge on which the unknown was made knowable. The acme of Turner's landscapes was the urban, neatly gridironed to shape a democratic civilization emerging from lessons learned on the frontier. Between the urban and the frontier landscapes lay the agrarian – the into-which the wilderness had ascended, the out-of-which the urban was made and fed. The evolution of frontier, agrarian and urban landscapes mirrored the simultaneous development of sciences like taxonomy, the naming, the attempting to make known, of all organic life that occupied the land.

Canadian historiography has been just as eager to celebrate landscapes of knowing, but it has had rather more difficulty than Turner in situating them. Our history attempted to foreground the agrarian landscape. Seigneurial rotures and the rectilinear survey ordered those elements of wilderness allowing the agricultural possibility, privileging the cultural baggage of the immigrant at the expense of Aboriginal cultures, indigenous plants and animals. Nature was made over into something measurable, quantifiable, saleable, a commodity. The problem with the agrarian landscape was its size. In America it was dominant; in Canada it was not. It could not, by itself, constitute an adequate measure of our involvement with the land. Other resource sectors were worked into the equation, but they involved brief return trips to the wilderness, selected properties of which were extracted and returned to the urban landscape, home to our cultural realities. In the "Metropolitan Thesis" of J.M.S. Careless, the urban landscape becomes the metropolis, the rural and wilderness landscapes dependent hinterlands. There is nothing that could be characterized as a frontier either in Careless, or in the Staples and Laurentian theses on which he built his analysis. There is no definable margin on which the organic process of making known can be said to occur. The wilderness is reduced to its constituent resources. We genuflect, in ritual deference, to the Group of Seven, but otherwise we attribute to resources no intrinsic value in the place where they exist. They find redemption, become knowable, only through their reconstitution into things other than themselves, in a landscape which they made possible but of which they are not part.

After wrestling with these contradictions for most of his professional career, W.L. Morton published his pathbreaking essay, "The 'North' in Canadian Historiography".[2] Himself a product of the west and of the agrarian landscape, Morton defined the North as "all that territory beyond the line of minimal growth of the known cereal grains." Morton reminded us that the wilderness was our dominant landscape, that it existed in the north of our imagination, and that it denied the agricultural possibility. It was a force, not of progress, but of limitation. The Shield was, he said, "an impenetrable as well as a permanent frontier. It may be vaulted; it cannot be removed." By no accident of fate this essay was written in 1970 just as myriad fragmenting processes following the Centennial began to articulate a political agenda dominated by aboriginal, gender, ethnicity and regional issues. This rebellious diversity reflected the imperatives of ecology, institutionalized, also in 1970, in the creation of Environment Canada. Morton was witnessing national debates surrounding the discovery of oil at Prudhoe Bay, the voyage of the *Manhattan*, Arctic Waters Pollution Prevention Legislation, Richard Rohmer's "Mid-Canada Corridor Plan", and, most importantly, the Trudeau government's ill-advised "White Paper" recommending the assimilation of Native people. For business and industry the North represented the new El Dorado, for ecologists it was a metaphor for limitation. To Native people – both those for whom it was home and those elsewhere – the North became a symbol of resistance. This resistance informed, for example, the creation of the Inuit Tapirisat in 1971. It has been mirrored ever since in the debates which will result, soon, in the birth of Nunavut. These debates centre on what those of us in the metropolis have been conditioned to call the wilderness landscape. A century after the publication of Turner's thesis, this wilderness asks through those to whom it is known, that its voice be heard.

Morton's permanent frontier is the meeting table for the discussion of ways of knowing. The dialogue which takes place there requires that the participants approach one another in a spirit of reconciliation. The language of staple and metropolis and hinterland may well explain what has been done to the land, but it need not dictate the future. There is a vast difference between knowing based on what is brought to the place and knowing that emerges from it. In the context of this conference, the real challenge lies not in "designating" natural heritage sites which are "protected" from the knowing of capitalism; the real challenge is, collectively, to accept the knowing of ecology, where order depends upon a relationship built from diverse but mutually dependant parts.

Each landscape contains elements of the others, however small. Similarly, there are micro landscapes – the places where people choose to live out the largest portion of their lives. Knowing these landscapes means reconciling their constituent urban, agrarian and wilderness elements, privileging neither human creation, nor natural creation but understanding both equally as creation.

In the north maple trees are scarce. But the loon is everywhere. Its haunting voice, the oldest of them all, calls us to the table. Urgently.

Canada does not exist. Rather, Canada is in a perpetual state of becoming. Its becoming is, and always has been, animated by hope. Hope for peace and health and joy, hope for lives lived richly and compassionately in a shared sense of belonging to something noble and exemplary. Historic sites and monuments are merely touchstones along our way. The forces once recommending their claim on our attention are often overthrown by evolving values, new knowledge. Plaques remain as yardsticks, subtle measures of our becoming, helping us to remember, selectively. They speak to us and we respond. Yet this dialogue occurs in only one of the places changed by events, people, or artifacts iconized. Many places may have been changed. These places constitute our environment; in their locales we are the environed. In changing, they change us. Why, then, do we identify our monuments to natural heritage – Parks, ANSIs, ESAs – in places distant from ourselves? Surely the only absolute, the unchallengeable arbiter of all our hopes, is the land itself. It is not remote.

No land, no monuments to celebrate its manipulation for creative human purpose.

Notes

1. Frederick Jackson Turner, "The Significance of the Frontier in American History", *Annual Report of the American Historical Association for the Year 1893* (Washington, D.C.: Government Printing Office, 1894), 199-227. See the essays by Richard White and Patricia Nelson Limerick in *The Frontier in American Culture: An Exhibition at the Newberry Library, August 26, 1994 - January 7, 1995*, ed., James R. Grossman. (Berkeley: University of California Press, 1994).
2. W. L. Morton, "The 'North' in Canadian Historiography", *Transactions of the Royal Society of Canada*, Series 4, 8(1970), 31-30.

JOHN HERD THOMPSON

Professional Historians and Heritage Commemoration

Abstract

The designation of academic historians as "professional" historians (and the implication that non-academic historians are "un-" or "non-professional") attests to the large and lamentable gap which has grown between university-based historians and their colleagues who work outside the academy in heritage commemoration. It was not always so. During the first half-century of the Historic Sites and Monuments Board, for example, academics actively shaped its agenda. Whatever the explanations for the growing gulf between two groups of Clio's Canadian servants, this division diminishes the efforts of both groups of professionals to explain Canada's pasts.

Les historiens « professionnels » et la commémoration du patrimoine - Résumé

Le qualificatif de « professionnel » attribué aux historiens d'université (qui donne à entendre que les historiens n'œuvrant pas en milieu universitaire ne sont pas professionnels) révèle le fossé énorme et déplorable qui s'est creusé entre les historiens rattachés à des universités et leurs collègues qui travaillent à la commémoration du patrimoine à l'extérieur du monde universitaire. Tel n'a pas toujours été le cas. Ainsi, au cours du premier demi-siècle d'existence de la Commission des lieux et monuments historiques, les universitaires ont largement façonné son programme. De quelque manière qu'on cherche à l'expliquer, cet écart croissant entre deux groupes de serviteurs canadiens de la muse Clio nuit grandement aux efforts déployés par l'un comme par l'autre pour faire comprendre l'histoire du Canada.

"Professional" Historians in a "Heritage Community"

Please observe that I have italicized the word "professional" in the title assigned to me: *"Professional* Historians and Heritage Commemoration". The italic in the title is my way of rejecting the implication that the adjectives "academic" and "professional" are synonyms when used to modify the noun "historian". As an academic historian I belong to but one of the sub-species of the "professional" historians.

The fact that the organizers have asked an academic historian to speak to this conference as the representative of "professional" historians seems to suggest that historians outside the academy are at best "*non*-professional", or at worst "*un*-professional". And, of course, the many excellent historians who work outside the university are neither of these things.

The two relevant definitions of the adjective "professional" in my *Webster's New Collegiate Dictionary* are:

> participating for gain or livelihood in...a field of endeavor...
> [and/or]
> characterized by or conforming to the technical or ethical standards of a profession.

Both of these definitions apply to the public-servant historians whose histories guide the commemoration, preservation and interpretation of historic sites in Canada. In my own area of interest for example, the history of the Canadian prairies, the fine work of Parks Canada historians such as Lyle Dick, Alan McCullough, Walter Hildebrandt, Robert Coutts, and Diane Payment "conforms to the [highest] technical or ethical standards" of written history. And although I realize that public service salaries are a highly charged topic in contemporary Canada, these estimable historians continue to "participate for gain or livelihood" in the field of writing history.

So I would like to start by changing the nomenclature. First, given that many historians who do not teach in universities are actually "professional" historians, I will use the more precise term to refer to historians like me who do teach in universities – *academic* historians. (After reading this introduction, some would no doubt suggest that "pettifogging professors" would be more appropriate.) To describe all historians collectively, I will adopt the term "heritage community", a term I discovered in the admirable historical survey of the Historic Sites and Monuments Board which was distributed to all the participants in this conference.

Each of us who creates hi[stories] of Canada for a living is (or should think of her/himself as) a member of this heritage community, whether s/he creates her/his histories in a university, in a secondary school, in a community college, in a museum, in an archive, or in heritage commemoration work.

I would now like to discuss the relationship between two groups of professional historians – academic historians and those historians who work directly with heritage commemoration, specifically the historians of Parks

Canada – and to discuss the relationship of academic historians to the Historic Sites and Monuments Board of Canada (HSMBC).

Academic Historians and Heritage Commemoration – the Past

Over the long durée of the seventy-five year existence of the Historic Sites and Monument Board of Canada, its relationship with academic historians has, in general, been excellent.[1] If in its first decade the HSMBC was typified by enthusiastic amateurs like Brigadier General E.A. Cruikshank, after the appointment of Fred Landon and D.C. Harvey in 1931, academics came more and more to dominate the Board and thus to shape the agenda for heritage commemoration in Canada. F.W. Howay, although technically an "amateur", was deeply imbued with the values of the academy, and regularly consulted colleagues in universities. After 1940, academics dominated not only the Board's philosophy but also its membership. A.G. Bailey, J.M.S. Careless, Donald G. Creighton, Arthur R.M. Lower, Margaret Ormsby, Walter N. Sage, Lewis H. Thomas, Marcel Trudel and Peter Waite: the names of the Board members are an honour roll of academic historians of Canada.

Not surprisingly, until the 1960s, most academic historians were well satisfied with the Board's approach to its mission. The Board simply designated "National Historic Sites", and marked each site chosen with a brief text displayed on a plaque. This choice of simple commemoration over more complicated and expensive preservation fit the academic historians' preferences. It also mirrored their reliance upon printed textual sources to create their own written histories, and suggested their academic indifference to material history.

The types of site the Board commemorated also reflected the preoccupations of academic historians. Of the 285 sites designated as of 1943, 105 represented military history, fifty-two fur trade and exploration, and forty-three famous individuals (mostly, but not exclusively, men). The ubiquity of War of 1812 sites at which Canada had been heroically preserved from the perfidious Americans has been attributed to General Cruikshank, but his choices fit well with the anti-American impulses emanating from the academy. In his 1963 Massey Lectures, Frank H. Underhill suggested facetiously that to celebrate the centenary of Confederation "there should be erected a monument to this American ogre" whose hostility had united British North America.[2] Underhill missed the point: the HSMBC had already erected more than 100 such monuments!

The preponderance of Ontario sites – 119 of 308, as of 1950, as compared to eight in Saskatchewan – also reflected the central-Canadian biases of Canadian academic historians. Significantly, in the mid-1940s, proposals to recognize

Jewish, Mennonite, Ukrainian and African-American settlement were all rejected by the HSMBC; academic historians did not write about those settlements either. Asked to identify Board priorities in 1952, Fred Landon of The University of Western Ontario listed discovery and exploration, French and English settlement, the loyalist defence of Upper Canada. During his tenure on the Board, Donald G. Creighton contributed an official guide to National Historic Sites which he entitled *Heroic Beginnings*. These "beginnings" were entirely Euro-Canadian: that the HSMBC had ignored the commemoration of Aboriginal prehistory troubled Professor Creighton not at all.

Things changed in the 1960s, however, with the beginning of what C.J. Taylor calls "The Era of the Big Project": Lower Fort Garry, Dawson City, the Halifax Citadel, and, most spectacularly, the Fortress of Louisbourg. In this new era, the HSMBC lost its central place in the process of historical commemoration. In Taylor's words, the Board "found itself in the role of a bystander" to the new process of preservation, recreation and interpretation. Academic historians had influenced commemoration through their influence on the Board; thus the Board's marginalization marginalized them as well. No academic historian, for example, would have chosen Dawson City as a site for massive investment in a National Historic Park; and once work began, the HSMBC was not consulted on the decision to demolish and reconstruct the Palace Grand Theatre rather than to restore it.

The important new historical players in the politics of commemoration were the rapidly increasing group of professional historians employed in the Historic Sites Division of the National Parks Branch. As the numbers and the technical expertise of this group grew throughout the 1970s, the Board became further "alienated": decisions about even "modest developments" in heritage commemoration "were too often taken without the Board's advice". But Taylor also explains that the Historic Sites Division was not an unambiguous "winner" of the commemoration game: professional historians at the Historic Sites Division found themselves supplanted by the "operational side" of the National Parks Branch. The professional historical researchers were never able to assert their control of the new "big projects", for example. Instead the engineers at National Parks "overshadow[ed] the historic sites division" at Halifax Citadel and the Québec fortifications. Thus professional historians as a group lost "the battle of Louisbourg" to engineers and politicians, with the result that the reconstructed Louisbourg came to represent a "single point in time" rather than demonstrating "the process of history and the changes wrought by time", as J.L. Herbert, chief of the Historic Sites Division had intended.

And as real budgets for commemoration shrank when the golden age ended, maintaining and staffing the large projects absorbed a larger proportion of them – as Christina Cameron reminded us.

Academic Historians and Heritage Commemoration – the Future

What will be, or what should be, the contribution of academic historians to heritage commemoration? And how will they make that contribution? To ask these questions in functional terms: what will be the relationship between academic historians and the HSMBC, and what will be the relationship between academic historians and the professional historians of Parks Canada?

It seems likely that the HSMBC will continue to be an important location in which academic historians "negotiate the past". In 1951, the Massey Commission proposed that the Canadian Historical Association (CHA) formally nominate two members of the HSMBC. Although the CHA lobbied vigorously for this privilege, the Commission's proposal was twice rejected by the government in the 1950s, and would no doubt be rejected today. And the CHA is today, unfortunately, probably less representative of the academic historical community than it was in the 1950s. But even without direct nomination by the CHA, membership of the HSMBC continues to tilt heavily toward historians based in universities. At present, seven of the appointees are academic historians,[3] and *ex officio* member Jean-Pierre Wallot was a distinguished academic historian before his appointment as National Archivist. The larger question, however, is how important the HSMBC will be in the larger process of commemoration. To rephrase slightly the alternatives C.J. Taylor poses, will the Board "emerge as an important conduit between public and government initiatives" in heritage commemoration, or "will it slide into obscurity?"

The "current concerns" that the Board lists in the "Introduction" (See Appendix 1a) suggest that "obscurity" is unlikely. Those "current concerns" are the history of Aboriginal Peoples, the history of women, and the history of "cultural communities other than...those of French and British stock." Not by coincidence, these identical priorities appear in Parks Canada's National Historic Sites Systems Plan. These same themes inspire many sessions at the Canadian Historical Association's Annual Meeting, and predominate in the *Journal of the Canadian Historical Association* and in the CHA's two series of historical booklets. The convergence of priorities among academic historians, historians at Parks Canada, and the HSMBC is of course more than coincidental; Parks Canada historians consulted the Women's History Group of the Canadian Historical Association and the CHA Council while it created the plan.

Since academic historians turned to the study of social history – the everyday lives of ordinary people – and to the study of "limited identities" of ethnicity, gender and class, they are probably as much of one mind with the professional historians who work in heritage commemoration as the two groups have ever been. The academic who coined the term "limited identities" was J.M.S. Careless, a member of the Historic Sites and Monuments Board from 1972 to 1985 and its chair for the last five of those years. But when we discuss the contemporary relationship between academic historians and those historians who work in heritage commemoration, we must also ask *which* academic historians are doing the relating. The academic historical community in Canada is more complex than it was in the days of Donald G. Creighton, Arthur R.M. Lower and Walter N. Sage. In many ways, like Canada, the academic historical community is not one "community" but an assortment of disparate historical sub-groups devoted to the intensive study of a proliferating number of specialized subjects.

There are outspoken dissenters among academic historians of Canada from the apparent consensus in favour of the social history of the "limited identities" of ethnicity, gender and class. The most outspoken of these are Professors J.L. Granatstein and Michael Bliss.[4] Granatstein's cranky dismissal of social history as "the history of housemaid's knee in Belleville in the 1890s" is oft-quoted, by Bliss among others. Granatstein and Bliss have eloquently lamented the "disintegration of Canadian history as a unified discipline," and the fact that "the world of the academic historian has become introverted to the point of ghettoization." Both deplore the failure of academic historians to "reach outside the academy" to a wider audience. Both deplore the lack of study of what they describe as "national" history, which they define as the study of national political, constitutional, diplomatic and military history. (Granatstein, in company with Norman Hillmer and Angelika Sauer, has formed a new "Organization for the Study of Canada's National History", which will have a new journal devoted to these topics.) Both also connect this "declining interest in the big questions" to "rising levels of national disunity", and to a "national plunge towards dissolution". (The very same sentiment is echoed in Thomas H.B. Symons' opening presentation.) "The Sundering of Canadian History" has led to "the Sundering of Canada", Michael Bliss says in the sub-title of his 1991 Creighton Lecture, subsequently published in *The Journal of Canadian Studies*.

Members of the social history consensus within Canadian academic history have dismissed these critics as old-fashioned, privileged, white male jeremiahs from Toronto, who are really lamenting the relative decline of old-fashioned, privileged, white males from Toronto; as Donald Creightons of the

1990s who pine for an imaginary golden past when Canada's academic historians were "national sages, ...definers and interpreters of the Canadian experience."

Without endorsing all of their arguments or their narrow definition of "national" history, however, I would timidly offer that Bliss, Granatstein and those who agree with them deserve the attention of other professional historians. We must remember that the original and enduring justification for heritage commemoration and preservation – and the justification for the expenditure of public funds upon it – was and is that heritage commemoration is a form of nation-building. From the beginning the HSMBC has been assigned a nation-building mission; this theme runs through the statements of Board members and through the legislation creating the Board.

C.J. Taylor concludes his *Negotiating the Past* by quoting a journalist's complaint that the reconstructed Louisbourg is "a symbol of our national puzzlement over what history is truly Canadian and how to possess it." "...If national historic parks cannot present a unified image of the Canadian past," Taylor suggests, "there are few historians and fewer cultural institutions that can." It is time for Clio's Canadian servants, in the academy and in heritage commemoration, to reconsider the "big picture" and to rededicate ourselves to portraying it.

Professional historians in the academy and those who work in historical commemoration must work together to invent a national, "unified image of the Canadian past" for Canadians. A "national" history does not have to be a nationalist history, a history with obvious "good guys" and "bad guys" (and mostly "guys") – the sort of history that E.A. Cruikshank was trying to invent with those omnipresent War of 1812 historic sites. And there is no reason why "limited identities" have to be limit*ing* identities.

There are two reasons why professional historians should undertake this task of creating a national vision of the past, reasons which reflect the two definitions of professional which began these remarks. The first is venal: if we do not, Canadian taxpayers and their elected representatives will stop paying us to be historians. A sharp contraction in the ranks of professional historians, virtually all of whom ultimately depend on governments for their salaries, is well underway. Fewer and fewer young historians find opportunities "to gain a livelihood" as part of the Canadian "heritage community".

The second reason derives from the other definition of "professional": our responsibility to meet the highest standards of our profession. It is our professional duty to answer the biggest historical question of them all: Why does Canada, and thus Canadian history, matter to Canadians?

Notes

1. My information about academic historians' relationships with the HSMBC and heritage commemoration, unless otherwise noted, is drawn from C.J. Taylor's *Negotiating the Past: The Making of Canada's National Historic Sites and Parks* (Montréal & Kingston, 1990).
2. Underhill, *The Image of Confederation* (Toronto, 1964) 4.
3. Francis Bolger, Margaret Conrad, Fernand Harvey, Charles Humphries, André Lalonde, Michael Kinnear, and, of course, the current Chair[man], Thomas H.B. Symons.
4. Michael Bliss, "Privatizing the Mind: The Sundering of Canadian History, the Sundering of Canada", *Journal of Canadian Studies*, 26:4 (Winter 1991-92), 5-17; J.L. Granatstein, "For a National History", Convocation Address, Memorial University of Newfoundland, 30 October 1993.

Brigadier General E.A. Cruikshank, FRSC (1853-1939), first Chairman of the HSMBC (1919-39), historian; designated 1943. / Le brigadier-général E.A. Cruikshank, FRSC (1853-1939), premier président de la CLMHC (1919-1939), historien ; désigné en 1943. (Photo: National Archives / Archives nationales, PA-66805, A.L. Hass)

Stoney Creek Monument and Gage homestead at the site of the Battle of Stoney Creek, War of 1812; designated 1960 / Le monument de Stoney Creek et la propriété Gage sur le lieu de la bataille de Stoney Creek, pendant la guerre de 1812 ; désigné en 1960. (Photo: National Archives, PA-86880; John Boyd collection, item 19296-6 / Archives nationales, PA-86880 ; collection John Boyd, pièce 19296-6)

Depiction of an historical reinactment passing by Benoist House, Porte Frédérick at the Fortress of Louisbourg, Nova Scotia. Designated in 1928, the eighteenth century French fortress was reconstructed during the 1960s and '70s / Reconstitution d'un défilé historique devant la maison Benoist, à Porte Frédérick, dans l'enceinte de la forteresse de Louisbourg (Nouvelle-Écosse). Désignée en 1928, la forteresse française du XVIIIe siècle a été reconstruite au cours des années 1960 et 1970. (Photo : Parks Canada / Parcs Canada, J. Steeves, 1987)

Whose Heritage? Whose Culture?
Quel patrimoine ? Quelle culture ?

"At the water's edge", Piegan Reserve, situated near Lethbridge in southern Alberta / « Au bord de l'eau », réserve piégane située près de Lethbridge, dans le sud de l'Alberta. (Photo: National Archives, C-19978; Edward Sheriff Curtis Collection, 1966-122 / Archives nationales, C-19978 ; collection Edward Sheriff Cutris, pièce 1966-122)

The Power of Place: Claiming Women's History in the Urban Landscape

Abstract

Women's history presents many possibilities for preservationists concerned with vernacular buildings and the urban landscape. This paper explores three projects undertaken in downtown Los Angeles, California, by The Power of Place, a non-profit corporation founded by the author in 1984. The Biddy Mason Project connected historians and artists in an effort to commemorate a nineteenth century African-American midwife's homestead where no physical traces remained, but two new works of public art were installed on the site. The Embassy Project utilized a public history workshop to reinterpret a union hall where three organizers gathered Latina women in the 1930s and 1940s. And the Flowergrowers Project, focusing on Japanese-American families running commercial flowerfields in the 1890s, helped to contribute to citywide support for the preservation of a historic district of Japanese-American family businesses in Little Tokyo, where preservation, public art, and a new ethnic history museum will contribute to the whole.

Le pouvoir du lieu : revendication de l'histoire des femmes en milieu urbain – Résumé

L'histoire des femmes offre de nombreuses possibilités aux partisans de la préservation de l'architecture populaire et du paysage urbain. Cette communication passe en revue trois projets exécutés dans le centre-ville de Los Angeles (Californie) par The Power of Place, société sans but lucratif fondée par l'auteure en 1984. Le projet Biddy Mason a réuni des historiens et des artistes dans le but de commémorer une propriété du XIXe siècle ayant appartenu à une sage-femme afro-américaine. Il ne subsistait aucune trace de la propriété, mais deux nouvelles œuvres d'art pour lieux publics ont été installées sur son emplacement. Dans le cadre du projet Embassy, on a utilisé un atelier sur l'histoire des lieux publics pour réinterpréter l'histoire d'une salle de réunion syndicale où trois organisateurs réunissaient des femmes d'origine latino-américaine dans les années 1930 et 1940. Enfin, le projet Flowergrowers, axé sur les familles nippo-américaines qui exploitaient des jardins commerciaux dans les années 1890, a contribué à mobiliser l'appui de toute la ville pour la préservation d'un quartier historique du Petit Tokyo regroupant des entreprises familiales nippo-américaines. Ce projet prévoit des travaux de préservation, des œuvres d'art pour lieux publics et l'aménagement d'un nouveau musée d'histoire ethnique.

Layered with the traces of previous generations' struggles to earn a living, raise children, and participate in community life, the vernacular urban landscape, as John Brinckerhoff Jackson writes, "... is the image of our common humanity – hard work, stubborn hope, and mutual forbearance striving to be love,"[1] a definition that carries cultural geography and architecture straight toward urban social history. At the intersection of these fields lies the history of urban space and its public meanings. How do urban landscapes hold public memory? And why should feminists and scholars of women's history struggle to create projects honouring and preserving women's history as part of public culture?

Every North American city and town contains traces of historic landscapes intertwined with its current spatial configuration. These parts of older landscapes can be preserved and interpreted to strengthen people's understanding of how a city has developed over time. But often what happens is something else. Cycles of development and redevelopment occur. Care is not taken to preserve the spatial history of ordinary working people and their everyday lives. Instead, funds are often lavished on the preservation of a few architectural monuments along with the celebration of a few men as "city fathers". For example, in New York City, many buildings designed by the architects McKim, Mead and White at the turn of the century are closely identified with an Anglo-Saxon, protestant, male elite who commissioned the private men's clubs, mansions, banks, and other structures from which many citizens were often excluded. In contrast, modest urban buildings that represent the social and economic struggles of the majority of ordinary citizens – especially women and members of diverse ethnic communities – have often been overlooked as possible resources for historic preservation. The power of place to nurture social memory – to encompass shared time in the form of shared territory – remains largely untapped for most working people's neighbourhoods in most American cities, and for most ethnic history, and most women's history. If we hear little of city mothers, the sense of civic identity that shared women's history can convey is lost. And, even bitter experiences and fights women have lost need to be remembered – so as not to diminish their importance.

To reverse the neglect of physical resources important to women's history is not a simple process, especially if preservationists are to frame these issues as part of a broader social history encompassing gender, race, and class. First, it involves claiming the entire urban landscape as an important part of American history, not just its architectural monuments. Second, it means identifying the building types – such as tenement, market, factory, packing shed, union hall – that have housed women's work and everyday lives. Third, it involves finding creative ways to interpret these modest buildings as part of the flow of contemporary city life. This means finding a politically conscious approach to urban preservation – complementary to architectural preservation – that emphasizes public processes to nurture shared memories and meanings. It also means reconsidering strategies for the representation of women's history and ethnic history in public places, as well as for the preservation of places themselves.

Early in the 1980s, when I was teaching at the Graduate School of Architecture and Urban Planning at UCLA, I founded The Power of Place as a small, experimental non-profit corporation, to explore ways to present the public history of workers, women, and people of colour in Los Angeles. It began as an unpaid, volunteer effort with a few student interns – I still had a full-time teaching job. Los Angeles is an ethnically diverse city. It always has been, since the day when a group of colonists of mixed Spanish, African, and Native American heritage arrived to found the pueblo in 1781, next to Yang-Na. It has remained so through the transfer of Los Angeles from Mexican to American rule in the mid-nineteenth century and on into the late twentieth century. Residents – more than one-third Latino, one-eighth African-American, one-eighth Asian-American, one-half women – cannot find their heritage adequately represented by existing cultural historic landmarks. (In 1985, 97.5% of all official city landmarks commemorated Anglo history and only 2.5% represented people of colour; 96% dealt with men and only 4% women, including Anglo women).[2] No one has yet written a definitive social history of Los Angeles. By the early 1980s, however, older works by Carey McWilliams and Robert Fogelson were being complemented by new narratives about ghettos, barrios, and ethnic enclaves, as Albert Camarillo, Mario Garcia, Vicki Ruiz, Richard Griswold del Castillo, Ricardo Romo, Rudolfo Acuna, Lonnie Bunch, Don and Nadine Hata, Mike Murase, Noritaka Yagasaki, and many others were creating accounts of Latinos, African-Americans, Chinese-Americans and Japanese-Americans in Los Angeles.[3] The new work suggested the outline the urban history of Los Angeles must one day fill. As a feminist scholar concerned with the history of the urban landscape, transplanted from New England to Los Angeles, I was tremendously excited by the new, ethnic urban history, and its potential to broaden my teaching in a professional school whose students were concerned with the physical design of the city, in areas such as preservation, physical planning, public art, and urban design. (I was looking for ways to enable students to take something back to their own communities.)

One of the first projects of The Power of Place in 1984-5 was a walking tour of downtown (co-authored with UCLA graduate students Gail Dubrow and Carolyn Flynn).[4] Organized around the economic development of the city, the tour looked at some of the working landscapes various industries had shaped over the previous two centuries. It highlighted the history of production, defining the historic core of the city, and emphasizing the skill and energy workers have expended to feed, clothe, and house the population. These workers included women, men, and sometimes children of every ethnic group employed in citrus groves, flower fields, flower markets, produce markets, oil fields, and prefabricated housing factories, as well as garment workers, midwives, nurses, and fire fighters. The State of California's on-going research on ethnic landmarks, eventually published as *Five Views*, was then available in manuscript form.[5] The Power of Place ran some public humanities workshops on topics such as Japanese-Americans in the flower industry, and African-American fire fighters. The published walking tour pamphlet finally identified an itinerary of nine downtown places (and twenty-seven minor ones): some were buildings eligible for landmark status because of their significant social history; some were buildings with architectural landmark status, needing reinterpretation to emphasize their importance to social history; and a few were vacant historic sites where no structures remained, but new public art or open space designs might be possible to commemorate the site's importance.

In 1986 The Power of Place launched into work of a much more experimental kind – combining public history and public art to commemorate an African-American midwife's homestead with no historic structure remaining – the site was one of the downtown's endless parking lots. In 1986 and 1987, the Los Angeles Community Redevelopment Agency was developing a plan for a ten-story commercial and garage building at 333 Spring Street. Because the material in the walking tour had been listed in their computer, the address popped out as Mason's historic homestead. The Power of Place was invited to propose a component for this new project involving both public history and public art. I served as project director and historian, and raised money from arts and humanities foundations. The team included art curator Donna Graves, artists Susan E. King, Betye Saar, and Sheila Levrant de Bretteville. The first public event was a workshop in 1987, co-sponsored by African-American studies at UCLA, and assisted by the California Afro-American Museum and the First African Methodist Episcopal Church, where the team came together with community members to discuss the importance of the history of the African-American community in Los Angeles, and women's history within it.

Using Biddy Mason's biography as the basis of the project was the key to finding a broad audience. One pioneer's life cannot tell the whole story of building a city. Yet the record of a single citizen's struggle to raise a family, earn a living, and contribute to professional, social, and religious activities can suggest how a city develops over time. This is especially true for Biddy Mason. Her experiences as a citizen of Los Angeles were typical – as a family head, homeowner, and churchgoer. Yet they were also unusual – since gender, race, and legal status as a slave increased her burdens.

Born in 1818, Biddy Mason was the lifelong slave of a master from Mississippi.[6] She had trekked west with his family and other slaves, including her three daughters, herding his livestock behind a Mormon wagon train, first to Deseret (Salt Lake City, Utah), and then to the Mormon outpost of San Bernadino, California. They arrived in Southern California in 1851. Biddy Mason brought suit for freedom for herself and thirteen others in court in Los Angeles in 1855. When she won her case and chose to settle in the small town of Los Angeles in 1856 as part of the very small African-American community there, her special medical skills, learned as a slave midwife and nurse, provided entry for her into many households. She became the city's most famous midwife, delivering hundreds of babies. She lived and worked in the city until her death in January 1891.

The Biddy Mason Project focused on the changing experience of being African-American in Los Angeles, the problems of earning a living as a free woman of colour in the city, and the nature of home as one woman created it. Although Mason at first lived with another family, and then rented on her own, the homestead she built in Los Angeles in the 1880s, a quarter-century after her arrival, was a surprisingly urban place: a brick commercial building with space for her grandsons' business enterprises on the ground floor, and for her own quarters upstairs, where the early organizational meetings of the Los Angeles First African Methodist Episcopal Church were held.

A working woman of colour is the ideal subject for a public history project because in her life all the struggles associated with class, ethnicity, and gender are intertwined. Although she herself was unable to read and write, the history of Biddy Mason was not lost. Through Mormon records of colonization, I was able to trace her journey west. Through the account of her suit for freedom in the local newspaper, I followed the legal proceedings. Some diaries and a photograph from the family her daughter married into provided personal details. Then using work in the history of medicine concerning other African-American midwives and women healers, I constructed an account of what a successful midwife's medical practice was probably like. (A few years later, Laurel Ulrich's *A Midwife's Tale*, a marvellous book about a Maine midwife's diary, confirmed some of my ideas about the social importance of women's medical work.) Finally, using detailed records of the built environment, I was able to unlock the narrative of how Biddy Mason created her urban homestead, beginning in 1866, although the building had been razed and the site turned into a parking lot. The records of her property happened to be particularly significant since the growth of the Spring Street commercial district in Los Angeles between 1866, when she bought her land, and 1891, when she died, proceeded right down her street and included her property. Thus her life story spans the wider themes of slavery and freedom, family life in pioneer times, women in the healing professions, and economic development in Los Angeles between the 1850s and 1890s.

The Biddy Mason Project eventually included five parts. First, Betye Saar's installation, "Biddy Mason's House of the Open Hand", was placed in the elevator lobby of the new structure. It includes a photomural, and motifs from vernacular architecture of the 1880s as well as an assemblage on Mason's life. Second, Susan E. King created a large format artist's letterpress book, *HOME/stead*, in an edition of thirty-five.[7] King incorporated rubbings from the Evergreen Cemetery in Boyle Heights where Mason is buried. These included vines, leaves, and an image of the gate of heaven. The book weaves together the history of Mason's life (drawing on my research and some by Donna Graves) with King's meditations on the homestead becoming a ten-story building. Third, an inexpensive poster, "Grandma Mason's Place: A Midwife's Homestead", was designed by Sheila Levrant de Bretteville. The historical text I wrote for the poster included midwives' architectural rituals for welcoming a newborn, such as painting the shutters blue, or turning the door around on its hinges. Fourth, "Biddy Mason: Time and Place", a black poured-concrete wall (81 feet long) with slate, limestone, and granite inset panels, was designed by Sheila Levrant de Bretteville to chronicle the story of Biddy Mason and her life, as well as the history of urban development in Los Angeles from 1818-1891. The wall includes a midwife's bag, scissors, and spools of thread debossed into the concrete. De Bretteville also included a picket fence, agave leaves, and wagon wheels representing Mason's walk to freedom from Mississippi to California. Both the deed to her homestead and her "Freedom Papers" are among the historic documents photographed and bonded to limestone panels. And fifth, there was prose in a journal. My article, "Biddy Mason's Los Angeles, 1856-1891", appeared in the Fall 1989 *California History*.[8]

Everyone who gets involved in a public history or public art project hopes for an expanded audience, beyond the classroom or the museum. The poster was widely distributed. The wall by Sheila Levrant de Bretteville has been especially successful in evoking the community spirit of claiming the place. Youngsters run their hands along the wagon wheels. Teenagers trace the shape of Los Angeles on historic maps and decipher the old-fashioned handwriting on the Freedom Papers. People of all ages ask their friends to pose for snapshots in front of their favourite parts of the wall. We who worked together on this project, which opened in late 1989, have had the satisfaction of seeing it become a new public place, one that connects individual women with family history, community history, and the city's urban landscape, developing over time.

If you lift your eyes above the wall, you will see a garment factory, and the next project which The Power of Place sponsored. It involved the Embassy Theatre as a site of union organizing and community organizing among Latina workers in the 1930s. This project was directed by Donna Graves while I remained as president of the organization. It suggests some ways an existing architectural landmark can be reinterpreted in terms of its importance to women's history, labour history, and ethnic history. Designated a Los Angeles Cultural-Historic Landmark (as part of a real estate deal) for its indifferent neo-classical architecture designed by Fitzhugh, Krucker, and Deckbar in 1914, the Embassy Theatre is far more important as the historic gathering place for labour unions and community organizations – including Russian-Jewish and Latina garment workers, Latina cannery workers, and Russian-Molokan walnut shellers. Unions, especially women's unions, met inside and marched outside the Embassy between the 1920s and the 1940s, as did El Congreso (the Spanish Speaking People's Congress), the first national Latino civil rights organization.[9] By the 1990s it had become a residential college for the University of Southern California.

The Embassy in its heyday was frequented by many of that era's most colourful organizers including Rose Pesotta of the ILGWU, who led the 1933 Dressmakers' strike, Luisa Moreno of UCAPAWA (United Cannery, Agricultural, Packing, and Allied Workers Association), and Josefina Fierro de Bright of El Congresso. All three reached Los Angeles after epic journeys of the same proportions as Biddy Mason's – from Russia for Pesotta, Guatemala, for Moreno, and Mexico for Fierro de Bright. All three experienced the height of their careers in Los Angeles, recruiting thousands of Spanish-speaking women into their organizations – but it must be added that their work was so controversial and disturbing that Pesotta resigned as ILGWU vice-president and Moreno and Fierro de Bright left for Mexico during the red-baiting years.

Graves's project highlighted these three organizers. Artist Rupert Garcia created a poster with their portraits to advertise a public humanities workshop, "La Fuerza de Union", held in the historic main auditorium in the spring of 1991. Participants included two artists, Garcia and Celia Alvarez Munoz, a restoration architect, Brenda Levin, and historians George Sanchez and Albert Camarillo (Moreno's biographer), as well as union leaders, students and retirees. (Historian Vicki Ruiz, whose wonderful book *Cannery Women, Cannery Lives* had first drawn attention to Moreno, also worked on the team briefly.)

Following the workshop, Celia Alvarez Munoz created an artist's book, *If Walls Could Speak*, which intertwined public and private story lines in English and Spanish, beginning: "If walls could speak, these walls would tell/ in sounds of human voices, music, and machines/ of the early tremors of the City of Angels." And on the same three pages, she wrote, "As a young child, I learned my mother had two families./ One with my grandmother, my aunt, and I./ The other at la fabrica, the factory." The end papers were union logos, and so was the conclusion. A typical spread included historic images of Rose Pesotta with her arm around a worker, and another worker stitching a banner reading, "Win the war", or Josefina Fierro de Bright organizing for El Congresso, and workers with linked arms. The small artist's book was distributed free to several thousand people, including union members, retirees, and students.[10]

At the same time, architect Brenda Levin proposed recreation of two traditional showcases in front of the Embassy Theatre to carry history text, as well as sculptural representations of the workers' sewing machines, spools, and hammers, while union logos were to be pressed into a new concrete sidewalk. In a storefront adjoining the sidewalk, the faculty hoped to open the "Luisa Moreno reading room" for students interested in social history. It was a disappointment to us all that, although the permanent art was fully funded, plans by the owners, the University of Southern California, to sell the building, prevented installation. Then the January 1994 earthquake hit the building so hard it had to be evacuated, so perhaps another site for a permanent commemoration is preferable.

Today, I and many of the people who worked with me in Los Angeles continue our work in other cities, but the work in Los Angeles goes on too. In Little Tokyo, a University of California at Los Angeles student, Susan Sztaray, working with me and The Power of Place, helped to plan a project for a public art sidewalk wrapping the First Street National Register Historic District. Sztaray wanted to recall the scale of small, traditional Japanese-American businesses flourishing there before the internment. The Los Angeles Community Redevelopment Agency has taken up this plan, and now runs a public art competition. Sheila Levrant de Bretteville, who designed the Biddy Mason wall, is the artist along with Sonya Ishii and Nobuho Nagasawa. Construction should have begun in 1995. Los Angeles will then have three cultural heritage projects – one African-American, one Latina, one Japanese-American – in three very different kinds of settings – ranging from a lost homestead, to a reinterpreted theatre building, to a National Register district – that demonstrate some of the new ways artists can work with preservationists and historians on parts of the public landscape.

The Biddy Mason, Embassy, and Flowergrowers/Little Tokyo Projects are all located in the area of our 1984 walking tour, close to the center of Los Angeles' downtown, set near the high-rise buildings of the Bunker Hill redevelopment area. They challenged the idea that only massive commercial development can provide a downtown with an identity, because The Power of Place presented an alternative account of the process of building a city, emphasizing the importance of people of diverse backgrounds and work – both paid work and work in family life – to urban survival. In a city where half the residents are women and over sixty percent are people of colour, these small projects struck a responsive chord.

The projects straddled several worlds, academic urban history and public history, urban planning, public art, preservation, and urban design. Every project had a multi-ethnic, multi-disciplinary team. Teamwork is difficult, especially across disciplines. But there are rewards. First, public space has a resonance for local history no other medium can match. Second, locking women's history into the design of the city exploits a relatively inexpensive medium. Over time, the exposure can be as great as a film or an exhibit. Third, as projects like Biddy Mason and Embassy show, when you have *one* significant public place, there is less pressure to divide history into academic categories (such as women, ethnic, or labour) that often trivialize and marginalize urban stories. For the university there are also benefits. A fieldwork program like The Power of Place connected students to urban history, and at the same time gave them the chance to work as interns on local projects with diverse organizations as co-sponsors.

For the city itself there are also rewards. Putting working people's history into downtown expands the potential audience for all urban preservation and public art. The recognition of important cultural heritage in diverse working people's neighbourhoods can support other kinds of community organizing – including neighbourhood economic development and affordable housing. Teachers can bring classes to the sites to launch educational projects on women's history. Last, but not least, public space dedicated to women's history and ethnic history, especially to projects focused on working women of colour, claims political territory in tangible ways. People can meet in these historic places and work together on new issues, with the collective knowledge of earlier struggles. And this fosters a public realm where, at last, women are free to be ourselves and to see ourselves as strong and wise people, because we have represented ourselves that way.

Across the United States today, I see many successful preservation projects focusing on women's history, such as the Seneca Falls Women's Rights National Park. And at the same time, promoting ethnic diversity in preservation has become a goal many organizations, including the National Trust, share, so projects involving African-American, Asian-American, and Latino history are receiving higher funding and visibility. Artists, too are working on many more public projects exploring spatial history. The 1990s offer many opportunities for reclaiming women's history and ethnic history in the urban landscape. Today there are hundreds of architects, landscape architects, and artists, as well as historians and preservationists, who enjoy these challenges. Finding the stories of diverse working women, and inscribing them in public space, is one small part of creating a public, political culture that can carry the North American city into the next century.

Notes

1. John Brinckerhoff Jackson, *Discovering the Vernacular Landscape* (New Haven: Yale University Press, 1984), xii.
2. Gail Dubrow made this count.
3. A pioneering work with a multiethnic approach is Carey McWilliams, *Southern California: An Island on the Land* (Salt Lake City, Utah: Peregrine Smith Books, 1983). This is a classic from the 1940s. Other recent overall treatments include Robert Fogelson, *The Fragmented Metropolis: Los Angeles 1850-1930* (Cambridge: Harvard University Press, 1967); Scott Bottles, *Los Angeles and the Automobile: The Making of the Modern City* (Berkeley: University of California Press, 1987); and Mike Davis, *City Of Quartz: Excavating the Future in Los Angeles* (New York: Verso, 1990). For a few examples of ethnic studies: Rudolfo Acuna, *A Community Under Siege: A Chronicle of Chicanos East of the Los Angeles River 1945-1975* (Los Angeles: UCLA Chicano Studies Center, 1980); Richard Griswold del Castillo, *The Los Angeles Barrio, 1850-1890: A Social History* (Berkeley: University of California Press, 1979); Ricardo Romo, *East Los Angeles: History of a Barrio* (Austin: University of Texas Press, 1983); Lonnie G. Bunch III, *Black Angelenos* (Los Angeles: California African-American Museum, 1989); and Noritaka Yagasaki, "Ethnic Cooperativism and Immigrant Agriculture: A Study of Japanese Floriculture and Truck Farming in California" (Ph.D. diss., Department of Geography, University of California, Berkeley, 1982).
4. Dolores Hayden, Gail Dubrow, and Carolyn Flynn, *Los Angeles: The Power of Place* (Los Angeles: The Power of Place, 1985).
5. State of California, Department of Parks and Recreation, *Five Views: An Ethnic Sites Survey for California* (Sacramento: Department of Parks and Recreation, 1988).

6. Dolores Hayden, "Biddy Mason's Los Angeles, 1856-1891", *California History*, 68 (Fall 1989), 86-99, carries the full documentation.
7. Susan E. King, *HOME/stead* (Los Angeles: Paradise Press, 1987).
8. Hayden, "Biddy Mason".
9. Mario Garcia, *Mexican Americans* (New Haven: Yale University Press).
10. Celia Alvarez Munoz, *If Walls Could Speak / Si Las Paredes Hablaran* (Arlington, Texas: Enlightenment Press, 1991).

Biddy Mason, Time and Place by Sheila Levrant de Bretteville with The Power of Place, located at 333 Spring Street, Los Angeles / *Biddy Mason, Time and Place*, par Sheila Levrant de Bretteville, du groupe The Power of Place, situé au 333, rue Spring, Los Angeles. (Photo: Jim Simmons/Annette del Zoppo for/pour The Power of Place.)

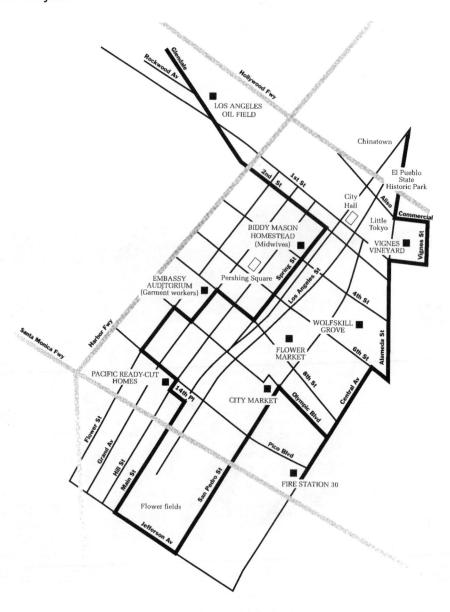

The Power of Place, itinerary of historic sites in downtown Los Angeles / parcours de lieux historiques dans le centre-ville de Los Angeles. From / tiré de Dolores Hayden, *The Power of Place: Urban Landscapes as Public History* (Cambridge, MA: The MIT Press, 1995). (Photo: Jim Simmons/Annette del Zoppo for/pour The Power of Place.)

BARBARA WYSS[1]

All My Relations:
Perspectives on Commemorating Aboriginal Women

Abstract

A definite lack of representations of Aboriginal women became evident through a review of some literature describing Parks Canada's Historic Sites and Monuments. The writer verified this perception while attending workshops sponsored by the Historic Sites and Monuments Board of Canada. This paper will provide perspectives on how Aboriginal women participated in their changing environment as Canada evolved as a nation; therefore the Aboriginal women's role should be part of any commemorative monument or site depicting the history of Canada.

Tous mes liens : perspectives sur la commémoration des femmes autochtones – Résumé

L'examen de certains documents décrivant les lieux et monuments historiques de Parcs Canada démontre nettement que les femmes autochtones y sont sous-représentées. L'auteure a confirmé cette constatation en assistant à des ateliers tenus sous les auspices de la Commission des lieux et monuments historiques du Canada. Sa communication montre comment les femmes autochtones ont agi sur leur milieu au moment où le Canada prenait forme en tant que pays. Leur rôle devrait par conséquent être souligné dans tout monument ou lieu rappelant l'histoire du Canada.

Untitled

i am the fire of time.
the endless pillar
that has withstood death.
the support of an invincible nation.
i am the stars that have guided
lost men.
i am the mother of ten thousand
dying children.
i am the fire of time.
i am an indian woman![2]

Introduction

The title, "All My Relations", refers to the belief held by Aboriginal people that everything in the universe has its own spirit. When Europeans arrived in North America, Aboriginal men and women offered supplications to the sun, the moon, a rock, a tree, or a bird, and called upon unseen forces to help with the processes of germination, birth, and healing. In this world view everything is interrelated and interdependent. Aboriginal women are very spiritual people who are keepers of the language of "all my relations".

Canada as a location in the world existed long before the arrival of Europeans and was populated by Aboriginal nations from coast to coast to coast. Although the French and British contributed much to the development of this country during the last three hundred years, the Aboriginal peoples have lived, loved, worked, hunted, fought, and died in Canada from time immemorial.

The literature circulated by the Historic Sites and Monuments Board in a recent workshop I attended reveals a definite lack of recognition of the role of Aboriginal women in the history of the area of the world we presently call Canada. Since Aboriginal women were, and are, major participants in the evolution of Canada as a nation, their story should be told in our historic sites.

What I propose to do here is review the current commemorative sites in Canada to determine the extent to which Aboriginal women are represented. Since the United States is often in the forefront of commemorative efforts, I will also examine the extent to which Aboriginal women are honoured in the American parks system as a basis for comparison. I will conclude with a survey of the role of Aboriginal women in the history of Canada and suggestions that might help the Historic Sites and Monuments Board in its future deliberations with respect to Aboriginal women.

The Context

The Historic Sites and Monuments Board was created in 1919 by Order-in-Council to advise the Parks Branch of the Department of the Interior on the commemoration of historic sites. In 1953, the present *Historic Sites and Monuments Act* was passed which outlined the process by which the Board advises the Minister responsible on matters relating to Canadian heritage. The Board makes recommendations to the Minister on people, places, and events deemed worthy of national recognition. It also advises on the level of recognition. A site can be marked by a plaque or monument, or can be developed into a national historic park/site.

The early years of the Board's activities reveal great enthusiasm for military sites and the fur trade. After the Massey Commission reported in 1951, the Board broadened its interests to include themes in economic and social history. More recently, the Board has made an effort to consider Aboriginal people, women, and cultural communities. Nevertheless, one has only to visit the 130 National Historic Parks spread across Canada to see the emphasis that is still placed on military commemorations. Although a few Aboriginal sites have been developed, no site can be said to represent Aboriginal women. Moreover, a review of the list of 524 people commemorated by the Board in the form of a plaque reveals only one Aboriginal woman. In 1969 the Board decided that Aboriginal languages should be used in the commemoration of Aboriginal sites with the result that some thirty plaques now include Native languages.

The United States has only a slightly better record on the commemoration of Aboriginal women. The National Registry lists seven Aboriginal women, and there is one National Historic Landmark and one Historical American Building which commemorate Aboriginal women. The publication *Notable American Women, 1607-1950: a biographical listing* includes at least fifteen Aboriginal women while some twenty-five Aboriginal women have been commemorated by family members, women's organizations, and a variety of other groups. A surprising fact is that an Indian woman, Sacajawea, is the most commemorated woman in the United States. At least seven states have statues and plaques dedicated to her. Born in 1786, Sacajawea was a Shoshoni Indian known for her role as guide and interpreter for the Lewis and Clark expedition to the Pacific in 1805-06. Her role in helping to forge a new frontier in American history has finally been recognized, but only after years of neglect.

Other Aboriginal women who have received recognition in the United States include Mary Musgrove (Bosumworth) who helped to cement relations between Native and newcomer. St Catherine's Island was designated a National Historic Landmark commemorating her success in claiming that piece of land for services rendered. Sometimes women are remembered because they are the last of their kind. Tragic as it may be, it is still important that their experience be recognized. Neither Canada nor the United States officially recognizes "Indian survivors" but they are not completely forgotten. Molly Locket, wife of Chief Sabattus, acted as midwife for the settlers in the area of present-day Maine in the eighteenth century. Her gravestone serves as a monument to her useful life. Another example of this kind is Juana Maria, who died in 1853. A plaque commemorating her life is located on a cemetery wall at the Santa Barbara Mission in California. It states that she was "an Indian woman the padres named Juana Maria...[who] lived for eighteen years without human companionship on the rocky, isolated island of San Nicholas... about sixty-five mile from the mainland."[3] Although most Aboriginal women are remembered in the United

States for their roles as sole survivors, warriors, guides and negotiators, a few reach "star" status as rulers. For instance, in the eighteenth century, the Hawaiian islands were ruled by an indigenous Hawaiian Monarchy that included women in its ranks. Given their prominent status, it is not surprising that a number of Hawaiian women have been commemorated for their roles as reformers, women's rights activists, and rulers.

One of the reasons that Aboriginal women are so neglected in North American commemorative programs is that there is great difficulty in finding written historical sources. As has been noted by Gretchen M. Bataille and Laurie Lisa, "The variety of gender roles and degrees of power experienced by Native American women is not easily represented in the pre-contact period or early colonial periods...because so little is know about individual lives."[4] Although it was clear that "in agricultural societies such as the Iroquois and Navajo, women were accorded more status than they received in the primarily hunting societies of the Great Plains,"[5] there were few "people, places or events" that can be singled out for commemoration.

In recent years more credibility has been accorded to oral traditions and archaeological evidence with the result that Aboriginal history has advanced considerably. As well, developments in women's history enable us to see more clearly the roles of women in past societies. It is now obvious that during the pre-contact period, the traditional roles of Aboriginal women varied with their particular cultural practices, geography and environment. Although men and women performed different tasks in Aboriginal communities, women, sometimes out of necessity, but, other times by choice or opportunity, exercised non-traditional roles as well. In the pre-industrial contact period Aboriginal women emerge as teachers, guides, diplomats, and captives. At all times, they were essential to the achievements of many prominent male leaders, both Aboriginal and non-Aboriginal. Unfortunately, these women "behind every great man" receive little or no attention in our texts and sites.

Scholarship has advanced to the point where it is no longer acceptable to justify the absence of Aboriginal women from our historic sites. Clearly, new historical criteria must be developed to permit the commemoration of the traditional roles of Aboriginal women prior to contact with Europeans as well as their roles in maintaining and adapting traditional Aboriginal values through the last five hundred years of resistance and renewal. There is also much more work to be done on the history of Aboriginal women and here too the Historic Sites and Monuments Board with its staff of historians can play an important role.

What follows is an outline of some of the major themes in the history of Aboriginal women in North America that might well serve the Historic Sites and

Monuments Board in making its recommendations to the Minister of Canadian Heritage. This survey does not dwell on the negative aspects of colonization on Native American women's traditional roles, but rather attempts to provide a re-evaluation of those roles in the context of considering Aboriginal women for commemoration.

Aboriginal Women's Spirituality

A common thread in Aboriginal history that has endured through pre-contact times to the present is spirituality. Native people who practice spirituality are sometimes called traditionalists. Although traditional rituals differ from one group to another, the essence of spiritual practices is clearly explained in Julian Rice's discussion of the Lakota traditionalists who believe in giving prominence to living a "full life on earth through ritual disciplines."[6] They believe that rituals "kept the people focused on the qualities of mind and body that made survival possible."[7] Through ritual the traditionalists maintain connection with all their relations. The element of fear provokes the conscience when "interfering with supernatural action by neglecting or improperly performing rituals."[8] This fear is accepted as a necessity in the evolution of the power to renew, give strength, or perpetuate growth. Even when hunting game, traditionalists are careful to thank the grandfathers for their gift of sustenance. It is equally important to leave "part of the individual carcass...as an offering to the generalized spirit of that species to show appreciation and to establish kinship, so that the particular species would agree to die for them."[9] In the Lakota tradition, the community is women-centred:

> [A]ll material aspects of the camp circle, apart from weapons and personal clothing 'belong' to the woman. But this is not to be equated with the Euro-American sense of possessions. The camp circle is under the influence of the feminine spirit and when the men are at home that spirit rules them there...the ceremonies celebrate the feminine in all human beings.[10]

Before contact with Europeans, traditional roles of Aboriginal women centred on the holistic well-being of their particular society. In the European sense, there is no historical record. However, the traditional and spiritual feminine nature is transmitted down through the oral tradition in Aboriginal communities.

83

Fur Trade And Early Settlement, 1600-1850

Before the fur trade the indigenous peoples had established intertribal trade routes. But in the wake of a new bartering economy some Aboriginal women took on new roles. These roles included interpreters, guides, negotiators, providers, protectors, nourishers of fur traders, explorers, missionaries, and settlers. Traditional women's roles began to change as contact intensified. For instance, a woman's role in traditional society included producing clothing and household items. However, with the introduction of European-made clothing this was no longer necessary. Her role now centred on processing furs for the fur market rather than for domestic use.

Such was the role of Madeleine Marcotte La Framboise [1780-1846]. Half French and half Ottawa Indian, she was held in high esteem by the garrison of Fort Mackinac (established by the French from Montréal) and its residents and other traders. She was raised in an Indian village and grew up unable to read or write. Yet she managed to converse in Ottawa and Chippewa dialects, and French and English. As an adult she taught herself to read and write French. Madeleine married Joseph La Framboise, a well-known French trader, and accompanied him on his fur-trading missions among the Indians. On one of his trips he was shot by an Indian, and Madeleine, after burying his body, continued his work. For fifteen years she wintered in the valley of La Grand Rivière buying furs, and returned to Mackinac Island for the summers. Madeleine was one of the most successful traders of her day. She was powerful enough to put some fear into the established fur companies, who were happy when she retired in 1821.[11]

Aboriginal women's traditional role also began to alter dramatically as various missionaries imposed Christian ideologies upon their communities. Aboriginal women struggled to preserve their languages, traditions, values, culture, status, and family unity. Not all Aboriginal women, of course, resisted Christianity.

In 1676, Kateri Tekakwitha, a twenty year old Algonquin, converted to Catholicism to the consternation of her relatives. Kateri's mother was Algonquin and her father, Mohawk. Kateri's life experience is one of surviving in times of great adversity. Her fascination with the precepts of Catholicism "manifested a spirit of great humility and charity [where upon she] . . . practiced continual mortification of the body – to show her love of Christ."[12] Kateri Tekakwitha's life story could be interpreted as one of experiencing joy and sorrow simultaneously. She chose chastity over a traditional marriage. Kateri chose Christianity over the traditional beliefs, values, and customs of her tribe. After threats on her life, because of her conversion, she fled from her birth place at Auriesville, New York, to St. Francis Xavier at Caughnawaga. In 1980, three hundred years after her death, Kateri "was the first North American Indian to be beatified by the Roman Catholic Church."[13]

The effect that colonization had on the relationship between the Aboriginal peoples and the land was one of forced separation. The colonists did not understand the attachment that Aboriginal people felt for their Mother Earth. "The [tie to the] land is [one of] the keys to the social, cultural and economic well being of Aboriginal people."[14] Other keys to the culture emphasize the importance of learning one's indigenous language and traditional history from the elders. Elders teach that our Aboriginal languages are unique to this continent – they live and die here. Elders are sometimes called the "Wisdomkeepers" because they guard the knowledge of the tribe or nation. Shawnaadithit is an example of such an educator.

Nancy is the Christian name for one of five Beothuk women captured by fur traders and taken to St. John's, Newfoundland. Her captivity began in 1823.[15] It is important to remember her by her Beothuk name, Shawnaadithit, because giving or receiving an Indian name is a very meaningful ritual in Aboriginal culture. Traditionally, an Indian name can only be inherited during a naming ceremony and its importance is to carry on the memories and traditions of the ancestors. So, a person receiving such an honour is also reminded to take care for the responsibilities (being an educator, provider, shaman, basketmaker) that comes with that name. Sometime after she was captured, "... [S]he helped Newfoundland scholar William Epps Cormack develop a Beothuk vocabulary, and she drew pictures representing the history and culture of her people as she knew them."[16]

Robert Wells, author of *Native American Resurgence and Renewal*, found that empirical research focusing on the status and sex roles of American Indian women is very limited. He also contends that the historical research that is available is flawed with inconsistencies and contains incomplete information. An immense value was placed on traditional female roles.

> Biologically, they valued being mothers and raising healthy families; spiritually, they were considered extensions of the Spirit Mother and keys to the continuation of their people...[17]

Wells conscientiously focuses on the "internal" activities of Indian women as non-Indian observers often overestimated male power within the tribe and they have little experience with women's spheres of power and activity. North American Aboriginal women share common ground with all their sisters. Women from the Cherokee Nation to the Navajo, the Haida Nation, the Plains Cree, the Métis, the Inuit and the Iroquois all enjoyed their spheres of autonomy.

> Realizing the importance of private power is critical to understanding Indian cultural systems because – in general – Indian women exercised almost complete control over the home, the children, and belongings [coming] inside the home.[18]

Wells states that, generally, the depictions of Aboriginal women "have been heavily influenced by stereotypical images, myths, and fantasies which limit Indian women to dichotomous princess/squaw roles."[19] It is therefore important to break through these stereotypical images perpetuated through these "male-centred biases of traditional social science research."[20] Just the name "Pocahontas" conjures up the popular myth of how a white man named John Smith, captured by Indians, was spared his life because of her intervention. Her story is important because it shows how these princess "images came to represent the discovery and settlement of the new world constrained by definitions of the old."[21] One Cherokee historical revisionist has put an Aboriginal twist on the life experience of Pocahontas:

> The European version would have you believe that Pocahontas saved him from her savage relatives, went to England and became English herself .... In the Indian version, Pocahontas, of course, was not turning English herself, rather she was trying to turn John Smith into an Indian. The ceremony he underwent was not his "salvation" from her savage relations, but an adoption ceremony in which he would be made a child of this New World. In the changes of that story that every school child knows, we hear the version that has replaced the Indian version.[22]

Rayna Green criticizes the European version of the Pocahontas story as "an intolerable metaphor for the Indian-White experience."[23] But her point is well taken if "we understood that the real version was to turn these [European] people who came to [America] into Indians and put them in a relationship of obligation, blood and history that we could live with now."[24] No matter which version is believed, Pocahontas is commemorated by the Memorial Window dedicated to her at St. John's Church in Hampton, Virginia. A bronze bust was also unveiled in 1965 at Jamestown, Virginia, gifted by the National Society of Colonial Dames.

Stemming from the missionary period in New France, but sounding a little contemporary was the charge by the men of a Montagnais band in 1640, "It is you women who are the cause of all our misfortunes." Frustrated and angry, the men blamed women's commitment to traditional beliefs as the stumbling block to the community's well-being.[25]

The gender conflict created by the women's refusal to accept European values is another theme that is often overlooked or misinterpreted in discussions of Aboriginal history.

Keeping a focus on maintaining the traditional way of life produced hardships for many Aboriginal women and men. However, Aboriginal women in early colonial times had a sense of place and belonging. David Thompson, working for the Hudson's Bay Company during the fur trade "was convinced that females were the stauncher traditionalists ... overall women expressed far more concern with ritual practices than did younger men."[26] An Ottawa woman called Net-no-kwa, was a powerful figure who lived among the Ojibwa. She belonged to a medicine society that practiced curing rituals. She also interpreted dreams and visions which "provided her and other women with an avenue both for communicating with supernaturals and for enhancing their authority."[27] Net-no-kwa was the foster mother of "captive John Tanner, whom she adopted in the 1780s as a replacement for her own dead son."[28] He said of her, "I have never met with an Indian, either man or woman, ... who had so much authority with the traders or the Indians...."[29] More research is required to flesh out her traditional role as a practitioner of medical knowledge, a shaman, a trader and foster mother.

Another medicine woman to emerge from the early the 1740s is a Mohawk woman named Coocoochee. She "was born into the Bear Clan at an Indian village southeast of Montreal but lived most of her life amongst Chief Blue Jacket's Shawnees" in Ohio. Coocoochee became adept as a healer and became "knowledgeable in the preparation of herbal medicines. She was also esteemed as a person of vision and wisdom and was often consulted before the start of a military expedition."[30] It was her "ability to successfully maintain her family and traditional way of life despite periodic removals and the ever-present threat of frontier warfare [that gives] Coocoochee's life a special significance within the annals of colonial and frontier Euro-Indian relations."[31]

Molly Brant [1770] is also a suitable candidate for commemoration. Molly was an Iroquois woman who had a traditional Indian marriage to Sir William Johnson, then Indian Superintendent. But on another level, she was "the hostess of his estate", his "mistress", the mother of eight children, and "political consort".[32]

> In part her power flowed from the traditionally influential position of women in the matrilineal society of the Iroquois, but Molly Brant parleyed her opportunities to the highest advantage.[33]

Molly helped to provision the Loyalists forces and kept them informed about rebel activities. She received a house and a pension for her efforts in helping the British during the American Revolutionary war.

Another notable woman is Amelia Conolly Douglas. As wife of Sir James Douglas, she became the First Lady of British Columbia. She was half Carrier and part Irish. Amelia was born around 1808. At sixteen years of age, she married James in the custom of the country.[34] A short time after their marriage, Douglas was attacked at Fort St. James. Through the courageous efforts of Amelia, he was spared his life. Amelia and James were the parents of thirteen children.

Industrialization

The industrialization of Canada created a cultural upheaval for the indigenous population. Aboriginal people were still reeling from the effects of being decimated by diseases, epidemics, environmental pollution, and alcoholism. They also suffered the breakdown of family traditions. An elder from British Columbia once commented that at this time in our existence, the Aboriginal peoples of Canada are entitled to declare a victory. We have survived.

Some of us have also successfully adapted. Christine Quintasket, a Salishan writer was noted for being the first Native American woman to publish a novel. Her pen name was "Mourning Dove". Christine was born around 1885 and lived much of her life among the Kootenay at Tobacco Plains, British Columbia She became a teacher on the Inkameep reserve at Oliver, British Columbia To achieve her goals she endured great difficulty in achieving a formal education. Her passion to learn made her sit at twenty-four years of age in a grade three classroom. She then succeeded in a business school education and went on to teach and write. Christine enjoyed her public image as a regional celebrity. But her public image did not reveal the harsh life she led. "...[A]fter backbreaking days in the orchards and fields, she would write for most of the night in a tent or cabin."[35] As a Salish woman, Mourning Dove, is notable for reaching for her dreams of becoming a writer and teacher.

Mary Capilano was another very industrious Salishan woman. "Three times a week she paddled across [Burrard] Inlet in her old dugout canoe with three hundred pounds ... [of produce and clams] to sell to the Hotel Vancouver." They paid her five cents a pound. Mary was the wife of Chief Joe Capilano, befriended by the Mohawk woman poet E. Pauline Johnson, and was a descendant from a very important family.[36] In 1913, Mary Capilano, " ... did a very unusual thing for an Indian woman – she gave a big Potlatch..."[37] in Stanley Park, Vancouver, that attracted 2000 people. Potlatch ceremonies were held upon occasion of deaths, marriages, births, divorces, naming ceremonies, and status changes. The event was also used to establish fishing territories and hunting rights, and to reaffirm the history of territorial boundaries. It was also a time to preserve connections with families, clans, and intertribal neighbours. The gift giving, for the Capilano family, was so extravagant that it entailed three days of giving away "lots of money and blankets." This event is all the more amazing because in 1884 the government banned the potlatch. Mary Capilano could have had all of her potlatch wealth confiscated, been fined, or sent to prison.

Madeleine, as she was known, was the Squamish wife of the infamous "Gassy Jack" Deighton, an early Vancouver pioneer. Madeleine is to be remembered not so much for marrying Gassy Jack, as for her determination to preserve her culture from the devastating effects of "whiskey" sold at Gassy Jack's Inn. Unable to endure the atmosphere at the Inn, Madeleine decided to leave Gassy Jack. It is said that he gave her a letter saying that he would provide for her for life, but upon marrying another man, this letter was to be destroyed. Madeleine remained in the background, as was expected of the women of the day.

Cedar Basket Making

Basketry has been part of Aboriginal women's traditional roles for over three thousand years. In British Columbia, the life of a cedar basket begins with the gathering and preparing of the materials. A cedar tree is selected and tobacco is offered thanking the tree, and all our relations, for its gifts. Cedar roots are then dug up, cleaned, split, and bundled for storage. Intricacies of basket making are bound up in the Aboriginal belief that they are a part of nature, and nature is a part of Aboriginal people. The greatest period of productivity in basket making, and the collecting of it, occurred in the late 1800s and continued into the early 1900s.[38]

Basket making is found in many Aboriginal cultures around the world. Coastal Salish women enjoyed a special knowledge of the cedar trees and sought to use its many applications in their daily lives. The art of cedar root basketry takes much patience, strength and stamina. Eva May Nahanee, for example, learned from her grandmother how to make baskets when she was ten years old. In her village, around the 1920s, the only lighting available was by coal oil lamp.

Conclusion

The women portrayed in this presentation deserve commemoration for maintaining their traditional roles and preserving the integrity of their culture and spirituality. The research and literature review conducted for this paper has been hampered by the limited information on Aboriginal female historical figures. A recommendation is that research funds be made available to document the historical contributions of those Aboriginal women who remain invisible and/or inaudible.

Many external factors have affected the lives of Aboriginal women. As stated above, whether by choice or design, these women endured and survived in times of adversity. It is hoped that Parks Canada will recognize that Aboriginal women have a vital history and a vibrant present.

All My Relations!

Notes

1. I would like to extend special thanks to my assistant, Rose Nahanee, for her help in researching this paper and to Christine Edington, for her editorial assistance.
2. Jane B. Katz, *I Am the Fire of Time: The Voices of Native American Women* (New York: E.P. Dutton, 1977).
3. These women are mentioned in Marion Tinling, *Women Remembered: A Guide to Landmarks of Women's History in the United States* (New York: Greenwood Press, 1986), p. 20, 625.
4. Gretchen M. Bataille and Laurie Lisa (eds.), *Native American Women: A Biographical Dictionary* (New York: Garland, 1993) p. xiii.
5. *Ibid.*
6. Julian Rice, *Black Elk's Story: Distinguishing Lakota Purposes* (Albuquerque: University of New Mexico Press, 1993) p. 65.
7. *Ibid.*, p. 65.
8. *Ibid.*, p. 65.
9. *Ibid.*, p. 141.
10. *Ibid.*, p. 141.
11. Tingling, p. 529.
12. Bataille and Lisa, p. 256.
13. *Ibid.*
14. Hugh and Karmel McCullum, *This Land is Not for Sale* (Toronto: Anglican Book Centre, 1975) p. 205.
15. Margaret Conrad, *et al.*, *History of the Canadian Peoples: Beginnings to 1867* (Toronto: Copp, Clark, Pitman Ltd., 1993) p. 318.
16. *Ibid.*
17. Robert N. Wells Jr., *Native American Resurgence and Renewal* (Metuchen, NJ: Scare Crow Press Inc., 1994) p. 466.
18. *Ibid.* p. 471.
19. *Ibid.* p. 465.

20. *Ibid.* p. 466.
21. Gary Farmer (ed.), *The Runner: Native magazine for communicative arts*, Vol. 1, No. 3 (Summer, 1994) p. 9.
22. *Ibid.*
23. *Ibid.*
24. *Ibid.*
25. Carol Devens, *Countering Colonization* (Los Angeles: University of California Press, 1992), p. 7.
26. Edward T. James *et al.*, *Notable American Women, 1607-1950* (Connecticut: Radcliffe College, 1971) p. 37.
27. *Ibid.* p. 42.
28. *Ibid.* p. 40.
29. *Ibid.*
30. *Ibid.* p. 37.
31. *Ibid.* p. 61.
32. *Ibid.* p. 36.
33. *Ibid.*
34. Robert Hamilton Coats and R.E. Gosnell, "Sir James Douglas", *The Makers of Canada* (Toronto: Morang & Co. Limited, 1908), p. 103.
35. Jay Miller (ed.), *Mourning Dove: A Salishan Autobiography* (Lincoln and London: University of Nebraska Press, 1990).
36. Mildred Valley Thornton, *Indian Lives and Legends* (Vancouver: Mitchell Press Ltd., 1966), p. 121.
37. *Ibid.*, p. 121.
38. Joan Megan Jones, *Western Indian Basketry* (Surrey: Hancock House Publishers Ltd., 1989), p. 4.

Portrait of Mary March or Desmasduit (ca. 1796-1820), aunt of Shawnaadithit. Portraits thought to have been of Shawnaadithit have since been proven to be copies of the original portrait painted by Lady Hamilton of Desmasduit, one of the five Beothuk women captured by the British. / Portrait de Mary March, ou Desmasduit (v. 1796-1820), tante de Shawnaadithit. On a établi que les portraits présumés de cette dernière étaient des copies du portrait original de Desmasduit, une des cinq femmes capturées par les Britanniques, peint par lady Hamilton. (Photo: National Archives / Archives nationales, C-87698; Artist/artiste: Lady Henrietta Martha Hamilton (1780-1857), 1819)

Mary Capilano – Lay-hu-lutte (1857-1940), wife of Chief Capilano Joe / femme du chef Joe Capilano. (Photo: City of Vancouver Archives / Archives de la Ville de Vancouver, P-430 ; 1939)

Madeleine or/ou Qwa-halia, second wife of Capt. John Deighton of Granville. She died 1948 / deuxième femme du capitaine John Deighton, de Granville. Elle est décédée en 1948. (Photo: Vancouver City Archives / Archives de la Ville de Vancouver, P-786; 1945)

Representation of / Portrait de Kateri Tekakwitha (1656-1680). (Photo: National Archives / Archives nationales, C-003313)

HARVEY A. McCUE

Native Culture and the Recording of History

Abstract
The history of Canada remains incomplete as long as the history of the Indians and Inuit is minimized or ignored by historians. Our identity as Canadians depends on how successful we are at recording our historical past including events and places which occurred well before Cartier, Cabot, and the inhabitants at L'Anse aux Meadows.

Les cultures autochtones et la consignation de l'histoire – Résumé
L'histoire du Canada restera incomplète tant que les historiens minimiseront ou écarteront celle des Indiens et des Inuit. Notre identité en tant que Canadiens dépend de la façon dont nous réussirons à consigner notre passé, y compris l'histoire de lieux et d'événements bien antérieurs à Cartier, à Cabot et aux habitants de L'Anse aux Meadows.

Native cultures around the world have recorded their histories by using a variety of techniques. Oral traditions, which include stories, legends, myths, and the simple transfer from one generation to the next of the significant events of the past by word of mouth are the most widespread. Mnemonic devices such as pictographs and petroglyphs, carvings, paintings, and wampum belts have also served to enable North American cultures to retain critical or important historical occasions within their social groups and societies.

I am most familiar with oral traditions. In my community and family, our history is handed down from one generation to the next in stories and memories kept alive through their retelling. Also, our reserve sustains a reservoir of legends and stories which help to reinforce and ground our values and spirituality. They also offer instruction and guidance based on traditional Ojibway knowledge to each new generation.

I had the good fortune to spend five years on the shores of James Bay in Northern Québec. During this residency, Cree friends offered me numerous opportunities to travel with them in their traditional territories, either on the coast or inland.

I recall travelling with different families along a 300 mile gravel highway which ran more or less parallel to the Grande Rivère, "Chisasibi" in Cree. Occasionally, the highway and river would converge and at certain sites where convergence occurred, people would tell me the story that accompanied that particular spot in the river.

I remember one site was known as the place where so-and-so smoked his last bit of tobacco (this was a well-known story which had been handed down in the village through six generations, at least, as twelve days remained between the spot and the coast; twelve long, hard days without tobacco!).

Another site marked the area where a woman lost her husband in the rapids. Or another, a site near the large flat rock where a giant wind (a tornado, probably) flattened the trees.

To countless generations of Cree, the river, which for hundreds of years, possibly thousands, continues to be a critical element in their lives, is more than a waterway, or a tumbling mass of giant rapids and waterfalls, or a constant source of fish and waterfowl. It is a vibrant, living element – in the Cree language it is an animate being. Cree history flows through it and along its banks. Cultural references abound as well.

I remember an earlier visit to Fort George, at the mouth of Grande Rivère, some twelve years before my five-year residency. Fort George, the historic village site of the Fort George Cree as they were known then, was situated on an island in the mouth of the Grande Rivère. It ceased to exist in 1979 when the residents relocated to the present village of Chisasibi, some two to three miles upstream from the island. The creation of a huge reservoir, really a large inland lake, some ninety miles further upstream as a result of the massive James Bay Hydro-Québec development led to an accelerated flow of water in the river which threatened the stability of Fort George Island, thereby forcing the relocation.

During that earlier visit I accompanied several families in their canoes to some of the small islands which lay some three to four miles off-shore for a Cree picnic. Before setting out for the half-hour or so trip out into the bay, the pilots of the four freighter canoes made their way up river about a quarter mile or so. At a spot marked by a huge gigantic rock, the four canoes stopped and everyone filled containers with fresh water from the river for drinking and for making tea, and to offer a gift to the Cree spirits of the river and the bay who, according to Cree history, caused the great rock to relocate to its present site as a result of a conflict with some other powerful entities. I am certain many other similar cultural sites exist throughout the Cree territory and environment.

These are several small and, perhaps to some, insignificant examples among many, many others which resonate throughout Aboriginal cultures in

Canada. Some are, indeed, very localized but countless others speak of events and occasions of vital importance, not to just a few, but to an entire nation.

The Cree of Northern Québec, some 350 years after recorded interaction with the old world, still maintain a rich and vibrant oral history which imbues their land and environment with distinctive life, vitality, and meaning. In this regard, the Cree are not unique among Indian and Inuit in Canada. The Mi'kmaq in Nova Scotia nurture many practices and beliefs similar to the Northern Cree.

Canadians, however, have not benefited from these histories nor are most Canadians aware of them. And the nation, as a whole, has lost or is losing quickly, with each passing generation, important historical details of Canadian Aboriginal people. More importantly, Canadians with some, but few, exceptions have yet to acquire the Aboriginal sensitivity to the connection between history and the land.

If we as a nation are to write, preserve, and teach a history which informs us, and others beyond, who we are and how we got here, then this history must include the distant as well as the recent past of this land and its people.

I referred earlier to the Cree practice of identifying sites or parts of the natural landscape with stories or events – local histories – which imbued the land with life and at the same time connected history to the one solid constant of our existence – the land.

If you will bear with me while I continue this idiosyncratic presentation, I would like to illustrate the next point with another personal observation.

One of my favourite pastimes is wilderness river canoeing, preferably on rivers which provide ample opportunities for navigating whitewater. Of the many aspects I appreciate about this activity – and some of you who share this interest may think I have missed too many vees when I say this – are the portages which inevitably appear on the banks of white water rivers.

Portages are something I hold dear and important. For when I am trudging along a portage, with either two large packs or an old town tripper above and on my shoulders, I embrace the knowledge and the history I am sharing with perhaps a thousand generations of travellers: ancient ancestors, courrier de bois, priests, voyageurs, and explorers whose feet, enclosed in moosehide or cowhide, have followed the very same trail for precisely the same reasons that I now travel it.

The exhilaration and connectedness with history one feels during such arduous journeys in my experience are seldom equalled elsewhere. Now, I am not suggesting or even hinting here that historical plaques should be erected along every portage trail – although some of you may gather from what I have expressed here that a small part of me would support such an action; however, the rest of me recoils at the thought of encountering such an object in an environment one seeks out to replace, however briefly, the urban landscape.

Rather, what this example attempts to illustrate is this: unlike Indian and Inuit societies which have valued and acquired meaning from this kind of historical detail, Canada, this modern nation, has been cut off from the rich minutiae on which our history, Canada's history, depends. The exhilaration which the land provokes and the visceral connection it provides with history are notably absent not only in our national history, but in how we teach it.

As a nation, we have yet to embrace fully the importance of an Aboriginal past, an Aboriginal history, if you will, to a national history. Nor have we embraced the importance of this history as a source of knowledge and possible instruction for survival on this great land.

I humbly suggest that the time for such an embrace is overdue. I humbly suggest that our history as a nation is incomplete without it. I humbly suggest that our identity as Canadians, our presence marked as it is and has been for aeons by this vast and magnificent geography demands nothing less.

Fort George, Québec: view from the landing, circa 1900 / vue du débarcadère, vers 1900. (Photo: National Archives, PA-135705, Jervois Arthur Newnhans collection, 1963-094 / Archives nationales, PA-135705, collection Jervois Arthur Newnhans, 1963-094)

Fort George, at the mouth of La Grande Rivière, Québec, ceased to exist in 1979. / Fort George, à l'embouchure de La Grande Rivière (Québec), n'existe plus depuis 1979. (Photo: HRS 911-1991)

Petroglyphs, Ontario Provincial Park, Peterborough, Ontario: situated on an outcrop of white marble on the Canadian shield, this site is one of the largest known concentrations of prehistoric rock carvings in Canada. They give evidence of the spiritual and intellectual life of the Algonkian Indians who carved them between A.D. 900-1400. This site is a sacred place; designated 1981. (Photo: Brian Morin, 1993)

Les pétroglyphes de Peterborough, dans le parc provincial Ontario, Peterborough (Ontario) : situés sur un affleurement de marbre blanc dans le Bouclier canadien, ces ouvrages constituent l'une des plus importantes concentrations de sculptures préhistoriques sur roc connues au Canada. Ils témoignent de la vie spirituelle et intellectuelle des Algonquiens, qui les ont sculptées entre les années 900 et 1400. Ce lieu est sacré. Il a été désigné en 1981. (Photo : Brian Morin, 1993)

MURIEL K. ROY

Les partenariats, base d'une commémoration efficace

Résumé

Cette communication examine le partenariat entre la collectivité acadienne et Parcs Canada relativement aux lieux historiques nationaux des Maritimes ayant un rapport étroit avec l'histoire du peuple acadien. Il s'agit de l'expérience du Comité consultatif acadien de Parcs Canada (région atlantique), créé en 1985.

La mise sur pied par Parcs Canada d'une structure officielle de consultation d'une collectivité sur les questions de son patrimoine et de ses lieux historiques était, nous a-t-on dit, une initiative pionnière. On décrit les conditions entourant la création du Comité, son mandat et son mode de fonctionnement. On retrace les principales étapes de son cheminement et on signale ses réalisations.

La mise en valeur et la promotion du patrimoine historique et culturel acadien, au cœur des préoccupations du Comité, ont suscité, dans un premier temps, des discussions parfois acerbes, voire des affrontements, quant aux moyens d'action. Avec le temps, les délibérations ont mûri et débouché sur une meilleure compréhension de part et d'autre et sur une saine collaboration dans le respect des besoins et des exigences de chacun. Le format tel qu'il se dégage aujourd'hui constitue, selon l'auteure, un modèle à prendre en considération pour les nouvelles structures de partenariat que veut établir le ministre du Patrimoine canadien.

En guise de conclusion, l'auteure propose quelques possibilités d'action à envisager pour enrichir davantage les rapports entre les gouvernements et les communautés dans des projets conjoints d'aménagement de lieux commémoratifs.

Partnership, Basis For Effective Commemoration – Abstract

In the context of the activity of the Parks Canada (Atlantic) Acadian Consultative Committee, created in 1985, this presentation examines the partnership between the Acadian community and Parks Canada with regard to the national historic sites in the Maritimes that are closely connected with the history of the Acadian people.

We were told that Parks Canada's establishment of a formal structure for consulting a community regarding issues pertaining to its heritage and historic sites was a pioneering initiative. This paper describes the conditions surrounding the Committee's creation, its mandate and its method of operation. It looks at the main steps it has taken along the way and points out its accomplishments.

Development and promotion of Acadian historical and cultural heritage, which are the Committee's focus, initially gave rise to discussions that were at times acerbic, and sometimes even to confrontations, regarding means of action. Over time, the deliberations matured, leading to better understanding and to healthy co-operation, in a context of respect for the needs and requirements of all. The author believes that today's format could serve as a model for the new partnership structures that the Minister of Canadian Heritage wants to develop.

By way of conclusion, the presentation proposes a few avenues for action with a view to further enhancing government-community relations in joint commemorative sites development projects.

Introduction

C'est avec plaisir et fierté que j'ai accepté de participer au symposium commémorant le 75ᵉ anniversaire de la création de la Commission des lieux et monuments historiques du Canada (CLMHC). Je remercie son président, le professeur Tom Symons, de son invitation et du privilège qui m'est accordé de partager ces quelques propos sur un partenariat qui s'est noué entre la collectivité acadienne et Parcs Canada, plus spécifiquement avec cette branche du service ministériel chargée de promouvoir le patrimoine historique canadien.

Le terme « partenariat », rapidement devenu presque un mot d'ordre dans le langage gouvernemental et d'affaires, n'a fait son entrée dans notre vocabulaire que tout récemment. En effet, ce n'est qu'à partir de 1991 qu'on trouve le mot « partenariat » au *Petit Robert*, qui le définit comme « une association d'entreprises, d'institutions en vue d'une action commune ».

C'est bien de partenariat, d'une action commune, que je vous entretiendrai ; un partenariat issu d'une expérience très concrète, d'un vécu qui s'étend sur les dix dernières années. Il s'agit des péripéties du Comité consultatif acadien de Parcs Canada en Atlantique, œuvrant en collaboration avec le secteur des lieux historiques de Parcs Canada.

D'abord, je vous ferai part des circonstances qui ont mené à la création du comité; je décrirai sommairement son mandat, sa composition et son fonctionnement. Mais je m'attarderai surtout aux réalisations de ce comité parmi lesquelles je sélectionnerai les plus probantes, afin d'illustrer toutes les possibilités qu'offre l'action concertée dans la poursuite d'un légitime objectif. Et pour terminer, je proposerai un nouveau défi à relever, pour célébrer davantage notre patrimoine et faire valoir le riche contenu de notre culture.

Les antécédents du partenariat

En mai 1983, à l'instigation de l'Acadien Yvon LeBlanc, architecte en résidence à la forteresse de Louisbourg, un comité *ad hoc*[1] est formé à l'Université de Moncton, sous l'égide de son Centre d'études acadiennes, pour examiner les rapports entretenus entre la section des lieux historiques de Parcs Canada et les groupes acadiens ayant la mission de promouvoir l'histoire acadienne. Monsieur LeBlanc, à la veille de quitter son poste pour la retraite, nous avait fait part de ses inquiétudes à l'égard du peu de communication entre ces deux parties et du besoin impératif d'une participation plus significative des instances acadiennes au développement de leurs lieux historiques.

Tout en reconnaissant la primauté des Autochtones au pays, faut-il rappeler que le peuplement européen en Amérique septentrionale s'est fait d'abord en Acadie par les colons venus de la France à la suite des explorations de Champlain, De Monts et Poutrincourt au début du XVIIe siècle; et qu'il n'est pas exagéré d'affirmer qu'aux Maritimes, au moins la moitié des principaux lieux historiques désignés d'importance nationale relèvent tout d'abord de cette présence française et acadienne comme en fait foi leur nom : Port-Royal, Fort Anne, Grand-Pré, Louisbourg, Port-la-Joye, Fort Beauséjour, Monument Lefebvre, Île Beaubears/Boishébert. D'où la nécessité d'une implication des Acadiens auprès de Parcs Canada dans ses travaux se rapportant aux lieux historiques frayés par leurs ancêtres.

Échanges ponctuels

Bien sûr, il y a eu à plusieurs occasions, des rapports ponctuels concernant les lieux historiques acadiens, entre le gouvernement du Canada et la société acadienne. Ceux-ci ont revêtu diverses formes, et certains remontent à un passé très lointain.

1. Entre autres, les pourparlers entre la Société nationale l'Assomption et le ministre fédéral Jean Lesage aboutissant au transfert du Parc de Grand-Pré au gouvernement canadien en 1956 ; puis, en 1961, les démarches qui ont précédé la désignation de Grand-Pré comme lieu historique national.

2. En 1978, Parcs Canada accordait au Centre d'études acadiennes un contrat pour la préparation d'une documentation en vue du montage d'un centre d'interprétation de la *Survivance du peuple acadien*. Le gouvernement canadien, à la recommandation de la Commission des lieux et monuments historiques du Canada, venait de désigner la survivance acadienne comme un fait

d'importance historique nationale précisant que la commémoration se ferait au moyen d'un centre d'interprétation. Fait à noter, les échanges entre les spécialistes de Parcs Canada, venus rencontrer ceux de l'Université de Moncton pour préciser les exigences documentaires du projet, ont dû se dérouler en anglais – aucun des participants fédéraux ne pouvant communiquer en français ! Enfin les textes rédigés dans le cadre de l'entente, colligés en recueil et publiés en versions française et anglaise, ont remporté un tel succès qu'une deuxième édition augmentée et mise à jour a paru en 1993, dix ans après l'originale. Cette dernière, intitulée l'*Acadie des Maritimes*, s'est méritée le prix France-Acadie 1994. La version anglaise verra le jour en 1995.

3. Une autre forme de collaboration sur les questions du patrimoine se fait par la présence d'Acadiens aux instances décisionnelles. Il y a eu, depuis une vingtaine d'années, la nomination, à la Commission des lieux et monuments historiques du Canada, de deux Acadiens, d'abord du regretté Jules Léger[2] et plus récemment de Jean Daigle, tous deux historiens et professeurs à l'Université de Moncton. Durant leur mandat, ils ont collaboré à l'œuvre de la Commission et sont intervenus dans des dossiers qui, parmi ad'utres, touchaient les sites acadiens.

4. Aussi, au sein de la fonction publique à Parcs Canada, quelques rares Acadiens ont fait carrière en tant que fonctionnaires professionnels à titre de cadres intermédiaires. Ils ont constitué une minorité difficilement influente dans la structure administrative de Parcs Canada en Atlantique.

5. Un autre fait à reconnaître est le souci de Parcs Canada, lors de ses projets d'aménagement des lieux qu'il gère, de consulter la population concernée au moyen d'audiences publiques. À certaines de ces audiences portant sur les sites acadiens, les participants ont pu exprimer leurs frustrations à l'égard de Grand-Pré et d'autres lieux historiques acadiens.

Analyse de la situation

L'étude menée en 1985 par le comité *ad hoc* de l'Université de Moncton[3] met en évidence une situation qui à l'époque faisait écho aux inquiétudes de l'architecte LeBlanc, et pour laquelle un important redressement s'imposait. Elle note en particulier que les francophones et les Acadiens sont faiblement représentés à Parcs Canada en Atlantique, et qu'ils sont totalement absents de la haute direction du bureau régional à Halifax. L'étude démontre aussi qu'à une exception près, les Acadiens sont absents aux postes de direction des principaux lieux historiques acadiens et absents des secteurs de recherche et d'interprétation de l'histoire acadienne (ils n'étaient pas là pour explorer, pour écrire et pour interpréter leur histoire).

Le comité juge anormal et inacceptable une telle situation, à savoir qu'un organisme gouvernemental fédéral qui gère autant de ressources portant sur l'histoire acadienne compte si peu de francophones et d'Acadiens au niveau administratif, et aucun historien acadien. Une intervention auprès du ministre responsable de Parcs Canada s'imposait. Parmi les nombreuses recommandations formulées et soumises par le comité, une seule fut retenue par le ministre, celle de la formation d'un comité consultatif.

Sous la tutelle de l'ancien directeur général régional, M. William Turnbull, Parcs Canada signe avec la collectivité acadienne, à l'automne 1984, une entente bipartite créant le Comité consultatif acadien de Parcs Canada en Atlantique, un partenariat à l'essai. Deux ans plus tard, le mandat du Comité est prolongé pour une période indéterminée.

Le Comité consultatif acadien : mandat, composition et fonctionnement

Les buts du Comité consultatif tels qu'ils sont définis dans l'entente peuvent se résumer comme suit :

D'une part, donner aux Acadiens des provinces Maritimes un moyen de participer aux décisions que prend Parcs Canada au sujet des lieux historiques liés à l'histoire du peuple acadien, notamment les décisions qui touchent à la recherche, à l'interprétation des faits et au développement des sites historiques.

D'autre part, instituer un forum d'échange d'idées où les participants s'instruiront mutuellement dans un esprit de compréhension et de collaboration et où ils pourront résoudre les problèmes qui touchent à leurs intérêts communs.

La Société nationale de l'Acadie est chargée de la sélection des six membres acadiens du Comité, dont deux représentants de chacune des provinces Maritimes. Y siègent aussi deux représentants de Parcs Canada[4]. Le Comité accueille en plus, à titre de membres d'office : le directeur général de Parcs Canada, région Atlantique, et le président de la Société nationale de l'Acadie.

Les délibérations se déroulent en langue française. Deux coprésidents dirigent les séances, soit l'agent de liaison de Parcs Canada et un représentant choisi par et parmi les six membres acadiens. Les membres participent au Comité bénévolement. Parcs Canada, pour sa part, assume les coûts de déplacement et d'hébergement des membres et fournit le nécessaire pour la tenue des réunions.

Les sujets à l'étude

Voilà institutionnalisé un mode de participation active des Acadiens aux décisions relatives aux questions acadiennes que prennent les spécialistes de Parcs

Canada. Au rythme de réunions semestrielles, le Comité peut tirer satisfaction de la somme considérable de travail réalisée au cours de ses dix années d'existence. Bien sûr, les dossiers ne se règlent pas d'un trait : il faut parfois plusieurs sessions de discussions et de dialogue avant de trouver des solutions aux problèmes soulevés.

Parmi les dossiers qui ont fait l'objet de longues et parfois de chaudes délibérations au sein du Comité, les suivants méritent d'être signalés :

1. Au lieu historique national de Grand-Pré, l'aménagement de l'église-souvenir s'est avéré une préoccupation absorbante. En particulier, le choix des artistes pour les œuvres commémoratives à l'intérieur de l'église fait l'objet d'un long processus, émaillé de vifs débats. Aujourd'hui, les efforts du Comité ont porté fruit et nous nous réjouissons de l'ambiance créée par les spécialistes de Parcs Canada, un aménagement propice à la réflexion sur les événements commémorés. On ne reste pas indifférent devant les émouvants tableaux de Claude Picard, les bas-reliefs de Claude Roussel, artistes et sculpteurs acadiens, et le vitrail qui domine l'entrée principale de l'église, une scène de l'embarquement des déportés sur les rivages de Grand-Pré, œuvre de Terry Smith Lamothe. Et les visiteurs ne manquent pas d'examiner à la loupe les plaques devant l'autel sur lesquelles sont inscrits les patronymes des familles souches acadiennes. Chacun s'y arrête espérant repérer l'ancêtre dont il porte le nom.

2. Autre fait à relever, lors d'une réunion du Comité à l'Île-du-Prince-Édouard, les membres ont pu explorer le lieu historique national du Fort-Amherst–Port-la-Joye où ils ont pris connaissance des fouilles archéologiques en cours à l'emplacement du vieux fort français. À la recommandation du Comité, les anciens drapeaux français et britanniques sont aujourd'hui déployés devant le Fort, alors que le centre d'accueil arbore le drapeau acadien.

3. Les membres du Comité s'affairent également à réviser les publications relatant les faits d'histoire des lieux acadiens et ce, tant pour le contenu historique que pour la qualité du français (la version anglaise est rarement fautive sur la qualité de la langue). Pour cet exigeant travail, le Comité fait appel aux historiens de l'Université de Moncton et aux spécialistes de son Centre d'études acadiennes.

4. Il faut souligner aussi les nombreuses interventions du Comité auprès de Parcs Canada en ce qui a trait à la représentation francophone et acadienne parmi ses fonctionnaires en Atlantique, en particulier aux échelons supérieurs et dans les secteurs de recherche et d'interprétation. Le Comité souhaitait la création d'un secteur acadien chargé de la gestion des activités et des programmes touchant les lieux historiques nationaux se rapportant

directement à l'histoire acadienne. Le Service des parcs n'est pas de cet avis et soutient qu'un secteur acadien séparé éloignerait les deux groupes linguistiques et créerait un doublement des tâches. Il soutient aussi qu'on ne peut dissocier l'histoire acadienne de celle des Anglais et/ou des Amérindiens qui les côtoyaient. Néanmoins, la toute récente refonte structurelle de plusieurs directions ministérielles sous la tutelle du ministère du Patrimoine canadien a prévu un bureau régional au Nouveau-Brunswick avec un personnel majoritairement bilingue. C'est une réponse partielle à nos recommandations. Le Comité n'écarte pas pour autant l'espoir de voir regroupés *sous une même direction* les principaux lieux historiques qui tracent les jalons de l'odyssée acadienne : Port-Royal, Fort Anne, Port-la-Joye, Grand-Pré, Fort Beauséjour, l'Odyssée acadienne, le Monument Lefebvre et autres. L'expérience probante de notre Comité nous a davantage conscientisés au fait que la dimension culturelle d'un peuple est difficilement saisissable par ceux de l'extérieur qui se voudraient aptes à la cerner. Soit dit en passant, l'équipe d'historiens de Parcs Canada compte maintenant, depuis un an, un historien acadien, mais à titre intérimaire seulement.

5. Parmi ses autres attributions, le Comité participe à l'examen des plans de réaménagement des lieux d'intérêt acadien tels ceux du Fort Anne, à Annapolis Royal, et du Fort Beauséjour, à la frontière Nouveau-Brunswick–Nouvelle-Écosse. Compte tenu des nouvelles orientations qu'endosse la CLMHC, le Comité suivra de près l'intégration de la dimension sociale dans la réinterprétation des lieux se rapportant à leur histoire et insistera sur l'importance de raviver et de mettre en valeur l'histoire, les traditions culturelles et la vie quotidienne des Acadiens et leurs rapports avec le milieu. Un projet éducatif collectif pour les écoles acadiennes conçu par l'ancienne directrice de Grand-Pré, Barbara LeBlanc, s'inscrit d'emblée dans cette optique. Nous souhaitons son adoption.

6. Enfin, le dossier le plus ancien et à la fois le plus actuel est celui du Monument Lefebvre, cet important édifice du patrimoine acadien venant tout juste de faire son entrée au temple des lieux historiques nationaux. Les péripéties du Monument Lefebvre constituent une véritable saga. En raison des événements récents, je m'attarderai un peu plus longtemps sur ce dossier afin que vous puissiez mieux apprécier la valeur du Monument comme lieu de commémoration de l'histoire et de la culture acadienne, et aussi l'importance du partenariat qui a sous-tendu les démarches faites en vue de sa reconnaissance.

Le Monument Lefebvre

Le Monument Lefebvre, à Memramcook (Nouveau-Brunswick) : symbole de la renaissance de la culture acadienne, ce bâtiment a été conçu par James C. Dumaresq et construit entre 1895 et 1897 à la mémoire du père Camille Lefebvre (1831-1895) ; désigné en 1994 / A symbol of Acadian cultural revival, it was designed by James C. Dumaresq and built in 1895-97 in memory of Father Camille Lefebvre (1831-1895); designated 1994. (Photo : Parcs Canada / Parks Canada, C. Cameron, 1987)

Il faut remonter au siècle dernier, à l'arrivée du père Camille Lefebvre dans la vallée de Memramcook, en 1864. Québécois et membre des religieux de Sainte-Croix, il est envoyé en Acadie pour fonder un collège, le premier en région acadienne qui offrirait aux jeunes Acadiens (au masculin seulement) une formation collégiale et universitaire en français. Trente ans durant, le père Lefebvre a œuvré au relèvement du peuple acadien. À son décès, en 1895, les Acadiens, voulant perpétuer la mémoire de ce valeureux pasteur et éducateur, érigent un imposant bâtiment en pierres taillées, où les générations d'étudiants à venir pourraient bénéficier de nouveaux services nécessaires à leur formation : classes et laboratoires de sciences, un auditorium pour les débats oratoires, concerts, théâtre, séances de fin d'année et autres activités propres au collège, et, pour la communauté acadienne, un lieu de rencontres, d'assemblées, de ralliements et de congrès. Au fil des ans, conférenciers, artistes, troupes de théâtre et chorales de renommée nationale et internationale ont foulé la scène du Monument, tous émerveillés par la qualité acoustique exceptionnelle de la salle. Les événements mémorables qui ont marqué la trajectoire séculaire du Monument constituent un long et important chapitre dans l'histoire du peuple acadien.

Après la création de l'Université de Moncton, en 1963, le gouvernement du Nouveau-Brunswick se porte acquéreur du collège pour en faire un centre de conférences et de formation pour adultes. Le Monument est compris dans la transaction, mais son entretien s'avère trop coûteux et on doit le laisser pour compte. Alors qu'on envisageait sa fermeture complète, une série d'événements fortuits dans les années 1970 vont changer le sort du Monument. En 1978, la Commission des lieux et monuments historiques du Canada faisait la recommandation exceptionnelle que la *Survivance du peuple acadien* soit reconnue comme un fait d'importance nationale et qu'un centre d'interprétation de cette survivance soit aménagé au Monument Lefebvre. L'inauguration du centre d'interprétation qui porte maintenant le nom de l'*Odyssée acadienne* a lieu quatre ans plus tard, soit en 1982. Par ce fait, Parcs Canada devient locataire du Monument, assurant ainsi un minimum de fonds pour son entretien. Mais à l'étage, la belle salle de spectacle, cet amphithéâtre à l'acoustique si enviable, restait vide, son utilisation condamnée par les règlements de sécurité de la province.

Par la suite, une entente fédérale–provinciale voit le Monument transféré au gouvernement fédéral, qui le désigne édifice classé, reconnaissant du fait même l'importance de son caractère patrimonial. En 1983, le ministre de Travaux publics Canada, l'honorable Roméo LeBlanc[5], annonce un projet pour la restauration complète de l'édifice. On pourrait enfin redonner à cette vénérable institution une vocation digne du peuple acadien et de sa vitalité renouvelée. Hélas, les travaux de restauration, amorcés au printemps 1984, sont suspendus quelques mois plus tard en raison de contretemps politiques.

À la première réunion du Comité consultatif acadien, en février 1985, les membres prennent connaissance du dossier et conviennent d'intervenir pour la reprise des travaux, afin que l'exposition de l'Odyssée acadienne, remisée dans une roulotte pour l'hiver, puisse bientôt réintégrer le Monument. S'ensuivent de longues et persistantes démarches auprès des instances gouvernementales; ce n'est qu'en juin 1989 que reprennent les travaux de restauration et qu'au printemps de 1994 que l'aménagement est terminé. Le 16 août 1994, durant le grand Congrès mondial acadien, devant une foule des plus exubérantes, l'honorable Michel Dupuy a présidé à la cérémonie de réouverture du Monument et a annoncé par la même occasion que le Monument Lefebvre, sur recommandation de la Commission des lieux et monuments historiques du Canada, serait désormais désigné *lieu historique national* et pris en charge par son ministère. Peut-on imaginer un plus heureux dénouement !

La Société du Monument Lefebvre Inc.

Depuis le début de cette saga, c'est la Société du Monument Lefebvre qui, avec l'appui des institutions acadiennes et de nombreuses personnalités intéressées et concernées, a piloté le projet à travers les dédales du temps et de l'appareil gouvernemental. Secondée par Parcs Canada, la Société entrevoit aujourd'hui un avenir des plus prometteurs pour le Monument et pour sa double mission de commémoration du passé et de devenir un véritable centre de foisonnement culturel en milieu acadien. Dans ce lieu bientôt centenaire, les Acadiens pourront raconter aux générations présentes et à venir ainsi qu'au monde entier ce qu'a été l'Acadie d'autrefois et ce qu'est l'Acadie vivante et vibrante d'aujourd'hui.

Conclusion

Voilà en bref quelques faits saillants de l'histoire d'un partenariat qui a mené loin. En rétrospective, la mise en valeur et la promotion du patrimoine historique et culturel acadien, toujours au cœur des préoccupations du Comité, ont suscité dans un premier temps des discussions difficiles, parfois acerbes, quant aux objectifs et aux moyens d'action. Mais, avec le temps, les délibérations ont mûri et les confrontations se sont atténuées. Aujourd'hui, une meilleure compréhension de part et d'autre se manifeste et une saine collaboration dans le respect des besoins et des exigences de chacun s'enracine. Le format tel qu'il émerge aujourd'hui constitue, croyons-nous, un modèle à considérer pour les nouvelles structures de partenariat que veut se donner le ministère du Patrimoine canadien.

Notes

1. Le comité regroupait le père Clément Cormier, recteur fondateur de l'Université de Moncton, M. Gilbert Finn, recteur de l'université, M. Jean Daigle, membre de la Commission des lieux et monuments historiques du Canada et professeur d'histoire à l'Université de Moncton, le père Anselme Chiasson, ancien directeur du Centre d'études acadiennes et auteur chevronné, M. André Vachon, premier titulaire de la Chaire d'études acadiennes, et Mme Muriel Roy, démographe, sociologue et directrice du Centre d'études acadiennes de l'Université de Moncton.
2. Le professeur Léger, participant à une réunion de la Commission en 1978, a perdu la vie dans l'écrasement de l'avion qui transportait des commissaires vers L'Anse-aux-Meadows (T.-N.). Parmi les autres victimes, on comptait le président de la Commission, Marc La Terreur et l'épouse de M. Léger, Jacqueline Bouchard, fondatrice de l'École de nursing de l'Université de Moncton.
3. Voir note 1.
4. Voir en annexe la liste des membres qui ont siégé au Comité depuis sa création.
5. Par la suite, M. Roméo LeBlanc est nommé sénateur, puis président du Sénat, et il occupe maintenant la haute fonction de gouverneur général du Canada.

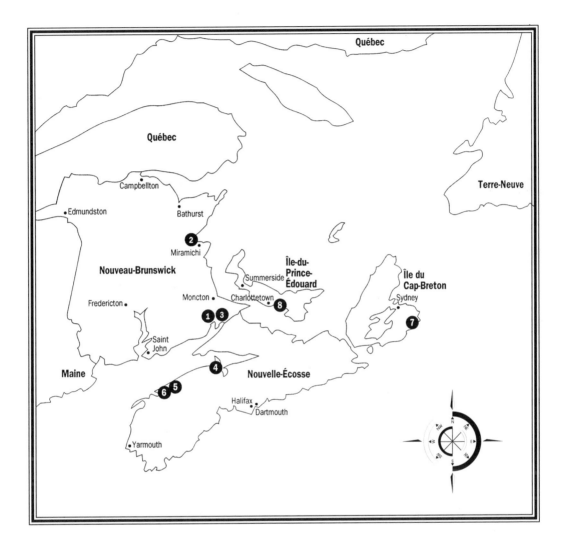

Légende de la carte

NOUVEAU-BRUNSWICK

1 Odyssée acadienne/Monument
  Lefebvre
2 Île Beaubears/Boishébert
3 Fort Beauséjour

NOUVELLE-ÉCOSSE

4 Grand-Pré
5 Fort Anne
6 Port-Royal
7 Forteresse de Louisbourg

ÎLE-DU-PRINCE-ÉDOUARD

8 Fort-Amherst – Port-la-Joye

MEMBRES DU COMITÉ CONSULTATIF ACADIEN DE PARCS CANADA DANS LES PROVINCES MARITIMES, 1985-1995

Île-du-Prince-Édouard
1. Francis Blanchard   1985 -
2. Georges Arsenault   1985 - 1986
    Cécile Gallant   1987 - 1990
    Reginald Porter   1990 - 1992

Nouvelle-Écosse
1. Neil Boucher   1990 -
2. Gabriel LeBlanc   1990 -
    Père Charles Aucoin   1985 - 1990
    Alphonse J. Deveau   1985 - 1990
    Yvon Samson (substitut)
    Paul Comeau (substitut)

Nouveau-Brunswick
1. Père Maurice Léger   1985 -
2. Muriel K. Roy   1985 - coprésidente

Parcs Canada
    William Turnbull, directeur général   1985 - coprésident
    Claude DeGrâce   1985 - 1994

Société nationale de l'Acadie (SNA)
    Roger Ouellette, président   1992 -
    René Légère, secrétaire général (substitut)
    Père Léger Comeau, ancien président   1985 - 1988
    Pierre Arsenault, ancien président   1988 - 1992
    Jean-Marie Nadeau, secrétaire général (substitut)

Autres participants au Comité
    Jean Daigle, membre de la CLMHC   1985 - 1987
    Jim Strew, Grand-Pré   1987 - 1988
    Barbara LeBlanc, Grand-Pré   1989 - 1992
    Jocelyne Marchand, Grand-Pré   1993 - 1994
    Gilles Babin, surintendant Kouchibougouac
    Lillian Stewart, surintendante Sud-Ouest, N.-É.
    Carmen Comeau-Anderson, Patrimoine canadien, N.-B.

Redress versus Commemoration

Abstract

There is no need for any sense of conflict between concepts of redress and commemoration. Many groups who have been part of Canadian culture, often pre-dating Confederation, have legitimate grievances resulting from discrimination in all of its forms. Black Canadians were once slaves in Canada. Chinese-Canadians faced a head tax on immigration. Japanese-Canadians were interned during World War II, as were German- and Italian-Canadians. This list is long. Above all, and first and foremost, Aboriginal Canadians have the most pressing need and cause for redress.

But redress is not necessarily a matter of money. Redress is concerned, above all else, with respect. It is the historical denial of dignity and respect that leads to the need for redress. Questions of payment arise, and become more urgent, as the cry for respect is ignored, delayed, and denied until it becomes a demand.

We cannot change the past, but we must develop strategies for acknowledging its wrongs and according respect and dignity to those to whom it has been denied.

Réparation vs commémoration – Résumé

La notion de réparation et celle de commémoration ne s'opposent pas nécessairement. De nombreux groupes qui ont participé à la formation de la culture canadienne, souvent même avant la Confédération, se plaignent à juste titre d'avoir été victimes de toutes les formes de discrimination. Il fut un temps où les Noirs étaient des esclaves au Canada. À une certaine époque, les immigrants chinois devaient payer une taxe pour être admis au pays. Pendant la Seconde Guerre mondiale, les Japonais canadiens ont été internés. Des Canadiens d'origine allemande et italienne ont subi le même sort. Et cette liste est loin d'être complète. Mais ce sont d'abord et avant tout les Canadiens autochtones qui ont le plus de motifs d'obtenir réparation et qui en ont le plus besoin.

Qui dit réparation ne dit pas nécessairement compensation financière. La réparation est par-dessus tout une question de respect. C'est le déni séculaire de dignité et de respect qui entraîne le besoin de réparation. Les questions d'argent interviennent, et deviennent plus pressantes, lorsque la demande de respect est laissée sans réponse, repoussée et rejetée. C'est alors qu'elle se transforme en exigence.

Nous ne pouvons modifier le passé, mais nous devons trouver des façons de reconnaître les torts qu'il a comportés et d'accorder respect et dignité à ceux qui en ont été privés.

*R*edress versus Commemoration is the title that was assigned to me for this talk and I suppose I'm going to cover those bases in ways that might surprise you. I might call this "From Pictou to Bond Street" or "From the Black Battalion to William Lyon Mackenzie" – some distance, some stretch, both in geography and in time.

I am shortly moving to Toronto to take up an office at 80 Bond Street, and those of you who know the city will know that right next door is the heritage house of William Lyon Mackenzie. Now I will be walking past that door daily over the next many years, and I will have some suggestions for you before I end about how to bring the plaque located there up-to-date.

Two summers ago, I had the extraordinary good fortune to be in Pictou, Nova Scotia, for the commemoration of the Second Construction Battalion in recognition of its work during World War I. I wonder if you know that story?

Blacks have been in Canada since the 1600s, and there has been a Black community in Nova Scotia for well over 200 years. The Blacks in Nova Scotia and across the country felt, during World War I, that this was their country and that they wanted to fight in that war to defend the principles, the standards, which we espouse in this country. But they were told that this was a "white man's war", and that they were not wanted. Although it happened in other places in the country in other ways, there was a strong movement in Nova Scotia amongst Blacks to participate in the war and, by so doing, demonstrate and lay claim to their right to be in this country and to be a part of it. Blacks tried very hard to enlist and they were told "no". After much lobbying they were told by people in Ottawa that if they could find a *white* commander to command their regiment, they would be allowed to enlist. It took a very long time to do that. But they persisted and finally found a man called Sutherland, who was from around here, who commanded what became the Second Construction Battalion which went over to France during World War I. They did not fight, of course; they were not allowed to have weapons; they were the construction crew and the ditch diggers and the support group, which was not out of tune with the times, I suppose. After the war they were returned to Canada and were demobilized; thereafter they virtually disappeared from history. Military history or any other

112

history of the country did not recognize that that event had taken place and that those 600 men had gone overseas in the cause of this country and the cause of what we like to think of as democracy.

It was many, many, years later that a man called Calvin Ruck discovered this story. He found some old men in some institutions around Nova Scotia – in hospitals and seniors' homes – who told stories of this event, and he took it upon himself as a personal crusade to see that this event got commemorated. I happened to be there as the host and narrator of a series of programmes, four one-hour programmes about the history of my people, Black people, in Canada, produced by an American immigrant to this country, now a Canadian, Almeta Speaks. Some of you may have seen it on TV Ontario or on Vision Television Network. It was called "Hymn to Freedom", and I had the remarkable experience of travelling this country and talking to people who had been here for generations and yet who were invisible as part of the landscape and historical record of this country. It was more through good luck than good planning that we were there with our film crew on the day that the "Black Battalion", the Second Construction Battalion, was commemorated in Nova Scotia. What a grand event on a wonderful day – the Premier was there, Senator Don Oliver was there, there were dignitaries from all over the country – and it was finally recognized, all of these years later, that these men had played a part in the war and deserved the right to claim full citizenship in this country.

Most of the history of this country, when you look at commemoration – the history books and at the building next door to my new office – reflect battles and politicians. There is a lot of bricks and mortar, lots of forts, a lot of stuff about 1812 when we whipped the Americans – kind of a testament to testosterone. This is understandable. Part of what your movement does and what this conference is about and what you are commemorating here and celebrating here this weekend, seventy-five years of trying to put on the map of our consciousness some of that history, is important. But it is important that the picture be complete – and it is not.

I chaired a conference in 1988 in Toronto called "Multiculturalism and the Media". "Reflections in the Mirror" was the sub-title, and someone said at that conference that on television if you do not see yourself, it is as if you do not exist; it is as if you are invisible. Now the same could be said about the monuments and other facilities, like institutions and parks, and the other things that we have across this country, and the recognizing of events and individuals and situations. Many Canadians do not see themselves as a part of this so we need to have a better, a fuller, more real picture. One could say that very often what one sees are snapshots. It's like the famous picture of the last spike, which

Pierre Berton has made famous, almost single-handedly: the picture of Donald Smith driving in the last spike in the Canadian Pacific Railway at Craigellachie, British Columbia. And I note from some research that I did for a project a long time ago that snapshots are very interesting; you see these men, with their stovepipe hats and their grand suits, doing this act of completion. But I also know that if you tilted the camera, perhaps thirty degrees in one direction, and zoomed the lens a bit, you would have seen way off in the corner, near the edge of the woods, a group of Chinese men who were stranded in this country. They were promised – after they were brought from China as indentured labour to do the dirty work of building that railroad – tickets home at the end of it. They did not get the tickets; they were left stranded. They then spread out across the prairies, alone or in groups of two and three, and set up laundries or restaurants, with names such as the "Canada Cafe" and the "Blue Bird Restaurant". They were not allowed to bring their wives; theirs was a bachelor society.

A friend and partner of mine, Dick Wong, still has his father's head tax certificate from 1913. His father had paid $500.00 which was a lot of money, even in Canadian dollars then, to come to this country. We do not see much about the Komagata Maru when we look at plaques and monuments and sites; not much acknowledges the fact that Sikhs have been in this country since the turn of the century. We, happily, only see a very small plaque in Victoria of Amor d'Cosmos, the founder of the *Victoria Colonist*, still alive as the *Times Colonist* I think, who, in the 1850s and '60s after the Fraser Valley gold rush, almost single-handedly led the battle against the "yellow peril" that he feared. We do not see – we are only beginning to see – a little bit about the Japanese internment.

When I was a kid growing up in Montréal, we all knew that Île Sainte-Hélène was where they kept some Italians and Germans, as well as Camillien Houde, former and later mayor of Montréal, for the duration of the War.

We do not hear about the history of Frank Oliver, publisher of the *Edmonton Bulletin* and later Minister of the Interior. He was part of that group, along with Sifton earlier, who told rather fanciful stories to Eastern Europeans about what the Prairies were like, and brought them here to fill up the country and create traffic for the railway.

There is a lot about railways, isn't there? It is almost as if the railway was, in my view, a way of staking a claim to the land by laying this line across it, and those wonderful railway hotels are almost like putting your stamp on the land.

We do not hear much, and there is not much to commemorate in the Prairies. A few places out where I live in Alberta commemorate Nellie McClung,

Ellie McMurphy, and their partners who fought in the 1920s and had to go to the Privy Council in London to prove that they were persons.

We do not hear very much, even now, about Thérèse Casgrain who almost single-handedly got the vote for women in Québec – in 1940! My mother, who was born and bred in Montréal, who lived there, could not own property or get a divorce without an act of Parliament in those days. And we have certainly expunged from our history the story of Africville, a part of Halifax, Nova Scotia.

On that same trip to Nova Scotia, I stood in that little park by the sea and tried to absorb the vibrations of people who had been there; where there had been a community of people with schools, and churches, and gardens, and clubs, and all of the things that make a community. It was bulldozed by the city of Halifax in the 1960s, not so very long ago. So if we are going to commemorate and recognize our history in this country, we had better tell the whole truth. That is the challenge.

I am with Professor Symons who said that this conference really needs to be about not where you have been but where you are going from here. I note in passing that I am the only Black man in the room. That, in my experience, is not unusual although it is becoming less and less the case. There is a Black woman, I think, somewhere in the room, and I note a few Aboriginal people, but I see no one of East Asian descent, or of Japanese or Chinese descent, and you may want to ask yourselves why that is.

We have this wonderful country that the United Nations says is the best in the world, and it is. It is kind of like Churchill's description of democracy: it is the worst system there is – except for all the others. And we are going through a period in our own history where we are beginning to question the remarkable strides that we have made in this country.

In spite of all that I have said which may sound negative to you, the fact that I am here saying it and that you have not left the room represents a tremendous advance. We have come a long way from the concept of *terræ nullius*, which was the old British Privy Council notion that these lands in this new world that Europeans discovered – as if the people already here did not know all about it – was really empty because the inhabitants were not civilized enough to have rights. *Terræ nullius* was finally defeated in 1992 by the Australian High Court; the first challenger was a group of Aboriginal people fighting over their land. These land fights only happen, as they do for the Lubicon in Northern Alberta, when there are resources at stake. A group of Aboriginal people, led by a man called Eddie Maboo, had been living peacefully in a part of Queensland for some time – until developers discovered some important resources there and then they tried to kick them out. Then the Aboriginal people went to court and they won.

115

That is a tremendous change; it is happening here of course. There is this notion that because we came here and we opened up the land, we did not conquer it, we negotiated it – in a good Canadian way and have treaties to prove it – we are better than the Americans. The reality is that we exterminated the Beothuk in Newfoundland, and you look at the lives of Big Bear, Riel and many, many others and it is not a pretty sight. So we have to, in the words of David Lowenthal, "make sure that the past is not a foreign country." We have a great distance to go and the challenge to you working in this field must be exciting.

❖ ❖ ❖

We are evolving with technology, and where snapshots were okay a generation ago now we want full motion video. We want to see ourselves in all of our diversity and in full colour and in full motion.

Now, putting up that monument in Pictou, Nova Scotia, in 1993, was redress. It heals wounds; it includes people; it says "yes you are Canadian, you have a right to your citizenship in this country." Putting up a plaque on William Lyon Mackenzie's house is commemoration, but what I say about it might surprise you.

We are engaged in this country in a debate in which some people think we ought to close our borders to immigrants, in which some people are wringing their hands publically and angrily about the diversity that has come upon us. We have people in my own province who question whether we ought to have a *Charter of Rights and Freedoms*, who are in the process of shutting down, in a defensive way, the Alberta Human Rights Commission and this debate is serious. It has the potential to do great damage to what this country has been and still is and must be in the future.

So when I talk about this "full motion video" it is because I want to see you reflect about our history, to see that this debate is taking place because we do not know who we are or where we came from. People, members of Parliament even, who talk about this as a white man's country, a Christian country, and "why can't we get back to the good old days", do not know our history. They are speaking out of ignorance. Media has a role to play in this, but your organization, by its charter and mandate, has an imperative to be advocates for the history of this country, and if you have to do that you have to do it as educators, using the media.

The job that I am taking up on the first of January (1995) is President of the Vision Television Network, in Toronto. What we try to do is to attempt to build bridges of information and understanding, and try to reduce the distrust and misunderstanding and fear between faiths and cultures. So we have some common cause here. But I want to end with a quote for which I thank Sheldon Godfrey, who is from the Heritage Canada Foundation. It is the quote which ought to be on the plaque on the house next door to 80 Bond Street. It is by William Lyon Mackenzie writing in York, Upper Canada, in the *Colonial Advocate*, "The population of the town and country consists of persons of many sects and denominations in respect to religious belief and who are either natives of Canada or immigrants from other parts of North America, or from Europe and Africa, a mixed race, neither amalgamated in manners, customs nor habits, doubtless containing many enlightened and well-informed men, as well as others of very different character." That is the plaque that should be on that house.

William Lyon Mackenzie House, Toronto, Ontario / La maison William-Lyon-Mackenzie, Toronto (Ontario). (Photo: Parks Canada, Canadian Inventory of Historic Building / Parcs Canada, Inventaire des bâtiments historiques du Canada, 1974)

Members of the Black Battalion: Private Joseph Alexander Paris, front row centre and Mr. Tom Reid were members of the No. 2 Construction Battalion. The other members are not identified; Battalion designated 1992. / Membres du Bataillon noir : le soldat Joseph Alexander Paris (première rangée, au centre) et M. Tom Reid étaient membres du Deuxième Bataillon de la construction. Les autres membres ne sont pas identifiés. Le bataillon a été désigné en 1992. [Photo: Ping Pong Studio, Islington, London, England; courtesy of the Black Cultural Centre, Dartmouth, Nova Scotia / gracieuseté du Black Cultural Centre de Dartmouth (Nouvelle-Écosse)]

CHARLES W. HUMPHRIES

The Past and the Culture of Compliance:
My History, Your History, No History

Abstract
The tendency to look at only very small portions, i.e. "studies history", of what should be a broad picture, and the development thereby of "exclusive language", needlessly hamper the task of historical examination. Context, too, is of utmost importance in the historical examination of events. Attempts have to be made to understand why – in what context – certain actions were taken, in order to properly evaluate the results. How we teach history now will determine the extent of the knowledge of those who will teach history in the future. Knowledge and understanding of our heritage can be advanced through open debate, particularly in matters of validity and context.

Le passé et la culture de la conformité : mon histoire, votre histoire, aucune histoire –
Résumé
La tendance à considérer seulement de très petits segments de ce qui devrait être un grand tableau (« l'histoire ramenée à des études ») et la création d'une « langue exclusive » qui en résulte entravent inutilement l'examen historique. Le contexte revêt par ailleurs la plus haute importance dans l'examen historique des événements. Des tentatives ont été faites pour comprendre pourquoi – c'est-à-dire dans quel contexte – certaines mesures avaient été prises, afin d'en évaluer convenablement les résultats. La façon dont nous enseignons l'histoire maintenant déterminera l'étendue des connaissances des professeurs d'histoire de l'avenir. Un débat ouvert, particulièrement en ce qui touche les questions de validité et de contexte, peut promouvoir la connaissance et la compréhension de notre patrimoine.

Let me begin by saying – as historians and myth-tellers are wont to say – once upon a time. Once upon a time there was a national historical society which met every year and the membership listened to a variety of papers dealing with a wide range of topics. Then, one year, the people interested in transportation pointed out that the annual programme paid insufficient attention to their subject, despite the obvious fact that their theme was an integral part of the story of nation-building. Consequently, they insisted, successfully, that a transportation section should be organized which would meet apart from the main meeting and deal exclusively with the subject of their interest. This separation was performed in a most congenial way, something akin to a bon voyage party.

Difficulties soon arose within the transportation ranks, however, because some wanted to look at canals, and some at trails, and some at railways. In an effort to be accommodating and not desiring any charge of discrimination, they agreed to divide the theme of transportation and have three sub-sections: canals, trails, and railways. This meant, of course, that no one had time to attend the general meetings on transportation.

Within the ranks of the railway enthusiasts, however, all was not calm because there were those who wanted to look at tracks and those who wanted to investigate trains; and there was a handful who had hopes of examining stations. Having gotten to this point through amicable breaks with the historical society and then with the transportation section, they cheerfully agreed to split into various groups according to their particular enthusiasms. The track people met and told tall tales of ties; the engine people met and got up their own head of steam; and the station people met and waited for their train to come in. And no one had time to go to the general meeting about railways.

This is not the end of the story, however, because the people who looked at tracks had an extremely civilized falling-out over the matter of gauge and divided themselves into standard, broad, and narrow gauge groups. So great was the subject interest in each of these bodies that, of course, no one could find those hours necessary to attend the general meeting about tracks. Meanwhile each of these sub-sub-sub-groups engaged in friendly but meaningful debates over whether they should be looking at rails or ties. To no one's surprise, and in a spirit of great goodwill, standard, broad, and narrow gauge all sub-divided to examine either the wood of the ties or the steel of the rails. No one attended the general meetings on gauge.

These scenarios, with slight modifications, were duplicated and then duplicated again throughout the entire transportation group. And as the sub-dividing went on and on, there was a further development: members of each of these rapidly expanding groups determined, by taking the lead from each other, that only they could speak about their subject of interest and they explicitly forbade any non-member from doing so. This meant, not surprisingly, that they only talked to each other within the narrow confines of their own sub-sub-sub-sub group. Such talk became known by the refined title of exclusive language.

The place of History / Les lieux de la mémoire

This situation continued – with sub-groups splitting as often as brooms in the Sorcerer's Apprentice – until the day when, after a thorough-going investigation of the consequences of the break-up of the old historical society, an economic historian was able to pronounce that the size of the grants each of these groups and sub-groups and sub-sub groups and sub-sub-sub groups and sub-sub-sub-sub groups received was in direct proportion to distance that the group in question was from the original theme of national transportation. That knowledge proved cold and comfortless to those who had originally thought it necessary to have a transportation section, because the present circumstances were not what they had had in mind with that initial break from the historical society. Thus chilled in their ardour for tribal accommodation, they thought they should try to find their way back to the national association and its annual meeting. So, with argument or threat – and translators to handle the exclusive languages – they tried to persuade the sub-groups, and the sub-sub-groups, and the sub-sub-sub groups, and the sub-sub-sub-sub groups to abandon their rarified get-togethers and to return to the larger body. But they failed, because their efforts foundered on those exclusive languages which now made the quest for unity fruitless. In failing, however, they made two discoveries which are also the morals of this tale. First, exclusive language makes understanding difficult and knowledge impossible; and second, the sum of the parts was considerably less than the whole.

I have told this tale because some recent developments in the field of Canadian history give me cause for concern; and these developments have occurred because, in the main, people have been too polite to ask questions that might be judged as sharp or possibly harsh or even prejudiced by those being quizzed.

These developments centre on the rise of "studies history" in which there is a historical examination of a particular group or a special theme. Now, I have no problem with this concept in general, but I do become concerned when I see signs of how it sometimes can be played out. It is in this area that we hear statements to the effect that someone cannot tackle these studies because that person's "voice" is wrong. Not that the research skills are deficient, not that the knowledge is weak, not that the writing is inadequate; but that the "voice" is wrong. And who makes this judgment? The person whose "voice" is right. It has also been remarked that because of cultural differences, the person from outside the culture can only proceed so far in understanding that culture and, therefore, cannot fully tackle some historical aspect of that culture. This deficiency has been described as only being able to climb half-way up the mountain, when the peak is the goal. Such talk – and it is often more in the nature of an immutable pronouncement than talk – is certainly exclusionary and can be intimidating. It means that not only does the "outsider" become an historical interloper whose business should be elsewhere, but it also serves as a buffer from outside criticism when the work of the insider is produced. In a present-day world which already suffers – and I mean suffers – from a nasty over-abundance of tribalism, I find such a development coming close to parallelling world affairs. I am not convinced that I can discover in such attitudes much that argues for the advancement of historical knowledge.

This would be troublesome enough if it were the only problem associated with "studies history", but there are others. One of these is the not insignificant matter of context. If some thing or some group is studied by an exclusive body of people, it is quite conceivable that those students will over-inflate the importance of the subject which they are studying, that is over-inflate it in its relationship to the larger context; or over-inflate to the exclusion of other matters in the larger context.

Or, worst of all, ignore the larger context. Let me provide an example of this problem. During the past summer I had a bright high school history teacher in my class, who was working on a master's degree – the course was war and society. At some point, he told me that he assigned his students the task of examining 1942 Vancouver newspapers at the time of the evacuation of Japanese-Canadians and Japanese nationals from the west coast. He said it provided the students with a better understanding of how these people had been treated. At the time, I did not think that much about it but, later, when we arrived at World War II in the course, I mentioned the internment of Mayor Camillien Houde of Montréal for four years. This student's hand shot up and he said to me somewhat incredulously, "You mean they interned the mayor of what was then Canada's largest city?" I replied affirmatively. He asked me what had been the reaction in Montréal; and I had replied that he had been spirited away so swiftly that there was not much chance for a public reaction, but there had been a big party when he returned to his home in 1944. Then, it hit me. He was having his students explore only one case, admittedly the largest case, but only one case of internment during the War as if it were the only case. And what became evident in the subsequent discussion was that the students were not only doing this but, also, that they were being given no context for the decision to evacuate those people: no mention of the fears; no mention of the Japanese successes to that point in the war; no mention of the wartime atmosphere. In sum, there was no attempt to provide a context and, obviously, no attempt to show that internment also happened to other people under the stress of wartime circumstances. None of this is said to justify the actions taken, but it is said to insist upon understanding why the actions were taken – that is where context is of paramount importance. If the context is not provided, then what frequently occurs is the application of present-day standards to historical events and, of course, the past events frequently cannot avoid looking bad. But this is not understanding the past; it is simply playing tricks upon the dead. Let me underline the point that understanding the past does not equate with sympathy for past actions; rather understanding the past means comprehending the forces that caused people to behave in the way in which they did. And context is what I fear can go missing when "studies history" is undertaken.

A quote from the past might be illustrative of the point which I am making. In 1913, Isabel B. Graham, living in Winnipeg, wrote a letter to the president of the National Council of Women in which she made a case for granting homesteads to women. In the course of this letter, she wrote:

> ... We <u>must people the West</u> with <u>British</u> subjects. We have far too many foreigners now.
> The Rev. Douglas Ellison, for twenty years past (and still is) an Anglican missionary, chiefly among the foreigners in the West says "there are not 25% of the population in the West Canadian born" and "the foreign element" he declares "is Canada's greatest menace at the present time." Who is going "to fuse" – ["]to assimilate" the foreign element, pouring into Canada annually by the thousands? – <u>all</u> coming to the West. (Look at our Jew, now in Montreal, refusing to recognize Easter). Are we Western farmers so cultured, so steadfast, so loyal, so philanthropic, that we can bear dilution by the ignorance, low idealism, and religious perversity of the average foreigner? <u>We</u> are too few to make this safe. Is it fair to keep back the Canadian, two or three generations, by surrounding him with neighbors that he is compelled to carry on his back? Keep back the foreigner. Give us good sound <u>British</u> stock – women already <u>British</u>, already civilized, already subjective to both earth and heaven for conduct ... [1]

Now, what are we to make of Isabel Graham? Was she an Anglo-Saxon supremacist whose opinions rested on her interpretation of social Darwinism? By most people's standards today she certainly was, but is that what we say about her? In the context of her day, a number of people would probably have judged her to be "politically correct", had such a phrase been then in use. It seems to me that we have to note, not only the manner in which she defined herself, and others like herself, by defining the foreigner, but also that this woman was, if not frightened, at least fearful. She was a Winnipeg resident in 1913; and what was 1913? It was the year in which this country accepted more immigrants than it ever had before or since – just over 400,000. In excess of 600,000 immigrants had arrived in the two preceding years of 1911 and 1912. A million newcomers in a country with a population of about seven and a half million. So many arrived that Isabel Graham thought they were all landing in Winnipeg.

Well, we know that they did not all land in Winnipeg, but a lot of these immigrants did. Isabel Graham saw in their faces, heard in their languages, noted in their dress, and witnessed in their religions, a profound threat to her way of life or, possibly, what she imagined as her way of life; and she wanted to do something about it. In her case, homesteads for British women was the answer. None of this means that we must like Isabel Graham, but it does mean that we must understand her in her context. And those who would simply write her off as an Anglo-Saxon supremacist, using homesteads for women as a cover for her racial views, are failing history by ignoring the context.

As an aside to this point, I should say that one of my problems with that much-debated docudrama (whatever a docudrama is; or maybe what it is not – it is not a documentary and it is not a drama), "The Valour and the Horror", was that it lacked context. Nowhere was that more evident than in that second segment when it appeared as if Hitler had invited the Allies to a Sunday school picnic and the British, Canadians, Americans all brought bombers. There simply was no meaningful context.

Finally, I think that one of the potential problems raised by "studies history" is made more acute by the population size of this country which is rather small. That in turn means that the numbers of students proceeding to do graduate work in history in this country is similarly quite small. Thus a shift in the direction of research need not be that large to have some very significant repercussions over a long period of time. If by virtue of grants or university offerings or social pressures, these students are directed down particular paths – especially "studies" paths, then we have the makings of two additional problems. First, we certainly will not be producing very many generalists – that group which could fill in some of the blanks in the larger context if they were permitted to do so. Secondly, we come to the matter of future staffing of universities. I realize that in a day and age when departments – including history departments – are shrinking on campuses regardless of the student enrolments, it is sometimes difficult to think that a bout of hiring will ever occur. But that hiring will occur – probably not on the scale of the 1960s – but it will happen. Now, if at that time, the graduate students in Canadian history are largely products of "studies history", then the hiring that occurs will certainly produce teachers with a very different slant on Canadian history and a narrowness that may well prove to be appalling. And I shudder to think about the knowledge which undergraduates may carry away from such an experience.

If I have painted an unappealing picture – or, possibly, overstated the case – I have done so to make a point. We cannot subdivide Canadian history to the point where specialists do not talk to each other but, rather, they talk past each other from their tribal enclaves. Secondly, we must keep on insisting that the broader context stand behind the narrower works. And, thirdly, we must avoid misshaping our offerings of Canadian history to the next generation of students.

We have arrived at this point because we have generally been polite and unquestioning when people – sometimes with an axe to grind – have opened up a new area for historical study. In other words, we have been compliant and, in some cases, advantage has been taken of that compliance. And we have started the sub-division of our history – not an irreversible process – sometimes without due regard for context. Consequently, we do run the risk of it being a case of my history, your history, no history.

At some point in the late sixties, I went to hear a lecture on the resurgence of Scottish nationalism in that day. The gist of the thesis presented by the lecturer was that this phenomenon was largely the result of the migration into Scotland of the Irish who had, thanks to their long experience, taken up someone else's concern with English dominance. And he buttressed his arguments with facts and figures about Scottish nationalist strength being most pronounced where Irish settlement was largest. But, before the lecturer, having stated the thrust of his argument, could proceed to a further elaboration, a Scottish voice from the rear of the assembled listeners yelled out: "Utter garbage; sheer tripe". In so doing, he set the stage for a free-swinging debate on the academic merits or otherwise of the now unfinished lecture.

I thought then – and I still think now – that the angry Scot had really behaved in a very un-Canadian way. Clearly, he had not been in this country long enough to absorb our capacity for accommodation and restraint – maybe even generosity – in the face of certain developments in the writing and re-writing of our history. In any event, it appears to me that we could do with a few more people in the field of Canadian history with that Scot's temperament. Why? To force those in the field to defend their ideas and their theses particularly in matters of validity and context. Not only would the debate be entertaining; but the knowledge and understanding of our heritage would be advanced.

Note

1. National Archives of Canada, MG28, I-25 (National Council of Women of Canada Papers), Vol. 67, File 4, letter from Mrs. Isabel Beaton Graham to Mrs. F.H. Torrington, President of National Council of Women of Canada, 1 March 1913.

Chilkoot Trail, British Columbia, was a transportation route to the Klondike gold fields; designated 1967. / La piste Chilkoot, en Colombie-Britannique, fut une route de transport vers les champs aurifères du Klondike ; désignée en 1967. (Photo: Parks Canada / Parcs Canada, W. Lynch, 1995)

Hartland Covered Bridge, Hartland, New Brunswick is by far the longest covered bridge extant in the world. It was built in 1921 and designated in 1977. / Le pont couvert de Hartland, au Nouveau-Brunswick, est le plus long du genre au monde. Il fut construit en 1921 et a été désigné en 1977. (Photo: Public Works and Government Services Canada/Travaux publics et Services gouvernementaux Canada, HRS, 1993)

Education, Communication, and Heritage
Éducation, communication et patrimoine

Country School, Aurora S.D. No. 1050, Saskatchewan, circa 1920 / École de campagne dans le district scolaire n° 1050 d'Aurora (Saskatchewan), vers 1920. (Photo: National Archives, PA-048660; National Film Board of Canada collection item, A-2483 / Archives nationales, PA-048660 ; pièce A-2483 de la collection de l'Office national du film du Canada)

JEAN DU BERGER

Le patrimoine vivant et l'éducation

Résumé
Après avoir retracé l'évolution du concept de patrimoine vivant, du folklore au patrimoine ethnologique, on décrit les transformations des pratiques culturelles traditionnelles dans le contexte technoculturel qui ont conduit L'Unesco à proposer des mesures pour la sauvegarde du patrimoine intangible. On aborde ensuite rapidement les différentes formes d'action culturelle se rapportant à cette forme de patrimoine au Canada, puis on traite des formes actuelles d'intervention, comme la planification, l'identification et la documentation, la conservation et l'analyse, la préservation, la diffusion et l'utilisation. On propose finalement des activités d'ordre pédagogique qui ont pour objet non seulement de faire prendre conscience du patrimoine d'une communauté, mais aussi de découvrir celui des autres communautés.

Living Heritage and Education – Abstract
After tracing the evolution of the concept of living heritage, from folklore to ethnological heritage, this paper describes the transformations undergone by traditional cultural practices in the techno-cultural context that led Unesco to propose measures for safeguarding intangible heritage. It then takes a quick look at the various forms of cultural action, in relation to this form of heritage in Canada. This is followed by a discussion of the current forms of intervention, such as planning, identification and documentation, conservation and analysis, preservation, dissemination and use. The author concludes by proposing educational activities aimed not only at increasing awareness of a community's heritage, but also at discovering the heritage of other communities.

Les actes de commémoration du passé sont à nos yeux évidents. Nous en connaissons les rituels. Des espaces collectivement reconnus comme « lieux de mémoire » sont désignés par des marques spéciales, aménagés ou remis en état, entretenus et animés par des visites guidées et des activités d'interprétation ; périodiquement, des cérémonies, des défilés (processions ou cortèges), des concerts, des discours, des banquets et des fêtes populaires y sont organisés. Dans ce champ de la commémoration au paradigme connu de tous, je dois traiter du patrimoine vivant dans l'éducation. Il faudra de toute évidence définir le terme de patrimoine vivant et celui d'éducation.

L'éducation

Je parlerai brièvement de l'éducation. Longtemps, pour beaucoup, l'éducation n'était qu'une étape dans l'existence, limitée dans le temps, qui conduisait à l'acquisition définitive d'un savoir permettant d'occuper un statut social. Dans le cadre d'un appareil hiérarchique, autoritaire et rigide, l'éducation n'encourageait pas l'expression d'opinions divergentes. Les apprentissages se faisaient par échelons ; les groupes d'âges étaient compartimentés. Évaluée quantitativement, la performance était prioritaire et permettait une opération d'étiquetage qui fixait le sujet sa vie durant dans une position immuable.

L'éducation devrait « apprendre à apprendre », à distinguer l'essentiel de l'accessoire, à s'orienter dans l'information, à suivre le développement des connaissances. Le savoir n'est pas une « chose », une substance figée, mais un apprentissage continuel par lequel le sujet s'adapte à son environnement. Cet apprentissage exige un climat de confiance : les personnes peuvent donc y exprimer leurs opinions et faire l'expérience d'une réelle autonomie. Les hypothèses, les opinions et les pensées différentes sont en effet les facteurs d'un processus d'apprentissage créateur. Par ailleurs, des structures d'apprentissage souples permettent l'intégration des groupes d'âges. Une personne n'est pas définie par son âge. Quant à la performance, l'image de soi en est le moteur. Enfin, le processus d'éducation a pour objet non seulement la rationalité, mais aussi l'intuition et la sensibilité. En définitive, toute éducation doit permettre à la personne de franchir les limites qu'elle s'est fait imposer. En ce sens, l'éducation est un apprentissage qui dure toute la vie.

Tel est le lieu où devraient être communiqués des savoirs et des savoir-faire que je désigne par le terme de patrimoine vivant.

Le patrimoine vivant

Le patrimoine vivant est constitué de traditions culturelles actives, dynamiques, inscrites dans la vie quotidienne d'une communauté. Dans toute communauté culturelle, ces traditions sont mises en œuvre par des artistes et des artisans reconnus comme porteurs de savoirs et de savoir-faire qui constituent la culture traditionnelle de cette communauté, pratiques transmises de génération en génération, sans interruption dans le temps, toujours actuelles dans la vie de la communauté dont elles atteignent la majorité des membres.

Le patrimoine vivant se trouve donc dans les communautés d'appartenance où les porteurs actifs de tradition en sont les témoins, mais surtout les praticiens. En ce sens, les pratiques culturelles traditionnelles constituent un patrimoine, parfois désigné sous le nom de patrimoine ethno-logique, qui s'inscrit dans l'héritage des hommes avec le patrimoine architectural, le patrimoine artistique, le patrimoine audiovisuel, le patrimoine écrit, le patrimoine enfoui, le patrimoine muséographique et le patrimoine musical[1].

Les patrimoines en redéfinition

Lors de l'Année du patrimoine en France, en 1980, un élargissement du concept de patrimoine apparut. En premier lieu, une liste constitua une première classe du patrimoine ethnologique :

> objets et ensembles mobiliers, immeubles, paysages aménagés par l'homme, bien fongibles tels que les espèces animales et végétales domestiquées et cultivées, ou les espèces sauvages devenues parties intégrantes de pratiques et de savoir (plantes médicinales, animaux classés, plantes servant de nourriture à certaines espèces ou de matière première pour l'artisanat)[2].

Par la suite, le champ du patrimoine s'est enrichi des témoins actifs de la tradition :

> Enfin, entrent dans le champ du patrimoine ethnologique des agents vivants (artisans, conteurs, musiciens), des phénomènes collectifs actuels (fêtes, cérémonies), des savoirs spécialisés. Ces derniers sont souvent indissociables d'une technique, comme dans le cas des artisans ou de l'exécution musicale. Ils peuvent être protégés par un consensus social ou un statut qui interdit de les révéler, comme dans le cas du savoir des guérisseurs, des rites d'initiation, de la vie interne des groupes de jeunes[3].

Ce patrimoine ne se laisse « voir » que dans la performance d'un conteur, d'un chanteur, d'un musicien, d'un danseur et même, dans le cas d'un artisan, dans l'acte même de création de l'objet. Ce qui est ici patrimoine est l'émergence esthétique au sein du groupe, instance qui par son jugement de valeur rend la performance légitime.

À plusieurs reprises, l'Unesco a posé le problème de l'extension du patrimoine. À Paris, en 1982, lors d'une rencontre organisée par cet organisme, fut défini le concept de sauvegarde des traditions folkloriques dans un contexte global :

> La sauvegarde a pour objet les traditions folkloriques car les peuples ont droit à leur culture propre que menace une culture industrialisée transmise par les media. Alors que la culture savante et la culture industrielle ont leurs propres moyens économiques, des mesures doivent être prises pour protéger et soutenir économiquement les traditions folkloriques à la fois dans et hors de leurs communautés[4].

Cette déclaration annonce les énoncés de la Conférence de Mexico, qui constitue une des premières instances internationales à se prononcer sur le patrimoine intangible. Après avoir affirmé que « le patrimoine culturel n'est pas seulement un ensemble de biens tangibles, mais aussi un ensemble de traditions, d'habitudes et de coutumes[5] », la Conférence a exploré le concept dans une série de considérations et de recommandations qui incitaient les États membres à assumer la totalité de leur patrimoine :

> La Conférence, considérant que le patrimoine d'une culture ne se limite pas à son héritage artistique mais est constitué par l'ensemble de ses expressions passées, notamment les arts et traditions populaires, les traditions orales et les pratiques culturelles [...] invite les États membres et les organisations internationales œuvrant dans ce domaine à élargir leur politique de protection du patrimoine à l'ensemble de la tradition culturelle ainsi qu'aux contributions à ce patrimoine de la création contemporaine[6].

La définition du patrimoine culturel comprend donc, en un premier temps, en plus de l'héritage artistique au sens strict, toutes les manifestations de la culture traditionnelle sous son aspect surtout esthétique. Puis la définition vint à inclure, en plus des « créations artistiques populaires [...] la langue, les traditions orales, les croyances, les célébrations, les coutumes alimentaires, la médecine, la technologie, etc. » Il fut par conséquent recommandé « d'accorder aux manifestations culturelles traditionnelles non encore consacrées le même rang qu'aux biens historiques ou artistiques, et à épauler, sur le plan technique et financier, les mesures tendant à préserver, développer et diffuser ces manifestations culturelles[7] ».

Une dernière recommandation justifie la préservation, le développement et la diffusion de ce patrimoine comme suit. Les « arts populaires traditionnels (folklore) » constituent en premier lieu un « élément d'identification de l'appartenance à un groupe ethnique et à une communauté nationale et [un] facteur prépondérant d'un patrimoine culturel ». Ils ne doivent cependant pas être considérés exclusivement sous cet aspect car, s'ils « reflètent [...] la spécificité d'une entité culturelle », ils témoignent aussi de « l'universalité des cultures ». Au-delà des contextes immédiats, les cultures de chaque communauté s'enracinent dans l'homme et s'inscrivent ainsi dans un dialogue interculturel qui peut contribuer à rapprocher les communautés. En ce sens, comme l'affirme la recommandation, « ils [les arts populaires traditionnels] peuvent par leur enrichissement mutuel et par leur mise en relief des valeurs communes, contribuer à rapprocher les cultures et les hommes[8] ».

Ces interventions ont imposé une nouvelle conception du patrimoine et, à la séance de clôture de la Conférence, le directeur général de l'Unesco, Amadou-Mahtar M'Bow, pouvait conclure :

> Les débats ont fait par ailleurs ressortir le fait que l'identité culturelle s'incarne dans le patrimoine, matériel et non matériel, des œuvres qu'elle a inspirées tout au long de l'histoire d'un peuple. C'est pourquoi le patrimoine culturel, comme point de repère et matrice, à la fois de la continuité de ce peuple et de sa force de création et de renouvellement, a fait l'objet d'une réflexion des plus approfondies. [...] Enfin, aux côtés des manifestations matérielles, tangibles du patrimoine, grandit l'importance de ses expressions immatérielles – traditions et coutumes, langues ou dialectes, musiques et danses, arts et artisanats, littérature[9].

Les positions adoptées lors de cette conférence de Mexico sont claires. Comment parler de patrimoine sans tenir compte de toute l'extension du terme?

La question des traditions culturelles fut de nouveau abordée lors d'une rencontre de l'Unesco, en décembre 1984, où l'on revint à une définition antérieure en la précisant :

> Il faut entendre par expressions folkloriques ces productions constituées d'éléments caractéristiques d'un patrimoine artistique

traditionnel, patrimoine constitué et conservé par une communauté ou par des individus répondant aux attentes artistiques traditionnelles d'une telle communauté ; en particulier :

I) les modes d'expression verbale comme les contes, la poésie populaire, les devinettes ;

II) les modes d'expression musicale comme la chanson folklorique et la musique instrumentale ;

III) les modes d'expression par l'action comme la danse, le théâtre populaire, les rites ;

IV) les modes d'expression qui prennent forme dans un objet comme :
   a) l'art populaire (dessins, peintures, sculptures, poterie, « terra-cotta », mosaïque, ébénisterie, fer forgé, bijoux, vannerie, broderie, tissage, tapis, costumes ;
   b) les instruments de musique ;
   c) les formes architecturales[10].

Il ressort de cette définition qu'il faut chercher les manifestations du patrimoine vivant, chez les conteurs, les poètes populaires, les maîtres de formes langagières comme les devinettes et les proverbes, les chanteurs, les instrumentistes, les danseurs, les comédiens, les détenteurs de rituels, les dessinateurs, les peintres, les sculpteurs, les potiers, les mosaïstes, les ébénistes, les forgerons, les orfèvres, les vanniers, les brodeurs et brodeuses, les tisserands, les fabricants de tapis, les couturiers et couturières, les fabricants d'instruments de musique, les constructeurs traditionnels. La liste n'est pas exhaustive. Dans ces hommes et ces femmes, dans leurs performances, dans leur présence active au sein de leur communauté, dans leur dynamisme traditionnel se trouve, à proprement parler, le patrimoine vivant.

L'organisme international a posé le problème de la sauvegarde du patrimoine en termes très larges. Pour l'Unesco, le patrimoine englobe plus que le patrimoine bâti. Comment aborder ce patrimoine ?

Pratiques culturelles et action culturelle
Au Canada, dans le domaine du patrimoine, la première démarche fut surtout constituée par la cueillette, l'analyse, la classification, la conservation en archives

et la diffusion par le livre de récits et de chansons traditionnels ainsi que de certaines pratiques coutumières ou pragmatiques.

La démarche qui doit la prolonger n'est pas une entreprise de conservation, ce qui se fait par les archives. Il s'agit d'une animation culturelle en profondeur dont un des effets secondaires sera de sauvegarder les pratiques signifiantes, reconnues comme telles par des communautés culturelles, de les faire connaître et de les faire « reconnaître ». Cette animation s'exerce d'abord au niveau de systèmes esthétiques traditionnels qui opèrent en fonction des valeurs des communautés ; dans un second temps, cette animation se produit au point où ces systèmes entrent en interaction avec des systèmes culturels qui opèrent à d'autres niveaux.

Cette animation profonde peut se faire par une opération de soutien de certaines activités culturelles au sein de la communauté culturelle dans un mouvement centripète de sensibilisation et de découverte, parfois de redécouverte (*in-reach*). Ce soutien peut se manifester par des outils de support et du matériel ainsi que par l'appui des activités. Il s'agit de favoriser l'action interne du groupe (*esoteric factor*) et de faciliter l'apprentissage, de fournir s'il y a lieu un soutien à la professionnalisation et de faciliter les rapports avec les industries culturelles.

Cette animation peut aussi se faire par une démarche de présentation et de mise en valeur de la culture traditionnelle en dehors de sa communauté d'origine elle-même (*out-reach*). Ce qui se réalise par des expositions, des enregistrements sonores, des festivals, des concerts, des publications, des films, des émissions radiophoniques et télévisuelles, des vidéos, des activités pédagogiques en milieu scolaire, des activités culturelles auprès des aînés, etc.

Un rapide examen des politiques de certains organismes permettra de mieux comprendre l'extension de cette animation profonde.

Propositions de l'Unesco et de l'American Folklife Center

Les propositions des comités d'experts convoqués par l'Unesco en 1982[11], 1985[12], 1987[13] et 1989[14] ainsi que celles de l'*American Folklife Center* de Washington[15] sur les politiques de sauvegarde et de mise en valeur vont remarquablement dans le même sens. Elles comportent en premier lieu une planification (1) qui doit tenir compte du patrimoine dans la mise en marche de projets de développement. Par la suite, les propositions touchent à la collecte et à la conservation (2,3), à la sauvegarde et à la protection (4), à la communication (5) et aux normes d'utilisation (6). Le tableau qui suit résume ces propositions. Il ne faut pas oublier que certaines de ces propositions s'adressent surtout à certains pays en développement.

1 **Planification** (*planning*)

2 **Identification** (catalogage et classification) – *documentation*
- inventaire des pratiques traditionnelles (identification des pratiques traditionnelles perçues comme objets de valeur)
- inventaire des collections et des dépôts d'archives
- établissement de protocoles de collecte et d'enregistrement
- cueillette (par le film, l'enregistrement, la photographie, la description)
- établissement d'une typologie du folklore (« *General Outline of Folklore* »)
- coordination entre les systèmes de classement

3 **Conservation et analyse**
- création de centres d'archives
- établissement de réseaux d'archives
- coordination entre les systèmes de classement
- harmonisation des méthodes d'archivage
- formation d'enquêteurs, d'archivistes, de documentaristes
- tenue d'un registre des institutions et des personnes

4 **Préservation** (sauvegarde et protection) – *maintenance*
- introduction de l'étude des traditions folkloriques dans les programmes d'enseignement[16]
- garantie aux différentes ethnies et communautés nationales, du droit à leur propre folklore
- établissement d'ateliers pour enseigner à une nouvelle génération des savoir-faire
- subventions à des témoins émérites de la tradition
- constitution de conseils nationaux du folklore ayant un caractère représentatif

5 **Diffusion** (communication) – *cultural encouragement*
- publication de livres, d'enregistrements, de films afin de faire connaître ces « *distinctive cultural features* » et d'éveiller l'intérêt du public
- création de programmes scolaires qui pourraient comporter des ateliers, des séminaires, des expositions, des cours, du matériel pédagogique et des démonstrations par des artistes populaires
- organisation de manifestations folkloriques à l'échelon régional, national et international : fêtes, festivals, films, expositions, séminaires, symposiums, ateliers, sessions de formation, congrès, etc.

- présentation d'événements qui pourraient recréer des activités traditionnelles : spectacles, activités dans le cadre de musées, expositions, festivals
- création de départements spécialisés à la télévision, à la radio
- encouragement aux régions pour favoriser la création de postes de spécialistes pour la consultation et la planification des activités régionales
- création de centres de production audiovisuelle pour la préparation de documents audiovisuels sur le folklore
- communication par les médias, les centres de documentation, les bibliothèques, les musées, les archives
- création de bibliothèques spécialisées
- organisation de rencontres entre individus, groupes, institutions tant sur le plan national que sur le plan international

6 Utilisation

- respect de la propriété intellectuelle
- protection des porteurs de traditions ainsi que des matériaux recueillis

Le concept de patrimoine vivant se comprend très bien dans le cadre d'une société traditionnelle. Au contact de la culture populaire occidentale et des valeurs véhiculées par les médias, nous savons que les cultures traditionnelles connaissent une érosion rapide et que des savoirs dans le domaine de la pharmacopée traditionnelle, par exemple, disparaissent avec les derniers témoins. Cet héritage, ce patrimoine, est perdu non seulement pour ces sociétés, mais aussi pour les autres sociétés qui y trouveraient leur profit.

Nous devons aussi nous interroger sur le patrimoine vivant dans notre propre milieu. Le champ des pratiques culturelles traditionnelles ne se limite pas à la chanson, à la musique ou à la danse. Dans le domaine des soins du corps, de l'alimentation, du vêtement, des arts et métiers, des loisirs et divertissements, des pratiques orales, des sciences populaires et des pratiques religieuses, des savoir-faire et des savoirs disparaissent. Il y a plus. Je songe aux métiers et professions. Je songe aux souvenirs des ouvriers et ouvrières, aux expériences des communautés religieuses, à l'histoire des familles, bref à toute cette histoire qui, dans les récits d'expériences personnelles, dans les récits de pratiques, dans les récits de vie, dans les *sagas* familiales, peuvent être communiquées. Ces récits qui ne se communiquent que dans le groupe d'appartenance constituent à leur manière un patrimoine d'expériences vitales qui ont une valeur pour tous les hommes et toutes les femmes et pourraient donner forme à une autre histoire. Derrière la mémoire fixée dans les documents officiels, derrière les statistiques qui permettent de définir des modes de vie, il y a en effet ces mémoires partielles et partiales, patrimoine vivant le temps de la vie de ceux et de celles qui les possèdent ou de ceux qui après eux en témoigneront. Là se trouve aussi le passé. Quelle part devrait prendre le projet éducatif dans cette entreprise d'attention au plus fragile des patrimoines.

L'action en milieu éducatif

Il faut en premier lieu faire prendre conscience du fait que les aînés possèdent un savoir. En des temps où ce qu'il faut savoir apparaît instantanément sur l'écran de l'ordinateur, est-il encore pertinent de se tourner vers les autres et d'être à l'écoute ? Le débat est ouvert.

Pour ma part, je souhaite que nous pratiquions une éco-ethnologie.

Je m'explique. Nous prenons conscience de l'urgence de prendre des mesures pour protéger les espèces végétales et animales. Deux plantes sauvages de Madagascar ont permis à des chercheurs de l'Institut Pasteur, à Paris, de développer des traitements pour deux formes de cancer. Dans les forêts tropicales, des plantes aux ressources encore inconnues disparaîtront avec les pratiques de « coupe à blanc » de bois. Or, dans les mémoires des aînés, que d'expériences toujours pertinentes pourraient prendre le chemin de la parole pour enrichir les générations qui suivent. Il n'y a pas que les aînés de notre milieu. Il y a les autres. Les hommes et les femmes d'autres communautés culturelles que nous n'écoutons pas, que nous n'entendons pas. L'ignorance des patrimoines intangibles transforme les communications interculturelles en un dialogue de sourds. Dans l'autre, dans celui qui est différent de nous, nous pouvons trouver ce qui peut nous compléter. Jusqu'ici, l'autre, celui qui est différent de nous, n'a été qu'un objet auquel nous pouvons nous opposer.

Je crois que l'éducation, au sens très large, devrait comporter une démarche d'apprentissage de l'autre, de l'autre par l'âge, par la langue, par l'origine, par la région, par les croyances. J'ai parlé d'une éco-ethnologie, car cette sensibilité à des cultures différentes permet de prendre conscience que mon destin est solidaire dorénavant de celui des autres. Que sur cette planète, votre destin est solidaire du mien.

En milieu scolaire, il faudrait amener les jeunes à entrer en contact avec des centres qui assurent la sauvegarde et la mise en valeur du patrimoine vivant, avec des groupes et des associations actifs dans le domaine de l'animation, et surtout de rencontrer des artistes comme des conteurs, des chanteurs, des danseurs, des instrumentistes et des artisans qui peuvent démontrer leur savoir-faire devant un public. Toujours en milieu scolaire, les jeunes pourraient procéder à des collectes auprès de conteurs, de chanteurs, de danseurs, d'instrumentistes et d'artisans de différentes communautés culturelles et collaborer avec des organismes régionaux pour identifier, conserver et sauvegarder ce patrimoine vivant. Il ne faudrait pas limiter cette démarche aux pratiques artistiques. Des étudiants et étudiantes pourraient recueillir le récit de vie de leurs parents et grands-parents ou, plus simplement, le récit des pratiques de leur métier.

À partir de ces collectes, ils pourraient enfin s'impliquer dans la diffusion, publier des recueils, produire des films, des cassettes, des disques, des documents vidéo, etc., et collaborer à la mise en valeur du patrimoine vivant par l'organisation de spectacles, de festivals de conteurs, de chanteurs, de danseurs, d'instrumentistes, de marionnettistes ainsi que par des expositions et des concerts. Il serait aussi possible de créer des fêtes de la parole où les aînés ainsi que tous ceux et celles que nous nommons les autres pourraient se dire, dire leur vie, dire leur histoire, dire leurs mythes, dire leurs contes. En ce sens, le Festival interculturel du conte de Montréal ouvre de magnifiques perspectives.

En définitive, il y a un patrimoine, un héritage, que lèguent à notre génération les conteurs, les poètes populaires, les maîtres de formes langagières comme les devinettes et les proverbes, les chanteurs, les instrumentistes, les danseurs, les comédiens, les détenteurs de rituels, les dessinateurs, les peintres, les sculpteurs, les potiers, les mosaïstes, les ébénistes, les forgerons, les orfèvres, les vanniers, les brodeurs et brodeuses, les tisserands, les fabricants de tapis, les couturiers et couturières, les fabricants d'instruments de musique, les constructeurs traditionnels.

Il y a aussi un patrimoine, un héritage, constitué des expériences de ceux et celles qui nous ont précédés, mais aussi de ceux et celles qui, différents et différentes, sont à nos côtés paradoxalement étrangers et qu'il faut entendre et comprendre.

Il faut faire l'apprentissage de la découverte et de la rencontre de l'autre en milieu scolaire mais cet apprentissage doit se poursuivre toute la vie, car l'homme et la femme de notre temps sont continuellement en présence de différences où ils peuvent trouver ce qui leur manque.

Notes

1. Voir _Culture et communication_, Paris, numéro hors-série, mars 1980.
2. _Culture et communication_, numéro hors-série, mars 1980, p. 17.
3. _Culture et communication_, numéro hors-série, mars 1980, p. 19.
4. Lauri Honko, « The Unesco Process of Folklore Protection. Working Document » _NIF Newsletter_, 12 (3), décembre 1984, p. 24.
5. Conférence mondiale sur les politiques culturelles, Mexico, du 26 juillet au 6 août 1982, _Rapport final_, [Paris], Unesco, [1982], recommandation 37.
6. Conférence [...] Mexico, du 26 juillet au 6 août 1982, recommandation 63.

7. Conférence [...] Mexico, du 26 juillet au 6 août 1982, recommandation 64.

8. Conférence [...] Mexico, du 26 juillet au 6 août 1982, recommandation 65.

9. Amadou-Mahtar M'Bow, directeur général de l'Unesco, « Allocution », Conférence mondiale sur les politiques culturelles, Mexico, du 26 juillet au 6 août 1982, *Rapport final*, [Paris], Unesco, [1982], p. 203.

10. Lauri Honko, *Op. cit.*, p. 14.

11. *Comité d'experts gouvernementaux sur la sauvegarde du Folklore (Maison de l'Unesco, 22-26 février 1982), rapport présenté par M. Bouadi Kindo, rapporteur général et adopté par le comité*, Paris, Unesco, 1982.

12. *Deuxième comité d'experts gouvernementaux sur la préservation du Folklore (Maison de l'Unesco, 14-18 janvier 1985), rapport présenté par M. Vilmos Voigt, rapporteur général et adopté par le comité d'experts gouvernementaux*, Paris, Unesco, 1985.

13. *Comité spécial de techniciens et de juristes sur la sauvegarde du Folklore (Maison de l'Unesco, 1ᵉʳ-5 juin 1987), rapport présenté par M. Daíthí O'hOgain, rapporteur et adopté par le comité*, Paris, Unesco, 1987.

14. *Projet de recommandation aux États membres sur la sauvegarde du folklore.* Original français, 5 juin 1989, Unesco, Vingt-cinquième session, Paris, 1989.

15. *Cultural Conservation; The Protection of Cultural Heritage in the United States. A Study by the American Folklife Center, Library of Congress, carried out in cooperation with the National Park Service, Department of the Interior.* Coordinated by Ormond H. Loomis. Washington, Library of Congress, 1983, viii+123 p. (Publications of the American Folklife Center: n° 10).

16. Non seulement des pratiques villageoises ou rurales mais aussi de celles qui ont été créées en milieu urbain par divers groupes sociaux, professionnels.

Bibliographie

« Culture et recherche scientifique [entretien avec Roland Barthes] », dans *Culture et communication*, numéro hors-série, mars 1980, p. 6 à 8.

« Dossier : 1980, année du patrimoine », dans *Culture et communication*, n° 23, janvier 1980, p. 2 à 49.

« L'objet, témoignage de permanence [entretien avec Georges-Henri Rivière] », dans *Culture et communication*, n° 23, janvier 1980, p. 42 à 43.

« L'Unesco et la protection du folklore », *Courrier de l'Unesco*, 38ᵉ année, avril 1985, p. 27.

« L'Unesco et les politiques culturelles », dans *Courrier de l'Unesco*, 35ᵉ année, juillet 1982, p. 12 à 13.

« La vitalité d'un sol fertilisé par le temps, entretien avec Jean-Philippe Lecat », dans *Culture et communication*, n° 23, janvier 1980, p. 10 à 11.

« Le patrimoine architectural », dans *Culture et communication*, numéro hors-série, mars 1980, p. 27 à 28.

« Le patrimoine artistique », dans *Culture et communication*, numéro hors-série, mars 1980, p. 23 à 24.

« Le patrimoine audiovisuel », dans *Culture et communication*, numéro hors-série, mars 1980, p. 46 à 47.

« Le patrimoine écrit », dans *Culture et communication*, numéro hors-série, mars 1980, p. 43 à 45.

« Le patrimoine enfoui », dans *Culture et communication*, numéro hors-série, mars 1980, p. 13.

« Le patrimoine ethnologique », dans *Culture et communication*, numéro hors-série, mars 1980, p. 17 à 21.

« Le patrimoine muséographique », dans *Culture et communication*, numéro hors-série, mars 1980, p. 37 à 39.

« Le patrimoine musical », dans *Culture et communication*, numéro hors-série, mars 1980, p. 48 à 49.

Artisanat et traditions orales, Paris, Unesco, 1975. (Développement culturel : dossier documentaire 5; SHC-75/WS/13).

BOURDIN, Alain, *Le patrimoine réinventé*, [Paris], Presses universitaires de France, [©1984], 240 p. (Collection « Espace et liberté »).

Comité d'experts gouvernementaux sur la sauvegarde du Folklore (Maison de l'Unesco, 22-26 février 1982), rapport présenté par M. Bouadi Kindo, rapporteur général et adopté par le comité, Paris, Unesco, 1982.

Comité intergouvernemental pour la décennie mondiale du développement culturel (première session), Paris, 12-16 septembre 1988. Rapport final. [Paris], Unesco, [1988].

Comité spécial de techniciens et de juristes sur la sauvegarde du Folklore (Maison de l'Unesco, 1ᵉʳ-5 juin 1987), rapport présenté par M. Daíthí O'hOgain, rapporteur et adopté par le comité, Paris, Unesco, 1987.

Conférence mondiale sur les politiques culturelles, Mexico, 26 juillet – 6 août 1982. Rapport final. [Paris], Unesco, [1982], 211+xxxix p.

Conventions et recommandations de l'Unesco relatives à la protection du patrimoine culturel. [Paris], Unesco, [1983], 248 p.

Cultural Conservation; The Protection of Cultural Heritage in the United States. A Study by the American Folklife Center, Library of Congress, carried out in cooperation with the National Park Service, Department of the Interior. Coordinated by Ormond H. Loomis. Washington, Library of Congress, 1983, viii+123 p. (Publications of the American Folklife Center: n° 10).

Culture plus, Lettre de la Décennie mondiale du développement culturel, Lettre n° 1, mars 1989.

Deuxième comité d'experts gouvernementaux sur la préservation du Folklore (Maison de l'Unesco, 14-18 janvier 1985), rapport présenté par M. Vilmos Voigt, rapporteur général et adopté par le comité d'experts gouvernementaux, Paris, Unesco, 1985.

DU BERGER, Jean, avec la collaboration de Simonne Dubois-Ouellet, *Pratiques culturelles traditionnelles* [Québec, Célat, 1989], 238 p. (« Rapports et Mémoires du Célat », n° 13, janvier 1989).

GABORIT, J.-R. et Ph. DUREY, « L'année du Patrimoine », dans *Universalia 1981*, p. 442 à 443.

GUILLAUME, Marc, *La politique du patrimoine*, Paris, Éditions Galilée, [1980], 196 p. (Collection « L'espace critique »).

HONKO, Lauri, « Do We Need an International Treaty for the Protection of Folklore? » *NIF Newsletter*, Nordic Institute of Folklore [Turku, Finlande], 12 (3), 1984, p. 1 à 3.

_____, « Possibilities of International Cooperation and Regulation in the Safeguarding of Folklore » *NIF Newsletter*, vol. 15, n° 1, May 1987, p. 10.

_____, « Protecting Folklore as Intellectual Property » *NIF Newsletter*, Nordic Institute of Folklore [Turku, Finlande], 11 (1), 1983, p. 1 à 7

_____, « The Final Text of the Recommendation for the Safeguarding of Folklore » *NIF Newsletter*, vol. 17, n° 2-3, juin 1989, p. 3 à 12.

_____, « The Unesco Process of Folklore Protection. Working Document » *NIF Newsletter*, Nordic Institute of Folklore [Turku, Finlande], 12 (3), décembre 1984, p. 10.

_____, « Unesco Work on the Safeguarding of Folklore » *NIF Newsletter*, Nordic Institute of Folklore [Turku, Finlande], 10 (1-2), juin 1982, p. 1 à 5.

_____, « What Kind of Instrument for Folklore Protection? » *NIF Newsletter*, Nordic Institute of Folklore [Turku, Finlande], 13 (1-2), 1985, p. 3 à 11.

Introduction aux études interculturelles : esquisse d'un projet pour l'élucidation et la promotion de la communication entre les cultures, Unesco, 1976-1980. [Paris], Unesco, [1980], 225 p.

JEUDY, Henri Pierre, *Patrimoines en folie*, Paris, Éditions de la Maison des sciences de l'homme, [©1990], 297 p.

L'aide-mémoire; répertoire pratique pour la mise-en-valeur du patrimoine québécois, version préliminaire, [Québec, Télé-université, 1978], 321 p.

La culture et l'avenir, [Paris], Unesco, [1985], 57 p.

LAMONTAGNE, Sophie-Laurence, *Le patrimoine immatériel : méthodologie d'inventaire pour les savoirs, les savoir-faire et les porteurs*, Québec, Les Publications du Québec, 1994, 135 p., Coll. Patrimoines, Dossiers.

Le développement culturel : expériences régionales, [Paris], Unesco, [1980], 454 p.

Le macro-inventaire : une banque de données sur les biens culturels du Québec [Québec], Ministère des Affaires culturelles, Direction générale du patrimoine, 1981, 15 p.

Le macro-inventaire du patrimoine québécois [Québec], Service du patrimoine du ministère des affaires culturelles, 1985, 150 p. (« Les publications du Québec »)

Le patrimoine, enjeu de notre lutte collective [Québec, Télé-université, 1978]. (Cahiers d'études, n° 4).

Le patrimoine, nouvelle dimension du changement [Québec, Télé-université, 1978]. (Cahiers d'études, n° 2).

Le patrimoine, un témoignage omniprésent [Québec, Télé-université, 1978]. (Cahiers d'études, n° 1).

Le patrimoine, une ressource à mettre en valeur [Québec, Télé-université, 1978]. (Cahiers d'études, n° 3).

Patrimoines, Québec, Ministère des Affaires culturelles, 1982, 29 p.

PICARD, François, *Le patrimoine maritime au Québec : état de la situation et recommandations* [Québec], Commission des biens culturels du Québec, [1983], 60 p.

Projet de recommandation aux états membres sur la sauvegarde du folklore. Original français, 5 juin 1989, Unesco, Vingt-cinquième session, Paris, 1989.

PROVENCHER, Jean, *Le patrimoine agricole et horticole au Québec : état de la situation et recommandations* [Québec], Commission des biens culturels du Québec, [1984], 94 p.

RIOUX, Jean-Pierre, « L'émoi patrimonial », dans *Le Temps de la réflexion*, VI, 1985, p. 39 à 48.

SKJELBRED, Ann Helen B., « The Nordic Perspective on Safeguarding Folklore » NIF's 4th Nordic Conference on Archives and Documentation in Bergen, 11-13 septembre 1986», *NIF Newsletter*, Nordic Institute of Folklore [Turku, Finlande], 14, n° 4, December-January 1986, p. 8 à 25.

TROTTIER, Louise, *Le patrimoine industriel au Québec : état de la situation et recommandations* [Québec], Commission des biens culturels du Québec, [1985], 85 p.

ANNETTE SAINT-PIERRE

Pour intéresser les jeunes et les moins jeunes à l'histoire

Résumé

Cette communication présente des d'expériences personnelles vécues au cours de l'enseignement de l'histoire au niveau secondaire et de la littérature régionale au niveau universitaire. Elle montre l'importance de familiariser les étudiants avec les lieux qui les environnent et de les mettre en contact avec ceux et celles qui peuvent susciter leur enthousiasme en les initiant à l'histoire orale – pages d'histoire jusque-là inconnues.

Par le biais du théâtre, l'histoire s'anime et déclenche des émotions susceptibles de nous sensibiliser aux valeurs de l'identité canadienne. Naîtra ensuite un intérêt plus aigu non seulement pour le vécu des personnages historiques de la scène théâtrale, mais aussi pour leur milieu respectif. Une fois la curiosité éveillée, les livres d'histoire seront plus invitants, car on s'identifiera naturellement aux faits et gestes des devanciers.

Il sera difficile de résister à l'écriture pour immortaliser son coin de pays ou encore le souvenir des intrépides pionnières et pionniers. Petit à petit, l'esprit s'ouvrira aux groupes de la mosaïque canadienne dont l'apport précieux a grandement enrichi le Canada. En entrant dans la grande mouvance de l'histoire, professeurs, écrivains, cinéastes et artistes – chacun à sa manière – racontent le passé aux jeunes et aux moins jeunes. Et si l'on sait apprécier la petite histoire de la grande histoire, la source de notre identité sera intarissable.

Turning Adolescents and Young Adults on to History – Abstract

This paper is a sharing of personal experiences from the teaching of history in secondary school and regional literature in university. It shows the importance of familiarizing students with the places around them and putting them in contact with those who can stimulate their enthusiasm by introducing them to oral history – pages of history until then unknown.

Through theatre, history comes alive and releases in us emotions that can make us more sensitive to the values connected with Canadian identity. This will lead to an increased interest not only in the experiences of the historic personages portrayed on stage, but also in their respective milieu. Once their curiosity is awakened, the young people will find history books more inviting, since they will naturally identify with the actions of those who came before them.

It will be hard for them to resist what has been written to immortalize their own part of their country or the memory of brave pioneers. Little by little, they will open their minds to the various groups in the Canadian mosaic whose contributions have greatly enriched Canada. Teachers, writers, film-makers, and artists, each in their own way can convey the past to young people. An appreciation for the footnotes of history can only strengthen our sense of identity.

Les Canadiens ne sont pas « un peuple sans histoire » et il leur appartiendra toujours de veiller à la conservation d'un héritage légué par ceux et celles qui ont fait le pays. Le symposium national auquel nous participons aujourd'hui témoigne d'un certain engagement en réunissant des personnalités qui, par amour et respect du patrimoine canadien, acceptent de tenir le flambeau de la mémoire.

Pour ma part, si l'on m'avait dit qu'un jour je m'adresserais à un auditoire de la Commission des lieux et monuments historiques du Canada et prédit que j'en arriverais à aimer l'histoire, j'aurais répliqué que l'on me connaissait mal. J'étais vraiment trop « présentiste » pour perdre du temps à examiner le passé. Au fil des ans, cependant, grâce à un cheminement plein de surprises, j'ai compris que rien ne valait l'histoire pour comprendre le présent et bâtir l'avenir. Mais comment oublier le jour où j'ai dû affronter l'enseignement de l'histoire ? J'avais entre les mains un manuel intitulé : *Canada, Land of the Beaver,* devant moi des gamins et gamines d'une douzaine d'années, et en mémoire une tout autre version de certains faits historiques.

La deuxième épreuve s'est présentée cinq ans plus tard. Un accident de parcours, puisque mon contrat stipulait clairement que je serais professeure de français dans un « High School » et non professeure d'histoire. L'historien que j'allais côtoyer au cours de cette année-là avait consacré un chapitre de son manuel à chaque province canadienne ; mais alors que l'histoire du Québec s'étendait voluptueusement sur soixante pages, celle du Manitoba était coincée entre trois pages. Une fois dans l'arène, j'ai donc décidé de me mouiller les pieds en annonçant à la classe mon intention de modifier le contenu du cours. Il y aurait deux pages sur le Québec et soixante pages sur le Manitoba.

L'entreprise était téméraire, mais une promesse est une promesse. En conséquence, le cours absorbait toute mon énergie, m'obligeant à fouiner à droite et à gauche et, le plus souvent, à traduire en français des textes que j'adaptais à mon auditoire. Je me mis à correspondre avec la plupart des ministères du

Manitoba : Santé, Pêcheries, Mines et Éducation, où l'on devinait mon cri d'alarme et m'expédiait feuillets et brochures.

Chose étonnante, cet enseignement à la pointe de l'actualité amena les élèves à ouvrir les yeux sur le passé. Par exemple, la présence d'un cairn à Sainte-Anne-des-Chênes dont personne ne pouvait dire qu'il rappelait le vieux chemin Dawson, et une vieille bicoque qui était bel et bien un ancien poste de fourrures de la Compagnie de la Baie d'Hudson. Peu à peu, des jeunes commencèrent à s'intéresser aux sites historiques et à annoncer à la classe qu'ils avaient vu un monument à telle entrée de village ou une plaque commémorative devant un quelconque édifice.

Après ces incursions sur des sentiers inconnus, j'entrai au Collège universitaire de Saint-Boniface pour entreprendre, le printemps suivant, des études doctorales en lettres françaises. Par quel hasard ai-je choisi comme sujet de thèse : « Cent ans de théâtre au Manitoba français » ? Des recherches m'obligeant à couvrir cent ans d'histoire me donnèrent accès à une littérature populaire et à des œuvres majeures publiées en France par des colons de l'Ouest canadien. De telles découvertes me conduisirent à la création d'un cours favorablement approuvé par le sénat de l'Université du Manitoba ; mais cette littérature régionale, avec ses profondes racines dans l'histoire, il m'était impossible d'en enseigner les premiers balbutiements sans consulter les archives.

Ce cours de littérature populaire marqua un point tournant dans mon évolution personnelle et dans celle de certains étudiants qui apprirent – moi aussi, d'ailleurs – que la naissance de notre littérature orale remontait à 1816 avec Pierre Falcon. En étudiant les chansons de ce « barde des prairies », les légendes des Métis, les récits des voyageurs et les poèmes de Louis Riel, la classe de littérature se transformait en laboratoire d'histoire. Des invitations furent lancées à des personnes âgées pour qu'elles nous racontent les faits véhiculés par la tradition orale et nous éclairent sur le mode de vie des anciens. Mais le point culminant de cette année inoubliable fut, sans contredit, le spectacle « Au pays des Bois-Brûlés ».

De cette aventure théâtrale, je garde le meilleur souvenir. Lors de la dernière représentation, je me tenais près d'un étudiant qui attendait de monter sur scène. Il devait interpréter *La Chanson de la Grenouillère* relatant une sérieuse escarmouche entre les deux compagnies de fourrures rivales. En me serrant la main, il murmura à mon oreille : « Madame, ça me fait de la peine de chanter pour la dernière fois. Mais je dois vous dire une chose. Maintenant, je sais ce que c'est que d'avoir une identité ».

Avoir une identité, se définir par rapport à quelque chose ou à quelqu'un, ne peut résulter que d'une meilleure connaissance de l'histoire et de ses semblables. C'est se sentir à l'aise dans son passé, vibrer à certains faits, former un groupe avec ceux de sa culture, trouver des modèles parmi ceux et celles qui partagent le même sol, être fier et satisfait de soi-même, avoir un sentiment d'appartenance à la grande nation canadienne. Ce jeune qui chantait du Falcon n'était pas un Métis, mais celui qu'il incarnait avec tant de cœur et de sincérité avait eu comme lui un père canadien-français et un grand-père français, un même sang coulait dans leurs veines, un même rêve les rapprochait et, pour ce, l'étudiant s'identifiait pleinement au personnage historique.

Aujourd'hui, il me semble que j'aurais pu faire davantage pour aider les étudiants à ressusciter leur passé, à retrouver leur dignité, à se redécouvrir une identité et à s'engager pour transformer le présent et édifier un avenir meilleur. Si j'avais fait une carrière en histoire... j'aurais sans doute réussi à faire se tenir debout un plus grand nombre d'hommes et de femmes, à les enraciner à leur sol et à les rendre fiers de leur histoire. Car l'histoire, il faut le dire et le redire, c'est une arme puissante. Elle nous permet de donner une mémoire durable à une génération d'étudiants, de leur fournir des repères, des jalons, de leur inculquer des valeurs leur permettant de faire pousser leurs racines loin dans la terre, des racines qui les empêcheraient de se déraciner et de perdre leur identité.

Un Manitobain qui réside au Québec depuis quelques années et à qui l'on demandait le pourquoi de son départ répondait : « Au Manitoba, je me suis toujours senti inférieur aux autres parce que j'étais francophone et je n'ai pas voulu que mes enfants connaissent le même sort ». S'il y avait eu chez cet homme, aujourd'hui professeur d'université, un meilleur ancrage de son identité, une profonde quête de son passé, aurait-il quitté le Manitoba ?

Après la réalisation du spectacle, « Au pays des Bois-Brûlés », j'avais le cœur dans l'histoire du Manitoba. Je n'allais jamais en guérir car, le cours de littérature populaire m'avait ouvert l'esprit sur un univers à mille fenêtres. L'année suivante, une fois initiés aux techniques de l'interview, certains étudiants allèrent rencontrer des personnes âgées. Je fus très étonnée de les voir s'abreuver avec autant d'empressement à la mémoire de leurs grands-parents, de les voir rapporter en classe, tel un trophée, un journal intime ou un chansonnier dont les compositions de circonstance étaient souvent émaillées de faits historiques.

Pour couronner cette année scolaire, une excursion permit à la classe de se rendre à l'ancienne terre du voyageur Jean-Baptiste Lagimodière, à la barrière érigée par les Métis pour interdire l'entrée du lieutenant-gouverneur dans une province encore non existante, ainsi qu'à la maison de la famille Riel, restaurée depuis par Parcs Canada. À une autre occasion, ce fut la visite des vestiges du Fort Garry d'En-Haut et le magnifique Fort Garry d'En-Bas, propriété de Parcs Canada. Plus tard, en compagnie de visiteurs étrangers, j'allais revoir, parmi les guides de sites historiques, des étudiants du Collège universitaire de Saint-Boniface.

Je reviens ici à une autre initiative enrichissante pour les étudiants : une tournée dans le vieux Saint-Boniface pour entendre une étudiante parler des maisons historiques. La recherche effectuée avec beaucoup de rigueur a produit une excellente documentation qui pourrait servir à la publication de feuillets touristiques. Il ne faut pas attendre l'annonce d'un projet de démolition pour se mettre à vanter le cachet particulier d'une maison, d'un hôtel ou d'un pont. Quand on songe à la démolition du Fort Garry d'En-haut dans le but d'obtenir une rue Main plus droite, on ne peut que déplorer l'ignorance et l'insouciance des témoins de ce temps-là.

Mes contacts avec les personnes âgées, et la satisfaction de découvrir du nouveau chaque fois que je jetais un regard en arrière, m'ont amenée à accepter l'animation d'un atelier de création littéraire au sein duquel des personnes du troisième âge allaient dire des choses qu'on ne retrouve pas dans les livres. Dans les traits de mes auditeurs et auditrices, je pouvais lire l'histoire de toute une vie, une vie qu'il fallait dire aux générations. C'était folie que de sacrifier un après-midi deux fois le mois à écouter de la petite histoire ; par ailleurs, l'atelier s'avérait une telle thérapeutique qu'il m'arrivait parfois de m'y présenter souffrant d'un mal de tête et d'en ressortir de fort bonne humeur.

Invités dans mes classes de littérature populaire, les membres de cet atelier faisaient la lecture de leurs textes ou répondaient à des questions sur la vie et les coutumes de leur temps. Ils suscitaient l'admiration des jeunes qui, tout en s'étonnant de la qualité de leur écriture, appréciaient la richesse de leurs témoignages. Laissez-moi raconter un fait survenu il y quelques mois, alors qu'une page du *Dictionnaire biographique du Canada* me rappelait du déjà vu, c'est-à-dire une aventure racontée par une de mes « élèves » de 84 ans. Je m'empressai de consulter les cahiers du club des Plumes d'Or pour vérifier les faits et découvrir qu'il s'agissait du même massacre dont traitait l'article du dictionnaire. Le voici en quelques mots. Une princesse crise massacrée par des Sioux et laissée pour morte avait survécu après avoir été secourue par des hommes de la Compagnie du Nord-Ouest. À cela, la dame des Plumes d'Or ajoutait que les sauveteurs avaient alors utilisé la peau fraîche d'une vessie d'animal pour replacer et greffer la peau de la victime sur son crâne. Et c'est de cette princesse crise, qui a vécu jusqu'à près de cent ans, que descendait mon « élève », Marguerite Trudel.

L'histoire orale a sa valeur, même si elle n'est pas toujours consignée par l'histoire écrite. Et s'il est vrai que les meilleurs philosophes sont ceux qui ont vécu, les meilleurs historiens ne seraient-ils pas ceux qui ont vécu l'histoire ? En écoutant les membres des Plumes d'Or, au soir de leur vie, raconter des anecdotes avec tant de lucidité, d'émotion et de précision, j'avais l'impression de faire de l'histoire et non de la littérature. Pierre-Joseph-Olivier Chauveau avait donc raison de dire que « la littérature, c'est son histoire ». En réalité, des ateliers de ce genre lancent parfois de sérieux défis puisque la mouche de l'édition peut nous piquer. Ce fut mon cas, car je m'engageai sérieusement dans le monde fragile de l'édition, un monde susceptible d'aiguiser la soif d'apprendre et le désir de partager les fruits de ses découvertes. Cinq ans après la fondation des Éditions du Blé sont venues les Éditions des Plaines, qui ont maintenant quinze ans. Cette deuxième maison ne se borne pas à la province du Manitoba mais se tourne vers les autres provinces de l'Ouest, ainsi que vers l'Ontario, où certains auteurs s'identifient mieux à l'Ouest qu'à l'Est du pays.

L'histoire du Manitoba est à l'image de la province, belle et jeune, tout comme ses sœurs de l'Ouest d'ailleurs. Mais que de ramifications ! On n'en finit plus de découvrir une aventure passionnante, un fait à publier ou un personnage à illustrer. Publier un livre dans l'Ouest est peu de chose dans la grande mouvance historique canadienne, mais c'est en semant régulièrement aux quatre vents que les porte-parole de l'Ouest canadien assureront une relève.

Il y a trois ans environ, un enseignant à la recherche d'un livre d'histoire sur le Manitoba me demanda un bouquin qui parlerait de tout avec des textes courts et illustrés. Puisqu'il allait accompagner une classe de trente élèves en Europe, il désirait que chacun d'eux présente un tel livre à sa famille d'accueil. Par-dessus tout, il souhaitait les voir répondre intelligemment aux questions des petits Français. Comment ses élèves allaient-il discourir sur le climat, la population, les industries ou le gouvernement, eux qui n'en savaient rien. Cette boutade m'a fait réfléchir et m'a incitée à écrire : *Le Manitoba au cœur de l'Amérique*. Le livre dirait le Manitoba aux Français, aux Canadiens, mais tout particulièrement aux Manitobains. En somme, je ferais d'une pierre trois coups. C'est le sort réservé à tout livre d'histoire issu de l'Ouest. En le lisant, les Français ne prennent plus pour des Martiens les francophones de l'Ouest qui s'aventurent sur leur sol, les

Canadiens font la connaissance de cette province et les habitants de cette dernière apprécient davantage leur coin de pays. Si Pierre Lalonde avait connu notre histoire, il aurait certainement chanté autre chose que : « À Winnipeg, les filles sont blondes / À Winnipeg, les nuits sont longues ».

Le Manitoba compte de bons historiens qui accueillent dans leurs rangs tout profane désireux de mettre la main à la pâte. À preuve, la contribution remarquable d'un Marcien Ferland, professeur de langue, musicien et directeur de chorale, qui a écrit et porté à la scène une trilogie historique : *Les Batteux, Au temps de la prairie* et *Le voyageur*. Les spectateurs ont applaudi les scènes historiques qui ressuscitaient leur passé et suscitaient leurs émotions. Un théâtre qui imprime des faits dans la mémoire collective ne peut que déclencher l'amour de l'histoire. Avant Ferland, Rosemarie Bissonnette, ancienne fonctionnaire du gouvernement fédéral, avait signé une pièce de théâtre historique pour la célébration du centième anniversaire de son village natal ; depuis, elle s'est lancée dans l'aventure d'un livre sur Marguerite Monnet, épouse de Louis Riel – autre cas de parcours allant de la petite histoire à la grande histoire.

J'aimerais parler d'un ecclésiastique qui, lors d'un stage d'études à Ottawa, confiait à quel point cela le gênait d'être interrogé sur le Manitoba quand il n'avait rien à répondre. Son alma mater, le Collège de Saint-Boniface, dont les professeurs étaient originaires du Québec, n'avait pu lui apprendre son histoire régionale si peu connue à l'époque. Un jour, cependant, il fit la lecture de *L'espace de Louis Goulet* et se mit à considérer comme une bible ce livre qui parlait du Manitoba. L'auteur, Guillaume Charette, avocat d'ascendance métisse, donnait des conférences, rédigeait des articles et recueillait précieusement les histoires de son peuple pour les raconter à son tour. Du vieux conteur de la station CKSB, sa fille religieuse écrivait : « Blottie dans l'escalier, j'écoutais, ravie, les aventures d'autrefois ». Si les récits de ce conteur exceptionnel sont passés à l'histoire, c'est grâce à celui qui les a confiés à un éditeur pour souligner l'existence d'une histoire vivante dans la mémoire des anciens, une histoire que nous nous devons de sauvegarder.

Grâce au programme, Exploration du Conseil des Arts du Canada, avant et après la création du Centre d'études franco-canadiennes de l'Ouest, nous avons obtenu des subventions pour des projets apparentés à l'histoire. En plus d'aider certains étudiants à « subsister jusqu'à la saison prochaine », de tels projets avaient l'avantage d'éveiller chez eux le goût de la recherche et la passion de l'histoire. En effet, parmi ces chercheurs en herbe, les uns ont poursuivi des études en histoire, les autres se sont engagés dans des organismes à vocation historique.

❖ ❖ ❖

De mon côté, la muse de l'histoire, Clio, vient de m'inviter à emprunter un sentier non battu : une chronologie du Manitoba. Mes nombreuses cueillettes risquent de me mener assez loin, car les pistes sont si nombreuses que le projet compte déjà deux cents pages. Pendant ce temps, il me faut avouer qu'une conversion s'opère en moi ; en effet, si ce travail avait été entrepris il y a une dizaine d'années, seuls les éléments de la francophonie auraient été retenus. C'est ainsi qu'au cours de la réalisation de *L'Almanach français du Manitoba*, l'équipe d'étudiants avait pour consigne de glaner seulement des faits se rapportant à la francophonie. Aujourd'hui, mon rayon d'observation s'élargit et mon respect grandit envers tous les pionniers, fussent-ils Allemands, Écossais, Français, Anglais, Ukrainiens, Polonais, Russes ou Américains. En promenant mon regard sur une plus grande surface et en observant l'apport de tous les Canadiens et Canadiennes, je ne peux qu'enrichir l'histoire manitobaine.

J'ai enseigné que Marie-Anne Gaboury était la première femme blanche à venir dans l'Ouest canadien et la mère du premier enfant blanc né dans les Prairies, jusqu'au jour où, en éditant un livre de Hugh McEwan, j'ai appris qu'elle avait eu une devancière. À ce moment-là, j'ai préféré croire que l'historien anglais manquait de rigueur et j'ai accepté les réprimandes d'un lecteur m'accusant d'avoir publié des mensonges. Eh bien! dans mon livre, *De fil en aiguille au Manitoba,* je dirai la vérité, quitte à entendre d'autres semonces parce que j'aurai quelque peu démystifié Marie-Anne Gaboury.

Voici les faits. Une Écossaise, Isabel Gunn, sous le nom de John Fubbister, suit son amoureux dans la terre de Rupert, en compagnie des hommes de la Baie d'Hudson. Au cours de son voyage en mer et de son séjour dans un poste de fourrure, Isabel remplit les tâches d'un garçon jusqu'au jour où elle entre dans le bureau du bourgeois et se jette par terre en poussant des cris. Après avoir accouché, à la surprise de tous, la pauvre fille va rejoindre le père du bébé dans un autre fort et, plus tard, rentre en Angleterre. Alors que la naissance de ce premier enfant blanc dans l'Ouest canadien remonte au 29 décembre 1806, celle du premier enfant de Marie-Anne Gaboury remonte au 6 janvier 1807. Mais, pour ne pas détrôner une héroïne manitobaine, il nous reste à affirmer que Marie-Anne Gaboury a été la première femme blanche à s'installer au Manitoba, puisque sa rivale est rentrée en Angleterre. On devrait élever un monument historique en son honneur, et pourquoi pas un autre à la mémoire de la pauvre Isabel ?

Si la vue d'un monument historique nous rappelle la mémoire d'hommes, de femmes ou d'événements, que dire d'une maison historique ? Au Manitoba, la maison de la romancière, Margaret Lawrence, fait l'orgueil du petit village de Neepawa, qui s'attire de nombreux touristes. Ce phénomène nous fait songer avec un peu d'amertume à la maison d'une autre écrivaine de réputation internationale, Gabrielle Roy, première auteure canadienne à recevoir un prix littéraire de la France, le prestigieux prix Femina. Actuellement, devant la maison Gabrielle-Roy, femme dont les œuvres sont traduites en plusieurs langues, une humble plaque historique marque le lieu de la naissance, de l'enfance et de la jeunesse de celle qui a tant contribué à faire connaître le Manitoba et ses habitants. La maison ayant été divisée en appartements, il faut se contenter de passer devant la porte et de dire au visiteur que « c'est là qu'a vécu Gabrielle Roy ».

Il y a une vingtaine d'années, un dossier présenté au ministère de la Culture du Manitoba avait été volontairement ignoré parce que l'auteure vivait encore. Dans les années quatre-vingts, l'achat de la maison très délabrée au prix de 36 000 $ aurait été possible, mais le manque de fonds pour la restaurer avait mis fin à nos rêves. Le troisième propriétaire a vendu la maison pour la somme de 115 000 $, et le quatrième, un Ukrainien, vient de la remettre sur le marché pour 151 000 $. Ces chiffres doivent faire se retourner dans leur tombe le bon monsieur Léon Roy qui la construisit au prix de 600 $ et la bonne madame Roy qui la vendit pour payer les impôts fonciers.

Mais un projet commun se dessine puisqu'un comité *ad hoc*[1] a décidé d'honorer la mémoire de Gabrielle Roy. C'est le temps ou jamais de passer à l'action. Une rencontre réunissant deux agents d'immobilier, trois administrateurs, un architecte, un artiste, une éditrice et une conservatrice de musée, a été suivie d'une réunion générale où s'est manifestée la volonté de réaliser un si beau projet. Le chemin sera long et difficile, mais c'est une « histoire que l'on ne saurait taire», en 1995, à l'occasion du colloque international sur Gabrielle Roy. Ne dit-on pas « qu'à force de désirer une fleur, on finit par la faire naître » ?

L'histoire d'une région ou d'un pays n'est jamais trop riche, et l'on n'en finira jamais d'y poser des jalons. Un autre projet pourrait voir le jour pour immortaliser un sculpteur de chez nous. Au petit village de Grahamdale, situé près de 500 km au nord de Winnipeg, nous avons vu une vingtaine de sculptures, abandonnées dans un champ où l'on ne se rend que pour faire les foins. Les sculptures de ciment installées sur de grands socles sont placées çà et là, à proximité de bâtiments désaffectés. On y voit Adam et Ève, Nixon, ancien président américain, un centaure, un singe, des dinosaures, un démon, une femme nue, etc., mais cinq des vingt sculptures ont été vandalisées. Quelle merveilleuse occasion d'intéresser les jeunes et les moins jeunes à la petite histoire en érigeant un parc à la mémoire du sculpteur belge, Armand Lemeiz.

La petite histoire! C'est ce qui motive l'artiste, Réal Bérard, si on lui demande le pourquoi de ses longues randonnées en canot pour faire le tracé de lacs et de rivières. Notons sa carte de la région de la Petite Poule d'Eau publiée par le ministère du Tourisme, lequel a fait ériger par la suite une plaque commémorative dans cette région sauvage si bien décrite par la romancière, Gabrielle Roy. Actuellement, Bérard revit la dangereuse aventure de l'artiste, René Richard, en suivant l'itinéraire de son voyage allant du nord de l'Alberta jusqu'au pays de l'Ungava.

On retrouve des jeunes et des moins jeunes, amoureux fous de l'histoire, au sein de la Brigade de la Rivière-Rouge, fondée il y a une quinzaine d'années. À sa tête, un bourgeois ou membre honoraire, un commis ou président, un guide, un chanteur et un interprète. Cette brigade, qui compte 130 membres, s'applique à faire revivre l'histoire du voyageur par le truchement d'expéditions allant du parc Quetico (Quebec Timber Company), situé au sud d'Atikokan (Ontario), jusqu'au Montana. Nous n'avons pas à parler longtemps avec ces « voyageurs » pour nous rendre compte à quel point ils connaissent leur histoire. À n'en pas douter, les chansons françaises doivent résonner pendant leurs longues heures de portage et de canotage puisque 90 % d'entre eux sont francophones.

Un autre groupe puise abondamment dans l'histoire du Manitoba en ranimant l'enceinte du fort Gibraltar, rebâti du côté est de la rivière Rouge. Les Associés du fort Gibraltar, transportés dans le temps et revêtus d'habits de l'époque, se mettent dans la peau des employés de la Compagnie du Nord-Ouest ; ils attirent les visiteurs, qui s'émerveillent à la vue des tisserandes et des ménagères, des forgerons et des fabricants de canots. C'est une affaire de famille puisque les enfants, aussi nombreux que les parents, sont recrutés parmi les scouts promus au grade de « pionniers » dans leur mouvement. Comme cette page d'histoire ajoute beaucoup à la couleur locale, les Associés du fort Gibraltar sont parfois les hôtes de visites officielles, telle celle des membres de la force policière venus dernièrement de tous les coins du Canada

L'histoire éclate de partout. En littérature, en peinture, en musique, en architecture et, bien sûr, dans la mémoire des moins jeunes qui l'ont vécue et parfois relatée. Dernièrement, tout un pan d'histoire a été découvert à la suite de la rencontre de deux dames voyageant en Égypte. La Française en apprenant que l'autre venait du Canada, a révélé que son arrière-grand-mère avait vécu au Manitoba et qu'un manuscrit retrouvé récemment parlait de sa vie sur un homestead à Sainte-Rose-du-Lac : *Soupe maigre et tasse de thé* est le titre de ce livre, publié en septembre dernier. C'est une première dans l'histoire du Manitoba. Que de lecteurs et lectrices vont maintenant revivre l'odyssée de leurs ancêtres et s'identifier à cette pionnière manitobaine !

✛ ✛ ✛

Cette œuvre d'identification peut être amorcée en faisant vivre à des jeunes des émotions fortes surgissant de leur pays natal ; au cours des ans, des occasions multiples se présenteront pour affiner cette même identité. Les étapes d'un cheminement personnel sont différentes, mais elles offrent aussi des images indélébiles, des sensations profondes où s'imprime et se conjugue une identité canadienne. Et l'histoire – la petite et la grande – restera toujours la source de cette identité.

Note

1. Depuis, la Corporation Maison Gabrielle-Roy a été fondée dans le but d'acheter et de restaurer la maison de cette auteure.

La maison natale, rue Deschambault, à Saint-Boniface

La maison de Gabrielle Roy au 375, rue Deschambault, Saint-Boniface, où l'auteure a vécu entre 1909 et 1937. / The home of Gabrielle Roy, located at 375 Deschambault Street in Saint-Boniface, where she lived from 1909 until 1937. (Photo : gracieuseté de / courtesy of La Société historique de Saint-Boniface)

153

Marie-Anne Gaboury (1780-1875), grand-mère de Louis Riel ; désignée en 1982 / grandmother of Louis Riel; designated 1982. (Photo : Marie-Anne Gaboury en compagnie du Père Norbert Provencher (détail) ; collée sur papier d'emballage par Pauline Boutal ; gratieuseté des archives du Collège universitaire de Saint-Boniface (Manitoba) / Marie-Anne Gaboury with Father Norbert Provencher (detail); pastel on brown paper by Pauline Boutal; courtesy of the Archives of Saint-Boniface College, Manitoba)

Louis Riel (1844-1885), chef des Métis, « père du Manitoba » ; désigné en 1956 / leader of the Métis, "father of Manitoba"; designated 1956. (Photo : Archives nationales / National Archives, C-18082)

Le couvent des Soeurs Grises à Saint-Boniface (Manitoba), constuit entre 1845 et 1851 ; désigné en 1958. / Grey Nuns' Convent, Saint-Boniface, Manitoba, was constructed between 1845 and 1851; designated 1958. (Photo : HRS, 1986).

Hôtel de ville de Saint-Boniface (Manitoba), construite en 1905 ; désigné en 1984 / Saint-Boniface city hall, Manitoba, was built in 1905; designated 1984. (Photo : HRS, 1986)

155

La route Dawson, voie de communication terrestre et fluviale entre le lac Supérieur et la rivière Rouge achevée en 1871, est marquée par un cairn installée à Sainte-Anne-des-Chênes (Manitoba), en 1939. / The Dawson Road, a land and water route from Lake Superior to Red River completed in 1871, is marked by a cairn that was erected in Sainte-Anne, Manitoba, in 1939.

KEN OSBORNE

Teaching Heritage in the Classroom

Abstract

This paper surveys the place of heritage education in the school systems of Canada. It focuses primarily on curricula, programmes of study, textbooks and other teaching materials, and on school and classroom activities. It looks mainly at work being done in the subjects of history and social studies, since this is where much teaching about heritage is concentrated, but it does not ignore other aspects of the curriculum, such as literature, drama, and the arts. It also takes account of the initiatives of teachers, archives, museums, and the heritage community generally. The paper includes a brief look at the past, but its main emphasis is directed towards what is being done in schools today. At the same time, the paper is more than descriptive. It presents an argument to the effect that: (1) heritage deserves a more prominent place than it generally receives in school curricula; (2) it should be seen as a vital part of citizenship, the development of which most schools do see as part of their mandate; and (3) more attention can be paid to heritage education than is now often the case without distorting or overloading the educational tasks of the schools.

L'enseignement du patrimoine à l'école – Résumé

Cette communication passe en revue la place de l'enseignement relatif au patrimoine dans les écoles du Canada. Elle porte essentiellement sur les programmes d'études, les manuels et les autres documents pédagogiques, ainsi que sur les activités organisées à l'école et dans la salle de classe. On y examine principalement le travail fait en histoire et en sciences humaines, car c'est dans ces domaines que se concentre une bonne part de l'enseignement relatif au patrimoine, sans négliger pour autant d'autres volets du programme, comme la littérature, le théâtre et les arts. On tient également compte des initiatives prises par les enseignants, les conservateurs d'archives, les musées et les défenseurs du patrimoine en général. On y jette un bref coup d'œil sur le passé, mais on s'attache surtout à ce qui se fait dans les écoles aujourd'hui. Mais cette communication n'est pas que descriptive. On y soutient en effet : 1) que le patrimoine mérite une place plus importante que celle qui lui est généralement réservée dans les programmes scolaires ; 2) qu'il devrait être considéré comme un élément fondamental de la citoyenneté, dont la plupart des écoles considèrent le développement comme faisant partie de leur mandat ; 3) que l'on peut accorder à l'enseignement relatif au patrimoine plus d'attention qu'on ne le fait souvent à l'heure actuelle sans dénaturer ni alourdir les tâches pédagogiques des écoles.

Introduction

This paper describes the way in which Canadian schools teach heritage. In view of the diversity of Canadian education and of the nature of the evidence, it is impossible to present a detailed and exhaustive report. Nor do limitations of space permit such a report, even if it were possible. Rather, the paper presents a broad, impressionistic, but not inaccurate, picture. At the same time, it is not simply a reflection of its author's personal likes and dislikes. It uses such data as there are and it is based on more than thirty years of working with and in schools around questions of heritage and history. The first part of the paper is intended to give an overall description of what schools and teachers are currently doing about heritage education, although the description is presented in broad terms and is necessarily short on detail. The second part of the paper attempts to draw some general conclusions from this evidence. The third part of the paper makes some suggestions for building on and enhancing the work currently being done in schools. Readers are asked to approach all three parts of the paper in the spirit of a statement made by Hilda Neatby when she surveyed the state of Canadian history for the Massey Commission: "It is difficult and dangerous to generalize in a field where very little exact information is available." [Neatby, 1951: 215]

Heritage Education in Canadian Schools

There is in fact a fair amount of information available, in both the education and the heritage literature, that describes what schools are doing about heritage education, but it is largely specific to particular schools and projects, and it is difficult to know how representative or typical it is, or to what extent it reflects more general trends. The abundance of trees makes it not only difficult to see the forest, but impossible to decide whether they constitute a forest at all, or only a copse, a spinney, or a modest woodlot. If part of the historian's task is to make general sense out of a mass of details, this is especially the case in trying to survey the state of heritage education in the schools. Thus, in what follows, many interesting and valuable projects and activities will be passed over in silence, in the interest of presenting a broad and comprehensive picture. To almost every general statement made in the pages that follow, there will doubtless be an exception somewhere in Canada, for such is the nature of the buzzing, blooming confusion of Canadian schooling.

All that can be said with any degree of certainty is that there is a considerable amount of heritage-related activity in Canadian schools. Whether it is enough, or whether there should be more, will obviously be matters of personal judgment. Whether, or to what extent, it is effective is impossible to decide, since we have neither criteria nor measures of what might constitute effectiveness in this area. It seems safe to say, however, that very few Canadian students will leave school without at least encountering some aspects of heritage at several points in their schooling, both through the authorized curricula and through a variety of special events and projects.

Some of this activity is generated from within the schools themselves, either through the work of committed and enthusiastic teachers or through opportunities afforded by the requirements of curricula and programmes of study. Some of it is generated in response to efforts that originate outside the schools, and usually from heritage organizations. Museums, local history societies, art galleries, cultural organizations, indeed most segments of the heritage community have over the years identified the schools as an important audience, largely on the reasonably founded assumption that, if young Canadians become interested in their heritage, they will maintain their interest in later life. There is also, of course, a certain amount of self-interest at work here, especially given the present climate of reduced public funding for culture and heritage, since students' interest might also translate into support for, and even membership in, the various organizations involved.

Perhaps the best way to describe what schools are currently doing about heritage is to survey the various kinds of heritage-related activities that students would typically encounter, often more than once, during their school careers. It should be emphasized that what follows describes a fairly typical school experience. It represents the norm rather than the exception. It is presented as a summary of activities or events that any given student would in most cases experience, or in some cases have at least the opportunity to experience. Readers should note also that the following description does not begin from some *a priori* definition of heritage which it then applies to the schools. Rather, it is based on looking at the schools and asking what they do that promotes some kind of awareness of or contact with heritage, and then asking what conceptions of heritage are contained in what they do.

Anniversaries and Festivals with Heritage Significance

These vary from region to region, but an obvious example is Manitoba Day, which falls on 12 May each year, and represents the date of the enactment of the Manitoba Act and thus the entry of that province into Confederation. Other provinces commemorate similar occasions. In all such cases, a certain amount of school time is devoted to marking the event, sometimes with special lessons, sometimes with some kind of assembly or special ceremony, sometimes with essay contests or debates or public-speaking. Provincial departments of culture, or heritage, or citizenship, often make available special educational materials. Many other such occasions present themselves throughout the school year. United Nations Day on 24 October, for example, is sometimes used to mark Canada's commitment and contribution to the United Nations, which can legitimately be seen as one element of Canada's heritage. Other opportunities for some reflection on history and heritage are provided by such anniversaries as International Women's Day, International Human Rights Day, Heritage Day, and various historical anniversaries. There is, of course, a long tradition in Canadian schools, as there is elsewhere, of using such events to try to influence students, as seen most obviously years ago in the case of Empire Day [Stamp, 1977]. One such event that is widely observed in schools, though more so in some provinces than others, is Remembrance Day, when very often a war veteran will be invited to speak at a school assembly, thus providing some opportunity for introducing students to Canada's military heritage.

It is impossible to say whether such events as these are widely commemorated or not. Certainly, Remembrance Day is, but in other cases much is left to the discretion of the teachers. And even when there are school-wide ceremonies or observances, they are unlikely to make much impact on students unless they are followed up in some way by teachers in the classroom. Perhaps the most that can be said is that the potential is there for teaching students about important aspects of Canadian heritage, and that some teachers take full advantage of it, but that in many cases the opportunity is not taken advantage of to the full.

Multicultural Festivals and Special Events

The combined impact of the 1971 adoption of multiculturalism as national policy, and of changing patterns of immigration, have made multicultural education a major undertaking in many Canadian schools [Gamlin, Berndorff, Mitsopulos & Demetriou, 1994]. In a remarkable turn-around from their long-established role as agents of assimilation and acculturation, Canadian schools in the 1970s quickly adopted multiculturalism as a guiding principle [Troper, 1978]. This meant much more than finding ways to educate immigrant children whose cultural backgrounds were new to Canadian schools. It also meant putting a major effort into educating for tolerance, for inter-cultural understanding, and, more specifically, for the elimination of racism. As part of this process, schools have increasingly adopted teaching materials that speak positively of students' varied cultural backgrounds; organized concerts, festivals and special events in which students and adults of varied backgrounds demonstrate or explain their cultural mores and values; and sought generally to find ways in which to acknowledge the diversity of their students.

All this activity has had a strong heritage flavour, seeking to emphasize that Canada is home to a wide variety of cultures, and that maintaining one's own culture is compatible with Canadian citizenship. Such activity, of course, has been able to draw on the venerable Canadian tradition that Canada has always been a mosaic, not a melting-pot. In any event, today a considerable amount of heritage education in Canadian schools is devoted to the promotion of the concept of multicultural heritage, although it seems fair to observe that much of this activity is concentrated on propounding the coexistence of separate cultural traditions, as opposed to seeking to harmonize them in a wider whole. Perhaps the two most obvious examples of this trend are the determination of Canada's First Nations to take control over their own education, including the cultural content of curricula, and the insistence of at least some Black Canadian students that schools have not treated their heritage and cultural traditions seriously, resulting in demands for courses in Black history and related subjects. This question of establishing unity in diversity has, of course, a considerable pedigree in Canada, and multiculturalism is simply its latest manifestation.

Visits to Historic or Other Sites that Connect with Heritage

Most students more than once during their school years are taken on field trips or visits to such historic sites as Lower Fort Garry, Fort Chambly, Fort Henry, Upper Canada Village, Fortress of Louisbourg, Fort Langley, and so on. They also go on more geographically related visits to study landforms, geology, forestry, flora and fauna, and other geographic features of the landscape. In some cases they go on the walking tours of the older sections of towns and cities that are organized by local history and heritage societies to draw attention to architectural heritage. There are also a variety of teaching kits and projects that focus specifically on the built heritage [Léveillé, 1982; Chuhay, 1988; Kisiow, 1992]. A variation of this practice is the walking tour that is designed to illustrate a particular historical event, such as Winnipeg's tour of the key sites connected with the history of the 1919 General Strike. There is obviously a rich variety of heritage sites across Canada, maintained and operated variously by agencies of the national government, such as Parks Canada, by provincial authorities, and by private local and cultural organizations. All except the most inaccessible are well used by schools, though anecdotal evidence suggests that they are more popular with elementary than with junior or senior high schools.

Visits to Museums, Art Galleries, Theatres, Archives, and Similar Institutions

Many schools organize visits to museums, art galleries, and other institutions, either as a matter of routine to see more or less permanent displays, or to take advantage of a special exhibit, play, or film. Except in the more remote areas of the country, most schools have an opportunity to visit a museum that has some educational potential, be it a small museum run by local volunteers, or a more sophisticated and better funded museum of provincial or regional importance [Cuthbertson, 1986; Tyler, 1986; Carter, 1986]. Bigger museums and art galleries often have skilled and active education staffs whose special task it is to work with schools and to provide suitable teaching and learning materials. Films and plays of historical significance also sometimes come accompanied by materials and activities for use in the classroom. In this regard, the efforts of the National Film Board and the Canadian Broadcasting Corporation are worthy of note, since both organizations obviously produce materials that are used in classrooms and are of significant potential for heritage education. In addition to all the activity that is initiated outside the school, it should be remembered that most history, geography, and social studies teachers receive as part of their training some instruction and encouragement about incorporating museums and other organizations into their teaching.

Visits to Sites of Contemporary Interest

In addition to the kinds of visits and field-trips described above, students are often taken to visit sites, not for reasons directly connected with heritage, but for more immediately contemporary purposes. Such sites include Hutterite colonies, First Nations communities, farms, industrial and commercial establishments, and so on. Students in remote communities are often taken to a town or city to get a flavour of urban life. Sometimes these visits are more than one-day affairs, lasting instead for several days, and sometimes taking the form of exchanges, in which, to take only one example, urban students live in a First Nations reserve community. There are also the better known and better funded exchange visits sponsored by the federal government between Anglophone and Francophone students.

It is true that all these visits and field trips are organized for reasons that have little explicitly to do with heritage. They are designed, for example, to increase inter-cultural understanding, to reduce racism, to enhance economic literacy, and so on. However, they also contain the potential to enhance awareness of heritage. It is difficult for students to experience a culture different from their own, for example, without asking why things are done differently and thus realizing that a different and historically rooted value system is at work, which in turn inevitably directs attention to heritage.

Participating in an Activity Connected with Local or Regional History

In many parts of Canada, local history societies or other heritage groups organize essay contests, young historians awards, debates, research projects, and so on, that are designed to stimulate students' and teachers' interest in local history. There are also history or heritage fairs, organized along the lines of the perhaps better known science fairs, in which participating schools require students to produce and display projects of all shapes and sizes, not only of the conventional written variety, but also including models, audio- and video-tapes, quilts, pictures, plays, and anything that students' imagination and creativity can encompass. Such fairs are sometimes accompanied by displays and presentations representing different aspects of local and regional history. Most recently, the Bronfman Foundation has been involved in sponsoring events of this type. By and large, however, it seems safe to say that only a minority of students participate in them, since much depends on the initiative and interest of teachers who find themselves increasingly hard-pressed on various fronts.

Writing Local or Family Histories

Many provincial and territorial curricula allow for, and in some cases require, the study of local history, either as a topic within a course or as a course in its own right. When they teach Canadian History or Canadian Studies, schools, for obvious reasons, are inclined to give some emphasis to local or regional matters. Thus, for example, Manitoba schools teach their students more about the Selkirk Settlement or the Winnipeg General Strike or the fur trade than do schools in other parts of Canada. By contrast, they neglect the history of Atlantic Canada, which of course appears prominently in the curricula of that region. In the same way, Québec schools teach more about the history of New France and the Conquest than do schools in other provinces. To take another example, the Yukon has produced some rich and interesting materials dealing with the history of the Aboriginal people of that region.

Archives have been involved in some of this activity and though, in the nature of the case, this applies to only a small number of students, it is not unusual to find some high school students doing some kind of archivally based research projects. Some archives have produced teaching kits for classroom use, though Canadian practice in this regard lags behind that in some other countries

[Osborne, 1986-7]. From time to time particular projects have been undertaken, as when the Saskatchewan Archives involved school students in conducting and collecting oral histories in connection with the seventy-fifth anniversary of that province.

In addition, as part of a general pedagogical move to require students to "do" history as well as study it, or, in other words, to get them to do some genuinely original research, history teachers across the country have turned to family history. The implications of this approach for heritage need no elaboration.

Heritage Opportunities in the Authorized Curricula

In addition to the various activities described to this point, students obviously learn about heritage in the context of their regular studies. In the nature of things, this is most likely to occur in the context of social studies and history, and to some extent geography, but it is not confined to these subjects. Literature, drama, art, and music have obvious heritage applications and all students are required to read some Canadian literature, to look at some Canadian art, to listen to some Canadian music, as they progress through school. The publication of Hodgetts' *What Culture? What Heritage?* in 1968 and the Symons Report, *To Know Ourselves,* in 1975, resulted in a vastly heightened awareness of the importance of ensuring that Canadian subject-matter and Canadian materials were included in curricula. In fact, there is no aspect of the school curriculum, from science to physical education, that does not contain some potential for dealing with matters of heritage. It is a rare student these days, for example, who is not taught that basketball was invented by a Canadian or that insulin was discovered by Canadian scientists. Most recently, this sort of knowledge has been reinforced by the "Heritage Minutes" sponsored by the Bronfman Foundation and Canada Post, which some teachers report as making an impression on students.

There is not space in this paper to report in detail on the state of Canadian history in the schools, but a recent investigation revealed that there is considerable room for improvement [Osborne, 1994]. Its conclusions are as follows:

- History has been largely subsumed under social studies so that it appears in curricula less as a systematic study of some part of the past, and more as a source of case-studies, examples and illustrative topics designed to illustrate social science concepts.

- The study of the past is seen as subordinate to the study of the problems of the present.
- When history is studied it is largely through themes, issues and concepts, and not through chronological narrative.
- In over half the provinces it is possible to graduate without having taken Canadian history in high school.
- There is very little required by way of the compulsory study of non-Canadian history.
- There is no clear sequence of historical study across the provinces and territories.
- Little attention appears to have been given to the question of what historical knowledge a person needs in order to cope with today's world.

To put this another way, the place of history in Canadian school curricula is justified largely in terms of the value of historical knowledge in understanding current problems, rather than of knowing or appreciating or understanding the past for its own sake, or for its value in conveying a sense of heritage. Thus, historical topics are selected for inclusion in curricula in terms of their ability to shed light on the issues of today rather than for their ability to give students a systematic knowledge of the past. To put it perhaps over-simply, there is a good deal of present-mindedness in school history courses [Macleod, 1982; Osborne, 1987; Davis, 1995].

This is not to be dismissed out-of-hand. Nor should we shed tears unnecessarily for the apparent demise of history. There never was a golden age of history teaching. When Hodgetts wrote *What Culture? What Heritage?* in 1968, based on his investigation of history teaching across the country, he was merciless in his criticisms. He described the state of affairs he found: curricula were boring and out-of-date; textbooks were inadequate at best; teaching was stiflingly dull and shallow; and students were bored and alienated. The teaching of history, he concluded, was counter-productive, turning students away from the story of their own country. A few years earlier, in a less well-known critique, Northrop Frye had concluded, in a study commissioned by the Toronto Board of Education, that it was "not at all self-evident that much would necessarily be lost if history, as presently prescribed and taught, were dropped entirely from the curriculum." [Frye, 1962: 86] Some years before that, in 1953, a survey of Canadian history teaching concluded that it "failed to bring about the creative reality in which the student might recognize the essential permanence of the Canadian story, nor at the same time understand the vision implicit in healthy change." [Katz, 1953: 13]

Indeed, it was this long-standing indictment of the nature of history in the schools that led teachers and policy-makers to replace it with courses that were oriented to contemporary problems and the social sciences. Such courses, it was believed, would prove more interesting to students, while at the same time preparing them for their roles as democratic citizens. And though history's traditional position as a separate course of study was eroded, a good deal of historical subject-matter remained, and remains, in school curricula. Most Canadian students, for example, will be taught about such elements of Canada's history as exploration; immigration; Confederation; the World Wars; relations with the United States; the history of the First Nations, particularly in their contacts with Europeans. History has not so much been eliminated as reorganized and different criteria of selection and relevance have been employed in the design of curricula. Where historical topics have been dropped from curricula, it is because they are seen as having little connection with contemporary concerns. As will be argued further below this also had the effect of reducing history's potential to address questions of heritage, but it does not mean that students are not introduced to a reasonable amount of historical subject-matter during the course of their schooling, although it is true that much of this is done before the high-school years.

Some Conclusions and a Paradox

As this all too brief survey suggests there is overall a fair amount of heritage activity in Canadian classrooms, despite the changes that have occurred in the way in which history is organized and approached. In fact, the 1970s saw a considerable increase in the amount of Canadian content in school curricula, in large part because of the concerns raised by Hodgetts and Symons, the work of the Canada Studies Foundation, and a general state of worry about the future of the country as it faced the challenges of Québec's "Quiet Revolution", constitutional change, the Americanization of culture, and an increasing provincial assertiveness. It is true that much of this new Canadian content addressed contemporary concerns but it also contained a good deal of material that had the potential to speak to issues of heritage and to create an awareness of the past.

Despite this Canadianization of curricula, however, complaints were increasingly heard that Canadians did not know enough about their own country and did not have a sufficiently strong attachment to, or understanding of, their heritage. The Royal Commission on Bilingualism and Biculturalism in the 1960s lamented the existence of two apparently exclusive views of Canada's heritage and culture, one in Québec and one in the rest of Canada. It was, of course, a duality with deep roots in the Canadian experience and one that was constantly rediscovered and lamented in the field of education. In the earlier words of a member of a 1940's committee investigating history textbooks:

> Dans l'ensemble, les manuels français se restreignent trop à la province du Québec et négligent l'histoire du Canada anglais, et réciproquement. On ne saurait reprocher à ces manuels de chercher à susciter de l'antipathie entre les races, mais ils tendent à réduire la part jouée par les citoyens de l'autre langue dans le développement du pays... Les reproches d'ignorance mutuelle entre les deux principaux groupes canadiens peuvent ainsi avoir leur origine à l'école [Bilodeau, 1951: 226].

This complaint of mutual ignorance was to be heard through the 1970s also, right up to the present, finding its most recent expression in Joe Clark's 1994 book, *A Nation Too Good To Lose*.

More is at stake here, however, than the mutual ignorance that exists between people in Québec and in the rest of Canada. The debates around the Meech Lake Agreement and the Charlottetown Accord gave rise to concerns that Canadians did not sufficiently understand their own history. This became a major theme of the Spicer Report and has been most recently voiced by Joe Clark: "While comparable nations rear their children on stories of the best of their past – from the glory that was Greece to the empire on which the sun never set, to the French Revolution, to the Declaration of Independence – we Canadians usually treat our history as though it did not happen." [Clark, 1994: 194-5]

Here, then, is a paradox, or at least a contradiction: schools are devoting a reasonable amount of time and effort to heritage but at the same time Canadians are found to lack a sufficiently developed sense of history and heritage. There are, of course, some simple, if hypothetical explanations. It could be, for example, that those who lament the lack of historical knowledge are wrong, or that what they really mean is that Canadians do not understand history in the way they are supposed to. However, there are enough signs that many Canadians do not know all that much about Canadian history to make this explanation unlikely.

A more plausible explanation is that schools can have at best a limited impact, even when what they do is effective and successful, especially if the messages they seek to deliver are drowned out by counter-trends in the media and the general culture. It is unlikely, for example, that schools can ever counteract the sophisticated and powerful Americanizing messages of the electronic media, no matter how much they concentrate on their Canadianizing role.

Perhaps the most intriguing explanation of the paradox, however, is to be found in the nature of the heritage activities undertaken by schools. An examination of these activities, as they have been described in the previous section of this paper, suggests that they have at least three elements in common. In the first place, the heritage on which they concentrate is overwhelmingly local and lacks any national focus. In the second, they are undertaken as discrete activities, lacking any uniting coherence. In the third, they lack any overarching rationale or philosophical commitment rooted in an awareness of heritage. All three points deserve some further elaboration.

As Taylor has pointed out, heritage activity in Canada has long faced a problem of reconciling the local with the national. In his words, there is a "tendency to regard national significance from regional perspectives." [Taylor, 1990: 152] In this regard, the local orientation of most school heritage activity is not surprising. So far as visits and field trips are concerned, the explanation is geographic. For obvious reasons, most such visits can be organized only to local sites and institutions, which, almost by definition, have a local significance. Even when they are of national importance, it is their part in local or regional history that attracts attention. Similarly, those non-school organizations that encourage heritage activity in the schools are overwhelmingly local in nature: local historical societies, provincial departments of education or culture, regional museums, and so on. The emphasis on multicultural education, with its accompanying interest in the diverse cultural heritages of Canadians, has reinforced this trend, perhaps not so much to the local as to the personal, but in any case not to the national. Constitutional proprieties and resource limitations constrain the involvement of federal institutions in education, though organizations such as the National Film Board, the Museum of Civilization, the Canadian Studies Directorate of the Department of Canadian Heritage, and others have had some influence, primarily in the production of teaching materials. Nonetheless, school heritage activity has for the most part reinforced the existence of "limited identities", whether local, cultural or personal, but without the articulation among them that Careless called for when he first elaborated the concept [Careless, 1969].

The one place where students might be introduced to a more national view of the past is in their courses in Canadian history, but here too there are problems. As already noted, in a number of provinces students are simply not required to take Canadian history after junior high school. Even when they do, the history they study is often governed by the criterion of contemporary relevance so that there is relatively little attention paid to the Canadian past as a whole. To take one particularly pointed example, few students outside Québec spend very much time studying the history of New France before the Conquest, and even less the history of Québec after the Conquest. As a result, they have at best a limited idea of the historical role of Québec in Canada and of the historical forces that have helped shape contemporary Québec. Often, in fact, when Québec is studied at all, it is studied as a problem or an issue. Québec is seen largely as a trouble-maker or a dissenting voice, as in the Riel affair, the Conscription crises, the Quiet Revolution and now separatism.

Beyond this particular issue of the portrayal of Québec in history courses, however, lies something larger: the inability of history courses and textbooks to convey the totality of the Canadian experience to students. Perhaps in this post-modernist age, it might be argued that the very idea of totality is a delusion. More politicized critics might ask whose view of totality should be taught, since it is certainly true that when Canadian history was taught more systematically in the schools, it often carried some heavy ideological baggage [Trudel & Jain, 1969; McDiarmid & Pratt, 1971; Pratt, 1975; Osborne, 1980]. Michael Bliss has recently argued that the fault lies with social history, which in his view has eroded even the idea of a national narrative [Bliss, 1991-92]. Whatever the reason, it seems reasonably clear that most students are not being led to think about the Canadian past, that is to say Canada's historical heritage, in any coherent or systematic way. When they engage in heritage activity or historical study, they do so with reference largely to local themes.

This emphasis on Canada's "limited identities" is obviously connected with the second problem identified above, namely the lack of any uniting coherence to pull together the many discrete activities undertaken in schools. Heritage education in schools seems to be largely *ad hoc*. It is a response to particular occasions: Remembrance Day, a museum exhibit, an anniversary, an initiative from some organization outside the school. Such activities are taken up for a variety of reasons. Sometimes they are seen as providing a worthwhile learning experience for students. Or they offer a chance to reinforce the curriculum. Or they are valued for primarily pedagogical reasons, for example as providing a break in the routine of the classroom or an opportunity for a different kind of learning, less oriented to books and more to direct observation. Again, they might be undertaken for more political reasons, perhaps to raise the public profile of a school, or to make connections with groups in the community. Whatever, the reasons, heritage activities in the schools are rarely seen as part of a long-term and deliberate effort to raise awareness of heritage. In a sense, heritage is treated as a means to another end.

This raises the third problem identified above: the failure to think of heritage education in terms of any overarching rationale or philosophical commitment. There is a certain tendency in teaching to value activity for the sake of activity. In a sense, this is understandable. It is no small task to keep students interested in their work over long stretches of time in the artificial surroundings of a school. It is easy to understand why teachers look for activities that will break the routine of the classroom, provide some variety for students, and still serve some educational purpose. Thus arises a situation where the question asked about an activity is not: what is it for? but, does it work? Field trips, visits, local history projects, multicultural festivals, and so forth, all fall into this category. The result can be that when heritage activities are taken up, the emphasis is on activity rather than heritage.

Heritage is not a word or a concept that often appears in educational or pedagogical discussion. Nor is it something that is at the forefront of teachers' minds. The word does not appear in the index to the 1965-1983 subject-guide to *The History and Social Science Teacher*, the national journal of anglophone Canadian history teachers. Few if any statements of provincial or territorial education policy speak explicitly of heritage, or for that matter deal with the concept even implicitly. An exception is to be found in the Saskatchewan Social Studies curriculum for Grades 1 to 5, where Heritage is specified as one of four themes binding together the programme, together with identity, interdependence and decision-making. This theme of Heritage is taught through a sequence of subject matter, beginning with the family, school and community in Grade 1, and ending with Canadian history in Grade 5, but the idea of heritage itself is not raised for discussion or examination [Saskatchewan Education, 1995].

Though they rarely speak of heritage, as such, provincial and territorial policy statements do, however, describe citizenship as a fundamental goal of schooling, by which they mean a combination of socially desirable values and dispositions (tolerance, cooperation, respect for others, and so on) and politically relevant behaviour (voting, participation in community affairs, and so forth). The central purpose is seen overwhelmingly as that of preparing students to participate in and contribute to society. As a 1982 survey of Canadian social studies curricula put it, their common goal was "to provide students with the knowledge, skills, values and thought processes which will enable them to participate effectively and responsibly in the ever-changing environment of their community, their country and their world." [Redden, 1982: 4; see also Pammett & Pépin, 1988; Sears, 1994]

As this quotation suggests, the view of citizenship taken in most education policy statements in Canada is curiously decontextualized. It could be applied almost anywhere and lacks any but the most general reference to any distinctively Canadian connotation. But, short of some sort of world citizenship of the sort once envisaged by H.G. Wells, citizenship inevitably involves membership in some sort of political community. It can be plausibly argued that compulsory public schooling was created in large part to create national citizens. It is, then, something of a puzzle to know why so much contemporary discussion of citizenship in Canadian education circles ignores its distinctively Canadian context. If students are compelled to attend school so that they will learn to become participating members of their community, it would seem to follow that they should learn a good deal about that community, and that this would require a solid grounding in the community's history, since this is one of the constitutive elements of any community. This, after all, is why nationalists have been so often determined to control the teaching of history.

However, no society that aspires to be democratic can tolerate one officially authorized version of history. History involves argument, interpretation and dispute. To some extent, the past is what we make it, as is heritage. The ideological motives inherent in any attempt to define history and heritage need no elaboration. To speak of heritage is to raise the questions of what heritage? and whose heritage? and who defines it? Such questions can be usefully explored with students, at their different levels, so that they learn to see heritage as something that is to some extent constructed (which is very different from claiming that it is invented), but that is at the same time integral to any sense of community. In other words, Canadian students need to learn about Canada's history and heritage and about the debates over what that history and heritage is. Without this, the citizenship that is envisaged by the schools will always be incomplete.

What Is To Be Done?

As this paper has sought to demonstrate, the main role of the schools in the field of heritage has been to organize specific events in order to achieve specific purposes. Such events have also provided the main link between schools and heritage organizations. Despite their *ad hoc* nature, they obviously serve a useful purpose. Indeed, since heritage education cannot take place in a vacuum, but instead has to be organized through some medium or other, events such as anniversaries, field trips, visits, and heritage days, offer a valuable vehicle. Thus, it is important that they continue and that schools and heritage organizations work together to ensure that they are as educationally useful as possible.

To be most useful, however, they need to be located in the context of a wider concern for heritage as an educational goal. The two subjects, heritage and

171

education, need to be brought into one integrated effort. Given the schools' traditional concern for citizenship, theoretically this should not be difficult, since, as suggested above, a sense of heritage is an indispensable element of effective citizenship, albeit one that often seems to get overlooked. Moreover, if one takes the usual descriptions of the goals of education – with their emphasis on citizenship, knowledge, literacy, understanding the world in which one lives, and behaving in socially acceptable ways – it seems obvious that heritage is not one more additional burden to be thrust on the schools, but rather something that can be naturally integrated into what they are already trying to accomplish. What is needed is, first, to produce the argument that shows how this can be done, and, second, the political and administrative mechanisms to do it.

The link between heritage and citizenship provides an obvious place to do this. The concept of citizenship is beginning to attract some attention from policy-makers and from theorists. The liberal-communitarian debate, for example, is at its heart a debate over the meaning of citizenship [Kymlicka, 1989 & 1992]. Political and educational theorists have also been devoting increasing attention to the topic [Heater, 1990; Turner, 1993]. Feminist theorists are also subjecting it to sustained analysis [Phillips, 1989 & 1993; Okin, 1992]. Here in Canada, the Senate Standing Committee on Social Affairs, Science and Technology has issued a report on the state of citizenship in Canada [Senate of Canada, 1993], and the Council of Ministers of Education has decided that citizenship education is to be nationally assessed. In other words, there is some potential for heritage to insert itself into an emerging debate over the meaning of citizenship [Osborne, 1991& 1994].

Putting heritage issues on one side, for a moment, such an effort would be worthwhile for strictly educational and social reasons. In the last few years, policy-makers in education have become preoccupied with what they see as the economic benefits of education [Osborne, 1992]. They have defined the role of schools as being to contribute to the entrepreneurial competitiveness of Canadians so that they can survive in the tough times facing us in the new global economy. Such is the message of document after document in Canadian education. In issuing a blueprint for school reform, Manitoba's Minister of Education emphasized that "We need to do everything possible to ensure that our children are prepared to compete successfully in today's competitive world." [Manitoba Education, 1994: 1] The Parti Québecois argues that the "schools will have to do better by becoming more closely linked to the job market" [Chodos, 1994: 23]. Similar statements can be found in almost all provinces. Despite the attention being paid to citizenship by theorists, in the world of daily practice the traditional goals of citizenship and all-round development are increasingly being down-graded.

Such a trend can only erode further the already declining sense of community and strengthen the view once explicitly stated by Mrs. Thatcher that "there is no such thing as society" [Kingdom, 1992]. In place of the view of society as community, or perhaps a community of communities, we are offered a view of life in which individuals and groups compete for their own self-interest, and in which political and social affairs become nothing more than the pursuit of advantage [Barber, 1984]. As Eric Hobsbawm has recently suggested, this is especially troublesome in the conditions of the late twentieth century. In his words:

> The destruction of the past, or rather of the social mechanisms that link one's contemporary experience to that of earlier generations, is one of the most characteristic and eerie phenomena of the late twentieth century. Most young men and women at the century's end grow up in a sort of permanent present lacking any organic relation to the public past of the times they live in [Hobsbawm, 1994: 3].

In this educational and social context, an awareness of heritage has more than an educational role to play. It can draw attention to to the importance of the concept of citizenship. It can reinvigorate a sense of community. There is a danger here that heritage and citizenship might be seen, as they have been in the past, as an opiate, blinding people to the problems of the present in a blaze of nostalgia for an imagined past and a community that never was. This use of heritage has been documented by Wright [1985], Hewison [1987], MacKay [1993], Samuel [1995], and others, but it is not what is intended here. In Hewison's terms, what we need is not a "heritage" but a "critical" culture, in which heritage plays an indispensable part. In Patrick Wright's words: "History should be the name of a future-oriented project: history-which-is-to-be-made rather than stately-history-which-is-already made and demands only veneration in what it also dismisses as an abjectly inferior and declining present." [Wright. 1985: 255]

Here is a valuable role for a critical awareness of heritage, and of the issues surrounding its definition, selection and presentation. It is a role which also connects heritage with the best traditions of education.

REFERENCES

BARBER, B. *Strong Democracy: Participatory Politics for a New Age*. Berkeley: University of California Press, 1984.

BILODEAU, C. "L'histoire nationale" in *Royal Commission Studies: A Selection of Essays Prepared for the Royal Commission on National Development in the Arts, Letters and Sciences*. Ottawa: King's Printer, 1951: 217-230.

BLISS, M. "Privatizing the Mind: The Sundering of Canadian History, The Sundering of Canada" in the *Journal of Canadian Studies*, 26 [4]. 1991: 5-17.

CARELESS, J.M.S. "'Limited Identities' in Canada" in the *Canadian Historical Review*, 50[1], 1969: 1-10.

CARTER, J.C. "Community Museums and Schools: An Annotated Bibliography of Resource and Reference Materials" in *The History and Social Science Teacher*, 21 [2], 1985: 89-93.

CHODOS, R. [translator]. *Québec in a New World: The PQ's Plan for Sovereignty*. Toronto: Lorimer, 1994.

CHUHAY, C. "Hooked on Heritage" in *The History and Social Science Teacher*, 23 [3], 1988:139-140.

CLARK, J. *A Nation Too Good To Lose: Renewing the Purpose of Canada*. Toronto: Key Porter, 1994.

CUTHBERTSON, S. "Museum Education: A British Columbia Perspective" in *The History and Social Science Teacher*, 21 [2], 1986: 80-85.

DAVIS, B. *Whatever Happened to High School History? Burying the Political Memory of Youth, Ontario: 1945-1995*. Toronto: Our Schools, Ourselves, 1995.

FRYE, N. [ed.]. *Design for Learning*. Toronto: University of Toronto Press, 1962.

GAMLIN, P.J., D. BERNDORFF, A. MITSOPULOS & K. DEMETRIOU, "Multicultural Education in Canada from a Global Perspective" in J.W. BERRY & J.A. LAPONCE [eds.], *Ethnicity and Culture in Canada: The Research Landscape*. Toronto: University of Toronto Press, 1994: 457-482.

HEATER, D.B. *Citizenship: The Civic Ideal in World History, Politics and Education*. London: Longman, 1990.

HEWISON, R. *The Heritage Industry: Britain in a Climate of Decline*. London: Methuen, 1987.

HOBSBAWM, E. *The Age of Extremes: A History of the World, 1914-1991*. New York: Pantheon Books, 1994.

KATZ, J. *The Teaching of Canadian History in Canada: A Survey Study of the Teaching of Canadian History in Junior and Senior High Schools*. Winnipeg: University of Manitoba Press, 1953.

KINGDOM, J. *No Such Thing as Society? Individualism and Community*. Buckingham: Open University Press, 1992.

KISIOW, E. "Manitoba Architecture Comes to the Classroom," in *The Manitoba Social Science Teacher*, 18 [4], 1992: 12-13.

KYMLICKA, W. *Liberalism, Community and Culture*. Oxford: Clarendon Press, 1989.

_____ *Recent Work in Citizenship Theory*. Ottawa: Multiculturalism and Citizenship Canada, 1992.

LÉVEILLÉ, C. "Architectural Heritage: An Experiment in Montreal's Schools" in *The History and Social Science Teacher*, 18 [2], 1982: 103-105.

MACLEOD, R.C. "History in Canadian Secondary Schools" in the *Canadian Historical Review*, LXIII [4], 1982: 573-585.

MANITOBA EDUCATION AND TRAINING. *Renewing Education, New Directions: A Blueprint for Action*. Winnipeg: Manitoba Education and Training, 1994.

McDIARMID, G. & D. PRATT. *Teaching Prejudice: A Content Analysis of Social Studies Textbooks Authorized for Use in Ontario.* Toronto: Ontario Institute for Studies in Education, 1971.

McKAY, I. *The Quest for the Folk: Antimodernism and Cultural Selection in Twentieth Century Nova Scotia.* Montreal: McGill-Queen's University Press, 1994.

NEATBY, H. "National History," in *Royal Commission Studies: A Selection of Essays Prepared for the Royal Commission on National Development in the Arts, Letters and Sciences.* Ottawa: King's Printer, 1951: 205-216.

OKIN, S.M. "Women, Equality and Citizenship" in *Queen's Quarterly,* 99 [1992]: 56-71.

OSBORNE, K.W. *"Hard-working, Temperate and Peaceable": The Portrayal of Workers in Canadian History Textbooks.* Winnipeg: University of Manitoba Education Monograph IV, 1980.

_____ "Archives in the Classroom" in *Archivaria,* 23 [Winter, 1986-87]: 16-40.

_____ "'To the Schools We Must Look for the Good Canadian': Developments in the Teaching of History since 1960" in the *Journal of Canadian Studies,* 23 [3], 1987: 104-126.

_____ *Teaching For Democratic Citizenship.* Toronto: Our Schools Ourselves, 1991.

_____ "The Emerging Agenda for Canadian High Schools," in the *Journal of Curriculum Studies,* 24 [4], 1992: 371-379.

_____ *"I'm Not Going To Think How Cabot Discovered Newfoundland When I'm Doing My Job": The Status of History in Canadian High Schools.* Paper delivered to the Canadian Historical Society Annual Conference, June 1994.

_____ *In Defence of History: Teaching the Past and the Meaning of Democratic Citizenship.* Toronto: Our Schools Ourselves, 1995.

PAMMETT, J. & J.-L. PÉPIN [eds.]. *Political Education in Canada.* Ottawa: Institute for Research in Public Policy, 1988.

PRATT, D. "The Social Role of School Textbooks in Canada" in E. ZUREIK & R. PIKE [eds.], *Socialization and Values in Canadian Society.* Toronto: McClelland & Stewart, 1975, Vol. I: 100-125.

REDDEN, G. *Social Studies: A Survey of Provincial Curricula at the Elementary and Secondary Levels.* Toronto: Council of Ministers of Education Canada, 1982.

SAMUEL, R. *Theatres of Memory.* London: Verso, 1995.

SASKATCHEWAN EDUCATION, TRAINING AND EMPLOYMENT. *Social Studies: A Curriculum Guide and Activity Guide for the Elementary Level.* Regina: Saskatchewan Education, 1995.

SEARS, A. "Social Studies as Citizenship Education in English Canada: A Review of Research" in *Theory and Research in Social Education,* XXII [1], 1994: 6-43.

SENATE OF CANADA. *Canadian Citizenship: Sharing the Responsibility.* Ottawa: Standing Senate Committee on Social Affairs, Science and Technology, 1993.

STAMP, R. "Empire Day in the Training of Young Imperialists" in A. CHAITON & N. MACDONALD [eds.], *Canadian Schools and Canadian Identity.* Toronto: Gage, 1977: 100-111.

TAYLOR, C.J. *Negotiating the Past: The Making of Canada's Historic Parks and Sites.* Montreal: McGill-Queen's University Press, 1990.

TROPER, H. "Nationalism and the History Curriculum in Canada" in *The History Teacher,* XII [I], 1978: 11-27.

TRUDEL, M. & G. JAIN. *L'histoire du Canada: Enquête sur les manuels.* Ottawa: Queen's Printer, 1969.

TURNER, B. [ed.]. *Citizenship and Social Theory.* London: Sage, 1993.

TYLER, B. "The Future for Museum Education Programs" in *The History and Social Science Teacher*, 21 [2], 1986: 86-88.

WRIGHT, P. *On Living in an Old Country: The National Past in Contemporary Britain.* London: Verso, 1985.

Egerton Ryerson (1803-1882), Methodist minister and editor of the *Christian Guardian*, he became Chief superintendent of education for Upper Canada (1844-1876), where he was largely responsible for shaping Ontario's present school system. He was designated in 1937. / Ministre méthodiste et rédacteur du *Christian Guardian*, Ryerson fut directeur général de l'instruction publique du Haut-Canada (1844-1876) et contribua largement à l'élaboration du système scolaire actuel de l'Ontario. Il a été désigné en 1937. (Photo: National Archives / Archives nationales, C-14235)

County Schoolhouse, Osgoode County, Ontario / École du comté d'Osgoode, en Ontario. (Photo: National Archives, PA-43579; Department of the Interior Collection, item 0-14-1-21 / Archives nationales, PA-43579; pièce 0-14-1-21 de la collection du ministère de l'Intérieur)

Twice Told Tales:
Researching and Teaching History in the 1990s

Abstract
Concerns about the status of history in the school curriculum and how well the subject is taught and received in the classroom have animated Canadian educational discussion for decades. This short presentation identifies four contemporary social trends that can be seen to influence how history is received by students, particularly at the secondary school level, and suggests strategies for dealing with each of them.

Double redécouverte : la recherche historique et l'enseignement de l'histoire dans les années 1990 – Résumé
Les préoccupations relatives à la place de l'histoire dans les programmes scolaires, à la qualité de l'enseignement de cette matière et à l'accueil que lui réservent les élèves sont au cœur des discussions sur l'éducation depuis des décennies au Canada. Cette brève communication met en lumière quatre tendances sociales actuelles dont on peut dire qu'elles influent sur la façon dont les élèves accueillent l'histoire, en particulier à l'école secondaire, et propose diverses façons de les aborder.

> Life is as tedious as a twice-told tale,
> Vexing the dull ear of a drowsy man
> Shakespeare, *King John*, III, iv. 108

Substitute "history" for "life" in this famous quotation from a not-so-famous Shakespearian play, and you have a fair encapsulation of what many think is the average student's opinion of the subject. Many commentators on the Canadian educational scene would claim this has long been the case. The question I want to ask is: do contemporary times offer new approaches to this old dilemma? Are there ways that we should be adapting the study of history to take advantage of current developments?

Underlying my response is the conviction that history as a discipline is not tedious and that it is undeniably important. How, then, do we encourage students to appreciate it? The answer, of course, is to demonstrate that history is both relevant and interesting. Easy to say, more difficult to do. Certainly accomplished teachers know how. A love of history is best instilled by teachers who can engage students' interest and bring the subject alive. Such teachers adapt pedagogical technique to different classroom situations. I will not presume here to tell them how to do their jobs.[1]

My object is simply to survey four current developments and suggest some new opportunities they present for teaching students the value of history. The target audience I have in mind throughout is the stereotypical adolescent whose inexperience of the world is reflected by his or her preoccupation with self and peer group. Adolescents are at a stage in life in which their identity is under construction. It extends outward to family and community, but has only tenuous links beyond to the national and international realms. Consequently, historical instruction should address these students first and foremost on a personal level. Once engaged, their interest can be teased out into a broader appreciation of the relevance of history to their place in their community, country, and the larger world.

Before going further, a caveat. In this format one cannot hope to cover all the complexities and implications of the contemporary trends I will here only touch upon. This should be regarded only as a quick inventory of points that bear further examination. These are preliminary observations.

Today we hear more and more about the aging of the Canadian population. Reports on this trend often include dire predictions about the baby boomers retiring en masse and draining pension funds. But for history, at least, the greying of Canadians is good news. As adults mature, they reflect more frequently on their roots. Anyone doubting this generalization, could look at the demographic profile of any local historical association. Older people also have more leisure to pursue historical interests. Many can be found in the archives tracing their family histories. Some even return to the classroom to study history.

However, most history students will continue to be young and, compared to their elders, less well equipped to study the past. Young people have a limited conception of the passage of time because they have so little experience of it. The history of far-off places, even the history of their own region, is difficult for most of them to grasp because they have lived in a relatively circumscribed world.[2] Given these factors, it is natural to ask whether there is a way to bring young and old together. Can the enthusiasm and knowledge of the elders be channelled into the historical education of the young?

One answer may be to make more use of genealogy in the teaching of history. It is a type of history in which old and young should be able to find common ground. The old are already pursuing genealogy in increasing numbers. A family interest in the past predisposes a student to benefit from the teaching of history in the classroom. For the young it offers a means of personalizing history by appealing to their curiosity about their own identity and place in the world.

While narrow in focus, genealogy provides a good starting point for the development of historical consciousness. It is also a good training ground for subsequent, broader historical studies. An archivist in the Genealogy Unit of the National Archives of Canada recently commented that:

> ... the most avid amongst [genealogists] are not content with merely obtaining names, dates and places of residence of their ancestors. They want to know how they lived, the special events that went on during their lifetime; in short, the history of the time. They are not only genealogists, they are amateur historians.[3]

Genealogy teaches the use of archives, the march of chronology, the inter-relatedness of generations, and the limits of historical knowledge. It leads to family history which in turn leads to social history. History teachers might do well to harness some of the growing interest in genealogy to help forward their pedagogical goals.

We also hear a lot today about the wonders of new computer and communication technologies. Often the facts are overlaid with a starry-eyed futurism that assures us that the boons of the information highway, user-friendly software and fibre-optic cable will revolutionize our lives. Perhaps. But in fact history shows that similar claims have been made during each media revolution of the past century first with the proliferation of popular newspapers, then mass circulation of magazines, film, radio, and television. With each new media technology we have heard promises about technology delivering a new age of enlightenment.

This does not mean that we should discount the impact of technology. Things will certainly change in ways we cannot predict. But the point is that we should not expect technology to solve problems that are pedagogical in nature. The ability to click on an icon on the screen and get an interactive, multimedia history tutorial will do little to change students' appreciation of history. And less positive results are also possible. Ultimately, the power of new media can also enhance the possibilities for distortion. Think, for a moment, of what Hollywood movies have done for Canadian history.[4]

While the information age may do little for history, history has an important contribution to make to the information age. New technologies make available more information than the individual can possibly use. It is hardly necessary to point out that this is an area where history teaches useful skills. Part of the challenge of historical research has always been, first of all, to find the right sources, and second, to reduce and transform the raw data they yield to a concise, meaningful form. Lest I be dismissed as an irredeemable Luddite, and technopeasant let me hasten to add that there are some ways in which new technologies may prove to be useful in historical instruction. They offer interesting possibilities both for teaching the basics of historical practice and for cultivating an historical consciousness.

Instructors' packages for American history textbooks now often include laser disks containing thousands of images – documents, photographs, illustrations – to assist in the presentation of lessons. As this practice becomes more established and technology lowers production costs, we can expect to see the same feature in the Canadian textbook market. Now that it is possible to duplicate documents electronically, we can also expect that archives will make records available by modem or disk.[5] If microfilm provides a precedent, we can anticipate that many important record groups will soon be reproduced electronically. Extensive primary sources will be available in the classroom and on students' home computers.

This development offers the opportunity to give more students hands-on experience working with original sources. Admittedly, they will not feel the texture of the old paper or sneeze from the dust in the records box. But they will be able to see what the originals look like, and may even come to grips with illegible handwriting, missing pages and other joys of research! The important fact is they may learn for themselves how history is done. It is a case where demystification may lead to deeper appreciation.

Of course, there are some types of knowledge that simply cannot be filtered through a computer screen. That is why the work of the Historic Sites and Monuments Board of Canada is so valuable. History presented "live" at reconstructed sites with interpretive programs makes quite a different impression on students than history in text or on film. Even the inexpensive interpretive plaque, properly deployed, prompts its reader to make an imaginative leap back in time. The student is usually separated from history by the dimensions of space and time; historical sites stimulate historical imagination by eradicating the former.

There is a danger, however, in implying that history is something that exists only at officially-sanctioned sites. Students should be made aware of all the ways in which the past is with them in the present: in monuments, headstones, landscapes, street names, buildings, ruins, and human memory. Helping them recognize history in their own communities is a way to show its relevance.[6] It demonstrates that history is in the living fabric of their surrounding environment; that history is always here, at the present moment. Like genealogy, local history connects with a world students understand and offers them a way to walk before they run.

A distinctive feature of public debate in Canada in the 1990s is the power of new voices with new perspectives. We hear strong opinions on important social issues from First Nations, ethnic minorities, women, workers, the disadvantaged, indeed, from a wide variety of alternative points-of-view. Many of these groups are unhappy with their experiences in the past. Old injustices are identified and named, blame is laid and justice demanded.[7] The result is what many commentators have described as a civic culture of guilt and grievance. In this context, it becomes more obvious than ever that teaching history is a political act.

Yet history, carefully taught, should moderate the stridency which often distinguishes today's public debate. It shows that the past is not a morality play. Instead it sets the context of bygone events and demonstrates that the values by which we judge issues now are not necessarily those which prevailed then. This is one of the most fascinating aspects of the discipline. It challenges the student to consider moral questions within the complexity of cultural contexts that change through time.[8]

Fortunately, over the past quarter-century, the Canadian historical profession has begun to respond to the emergence of new viewpoints in our society with new scholarship.[9] As a result we now have a national history in which sex, class, and ethnicity are important categories of analysis. The revisionism is not finished – what branch of scholarship ever is? – but there is enough good material in print to keep students busy from high school well into university.

In fact, there has been so much specialization of historical inquiry in the past two decades that the big challenge at the moment is to synthesize the new history.[10] However, as the reconstruction of our national history gets underway, our object should not be a new orthodoxy. Instead, we should aim for an on-going debate and dialogue. A history agreed upon is dead and boring; a history disputed is lively and engaging.

And, that I would suggest, is why we should be teaching not just history, but historiography. Historiography offers students an academic exercise that has an obvious relevance in our contemporary society. It introduces conflicting interpretations on a variety of issues, suggests the ideological origins of each, and teaches how to evaluate them. Attentive students can acquire from it an array of critical skills that will help them to draw their own conclusions on controversial contemporary social issues.[11] Best of all, historiography dispels the myth that history is a dull, immutable litany of facts and dates. Perhaps we should even borrow a phrase from American historian William L. Burton, and say to our students: "If you do not like the past, change it."[12]

In the 1990s we are increasingly aware of and involved with the world beyond our national borders. The same thing is happening to some degree in all countries in the world. Technological progress has lowered the cost and improved the quality of communications and transportation. The end of the Cold War has transformed international relations. Meanwhile, developing nations – particularly those in the Asia-Pacific region – are growing more prominent in world affairs.[13]

One consequence of this trend toward globalization has been an international trade regime defined by a variety of new regional trade arrangements and an improved GATT. Canada, like it or not, has entered an era of continental free trade with expanding opportunities for stronger commercial relationships around the globe.

Globalization is important to Canadian students because it is defining the world in which they will live and work. Yet it is impossible for them to fully appreciate it if they do not know that the struggle of economic and cultural nationalism versus free trade is a fundamental theme of our own history. Students will be much more interested in the elections of 1891 and 1911 if they are reminded of the free trade election of 1988. Even those who are too young to remember 1988 have heard about NAFTA, and can be led from it to an appreciation of the Repeal of the Corn Laws, Reciprocity, the National Policy, even the Ogdensburg Agreement. To teach students these precedents is to awaken them to the connections between past and present.

Yes, there are dangers with this sort of approach. The past deserves to be appreciated on its own terms, and present-mindedness always colours historic issues with current concerns. But even professional historians who pride themselves in their objectivity admit that contemporary relevance motivates their work. When students have historical insights which reflect back on issues which are important to them in the present, they too will truly be engaged by the discipline. Suddenly our history, far from being parochial and irrelevant, bears directly on contemporary world events.

These are all approaches to enhance the teaching of history in the 1990s. We want to reach adolescents, a group whose interest in anything that does not affect them directly is often extremely limited. That is why I advocate some consideration for approaches which first appeal to them on their own terms by engaging their family and their community, then moves on to the wider realms of nation and world.

The contemporary trends I have touched upon – our aging population and its interest in genealogy, the potential and limitations of electronic information, the usefulness of historiography in a civic culture distinguished by multiple perspectives, and the globalization of communications and commerce – all offer opportunities for advancing different stages in this process. Now I admit that some of what I suggest is opportunistic. Perhaps it has to be. Much as we love history, we cannot expect the average student to naturally share our passion. If they are ever to be initiated, they must first be attracted, perhaps even enticed. However, we can adapt the teaching of history to present interests and conditions without compromising the essentials of the discipline. And when we do that we ensure that our past will continue to inform and enrich future generations.

Notes

1. For an exposition of contemporary teaching methods see Peter J. Frederick, "Motivating Students by Active Learning in the History Classroom", *Bulletin* (Canadian Historical Association), 15-16 [rpt. From American Historical Association *Perspectives*, (October 1993).
2. Geoffrey Partington, *The Idea of an Historical Education* (Windsor: NFER, 1980), 26-31.
3. Lorraine St-Louis-Harrison, "Family Footprints", *The Archivist*, 107, (1994), 7. See Also David Lowenthal, *The Past is a Foreign Country* (New York: Cambridge University Press, 1985), 409.
4. Pierre Berton, *Hollywood's Canada: The Americanization of our National Image* (Toronto: McClelland and Stewart, 1975).
5. In recent years, of course, the original format of many records has been electronic.
6. Mary Joan Cook, "Finding the Layers in Your Town" in Robert Blackey (ed.), *History Anew: Innovations in the Teaching of History Today* (Long Beach, California: California State University Press, 1993), 289-91.
7. In a recent editorial in *The Beaver*, Christopher Dafoe raised the question of whether society as a whole owes restitution to all of history's victims. See Christopher Dafoe, "Are We All Guilty?", *The Beaver*, 74, 5 (October/November 1994), 2-3.
8. On how to get students to empathize with historical subjects, see A.K. Dickinson, P.J. Lee and P.J. Rogers, *Learning History* (London: Heinemann, 1984), 50.
9. See Greg Kealey, "Writing About Labour", Veronica Strong-Boag, "Writing About Women"; and Roberto Perin, "Writing About Ethnicity" in John Schultz (ed.), *Writing About Canada: A Handbook for Modern Canadian History* (Scarborough: Prentice Hall, 1990).
10. Michael Bliss, "Privatizing the Mind: The Sundering of Canadian History, the Sundering of Canada", *Journal of Canadian Studies*, 26 (Winter 1991-92), 5-17.

11. Robert F. Berkhofer, Jr. "Demystifying Historical Authority: Critical Textual Analysis in the Classroom" in *Blackey*, 23-6.

12. William L. Burton, "The Use and Abuse of History", *American Historical Society Newsletter*, 20, 2 (1982).

13. Outlines of globalization from opposing camps are available in Richard G. Lipsey, "Globalization, Technological Change and Economic Growth", *Canadian Business Economics* (Fall 1993) 3-17 and James Laxer, *False God: How the Globalization Myth has Impoverished Canada* (Toronto: Lester, 1993), 10-13.

Canada Hall, Canadian Museum of Civilization: Staff members in period dress are available to tell school outings about life in bygone eras and to answer the children's questions. / Salle du Canada, Musée canadien des civilisations : des membres du personnel en costumes d'époque parlent de la vie d'antan aux groupes d'élèves qui visitent le musée et répondent à leur questions. (Photo: Canadian Museum of Civilization / Musée canadien des civilisations, S94-37679)

Computer programs on history and civilization are another way to stimulate a child's curiosity. / Des programmes informatiques sur l'histoire et la civilsation offrent un autre moyen de stimuler la curiosité des enfants. (Photo: Canadian Museum of Civilization / Musée canadien des civilisations, S94-37822)

DOROTHY DUNCAN

Heritage as Classroom: Teaching Teachers to Teach Using Heritage Commemoration

Abstract

The classroom teachers in Canadian schools face many challenges. One of the most important is the formidable task of motivating students to research, discuss and explore every aspect of our history, spanning the centuries from First Nations to newcomers arriving daily from around the world.

There are many ways of learning about the past. The history book, the descriptive label, the historical plaque, and the museum interpreter are just a few of the recognized sources of information. Teachers must link that information about the often unknown people, places and events of the past to the known people, places and events of the present. If they are successful their students will recognize and respond to the rich resources that surround them, often hidden in the everyday objects and buildings that served the everyday needs of our ancestors.

Le patrimoine à l'école : apprendre aux enseignants à enseigner à l'aide de la commémoration du patrimoine – résumé

Au Canada, les enseignants font face à de nombreux défis dans la salle de classe. Une de leurs tâches les plus difficiles consiste à donner à leurs élèves le goût de fouiller, d'examiner et d'explorer tous les aspects de notre histoire, à partir des temps anciens où le territoire était occupé par les Premières Nations jusqu'à l'époque actuelle, où des immigrants du monde entier arrivent quotidiennement chez nous.

Il existe de nombreuses façons de s'instruire sur le passé. Le livre d'histoire, l'étiquette descriptive, la plaque historique et le guide de musée ne sont que quelques-unes des sources d'information reconnues. L'enseignant doit faire le lien entre cette information sur des gens, des lieux et des événements – souvent inconnus – du passé, et des gens, lieux et événements connus du présent. S'il y réussit, ses élèves sauront reconnaître et apprécier la richesse qui les entoure, souvent cachée dans des objets courants et des bâtiments qui sont des vestiges de la vie quotidienne de leurs ancêtres.

Classroom teachers face many challenges in this rapidly changing world. Students in our modern classrooms have very diverse racial and cultural backgrounds, interests, abilities, skills, knowledge, needs, and values. Teachers must find ways of motivating those students to love history while coping with decreasing budgets, rising expectations from the students themselves, their parents and the community, restrictive time tables, bus schedules and much, much more. Add to this the changing courses of study in many provinces. Ontario has a new common curriculum for Grades 1 to 9, where History has vanished as a subject and the core programme areas are: language, arts, self and society, mathematics, science and technology.

Despite these obstacles there are many innovative and diverse programmes being designed and presented by teachers, youth leaders, museum workers, and historical society members across Canada where students of all cultural backgrounds are making vital links between themselves, their communities, the events that make up their daily lives and the people, places, and events of the past. The living history of neighbourhoods, villages, and towns is being discovered, and the "long ago and far away" is becoming the "here and now" – something that every student, of every cultural background, can understand.

As a heritage community we must insert ourselves into the educational process wherever and whenever possible: Ministry of Education, Board of Education, local schools, teaching profession, professional development days, the selection of reading materials and the current courses of study, and provision of resources such as reproduction artifacts and documents, books and articles, videos, films, slide sets, and speakers for our schools. Many community museums across Canada already have well-developed educational programmes that provide cross-cultural and cross-curriculum development while focusing on the heritage and history of the community.

As we all know, many teachers do not have a recognized national or provincial historic site in the community. They may, or may not, have local heritage resources such as a plaque, museum, archives, or resource centre. However, every teacher has two priceless resources – the students and the local community. Each community is as individual as each human being. By studying themselves and their community, students learn what role they, their families, and earlier residents have played in Canada's larger history and how national events have affected them locally.

Young people must first be motivated to become detectives, to explore the history of the people, the streets, and the buildings that make up the community, and to compare, discuss, and analyze their findings. An introduction to the topic can begin in the classroom and should capture the imagination of every student. Do you remember the Peanuts cartoon that showed Lucy in her classroom telling her fellow students, "For show and tell today I have something unique. I'm not going to tell about a pet or show you a toy or a book or something like that. Instead I'm going to tell you all about someone I consider quite fascinating – MYSELF!!!" Begin with the students and their own history.

Young people will have heard their first history without realizing it – at a family reunion, birthday party, wedding, or sitting on their mother's knee. Students should be encouraged to explore that history using not only oral history, but family Bibles, documents, cemetery records, whatever is available. Has the family always lived here? Why did they come here? Why did they stay? Ancestors will take on form and substance, traditions and lifestyles will emerge, and pride of ancestry and of being a Canadian will acquire a new meaning. Discussions about special events such as birthday parties, religious observances, special days lead naturally to discussions about the observances and ceremonies that are part of our life together as a nation.

The study of artifacts will also provide both teacher and students with some of the most tangible and concrete clues about the everyday life of the community and how it has changed over time. As the group learns to really LOOK at an object, the skills of a detective come into play and something as simple as a penny can be used for the first exercise. As the students become efficient detectives, they should move out into the community, for the school building and the structures that surround it are links with the past that can be seen, felt, and touched. In our Canadian climate structures have, for centuries, provided shelter for living and working and have reflected the resources available – mud, sticks, stones, hides, bricks, sandstone, timber, steel. Research may reveal that the present community is constructed on the site of a previous one that has now vanished due to lifestyles, climate, or a natural or economic disaster. Students must be encouraged to examine structures with the eyes of a detective asking who? why? when? what for? changes? additions? Why, in some Canadian communities are we demolishing buildings to replace them with others?

The local cemetery is an outdoor classroom where art, language, genealogy, mathematics, health and social history can be explored. From the simple wooden crosses of the First Nations to the carved sandstone, granite, and marble stones of the newcomers, many Canadians believe that our burial places are mirror images of our communities. Is that true?

This land mass that is known today as Canada has for centuries been the destination of newcomers. The First Nations, explorers, fur traders and the first settlers from France, Great Britain and Europe used the waterways as their highways. Paths and roads were eventually carved through the forests, marshes, and meadowlands. Wagon roads, stagecoach routes, paved highways, canals, railways and airports have been built and already some are obsolete. What happened in this community? As the students walk the present streets they may see traces of change: old paths overgrown, roads to mine sites closed, streets diverted. Why? What does that have to do with the history of this community?

Every aspect of everyday life – food, clothing, songs, stories, legends, methods of communication, crafts, and industries – reveal Canada's history: who came, why they came, what was the invisible and visible baggage that they brought with them, what have they made, built, changed to serve their needs, and what contributions have they made to our development as a nation. The Ontario Historical Society has developed a bilingual resource for teachers, youth leaders and parents to use with young people called *Discovering Your Community*, in partnership with *Regroupement des organismes du patrimoine franco-ontarien*. We believe this is the first resource developed in Canada that encourages young people to examine the world around them with the eyes and skills of a detective, to analyze their findings, and to make deductions based on the clues that they have discovered.

If the students are good detectives and the teacher has motivated the students to explore their own community and the people who lived there, a visit to a recognized national or provincial heritage site can be put into the context of our larger history. Freeman Tilden in *Interpreting Our Heritage* expresses it best:

> Visiting the places that have been made famous and treasurable by the acts of men and women, where the story is told of courage and self-sacrifice, of dauntless patriotism, of statesmanship and inventive genius, of folkways, of husbandry or of the clash of armed men following their ideals to the valley of the shadow – all this offers a very different kind of experience. These places... represent the life and acts of people.
>
> The prehistoric ruin must somehow manage to convey the notion to the visitor that the ancients who lived there might come back this very night and renew possession, and that there will be a renewal of the grinding of corn, the cries of children, and the making of love and feasting. ... The battlefield...is not merely a place of strategy and tactics; not a place where regiments moved this way and that like checkers on the board; not merely a spot where something was decided that would lead to another decision. It is a place of the thoughts and acts of men, of their ideals and

memories; a place where on the evening of a fatal tomorrow men could joke and sing; a place of people, not armies.[1]

That is the key to any study of Canada's history that teachers, youth leaders, and parents can explore and exploit. Canadians are not descendants of a regiment, Canadians are descendants of men and women who had all the strengths and weaknesses we have, who faced dangers, hardships, joys, and sorrows, just as we do. Students must confront that reality and must always be challenged to answer the questions: What would I have done, if I had been there? How would I have acted? Would I have solved that problem in another way? What would have been my fate?

I believe everyone in this room is hooked on history. If we want our children, grandchildren, the generations that follow us to love history as we do we must all, not just classroom teachers, strive to bring our history, the good, the bad, the terrible, to life so that our young people will better understand themselves as individuals and as proud citizens of a nation that is moving into a new century.

Note

1. Freeman Tilden, *Interpreting Our Heritage*, American Association for State and Local History, Nashville, Tennessee (© 1967, renewed 1985, Chapel Hill, The University of North Carolina Press) p. 69.

Shaver Family Cemetery, Ancaster, Ontario, designated by the Ontario Ministry of Culture and Communication under the *Ontario Heritage Act* in 1993. / Le cimetière de la famille Shaver, à Ancaster (Ontario), désigné en vertu de la *Loi sur le patrimoine de l'Ontario*, en 1993. (Photo: Marjorie Stuart)

Burial site of William Shaver, 28 April 1830. The last internment in this graveyard took place on 13 November 1938. / Lieu de sépulture de William Shaver, 28 avril 1830. La dernière inhumation faite dans ce cimetière eut lieu le 13 novembre 1938. (Photo: Marjorie Stuart)

Heritage as Sound Bites

Abstract

History in "60 seconds": that is the concept that was developed to make use of media to bring history to life. "La petite histoire" of those who make up Canada is examined and, if possible, developed into a micro-movie. How Canada got its name, innovation, the first female medical student, the growth of an industry – all have been subject to the "60 second" snapshot of one incident that has led to so much more. History gains life and relevance through these productions.

Le patrimoine en capsules – Résumé

L'histoire en 60 secondes : telle est l'idée conçue pour faire revivre l'histoire par le truchement des médias. On examine « la petite histoire » de la société canadienne et, si possible, on la reconstitue dans un minifilm. L'origine du nom du Canada, l'innovation, la première étudiante en médecine, la croissance d'une industrie sont autant des sujets « croqués » dans ces instantanés d'événements isolés qui ont été suivis de tant d'autres. Ces minifilms animent l'histoire et lui donnent un sens.

My purpose is to introduce you formally to something that virtually all of you have met informally on your televisions and in the cinema: the *Heritage Minutes*. I want to explain what these 60 second micro-dramas are, how they came about, and what they mean. The *Minutes* are history, but they are history presented in an entirely original form.

The *Minutes* are part of the Heritage Project of the CRB Foundation. The idea to create the project came to Charles Bronfman, Chairman of the Foundation, at the ceremony at which he received the Order of Canada. Struck by the wonderful stories told by each of his fellow laureates, Canadians of many different backgrounds, Mr. Bronfman realized that the history of Canada was full of such stories. These – as we call them in French *la petite histoire* – needed to be told, and the *Heritage Minutes* were invented to tell them.

The Heritage Project extends beyond the *Minutes*. The television shows "Just a Minute" and "D'une minute à l'autre" give viewers a broader context for the tantalizing micro-dramas. Sixty thousand classrooms receive the *Heritage*

Post/Courrier du Patrimoine magazine, which expands on the ideas introduced in the *Minutes*. Heritage Fairs have been held in seven provinces. The CRB Foundation's Learning Resources Program will provide curriculum-based supplementary materials to link what students see on television to what they learn in school, and help students learn about the past by living it through simulations, role-playing, and participatory exercises.

But the *Heritage Minutes* are the critical first step to introducing Canada's history to Canadians. The program began with *"un préjugé favorable"* for the young. Kids are more media literate than older generations, and they are very demanding viewers, impatient to get to the bottom of things quickly and to move on. Patrick Watson and I, the creative directors, knew that we had to compress our histories into sixty-second scripts, to squeeze *"l'infiniment grand dans l'infiniment petit"*, as Pascal once said. This proved very, very difficult. I cannot tell you the number of excellent stories suggested to us that have had to be rejected because they could not fit into a 60 second format or would have been far too expensive to produce if they could.

What started as a project aimed at young people has now been watched by all generations. Twenty-three million Canadians see the *Minutes* in cinemas annually, and uncounted millions watch them at home during the thirteen hours per month of national television devoted to the *Minutes*.

Ideas for *Minutes* come from many places, including suggestions from viewers. The creation of each micro-movie begins with a brainstorming session which leads to traditional historical research. Two academic historians, Jean-Claude Robert and John Herd Thompson, work on every script. We adapt dialogue from historical record whenever possible, but occasionally we must create a conversation to convey the story line of an event.

For example, one *Minute* turns on an invented conversation between Jacques Cartier, a priest, and an Iroquoian chieftain. Cartier and the priest mistakenly assume that the Iroquoian word for village, *Kanata*, is the name for the country of the Iroquois. But although the specific historical situation may not have taken place, the scenario is a plausible way to transmit many valid historical messages. The word *Kanata* is the most generally accepted source of the word Canada, and we know from Cartier's journals that he was aware of it.

We try to place viewers in a position in which the sweep and the contradictions of history become suddenly obvious to them. I offer as *la première minute que je vais vous présenter, qui représente une contradiction fascinante, notre hymne national, le "Ô Canada" – et c'est Tom Axworthy à la tête de la Fondation qui avait pensé à ça – a été donné la première fois en 1880 à un grand gala le jour de la Saint-Jean-Baptiste, le 24 juin.* This is an incontrovertible fact. The army was responsible for that concert in Québec City and had commissioned a song – although they hadn't commissioned a national anthem – by Calixa Lavallée which was played at the concert on Saint Jean Baptiste Day. And so the historical but amusing part of it, to us, was central. It is at once amusing and moving. As we did not want to be solemn about a *Minute* that would deal with the national anthem, our script writers had to bridge the gap between history and entertainment, and to do it in 60 seconds. Our script writers had a very hard time with this one. "Les Voltigeurs", a Québec Regiment, played the song on Saint Jean Baptiste Day in 1880, but what then? Someone came up with a Felliniesque idea, borrowed from "Provo d'orchestra" in which Fellini suggests that the bickering at an orchestra rehearsal is perhaps a mirror for the rest of society. So the script writer took off from that and we had our *Minute* on "les Voltigeurs" and "Ô Canada".

We assume that there was a rehearsal. The way the script writer set it up, the band members do not want to rehearse; they want to go home, have a beer, so they have some fun with the band leader, they mock him. We do not know if this actually happened, but it is legitimate to suppose that it could have happened. One thing is certain: on 24 June 1880 the song that was to become our national anthem was played at a concert to celebrate *la fête de Saint-Jean-Baptiste*.

Another example of how we tried to take a historical moment and project it and give it more is our *Minute* on Étienne Parent. This was another idea from Tom Axworthy, who noted that in nineteenth century French-Canadian thought there was a great variety of opinion. Parent and a few others argued that nationalism and political institutions were all well and good, but that education and commerce were the ways of the future. Now of course, that rings a bell today because of the "Quiet Revolution"; there has been *Québec incorporé*; there has been a number of things, but it is astounding, especially to a French-language audience, to think that this was said in the early nineteenth century by a patriot. And that is what Étienne Parent was: a patriot and a journalist who was jailed in 1837 for his ideas. What we wanted to do was to hold up a mirror between the two centuries.

Now again, the ironies or the contradictions of history are of great interest to us, also that which is relatively unsaid, unspoken. One *Minute* that has a large retention factor with kids is the "Jenny Trout" *Minute* because it is about the first woman licenced to practice medicine in Canada. It was taken from an incident described in a friend's diary. We had to recreate the incident and give it dramatic depth. It deals with an anatomy class being given at the University of Toronto. The male-dominated lecture hall is resounding with the calls of "Get them out!" The professor panders to the men, saying that he cannot describe the male anatomy "due to the presence of certain members of the 'weaker sex'". It is astounding how many kids will come up to me and say, "Well, I didn't realize there was any problem with women doctors, or that women could not study medicine. I can't imagine that, is that true?" And so we have pointed out broader historical issues not specifically pointed out in the *Minute* – the unspoken.

At Charles Bronfman's suggestion, when producing *Minutes*, French Canadians are responsible for the French-language *Minutes*. This helps us to get away from "*le folklore*"; we can concentrate not only on explorers, but also on people who have done great things, thus we avoid enshrining clichés. Mr. Bronfman then said, "How about the entrepreneurs? How about the people who are doing things now?" Always, in keeping with our goal to introduce people who are not generally known, we have chosen true historical characters and brought them alive for the first time.

This is how we thought of Joseph-Armand Bombardier. There was an exciting series on Bombardier by François LaBonté, who is the director of the "Étienne Parent" *Minute* that I mentioned earlier, but there were still some incidents that had not been put into that series. We got Vincent Bolduc, one of the great young actors in Québec, to act the part. In this film we again project into the future, because now Bombardier, the company, is far more than the snowmobiles it started with. This is a true fact – I have this from André Bombardier, his son, and the biographers – Joseph-Armand Bombardier did actually use his pocket money to go to the jewellers, but he did not want to buy jewellery, he wanted to buy the jeweller's tools. The jeweller was astounded at this fourteen year old's unusual request, but Bombardier took the tools home and began his tinkering. We do not know if he left that little toy snowmobile on his desk for the rest of his life, but we know that he did build one that worked. Reaction to this *Minute* is largely favourable. People are amused and intrigued that the lives of the famous can be like their own lives, and that little things can lead to great things.

Those of us who collaborate to create the *Heritage Minutes* have great hopes for our historical micro-movies: that Canadians will not only learn more about their history and learn to appreciate it, but that they will, as well, be entertained and moved by these *Minutes*.

Scene from the "Jacques Cartier/Naming of Canada" *Minute*. / Scène de la « minute » sur Jacques Cartier et le choix du nom Canada. (Photo by Claude Charlebois courtesy of The CRB Foundation Heritage Project / photo de Claude Charlebois ; gracieuseté du programme Reflets du patrimoine de La Fondation CRB)

Scene from "Les Voltigeurs" *Minute* / Scène de la « minute » sur Les Voltigeurs. (Photo by Claude Charlebois courtesy of The CRB Foundation Heritage Project / photo de Claude Charlebois ; gracieuseté du programme Reflets du patrimoine de La Fondation CRB)

195

Scene from the "Étienne Parent" *Minute* / Scène de la « minute » sur Étienne Parent. (Photo by Claude Charlebois courtesy of The CRB Foundation Heritage Project / photo de Claude Charlebois ; gracieuseté du programme Reflets du patrimoine de La Fondation CRB)

Scene from the "Joseph-Armand Bombardier" *Minute* / Scène de la « minute » sur Joseph-Armand Bombardier. (Photo by Claude Charlebois courtesy of The CRB Foundation Heritage Project / photo de Claude Charlebois ; gracieuseté du programme Reflets du patrimoine de La Fondation CRB)

Knowing and Communicating a Sense of Place

Abstract
Should we have the right to introduce our children to the places we ourselves knew as children? Or are old buildings mere nostalgia, and nostalgia the breeding ground of conflict? The answer lies in the deepest of human needs: the built heritage has an impact on our sense of self, our sense of safety, the way we interact with one another and function as citizens in a democracy.

Posséder et communiquer le sens du lieu – Résumé
Devrions-nous avoir le droit de présenter à nos enfants les lieux que nous avons connus nous-mêmes lorsque nous étions enfants ? Ou les vieux édifices sont-ils simplement un sujet de nostalgie et celle-ci, une source de conflits ? La réponse se trouve dans le plus profond des désirs humains : le patrimoine architectural a une incidence sur notre sentiment d'individualité, sur notre sentiment de sécurité, sur notre façon d'agir les uns envers les autres et sur notre comportement comme membres d'une société démocratique.

History is becoming too small to share, writes Rem Koolhaas, the Dutch architect and urban thinker. The world is producing too many people for the built heritage that remains.

> To the extent that history finds its deposit in architecture, present human quantities will inevitably burst and deplete previous substance. Identity conceived as this form of sharing the past is a losing proposition. Not only is there . . . proportionally less and less to share, but history also has an invidious half-life: as it is more abused, it becomes less significant, to the point where its diminishing handouts become insulting.

Reading Koolhaas's comments, I find my mind speaking Ebenezer Scrooge's words to the Ghost of Christmas Yet to Come: "Are these the shadows of the things that Will be, or are they shadows of things that May be only?"

Disney is taking charge of our history. Disney markets the RCMP. "The people at Disney," says the American architect Frank Gehry, "are the people who really count in America." The Europeans call EuroDisney a cultural Chenobyl. The Europeans, says Koolhaas, are in massive denial, behaving like dead parents deploring the mess their children have made of their inheritance.

The Japanese architect Arata Isosaki likes designing buildings for Disney. Disney, he says, is the clean slate, the *tabula rasa*. Old buildings are mere nostalgia, and nostalgia breeds conflict. "At Disney World, there is no conflict, no history, no context through which it can bond with the existing community. There is no friction. There is only fiction. Pure space."

And no meaning.

Kate taught me my idea of Canada.

Kate, my maternal grandmother, at the age of eight, in the year 1886, travelled with her family on one of the CPR's first through trains from Toronto to Vancouver. She engaged me from childhood with accounts of that train ride: what the interior of the old colonist cars looked like; how the passengers brought their own bedding; how the Plains Indians rode up to the train on their horses and peered curiously through the windows at frequent stops where the line was still under construction.

She told me stories of pioneer life in Vancouver and on Vancouver Island. For every turn-of-the-century building she had a story. She took me aboard a chartered CPR ferry every year to the annual pioneers' picnic on a small island off Nanaimo.

She told me about campaigning with her second husband for the United Farmers Party in the province's interior before World War I, where young ranchers fresh from England served them tea, with the finest china and linen napkins, in sod huts.

When I grew up and worked briefly in Peterborough – where my grandmother was born – she wrote a letter to me with a description of the house built by her father where she had lived as a child, a description so vividly detailed that I was easily able to find the house with the help of municipal records. I called on its occupants, who were in love with this house, and who boasted to me – the great-grandson of its builder, a carpenter – about the artistry of its construction.

"Our relationship with the places we know and meet up with," wrote Tony Hiss in his wonderful book, *The Experience of Place*, "is a close bond, intricate in nature, and not abstract, not remote at all. It is enveloping, almost a continuum with all we are and think." Shouldn't we have a right, Hiss asks wistfully, to introduce our children to the places we as children knew?

Because of my grandmother's stories, I will forever in my lifetime conceive of Canada as The Land. I travel it today – 10,000 metres above the ground in a jet aircraft – touched by the romance of my grandmother's train journey of more than a century ago.

I know the places in British Columbia's mountain valleys – like Walhachin – where the young settlers came, homesteaded, went off to the Great War and never returned, leaving ghost towns behind. I make time for the old buildings when I'm in Vancouver. I stop on the sidewalk to look at them, go inside those that are public, to reconnect myself with my past, my family's past and with Kate, the woman I loved.

History's deposit in architecture, says Koolhaas, is a losing proposition. And the more history is abused, the less significant it becomes to the point where its diminishing returns become insulting.

We humans are a species in massive global churn, reproducing in frightening numbers, shrinking the planet with our technology, overwhelming the notion of tribal culture and homeland. Yet the fact that human beings are forever an unfinished species – a succession of families, tribes and societies in continuing transition to a new awareness – necessitates the preservation of the built past as markers for where we have been and where we are going.

"These places," says Tony Hiss, "have an impact on our sense of self, our sense of safety, the kind of work we get done, the ways we interact with other people, even our ability to function as citizens in a democracy."

We cannot all claim relationship to heritage that sinks its roots in the land a century, two centuries, a millennium deep. Yet in a land as multicultural as Canada, as forever subject to re-invention as Canada, these places of built heritage are more than the markers of any one particular culture. They are markers of the nation itself, and the nation itself has a history, a past that has shaped its present.

"As places around us change – both the communities that shelter us and the larger regions that support them – we all undergo changes inside," says Hiss. "The danger, as we are now beginning to see, is that whenever we make changes in our surroundings, we can all too easily shortchange ourselves, by cutting ourselves off from some of the sights and sounds, the shapes or textures, or other information from a place that have helped mould our understanding and are now necessary for us to thrive." It is a danger each new generation inherently recognizes as it slips loose its moorings from childhood.

My daughter was baptised in a tiny village church near our farm on Georgian Bay. The church had no longstanding connection to our family; our attendance at Sunday services was occasional. Yet my daughter's sadness was immense when the half-dozen remaining members of the congregation voted to pull it down rather than see it sold as some chi-chi weekend residence for city folk. One day, she took a rock from a fenceline, painted it white, lettered her name and the date of her baptism on it and placed the rock in a secluded corner of the churchyard. It has been there for years, unmoved, her personal heritage, her marker.

Scrooge, enlightened by his revisit to the Past, remorseful for his Present and terrified of the Future to which his Present is leading him, begged of the last Spirit who commanded his attendance: "Assure me that I yet may change these shadows you have shown me, by an altered life. I will live in the Past, the Present and the Future. The Spirits of all Three shall strive within me."

Disney World – and nothing but Disney World – is the alternative.

St. Matthew's Anglican Church, Bognor, Ontario, constructed in 1901, demolished in 1981. A cairn was built from bricks and stone taken from St. Matthew's Church and the church bell was hung in the cairn. A plaque has been placed on the cairn giving details of the former church. / L'église anglicane St. Matthew, à Bognor (Ontario), constuite en 1901 et démolie en 1981. Un cairn, où est suspendue la cloche de l'église, a été fait de briques et de pierres provenant de celle-ci. Une plaque donnant des précisions sur l'ancienne église y a été apposée. (Photo courtesy of / gracieuseté de Jim Thomson, Bognor)

Politics, Society, and Commemoration
Politique, société et commémoration

Original Parliament Buildings, Ottawa: the construction work begun in 1859 was completed in 1866. An iron crown was added to the tower between 1876 and 1878. Fire destroyed all but the library of the Central Block in 1916. The new Centre Block was completed in 1919 with the Peace Tower added afterwards; designated 1976. / Premiers édifices du Parlement, Ottawa : les travaux, entrepris en 1859, furent achevés en 1866. Une flèche en fer fut ajoutée à la tour entre 1876 et 1878. Un incendie détruisit tous les bâtiments, sauf la bibliothèque de l'édifice du Centre, en 1916. Le nouvel édifice du Centre fut achevé en 1919 et la tour de la Paix fut ajoutée par la suite ; ensemble désigné en 1976. (Photo: National Archives / Archives nationales, C-3760, Samuel McLaughlin, ca / v. 1880)

ALBINA GUARNIERI, M.P.*

The Creation of the Department of Canadian Heritage

Abstract

The Department of Canadian Heritage was created in 1992 to bring together the elements essential to preserving the symbols of our nation and its people. It was designed to promote a better understanding of our diversity, active participation in Canadian society, and an awareness of our cultural and natural riches.

The system of national historic sites and monuments is an important aspect of this Department as it commemorates the multiple and diverse aspects of the Canadian experience.

La création du ministère du Patrimoine canadien – Résumé

Le ministère du Patrimoine canadien a été créé en 1992 afin de réunir les éléments essentiels à la conservation des symboles de notre pays et de ses habitants. Il a pour mission de promouvoir une meilleure compréhension de notre diversité, la participation active à la société canadienne et la prise de conscience de nos richesses culturelles et naturelles.

Le réseau des lieux et monuments historiques nationaux constitue un volet important de ce ministère, car il met en lumière la multiplicité et la diversité de l'expérience canadienne.

The birth of the Department of Canadian Heritage almost a year and a half ago caused a few pangs at the time due in large part to its extraordinary size. The creation of such a large department immediately posed a challenge. How could we justify gathering together in one federal department, such diverse elements as Cultural Industries, Official and Heritage Languages, National Parks and Historic Sites, Canadian Studies, Youth, Voluntary Action, Human Rights, Multiculturalism, Amateur Sport, and State Ceremonial? I must admit, parenthetically, it does seem like a good question. But it does not necessarily follow that large size is an impediment to efficient government. The Department of Canadian Heritage is about to be expressed in three main themes: Culture, Heritage, and Canadian Identity, and it makes eminent sense to bring these elements together in one department called Canadian Heritage.

After all, what does the word heritage really mean? In its broadest sense heritage is a set of signposts that enables us to recognize ourselves as individuals who belong to a particular group or country. In that sense the Department's name is fitting and succinct. Today we can no longer restrict the meaning of heritage to the legacy of the past. Far more than a simple collection of traces left by history, a country's heritage is the manifestation of the connection among members of the community and of a distinctive character inside the global environment. Thus, heritage is closely linked to questions of individual and national identity. The elements which help us to identify, strengthen, and celebrate the symbols of our nation are thus brought together in the Department of Canadian Heritage.

The Department combines all or some parts of five strong, former departments: Secretary of State, Multiculturalism and Citizenship, Fitness and Amateur Sport, Parks Canada, and the Cultural Broadcasting and Heritage components of Communications Canada. These departments varied in size and complexity from Parks, which was the largest, to Amateur Sport, the smallest. We had to consider how to position the new department; how to amalgamate a variety of traditions, mandates, and visions; and how to handle the rising profile of the new department as it achieved its present highly visible and powerful role. And once the Department was underway we had to establish priorities. We had to determine, in these difficult and challenging times, what our most important priorities and issues are. Therefore, the exchange of ideas and gatherings such as this one is crucial. Through such dialogue we can benefit from your work and advice in the programme areas in which you connect with us. We can learn, from your perspective, what we need to do at this time, whether there is some fundamental shift that can make us better and more effective as a government. In fact, the establishment of the Department of Canadian Heritage reflects the commitment to more effective and efficient government.

We like to use the term synergy because we feel that the combined impact of the whole of the Department of Canadian Heritage exceeds the effects of its individual parts. We feel that the formation of this new department has enhanced the future strength and effectiveness of its many programmes. In addition, this synergy provides many benefits that flow into the cultural and heritage aspects of the Department's mandate. The Department of Canadian Heritage brings together those elements which define Canada as a multi-faceted, dynamic nation, with a rich cultural and national heritage. The Department is responsible for everything relating to Canadian identity and values, cultural development, heritage, and areas of natural or historical significance to Canada and to Canadians.

The reorganized Department has brought together many programmes that share a common ground, whether in terms of their mandate, clients, or stakeholders. The Department of Canadian Heritage has been designed to promote a better understanding of our diversity, active participation in Canadian society, and an awareness of our cultural and natural riches. It does so through the application of policies and programmes that assist in solving the problems facing a modern society, in clearing up the misunderstandings, and in instilling a pride in ourselves as individuals and as a nation. The Historic Sites and Monuments Board of Canada is an important contributor to achieving this vision of Canadian heritage. Our national historic sites are part of a heritage that is as varied as this land and the people who live here now and in the past. Canadians across this land share a strong interest in commemorating aspects of our past. Historic sites and monuments provide a tangible, geographic connection to our historic past and they help encourage a feeling of national identity.

The Department of Canadian Heritage encompasses a vision of Canada's past, present, and future, building on the ancestral values of its founding departments and bringing the country into the future. The Department improves the quality of life in Canada by strengthening Canadian identity and pride in our nation, and this can be very beneficial in a multicultural society like our own.

The increasing diversity of our population is only one of the dramatic challenges we are facing as a nation. Addressing issues of diversity is one of the many responsibilities of the Department of Canadian Heritage. The Department does this through programmes such as human rights, voluntary action, native citizens, as well as multiculturalism. Frank Rutter, a writer with the *Vancouver Sun*, has described multiculturalism as, and I quote, "trying to balance a multicultural heritage with the national soul." It is the Department of Canadian Heritage that can achieve that balance. Each and every unit of the Department reflects some aspect of the visceral relationship between Canadians and their country. This is the Department that can strengthen those ties and thus strengthen Canada.

The system of national historic sites and monuments is fast becoming a success story in reflecting the diversity of Canadian experience. Sites and monuments commemorate such accomplished Canadians as Fanny Rosenfeld, Canada's woman athlete of the half-century; E. Pauline Johnson, poet and cultural ambassador; and Sir William Osler, physician and educator. They commemorate the contributions to Canada made by people of Chinese heritage who helped to build the Canadian Pacific Railway, as well as the historic importance of Canada's First Black Battalion, in Pictou County, Nova Scotia. We are continuing to develop new themes for national historic sites focusing on the accomplishments and contributions of women and the Aboriginal peoples of Canada.

This important work would have been more difficult before the creation of the Department of Canadian Heritage. Now our national historic sites and monuments are not only illustrating our history but it is in places like Port aux Choix in Newfoundland, where documents of a 4000 year-old Aboriginal site fill in missing chapters in our history.

We are proud of what can be achieved when the diverse programmes of the Department work together. Within the Department, as it is now structured, we have the tools, expertise, and vision to develop initiatives and to use resources that reflect the reality of the Canadian experience. We will do so effectively, efficiently, and creatively. Whether it is our historic sites, our monuments, our national parks, the achievements of our athletes, the influences of our artists, the diversity and scope of our population, or the success of our cultural industries, all of these elements highlight our drive to excel as a people.

The custodians of our national heritage are the visionaries and administrators of the Historic Sites and Monuments Board of Canada. Their charge is a heritage that must never be lost because it is a heritage rooted in Canada and in the lives of Canadians. Only two years ago (1992), the 75th anniversary of the establishment of Canada's first National Historic Site (Fort Anne, Nova Scotia) was celebrated, while Canada celebrated 125 years as a nation. It seems fitting that both Canada and the National Historic Sites system marked major anniversaries in concert. The Board, through the national historic sites and monuments which result from its deliberations, reflects the heritage of Canada and the diversity of the Canadian experience. Similarly, whether it is in preserving our natural heritage, promoting our official languages, encouraging involvement in sport, or supporting cultural development, the Department of Canadian Heritage reflects the diversity of Canadian experience. The Department is working to foster a sense of shared values that will enable us to realize the democratic ideals on which this country was founded. That is the kind of synergy which has kept Canada together and which will strengthen our ties in the future.

* In the absence of Ms Guarnieri, her paper was delivered by John English, M.P. for Kitchener, Ontario. / En l'absence de Mme Guarnieri, sa communication a été donné en anglais par M. John English, député de Kitchener (Ontario).

E. Pauline Johnson (1861-1913), the internationally acclaimed Mohawk poet and author; designated 1983 / la poétesse et écrivaine mohawke de renommée internationale ; désignée en 1983. (Photo: National Archives / Archives nationales, C-85125)

Sir William Osler (1849-1919), medical researcher and educator; designated 1950 / chercheur médical et professeur ; désigné en 1950. (Photo: National Archives / Archives nationales, C-7105).

207

Point Riché Lighthouse, Port au Choix, Newfoundland: near the location of prehistoric burial and habitation sites that were designated in 1970. / Phare de Point Riché, Port au Choix (Terre-Neuve) : situé près de l'emplacement du cimetière et du lieu d'habitation préhistoriques qui ont été désignés en 1970. (Photo: Parks Canada / Parcs Canada, A. Cornellier, 1989)

JOHN GODFREY, M.P.

The Missing Pieces: Heritage Commemoration and Public Policy

Abstract
The missing piece is money! However worthy a project may be, it needs the funds to support it and in this time of fiscal restraint the reality is that the funds are limited.

Les pièces manquantes : commémoration du patrimoine et politique gouvernementale –
Résumé
L'élément manquant est l'argent ! Aussi valable que soit un projet, il faut des fonds pour le soutenir et, en cette période de compressions financières, ceux-ci sont limités.

There is something a little unnerving about reproducing a speech that was never given. Would I have altered my text in the light of remarks made previously? Would they have laughed at my jokes?

As I sat in Pearson Airport waiting for the "Plane That Never Came", I began wondering about the greatest piece of Canadian Heritage of all: weather. With Gilles Vigneault, I found myself humming under my breath, *"Mon pays ce n'est pas un pays, c'est l'hiver"*.

Idly, my mind turned to the subject at hand: airport lounges. Perhaps, I reflected, these could be the next group of heritage spaces to be "plaqued". "Plaqued": a strange vaguely dental verb, I mused.

Had I the opportunity of speaking at this Symposium, I might well have begun by asking: "How's your health?" Having read your early history, I wasn't sure you were a group with which I wished to associate. I had read with alarm about the first members of the Board appointed in 1919: Benjamin Sulte, from Quebec, "78 years of age and infirm, he had limited influence on the Board, he died in 1923; Archdeacon Raymond from New Brunswick, an acknowledged expert on his province's early history, was already suffering from the illness from which he would die and never attend a Board meeting.... After the death of Raymond the Maritimes were most strongly represented by J. Clarence Webster.... He was a distinguished physician and surgeon with an international reputation when he retired to Shediac in 1920 because of ill health."

As for my assigned topic, "The Missing Pieces, Heritage Commemoration and Public Policy", I assumed that you had heard from Heritage Minister Dupuy and Parliamentary Secretary Albina Guarnieri about the policies and intentions of the Department of Canadian Heritage. For my part, I would have told you that the "Missing Pieces" of my assigned title were primarily dollar bills.

I found it instructive to read through the history of your seventy-five year old organization. My first impression was the modesty of your early efforts, which consisted mainly of putting plaques on military and fur-trade monuments. I also think it is useful to recall that the Board virtually suspended operations for four years during World War II.

In these early days, there was no money for preservation, restoration, or reconstruction. Indeed, D.C. Harvey, the great director of the Archives of Nova Scotia and a long-time Board member, vigorously opposed the whole concept of colonial Willamsburg in the United States when it first came into being in the 1930s.

It was only after World War II, with the Massey Commission in 1951, that the role of the Board changed significantly. There was a new emphasis on preserving the built heritage. And as time passed, there was an ever-expanding list of categories of buildings and spaces to be preserved: court houses, town halls, theatres, gardens, streetscapes, districts, churches, engineering works, and railway stations. With this expansion came increasing demands for federal funding. In more recent times, industrial sites, Aboriginal sites, cultural communities, and places closely identified with women's history have been added to the list.

Clearly, there is much to be said for recognizing greater numbers of worthy categories of buildings and spaces as our sense of what is significant for our national history evolves. One might say the more plaques the merrier. The problems come when recognition implies funding for preservation, let alone restoration or reconstruction. The Department of Canadian Heritage, like all federal government departments, has been subjected to both the programme review process and severe budget cuts.

What I did not know for certain in November 1994, but which I predicted in my initial text, was that the Department of Canadian Heritage would be subject to annual cuts of 5% for three years, which, indeed, became the case.

So what do these cuts mean for the Historic Sites and Monuments Board of Canada and its ever-expanding list of worthy sites, accompanied by ever-increasing demands for funding to preserve them? In practical terms, it means mothballing many worthwhile projects until better times return. After all, viewed from the perspective of the last seventy-five years, the least an economic historian like myself can do is remind you of economic cycles!

No trend, down or up, is eternal. I am convinced that an era of sustained high economic growth *will* return (under Liberal government, I hope!) But in the meantime, this government simply can't undertake new heritage projects, however worthy. In saying this, I do not claim to represent official government policy, but I think it *does* represent fiscal reality.

On my early morning runs around Ottawa, I pass by the Parliament buildings, the locks, and former industrial buildings which have been preserved as historic sites. It would be a false economy to allow these historic sites to deteriorate. Equally, however, our straitened circumstances mean doing the bare minimum to keep things going.

I did not intend to be the skunk at your garden party, but that is the way the world seemed to me last November. The subsequent budget of February 1995 has only served to reinforce my convictions.

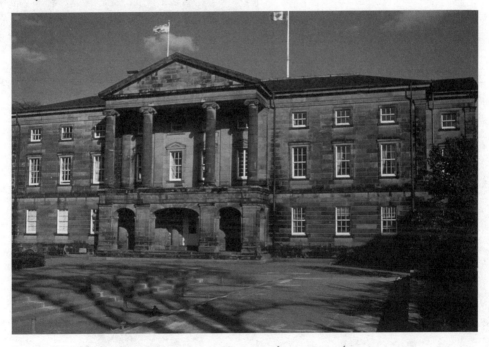

Province House, Charlottetown, Prince Edward Island / Île-du-Prince-Édouard : Construction of the neoclassical edifice was completed in 1847; the birthplace of Confederation; designated 1966. / La construction de cet édifice de style néo-classique fut achevée en 1847 ; il est célèbre en tant que berceau de la Confédération ; désigné en 1966. (Photo: CIHB / IBHC, M. Cullen, 1976)

Parliamentary Library, Ottawa: built in 1866, it is the only original part of the Centre Block still in existence; designated 1976. / La Bibliothèque du Parlement, Ottawa : construite en 1866, c'est la seule composante initiale de l'édifice du Centre qui existe encore ; désignée en 1976. (Photo: Parks Canada / Parcs Canada, HRS-28, 1982)

Lower Brewer Locks, Rideau Canal: Construction of the canal began in 1826 under the direction of Lieutenant Colonel John By; designated 1925. / Écluses inférieures Brewer, sur le canal Rideau : La construction du canal Rideau débuta en 1826 sous la direction du lieutenant-colonel John By ; désigné en 1925. (Photo: Parks Canada / Parcs Canada, F. Cattroll, 1983)

Caught in the Act: Legislating Heritage Protection

Abstract

Since the early days of railway transportation in Canada in the mid-nineteenth century, settlements were located along rail lines. The layout of many towns took its cue from the placement of the station, offering grand vistas and unimpeded traffic for passengers and freight. Most communities in Canada are, or were, connected to most others by a thread of steel rails, bringing Canadians together in a very real sense. The stations along those railway lines connected Canadians, in turn, to the world. The station became the central focus of a town's social life as well as its economy.

Demolition of railway stations, therefore, cut deeply into Canadians' sense of themselves and their communities. Preservation battles fought over these buildings led to the passing of the only legal architectural protection at the national level in Canada, *The Heritage Railway Stations Protection Act*. The success of the legislation lies largely in the intense consultation that has been part of the process since its inception. Participation by all those concerned with and concerned about each station in the country which falls under the purview of this Act was part of the Act's creation, and remains central to its implementation.

This paper examines the creation of the legislation, the process of its implementation, and the lessons which may be learned from it – lessons which may assist the protection of other facets of Canada's past. As presented, the paper was illustrated by slides of dozens of Canadian railway stations, rural and urban, opulently decorated and basic standard plans, abandoned and in sad states of decay, or beautifully restored and actively used.

Le cadre législatif pour la protection du patrimoine – Résumé

Dès les débuts du transport ferroviaire au Canada, au milieu du XIXe siècle, les collectivités se sont implantées le long des voies ferrées. Le développement de nombreuses villes s'est articulé autour de la gare, qui offrait un point de vue dégagé et facilitait le transport des voyageurs et des marchandises. La plupart des communautés du Canada sont ou étaient reliées aux autres par le fil conducteur que constitue la voie ferrée, véritable instrument de rapprochement des Canadiens. Les gares situées le long des voies ferrées reliaient à leur tour les

Canadiens au monde entier. Elles sont devenues les foyers de la vie sociale et de l'économie des villes.

La démolition de gares ferroviaires constitue donc pour les Canadiens une grande perte sur le plan de leur identité et de leur vie communautaire. Les batailles pour la préservation de ces bâtiments ont mené à l'adoption de la *Loi sur la protection des gares ferroviaires patrimoniales*, seul instrument législatif permettant d'assurer la protection de l'architecture à l'échelle nationale au Canada. Le succès de cette loi repose, dans une large mesure, sur un processus systématique de consultation. La participation de toutes les personnes qui s'intéressent à chacune des gares visées par cette loi a été un élément essentiel de sa création et continue d'être au cœur de son application.

Cette communication examine la création de la loi, sa mise en œuvre et les enseignements qu'on peut en tirer pour aider à protéger d'autres aspects de l'histoire du Canada. Elle a été présentée à l'aide de diapositives représentant des douzaines de gares ferroviaires canadiennes, tant en milieu urbain qu'en milieu rural, certaines richement décorées, d'autres conçues selon un plan de base normalisé, certaines abandonnées et dans un triste état de détérioration, d'autres magnifiquement restaurées et largement utilisées.

Heritage colleagues, I have a confession to make. I do not like snakes. When I go for a walk in the dry grass prairie of southeastern Alberta, I can be quite sure that there are snakes somewhere nearby. If a snake suddenly slithers over my foot, I am likely to panic. I do not like the situation at all, to put it mildly. I do not like surprises when I am out for a walk. On the other hand, if someone says, "Oh look, there is a snake," I am prepared. I can examine the colour, the way it glides through the grass – I can deal with the situation calmly.

To bring this analogy to my topic, "Caught in the Act: Legislating Heritage Protection", let us say that I am an ordinary business person, not particularly interested in "old stuff". I have purchased a piece of land which I intend to develop. I have calculated that the profit from this project will finally let me retire. With paid-for architectural plans in hand, I apply for the permit to demolish the old heap on the property, and am suddenly met by the "snake-in-the-grass", the surprise. It slithers over my foot in the form of the refusal of my demolition permit because the building is on somebody's heritage list. Nobody ever told me that old heap of lumber was "heritage". I do not like the situation at all, to put it mildly. I do not like surprises when I go about my legitimate business with my own property.

Oversimplified? Of course. However, in both cases, and in the broader context of Canadian heritage preservation, it is "before-the-fact" knowledge versus surprise that is the crucial element in maintaining the ability to deal with the situation calmly.

I would like to describe the process of creating and implementing a major, and impressive, piece of Canadian heritage legislation that works. It works because the element of surprise has been removed. Property owners, legislators, implementers of the process, and the public all have a role to play, all are aware of their role – before the fact. All the players can agree with the result because they have been part of the creation of the process by which the result is achieved: *The Heritage Railway Stations Protection Act.*

Since the 1850s, we Canadians have had a love affair with our railways. Almost every community in Canada is, or was, connected to almost all others by cobwebs of steel rails. Stations along those railway lines connected us to the world, as people and goods arrived or departed. Travel by train is part of the Canadian heritage ethos, our "national dream", although I believe most Canadians today have never travelled by train, at least not here in Canada.

Even the names of the larger companies are evocative of Canada's geography and Canada's past: Canadian Pacific Railway, Canadian National, Grand Trunk Pacific, Canadian Northern, the Newfoundland Railway, the Intercolonial, the National Transcontinental, the Great Western. Towns and cities across Canada were created by and for railway companies. Their fortunes, and that of the nation, rose and fell with the strength and decline of rail company fortunes.

Railway stations were, and still are, often the most substantial buildings in town – planned by fine architects, and incorporating the newest designs and materials, construction and engineering techniques. Although there were standard plans created by some companies on some lines, there were also "variations on a theme" and special designs for special locales. Often with elegantly decorated interiors, as well as grand exteriors, the railway station was the focus of community life – economic, certainly, but also social, political and cultural – in good times and bad.

In the 1960s, competition from highway and air transportation began to force railway companies to abandon financially unproductive rail lines, or cancel passenger service to selected stations. People were disappointed, saddened. But when those same companies began to demolish redundant railway stations, people were angry and frustrated. Angry because they were losing significant chunks of their sense of themselves, their communities, their past; and frustrated because there did not seem to be anything they could do about it. No matter how strong their provincial protective heritage legislation, provincial legislation had no impact on the property of railway companies regulated under the federal *Railway Act*. Sold by the railway companies, many stations found new uses as community centres, libraries, town halls, and even liquor stores. Many were moved to become specimens in the architectural zoos that Canadians call "heritage parks". But many were being simply demolished; some, such as the station in Kentville, Nova Scotia, immediately prior to the enacting of protective legislation. The situation had come to a head following the early morning demolition of CPR's 1912 West Toronto Station in November 1982.

Railway station preservation efforts, coordinated largely by Heritage Canada, resulted in a Private Member's Bill presented by MP Jesse Flis. That old snake was slithering over the foot of the railway companies, who had seen selected demolitions as a way of decreasing costs in times of decreased revenues. Introduced late in the session and facing opposition, the bill died on the order paper.

Gordon Taylor, an Alberta MP, picked up the issue, presented a revised Bill (the result of a lot of behind-the-scenes hard work by Heritage Canada's Doug Franklin and others, and Parks Canada's National Historic Sites Directorate staff), and guided it through the legislative process. *Bill C-205, An Act to Protect Heritage Railway Stations* was passed by the House of Commons and the Senate, and came into force with Royal Assent on 22 September 1988.

Basically, to quote the legislation, the Act "provides a mechanism whereby citizens may make objections when railway companies plan to alter or in any way dispose of heritage railway stations under their control – a Heritage Railway Station being one designated as such by the Federal Minister [responsible] on the recommendation of the Historic Sites and Monuments Board of Canada."

In procedural terms, the research, the coordination, the secretariat duties, and a great deal of consultation and negotiation are done, or coordinated, by the staff of Parks Canada's National Historic Sites Directorate and seconded staff of the Public Works Department's Architectural Division.

Both research material for evaluation purposes and applications for permission to alter a designated station are presented to the Board's Heritage Railway Stations Committee, which I have had the pleasure and honour of chairing since its inception in 1988. Committee recommendations are taken to the full Board, and the Board takes its final recommendations to the Minister for action.

Important factors in the success of this legislation are that the creation of the implementation process began well before the legislation was finally enacted, and that intense consultation with the railway companies and with Heritage

Canada, on behalf of the public, were included from the beginning. Criteria were established to determine which stations were to be designated "heritage" stations, and which were not.

It was agreed that the criteria would include three sections: history, architecture, and community impact. The full descriptive wording of the criteria was carefully crafted to ensure as much equanimity in the evaluation process as possible. It was vital that a small station – even a whistle stop – in a remote rural area be examined by the same criteria, but not in comparison to, a large station in a major urban centre. The process, agreed upon by all players, has now been followed for some six years.

Research has been undertaken on contract, almost line by line, station by station, across Canada – all stations still owned by railway companies operating under the *Railway Act*. Stations that had been referred by individuals, organizations and/or government agencies, were dealt with first, beginning with those at least forty years old.

Each station, even those already designated as National Historic Sites, has been evaluated following the same criteria, and the recommendation for designation, or not, made. Out of approximately 250 stations researched and evaluated, 148 have been designated. Research is continuing to prepare reports on the balance of the older stations (approximately eighty) as well as for inventories of contemporary stations that will also have to be reviewed at some point.

For each of the designated stations, Heritage Character Statements (HCS) have been written. The HCS identifies heritage features and guides future work for each building. From the time of designation, a station's owners are required to make application for alteration or disposal; post notice of intention, describing the proposed change of status; and wait the required sixty days, giving the public time to respond. Each application must be reviewed by the staff and the Board, including consultation and even negotiation. A recommendation is then made to the Minister. If there is no objection from the staff, the Board or the public, authorization is given through Order-in-Council, and the work or sale proceeds. If there is objection, there is provision for representations to be made to the Board, and a public meeting may even be held.

The only time this provision has been used occurred in November 1991 with regard to plans by Canadian Pacific, Molson's Brewery, and *Les Canadiens* hockey team to redevelop the Windsor Station property for Montréal's new Forum and an office complex. Not only a designated National Historic Site, but also a station designated under the HRSPA, Windsor Station is an icon in the history of Canadian railroading. Although the proponents' plans included a multi-million dollar restoration and rehabilitation of Windsor Station's 1888-

1914 Price, Maxwell and Painter wings, they also included demolition of two other sections of the complex, and impact on the remaining passenger sheds and underground structures supporting the tracks. These features had all been included in the Heritage Character Statement, and "alterations" had to be considered and a ministerial ruling given before work could proceed.

Three days of public meetings brought the issue of preservation of railway stations in general, and Windsor Station in particular, a great deal of media and public attention. People were passionate in their presentations, pro and con, detailed and wide-ranging, professional and amateur. A report was drafted by the Board and forwarded to the Minister. Ultimately, certain portions of the corporate proposal were approved, others were not, and still others were amended. The "Great Canadian Compromise" perhaps, but I feel that heritage was well served, on many levels.

Communication and consultation are important aspects of the implementation of the HRSPA. Staff and Board members are in touch with railway and development companies; provincial and municipal governments, and heritage counterparts; and interested individuals, agencies and organizations. Yes, this is time-consuming. Yes, it is staff-intensive. But it makes the process, and thus the legislation, work.

One major concern of the railway companies was that they would be hindered in undertaking routine maintenance such as repainting or replacement of broken windows, as the Act is clear that any "alteration" of historic fabric described in its Heritage Character Statement requires the company to apply, post notice, and receive approval before proceeding. A minimum maintenance approach was established, again in consultation, to allow the everyday business of the companies to continue, while respecting both the legislation and the historic character of the designated stations.

Despite the successes and the generally positive response to the legislation from both the railway companies and the public, some drawbacks remain:

1. Only the station itself is protected – not outbuildings, not gardens, not tracks, not roundhouses, not the station's setting as the focus for town planning – only the station.
2. There is no incentive to preserve or restore station buildings once designated. Demolition by neglect and demolition by vandalism, often a partner of neglect, continue to take their toll.
3. A number of instances exist in which the railway companies have sold the building, but leased the land. These stations face an uncertain future – does this sale/lease situation constitute a legal sale of "property"? No, not in terms

of land-based property, merely the sale of an object. Can the company at some point say, "get your building off my land"? Potentially, yes. Can provincial legislation, which is tied to the land protect this building? No. Can *The Heritage Railway Stations Protection Act*, which requires ownership by a railway company, protect this station? Also no.

4. Another drawback is the length of time it takes to complete the Order-in-Council process to give approval for "alterations". For example, railway company "X" wants to repaint station "Y". The company agrees to respect the Heritage Character Statement and return the station to its original colour scheme; applies to the Minister for permission; gives notice to the public; and waits the required sixty days. The Board recommends approval, the Minister approves. Then, the Order-in-Council must be placed on the government's busy agenda. Sometimes months go by; a frustration for all concerned.

    In the current federal exercise of streamlining government operations, consideration is being given to allowing the Minister to authorize approvals that the staff, the Board and the public agree are appropriate, rather than requiring Governor-in-Council authorization, as the legislation now states. This may be a positive measure.

5. The last drawback is that people tend to see the HRSPA as the ONLY way to save railway stations. Just because a station does not meet the criteria for designation, there is nothing to stop a concerned group, or community, from going directly to the railway company, as was the case before the legislation. A negotiated, creative alternative to demolition can still be found.

That focus on individual responsibility for preservation leads to my conclusion. I feel that there are three inter-related lessons to be learned from *The Heritage Railway Stations Protection Act*. First, if they have not done so already, local, regional, provincial, and national heritage agencies and organizations need to do more to establish criteria, evaluation systems, and the processes by which they will determine what is significant to them and what is not. Second, they must communicate more and better about the value of preserving the past, about their criteria for evaluating heritage properties, and about their heritage inventories. And third, they must create better, stronger, and broader communication networks. These networks must include not only heritage organizations and agencies, but also property owners and managers, realtors, developers, renovation contractors, construction unions, even demolition companies.

Only dedicated communication and consultation will ensure that there are no snakes, no surprises, lurking in the grassy future of protecting and commemorating Canada's past.

Windsor Station, Montréal, Québec: Canadian Pacific Railway Station built in 1886 by architect Bruce Price, with additions by E. Maxwell in 1900 and W.S. Painter between 1910 and 1913; designated 1975. / La gare Windsor, Montréal (Québec) : gare du Canadien Pacifique construite en 1886 par l'architecte Bruce Price ; ajouts réalisés par E. Maxwell en 1900 et par W.S. Painter entre 1910 et 1913 ; désignée en 1975. (Photo: Parks Canada / Parcs Canada, HRS 1991).

McAdam Railway Station, McAdam, New Brunswick: Canadian Pacific built the large château-style railway station in 1900. It is now in the hands of the McAdam Historical Restoration Commission; designated 1976. / La gare de McAdam (Nouveau-Brunswick) : le Canadien Pacifique construisit cette grande gare de style Château en 1900. Elle est maintenant entre les mains de la commission de restauration historique de McAdam ; désignée en 1976. (Photo: RSR-20)

Prescott Railway Station (Grand Trunk), Ontario: 1855 monument to early Canadian railway enterprise; designated 1973 / La gare de Prescott (Ontario) : cette gare du Grand Tronc datant de 1855 est un monument aux premiers constructeurs de chemins de fer du Canada ; désignée en 1973. (Photo: Parks Canada / Parcs Canada, HRS, 1991)

221

Qualicum Beach Railway Station, British Columbia: the former Canadian Pacific Railway Station was built by the Esquimalt and Nanaimo Railway in 1914. It has been designated a Municipal Heritage Site and the property around the station and along the rails has been landscaped and designated as a Heritage Core Park. / La gare de Qualicum Beach (Colombie-Britannique) : cette ancienne gare du Canadien Pacifique fut construite par l'Esquimalt and Nanaimo Railway en 1914. Elle a été désignée lieu du patrimoine municipal, et le terrain entourant la gare et longeant la voie ferrée a été aménagé et désigné parc du patrimoine. (Photo: RSR-151)

ROBERT GARON

Le point de vue du Québec sur la politique du patrimoine[1]

Résumé

La société québécoise s'intéresse à son patrimoine depuis plus d'un siècle, mais cet intérêt est resté longtemps celui d'une élite avant de connaître son premier véritable essor, au début des années 1970. C'est également à partir de ce moment que le gouvernement du Québec s'est donné de véritables instruments d'intervention, dont une loi de portée beaucoup plus large que celle de 1922 en matière de protection des biens culturels. Au fil des années, cependant, le ministère des Affaires culturelles a orienté de plus en plus ses efforts vers la sensibilisation de la population et la recherche de partenaires. À cette fin, il a mis de l'avant certaines mesures de soutien et tiré parti de diverses autres lois et politiques liées à des secteurs connexes. En 1992, il se dotait enfin d'une véritable politique culturelle et se propose d'adopter sous peu une politique sectorielle en matière de patrimoine.

Quebec's Point of View on Heritage Policy – Abstract

Quebec society has been interested in its heritage for over a century. For most of that time, however, it was only an elite that took an interest; it was not until the early 1970s that the interest in heritage became widespread in Quebec. This was also the point at which the provincial government gave itself the tools to intervene meaningfully, including an act with much wider scope than the old 1922 act to protect cultural property. Over the years, however, the Department of Cultural Affairs has focused more and more of its efforts on raising awareness among the general public and on finding partners. To that end, it established certain support measures and took advantage of various acts and policies pertaining to related sectors. In 1992, it finally developed a real cultural policy and plans to adopt a sectoral heritage policy in the near future.

D'abord un mouvement d'affirmation

On a souvent tendance, à tort, à résumer l'histoire des actions menées au Québec pour la sauvegarde et la protection du patrimoine en se contentant d'évoquer le rôle traditionnel de l'État, et plus particulièrement deux jalons de sa législation : 1922, année de l'adoption d'une première *Loi relative à la conservation des monuments et des objets d'art*, et 1972, celle de l'entrée en vigueur de l'actuelle *Loi sur les biens culturels*. Sans nier l'importance de ces deux gestes significatifs posés à un demi-siècle d'intervalle, qui ont témoigné d'une volonté des élus d'intervenir de façon tangible et ont su rassurer dans une certaine mesure les citoyens déjà sensibilisés à la « cause », on doit toutefois reconnaître qu'ils sont venus couronner, l'un et l'autre, des décennies d'efforts individuels et d'actions concertées de certains regroupements.

Déjà au XVIIIᵉ siècle, et même avant, comme nous le rappelle un répertoire chronologique publié par la Commission des biens culturels[2], des individus, des congrégations religieuses et des sociétés savantes font œuvre de conservation en constituant et protégeant des collections diverses de notre patrimoine artistique et scientifique. Au siècle suivant, à leur tour, les littérateurs et illustrateurs du terroir, avec en tête Philippe Aubert de Gaspé et quelques autres, attirent l'attention d'un certain public sur la réalité du folklore et tracent à leur façon la voie aux ethnologues qui suivront, les Massicotte – Édouard-Zotique et son frère Edmond-Joseph –, Marius Barbeau, Luc Lacourcière...

À travers les initiatives de personnes et de groupes plus sensibilisés – pensons entre autres aux clubs sociaux de toutes sortes qui voient graduellement le jour, en milieu anglophone notamment –, c'est tout un courant de prise de conscience et d'affirmation collective qui se dessine, d'abord au niveau d'une élite, soit intellectuelle soit socio-économique, puis graduellement auprès d'un public élargi. À cet égard, les autorités religieuses et politiques du tournant du siècle et des décennies qui suivront ne seront pas étrangères à la promotion des valeurs traditionnelles et d'un nationalisme renaissant, spécialement chez certaines classes de la société québécoise francophone.

C'est d'ailleurs ce mouvement d'affirmation, associé tout d'abord à la notion de survivance et plus tard davantage à celle du rayonnement culturel, qui inspirera et guidera dans une large mesure le sentiment populaire, mais aussi l'action gouvernementale en ce qui a trait à la protection et à la mise en valeur des divers patrimoines, qu'il s'agisse de monuments, d'œuvres d'art, d'archives et de biens archéologiques, de paysages et de sites ainsi que de traditions immatérielles. Encore aujourd'hui c'est, croyons-nous, cette volonté d'affirmation de l'identité nationale qui représente sans doute le principal dénominateur commun pour l'ensemble des intervenants du patrimoine au sein de la collectivité québécoise, et le gouvernement entend bien continuer d'y souscrire à travers ses orientations et ses interventions futures.

Des visions différentes du patrimoine

Mais l'intérêt porté au patrimoine et surtout les façons d'envisager son utilisation et son intégration dans la vie contemporaine varient considérablement, nous le savons tous, selon les milieux, les instances et les groupes d'intérêt mis en sa présence. Au Québec comme partout ailleurs, le patrimoine a été et demeure, suivant les circonstances et les acteurs, objet de contemplation, de fascination, de respect, de curiosité, de fierté, de convoitise ou de spéculation. Ce qui explique que trop souvent, loin d'être un facteur de cohésion sociale, il peut être un motif de division, de lutte et d'opposition, à l'instar de ce que l'on observe à l'égard du patrimoine écologique et de l'environnement naturel depuis déjà bon nombre d'années.

Dans le cas du patrimoine historique ou culturel, et notamment au Québec, cette diversification des perceptions et des attitudes remonte assurément à plus d'un demi-siècle, alors que s'intensifiaient l'urbanisation du territoire et la volonté de renouvellement de certains équipements et infrastructures. C'est également à cette époque que les campagnes québécoises se vident de leurs plus belles « antiquités » au bénéfice d'une nouvelle élite en quête de « rusticité » ; que de nombreuses demeures bourgeoises d'une autre époque sont subdivisées, modernisées, banalisées ; que les premières agressions majeures sont causées à la trame et au tissu de certains quartiers anciens. Ainsi, durant quelques décennies, l'essentiel du débat se situera entre tenants et adversaires de la conservation, les uns au nom du respect d'un héritage et les autres en celui du progrès économique et technologique.

Depuis une vingtaine d'années, toutefois, la dynamique et la problématique du patrimoine se sont complexifiées. Outre l'éternel conflit opposant protectionnistes et développeurs, on a pu assister à l'émergence de conceptions différentes – souvent complémentaires, mais parfois aussi divergentes, voire contradictoires – chez les partisans mêmes de la cause patrimoniale. Ces points de vue sont d'abord ceux des spécialistes des différents champs disciplinaires : historiens, archivistes, archéologues, ethnologues, historiens de l'art et de l'architecture, architectes, ingénieurs et restaurateurs. Au sein de ces spécialités, on retrouve également des approches et des tendances qui, tout en étant scientifiquement comparables, concilient à des degrés variables le recours à des principes et à des procédés plus souples de conservation et d'intégration au cadre contemporain.

Plus récemment encore, de nouveaux intervenants se sont ajoutés ou, tout au moins, ont réévalué leurs modes d'intervention vis-à-vis du patrimoine. Parmi ceux-ci, certaines administrations municipales ont effectué un virage en faveur de la conservation préventive et de l'harmonisation du

225

moderne et de l'ancien. Des entreprises et des promoteurs ont aussi emboîté le pas dans le sens de la réutilisation d'un patrimoine corporatif ou privé. Des communicateurs et des artisans de la mise en marché s'intéressent également de plus en plus au patrimoine, en termes de sujets cinématographiques et d'émissions télévisées, de destinations de voyages et de forfaits touristiques, de produits de consommation de toutes sortes. Le patrimoine devient dès lors objet d'inspiration, d'éducation populaire et de loisir, quand il n'est pas tout simplement prétexte à la découverte du territoire et de ses habitants.

Tous ces intervenants, de longue date ou de venue plus récente, n'ont pas forcément des visions toujours compatibles, et leurs intérêts soit de propriétaires, de simples usagers, de « facilitateurs » ou encore d'arbitres demandent à s'ajuster. Or, c'est précisément à ce défi de la concertation entre de si nombreux partenaires potentiels que le gouvernement du Québec, et spécialement son ministère de la Culture, a consacré progressivement ses efforts au cours des dernières décennies ; il n'y est toutefois parvenu véritablement qu'au terme d'un long processus et au prix d'expériences pas toujours concluantes, du moins à leurs débuts.

Le rôle de l'État au fil des ans

Suivant de peu le gouvernement d'Ottawa, qui avait commencé à se doter de mesures législatives concernant le patrimoine culturel peu avant la Première Guerre mondiale, notamment par sa *Loi des champs de bataille nationaux à Québec* (1908) et sa *Loi sur les archives publiques* (1912), le Québec a été la première province canadienne à légiférer en la matière. Il s'y est tout d'abord appliqué en 1922, en procédant à l'adoption de la *Loi relative à la conservation des monuments et des objets d'art ayant un intérêt historique ou artistique*, loi qui instituait par la même occasion une Commission des monuments historiques chargée d'assurer, au nom de l'État, la sauvegarde du patrimoine. Le mandat de cette nouvelle commission venait en fait compléter, dans un secteur connexe, celui d'une autre instance créée à peine deux ans plus tôt, soit les Archives de la province de Québec.

Ensemble, ces deux institutions naissantes allaient poser les premiers jalons d'une entreprise d'identification, de protection et de promotion du patrimoine, grâce entre autres à des pionniers et chefs de file tels que Pierre-Georges Roy et, un peu plus tard, Gérard Morisset. Par leur initiative et celle de leurs équipes fort restreintes, des travaux d'inventaire seront graduellement entrepris et des publications de type « répertoires » verront le jour, plaçant évidemment l'emphase sur un patrimoine hautement valorisé par nos élites, celui des églises et œuvres d'art, des manoirs et habitations témoignant du

Régime français. La Loi elle-même s'inspire abondamment de la législation française alors en vigueur, mettant l'accent sur les mesures de protection ponctuelle, plus spécialement celle du classement. De fait, trois premiers édifices seront classés à titre de monuments quelques années plus tard, plus précisément en 1929 : il s'agira de l'église Notre-Dame-des-Victoires, à Québec, de la maison des Jésuites, à Sillery, et du Château de Ramezay, à Montréal.

Au même moment, le Musée de la province de Québec ouvrira ses portes au cœur de la Vieille Capitale, prenant ainsi en charge un autre mandat essentiel pour cette époque, celui d'assurer le sauvetage et la conservation des œuvres les plus précieuses de nos artistes et artisans ; en réalité, cette première institution muséale d'État élargira bientôt son champ d'intérêt à des collections beaucoup plus vastes et diversifiées, relevant tantôt de l'histoire de l'art et de la numismatique, tantôt de l'ethnologie et même de la zoologie. C'est d'ailleurs dans cette foulée que Gérard Morisset entreprendra, en 1937, son *Inventaire des œuvres d'art*, opération que d'autres poursuivront au moins jusque dans les années soixante-dix, à l'intérieur des nouvelles structures mises en place par le ministère des Affaires culturelles.

En effet, un premier ministère québécois dédié exclusivement au secteur de la culture verra le jour en 1961, dans l'effervescence de cette période de vastes réformes que les historiens, journalistes et politiciens qualifieront de « Révolution tranquille ». La mise en place d'une telle structure, tout en facilitant dorénavant la coordination et l'harmonisation des interventions gouvernementales en matière de patrimoine aussi bien que d'arts et de lettres, permettra en outre de concentrer et de consolider peu à peu les ressources de tous ordres qui leur sont affectées. Dans le champ plus précis de la protection des biens culturels, par ailleurs, on assistera successivement à deux opérations de révision de la législation de 1922 : une première fois en 1952, alors que l'on étend la portée de la loi aux *monuments (sic) préhistoriques* ainsi qu'aux *paysages* et aux *sites*, et une seconde en 1963, alors qu'est introduite la notion d'*arrondissement historique*.

Quant à la Commission des monuments historiques, qui voit ses pouvoirs élargis dès la première de ces refontes, elle ajoute à ses activités d'inventaire, d'apposition de plaques et de classement l'acquisition de biens meubles et immeubles jugés d'intérêt national. C'est du reste ainsi que se constituera le noyau d'un parc immobilier patrimonial qui, bon an mal an, ira en s'accroissant durant près de deux décennies. C'est aussi au cours de cette période s'étendant de la fin des années cinquante au milieu des années soixante que l'État, par le biais de sa Commission, accentuera de façon notable son intervention à l'égard de la protection des biens culturels, en procédant notamment au classement de près de 200 monuments et de plus de 400 œuvres d'art, réunies en une vingtaine de collections ; il protégera de plus, par classement ou par décret, une dizaine de sites et d'arrondissements.

Mais, c'est 1972 qui marquera le premier tournant véritable quant au réalignement de l'action gouvernementale dans le secteur du patrimoine au Québec. Ainsi, la législation existante, dont l'administration a été jusque-là confiée pour l'essentiel à la Commission des monuments historiques, cède sa place à la *Loi sur les biens culturels*, beaucoup plus complète et articulée et dont la gestion revient au Ministre et à ses mandataires, la Commission – rebaptisée Commission des biens culturels – étant appelée désormais à exercer un rôle essentiellement consultatif. Les quelques années qui vont suivre donneront d'ailleurs lieu à une augmentation considérable du nombre d'œuvres d'art et de monuments classés, auxquels s'ajouteront une centaire d'*aires de protection* et une proportion substantielle d'œuvres et de monuments *reconnus*, ces additions correspondant à quelques-unes des nouvelles mesures dorénavant prévues par la Loi.

Dans des champs connexes au patrimoine culturel, les années soixante-dix et, dans une moindre mesure, les années quatre-vingt verront également l'entrée en vigueur d'une série de lois, politiques et réglementations qui ne seront pas sans conséquences, bien au contraire, sur la gestion et la préservation des ressources patrimoniales. La *Loi sur la qualité de l'environnement* (1972), la *Loi sur les réserves écologiques* (1974), la *Loi sur les parcs* (1977), la *Loi sur la protection du territoire agricole* (1978), la *Loi sur l'aménagement et l'urbanisme* (1979), la *politique de gestion des terres publiques* (1980), la *réglementation relative à l'évaluation et à l'examen des impacts sur l'environnement* (1982) et, enfin, l'établissement de normes particulières concernant les coupes forestières sur les terres du domaine public (1988) sont toutes des actions qui ont eu et ont toujours une incidence non négligeable dans la mesure où elles assurent non seulement la protection de ressources complémentaires, mais également la neutralisation en quelque sorte de certaines sources de conflits préjudiciables au patrimoine culturel – l'urbanisation, la spéculation foncière et la pollution notamment – de même que la conservation préventive indirecte de ressources plus spécifiques telles que les sites archéologiques et les paysages humanisés.

La *Loi sur l'aménagement et l'urbanisme* aura eu une influence encore plus marquante en introduisant, dans le cadre de la gestion du territoire et du développement régional, des mécanismes à la fois de décentralisation et de concertation tout en obligeant de nouvelles entités administratives, les munici-palités régionales de comté (MRC), à tenir compte de la dimension patrimoniale dans l'élaboration de leurs schémas d'aménagement et la planification des infrastructures et des équipements de leurs communautés constituantes. Cette idée de concertation et de planification en association avec le monde municipal, le ministère des Affaires culturelles la reprendra du reste à son compte en modifiant à deux reprises, soit en 1978 et en 1986, sa *Loi sur les biens culturels* de manière à permettre la conclusion d'ententes de mise en valeur entre le Ministère et les administrations municipales et à favoriser la prise en charge de leur patrimoine immobilier par les collectivités.

On estime ainsi à un peu plus de 400 le nombre d'ententes à portée culturelle conclues avec des municipalités entre 1984 et 1989, dont plus de 250 s'adressant directement au patrimoine et une trentaine mettant plus spécifiquement en cause des municipalités régionales de comté. Parallèlement, et afin de faciliter la concrétisation de pareilles ententes, le ministère des Affaires culturelles se dotera de programmes d'aide financière normalisés ainsi que d'expertises additionnelles, dont il s'efforcera de rapprocher la gestion des clientèles en accentuant la déconcentration en région d'une partie importante de ses effectifs. Durant la même période de 1984 à 1989, à titre indicatif, on évalue à quelque 120 millions de dollars le montant global des engagements financiers contractés par le gouvernement québécois et les municipalités dans le cadre de ces ententes en patrimoine, une large majorité d'entre elles ayant été orientées vers l'acquisition et la diffusion des connaissances et une proportion moindre, mais néanmoins significative, vers des activités et des projets d'aménagement, de restauration et d'interprétation.

Les amendements apportés en 1986 à la *Loi sur les biens culturels* visaient, en outre, à responsabiliser davantage les municipalités locales en les habilitant à protéger elles-mêmes des sites ou des monuments situés sur leur territoire – on parlera, dans ce second cas, du pouvoir de *citation* – et à contribuer financièrement à l'entretien et à la restauration de tout immeuble protégé en vertu de la même loi. En 1991, une quarantaine de municipalités s'étaient prévalues du pouvoir de protéger des immeubles patrimoniaux, le nombre de monuments *cités* s'élevant alors à une centaine et celui des *sites du patrimoine* à plus d'une douzaine. La quantité d'immeubles ainsi protégés annuellement dépasserait désormais, et ce de façon appréciable, celle des biens immobiliers classés ou reconnus par le gouvernement lui-même au cours d'un intervalle équivalent. Bon nombre de municipalités allaient répondre de la sorte à l'invitation du Ministère et s'inscrire résolument comme maîtres d'œuvre d'une mise en valeur adaptée aux attentes et aux besoins de leur communauté. Ce nouveau constat porteur d'avenir incitait monsieur Michel Dufresne, alors directeur des Biens culturels, à conclure ainsi l'une de ses

229

interventions lors du Colloque international des villes du patrimoine mondial, tenu à Québec à l'été de 1991 :

> Le Québec, disait-il, a su développer ces dernières années une approche de partenariat originale et prometteuse en matière de patrimoine. Il a convié en particulier le monde municipal à la partager, voire à se l'approprier. La réponse fut d'abord hésitante, puis de plus en plus significative. L'implication des municipalités dans la conservation ne constitue certes pas encore une pratique généralisée, mais de nombreux indices nous permettent de tracer un bilan malgré tout positif. C'est pourquoi notre ministère, ajoutait-il, croit maintenant le temps venu de consolider cette approche afin que s'accélère un processus devenu inévitable et, espérons-le, irréversible.

La lecture que j'ai pu faire moi-même de l'actualité patrimoniale au cours des quelques dernières années m'amène à tirer des conclusions analogues, et j'ose affirmer que le monde municipal est devenu à cet égard un partenaire incontournable, tout comme le monde associatif et celui de la recherche d'ailleurs. Et, en ce sens, je m'en voudrais de passer sous silence les mesures adoptées par le Ministère à l'égard des autres volets du patrimoine culturel. Je pense ici notamment à la *Loi sur les archives publiques* et à la *Loi sur les musées nationaux*, toutes deux adoptées en 1983 et qui reconfirmaient le rôle de premier plan des grandes institutions d'État dans le domaine de la conservation et de la diffusion du patrimoine.

En matière d'archives, en particulier, la législation québécoise consacrait le principe d'une conservation préventive et d'une sélection progressive des documents d'intérêt historique à travers le processus de leur constitution et de leur cheminement depuis le stade *actif* jusqu'à l'état *inactif* ; là aussi, des partenaires étaient conviés, dont les ministères et organismes gouvernementaux bien sûr, mais également les organismes publics décentralisés et les organismes privés, des programmes d'aide financière et d'agrément étant de surcroît prévus pour ces derniers. En matière de muséologie, de même, le Ministère a recherché l'émergence d'établissements de moindre taille susceptibles de compléter les musées de statut national et de constituer un réseau cohérent à l'échelle de l'ensemble des régions ; à cette fin, il a mis de l'avant toute une série de mesures, dont une politique d'accréditation, des programmes d'aide financière à l'équipement et au fonctionnement ainsi que des services spécialisés d'expertise et de restauration par le biais de son Centre de conservation.

Nouvelles attentes et partenariat

La voie recherchée de plus en plus par le ministère et le gouvernement au cours de la dernière décennie aura été celle du partenariat. Celui-là même auquel faisait encore référence, il n'y a pas si longtemps, un ancien sous-ministre des Affaires culturelles et actuel directeur général du Musée de la civilisation du Québec, monsieur Roland Arpin, alors qu'il expliquait ainsi les réussites de l'institution qu'il dirige[3] :

> Ce succès illustre une conception moderne et dynamique du développement. Un développement fondé sur le partenariat avec les universités, les centres de recherche, le réseau scolaire, les médias, les organismes culturels, le secteur privé, le réseau des musées et j'en passe ; un développement qui n'a pas craint de s'ouvrir au monde et de tabler sur l'action internationale.

Il me plaît de faire référence à ce passage du propos de Roland Arpin et surtout au cas exemplaire du Musée de la civilisation, car ils me semblent bien marquer l'un et l'autre le nouveau virage qui doit être opéré en matière de culture et de patrimoine si l'on désire répondre, de façon adéquate et satisfaisante, aux nouvelles attentes et tendances qui se manifestent de plus en plus chez nos partenaires et dans la population.

Parmi ces attentes, il y a sûrement celle au premier chef de l'accessibilité du patrimoine, trop longtemps réservé, plus ou moins consciemment, à une élite intellectuelle ou socio-économique. Puisque le patrimoine doit contribuer à la connaissance et à l'affirmation de l'identité collective, on s'attend bien sûr à ce qu'il soit accessible au plus large public possible, selon des formules qui pourront néanmoins varier selon les types de patrimoine et les milieux concernés. Cette accessibilité accrue ne doit d'ailleurs pas être que physique – c'est-à-dire pouvoir se mesurer en termes de distances, d'infrastructures ou d'heures d'ouverture –, mais également didactique, ce qui implique un minimum de mise en contexte historique et de vulgarisation. À cet égard, l'approche muséologique et la diffusion en général peuvent suppléer dans bien des cas au contact direct et tangible avec le site ou l'objet.

Dans le prolongement de ce principe d'accessibilité du patrimoine, et spécialement pour le patrimoine immobilier, le contribuable insiste de plus en plus pour une utilisation optimale du lieu ou de l'édifice qu'on entend protéger et mettre en valeur de quelque façon. Et ce citoyen, dans la mesure du possible, espère pouvoir profiter de cette utilisation ou, tout au moins, de ses retombées directes ou indirectes, qu'il s'agisse d'utilité publique ou communautaire ou encore de rentrées fiscales ou de location. Dans ce sens également, le contribuable s'estime en droit d'exiger une saine gestion des programmes et des projets patrimoniaux au financement desquels il participe, ce qui peut signifier le droit d'interroger et de remettre en cause le coût d'une restauration, d'un équipement muséal ou de son fonctionnement, celui d'une activité commémorative ou d'un événement majeur de diffusion. En somme, le citoyen en général s'attend à ce que la ressource patrimoniale ne serve pas qu'à des fins contemplatives ou de culte des ancêtres, mais contribue tout comme d'autres à la richesse économique et à la qualité du cadre de vie.

En ce qui regarde le rôle de l'État, par ailleurs, le même citoyen ainsi que les partenaires publics et privés auxquels j'ai déjà fait largement allusion expriment des attentes additionnelles tout aussi élevées. Plusieurs intervenants souhaitent notamment que le gouvernement du Québec, et particulièrement le ministère de la Culture et des Communications, manifeste plus ouvertement et fermement son leadership en termes de politiques et d'orientations. D'autres questionnent l'opportunité et la qualité de certaines interventions gouvernementales à l'intérieur de son propre champ d'activités mettant en cause des biens patrimoniaux qu'il possède ou qu'il a la charge d'exploiter ; ceux-là s'attendent, en quelque sorte, à ce que l'État s'affirme par l'exemplarité de ses gestes. D'autres enfin, et ils sont sans doute les plus nombreux, réclament désormais de l'appareil gouvernemental qu'il leur facilite la sauvegarde et la gestion des patrimoines dont ils sont déjà les propriétaires ou les usagers, en somme qu'il les accompagne et les soutienne au lieu, comme ce fut parfois le cas autrefois, de les déposséder et de les « déresponsabiliser ».

Vers un renouvellement de la politique du patrimoine

Ces attentes et ces besoins maintes fois ressentis chez nos partenaires et que je me suis contenté de vous résumer à grands traits ont été réitérés en 1991, à l'occasion de la consultation menée par le Groupe-conseil sur la politique culturelle et qui donna lieu au dépôt de ce que l'on a appelé le « Rapport Arpin ». Ces attentes ont également été exprimées la même année, puis annuellement, par le Forum québécois du patrimoine, un regroupement des forces vives associées à ce secteur et qui vient tout juste de tenir ses 4ᵉ Assises, il y a deux jours à peine, à Montréal.

Essentiellement, les milieux du patrimoine, outre le besoin de confronter leurs visions respectives et – pour user d'une expression propre à notre folklore – d'« accorder leurs violons », demandent au gouvernement québécois de leur faire connaître ses nouvelles couleurs à travers un énoncé de politique spécifique à ce volet. Il peut d'ailleurs paraître étrange que nos administrations successives ne se soient jamais dotées officiellement d'une telle politique sectorielle avant ce jour, et ce en dépit des quelques *livres vert* ou *blancs* déposés précédemment par des ministres des Affaires culturelles, soit tour à tour en 1965, 1976 et 1978. De fait, le Ministère a toujours considéré que l'essentiel de ses principes directeurs et de ses moyens d'intervention se trouvait inscrit dans sa *Loi sur les biens culturels* et que les modalités d'application en étaient précisées dans certains règlements ainsi que dans ses différents programmes d'aide financière.

La réalité politique et administrative ayant toutefois évolué vers un nécessaire « repartage » des rôles et une « redéfinition » même de l'objet d'intervention, il apparaît maintenant opportun de consigner dans un discours plus officiel les règles d'exercice et les conditions d'accompagnement de ce nouveau partenariat. Du reste, la *Politique culturelle du Québec* rendue publique en 1992 ouvrait déjà grande la porte à l'idée de politiques sectorielles en matière de patrimoine et de muséologie. Aussi, avec l'appui de la Commission des biens culturels, un groupe de travail interne s'est consacré au cours des deux dernières années à l'élaboration d'un projet de politique du patrimoine que le ministère espère pouvoir rendre public sous peu. Bien qu'il ne soit pas de mon ressort de vous dévoiler pour l'instant le contenu détaillé des mesures de mise en œuvre susceptibles d'être adoptées, je puis néanmoins vous confier, sans risque de changement majeur, que ce projet de politique proposera dans ses grandes lignes une décentralisation accrue des interventions et un renforcement du partenariat, tout en replaçant l'objet patrimonial dans une perspective de développement durable et d'intégration au cadre de vie.

En raison de l'affirmation vigoureuse de groupes qui s'intéressent à un patrimoine jusqu'ici négligé, comme le patrimoine vivant, la future politique devra reposer sur une définition du patrimoine actualisée qui englobera une réalité débordant largement l'architecture et la production ancienne. De plus, l'accueil unanimement favorable réservé à la Politique culturelle orientera la politique du patrimoine vers une association avec le plus grand nombre possible de partenaires, non seulement pour la conservation et la mise en valeur du patrimoine, mais aussi et d'abord pour son *identification*. La nouvelle *Loi sur le ministère de la Culture* force d'ailleurs ce virage ; le ministère doit en effet abandonner la maîtrise d'œuvre pour soutenir et harmoniser les interventions de ses partenaires.

Concrètement, la politique devra affirmer la dimension collective du patrimoine, de façon à faire comprendre qu'il est l'affaire de tous ceux qui peuvent en profiter : les propriétaires, les collectivités et leurs gouvernements locaux, tout autant que le gouvernement québécois. Elle devra prévoir des mesures destinées à éveiller les jeunes publics à la mémoire des lieux, des personnes et des choses de toute provenance, de façon à leur faire découvrir à la fois leurs racines et leur diversité ; mettre en valeur les réussites exemplaires en matière de conservation, et d'exploitation judicieuse du patrimoine; soutenir la tenue d'événements propres à faire valoir son importance et son utilité, telles la valorisation d'individus, d'entreprises et de groupes performants ; favoriser l'enrichissement de la programmation des réseaux de radio et de télévision.

Cette politique devra aussi associer le patrimoine au développement durable, c'est-à-dire ce développement qui vise à satisfaire les besoins d'aujourd'hui sans compromettre la possibilité pour les générations futures de satisfaire leurs propres besoins.

Elle devra laisser entendre qu'il en est des biens patrimoniaux comme des personnes : mieux vaut les maintenir en service, les garder dans le circuit économique, éducatif ou autre, quitte à les recycler, que d'investir des efforts importants pour les réhabiliter après dix ou vingt ans d'abandon. Elle devra favoriser la conservation en bon état et l'utilisation rationnelle de ce que les Européens appellent « patrimoine de proximité », cette multitude de connaissances, de biens mobiliers et immobiliers que seuls les citoyens et les groupes locaux peuvent identifier et qui préviennent la banalisation des villes et des villages.

La politique du patrimoine, destinée à convaincre citoyens et municipalités de faire les efforts nécessaires pour tirer parti de leur originalité, devra prévoir l'exemplarité du geste gouvernemental et amener le gouvernement du Québec à bien gérer son propre patrimoine.

En d'autres termes, la politique devra concrétiser par ses mesures que le patrimoine est à la charge et à la disposition de tous et que son entretien exige plus de ressources que celles qui lui sont présentement consacrées. Le gouvernement devra donc maintenir son effort et faire en sorte que ses partenaires accroissent le leur. Il y parviendra en s'inspirant du milieu de l'environnement qui, en vingt ans, a fait passer la société de l'indifférence générale aux bacs de recyclage en convainquant les citoyens de deux choses : 1) c'est leur affaire et ils peuvent poser des gestes utiles et 2) ils y trouveront leur profit.

De plus, la politique devra reconnaître que le patrimoine, comme tout héritage personnel ou familial, appartient à ses détenteurs actuels, qui peuvent l'utiliser, mais qui doivent aussi l'enrichir, et non le dilapider. C'est une ressource, un actif, non un passif. Une telle vision nous autorise à utiliser notre héritage, notre patrimoine, comme artefact dans les musées, comme source d'information dans les archives et les bibliothèques, comme logement pour des services communs et même, à l'occasion, pour des groupes ciblés de citoyens. Une telle vision nous autorise même à considérer comme acceptable l'usure de certains biens patrimoniaux, si c'est le prix à payer pour augmenter et améliorer l'héritage que nous léguerons. Nous rendons service à nos héritiers en utilisant notre patrimoine, si cette utilisation nous conduit à mieux l'entretenir.

Enfin, cette politique devra reconnaître que le patrimoine n'est pas d'abord ce que nous avons reçu, mais surtout ce que nous laisserons à nos héritiers et, qu'en conséquence, nous devons accorder autant d'importance à ce que nous produisons qu'à ce que nous avons reçu de nos prédécesseurs. Le patrimoine est un actif à utiliser de façon judicieuse, responsable et multiforme.

En procédant à la mise en place des nouveaux moyens que supposera l'adoption d'une telle politique, le ministère de la Culture et des Communications cherchera, entre autres à favoriser l'insertion du patrimoine dans les valeurs des citoyens. Il cherchera à stimuler la qualité des interventions des milieux culturels qui s'intéressent au patrimoine, en prenant appui notamment sur le caractère exemplaire des gestes gouvernementaux à cet égard. Il accentuera par ailleurs ses efforts auprès des gouvernements locaux et régionaux pour que ceux-ci tiennent davantage compte de la dimension patrimoniale dans la gestion, le contrôle et l'exploitation de leur cadre de vie. Il recherchera, en outre, l'association des propriétaires privés à la conservation et à la mise en valeur des biens patrimoniaux.

En somme, grâce à cette nouvelle approche, le Ministère croit fermement que le patrimoine culturel des Québécois pourra continuer de s'enrichir et de s'inscrire parmi nos ressources les plus précieuses et les plus durables, et ce pour le bénéfice des générations futures aussi bien que de la société d'aujourd'hui. Le défi est grand, mais nous croyons le moment propice et le milieu plus disposé que jamais à effectuer avec nous ce nouveau virage !

Notes

1. Je remercie M. Michel Dufresne, chef des Services aux ministères et aux organismes gouvernementaux de la Direction des Archives nationales de l'est du Québec, de son importante collaboration à la rédaction de ce texte.
2. *Patrimoine muséologique au Québec : repères chronologiques.* Commission des biens culturels, Québec, 1992. 114 p.
3. Allocution prononcée par R. Arpin, le 4 novembre 1994, lors de la réception du doctorat honorifique que lui décernaient conjointement l'Université du Québec et l'Institut national de recherche scientifique (INRS).

La maison des Jésuites, Sillery (Québec) : construite vers 1730 ; désignée monument historique en 1929. / The Jesuit House, Sillery, Québec: built around 1730; named an historic monument in 1929. (Photo : IBHC / CIHB, 1972).

Le Château de Ramezay, Montréal (Québec) : Construit en 1705 par Pierre Couturier pour le gouverneur de Montréal, il fut rebâti et agrandi en 1756 selon les plans de Paul Tessier, dit Lavigne ; désigné en 1949. / Built in 1705 by Pierre Couturier for the Governor of Montréal, it was rebuilt and enlarged in 1756 according to the plans prepared by Paul Tessier called Lavigne; designated in 1949. (Photo : Parcs Canada / Parks Canada, HRS, 1992).

Finding the Funding and Other Provincial Responsibilities: The Alberta Experience

Abstract

The Alberta government experience in heritage commemoration is relatively recent, becoming in 1967 one of the last provinces to develop an official provincial museum. With the passage of *The Alberta Heritage Act* in 1973, however, it rapidly implemented a proactive policy of first preserving and then presenting a wealth of materials reflecting this province's unique natural and human history. Over the past fifteen years it has opened some seventeen new museums, historic sites, and interpretive centres in an integrated network of public facilities dedicated to the promotion of an appreciation of Alberta's history. In developing this comprehensive system at a time of increasing economic pressures and social change, innovative approaches have been developed to meet the many challenges.

Recherche du financement et autres responsabilités provinciales touchant le patrimoine : l'expérience de l'Alberta – Résumé

L'expérience du gouvernement de l'Alberta dans le domaine de la commémoration du patrimoine est relativement récente. Cette province a été une des dernières à se doter d'un musée officiel, en 1967. Toutefois, après l'adoption, en 1973, de l'*Alberta Heritage Act*, elle n'a pas tardé à mettre en œuvre une politique dynamique visant d'abord à protéger, puis à présenter au public une multitude d'objets et d'entités caractéristiques de son patrimoine naturel et de son histoire propres. Au cours des quinze dernières années, l'Alberta a ouvert quelque dix-sept nouveaux musées, lieux historiques et centres d'interprétation s'insérant dans un réseau intégré d'installations publiques destinées à faire apprécier l'histoire de la province. On a trouvé des façons innovatrices de relever les nombreux défis rencontrés lors de la mise sur pied de ce vaste réseau dans une période de tensions économiques croissantes et de changement social accéléré.

Barely more than thirty years ago it was observed by at least one critic that Alberta as a province had "shown less interest in museums than any of the other eight provinces on the mainland of Canada".[1] Although Newfoundland was conspicuous by its absence in this reference, I suspect that this condemnation would have been equally valid if the comparison had been extended offshore to include all nine other provinces. Indeed it is notable that Alberta was virtually the very last province to establish an official provincial museum, with the opening of the Provincial Museum and Archives of Alberta only taking place on 6 December 1967.

Since then, great strides have been taken. Epitomized in some sense by the opening of this museum, in the 1960s the Alberta provincial government began to increase through programmes and legislation its direct participation in the growing heritage movement evident throughout Canada during the latter part of that decade. Historic property acquisitions, roadside point-of-interest signage, and provincial park initiatives featuring significant historic resources characterized the early steps, culminating in 1973 in the passage of *The Alberta Heritage Act* (now known as *The Alberta Historical Resources Act*). This last step heralded a revolution in Alberta's position in the heritage movement, for through this Act it declared legislative authority over all physical remains relating to the province's human and natural history. It also declared ownership of all archaeological and palaeontological remains still lying in the ground.

The remainder of the 1970s saw a rapid escalation in provincial activity in the heritage community, with a variety of agencies and offices being created to exercise the newly created mandate. This was also the era of the greatest development boom in the province's history, and the immediate consequence was that the primary emphasis in all government heritage programmes was placed on simply identifying and protecting the various palaeontological, archaeological, and historic site resources which were now being threatened by the development juggernaut. Regrettably, there were few commensurate provincial initiatives at this time to increase public access to the history being protected.

In the early 1980s this changed dramatically. Driven in equal measure by a desire to present the emerging wealth of historical resources to its citizens, and in an effort to diversify the provincial tourism base beyond Edmonton, Calgary, and the Rocky Mountain Parks, the province decided to develop a series of major and minor museums, interpretive centres, and historic sites throughout Alberta. Over the next ten years some $120 million was allocated to this purpose, none of which was derived from the province's "Heritage Savings Trust Fund".

The result was the creation of a province-wide network of eighteen historic facilities.[2] Scattered from Fort McMurray in the far northeast to the Crowsnest Pass of southwestern Alberta, they range in scale from the 120,000 square foot Royal Tyrrell Museum of Palaeontology at Drumheller, to the tiny nineteenth-century farmhouse of the Icelandic immigrant poet, Stephan

Stephansson, at Markerville. All, however, are based on unique historical resources of significance to the development of the province of Alberta.

The basis of this policy of development should be clearly understood. With no apologies but rather with pride in the foresight, I would emphasize that the decision to proceed with the various developments was predicated in good measure on the anticipated economic return on the investments. At the same time this was not a far-fetched attempt to compete with the Disney Corporation for entertainment dollars. Rather it was a reasoned decision which recognized that one could take important historic resources and develop them in such a fashion that they would not only serve a major cultural purpose by educating visitors about Alberta's history, but also they could become significant generators of tourism spending in the local service economies. In attempting to bring people into parts of the province beyond Banff, Jasper, and the two largest cities, it was nothing less than a conscious attempt to alter tourism travel patterns on a province-wide scale.

From the outset it was believed that to make this development strategy work you must have legitimate historical values to present, appropriate physical resources reflecting these significant values, and a high quality presentation venue and system. But by recognizing that at least part of the provincial purpose was economic, it is no accident that none of these developments were placed in the major urban centres or the Mountain Parks. At the same time, it was also no accident that all are conveniently located on or near major transportation corridors. While limitations of access meant that some sites of major historical interest would not be developed, only sites and subjects of legitimate historical value were identified for public presentation and promotion.

As the system developed, we were immediately concerned that the "parachuting" of major government initiatives into the generally rural communities could have disastrous consequences. That is, we believed that the success of these ventures was absolutely dependent on community commitment and participation, and therefore engineered, from the outset, mechanisms to give a strong community presence. A major component of this approach was to establish local Ministerial Advisory Boards for each facility, initially to provide input on the capital development decisions but subsequently to continue as operational advisory mechanisms. Appointed directly by the Minister, these bodies generally incorporate representatives of local governments, economic and tourism agencies, historical interest groups, and other key community players.

At the same time we also became increasingly concerned by growing fiscal restraints. During the latter part of the 1980s and early 1990s the capital budgets for the development of the various projects generally survived essentially intact, but the operational dollars were reduced dramatically, sometimes by as much as 50% before the doors of a new facility even opened. The problem was that these museums, historic sites, and interpretive centres were expected to become significant regional economic generators by being attractive enough to increase tourism, but they could only do so if they were operated at or near their initial design levels. On a global scale, cultural tourism is becoming a highly competitive business, and world-class audiences require world-class standards.

To address this dilemma we engineered throughout the organization a commitment to exploring any and all opportunities to have community and corporate partners assume responsibility for a wide range of activities associated with the facility promotions and operations. In addition, we encouraged all staff to explore entrepreneurial opportunities within the system which could generate a revenue stream which could contribute to operations.

A major component of this approach consists of the so-called "Affiliated Cooperating Societies". These are independently chartered societies which enter into a formal contractual relationship with a particular facility. Sometimes these organizations have a prior life as the local historical or other society, but more often than not they were created anew through interested community volunteers as the capital work progressed. In either case they enter into "master cooperating agreements" defining their legal relationship with the facilities, then into any number of sub-agreements which sees them assume responsibility for various parts of the institution's operations. These responsibilities can range everywhere from collecting admissions to delivering interpretive programming to developing new exhibits.

The University of Calgary Intern Programme is another partnership programme. Through a joint venture with the Faculty of Environmental Design we have developed a programme leading to a Certificate in Historical Research Management. A critical component of this programme is the placement of interns in the various historical facilities in the system, resulting in anywhere from thirty to sixty individuals being available to assist in-site operations at any given time. Although we pay wages for these interns, the mechanism allows a great deal of flexibility in hiring beyond the traditional government strictures, without fear of compromising contractual relationships. As a side benefit, graduates of the programme have a high employment placement rate throughout the province and Western Canada.

Corporate partnerships can take a wide variety of forms, generally involving joint ventures of some sort. Probably our most spectacular foray into this world was working with the Gakken Corporation of Japan, which saw the development of a 70,000 square foot exhibit of Alberta dinosaurs at Makuhari

Messe, a major exhibit and convention centre near Tokyo. Through this mechanism we were able to deal with a ten-year backlog of palaeontological specimens which had been accumulating at the Tyrrell Museum, all of the work being funded by our Japanese partners. In addition, through the exhibitry we were able to present an invitation to the more than one million Japanese visitors to the show, as well as to the many millions more exposed to the intensive advertising campaign launched throughout Japan in conjunction with the show, to themselves come to Alberta to enjoy our many historical attractions.

As was the case with Gakken, most of our corporate partnerships involve marketing and promotions of some sort. In a critical departure from traditional museum/business relationships, the corporate partners are not being asked for charitable contributions. Rather, approaches are made on a truly business-like basis in which it is anticipated that both partners will derive some net economic benefit. Frequently the deals which are struck sees one or more of the heritage facilities enter into an association with a particular partner, which then uses our historical facilities as part of their advertising campaign. This has been a very useful vehicle, involving everything from local merchants to major companies like Eaton's, Mac's Milk, and Husky Oil to increase our public awareness and profile.

Other relationships can take a wide variety of forms, involving community partners, corporate partners, or both. The key is that we will play "let's make a deal" with anyone, on anything that we do, if it proves mutually beneficial and workable. Flexibility throughout the system, with specific arrangements which make sense to the local situation rather than rigid adherence to a province-wide standard approach, is critical to making this work.

Coupled with this partnership arrangement, increasingly, is the reliance on facility-earned income (admissions fees and other activities) to keep the doors open. Exploration of entrepreneurial opportunities is actively encouraged throughout the organization, whether initiated and implemented by staff or by one of our partners. From building dinosaurs for other heritage institutions around the world to providing accoutrements for Victorian-era funerals for local pioneers, we examine the practicality of providing historically accurate goods and services for a fee, whenever there is a customer willing to pay.

Lest this sound completely crass, I would emphasize that the initiation of new programmes at the various facilities is not based simply on their revenue generating potential. We are first and foremost dedicated to the preservation and promotion of public appreciation of Alberta's rich and diverse human and natural history, and everything we do must have this mission as its primary characteristic. At the same time, when it comes to making these programmes available, the principle we rigorously pursue is that we will operate in a business-like fashion everywhere, and like a business whenever it is practical.

The final factor which makes all of this work is that we have been granted a fiscal mechanism traditionally denied to line operations of the provincial government. As a result of the creation of the Historical Resources Regulated Fund, we are able to retain in this non-lapsing fund all of the revenues we generate through institutional programming and to use these monies for operations, maintenance, and enhancements to the system. This very non-traditional approach to handling programme income has opened a vast array of possibilities to the organization. It has also resulted in some rather startling initiatives by staff, including the revelation of a side to the characters of individual employees hitherto completely unsuspected. As a case in point, one of our most aggressive – and successful – new entrepreneurs is an archivist at the Provincial Archives of Alberta.

In assessing how successful this approach has been overall it should be noted that at a time when our normal government operating budget has been shrinking dramatically, we have been able to increase the scale and scope of public programming and services throughout the system. For example, in 1985/86 we operated nine facilities using a government staff of approximately 330, plus slightly over 200 seasonal staff from a government student summer employment programme. By way of comparison, in the summer of 1994 we operated eighteen facilities using 230 government staff, and less than twenty summer students. The rest of the programming and staffing at these facilities was provided through our various community partners. In fact, a recent audit at the Ukrainian Cultural Heritage Village revealed eight different categories of employees, only one of which was traditional civil service employment.

Of course, none of the individual operational mechanisms in use are completely new. What is perhaps somewhat innovative, however, is the breadth and depth of these arrangements in the organization. In addition to individual facility responsibilities such as gift shop operations and staffing of interpretive programmes, such mechanisms are also used to operate the government geographical names programme, to facilitate archaeological monitoring for regulatory purposes, and to develop the resources of the Provincial Archives. In truth there is virtually no longer any portion of our comprehensive historical programme responsibilities which does not involve some non-traditional partnerships or co-operative ventures to facilitate programme delivery. At the same time, the partners have been deliberately integrated into the system so that the service delivery is source-neutral or seamless, meaning that the visitors know only that they are being treated properly, without knowing if the service is being provided by government staff or one of our partners.

One of the great side benefits of this approach has been the significant degree of community identification it has generated for the facilities and their programmes. Through this means there has developed a large cadre of community and corporate partners, each acting as ambassadors and promoters for the programmes and facilities. Also, through this means, the scattered museums and historic sites have become thoroughly integrated into the regional societies and economies. At a time when governments are increasingly asking themselves just what business they should be in, it is not a bad thing to be considered part of the core business of Alberta's many communities.

Notes

1. C.P. Wilson, "Modern History Museums", *Alberta Historical Review* 8 (Summer 1960): 27.
2. The eighteen facilities in the provincial system include the Provincial Museum of Alberta, the Remington-Alberta Carriage Centre, the Frank Slide Interpretive Site, Leitch Colleries, Head-Smashed-In Buffalo Jump, Cochrane Ranche, the Royal Tyrrell Museum of Palaeontology, the Field Station of the Royal Tyrrell Museum, Brooks Aqueduct, Stephansson House, the Reynolds-Alberta Museum, Rutherford House, Father Lacombe Chapel, the Ukrainian Cultural Heritage Village, Fort Victoria, Buckingham House/Fort George, Fort McMurray Oil Sands Interpretive Centre, and Fort Dunvegan Historic Site.

Royal Tyrrell Museum of Palaeontology / Le musée de paléontologie Royal Tyrrell, Drumheller, Alberta

R. SCOTT JAMES and RICHARD L. STROMBERG

Preservation Policy from the Municipal Perspective: A Focus on Tax Issues

Abstract

All levels of government espouse heritage preservation. However, many planning and tax measures encourage the demolition rather than the preservation of existing buildings. Structural changes to the economy and eroding urban tax base are increasing the threat. Although municipalities can take steps to improve preservation efforts, tax incentives remain the most effective tool for inducing the continued use of existing buildings. Only the federal and provincial governments can make the changes in taxation that would help Canadian municipalities preserve their past.

Le point de vue des municipalités sur la politique de conservation : les questions fiscales – Résumé

Tous les niveaux de gouvernement sont voués à la cause de la conservation du patrimoine. Cependant, un grand nombre de mesures fiscales et d'urbanisme encouragent la démolition plutôt que la préservation des bâtiments existants. Les modifications structurelles de l'économie et le rétrécissement de l'assiette fiscale des villes amplifient la menace. Les municipalités peuvent prendre des mesures pour améliorer les efforts de conservation, mais les stimulants fiscaux demeurent l'outil le plus efficace pour encourager l'utilisation continue de bâtiments existants. Seuls les gouvernements fédéral et provinciaux peuvent modifier les règles d'imposition afin d'aider les municipalités canadiennes à préserver leur passé.

It is a pleasure to join so many heritage professionals and old friends in celebrating the 75th anniversary of the Historic Sites and Monuments Board of Canada, and to bring greetings from the City of Toronto and the Toronto Historical Board.

This paper addresses problems faced by municipalities. Canada's local governments are on the front line of heritage preservation – they approve permits, establish zoning, and collect taxes – all of which affect heritage buildings and efforts to preserve them. At the same time, municipalities by themselves do not have the legal authority to ensure Canada's historic sites and structures survive. We propose to discuss some of the things that we at the municipal level can do and to ask for your help across the country and at all levels of government to strengthen the commitment to heritage preservation.

We would like to begin with a story. In early 1994, Toronto City Council refused to designate the Dora Mavor Moore house and, in so doing, paved the way for its demolition. The house had many unique features. It was a log structure, it was Toronto's oldest continuously occupied residence, and it had been the home of three significant Canadians: interior design expert Jeanne Minhinnick; famed actor and theatre innovator Dora Mavor Moore; and Moore's son, Mavor Moore, professor and former head of the Canada Council. One must ask what *could* have been done to save this significant part of Toronto's, and indeed Canada's, history?

It should come as no surprise that the principal argument put forth for demolition was economic. The old house occupied a double lot and demolition would permit the new owner to build two houses, thus maximizing the return on his investment. Again, it probably will not come as a surprise that the principal argument for preservation was the intangible appeal to respect history and culture. When the time came for Toronto City Council to make its decision, preservationists did not have the economic tools to encourage the Moore house to be kept and reused. The inability to increase the return on a heritage property is still the largest single impediment to preservation today. That is especially true for commercial properties.

This paper is a brief discussion of the economics and politics of preservation.[1] It alludes to previous attempts to secure tax incentives for preservation and it presents several actions that, if implemented, could encourage the private sector to preserve and reuse our heritage buildings stock. It also reminds us of the constraints municipalities face. Removing disincentives to preservation must occur at all levels of government, but especially the federal, and we conclude with a proposal to engage the officials at Finance Canada in renewed discussions.

The nineties have not been kind to our cities and their heritage. The recession has hit all parts of the country: businesses have closed, jobs have left Canada, and governments are faced with mounting deficits. Structural changes in the global economy are leading to permanent changes in Toronto's traditionally broad-based economy. It is especially unlikely that manufacturing jobs will return to the city. As a result, the tax base has eroded. Demand for municipal services, however, remains high and has even grown. This picture is repeated at various scales from coast to coast.

At first glance, one would expect a recession to benefit heritage because no new construction would mean fewer buildings are threatened.[2] Exactly the opposite has occurred. During the boom years of the eighties, developers were willing to preserve heritage structures in exchange for density transfers and bonuses. They calculated they could absorb the extra costs associated with restoration because they would easily make up the difference by renting out the extra space. Rehabilitating heritage space was one of the costs of doing business. However, the recession and resulting "office glut" have led to projects being cancelled and legal restoration agreements being waived. In the fall of 1994, for example, Toronto City Council released one developer from its obligation to restore a designated 12-storey office building even though the developer had provided a two million dollar letter-of-credit to guarantee restoration would be completed. The rationale was that forcing compliance would be onerous given the unforeseen downturn in business activity. The penalty for release from the agreement was $100,000.00.

High property taxes discourage owners from keeping older buildings. With tighter margins and less certainty on returns, several older downtown Toronto office buildings have been, or are slated to be, demolished for parking lots. Parking lots are assessed for business taxes at a lower rate so one can reduce short-term costs and liability by demolishing an underused building. Add to that the ability to deduct the costs of demolition against income and one has a powerful incentive to dispose of unprofitable buildings. The Toronto Historical Board hears repeatedly that commercial property taxes are too high and that tax relief should be forthcoming if owners are going to maintain older buildings willingly.

It is discouraging to recall just how long taxation has been discussed by preservationists. Marc Denhez, speaking in 1978 at the "Conserving Ontario's Main Streets" conference in Peterborough, noted inequities in the tax code that permitted businesses to write-off the full book value of properties they chose to demolish while there were no corresponding tax breaks available to owners who wished to restore and rehabilitate buildings.[3] He could say the same today. The sad thing is that a workable model existed in the United States after 1976.

The American federal government offered tax incentives for approved restoration to older structures. Between 1976 and 1988, thirteen billion dollars was spent on 20,000 projects. Half were for housing and three-fourths of respondents sampled indicated they would not have chosen to rehabilitate an historic structure if tax credits had not been available.[4] From a preservation perspective, the American tax credits were very effective. They also brought much needed investment into downtown areas. Many may remember that in Canada in the mid-1980s the Buildings Revival Coalition submitted a brief to the Parliamentary Committee on Finance and Economic Affairs containing proposals that would stimulate Canadian restoration and rehabilitation by offering tax credits for approved work and hiring skilled trades. The Toronto Historical Board and Toronto City Council supported the Buildings Revival Coalition, as did many other municipalities. However, then Finance Minister Michael Wilson responded:

> In the context of tax reform, introducing a preference for the renovation of old buildings would not be appropriate. Tax reform involves reducing the number of highly targeted selective incentives. Concerns about heritage property are more appropriately dealt with outside of the tax system. The government does not intend to proceed with this proposal.[5]

The inconsistencies in Mr. Wilson's response are numerous. Western governments regularly use taxation to achieve desired social ends. Moreover, he could have removed tax measures that favour demolition over reuse, thus creating a "level playing field", but he chose not to. Mr. Wilson's refusal to consider heritage tax incentives closely followed the Reagan administration's *Tax Reform Act* of 1986 which sharply curtailed the American tax incentives.[6] Not to appear partisan, one need only imagine the response Mr. Paul Martin would give today when every level of government is espousing "deficit reduction". At the provincial level, Alberta and Saskatchewan have enacted enabling legislation to permit municipalities to lower local property taxes on heritage buildings, but Ontario has not. Even if it did, discussions with both City of Toronto Finance Department staff and City Council's Budget Chief reinforce the expectation that any programme resulting in the loss of tax revenue at this time would be opposed. It is doubtful that any municipality in the country would respond any differently today.

Does it necessarily follow, though, that tax abatement for heritage buildings results in a net loss to city treasuries? A 1986 study for Canada Mortgage and Housing Corporation showed that 27.8 direct jobs were created for every one million dollars spent on renovation. Much of that money is spent locally so it is estimated that each million actually leads to 59.5 jobs when its full effect is measured.[7] One could also take a "revenue neutral" approach to altering the assessment formula so that some would pay more while all owners of older buildings paid less. For example, municipalities could lower property taxes on vacant buildings while raising taxes on parking lots. This would encourage owners to mothball rather than demolish.

If governments are reluctant to offer tax relief, what other options should be pursued? We can try to improve for property owners their rate of return on investment and their property value.[8]

We suggest there are four ways that Municipalities can improve returns by:

i) lowering the owner's costs through grants and seed money. The Toronto Historical Board is considering expanding the use of its Toronto Heritage Fund, currently limited to restoration work, to allow funding for feasibility and technical studies – studies that could demonstrate the potential benefits and types of reuse;

ii) increasing the owner's income by helping to find occupants, e.g., governments could adopt as policy a preference for locating their offices and employees in heritage buildings;

iii) acting as an information clearing house e.g., on the market and on rehabilitation technology; and

iv) helping to secure financing and lower interest rates through loan guarantees.

There are also four ways in which municipalities can help increase value, by:

i) altering zoning to expand the range of permissible uses in heritage buildings;

ii) offering owners of heritage properties exemptions from requirements, e.g., the need to provide parking;

iii) creating heritage districts in which older buildings reinforce one another to provide a desirable and usable environment that can be marketed; and

iv) developing educational programmes that convey the importance of heritage to a community's sense of identity, and induce greater personal pride in ownership of heritage properties.

Exemptions have worked well in Toronto. "Use bonuses" have been used only in the King-Parliament industrial area, but we are now discussing with the City Planning and Development Department extending them to the King-Spadina "Fashion District". The garment industry has lost many jobs so there is considerable vacant space. If adopted by City Council, owners would be able to convert existing structures to what is being called "live-work" space. New construction would not be eligible.

The conversion to live-work space is an example of a solution that attempts to address both the preservation and economic problems. Limiting the "bonus" to buildings existing at the time the by-law was drafted discourages demolition. Allowing new uses helps to increase the number of potential tenants which should make the buildings more viable. This is a creative solution that helps many parties at no additional cost to local government. If anything, one can expect more tax revenue if the area remains a dynamic part of the city.[9]

As was noted in the introduction, municipalities are on the front line of preservation. Municipalities issue permits and establish zoning. Heritage advocates must lobby and keep up the pressure to ensure that our cities do not cave-in to short-term pressures but commit themselves to preserving our past over the long-term.

We are ready at the municipal level to take up the challenge and to do what we can. Our municipal politicians have stated their support for legislation that would permit heritage tax relief once the local economy improves, but municipalities also have limited authority and limited resources. They cannot do the job by themselves. In principle it is not the responsibility of municipalities (or provinces) to counterbalance the negative effects of federal tax laws.

With the economy apparently on the rebound, now is a good time to take up the challenge left by the Buildings Revival Coalition's work in 1987. Let us bring together a new coalition – the heritage community, municipalities, the housing and renovation industries, and tax and accounting experts from both the academic and private sectors – and bring Finance Canada to the table again to attempt to achieve a "level playing field" for our existing building stock.

Is there a role for the Historic Sites and Monuments Board of Canada in facilitating such an exercise? We hope so. It would be a practical and eminently fitting exercise of the Board's important national advisory function, in this especially significant 75th anniversary year.

Notes

1. The economics of preservation has an extensive literature. See, e.g., "Economic Benefits of Preserving Old Buildings", National Trust for Historic Preservation, Washington, 1976; Ann Falkner, *Without our Past?*, University of Toronto Press, Toronto, 1977, ch.9; "Conserving Ontario's Main Streets", Ontario Heritage Foundation, Toronto, 1979, pp. 66-70; Marc Denhez, "Income Tax Policies Pertaining to the Care of Buildings", *ICOMOS Canada Bulletin*, Vol. 1, No. 3, 1992, pp. 29-33.
2. For a view emphasizing heritage opportunities during a recession, see Donovan Rypkema, "The Recession: Good News in Bad Times", *Historic Preservation Forum*, May/June 1991, pp.15-25.
3. "Conserving Ontario's Main Streets", 1979, pp. 69-70
4. Betsy Chittenden, "Tax Incentives for Rehabilitating Historic Buildings: Fiscal Year 1988 Analysis", National Park Service, Washington, 1988.

5. Cited in Buildings Revival Coalition memorandum, 1 September 1988. On file with the Toronto Historical Board.

6. In 1993, private investors received credits for rehabilitation totalling less than $475 million – approximately 20% of the amount received at the programme's height in 1985. Harry K. Schwartz, "A Federal Historic Rehabilitation Tax Credit for Home Ownership", *Historic Preservation News*, October/November 1994, p. 12.

7. Mary Jane Copps, "Getting a Fair Deal for Rehab Investors in Canada", *Building Renovation*, March/April, 1987, p. 24.

8. For a good discussion of the concepts of "return" and "value" in heritage properties, see Donovan Rypkema, "The Economics of Rehabilitation", National Trust for Historic Preservation Information Series No. 53, Washington, 1991.

9. Since this paper was first presented, the City of Toronto has adopted new zoning for both the King-Parliament and King-Spadina areas. The new zoning is designed to stimulate economic activity by expanding permissible uses on all properties, including new construction. Heritage buildings are exempted from providing parking, but our overall sense is that the new zoning is at best neutral towards heritage. We still think a form of bonusing that only applies to extant structures would be worth pursuing.

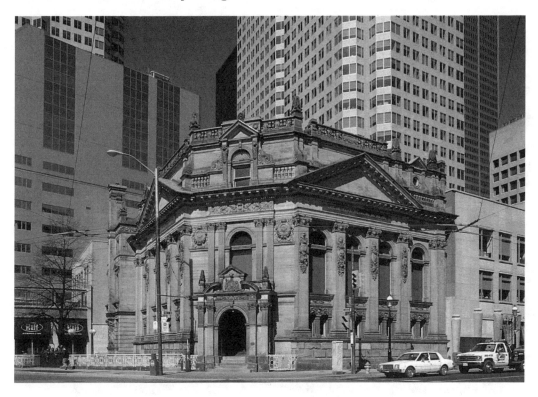

This branch of the Bank of Montreal, built in 1885, is now the Hockey Hall of Fame. It is a good example of restoration and adaptive re-use. / Cette succursale de la Banque de Montréal, constuite en 1885, abrite maintenant le Temple de la renommée du hockey. C'est là un bel exemple de restauration et d'adaptation d'un bâtiment à un nouvel usage. (Photo: Toronto Historical Board)

The Dora Mavor Moore house being dismantled and recorded prior to removal from the site. Stucco and clapboard have been removed to reveal the log construction. / Démontage de la maison Dora-Mavor-Moore et prise de notes avant sa disparition. L'enlèvement du stuc et du bardeau révèle la construction en rondins. (Photo: Michael McClelland)

The 1845 Commercial Bank was moved and incorporated in the interior of BCE Place. Beneath a breathtaking modern steel and glass galleria, it showcases successful preservation made possible by bonusing. / Le bâtiment de la Banque commerciale de 1845 a été déplacé et intégré à l'intérieur de la Place BCE. Sous une impressionnante arcade moderne en acier et en verre, il illustre une réussite de conservation rendue possible par une gratification. (Photo: Toronto Historical Board)

Création d'une icône architecturale

Résumé

En 1892, lorsque l'architecte américain Bruce Price reçut la commande d'un hôtel prestigieux pour la ville de Québec, il choisit non seulement le site, mais le style Château, pour un établissement qu'il allait appeler Château Frontenac.

Quels antécédents influencèrent Price dans la création de l'hôtel ? Fut-il le seul à avoir instauré ce qui devint la marque de commerce des grands hôtels des compagnies ferroviaires au Canada ? Entre l'époque de Champlain et celle de Bruce Price, de grands architectes avaient déjà dessiné des bâtiments d'allure médiévale pour le site, et de nombreuses constructions avaient été érigées dans le même style, tant aux États-Unis qu'au Canada.

Toutefois, c'est avec l'avènement du Canadien Pacifique que le style Château pour les grands hôtels devint une icône architecturale reconnaissable de l'est à l'ouest du Canada.

Creation of an Architectural Icon – Abstract

In 1892, when American architect Bruce Price was given the commission for a prestigious Quebec City hotel, he chose not only the site, but also the château style for an establishment he would name Château Frontenac.

What inspired Price in the creation of this hotel? Was he alone in establishing what was to become the trademark for the great railway hotels in Canada? Between the times of Champlain and of Bruce Price, great architects had already proposed medieval-style buildings for the site, and this style had been adopted for many structures in both the United States and Canada.

However, it was with the advent of the Canadian Pacific that the château style for the big hotels became a recognizable architectural icon across Canada.

Lorsque Samuel de Champlain s'installe au pied du Cap-aux-Diamants, en 1608, il a remarqué l'avantage extraordinaire du site en hauteur qui protège la basse ville. La valeur stratégique du lieu a été reconnue par le fondateur et, dès 1620, il y construit une première forteresse qui abritait les sentinelles et son modeste logis. En 1636, à l'arrivée de Charles Huault de Montmagny, premier gouverneur de la Nouvelle-France, de nouveaux travaux sont entrepris et le fort de Québec est désormais baptisé « *Château Saint-Louis* ».

Détruit par l'attaque de Sir William Phipps, le 16 octobre 1690, le Château Saint-Louis est érigé sur le même site par le comte de Frontenac en 1692. Après plusieurs campagnes de reconstruction, le bâtiment est détruit par un incendie le 25 janvier 1834.

L'intérêt et la convoitise suscités par ce site, d'une beauté naturelle remarquable, n'ont eu de cesse pendant près de trois siècles. C'est alors que sir Donald Alexander Smith, sir William Van Horne, sir Thomas Shaughnessy et quelques-uns de leurs amis financiers de Montréal forment la Compagnie du Château Frontenac pour financer l'érection d'un hôtel de grand luxe sur l'emplacement de l'historique Château Saint-Louis. L'architecte choisi par les barons de la haute finance est l'Américain Bruce Price. Celui-ci entreprend de réhabiliter les formes de la Renaissance de façon éclatante lorsqu'il dessine le Château Frontenac. À l'origine, l'hôtel devait être une structure contemporaine. Or, Bruce Price déclarait à l'époque :

> Le style est, bien sûr, celui des anciens châteaux français adapté aux besoins d'aujourd'hui. Ce style est en accord avec les traditions de l'ancienne ville française, les matériaux de calcaire bleu et de brique d'Écosse sont en harmonie avec l'environnement ; ce sont des matériaux rendant possibles les effets de couleur et de lumière. Cet hôtel est placé au centre d'un paysage grandiose ; par conséquent il se doit d'être grandiose tant par ses matériaux que par la simplicité de sa conception. (Barr Ferree, "A talk with Bruce Price" dans *Architectural Record*, juin 1899)

L'architecte américain s'était même rendu en France, à Saint-Germain-en-Laye sur les lieux d'origine de Louis de Buade, comte de Frontenac. Dessiné par Bruce Price et construit par Félix Labelle, le Château Frontenac empruntait la forme de fer à cheval autour d'une véritable cour d'honneur. Quatre ailes de proportions différentes logeaient les salles et les chambres alors, que les tours qui reliaient ces ailes abritaient les grandes suites. Le jour de l'ouverture du complexe hôtelier, le 18 décembre 1893, le *Quebec Morning Chronicle* publiait :

> Sans aucune hésitation, il faut affirmer que le plus beau site dont on puisse rêver pour construire un hôtel de prestige est celui où se trouve aujourd'hui le Château Frontenac. Les hauts toits de cuivre, les tours et les tourelles donnent au bâtiment l'allure d'un château médiéval perché au-dessus d'un précipice. À travers une arche de pierre supportée par des colonnades, on pénètre dans la cour

intérieure et dès l'entrée, le visiteur est frappé par la beauté des tableaux, des parquets de mosaïque et par les lambris et les décors des murs de chêne sculptés, le grand escalier du hall, les armoiries de Frontenac peintes sur écusson, les portraits en pied de Frontenac et de Montmagny qui décorent les murs.

Le Château Frontenac a établi le style Château pour le Canadien Pacifique et, dès sa construction, il répond au désir de Van Horne, qui voulait en faire l'hôtel dont on parlerait le plus au monde. Le Château Frontenac était grandiose. Cette composition asymétrique était marquée par des tours, des lucarnes, des toits pointus recouverts de cuivre avec des murs polychromes de brique d'Écosse allégés par la pierre de Lachevrotière qui composait les fondations, les tourelles et toutes les corniches.

On s'est plu à inscrire dans l'histoire Bruce Price comme l'instigateur du style *Château* au Canada et le créateur d'une icône architecturale exceptionnelle dans le paysage architectural canadien. Qu'en est-il ?

Au moment où Bruce Price se présente à Québec, la vieille ville est en soi un témoignage marqué au sceau de l'architecture militaire et le style de ses bâtiments reprend souvent le vocabulaire des châteaux de la mère patrie. Les murs d'enceinte sont ponctués de portes massives, et la citadelle de plan Vauban comme le Manège militaire dessiné par Étienne Taché en 1888 sont des bâtiments de pierre massive ponctués de tours, d'échauguettes et de coursives.

Autres faits intéressants que devait connaître Bruce Price, plusieurs architectes québécois et européens avaient déjà dessiné des plans de style Château pour l'érection d'un grand hôtel au-dessus de la vieille ville. Dès 1878, l'architecte irlandais W.H. Lynn dessine des plans et les publie dans le *Building News*. C'est une immense forteresse s'inspirant des châteaux de la Renaissance française. Quinze ans plus tard, soit en 1890, les architectes Rotch et Tilden dessinent le *Fortress Hotel* dans le style des châteaux de la Loire pour répondre à la commande des fondateurs d'une compagnie créée pour doter la ville d'un hôtel de prestige. Enfin, en 1890, Étienne Taché, qui vient de terminer le Manège militaire sur la Grande-Allée dessine également un château médiéval. Et, si l'on compare ce plan à celui qu'adoptera Bruce Price pour l'aile Riverview de son Château Frontenac, la similitude est beaucoup trop évidente pour croire à une simple coïncidence. Il est certain que tous ces plans ont concourru à la création de l'icône architecturale, le style Château.

Quant à Bruce Price, quelques années avant de se retrouver à Québec, il travaillait pour William Van Horne à développer les premiers grands hôtels de la ligne du Canadien Pacifique et faisait construire au cœur des montagnes

Rocheuses le plus grand château de la ligne ferroviaire, le fameux *Banff Springs Hotel*. Bien que construit entièrement de bois le *Banff Springs Hotel* était véritablement un château avec ses ailes asymétriques recouvertes de hauts toits et de tours multiples. Bruce Price avait aussi dessiné le bâtiment qui abritait l'hôtel et la gare Viger ainsi que la gare Windsor à Montréal.

Les châteaux prestigieux américains ont précédé de loin la construction d'édifices de même type au Canada. Que l'on se rappelle le fameux château de Vanderbilt, *Biltmore*, près d'Asheville, en Caroline du Nord, et tous ceux que les barons de la finance américaine feront bâtir sur la côte est des États-Unis et au cœur de la Cinquième Avenue, à New York. Au Canada, ce fut la firme prestigieuse d'Edward et William Maxwell qui se vit confier l'exécution de quantité d'hôtels, de gares, de bâtiments pour le compte de la compagnie ferroviaire, de St. John's (Terre-Neuve) à Vancouver (Colombie-Britannique), en passant par l'élément marquant de la ville de Québec, la grande tour centrale de l'hôtel Château Frontenac.

Bruce Price, qui s'extasie devant le site prestigieux de la terrasse Dufferin et se sent inspiré par l'architecture de la vieille ville française, n'a donc pas inventé de toutes pièces ce style château, comme ses biographes tentent de nous le faire croire.

L'icône architecturale, le symbole des hôtels de la grande compagnie ferroviaire demeure; c'est le Canadien Pacifique qui a adopté ce style et en a créé une icône architecturale que l'on retrouve dans tout le Canada et qui a marqué une longue période de construction. Les hôtels prestigieux comme l'*Empress*, à Victoria, le *MacDonald*, à Edmonton, le *Château Whistler*, dans les Rocheuses, le *Laurier*, le *Royal York*, en Ontario, les édifices publics tels le *Palais de Justice*, dans la capitale nationale, et des quantités de gares de pierre comme *Sicamous Junction*, *Moose Jaw*, dans l'Ouest, et *McAdam*, dans les Maritimes. Sans oublier la gare Viger et la gare Windsor, qui reprendront les compositions ponctuées de tours, de tourelles, de hauts toits de cuivre ou d'ardoise.

Ainsi fut créée une icône architecturale qui démarquera le paysage architectural canadien et qui rappelle une série de grands architectes tels qu'Étienne Taché, W.H. Lynn, Bruce Price, Edward et William Maxwell. Icône architecturale dont le bâtiment le plus significatif est sans contredit le grand hôtel de Banff Springs, au cœur des montagnes Rocheuses canadiennes.

Le « nouveau » Château Saint-Louis, Québec : « Vue d'ensemble face à la rivière », gravure de W.H. Lynn, architecte, publiée dans *The Building News*, 1878. / The new Château St. Louis, Québec, "General View, Front towards the river", engraving by W.H. Lynn, Architect, *The Building News*, 1878. (Photo : Archives nationales du Québec)

Plan de Château Frontenac par Bruce Price, 1893 / Design by Bruce Price for the Château Frontenac. (Photo : Archives nationales de Québec)

The Role of the Citizen Activist in Policy-making or "the space between"

Abstract

Drawing on over a century of collective experience, this presentation will explore the nature and impact of the volunteer citizen activist, focusing on the activist's influence on public programmes and policy. Following analysis of the anatomy of the gadfly, the wasp, and the barnacle, we will examine the activist as visionary, innovator, conscience, and supporter in the world of heritage conservation and commemoration. We will explore the role of the volunteer in the new century, concepts of training, and appreciation of effective partnerships between volunteers and professionals.

Le rôle des citoyens militants dans l'élaboration des politiques – Résumé

À la lumière de plus d'un siècle d'expérience collective, cette communication étudie les caractéristiques du citoyen bénévole militant et plus particulièrement son influence sur les politiques et les programmes publics. Après avoir analysé les cas de « mouches du coche », d'enquiquineurs et d'importuns, on examine le militant en tant que visionnaire, innovateur, conscience et partisan dans le milieu de la conservation et de la commémoration du patrimoine. On étudie en outre le rôle du bénévole au cours du prochain siècle ainsi que la notion de formation, et on évalue l'efficacité des partenariats entre bénévoles et professionnels.

As part of a cycle of poems related to our earth, our place, our land, on November 11th I wrote one named for that poignant unforgettable area known as "no man's land". This piece reflects images evoked by a space that has become a symbol:

> The space between, waste, barren, still yielding
> Iron harvest from death-dealers; this is land
> Held sacred now, a foreign poppy field
> For some forever home.

Space between, a silent bleak memorial
Where dead air stifles messages
Between believers, each with fragile faith
In equal and ironic truth.

Intertidal space, the unclaimed area between
The water and the shore, the ebb and flow,
Where footprints can be seen, of bold adventurers
Recorded briefly on the sand.

The space between the hostile lines is there
To be acknowledged as reality. Then speak in tongues,
And make a treaty; you have found
The ultimate in common ground.

The "space between" is a metaphor for that yawning distance between antagonists, the unclaimed territory that could belong to either side, the distance separating people in an argument, families at odds snarling across a room, the unsolved items in a crucial agenda.

In the context of citizen activism, the space between represents the above and also the differences between knowledge and understanding, between listening and hearing, between those who speak in one language and those who comprehend in another, between valid arguments on either side where the desirable goal is reconciliation and mutually beneficial progress.

This symposium has examined loons, landscapes, partnerships, native culture, recognition of and communication about "The Place of History". Permeating all discussion of our heritage is the reality of the citizen activist, the role of the activist in shaping public policy, influencing political decision-makers toward building a better country.

The activist is a relatively familiar figure. Each of us can draw upon about half a century of our own experience and another half of borrowed expertise to recognize the stereotypes: the little-old-lady-in-running shoes, the earnest and eager student representative, the all-knowing retired civil servant hinting at dark secrets, the incipient politician hungry for a platform and media coverage, the certifiable weirdo, the solid conservative who has suddenly realized something horrendous is happening in HIS back yard....

Or they can be seen as creatures of nature. The gadfly, or deerfly, is ubiquitous, bothersome, persistent, extremely irritating. The wasp has two relevant characteristics: it is an authoritative social insect capable of frightening creatures much larger than itself and of inflicting a venomous sting, and it is the original Great Communicator as any picnic-goer can attest. Let the word go out, "Announce it, and they will come!"; wasps assemble their friends and relations in powerful numbers with incredible speed. As incidental intelligence, among the species are both paper wasps and so-called mud-daubers, but let us not belabour the parallel.

The activist may also be recognized as a barnacle, defined as "a tenacious attendant who cannot easily be shaken off." Research also reveals that while the barnacle is in the process of developing its hard outside shell or carapace it is known to "stand on its head while kicking vigorously."

Here is our prototype of the ideal activist:

- a thoughtful citizen devoted to the public good (and a realist who knows it costs money);
- one who has worked hard and consistently to "earn the right" to be heard (and is reasonably articulate);
- one prepared to study, to learn from history and from one's contemporaries (and that one could be wrong);
- one willing to work with others, in partnership (and expecting small thanks);
- one blessed with passion, patience, and civility (to say nothing of good physical and mental health).

These are the outriders of the democratic system, the scouts, and guardians. They have earned the trust of their travelling companions; they are known to be consistent, indefatigable, and dependable. The journey is more fun if they have a sense of humour.

As a basic premise, this primer of effective activism presupposes that there are honest, decent, idealistic men and women in Municipal Councils, Provincial Government, and in the House of Commons. God help if the cynics prevail and we allow doubt and despair to poison our appreciation of politics and politicians. The intelligent activist will always first seek out, cultivate, and support honourable candidates, and secondly enlist them as crucial to the success of good causes.

Also basic to our theme is rejection of a prevailing perception of "special-interest" groups as a contemptible swarm of trouble-makers. Of course people have special interests; being a woman is a special interest for over half the population, any citizen will have expertise and concern in some specific field of endeavour. Advocacy by the electorate is essential in the operation of the democratic system; the fact that "lobbying" is vulnerable to abuse does not justify dismissing it as a nuisance, or, worse, a danger to that system.

Our paragon activist has two cardinal virtues: vision and political pragmatism. As Longfellow would have it:

> Thine was the prophet's vision, thine,
> The exaltation, the divine
> Insanity of noble minds.

Vision is an essential ingredient in all great human achievements, even those that seem insane. Resigned sighs and raised eyebrows notwithstanding, it is imperative to see into the future, to have foresight. Our very country is the fruit of that splendid vision of noble minds in Charlottetown in 1864. The United Nations is a vision; peace on earth is a vision. That we fail to achieve perfection is no reason to abandon the ideal.

The second essential in the process of shaping public policy is a tough sense of practical reality, political acumen. Naïveté is charming but pathetically ineffective. A clear understanding of the workings of the political system and the ways of influencing public debate is vital to the art of the activist.

It may be impossible to teach vision; it is not hard to teach visionaries. It is incumbent on our educational institutions to prepare students to be good citizens, to understand the intricacies of our systems of government, to feel involved and responsible in public affairs, and to acquire skills in debate and communication.

Refining the prototype of the ideal activist, we see the well-educated visionary identifying essentials for successfully influencing and shaping public policy. It is imperative that relevant laws be understood, bureaucratic language and technology mastered, a communications system in working order, facts in focus, goals clear and articulated.

Among the facts that must be in focus are three realities of government in the twenty-first century. These are the public's perception of politics, financial reality, and the phenomenon of citizen participation.

Mistrust, skepticism, crankiness, cynicism, anger, despair... these are all deterrents to the achievement of peace, order, and good government. And their backlash is that it becomes increasingly difficult to recruit competent, qualified men and women to run for public office. Unhappily for the future of our country too many reject the bear-pit, steer clear of the jungle. We are in danger of wasting great talent, of diminishing into fearful mediocrity. We need to fight against this cynicism, spread the gospel of good works by encouraging voluntarism, demonstrate the virtues of civic responsibility.

A second reality is financial. The mess of debt in which we wallow will be with us for at least the next decade. This in a world which has increased by twenty million people in the course of this very weekend, with the numbers of sick, starving, and homeless increasing in direct and tragic proportion. Uncontrolled population growth is the real and universal "cost of living", and every aspect of public policy is related to this awesome reality.

The Pollyanna flip is that in times of shortage of funds, governments review policies. While this can be carried to unpalatable extremes, it can also work to the advantage of the activist. In the heritage business, for example, we have a superb opportunity to pursue arguments for a clear, positive, national conservation and preservation policy, following up on the conference in Edmonton in 1991, and this symposium. We can work together with the provinces, assembling the goodwill of Premiers and Ministers, marshalling the energy and enthusiasm of hundreds of thousands of volunteers. We can also get our act together and share with policy- and decision-makers the fact that heritage infrastructure is good business, that it creates jobs, and is a vital element in our lucrative tourist industry. Every dollar invested in heritage conservation generates profit for Canada.

A third reality is the complex and costly process of citizen participation, now accepted as being integral to every level of government. It can be a monster of sorts; too little signals autocracy and disdain for public opinion. Too much suggests indecision at best, incompetence at worst. Bungled efforts to consult the people are almost worse than none at all, as they reinforce and feed the cancer of cynicism.

How not to bungle? Let me count some ways, as a guide to politicians:
- make best use of helpers competent in group process
- agree on specific terms of reference for the issue at hand
- distribute in advance clearest possible background material
- determine time frames and deadlines for recommendations
- listen with patience and respect
- promise only what can be delivered
- create an atmosphere of honesty, civility, and good faith

Permeating these realities of twenty-first century government is the spectre of instant information. As the pace of our world accelerates and we learn more at the speed of light, as the goat appetite of the media must be fed, the role of both the activist and the politician becomes increasingly difficult. The need for balance and wisdom presses hard. We are almost in gridlock on the Information Highway, with little relief in sight, jammed as we are with opinions, ideas, polls, and commentary. This further reality reinforces the contention that the good citizen must prepare for intelligent intervention in the affairs of state.

Preparation for activism requires a sustained study and understanding of communities, knowing how demographics influence our actions. It must include surefootedness in Parliamentary procedure; rules of order and debate; and understanding of how groups work and how leadership and chairmanship function, how people act, interact and react. It demands skills in writing clearly, speaking effectively, recording accurately, and being able to perform at least adequately on radio and television.

But our paragon is not yet ready for cap and gown. The successful activist is either a planner by profession or by osmosis, and in either case respects the planning process and makes maximum use of available expertise in the field. The successful activist also has a healthy respect for the career public servant, and is prepared to develop and nourish mutually helpful partnerships. It behooves the intelligent professional both in government and non-governmental organizations to learn all there is to know about working with volunteers; they are the richest resource in our social fabric and must be cherished accordingly.

We have evolved over the past two decades from vociferous confrontation, moving toward consultation, reaching for consensus. There are still mass rallies and protest marches and these may still be necessary. There will be, if need arises, avalanches of free post cards, floods of faxes flowing up Parliament Hill, blistering letters to editors, filibusters at municipal council meetings. But we are beginning to learn. We realize it is better to anticipate crises and circumvent them. It is better to find alternative ways to resolve conflict than to resort to fisticuffs. We are getting better at projecting options and consequences, enabling more intelligent choices, seeking ways to compromise within the range of accepted principles.

One irony of "no man's land" was that both sides thought they were right and that God was on their side. In every battlefield something of this prevails. This "space between" has become a symbol for our differences, for all that separates and aggravates – that which can and should be reconciled.

The space between is also dead space, where communication has been stifled; where contact of mind-to-mind or cause-to-cause has been aborted. This interstitial area can be compared to intertidal space in the ebb and flow of oceans – a brief time and space when something important can happen, lives can be saved, a rocky promontory reached, or a truth found.

The space between the hostile lines is there
To be acknowledged as reality. Then speak with tongues
And make a treaty; you have found
The ultimate in common ground.

To reach that common ground we must recognize the space between, acknowledge the gap, examine the differences with respect. Then "speak with tongues" as eloquent as those at Pentecost, finding the languages that can be understood by all the participants, not assuming that because it has been said it is automatically true or accepted. These precious words are the way through negotiations toward understanding, toward bridging the "space between" and finding a creative solution to the problem.

Those who do this are the citizens who affect public policy and whose footprints will be recorded. They are the gadflies and the critics, the conscience of our society. They bring their divine insanity to good works; they are essential outriders in the democratic process and have their place not only in history but in the rich and exciting future of our country.

Royal Alexandra Theatre, Toronto, Ontario: This lavish 1906-1907 Beaux-Arts playhouse was saved from demolition by Ed Mirvish in 1963; designated 1985. / Le théâtre Royal Alexandra, Toronto (Ontario) : Ce somptueuse théâtre de style Beaux-Arts construit en 1906-1907 fut sauvé de la démolition par Ed Mirvish en 1963 ; désigné en 1985. (Photo: CIHB / IBHC, W. Duford, 1987)

Volunteerism and Heritage Commemoration

Abstract

The post-recession economy and fiscal restraint at all levels of government has produced significant budgetary and operational challenges for heritage organizations. The major points discussed are: 1) not-for-profit organizations in the cultural sector are being forced to operate less like institutions and more like businesses; 2) their volunteer governing boards and staff are not well-prepared to deal with this change; and 3) we need to get people on our boards who have a talent for running things well rather than a passionate dedication to culture or heritage. The Newfoundland Historic Parks Association is described as a model organization with many of the characteristics needed to face the new economic realities confronting us.

Bénévolat et commémoration du patrimoine – Résumé

La situation économique de l'après-récession et les compressions financières effectuées à tous les niveaux de gouvernement se sont traduites par des défis budgétaires et opérationnels considérables pour les organismes voués à la protection du patrimoine. Les principaux points traités dans cette communication sont les suivants : 1) les organisations culturelles sans but lucratif sont forcées de fonctionner comme des entreprises plutôt que comme des institutions ; 2) les bénévoles qui composent leur conseil d'administration et leur personnel ne sont pas bien préparés à faire face à ce changement ; 3) nous devons recruter dans nos conseils d'administration des personnes possédant la capacité d'assurer la bonne marche d'une organisation, plutôt qu'un dévouement passionné à la culture ou au patrimoine. L'Association des parcs historiques de Terre-Neuve est présentée comme un organisme modèle doté d'un bonne nombres des caractéristiques nécessaires pour faire face aux nouvelles réalités économiques.

I welcome the opportunity to share some thoughts with you today on the topic of volunteerism and the governance of cultural organizations. We are at a time when economic conditions are forcing us to rethink long-held assumptions about not-for-profit organizations dedicated to the preservation of our heritage and culture. I have three observations for your consideration:

1) not-for profit organizations in the cultural sector are being forced to operate less like institutions and more like businesses; 2) their volunteer governing boards are not well-prepared to deal with this change and the unfamiliar challenges facing them; and 3) it is time to get people on our boards who have a talent for running things well rather than a passionate dedication to culture or heritage. I will end by describing the workings of one organization, the Newfoundland Historic Parks Association, which I believe exemplifies many of the characteristics needed to rise to the challenges facing us.

1. Not-for-profit organizations are being forced to operate less like institutions and more like businesses

The economic shocks imposed by the worst recession of our times are still reverberating in both public and private sectors. Private-sector companies have been forced to restructure and realign to become more efficient, to focus on quality in both products and services, to become customer-driven, to harness the power of an ever-expanding computer-based technology, to be globally competitive, and above all to sustain their profitability.

Our debt-ridden federal and provincial governments, meanwhile, are undergoing a fundamental shift in focus, from direct manipulation of the economy through subsidization and job creation, towards moulding an economic environment which encourages and supports private enterprise. Through privatization, contracting out, and downloading onto other agencies, governments are backing away from being providers of non-essential services and are moving in the direction of cost-recovery in the services they do provide.

As far as not-for-profit organizations are concerned, the trend is clear. There are pressures now to balance revenues and expenses and even to show a profit. There are pressures to identify exactly what it is we are doing and to market our services competitively. There are pressures to view the people coming through the door as customers and to look at ways in which they can be better served. There are pressures, in other words, to become fiscally responsible, more efficient, and more entrepreneurial in nature.

2. The governing boards of not-for-profit organizations are not well-prepared to deal with these changes

Board members and, in many cases, staff will find themselves part of an organizational culture that will come to resemble a business more than a government department, a situation not at all like the environment in which they have found themselves up to now. Management has too often been inward-looking and defensive, placing a higher value on playing it safe than on finding ways to bring about success. Management in an entrepreneurial environment involves measured risk-taking to accomplish objectives. The question is "What can we do today to succeed?" rather than "What do we have to do to avoid failure?"

This is a major challenge to governing boards, and is going to require changes in the way they function and especially in how they go about recruiting new board members. Our boards have typically been comprised of people who have shown an interest in or dedication to the cause of the organization. I am not being critical of their contribution. Quite the contrary, they are altruistic, dedicated individuals whose efforts have energized and sustained Canada's cultural heritage. In 1987 the Department of the Secretary of State carried out a National Survey on Volunteer Activity. They reported that there were 335,000 volunteers in the arts, culture, and humanities area – about 7% of the total of five million volunteers throughout the country. The typical volunteer in the arts and culture sector was an older, well-educated, urban person, more likely female than male, and with a higher than average income. Our board members have come from this pool of dedicated volunteers.

When those surveyed were asked why they got involved as a volunteer, most said it was because "Someone in the organization asked me." In searching out new board members, we have invited people who share our commitment to the cause. So we look for people like ourselves – patrons of the art gallery, visitors to the museum, someone who has restored an historic property, volunteers who have worked in the gift shop. This will have to change, which brings me to the third point.

3. It is time to get people on our boards who have a talent for running things well rather than a dedication to the cause

The increasingly entrepreneurial demands on cultural organizations means that we are going to have to seek out board members with the background and skills necessary to the task. We will need to recruit individuals who understand how organizations work – who understand planning and budgeting and how to operate in the black, who understand marketing and promotion and customer service, who understand the need to be proactive rather than reactive in the marketplace. Most of these people will come from the private sector.

I am not suggesting that governing boards should be taken over by business people and our organizations converted to businesses. They are not businesses, even though they will have to become more businesslike in the way they operate. They have a responsibility that goes well beyond the responsibility of business. They are custodians and promulgators of our culture, and board members must have an appreciation of this fact. What I am suggesting is that there has to be a healthy balance of board membership between those individuals with a passion for the cause and those who have a passion for seeing things run well.

The good news is that, with the ageing population, there is a growing pool of talent like this available to us. The leading edge of the celebrated "baby boom" generation has just passed the mid-40s and begins to turn 50 in 1996. They are at an age when people are known to take a greater interest in, and are more willing to participate in, cultural activities. These people are out there now waiting to be asked, and there are going to be more of them. We just have to make an effort to get them involved.

I would like now to turn to one organization that I have been involved with for the past ten years. The Newfoundland Historic Parks Association has, over that time, excelled in achieving its mandate and objectives. A description of how it operates will reinforce some of the points I have been making up to now. First, a sketch of what it does...

The NHPA was established in 1984 as a cooperating association with Parks Canada with a mandate to preserve, protect, promote, and interpret the history and heritage of Newfoundland and Labrador especially as it relates to the five National Historic Parks in the province. Its core activity, and the main source of its revenue, is the operation of gift shops at the Historic Parks plus another at a commercial shopping centre in St. John's.

The Association also has an active awards program which recognizes the work of other groups and individuals in restoration and maintenance of historic places throughout the province. As well, it has sponsored essay and poster contests in the schools on topics with an historic theme. And it has undertaken several major fundraising campaigns for special projects in the Parks.

Apart from Canada Employment grants for summer workers, the Association has never received government funding for its operations, and it has never incurred an operating deficit. In fact, it has an accumulated cash surplus, including funds in trust, of over $500,000. On top of this, it has contributed, directly and indirectly, in excess of $1.3 million to Parks operations in Newfoundland during its ten year history. A major objective over the next year is to identify new projects within its mandate to which it can lend financial support. In other words, it is looking for ways to spend its money.

Let me put this in context. Even though the people of Newfoundland on a per capita basis contribute more to charitable organizations than Canadians generally, it is by no means an easy place to raise money, particularly for causes that do not tug the heart strings. It is also not an easy place to run a gift shop operation, or for that matter, any kind of business. The economy of Newfoundland is not exactly booming. Add to that the fact that the NHPA has a very low public profile, and really no distinctive identity. It is continually confused with other heritage organizations, even with Parks Canada itself.

Why then has it had such an unusual degree of success? I can suggest the following reasons:

1. It has an excellent relationship with the sponsoring government agency.
From the beginning, the relationship that the Association has had with the Regional Office of Parks Canada has been cooperative and mutually supportive. Communication has been honest, open, direct, and cordial. There has always been advance consultation on policy changes that might affect either partner, and problems with the partnership have not been allowed to go unaddressed. We have worked at getting on well together.

2. There has been careful and balanced selection of board members.
The founding board members were brought in because they had the experience, reputation, connections, and ability to get things done. A demonstrated interest in heritage was not really considered. We assumed that someone who would agree to devote time to the Association would have some interest in its mandate. Most people who are active in business and in the community do value cultural preservation. The important point is that good board members are attracted to an organization that is doing something and doing it well.

We have since balanced the board with members recruited because of a primary interest in the mandate and they have been instrumental in helping us to expand our activities. We also achieve a balance by drawing on volunteers outside the board and on past members for help with specific projects.

3. A specific plan was put in place and followed.
Early on, the Association ran into problems with some of the gift shops and with sales of an art print portfolio. Financial difficulties ensued. The board decided to sit down at a one-day planning session to set a course of action and put things back on track. That is probably the single most important decision we have made. With the help of an outside facilitator, board members came away from that session with a clear idea of what the organization was, and what it should and should not be doing, plus a set of objectives and ways to achieve them. Yes, we followed the well-worn path to a mission statement, but that only provided the basis for the most important part of the exercise – the development of an action plan. A few years later, the same process was followed again to make sure

we were still on course and to make necessary adjustments, but it was the focused drive that came from the original planning day that caused the organization to thrive.

4. The organization is run like a business.

In fact, it is run far better than most businesses. Accounting functions are under tight control. The Executive Director works from a detailed budget and the board receives monthly financial statements. Job descriptions and salary ranges have been put in place for each staff position. The organization knows exactly where it is financially at any point in time and is able to make adjustments quickly and effectively. Three years ago, because of rapid expansion of product lines in the gift shops the board again faced the prospect of running a deficit on operations, but was able to move quickly to make the adjustments needed to bring in a profit at the end of the year.

5. The organization is entrepreneurial in spirit and outlook.

The Association is not afraid to take on new ventures once we have weighed the risks and potential rewards. There is an organizational instinct to move ahead and expand, coupled with a belief in "making haste slowly". There is also something approaching absolute fanaticism about not operating in the red. I sometimes think that, rather than "not-for-profit" the organization should be called "not-for-loss" – not such a bad guiding principle. (Do not-for-profit organizations interpret the term literally and start out with the objective not to make a profit and therefore not make one?) There is nothing wrong with making a profit in a not for-profit organization, as long as the profits are used to further the aims of its mandate.

6. There is a relaxed board environment.

The NHPA goes out of its way to make sure that board members have opportunities to enjoy themselves. There is always a Christmas party, and we have made a practice of holding our Annual General Meeting at a location outside St. John's so that the board can travel together at least once a year. There are tales of these excursions that are better left untold, but the point is that board members need an opportunity to have fun together. Being relaxed with one another carries over to good decision-making.

7. There is an atmosphere of excellence.

It is understood that whatever the Association takes on, it will do in the very best way possible, and conversely, if a project cannot be done well, it will not be attempted at all. This is a guiding principle for decision-making by staff and by the board, and permeates the whole organization. I cannot pinpoint how this came about, but I can tell you that once this principle becomes entrenched, it is almost impossible to lose, since everyone has a stake in keeping the standard high.

When you look at the list of characteristics which make this organization work, though, it all comes back to one overriding factor – the people who are involved. None of these factors would apply without the right people and the right mix of people on the board. And the same is true of any organization. Organizations are not good, bad, or mediocre in and of themselves – the people running them are. It is the responsibility of the board of a not-for-profit organization to see that it runs properly – not the staff, not the funding agency, but the board. The organization is accountable to the board, and the board has the obligation to see that the organization functions in the best possible manner, whatever the circumstances.

Governing boards throughout the country today are being challenged to this task as never before. They are going to have to change the way their organizations do business. The people who will help effect this change are waiting to be asked to get involved. We can rise to the challenge. Indeed, we must, for the alternative cannot be contemplated.

Winterholme, Rennie's Mill Road, St. John's, Newfoundland: built by Sir Marmaduke Winter in 1905-1907, it is a Queen Anne revival style mansion; designated 1991. / Winterholme, chemin Rennie's Mill, St. John's (Terre-Neuve) : cette résidence de style néo-Queen Anne fut construite par sir Marmaduke Winter entre 1905 et 1907 ; désignée en 1991. (Photo: HRS, 1984).

Heritage in the Future
L'avenir du patrimoine

"Inuksuk", Enukso Point, Northwest Territories / (Territoires du Nord-Ouest); designated 1969 / désigné en 1969. (Photo: Parks Canada / Parcs Canada, Photothèque, 1996)

STEPHEN M. SMITH

Does The Past Have A Future?

Abstract

There can be no doubt about the answer to the question of whether the past has a future: the past *must* have a future. What we have to ask ourselves is how we want to put it to use, in what ways we are willing to allow it to amplify and enrich our lives.

When you talk about the past, you can of course choose your own terms of reference. But too often we talk about the past as some kind of antiquity, as delicate as papyrus, likely to disintegrate if it is so much as looked at too intently. But what if we think of the past in terms of sturdy stuff – in terms of nature, say, in terms of a resource, a rich, hardy, self-perpetuating mineral that is nightly renewed underfoot, in the dark hours when today becomes yesterday, when present turns into past.

To make use of this resource, we have to be aware of it. And we are; it shows in our museums, our archives, our literature, our classrooms, and when historically significant properties are protected or commemorative plaques raised. These are all valuable technologies for memory. But what if we could somehow press on a step further with awareness; what if we could find a way to regard our past, in both its concrete representations and its more indistinct filaments, in the same way we have come to regard our environment? And what if we were to extend the duties associated with active citizenship to include responsibility for and stewardship of our history? If we talk about the future of the past, we have to talk about passing from one generation to the next the imagination and the will to manage and develop it as a resource. What is needed, perhaps, is not so much a call to arms as a call to imagination.

Le passé a-t-il un avenir ? – Résumé

La réponse à cette question ne fait aucun doute : le passé *doit* avoir un avenir. Ce qu'il faut nous demander, c'est comment nous voulons l'utiliser, c'est-à-dire de quelle façon nous sommes disposés à le laisser enrichir notre vie.

Lorsqu'il est question du passé, chacun peut, bien entendu, choisir ses propres points de repère. Trop souvent, cependant, nous en parlons comme d'une sorte d'objet ancien, de papyrus fragile, qui risque de se désintégrer si on le regarde trop intensément. Mais si on le considérait plutôt comme quelque chose de solide, d'étude, comme une matière issue de la nature, autrement dit comme une ressource, un minerai riche, résistant et autorégénérateur, qui se renouvelle chaque nuit sous nos pieds, pendant les heures sombres où aujourd'hui devient hier et où le présent se transforme en passé ?

Pour bien utiliser cette ressource, nous devons être conscients de sa valeur. Nous le sommes d'ailleurs : cela est évident dans nos musées, nos archives, notre littérature, nos salles de classe, et lorsque des lieux présentant un intérêt historique sont protégés ou que des plaques commémoratives y sont installées. Ce sont là autant de moyens de commémoration précieux. Mais que se passerait-il si nous pouvions pousser la prise de conscience un peu plus loin ? Si nous pouvions trouver un moyen de considérer notre passé, aussi bien dans ses représentations concrètes que dans ses ramifications plus indistinctes, de la même manière que nous en sommes venus à regarder notre environnement ? Et si nous élargissions les devoirs associés au civisme pour assumer, en plus, la réappropriation et la mise en valeur de notre histoire ? Lorsque nous parlons de l'avenir du passé, nous devons parler de la transmission de l'histoire entre les générations, ainsi que de l'imagination et de la volonté nécessaires pour la gérer et l'exploiter comme une ressource. Ce qu'il faut, ce n'est peut-être pas tant un appel aux armes qu'un appel à l'imagination.

I would like to take as a setting for these remarks a place that lies to the west of Parliament Hill, a low-lying, lakeside place bounded by willows and reeds and rushes, where in the summer the air is sweetly savoury and the world is sharp-edged in the sunlight. There is a house at this place, a whimsical, heavy-lidded, stuccoed structure. It is a place that has long been lodged in my heart and it is a place, this past summer, that the Historic Sites and Monuments Board of Canada recognized with commemorative plaques. It was, still is, Stephen Leacock's place, the house and property in Orillia, Ontario, to which each year, early this century, he removed himself so that he could write far from the stresses and strictures of society.

I will ask you to step for a moment out onto Leacock's verandah. Our purpose on this porch is not to focus too narrowly on Leacock, or Mariposa, the town that his imagination fashioned from Orillia in *Sunshine Sketches of a Little Town*. There are, as we well know, many other National Historic Sites worthy of focus, as well as many other sites that, for whatever reason, have not yet been officially recognized. Fil Fraser writes of absorbing the vibrations of a place. For me, Leacock's property at Orillia is a place where the vibrations verge on the seismic. There are other places that have the same effect: two examples are the cairn to Tom Thomson on Canoe Lake in Algonquin Park and the place that used to be called Smith's Creek, where an ancestor of mine laid the foundation of what is today Port Hope, Ontario. I don't think we should discount or underestimate these kinds of personal and intangible connections to the past, this electricity of place.

But why should Leacock's house, as a representative National Historic Site, a representative place from our past, have a place in our future? Because in this place an inimitable imagination bloomed. The architecture here is important because of its associations with Leacock and his singular comic vision. Leacock's house is a place where our collective memories of him can coalesce. If you visit the house, there are guides to help you navigate a way into Leacock's world, but in large part this place is connected to the past by a current of imagination. Yes, we need money and legislation and will to steward our history into our future. But we also need imagination, not least to understand just what the past is and how we can put it to use. Like other worthy sites across the country, Leacock's house is a kind of seed-bed: a place for the past to alight, earth in which our own present-day imaginations can take root.

When we talk about the past we tend to choose frames of reference that apply to the most fragile of long-buried artifacts. Too often, history becomes in our minds an all too delicate substance, as frail as ancient papyrus, likely to powder if we so much as look at it intently. But what if we project to young minds the idea of history as a sturdier, lively stuff – in terms, say, of a natural airborne element, rich, tenacious, and self-perpetuating – something like, say, imagination. Then it can be more easily represented that imagination does not just alight in the sanctuaries we set aside, on sanctioned properties like Leacock's; it is abroad everywhere.

And if we agree also that this is an organic element, like a language, a language of stories? Then we need to remind ourselves that we need it to communicate among ourselves, and that, if we are not careful, it can be blunted or brutalized.

As Professor Symons has written so memorably in his opening chapter, we have an imperative in integrating heritage values into the environmental ethic. We have learned that we cannot trifle with the air we breath, the water we drink, the earth we tread. We have shown that as a society we can adjust our sights in order to survive. And yet as a community, we can still be willfully heedless when it comes to this other critical question of environment. History is very definitely environment. Too often, too many of us do not hear the vibrations that confirm this. Maybe it is partly because the past and the history we draw out of it cannot be quantified – we cannot talk about parts per million when it comes to history; we cannot estimate its value in dollars – just as we cannot exactly measure ignorance.

We are not entirely cavalier with the past; there is proof of commitment here today, in this auspicious assembly and in the work the Board does, as well as in the other valuable technologies we have for putting the past to use. The technologies I am talking about – the ones we use to engage this element, to help us speak in this language – these technologies do not look like a dehumidifier, or a Geiger counter. The technologies I am thinking of are museums and archives, our literature, our classrooms. With these, we cull the stories of ourselves from the air. We have to go on identifying these technologies, making sure they are in working order, and protecting them when they are threatened. And we should be passing on to younger minds and imaginations the ideals by which they are are informed, by which they operate, by which they develop. But we should also be promoting the idea that history can alight, that it can grow, in any receptive soil – that it is alive among us. If we are constantly assessing its place and its effects – then I think we would not find ourselves so often having to justify the need to shield from neglect or destruction our historic buildings, our old-growth forests, our oral histories.

All this is to say the past does emphatically have a future – but we have to be sure that we are attuned not just to its physical manifestations. That, I suppose, leaves a challenge in the air, a challenge to us all to take a wider view. But maybe the challenge is mainly to my generation and the ones immediately following mine. Mine is often depicted as a generation wired to computers, feeding off the etherworld of the Internet. I do not say we should shun that technology and the future it promises. As we have heard here, these technologies do not cancel each other out. And I do not think the generation of which I am part – not to mention the ones following on my heels – has floated so far into what gets called cyberspace that we cannot be animated and engaged by historical imagination. The young do need to be encouraged, to be incited – well, so do the post-young and post-post-young, while we are at it – to keep thinking creatively about the past, how it lives in literature as well as in landscape, and how it feeds us. This symposium has been a very valuable call to imagination; as ever, the next order of business is to get the many wise and inspiring words heard here out to imaginations at large. Especially, I submit, to the young, whose present represents our future, which is to say our past. If you take my meaning.

I started with a writer; I would like to end echoing one. In November 1994, in Montréal, the Alberta novelist Rudy Wiebe accepted that year's Governor General's Award for English fiction. His prizeworthy novel, *A Discovery of Strangers*, is a triumph of historical imagination that tells a story of Sir John

Franklin's first journey through our Northwest Territories in 1819-21. In accepting his prize, Wiebe began with gratitude but quickly moved on to lament two particular instances of the flippant self-negation that too often gets into us in this country. He mentioned a Canadian politician who said that we have too much geography and not enough history; he mentioned a Canadian poet who said that we are haunted by our lack of ghosts. Fie, Wiebe said, fie on both of them. If anything, he argued, we are haunted by our ignorance. "We know too little about ourselves", he continued, pointing out that people have been living in our country for more than 11,000 years, or about 550 generations.

> In this enormous, beautiful land we inhabit, we seem to have no eyes to see, no ears to hear, the stories that are everywhere about us and clamouring to be told.
> I say, only the stories we tell each other – about ourselves, about each other – can sustain us. Because only the stories we tell each other about ourselves create us as a society, as a nation.
> Only the stories we tell each other will create us as a true Canadian people.

Stephen Leacock Home, Old Brewery Bay, Orillia, Ontario, built 1928; designated 1992 / La maison Stephen-Leacock, Old Brewery Bay, Orillia (Ontario), construite en 1928 ; désignée en 1992. (Photo: Parks Canada / Parcs Canada).

L'Anse aux Meadows, Newfoundland / (Terre-Neuve): the first authenticated Viking settlement in North America; designated 1968 / le première établissement viking reconnu en Amérique du Nord; désigné en 1968. (Photo: C.P.S. Archaeology, Parks Canada / Archéologie-S.C.P., Parcs Canada, 1975)

Le passé a-t-il un avenir ?

Résumé

La constitution d'un patrimoine national s'effectue par le biais d'un processus de sélection, en fonction de critères qui évoluent selon les époques. Cette constatation est particulièrement pertinente dans le cas du Canada, un pays où coexistent une multitude de traditions et d'interprétations de l'histoire. Pour l'avenir, la réinterprétation du patrimoine passe par un élargissement des critères d'analyse, par une reconnaissance plus grande de l'importance de la tradition orale ainsi que par la participation des communautés culturelles, et par une meilleure éducation du public en général et des jeunes en particulier dans un monde où les technologies de l'information rendent disponible une masse sans cesse croissante de données.

Does the Past Have a Future? – Abstract

The building of a national heritage is the result of a selection process based on the criteria that evolve over time. This observation is especially relevant in the case of Canada, a country where a multitude of traditions and interpretations of history are found. The reinterpretation of our heritage for the future will require an extension of the analysis criteria, increased recognition of the importance of oral tradition, participation by the cultural communities, as well as measures to better educate the public in general, and the young in particular, in a world where information technologies are making available an ever increasing quantity of data.

After two days of discussions where we have been travelling in our past and present history, the history of our country, history of our communities, history of our regions, I have been given the challenging task to do a kind of wrap-up session and to project the past into the future. This is challenging because so many interesting things have been said that I had to make a choice.

Vous me demandez de me projeter dans le futur et de chercher à trouver de nouvelles voies pour l'avenir. Mais, avant d'en arriver là, nous devons nous demander quel est donc ce passé auquel nous voudrions donner un avenir. Si vous demandez au grand public ce qu'est le patrimoine, il vous répondra que ce sont de vieilles pierres, le passé, le vieux. C'est la première image qui vient à l'esprit ; ce qui est vraiment dommage, car cette perception populaire va à l'opposé de tout le travail qui est fait pour commémorer le passé. En effet, bien que ce qui nous a été légué du passé soit inépuisable, nous avons créé un patrimoine par la sélection de ce qui est important pour chaque période de notre histoire. Notre patrimoine est en perpétuelle évolution, et le passé est en quelque sorte reconstitué sans cesse à notre image. Plus encore, les discussions qui ont eu lieu lors de ce symposium ont mis en évidence la multiplicité des interprétations de notre passé.

Le Canada est un pays bilingue à l'identité multiple où le Québec a une place particulière et où les Autochtones ont des traditions qui leur sont propres. Aussi, ce foisonnement d'interprétations n'a rien de choquant, bien au contraire. Il fait partie de notre vie quotidienne de Canadiens et reflète les valeurs et la culture de notre société. Cependant, le discours public a trop souvent tendance à oublier que ce passé est un trait d'union entre nos différences, un espace ouvert où chacun vient puiser les éléments essentiels à l'affirmation de ces valeurs.

La deuxième question que j'aimerais me poser avant de me projeter dans le futur fait référence à la nécessité de comprendre pourquoi le passé est si important dans notre vie. Notre patrimoine nous permet de mieux comprendre d'où nous venons et où nous allons. Notre quête d'identité est renforcée aussi par le contexte dans lequel nous vivons. Notre monde est en pleine mutation, comme l'illustrent la révolution technologique, l'autoroute électronique et la révolution des transports, laquelle raccourcit les distances entre les pays et les cultures. Nous vivons aussi à l'ère de la mondialisation, où la terre est devenue un village global à la Marshall McLuhan. Dans ce monde mouvant, nous avons besoin de points de repère d'une part, et de pouvoir avoir prise sur quelque chose, d'autre part. Par notre travail, nous contribuons au développement futur de notre patrimoine, et tout en préparant l'avenir, nous pouvons mieux définir notre identité. Dans cette perspective, le travail d'Annette Saint-Pierre en rapport avec l'histoire manitobaine, qui consiste à aider ses étudiants à renforcer leur identité culturelle, m'apparaît particulièrement intéressant.

Après ces quelques observations préliminaires, nous arrivons donc à nous poser la question centrale : quel avenir pour le passé ? S'il est vrai que le passé, tel qu'interprété par le patrimoine, est en perpétuelle évolution, la participation à ce processus de sélection nous aide à préparer l'avenir. Dans cette perspective, il convient de se demander quelles sont les orientations à prendre pour optimaliser ce processus de sélection pour l'avenir. Sans prétendre à l'exhaustivité, j'ai relevé parmi les interventions au symposium quelques orientations et défis pour l'avenir.

Dans un premier temps, il convient de rappeler que le futur passe de toute évidence par le développement de nouvelles attitudes et l'élargissement des critères d'analyse qui permettent la sélection des éléments constitutifs du patrimoine. Comme l'a affirmé le professeur Mathieu, la thématisation et la contextualisation constituent deux de ces critères. Selon lui, un objet qui n'a qu'une valeur patrimoniale modeste peut néanmoins contribuer à quelque chose de plus vaste. La professeure Hayden a elle-même fourni un exemple très intéressant dans ce sens. Le groupe qu'elle a mis en place sous le nom de « *Power of Place* » a trouvé une approche novatrice pour interpréter des immeubles présentant, au départ, un intérêt relativement modeste. L'architecture a ainsi été réinterprétée en fonction du vécu des femmes africaines-américaines, latino-américaines et japonaises-américaines.

Dans un deuxième temps, j'aimerais mentionner que le développement de nouvelles attitudes fait référence à la reconnaissance de l'importance croissante de la tradition orale, particulièrement dans un pays comme le Canada. Je reviens aussi à l'expérience d'Annette Saint-Pierre qui faisait des entrevues avec de vieux Métis racontant l'histoire. Ma propre expérience m'a aussi convaincue de l'importance de cette tradition orale. Un jour que je travaillais à un projet de recherche dans le nord du Canada, j'ai rencontré Léa Naturak, une femme absolument merveilleuse âgée de 104 ans. Dans sa maison, je me souviens d'avoir aperçu une assiette avec la cervelle fumante d'un phoque, un de ses mets favoris. Elle s'était aussi aménagé son petit musée du passé, car sur les murs on pouvait apercevoir des photos de pasteurs anglicans et de capitaines de navires qui avaient jalonné la vie de sa communauté dans le Nord. C'était, en quelque sorte, son lieu du souvenir et elle s'était mise à nous raconter comment, lorsqu'elle était jeune, elle était allée à la chasse avec son mari aux limites de la Baie d'Hudson. Elle avait alors entendu un bourdonnement étrange et continu et croyant qu'elle était attaquée par des abeilles géantes et monstrueuses, elle s'était cachée derrière sa tente. C'est là que son mari l'avait retrouvée tremblante et lui avait expliqué que ce qu'elle venait d'entendre était le premier avion qui arrivait dans la communauté pour livrer des provisions. Ainsi, l'arrivée de ce premier avion avait été pour Léa Naturak, et pour les gens de sa communauté, l'événement le plus marquant de leur vie.

Outre la reconnaissance de la tradition orale, notre société canadienne fait face au défi de la reconnaissance de la participation des communautés culturelles. Sans vouloir clore ici le débat lancé par le professeur Humphries, il importe de réfléchir sur les enjeux de cette question tout à fait fondamentale, si j'en juge par les réactions suscitées. Comment intégrer toutes ces contributions à notre histoire nationale, tout en évitant le piège d'une fragmentation de l'histoire et de l'identité ?

Le quatrième défi qui se pose à nous est celui de l'architecture moderne : comment pouvons-nous planifier dès maintenant ce qui sera important pour les vingt, trente et quarante prochaines années ? Je sais que la Commission des lieux et monuments historiques du Canada se préoccupe de cette question très importante, qui conditionne l'héritage que nous voulons transmettre à nos enfants.

J'aimerais maintenant soulever la question de la réinterprétation des lieux et des événements du passé à la lumière des nouvelles sensibilités. Je prendrais ici le cas de Skookum Jim, tel que présenté par Daniel Tlen. Après avoir été laissé dans l'ombre, Skookum Jim a finalement été reconnu comme le seul et unique découvreur du premier filon d'or du Klondike ; ce qui jette un éclairage très intéressant sur cette question de la réinterprétation du passé. Pour sa part, Christina Cameron a bien mis en évidence la nécessité de respecter les choix du passé sans chercher à les transformer ou à les camoufler, car ces interprétations sont elles-mêmes significatives du contexte d'une époque. Et sans doute faut-il aussi aller au-delà des interprétations toutes faites. Dans sa communication au symposium, Robert Scully expliquait son travail de diffusion de l'histoire réalisé avec La Fondation CRB dans le cadre des «Minutes du patrimoine» et qui mettait en évidence un travail qui a permis de soulever certaines contradictions intéressantes et de jeter ainsi un nouvel éclairage sur l'histoire.

De son côté, Robert Garon, citant Roland Arpin, affirmait qu'il faut en arriver à développer un partenariat avec différents intervenants ; notamment les municipalités, les universités, les centres de recherches, les réseaux scolaires, les organismes culturels, le secteur privé, les musées et tous les acteurs sociaux impliqués dans l'interprétation du passé et la création du patrimoine.

En terminant, j'aimerais soulever un défi de taille auquel nous faisons face : celui de l'éducation du public dans un monde où les nouvelles technologies sont en constante évolution. En effet, l'éducation du public nous oblige à poser la question de l'adaptation aux nouvelles technologies. Puisque mon temps de parole s'écoule, je me contenterai ici d'un exemple rapide. Il y a quelque temps, alors que je visitais le Salon du Livre, à Montréal, avec mes enfants, nous avons aperçu à un kiosque un ordinateur équipé d'un lecteur de CD-ROM. On présentait les voyages de Jacques Cartier au moyen de textes écrits et parlés, de cartes magnifiques et de diverses photos de lieux historiques, le tout incluant de la musique et des images d'une grande qualité. Dans le cadre de cette présentation interactive, l'enfant était situé au lieu de départ de Jacques Cartier et pouvait choisir différentes routes ou différentes époques, compte tenu de ses désirs. Cette expérience m'a permis de confirmer que l'approche de l'histoire de ces enfants va de plus en plus passer par l'ordinateur. Les enfants de l'informatique, du CD-ROM et de l'Internet auront ainsi à leur disposition une masse d'information concernant l'histoire. Il importe donc de nous demander, dès maintenant, de quelle façon nous pourrons les aider à trouver un fil conducteur et à se bâtir une identité à travers cette masse de données.

Telles sont les quelques réflexions que je voulais vous livrer au terme de ce symposium car, comme le disait Sénèque, il n'y a point de vent favorable pour celui qui ne sait où il va.

Grand-Pré (Nouvelle-Écosse) : Le lieu historique national est situé dans l'ancien établissement acadien de Grand-Pré et renferme l'église construite par les Acadiens entre 1922 et 1930 à titre de monument commémoratif de leur Déportation, ainsi que la statue d'Évangéline, immortalisée par le poète Longfellow. / Grand-Pré, Nova Scotia: The National Historic Site is located within the former Acadian settlement of Grand-Pré and contains the Church built by the Acadians between 1922-1930 as a memorial to their Deportation, as well as the statue of Evangeline, immortalized by the poet Longfellow. (Photo : Lieux historiques nationaux / National Historic Sites)

Le couvent des Ursulines, Québec ; désigné en 1972 / Ursulines Convent, Québec City; designated 1972. (Photo : Parcs Canada / Parks Canada, A. Guindon, 1986).

Fort Qu'Appelle (Saskatchewan) : fort de la Compagnie de la Baie d'Hudson ; désigné en 1953 / Fort Qu'Appelle, Saskatchewan: Hudson's Bay Co. Fort; designated 1953. (Photo : Parcs Canada / Parks Canada, Photothèque, 1974).

Closing Remarks
Allocution de clôture

DWELLING HOUSE.

A PLAN
of
SPRING PARK
in
PRINCE EDWARD ISLAND
The PROPERTY of ROBERT GRAY, Esq.

Spring Park, Charlottetown: The birth place in 1811 of John Hamilton Gray, Premier of Prince Edward Island and chairman of the Charlottetown Conference of the Fathers of Confederation in 1864. Demolished 1996. / John Hamilton Gray, premier ministre de l'Île-du-Prince-Édouard et président de la conférence des pères de la Confédération tenue à Charlottetown en 1864, naquit ici en 1811. Bâtiment démoli en 1996. (Photo: Prince Edward Island Public Archives and Records Office, 0,642 C).

A Race Against Time

By way of "Closing Remarks", may I offer just a few thanks, and a few observations?

First, I must thank the various speakers, who have given us such a feast of interesting, informative, and, sometimes, provocative papers. There have been, in fact, some thirty presentations made to the Symposium which have ranged over a wide spectrum of topics. There have been, as well, many perceptive questions and interventions from the floor.

Ensemble, ces communications et les questions et discussions qu'elles ont provoquées nous ont donné amplement de matière à réflexion. Ensemble, elles ont éclairé de nombreux aspects du dossier du patrimoine. Elles ont en outre souvent suscité des suggestions d'approches, de politiques, de priorités et de programmes nouveaux ou différents. Ceux-ci ont à leur tour été discutés et examinés lors des activités sociales du symposium – à la réception d'ouverture tenue au Musée canadien des civilisations, au cours des repas et des pauses café, ainsi qu'à la réception organisée par l'Office national du film à la Bibliothèque nationale et à l'exposé qui l'a suivie.

There has clearly been a remarkable and extensive exchange of information and ideas. For this, I thank every participant.

The Parliamentary Channel has filmed and recorded most of the Symposium. By this means, it will be available to a wider public.

In addition, arrangements have been made for a publication of the proceedings, under the auspices of the Royal Society of Canada, which will be, I hope, of continuing service to the heritage community, to teachers, and to the planners and makers of public policy, for years to come.

It is, of course, impossible to offer, on the spot, a summary or even an overview of the highlights of such a broad-ranging and substantive Symposium. A great many issues were aired and themes underlined. But perhaps I can venture just a few observations and impressions.

1. It is not surprising that, in this gathering, there was strong consensus on the value and importance of heritage. Of course, I agree. But I wondered, from time to time, if it might not be useful to have some more explicit discussion on this subject? The rationale for heritage needs constant review and exposition.

2. If heritage conservation is important, it is also urgent. Again, this theme was always present but not very often made explicit.

3. It appears that many aspects of the Canadian experience are still receiving little, or comparatively little, attention in terms of the study and exposition of their heritage significance. Examples of this include sports, recreation, and popular culture.

4. The interdependence of the many elements making up the heritage community was noted, as was the need for all these elements to learn to pull together. Going beyond this, the scope and the need for co-operation between the heritage community and other communities, such as the environmentalists, were noted.

5. There were calls for both vision and practicality, and for the need to keep these in balance.

6. It was frequently emphasized that heritage commemoration is not something confined to the past, that it should not be dead. On the contrary, it must deal with the present and the future, as well as the past, by promoting knowledge and understanding and an awareness of the on-going significance of significant things.

7. There was recognition of the special challenge involved for the processes of heritage recognition in dealing with the intangible parts of history – for example, oral histories, and influences and consequences in the human experience.

8. The need for historical honesty was noted and debated. Historical truth is often, clearly, whatever is in the eye of the beholder. None the less, the need for knowledge of historical context was underlined. So, too, was the need to recognize squarely the injustices of the past. On both counts, and many others, care must be taken to ascertain the facts.

9. The utility of in-depth studies of many special subjects was recognized. But there was concern that attention to, and understanding of, the whole be not lost sight of in the examination of the parts. History should be inclusive, not exclusive.

10. Accessibility to heritage was emphasized.

11. Somewhat in tandem with the arguments for accessibility, but in a more gingerly fashion, we heard arguments for opening the doors to a greater public participation in the whole of the heritage enterprise – including a fuller public participation in the planning and governance arrangements for heritage preservation and use. After all, it is the public that is paying for it!

12. There was some discussion about funding but not, I think, nearly enough. Questions about the ways and means for financing heritage deserve and require more attention.

13. Similarly, tax reform was mooted but not really explored. Changes are needed in definitions and in the tax treatment of the repair and maintenance of historic buildings. Incentives to demolition should be removed and replaced with incentives to preserve and make good use of heritage structures.

14. The lead responsibility of government in heritage preservation was, of course, noted. But so, too, was the importance of the role of the private citizenry and of associations, and of the rest of the private sector.

15. There are problems of mixed or uncertain jurisdiction in many heritage areas, underwater archaeology is one example, which need federal-provincial agreement.

16. The dangers of the Disneyland syndrome were noted.

17. There appears to be a movement away from the "monument culture" of built heritage towards a greater focus on the significance of the place, the person, the idea, and the event.

18. The utterly crucial role of heritage education, at every level and at every age, was apparently well-recognized, at least in this gathering. The challenge now is to achieve a better recognition amongst educators of the place of heritage in education.

From these, and many other themes, the conclusion is clear: We must all plough on, to do the job that needs to be done. However, in doing this, we must have in mind at all times both its urgency and its complexity. In all this, there should be few surprises. It is because heritage is so fundamental that the task of identifying, preserving, and deploying it can, at times, be so very difficult.

Dans l'ensemble, ce symposium a, je pense, contribué utilement à mieux faire comprendre le besoin d'agir pour préserver le patrimoine bâti du Canada et, en fait, tous les aspects de notre patrimoine. Il a en outre aidé à développer les fondements de cette préservation.

Some forty-five years ago, the Report of the Massey-Lévesque Commission reminded us of St. Augustine's definition of a nation as "an association of reasonable beings united in a peaceful sharing of the things they cherish; therefore, to determine the quality of a nation, you must consider what those things are." The information and views conveyed at this Symposium indicate, despite manifold concerns, that there is a growing consciousness of a Canadian heritage in all its diversity.

Yet, an examination of the record should remind us that ours has proven to be, thus far, a remarkably destructive society. The plundering of natural resources, the ravaging of nature, the abandonment of rail lines and of railway stations, the many mining and other company ghost towns, the silent lumber mills, the rotting grain elevators, the empty town centres, the destruction of landmarks, the displacement of native peoples, and much more, speak to this fact. The fate of much of our heritage reflects the wry comment that the history of Canadian technology embraces an advance from the axe to the bull-dozer.

Much of this loss has come more through sins of omission than sins of commission. Absent-mindedness, thoughtlessness, ignorance, and cultural amnesia all play a part, but so does rampant me-firstism. Very frequently those who care about heritage face the conundrum posed by individuals and organizations acting within their legal rights but in opposition to the broader public interest. This, in turn, leads to demands for government action to preserve heritage through regulations and various kinds of controls. Steps in this direction are clearly needed. But caution and balance are needed in trying to find solutions based upon the creation of bureaucracies. Excessive controls that mortgage the future to the past are no panacea. Not everything can or should be preserved. Humankind can only build for the future by ridding itself of some of the accumulations of the past. The key is education and research, areas in which the heritage movement, given the scale of the need, has so far made only a modest start.

The destructiveness which has marked so much of Canadian history is offset by what may be an advantage, that is, the essential conservatism of Canadian society. Canada's history, despite the changes of régime and varied experiences, features a remarkable degree of continuity which is perhaps the most fundamental characteristic of our society. It is a characteristic that the heritage-minded community needs to harness and to build upon. Given its innate conservatism, Canadian society should readily understand and relate to the conserver society ethic, but it has not yet quite done so.

L'étude de notre patrimoine bâti dans toute sa diversité devrait souligner le fait que la prise de conscience et l'appréciation mutuelles des cultures et patrimoines différents de notre pays sont à la base de tout sentiment du patrimoine canadien. Elles constituent, en fait, le patrimoine canadien. Et celui-ci est mieux servi par les thèmes du partenariat et de la bonne gestion, qui sont des fils essentiels du tissu fortement tendu de la société canadienne.

It must be faced that, despite some gains in recent years, heritage is still low in the priorities of Canada. Yet it has much to tell Canadians about themselves and to tell the world about Canada. Heritage has so much to contribute to our sense of community and to our sense of purpose in these troubled times, it is amazing that it has been so underfunded and so neglected as an area of public policy. Indeed, because heritage is so fundamental to our survival and progress as a society it needs to become the business of all Canadians.

We are involved in a race against time to save our heritage. It is a race we cannot afford to lose.

Sparks House, Ottawa: Nicholas Sparks, a Bytown pioneer, owned the land from Wellington to Laurier Street and from Waller to Bronson. His free-stone Georgian or Neo-Classical house was built in 1830. During the early part of the twentieth century its address was 359-361 Sparks Street. It was demolished in 1954 to make way for the Department of Trade and Commerce Building, now called the West Memorial Building, completed in 1955. / La maison Sparks, Ottawa : Nicholas Sparks, un pionnier de Bytown, était propriétaire des terres allant des rues Wellington à Laurier et Waller à Bronson. Sa maison en pierre franche de style anglais d'inspiration classique, ou néo-classique, fut construite en 1830. Au début du XXᵉ siècle, son adresse était le 359-361, rue Sparks. Elle fut démolie en 1954 pour faire place à l'édifice du ministère du Commerce, maintenant appelé Édifice commémoratif de l'Ouest, qui fut achevé en 1955. (Photo: courtesy of The Heritage Canada Foundation / gracieuseté de la Fondation canadienne pour la protection du patrimoine)

Kitchener City Hall, built in 1923 and demolished in 1973 / L'hôtel de ville de Kitchener, construit en 1923 et démoli en 1973. (Photos: Kitchener-Waterloo **Record** Photographic Negative Collection, Dana Porter Library, University of Waterloo)

The Thomson Building, Timmins, Ontario, built by Roy Thomson in 1939, was designated a national historic site in 1987 for both its architectural and historical significance. One of Canada's finest examples of unaltered Moderne architecture, the building housed newspaper offices and a pioneering Northern radio station which became the nucleus of the communication empire of Lord Thomson of Fleet. It was demolished in 1995. (Photo: courtesy of The Heritage Canada Foundation)

L'édifice Thomson, Timmins (Ontario), construit par Roy Thomson en 1939, a été désigné lieu historique national en 1987 en raison de son importance architecturale et historique. C'était un des plus beaux exemples d'architecture moderne non modifiée. Le bâtiment logeait les bureaux de journaux et la toute première station de radio du Nord, qui devint le noyau de l'empire de communications bâti par lord Thomson, baron de Fleet. Il a été démoli en 1995. (Photo : gracieuseté de la Fondation canadienne pour la protection du patrimoine)

St. Isidore Convent, Montréal, Québec: The last remnant of one of Montréal's earliest French settlements, the 150-year old convent situated on Notre Dame East, near the port in what was once Longue Pointe village, was demolished in 1996. It had been declared an historic site by the City of Montréal in 1990. / Le couvent Saint-Isidore, Montréal (Québec) : Dernier vestige d'un des premiers établissements français de Montréal, le couvent vieux de 150 ans situé dans la rue Notre-Dame est, près du port, dans l'ancien village de Longue-Pointe, a été démoli en 1996. Il avait été déclaré lieu historique par la Ville de Montréal en 1990. (Photo: *The Gazette*, Montréal)

297

Fire Hall No. 1, Saskatoon, Saskatchewan: One of the city's earlier brick structures (built 1908), this building facing the City Hall was a familiar landmark until it was demolished in 1965. / La caserne de pompiers n° 1, Saskatoon (Saskatchewan) : l'un des premiers pâtiments en brique de la ville (construit en 1908), cet édifice situé en face de l'hôtel de ville fut un point de repère familier jusqu'à sa démolition, en 1965. (Photo: LH448 gracieuseté de / courtesy of the Saskatoon Public Library Local History Room)

The charred remains of the historic Berube House, Beaumont, Alberta, used for fire practice by local firefighters, despite an offer to purchase by the Beaumont, and District Historical Society. "We thoroughly enjoyed using it," the Fire Chief told *LaNouvelle*, the town newspaper. / Les restes carbonisés de l'historique maison Bérubé, de Beaumont (Alberta), que les pompiers de la localité utilisaient pour leurs exercices d'évacuation, malgré l'offre d'achat faite par la Beaumont and District Historical Society. « Nous aimions beaucoup l'utiliser », a déclaré le capitaine de pompiers au journal local, *LaNouvelle*.

NOTES ON THE AUTHORS /
NOTICES BIOGRAPHIQUES DES AUTEURS

RICHARD M. ALWAY
President / Président, St. Michael's College, University of Toronto

Richard Alway was born and received his early education in Hamilton, Ontario. He was a gold medalist in philosophy at St. Michael's College and graduated from the University of Toronto *summa cum laude* in 1962. He has two graduate degrees in Modern History from the University of Toronto.

A long time Warden of Hart House, at the University of Toronto, he presently serves as the first lay President and Vice-Chancellor of the University of St. Michael's College, Toronto, a position he has held since 1990. He is also currently Chairman of the Montréal-based C.D. Howe Institute.

In the past Dr. Alway has served on a number of national cultural boards and advisory committees. A member of the Board of Trustees of the National Museums of Canada from 1979 to 1986, he was Chairman of the National Gallery of Canada, of the National Programmes Committee of the National Museums, and, at one point, Acting Chairman of the National Museum of Natural Sciences, as well as a member of the Board of the National Postal Museum.

Dr. Alway was appointed as a Member of the Order of Canada in 1989 in recognition of his work in educational, cultural, and ecumenical affairs. He was the founding Chairman of the Parish Council at St. Michael's Cathedral, and is a Knight of Malta and a Knight of the Holy Sepulchre.

Richard Alway est né à Hamilton (Ontario) et y a fait ses premières études. Il a reçu la médaille d'or en philosophie du St. Michael's College et a obtenu son diplôme de l'université de Toronto avec très grande distinction en 1962. Il est par ailleurs titulaire de deux diplômes supérieurs en histoire moderne de l'université de Toronto.

M. Alway a été directeur de la Hart House, à l'université de Toronto, pendant de nombreuses années. Il est, depuis 1990, le premier président et vice-recteur laïc du University of St. Michael's College, à Toronto. De plus, il occupe actuellement les fonctions de président de l'Institut C.D. Howe, qui a son siège à Montréal.

Par le passé, M. Alway a siégé à plusieurs conseils culturels et comités consultatifs nationaux. Membre du conseil d'administration des Musées nationaux du Canada de 1979 à 1986, il a été président du Musée des beaux-arts du Canada, du Comité des programmes nationaux des Musées nationaux et, pendant un temps, président suppléant du Musée national des sciences naturelles, ainsi que membre du conseil du Musée national de la poste.

M. Alway a été reçu Membre de l'Ordre du Canada en 1989 en reconnaissance de ses travaux dans les domaines de l'éducation, de la culture et des affaires œcuméniques. Il a été président fondateur du conseil paroissial de la St. Michael's Cathedral et est par ailleurs chevalier de l'ordre de Malte et chevalier de l'ordre du Saint-Sépulcre.

MARY ELIZABETH BAYER

Past Chair, Heritage Canada / Ancienne présidente de la Fondation canadienne pour la protection du patrimoine

Descendant of Red River settlers, born in Alberta, educated at St. Andrews, Manitoba, and the University of Manitoba, Mary Elizabeth Bayer has worked as Executive Director of the Central Volunteer Bureau in Winnipeg; as writer, researcher, and performer with CBC radio and television; as Executive Director of the Manitoba Centennial Corporation; and as Assistant Deputy Minister with the Government of Manitoba, responsible for culture and heritage.

Volunteer activities include Manitoba Historic Sites Advisory Board, founding Chair of Heritage Winnipeg, Governor for British Columbia and Chair of Heritage Canada, thirteen-year member and Life Member of the Heritage Society of British Columbia, on Board of Confederation Centre of the Arts, and Director of B.C. Heritage Trust. She is a poet, activist, living in Victoria.

Descendante de colons de la rivière Rouge, Mary Elizabeth Bayer est née en Alberta et a fait ses études à St. Andrews (Manitoba) et à l'université du Manitoba. Elle a été directrice générale du Central Volunteer Bureau, à Winnipeg, rédactrice, documentaliste et interprète aux réseaux de radio et de télévision de la CBC, directrice générale de la Société du Centre du centenaire du Manitoba et sous-ministre adjointe chargée de la culture et du patrimoine auprès du gouvernement du Manitoba.

À titre bénévole, elle a siégé au Conseil consultatif sur les sites historiques du Manitoba, a été présidente fondatrice d'Heritage Winnipeg ainsi qu'administratrice pour la Colombie-Britannique et présidente de la Fondation canadienne pour la protection du patrimoine. Elle fait partie depuis treize ans et est membre à vie de la Heritage Society of British Columbia. Elle siège par ailleurs au conseil du Centre des arts de la Confédération et est directrice de la B.C. Heritage Trust. Poétesse et militante, elle réside à Victoria.

WILLIAM J. BYRNE

Assistant Deputy Minister, Cultural Facilities and Historical Resources Division, Alberta Community Development / Sous-ministre adjoint, Division des installations culturelles et des ressources historiques, Développement communautaire de l'Alberta

Born in Raymond, Alberta in 1945, William J. Byrne received his B.A. in Archaeology from the University of Calgary and his M.Phil. and Ph.D. from Yale University. After three years with the National Museum of Man in Ottawa, he returned to Alberta as the founding Director of the Archaeological Survey of Alberta, a position he held from 1974 to 1980. In 1980 he became the Assistant Deputy Minister for the Historical Resources Division, and has since held that post. He has been Chairman of the Heritage and Legislation Policy Committee of the Canadian Archaeological Association since 1985.

Né à Raymond (Alberta), en 1945, William J. Byrne est titulaire d'un baccalauréat ès arts en archéologie de l'université de Calgary ainsi que d'une maîtrise et d'un doctorat en philosophie de l'université Yale. Après avoir travaillé trois ans au Musée national de l'homme, à Ottawa, il retourne en Alberta, où il devient directeur fondateur de l'Archaeological Survey of Alberta, poste qu'il occupe de 1974 à 1980. Cette année-là, il est nommé à son poste actuel de sous-ministre adjoint de la Division des ressources historiques. Il est par ailleurs président du comité de la politique du patrimoine et de la législation de l'Association canadienne d'archéologie depuis 1985.

CHRISTINA CAMERON

Director General, National Historic Sites Directorate, Department of Canadian Heritage / Directeur général, Direction générale des lieux historiques nationaux, ministère du Patrimoine canadien
Secretary, Historic Sites and Monuments Board of Canada / Secrétaire de la Commission des lieux et monuments historiques du Canada

Currently Director General of the Department of Canadian Heritage's National Historic Sites programme, Christina Cameron has had an extensive career as an architectural historian and senior manager in Canada.

After undergraduate studies in English Language and Literature at the University of Toronto, she obtained a Master of Arts degree from Brown University in the History of Art and Museology. In 1982, she completed her Ph.D. at Université Laval in the History of Architecture.

Since 1970, Christina Cameron has held a succession of posts in Parks Canada. She is now responsible for the policy development and functional direction of a national system of Canadian historic sites, the protection of heritage railway stations in Canada, and the implementation of the Federal Heritage Buildings policy. She also serves as Secretary to the Historic Sites and Monuments Board of Canada.

Christina Cameron has served as President of the Society for the Study of Architecture in Canada, Rapporteur and Chairman of the World Heritage Committee of Unesco, a member of the Advisory Board of the Canadian Centre for Architecture in Montréal, and a member of the Editorial Board of the *Journal of Canadian Art History*.

Christina Cameron est actuellement directeur général du Programme des lieux historiques nationaux du ministère du Patrimoine canadien. Elle a eu une carrière bien remplie à titre d'historienne de l'architecture et de cadre supérieur au Canada.

Après avoir réussi des études en langue et en littérature anglaises à l'université de Toronto, elle a obtenu une maîtrise en histoire de l'art et en muséologie de l'université Brown. En 1982, elle recevait un doctorat en histoire de l'architecture de l'Université Laval.

Depuis 1970, Christina Cameron a occupé divers postes à Parcs Canada. Elle est actuellement responsable de l'élaboration de la politique et de la direction fonctionnelle d'un réseau national de lieux historiques au Canada, de la protection des gares ferroviaires patrimoniales du Canada et de la mise en œuvre de la politique sur les édifices fédéraux à valeur patrimoniale. Elle est par ailleurs secrétaire de la Commission des lieux et monuments historiques du Canada.

Mme Cameron a été présidente de la Société des études architecturales au Canada, rapporteur et présidente du Comité du patrimoine mondial de l'Unesco, membre du comité consultatif du Centre Canadien d'Architecture à Montréal et membre du comité de rédaction des *Annales d'histoire de l'art canadien*.

TRUDY COWAN
Heritage Consultant / Consultante en matière de patrimoine, Calgary
Former Alberta Member, Historic Sites and Monuments Board of Canada / Ex-membre de la Commission des lieux et monuments historiques du Canada pour l'Alberta

Educated at the universities of Toronto and Calgary, Trudy Cowan has more than twenty-five years experience in the museum, historic site, heritage preservation, and broader cultural fields. During this time she has been head of educational programming at the Glenbow Museum; Curator/Director of Fort Calgary while that historic site was being developed from an under-used railway yard into an interpretive centre and park; Executive Director of the Alberta Historical Resources Foundation; and for ten years has successfully operated her own consulting business. Ms. Cowan has also created two theatrical "In-Person-Ations" of significant women from Canada's past, and she chairs a project to rehabilitate Calgary's Beaulieu, the historic Lougheed House. An author and editor, she has served on many boards at the local, provincial, and national levels.

Trudy Cowan a fait ses études à l'université de Toronto et à l'université de Calgary; elle possède plus de vingt-cinq années d'expérience dans les domaines des musées, des lieux historiques, de la conservation du patrimoine et de la culture en général. Au cours de sa carrière, elle a été directrice du programme d'éducation du musée Glenbow; conservatrice-directrice du fort Calgary lors des travaux d'aménagement de ce lieu historique, qui était auparavant une gare ferroviaire sous-utilisée, en un centre d'interprétation et un parc; et directrice générale de l'Alberta Historical Resources Foundation. Elle exploite maintenant avec succès sa propre entreprise de consultation depuis dix ans. Auteure et rédactrice, Mme Cowan a incarné à la scène deux femmes célèbres de l'histoire du Canada dans des pièces de sa propre composition. Elle est par ailleurs présidente d'un projet de remise en état de la maison historique Lougheed (Beaulieu), à Calgary, et a siégé à de nombreux conseils aux paliers local, provincial et national.

JEAN DU BERGER

Professeur d'ethnologie au Département d'histoire / Professor of Ethnology, Department of History, Université Laval

Docteur ès lettres de l'Université Laval de Québec (1980), Jean Du Berger fut d'abord professeur de littérature canadienne et de folklore à l'Université Laval à partir de 1964, puis professeur d'ethnologie à partir de 1971. Depuis 1981, il est chercheur au Centre d'études sur la langue, les arts et les traditions populaires des Français d'Amérique (CELAT) de l'Université Laval. Il a été président de l'Association canadienne d'ethnologie et de folklore (1989-1990) ainsi que du Centre de valorisation du patrimoine vivant de Québec (1988-1993). Il a par ailleurs été président du Comité organisateur des États généraux du Patrimoine vivant (juin 1992). Dans le domaine du patrimoine vivant, il a dirigé une mission auprès du ministère de l'Enseignement supérieur et de la Recherche scientifique du Rwanda par l'entremise du Programme spécial de développement de l'Agence de coopération culturelle et technique (ACCT) pour la mise sur pied de la Collecte globale et systématique de la tradition orale (juillet-août 1987). Il a animé plusieurs séries d'émissions à la radio MF de la Société Radio-Canada : *Traditions et chansons* (1981-1982), *Démons et merveilles* (1984-1985), *Les Héros qui nous habitent* (1985-1986) et *Voyage au centre de la ville* (1990-1991). De plus, il a participé à deux films de Gilles Carle : *Vive Québec !* et *Le Diable d'Amérique*.

Jean Du Berger holds a Ph.D. in Literature (1980) from Université Laval where he also taught Canadian Literature and Folklore (1964-1971) and Ethnology (1971-1981). Since 1981 he has been a researcher at the University's Centre d'études sur la langue, les arts et les traditions populaires des Français d'Amérique (CELAT). He has been president of the Folklore Studies Association of Canada (1989-1990) and of the Centre de valorisation du patrimoine vivant de Québec (1988-1993), and chaired the Organizing Committee of the États généraux du Patrimoine vivant, held in June 1992. In the field of living heritage, he led a delegation to Rwanda's Department of Higher Education and Scientific Research through the Special Development Program of L'Agence de Coopération Culturelle et Technique (ACCT) for the establishment of a Global and Systematic Collection of Oral Tradition (July-August 1987). Mr. Du Berger has hosted several series on the FM radio network of La Société Radio-Canada, namely *Traditions et Chansons* (1981-1982); *Démons et Merveilles* (1984-1985); *Les Héros qui nous habitent* (1985-1986); and *Voyage au centre de la ville* (1990-1991). He also took part in two films produced by Gilles Carle: *Vive Québec !* and *Le Diable d'Amérique*.

DOROTHY DUNCAN
Executive Director, The Ontario Historical Society / Directrice générale de l'Ontario Historical Society

Dorothy Duncan is currently the Executive Director of The Ontario Historical Society, and a contributing editor to *Century Home* Magazine, published in Port Hope, Ontario. Dorothy writes the "Country Fare" column that covers Canadian food traditions.

Mrs. Duncan has served as a Board Member for Heritage Canada and for the American Association for State and Local History. She has also served as a Board member for the Ontario Heritage Foundation and as Chair of the Foundation from 1992 to 1994.

Mrs. Duncan is a former Curator of Black Creek Pioneer Village in Metropolitan Toronto and Museums Advisor for the Province of Ontario.

Dorothy Duncan est actuellement directrice générale de l'Ontario Historical Society et collabore à titre de rédactrice à la revue *Century Home*, publiée à Port Hope (Ontario). Elle y rédige la chronique intitulée « Country Fare », qui porte sur les traditions alimentaires canadiennes.

Mme Duncan a été membre du conseil d'administration de la Fondation canadienne pour la protection du patrimoine et de l'American Association for State and Local History. Elle a également siégé au conseil de la Fondation du patrimoine ontarien et a occupé la présidence de l'organisme de 1992 à 1994.

Elle a par ailleurs été conservatrice du Black Creek Pioneer Village, dans le Grand Toronto, et conseillère en matière de musées auprès de la province de l'Ontario.

ANGÉLINE FOURNIER
Chercheure et associée senior / Researcher and Senior Associate, FTTG, Montréal

Angéline Fournier est chercheure et associée senior de FTTG à Montréal, groupe de consultation dans le domaine de la prospective et de la planification stratégique (gouvernance).

Mme Fournier est auteure d'analyses touchant au développement social, économique et culturel du Canada et du Québec. Elle a traité, entre autres, de questions touchant à l'identité canadienne, à l'identité québécoise, à l'identité culturelle canadienne et québécoise, à l'avenir de la langue française. Conférencière, elle a aussi traité de sujets portant sur la réforme constitutionnelle, de la place du Québec dans la Confédération, de la place du Canada dans le monde, de la question de l'identité canadienne. Elle a publié au Canada, en France et aux États-Unis, dans *La Presse*, *Le Devoir*, *The Globe and Mail*, *The Christian Science Monitor*, *Politique Internationale* et *World Affairs*.

Mme Fournier est juriste de formation et a travaillé comme avocate à Paris (dans le domaine des droits d'auteur) et à Montréal. Elle est titulaire d'une maîtrise en droit de l'Université McGill et d'une maîtrise eu droit commercial de l'Université de Paris V.

Angéline Fournier is a researcher and senior associate at FTTG in Montréal. This consultative group specializes in prospects and strategic planning (governance).

Madame Fournier has written essays on the social, economic and cultural development of Canada and Québec. She has discussed, among other things, issues relating to the Canadian identity, the Québécois identity, the Canadian and Québécois cultural identity, and the future of the French language. She has also given lectures on constitutional reform, Québec's place in Confederation, Canada's place in the world, and the issue of Canadian identity. She has published articles in Canadian, French, and American newspapers and periodicals including *La Presse*, *Le Devoir*, *The Globe and Mail*, *The Christian Science Monitor*, *Politique Internationale* and *World Affairs*.

Madame Fournier trained and worked as a lawyer in Paris (where she specialized in copyright law) and in Montréal. She is a graduate of McGill University (Master of Law) and holds a master's degree in commercial law from Université de Paris V.

FELIX (FIL) FRASER
Former Chief Commissioner, Alberta Human Rights Commission / Ancien commissaire en chef de la Commission des droits de la personne de l'Alberta

Fil Fraser has been a life-long journalist, a radio and television programme director and administrator, and a television and feature film producer. His (dramatic) films include *Why Shoot The Teacher*, *Marie Anne*, and *The Hounds Of Notre Dame*. He has been involved in the development of public policy as a member of the Alberta Task Force on Film, the Canadian Multiculturalism Council, and the Federal Task Force on Broadcasting Policy (Caplan/Sauvageau).

Between 1989 and 1992, Fraser served a three-year term as Chief Commissioner of the Alberta Human Rights Commission. During that time, between November 1990 and June 1991, he served as a member of the Citizens' Forum on Canada's Future (the Spicer Commission).

In the fall of 1994 he began a series as host/presenter of "Other Voices", Wednesday evening programming on VISION-TV. He is now the President and Chief Executive Officer of VISION-TV, a national specialty channel.

Fil Fraser a travaillé toute sa vie comme journaliste, directeur et administrateur d'émissions de radio et de télévision, réalisateur de télévision et producteur de longs métrages. Parmi ses films (dramatiques) figurent *Why Shoot the Teacher*, *Marie Anne* et *The Hounds of Notre Dame*. Il a participé à l'élaboration de la politique gouvernementale à titre de membre de l'Alberta Task Force on Film, du Conseil canadien du multiculturalisme et du Groupe de travail fédéral sur la politique de la radiotélévision (groupe Caplan-Sauvageau).

De 1989 à 1992, M. Fraser a rempli un mandat de trois ans à titre de commissaire en chef de la Commission des droits de la personne de l'Alberta. Au cours de cette période, il a siégé au Forum des citoyens sur l'avenir du Canada (commission Spicer) de novembre 1990 à juin 1991.

À l'automne de 1994, il avait entrepris, à titre d'hôte et de présentateur, une série d'émissions intitulée « *Other Voices* », qui était diffusée le mercredi soir sur les ondes de VISION/TV. Il est actuellement président et chef de la direction de la chaîne nationale spécialisée VISION/TV.

FRANCE GAGNON PRATTE
Présidente / Chairperson, Conseil des monuments et sites du Québec

France Gagnon Pratte est historienne de l'architecture et présidente du Conseil des monuments et sites du Québec et de la Fondation québecoise du patrimoine, organismes privés fondés en 1975 pour la protection et la défense du patrimoine.

Elle est l'auteure d'un ouvrage sur les villas anciennes de Québec intitulé *L'architecture et la nature à Québec au XIXe siècle : Les villas*, et d'un ouvrage sur les architectes Maxwell, *Maisons de campagne des Montréalais 1892-1924 : L'architecture des frères Maxwell*. Elle est coauteure du catalogue sur l'exposition canadienne sur l'architecture des Maxwell, *L'architecture d'Edward et William Maxwell*, d'un livre publié lors du centenaire du Château Frontenac, *Le Château Frontenac : Cent ans de vie de château* et d'un livre sur l'hôtel Royal York.

France Gagnon Pratte est vice-présidente des Éditions Continuité, qui publient le seul magazine en français sur le patrimoine au Québec, *Continuité*.

France Gagnon Pratte is an architecture historian and chairperson of Le Conseil des monuments et sites du Québec and the Heritage Québec Foundation, two private heritage preservation and conservation organizations established in 1975.

Her publications include a book on Québec City's early villas, *L'architecture et la nature à Québec au XIXe siècle : Les villas*, and a book on the architecture of the Maxwell brothers, *Maisons de campagne des Montréalais, 1892-1894 : L'architecture des frères Maxwell*. She is a co-author of *L'architecture d'Edward et William Maxwell*, the catalogue for the Canadian exhibition on the two architects' work; of *Le Château Frontenac : Cent ans de vie de château*, a book published for the hotel's centenary; and of a book on The Royal York Hotel.

France Gagnon Pratte is vice-president of Les Éditions Continuité, publisher of *Continuité*, the only French-language magazine on Québec heritage.

ROBERT GARON
Archiviste national du Québec / National Archivist of Québec

Professeur d'archivistique et d'histoire à l'Université Laval de 1969 à 1975, Robert Garon est ensuite passé au service du gouvernement du Québec. Après deux années au ministère des Affaires intergouvernementales, il est entré aux Archives nationales du Québec à titre de conservateur adjoint, puis de conservateur. De septembre 1991 à avril 1994, il a aussi été directeur général du patrimoine au ministère de la Culture et des Communications du Québec. Il a présentement la responsabilité des Archives nationales et du Centre de conservation du Québec.

Sous sa direction, les Archives nationales du Québec ont complété leur déconcentration, en ouvrant en 1980 leur neuvième et dernier centre régional ; l'Assemblée nationale du Québec a adopté, en 1983, la *Loi sur les archives*, modèle d'ouverture sur le partenariat, qui a inspiré nombre de législatures ; les Archives nationales du Québec ont réglé l'épineux problème des archives judiciaires. Son passage à la Direction générale du patrimoine a permis de jeter les bases d'une nouvelle approche de gestion du patrimoine dont les assises seront le partage des responsabilités, l'engagement de la population, l'insertion du patrimoine dans le cadre de vie et le patrimoine contemporain.

Robert Garon taught archival science and modern history at Université Laval from 1969 to 1975 before joining the Québec public service. After working for two years in the Department of Intergovernmental Affairs, he moved to the National Archives of Québec where he became Assistant Curator and later Curator. From September 1991 to April 1994, he was also Director General of Heritage in the Québec Department of Culture and Communications. He is currently responsible for the National Archives and the Centre de conservation du Québec.

During his tenure, the National Archives of Québec opened their ninth regional centre in 1980, thus completing their decentralization program; in 1983, the Québec National Assembly passed the Archives Act, which provides a model of a partnership focus that has inspired many other legislatures; and the Québec National Archives dealt with the difficult problem of judicial archives. As head of the Heritage Directorate, Mr. Garon lay the foundations of a new approach to heritage management based on the sharing of responsibilities, the involvement of the public, the inclusion of heritage issues in everyday life, and contemporary heritage.

JOHN FERGUSON GODFREY

Member of Parliament, Parliamentary Secretary to the Minister for International Cooperation and Minister Responsible for la Francophonie / Député, secrétaire parlementaire du ministre de la Coopération internationale et ministre responsable de la Francophonie

John Godfrey was first elected as a Liberal Member of Parliament for the Toronto riding of Don Valley West in the General Election of October 1993. He was appointed Chairman of the Standing Committee on Canadian Heritage by Prime Minister Jean Chrétien in January 1994. In September 1995, he was appointed Chairman of the Standing Committee on Industry. In February 1996 he was appointed as the Parliamentary Secretary to Pierre Pettigrew, Minister of International Cooperation and Minister Responsible for la Francophonie.

Mr. Godfrey was educated at the University of Toronto and earned his M.Phil and D.Phil. from the University of Oxford. He began his working career as an academic at Dalhousie University in Nova Scotia where he taught for seventeen years as a professor of history, ten of which he also served as President of the University of King's College, Halifax.

John Godfrey is familiar to many as the Editor of *The Financial Post*, a position he held from 1987 to 1991. Before becoming the Member of Parliament for Don Valley West, he was Vice-President of the Canadian Institute for Advanced Research, one of Canada's leading research institutes, with programmes studying social, economic and scientific issues of major importance for Canada.

John Godfrey a été élu député libéral de la circonscription de Don Valley-Ouest lors des élections générales d'octobre 1993. Le premier ministre Jean Chrétien l'a nommé président du Comité permanent sur le patrimoine canadien en janvier 1994. En septembre 1995, il est devenu président du Comité permanent de l'industrie. En février 1996, il a été nommé secrétaire parlementaire du ministre de la Coopération internationale et ministre responsable de la Francophonie, M. Pierre Pettigrew.

M. Godfrey a fait ses études à l'université de Toronto et est titulaire d'une maîtrise et d'un doctorat en philosophie de l'université d'Oxford. Il a commencé sa carrière à l'université Dalhousie, en Nouvelle-Écosse, où il a enseigné l'histoire pendant dix-sept ans ; au cours de cette période, il a également été président du University of King's College, à Halifax, pendant dix ans.

M. Godfrey est bien connu de nombreux Canadiens à titre de rédacteur du *The Financial Post*, fonction qu'il a occupée de 1987 à 1991. Avant son élection au Parlement, il était vice-président de l'Institut canadien de recherches avancées, l'un des principaux instituts de recherche du pays, dont les programmes d'étude touchent des questions sociales, économiques et scientifiques d'importance capitale pour le Canada.

ALBINA GUARNIERI
Member of Parliament, Former Parliamentary Secretary to the Minister of Canadian Heritage / Députée, ancienne secrétaire parlementaire du ministre du Patrimoine canadien

Albina Guarnieri was first elected to represent the riding of Mississauga East in the House of Commons in 1988. Prior to taking public office, her private sector experience included *Time Magazine*, *The Globe and Mail*, the Ontario Institute for Studies in Education, and the Ontario Waste Management Corporation. She was also Press Secretary to a Solicitor-General of Canada, Ontario Liberal Leader Stuart Smith, and Toronto Mayor Art Eggleton.

Albina Guarnieri was a member of the Standing Committee on Canadian Heritage and has served on the Standing Committee on Health and Welfare and the Sub-Committee on Poverty. She was also a member of the Canadian Delegation to the conference of the Association of South East Asian Nations in Jakarta, Indonesia (September 1992).

On 25 October 1993, Ms Guarnieri was re-elected to Parliament. In December 1994 she was appointed Parliamentary Secretary to the Minister of Canadian Heritage, a post that she held until February 1996 when she was elected as Chair of the Standing Committee on Government Operations. She is currently Co-Chair of the Joint Standing Committee on Official Languages.

Albina Guarnieri a été élue députée de la circonscription de Mississauga-Est à la Chambre des communes pour un premier mandat en 1988. Elle avait auparavant travaillé dans le secteur privé pour le compte de la revue *Time*, du *The Globe and Mail*, de l'Institut d'études pédagogiques de l'Ontario et de la Société ontarienne de gestion des déchets. Elle a par ailleurs été secrétaire de presse d'un solliciteur général du Canada, du chef du Parti libéral de l'Ontario, M. Stuart Smith, et du maire de Toronto, M. Art Eggleton.

Mme Guarnieri a été membre du Comité permanent sur le patrimoine canadien. Elle a par ailleurs siégé au Comité permanent de la santé et du bien-être et au Sous-comité sur la pauvreté et a fait partie de la délégation canadienne à la conférence de l'Association des Nations de l'Asie du Sud-Est, tenue à Djakarta (Indonésie), en septembre 1992.

Réélue au Parlement le 25 octobre 1993, elle a été nommée secrétaire parlementaire du ministre du Patrimoine canadien en décembre 1994. Elle a occupé ce poste jusqu'à son élection à la présidence du Comité permanent des opérations gouvernementale, en février 1996. Elle est actuellement co-présidente du Comité mixte permanent des langues officielles.

DOLORES HAYDEN
Professor of Architecture, Urbanism and American Studies / Professeure d'architecture, d'urbanisme et d'études américaines, Yale University

Dolores Hayden, historian and architect, is Professor of Architecture, Urbanism, and American Studies at Yale University. She writes about the social and political history of American built environments, and about the politics of design. Her books include *Seven American Utopias: The Architecture of Communitarian Socialism, 1790-1975* (MIT Press); *The Grand Domestic Revolution: A History of Feminist Designs for American Homes, Neighborhoods, and Cities* (MIT Press); and *Redesigning the American Dream: The Future of Housing, Work, and Family Life* (Norton). As founder and president of The Power of Place, she spent eight years developing collaborative projects with historians, artists, and designers to celebrate the history of women and ethnic groups in public places in Los Angeles, the subject of her latest book, *The Power of Place: Urban Landscapes as People's History* (MIT Press, 1995).

She has received numerous awards, including Guggenheim, Rockefeller, NEH, NEA, and ACLS/Ford Fellowships. Her work on cities has been translated into French, German, Italian, Spanish, Swedish, Danish, Japanese, and Chinese. She has taught at MIT, UC Berkeley, and UCLA, as well as Yale.

Historienne et architecte, Dolores Hayden est professeure d'architecture, d'urbanisme et d'études américaines à l'université Yale. Elle écrit des ouvrages sur l'histoire sociale et politique des milieux bâtis américains et sur la politique de l'architecture. Elle a notamment publié *Seven American Utopias: The Architecture of Communitarian Socialism, 1790-1975* (Presses du MIT); *The Grand Domestic Revolution: A History of Feminist Designs for American Homes, Neighborhoods, and Cities* (Presses du MIT), et *Redesigning the American Dream: The Future of Housing, Work, and Family Life* (Norton). À titre de fondatrice et présidente du groupe The Power of Place, elle a passé huit ans à élaborer, avec des historiens, des artistes et des dessinateurs, des projets coopératifs destinés à mettre en lumière l'histoire des femmes et des groupes ethniques dans les lieux publics de Los Angeles, sujet sur lequel porte son dernier livre, intitulé *The Power of Place: Urban Landscapes as People's History* (Presses du MIT, 1995).

Mme Hayden a reçu de nombreux prix, dont des bourses de la fondation Guggenheim, de la fondation Rockefeller, de la NEH, de la NEA et de l'ACLS/Ford. Ses ouvrages sur les villes ont été traduits en français, en allemand, en italien, en espagnol, en suédois, en danois, en japonais et en chinois. Elle a par ailleurs enseigné au MIT ainsi qu'à l'université de la Californie à Berkeley et à Los Angeles.

CHARLES W. HUMPHRIES
Professor of History / professeur d'histoire, The University of British Columbia
Former British Columbia Member, Historic Sites and Monuments Board of Canada / Ex-membre de la Commission des lieux et monuments historiques du Canada pour la Colombie-Britannique

Charles W. Humphries, from the History Department of The University of British Columbia, was the British Columbia member of the Historic Sites and Monuments Board of Canada from 1979 to 1993. His chief historical interests are twentieth century Canadian history and the study of war and society.

Professor Humphries has published in the field of Ontario political history, most notably a biography of Premier James P. Whitney, *Honest Enough to be Bold*. He has also delivered a wide range of papers on the subject of Canadian society, during World War I; these include studies on the significance of wartime rumour, the importance of volunteerism in British Columbia, the causes of the Victoria *Lusitania* riots, and the contribution of Canadian craftsmen who laboured in British munition factories. He is currently preparing a book-length study of these workers and a manuscript on the social history of British Columbia during World War I.

He was one of the first five recipients of the Excellence in Teaching Award at UBC in 1990. When not busy with students, research, and writing, Professor Humphries has frequently been a political panellist on CBC radio.

Charles W. Humphries, du Département d'histoire de l'université de la Colombie-Britannique, a été le représentant de la Colombie-Britannique à la Commission des lieux et monuments historiques du Canada de 1979 à 1993. Il s'intéresse principalement à l'histoire du Canada au XXe siècle et à l'étude de la guerre et de la société.

M. Humphries a publié des ouvrages relatifs à l'histoire politique de l'Ontario, et notamment une biographie du premier ministre James P. Whitney intitulée *Honest Enough to be Bold*. Il a en outre présenté un grand nombre de communications traitant de la société canadienne pendant la Première Guerre mondiale, dont des études sur la signification des rumeurs en temps de guerre, l'importance du volontariat en Colombie-Britannique, les causes des émeutes du *Lusitania* à Victoria et la contribution des hommes de métier canadiens qui peinèrent dans les usines de munitions britanniques. Il prépare actuellement un livre sur ces travailleurs et un manuscrit sur l'histoire sociale de la Colombie-Britannique durant la Première Guerre mondiale.

Le professeur Humphries a été l'un des cinq premiers récipiendaires du prix d'excellence en enseignement de l'université de la Colombie-Britannique en 1990. Lorsque ses occupations universitaires, ses recherches et son travail d'écrivain lui en laissent le loisir, il participe souvent à des tables rondes au réseau radiophonique de la CBC.

R. SCOTT JAMES
Former Managing Director / Ancien directeur général, Toronto Historical Board

Mr. James was born in Oxford, U.K. and educated at the University of Wales, 1962-1965 (B.A. Honours, History), and London University, 1965-1966 (Post Graduate Certificate in Education). After a year in the M.A. History programme of Dalhousie University, Halifax, N.S., he joined the City of Toronto Archives in 1967 serving as Archives Assistant, Supervisor of Archives, and finally as Director of Records and Archivist, 1975-1984.

From 1984 until his retirement in 1995, he served as Managing Director of the Toronto Historical Board, an agency of the City of Toronto dedicated to the promotion, preservation, and interpretation of Toronto's heritage. The Board manages five historic site museums and serves as City Council's advisor on heritage preservation matters in its capacity as the Local Architectural Conservation Advisory Committee under the *Ontario Heritage Act*.

Né à Oxford (Grande-Bretagne), M. James a fait ses études à l'université du pays de Galles (1962-1965 ; licence en histoire) et à l'université de Londres (1965-1966 ; diplôme supérieur en éducation). En 1967, après une année d'études en vue d'une maîtrise en histoire à l'université Dalhousie, il entre au Service des archives de la ville de Toronto, où il occupe successivement, entre 1975 et 1984, les postes d'adjoint aux archives, de surveillant des archives, puis de directeur des documents et archiviste.

De 1984 jusqu'à sa retraite, en 1995, il a été directeur général du Toronto Historical Board, organisme de la ville de Toronto voué à la promotion, à la protection et à l'interprétation du patrimoine torontois. Cet organisme gère cinq musées faisant partie de lieux historiques et donne des avis au conseil municipal touchant les questions de protection du patrimoine à titre de Comité consultatif local pour la conservation de l'architecture, conformément à la *Loi sur le patrimoine de l'Ontario*.

JACQUES MATHIEU
Professeur d'histoire / Professor of History, Université Laval

Jacques Mathieu est professeur d'histoire à l'Université Laval, à Québec, depuis 1970. Il a été membre de la Commission des biens culturels du Québec, directeur du Centre d'études en arts et traditions populaires et responsable des séminaires de la Chaire d'études des francophones en Amérique du Nord portant sur « les dynamismes de la recherche au Québec » et « la mémoire dans la culture ». Il est maintenant titulaire de cette chaire et il a été élu membre de l'Académie des lettres et des sciences humaines de la Société royale du Canada en 1988.

M. Matthieu a conçu et dirigé la recherche pour l'exposition inaugurale et permanente *Mémoires*, au musée de la civilisation à Québec, qui a donné lieu à une publication, *Les mémoires québécoises*, aux PUL. Il a dirigé des recherches pour la mise en valeur du musée de Pointe-à-Callière, site fondateur de Montréal. Il a également publié *Les Plaines d'Abraham, le culte de l'idéal* (aussi en version anglaise), étude qui a servi à la conception d'un programme de mise en valeur. En somme, plusieurs de ses travaux récents rejoignent la problématique de la commémoration.

Jacques Mathieu has been Professor of History at Université Laval since 1970. He was a member of the Cultural Property Commission of Québec, Director of the Centre d'études en arts et traditions populaires, and was in charge of the seminars organized by the Chaire d'étude des francophones en Amérique du Nord on the themes *"Les dynamismes de la recherche au Québec"* and *"La mémoire dans la culture"*. He is presently the holder of this Chair and is a Fellow of the Académie des lettres et des sciences humaines of the Royal Society of Canada (elected in 1988).

Mr. Mathieu developed and directed the research for the inaugural and permanent exhibition "Mémoires" at the Musée de la civilisation in Québec City. This work resulted in a publication, *Les mémoires québécoises* (Les Presses de l'Université Laval). He lead a research project relating to the development of the Pointe-à-Callière Museum, site of the foundation of Montréal. He has also published *Les Plaines d'Abraham, le culte de l'idéal* (translated in English as *The Plains of Abraham: The Search for the Ideal*), a study which formed the basis of a development programme for the site. In short, several of his recent activities have related to commemoration issues.

HARVEY A. McCUE
Consultant, Nova Scotia / Nouvelle-Écosse

Harvey McCue is a consultant in Aboriginal self-government, health, and education. He served recently as the first Director of Education and CEO of the Mi'kmaq Education Authority in Nova Scotia. A member of Canada's First Nations, Mr. McCue studied at Trent University and McMaster University where he received a M.A., and has worked with and on behalf of Canada's aboriginal peoples both in the private and public sector. He taught at Trent for fourteen years and served on its Senate before becoming Director of Education at the Cree School Board in James Bay. He then became Director of Policy & Planning, Education Branch, for the Department of Indian Affairs and Northern Development, becoming Director General of the Branch in November 1990. His founding work with the Mi'kmaq Education Authority concluded in July 1995. Mr. McCue served on the National Task Force on Native Issues for SSHERC, and is author, editor and contributor to several publications. In 1994, Mr. McCue was appointed to the National Advisory Board on Science and Technology.

Harvey McCue est consultant en matière d'autonomie gouvernementale, de santé et d'éducation des Autochtones. Il a occupé jusqu'à récemment le poste de premier directeur de l'éducation et président de la Mi'kmaq Education Authority en Nouvelle-Écosse. Membre des Premières Nations du Canada, il a fait ses études aux universités Trent et McMaster. Il est titulaire d'une maîtrise de cette dernière université et a travaillé avec les peuples autochtones du Canada et pour leur compte dans les secteurs privé et public. Il a enseigné à Trent pendant quatorze ans et a siégé au conseil de l'université avant de devenir directeur de l'éducation au conseil scolaire cri de la Baie James. Il a ensuite occupé, au ministère des Affaires indiennes et du Nord canadien, le poste de directeur des politiques et de la planification à la Direction générale de l'éducation, dont il est devenu directeur général en novembre 1990. Il a achevé son travail de fondateur auprès de la Mi'kmaq Education Authority en juillet 1995. M. McCue a siégé au Groupe de travail national sur les questions autochtones du Conseil de recherches en sciences humaines et a contribué, à titre d'auteur, de rédacteur ou de collaborateur, à plusieurs publications. En 1994, il a été nommé au Conseil consultatif national des sciences et de la technologie.

KEN OSBORNE
Professor, Faculty of Education / Professeur à la Faculté d'éducation, The University of Manitoba

Educated at the universities of Oxford, Birmingham and Manitoba, Ken Osborne began teaching in the Winnipeg school system in 1961. He recently retired from the Faculty of Education at The University of Manitoba, where he also served as Coordinator of Canadian Studies for the University. He has been the editor of the national journal, *The History and Social Science Teacher*, and was on the advisory board of the magazine, *Horizon Canada*. He has won various awards at The University of Manitoba for excellence in teaching, community service and interdisciplinary scholarship. He is the author of many articles on education and history and has edited and written various books, among them *The Teaching of Politics*; *The Prairies: Selected Historical Sources*; *R.B. Russell and the Labour Movement*; and *Hard-Working, Temperate and Peaceable: The Portrayal of Working People in Canadian History Textbooks*.

Après avoir fait ses études aux universités d'Oxford, de Birmingham et du Manitoba, Ken Osborne a commencé à enseigner dans les écoles de Winnipeg en 1961. Il s'est retiré récemment de ses fonctions de professeur à la Faculté d'éducation de l'université du Manitoba et de coordonnateur des études canadiennes. Il a été rédacteur de la revue nationale *The History and Social Science Teacher* et a siégé au conseil consultatif du magazine *Horizon Canada*. Il a remporté plusieurs prix d'excellence en enseignement, en service communautaire et en érudition interdisciplinaire à l'université du Manitoba. Il a par ailleurs publié de nombreux articles sur l'éducation et l'histoire, ainsi que plusieurs livres à titre d'auteur ou de rédacteur, dont *The Teaching of Politics* ; *The Prairies: Selected Historical Sources* ; *R.B. Russell and the Labour Movement* ; et *Hard-Working, Temperate and Peaceable: The Portrayal of Working People in Canadian History Textbooks*.

TED ROWE
Past Chairman / Ancien président, Newfoundland Historic Parks Association

A real estate broker in St. John's, Newfoundland., Ted Rowe is President of RE/MAX Realty Specialists Ltd., RE/MAX United Inc. and related companies. His community activities include President of the Newfoundland Historic Trust (1979-1981), Chairman of the Newfoundland Historic Parks Association (1990-1992), President of the St. John's Rotary Club (1993-1994), and Chairman of the Art Gallery of Newfoundland and Labrador (1994-present). He represented the Province of Newfoundland on the Board of Governors of the Heritage Canada Foundation (1982-1986) and on the Board of the Fathers of Confederation Buildings Trust, Charlottetown (1993-1996).

Courtier en immeubles à St. John's (Terre-Neuve), Ted Rowe est président de RE/MAX Realty Specialists Ltd, de RE/MAX United Inc. et de compagnies affiliées. Sur le plan communautaire, il a été président de la Newfoundland Historic Trust (1979-1981), de la Newfoundland Historic Parks Association (1990-1992), du club Rotary de St. John's (1993-1994) et occupe depuis 1994 la présidence de l'Art Gallery of Newfoundland and Labrador. Il a par ailleurs représenté la province de Terre-Neuve au conseil d'administration de la Fondation canadienne pour la protection du patrimoine de 1982 à 1986 et au conseil du Groupe fiduciaire des édifices des pères de la Confédération, à Charlottetown (1993-1996).

MURIEL K. ROY
Professeure émérite / Professor Emerita, Université de Moncton (Nouveau-Brunswick)

Muriel Roy est diplômée de l'Université de Montréal et de la Sorbonne. Elle a été professeure de sociologie et de démographie à l'Université de Moncton et directrice du Centre d'études acadiennes. Professeure émérite de cette même université, elle a siégé à l'exécutif de plusieurs commissions, conseils consultatifs et associations professionnelles en Atlantique, à l'échelle nationale et internationale. Elle est coauteure du « Que sais-je ? » intitulé *Les Acadiens*.

Membre de l'Ordre du Canada, elle s'est mérité, entre autres distinctions, le prix du Mérite patrimonial du Service canadien des parcs pour son engagement au projet de restauration du Monument Lefebvre, important édifice du patrimoine acadien. Sur la recommandation de la Commission des lieux et monuments historiques du Canada, le ministre du Patrimoine canadien, l'honorable Michel Dupuy, a déclaré le Monument Lefebvre lieu historique national en août 1994, durant les grandes fêtes du Congrès mondial acadien.

Muriel Roy is a graduate from Université de Montréal and the Sorbonne. She has taught sociology and demography at Université de Moncton and was Director of the Centre d'études acadiennes. She is also a Professor Emerita at that University and has sat on the board of several commissions, advisory boards and professional associations in Atlantic Canada, both at the national and international levels. She is a co-author of a volume on Acadians published in the series "Que sais-je ?".

Madame Roy is a Member of the Order of Canada and has received several other distinctions, including the Heritage Award of the Canadian Parks Service for her commitment to the restoration of Monument Lefebvre, an important Acadian heritage building. On the recommendation of the Historic Sites and Monuments Board of Canada, the Minister of Canadian Heritage, the Honourable Michel Dupuy, declared Monument Lefebvre a national historic site in August 1994, during the celebrations of the Congrès mondial acadien (Acadian World Congress).

ANNETTE SAINT-PIERRE
Auteure et éditrice / Author and Publisher, Saint-Boniface (Manitoba)

Annette Saint-Pierre a enseigné dans les écoles du Manitoba et au Collège universitaire de Saint-Boniface. Elle est la fondatrice du Centre d'études franco-canadiennes de l'Ouest et la cofondatrice des Éditions du Blé. Elle dirige actuellement Les Éditions des Plaines dont elle est la cofondatrice et la copropriétaire. Elle a publié : *Gabrielle Roy sous le signe du rêve* (essai), *Le rideau se lève au Manitoba* (essai), *La fille bègue* (roman), *Répertoire littéraire de l'Ouest canadien*, *Sans bon sang* (roman), *Coups de vent* (roman), *Le Manitoba au coeur de l'Amérique* (histoire), *De fil en aiguille au Manitoba* (chronologie), ainsi que des articles parus dans des livres ou des revues universitaires.

315

Annette Saint-Pierre est la récipiendaire du Prix Alliance-Française-Canada et de la médaille d'honneur offerte par le Conseil de la vie française en Amérique ; elle est en outre membre de l'Ordre des Francophones de l'Amérique du Nord et titulaire d'un doctorat *honoris causa* de l'université du Manitoba.

Annette Saint-Pierre has taught in the Manitoba school system and at the Collège universitaire de Saint-Boniface. She founded the Centre d'études franco-canadiennes de l'Ouest and was a co-founder of Les Éditions du Blé. She currently manages Les Éditions des Plaines, of which she is a co-founder and co-owner. Her publications include two essays, *Gabrielle Roy sous le signe du rêve* and *Le rideau se lève au Manitoba*; three novels, *La fille bègue*, *Sans bon sang* and *Coups de vent*; an anthology, *Répertoire littéraire de l'Ouest canadien*; a history work, *Le Manitoba au cœur de l'Amérique*; and a chronology, *De fil en aiguille au Manitoba*. She has also published articles in books and academic journals.

Annette Saint-Pierre is a recipient of the Alliance Française Canada Award and of the Medal of Honour awarded by Le Conseil de la vie française en Amérique. She is a member of the Ordre des Francophones de l'Amérique du Nord and holds an honorary doctorate from The University of Manitoba.

ROBERT SCULLY
Directeur des services de création en français du projet Reflets du patrimoine de La Fondation CRB / French Creative Director, The CRB Foundation's Heritage Project

Personnalité de la télévision canadienne, Robert Scully anime trois émissions nationales, en anglais et en français, qui atteignent un million de téléspectateurs par semaine au Canada et sont rediffusées dans plus de 60 pays étrangers. En plus des émissions *Scully/The World Show*, *Scully rencontre* et *Venture*, M. Scully a participé à de nombreuses séries et émissions spéciales de la CBC et de la Société Radio-Canada à titre de réalisateur, d'animateur ou de coanimateur, notamment *Scully en direct*, *Racing the Rising Sun*, *Démocraties*, *A Time for Children* et *Héritiers de l'Histoire*.

Depuis 1990, il occupe les fonctions de directeur des services de création en français du projet Reflets du patrimoine de La Fondation CRB, qui vise à sensibiliser davantage les Canadiens et Canadiennes à leur histoire, à leur culture et à leur progrès collectif. Ce projet comprend 52 « Heritage Minutes », ou films d'une durée de 60 secondes (dont certains ont été réalisés par monsieur Scully) qui sont diffusés sur tous les réseaux ; *Le Courrier du Patrimoine*, revue diffusée dans les écoles de tout le pays ; un programme national multimédia d'enseignement de l'histoire en dix unités intitulé *We are Canadians* ; et un important programme d'extension.

M. Scully a travaillé dans un certain nombre de langues qu'il parle couramment : l'anglais, le français, l'allemand et l'espagnol. Sa carrière a débuté en 1969, en Amérique du Sud, où il était correspondant du journal *Le Devoir*. Il a également publié des articles dans *La Presse*, *Die Welt*, le *Washington Post*, la *Gazette* (Montréal) et d'autres organes d'information.

Né à Ottawa en 1950, il est titulaire d'un baccalauréat ès arts (avec mention très bien) et d'une maîtrise de l'Université McGill.

Robert Scully is a Canadian TV personality, the host of three national programmes, in English and in French, reaching a million viewers a week in Canada, in addition to rebroadcast audiences in over sixty countries. In addition to *Scully/The World Show*, *Scully rencontre*, and *Venture*, Mr. Scully has also been associated with many CBC/SRC series and specials, as producer, host or co-host, such as: *Scully en direct*, *Racing the Rising Sun*, *Démocraties*, *A Time for Children*, and *Héritiers de l'Histoire*.

Since 1990, he has served as French Creative Director for The CRB Foundation's Heritage Project, a major initiative which aims to give Canadians greater awareness of their history, culture, and progress as a nation. The Project includes 52 *Heritage Minutes*, 60 second mini-movies (some produced by Mr. Scully) broadcast over all networks; *The Heritage Post*, a magazine distributed in schools across the country; *We are Canadians*, a national, multimedia history curriculum in ten units; and an extensive outreach programme.

Robert Scully has worked in a number of languages which he speaks fluently: English, French, German, and Spanish. His career began in 1969 in South America, where he corresponded for *Le Devoir*. His pieces have also appeared in *La Presse*, *Die Welt*, *The Washington Post*, *The Gazette* (Montréal), and elsewhere.

Born in 1950 in Ottawa, he holds a B.A. (First Class Honours) and an M.A. from McGill University.

STEPHEN M. SMITH
Freelance writer and editor / Auteur et rédacteur indépendant

Stephen Smith lives in Toronto, where he is a freelance writer and editor. He was the book review editor at *Quill & Quire*, Canada's national magazine of book news and reviews. He has written about books, travel, and cultural matters for *The Globe and Mail*, *The Gazette* (Montréal), *The New York Times*, *Saturday Night*, and *Toronto Life*.

Stephen Smith habite à Toronto, où il travaille comme auteur et rédacteur indépendant. Il a été critique littéraire pour le compte de la revue nationale canadienne de nouvelles et de critique littéraires *Quill & Quire*. Par ailleurs, il a publié des articles sur les livres, les voyages et les questions culturelles dans le *Globe and Mail*, la *Gazette* (Montréal), le *New York Times*, *Saturday Night* et *Toronto Life*.

RICHARD L. STROMBERG
Manager, Inventory and Research / Directeur de l'Inventaire et de la Recherche, Toronto Historical Board

B.A., Economics, George Washington University (1977); M.A., Anthropology, University of Toronto (1980), Stromberg has been at the Toronto Historical Board since 1987, where he oversees architectural and historical research to support the Toronto Historical Board's preservation programme on behalf of the City of Toronto.

Titulaire d'un baccalauréat ès arts en économique de l'université George Washington (1977) et d'une maîtrise en anthropologie de l'université de Toronto (1980), M. Stromberg fait partie du personnel du Toronto Historical Board depuis 1987. Il supervise la recherche architecturale et historique à l'appui du programme de conservation de cet organisme pour le compte de la ville de Toronto,

THOMAS H. B. SYMONS
Founding President and Vanier Professor Emeritus / Président fondateur et professeur émérite de la chaire Vanier, Trent University
Chairman, Historic Sites and Monuments Board of Canada / Président de la Commission des lieux et monuments historiques du Canada

Professor Symons is a teacher and writer in the field of Canadian heritage studies. He is the author of *To Know Ourselves*, the Report of the Commission on Canadian Studies, and of numerous studies and articles dealing with education, human rights, cultural pluralism, Aboriginal and northern studies, and other aspects of public policy in Canada.

Educated at Toronto, Oxford, and Harvard, Professor Symons has served as Chairman of the Commission on Canadian Studies (1972-1984), Vice-President of the Social Sciences and Humanities Research Council (1978-1984), Chairman of the National Library Advisory Board (1987-1990), Chairman of the Ontario Human Rights Commission (1975-1978), Chairman of the International Board of United World Colleges (1980-1986), Chairman of the Association of Commonwealth Universities, Chairman of the Canadian Polar Research Commission Study (1988), Chairman of the Canadian Educational Standards Institute (1986-1991), as a member of the Canada Council (1976-1980), of the Federal Cultural Policy Review (1979-1982), and of the Advisory Committee on Academic Relations for the Department of External Affairs, and as a Special Advisor on Education and Human Rights to the Secretary of State (1982-1990).

Professor Symons' work has been recognized by a number of universities and colleges in Canada and elsewhere. He is a Fellow of the Royal Society of Canada and an Officer of the Order of Canada. In 1993, he received the Award of Merit of the Canadian Bureau for International Education. He was elected an Honorary Fellow by Oriel College,

Oxford University, in 1988, and a Visiting Fellow by Robinson College, Cambridge University, in 1993.

Le professeur Symons enseigne et écrit dans le domaine des études patrimoniales canadiennes. Il est l'auteur de *To Know Ourselves*, rapport de la Commission des études canadiennes, et d'un grand nombre d'études et d'articles traitant de l'éducation, des droits de la personne, du pluralisme culturel, des études autochtones et nordiques et d'autres aspects des politiques publiques du Canada.

Le professeur Symons a fait ses études aux universités de Toronto, d'Oxford et d'Harvard. Il a été président de la Commission des études canadiennes (1972-1984), vice-président du Conseil de recherches en sciences humaines (1978-1984), président du Conseil consultatif de la Bibliothèque nationale (1987-1990), président de la Commission des droits de la personne de l'Ontario (1975-1978), président du conseil d'administration des Collèges du monde uni (1980-1986), président de l'Association des universités du Commonwealth, président de la Commission d'enquête sur la recherche polaire canadienne (1988), président du Canadian Educational Standards Institute (1986-1991), membre du Conseil des Arts du Canada (1976-1980), membre de la Commission d'examen de la politique culturelle fédérale (1979-1982), membre du Comité consultatif sur les relations universitaires du ministère des Affaires extérieures, et conseiller spécial du secrétaire d'État en matière d'enseignement et de droits de la personne (1982-1990).

Ses travaux ont été reconnus par plusieurs universités et collèges du Canada et d'autres pays. Le professeur Symons est d'autres part membre de la Société royale du Canada et Officier de l'Ordre du Canada. Le Bureau canadien de l'éducation internationale lui a décerné le prix d'excellence en 1993. Il a par ailleurs été élu membre honoraire du collège Oriel de l'université d'Oxford en 1988 et membre associé du collège Robinson de l'université de Cambridge en 1993.

JOHN HERD THOMPSON
Professor of History / Professeur d'histoire, Duke University

John Herd Thompson teaches Canadian History and directs the Canadian Studies Program at Duke University. Before he accepted the Sisyphean task of explaining Canada to Americans, Thompson taught for eighteen years at McGill University. He is best known for *Canada 1922-1939: Decades of Discord* (1985), volume 15 of *The Canadian Centenary Series*, a Governor-General's Award Finalist. His most recent book, *Canada and the United States: Ambivalent Allies*, (with Stephen J. Randall) appeared in 1994 from McGill-Queen's University Press and the University of Georgia Press. His *Oxford Illustrated History of the Canadian Prairies* will be published soon.

Thompson also serves as the English-language historian for The CRB Foundation's Heritage Project and works as part of the team which creates the "Heritage Minutes". He was a Councillor of the Canadian Historical Association from 1991-1994.

John Herd Thompson enseigne l'histoire du Canada et dirige le programme d'études canadiennes à l'université Duke. Avant d'accepter le défi d'expliquer le Canada aux Américains, il avait enseigné à l'Université McGill pendant dix-huit ans. Il est mieux connu en tant qu'auteur de *Canada 1922-1939: Decades of Discord* (1985), qui constitue le volume 15 de la série *The Canadian Centenary* et avait été sélectionné pour un prix du Gouverneur général. Son livre le plus récent, *Canada and the United States: Ambivalent Allies* (écrit en collaboration avec Stephen J. Randall), a été publié en 1994 par la McGill-Queen's University Press et par la University of Georgia Press. Son ouvrage intitulé *Oxford Illustrated History of the Canadian Prairies* paraîtra bientôt.

M. Thompson est en outre l'historien de langue anglaise du projet Reflets du patrimoine de La Fondation CRB et fait partie de l'équipe de conception des « Heritage Minutes ». Il a été conseiller de la Société historique du Canada de 1991 à 1994.

DANIEL L. TLEN
Aboriginal Language Consultant, Yukon Territory / Consultant en matière de langues autochtones au Yukon
Historic Sites and Monuments Board of Canada Yukon Member / Membre de la Commission des lieux et monuments historiques du Canada pour le Yukon

Daniel Tlen was born in 1949 at Burwash Landing, Yukon Territory. He attended primary school at the Lower Post Indian Residential School in British Columbia. In the Yukon he attended Christ the King High School and F.H. Collins Secondary School in Whitehorse where he graduated in 1968. Mr. Tlen studied at Camosun College and at the University of Victoria from which he graduated with a B.A. (Honours) in linguistics.

Mr. Tlen has been a Chief for the Kluane First Nation, and Chairman of the Council for Yukon Indians. He has been teaching at Yukon College and has instructed Southern Tutchone, Northern Studies, and First Nations History. Mr. Tlen is presently the consulting linguist for Aboriginal Language Services, Government of Yukon. He has recently published *Kluane Southern Tutchone Glossary* through the Northern Research Institute.

Daniel Tlen est né à Burwash Landing (Yukon) en 1949 et a fait ses études primaires au pensionnat indien Lower Post, en Colombie-Britannique. Au Yukon, il a étudié à l'école supérieure Christ the King et à l'école secondaire F.H. Collins, de Whitehorse, où il a reçu son diplôme en 1968. Il a ensuite poursuivi ses études au collège Camosun et à l'université de Victoria, où il a obtenu un baccalauréat en linguistique.

M. Tlen a été chef de la Première Nation Kluane et président du Conseil des Indiens du Yukon. Il a enseigné le tutchoni du sud, les études nordiques et l'histoire des Premières Nations au collège du Yukon. Il occupe actuellement le poste de linguiste conseil auprès des Services de langue autochtone du gouvernement du Yukon. Il a publié récemment un ouvrage intitulé *Kluane Southern Tutchone Glossary*, par l'entremise du Northern Research Institute.

MICHAEL VALPY
Columnist for "The Globe and Mail" / Chroniqueur au « Globe and Mail »

A columnist on social and political affairs for *The Globe and Mail*, Michael Valpy began his journalism career at *The Vancouver Sun* in 1961 while still a student at The University of British Columbia. He became that newspaper's associate editor and national affairs columnist.

For *The Globe and Mail*, he has been a member of the editorial board, Ottawa national affairs columnist, Africa correspondent and deputy managing editor.

He has co-authored a book on the Constitution, produced numerous public affairs documentaries for CBC Radio, and won three National Newspaper Awards – two for foreign reporting and the most recent for an examination of how the schools cope with children from dysfunctional families.

Michael Valpy rédige la chronique des affaires sociales et politiques du *Globe and Mail*. Il était encore étudiant à l'université de la Colombie-Britannique lorsqu'il a commencé sa carrière de journaliste au *Vancouver Sun*, en 1961. Il devint rédacteur adjoint et chroniqueur des affaires nationales de ce journal.

Au *Globe and Mail*, il a été membre de l'équipe de rédaction, chroniqueur des affaires nationales à Ottawa, correspondant en Afrique et rédacteur en chef adjoint.

Coauteur d'un livre sur la Constitution, il a par ailleurs réalisé de nombreux documentaires d'affaires publiques pour le compte du réseau radiophonique de la CBC et remporté trois prix nationaux de journalisme, dont deux pour des reportages à l'étranger et le troisième, de date récente, pour un examen de la façon dont les écoles s'occupent des enfants venant de foyers désunis.

JOHN WADLAND
Director / Directeur, Frost Centre for Canadian Heritage and Development Studies, Trent University

John Wadland is a graduate in History of McMaster (B.A. 1965), Waterloo (M.A. 1968), and York (Ph.D. 1976) universities. He has taught in the interdisciplinary Canadian Studies Program at Trent University since 1972. He was Chair of the Program from 1984 to 1993 and Editor of the *Journal of Canadian Studies* from 1980 to 1984. He concentrates his teaching in the fields of environmental history, art history, land policy, bio-regionalism, and interdisciplinary methods. He has published a book-length academic biography of the Canadian artist and naturalist Ernest Thompson Seton (New York, 1979), and numerous articles and book reviews. Most recently he completed, with Margaret Hobbs, two folio plates for Volume II of the *Historical Atlas of Canada* (Toronto, 1993). In 1993 Professor Wadland received both the Ontario Council of University Faculty Associations and the Lieutenant Governor of Ontario Awards for Excellence in Teaching.

John Wadland est diplômé en histoire de l'université McMaster (B.A., 1965), de l'université Waterloo (M.A., 1968) et de l'Université York (Ph.D., 1976). Il donne des cours dans le cadre du programme interdisciplinaire d'études canadiennes à l'université Trent depuis 1972. Il a été directeur de ce programme de 1984 à 1993 et rédacteur du *Journal of Canadian Studies* de 1980 à 1984. Il concentre son enseignement dans les domaines de l'histoire de l'environnement, de l'histoire de l'art, de la politique des terres, du biorégionalisme et des méthodes interdisciplinaires. Il a publié une biographie savante du naturaliste et artiste canadien Ernest Thompson Seton (New York, 1979) et de nombreux articles et critiques de livres. Il a achevé dernièrement, en collaboration avec Margaret Hobbs, deux planches in-folio destinées au volume II de l'*Atlas historique du Canada* (Toronto, 1993). En 1993 également, il a reçu deux médailles d'excellence en enseignement, soit celle de l'Union des associations des professeurs des universités de l'Ontario et celle du lieutenant-gouverneur de l'Ontario.

BARBARA WYSS
British Columbia Native Women's Society

Barbara Wyss is a Coast Salish and a member of the Squamish First Nation. She is a college graduate of the Open Learning Agency and she also attended Simon Fraser University for three years. Although her major at the University was economics, she had a strong interest in history.

Her career has centred on native people. In the political realm, her work, both paid and volunteered, has included promoting the rights of Aboriginal women and securing funds to document the roles and history of Aboriginal women. In the area of socio-economic improvement, she has assisted Native people in training, job creation, economic development, and policy plan formation. She has also written documents or advised on documents pertaining to the history of Aboriginal people in Canada and their role in the shaping of Canada over the past 150 years.

Salish de la côte, Barbara Wyss est membre de la Première Nation squamish. Elle est titulaire d'un diplôme d'études collégiales de l'Open Learning Agency et a étudié trois ans à l'université Simon Fraser. Elle s'y est spécialisée en économique, mais s'est aussi vivement intéressée à l'histoire.

Sa carrière a été axée sur les peuples Autochtones. Son travail dans le domaine politique, tant rémunéré que bénévole, a englobé la promotion des droits des femmes Autochtones et la collecte de fonds pour recueillir des documents sur leur rôle et leur histoire. Dans le domaine du progrès socio-économique, elle a aidé les peuples Autochtones en matière de formation, de création d'emplois, de développement économique et de planification de politiques. Elle a par ailleurs écrit des textes relatifs à l'histoire des peuples Autochtones du Canada et à leur rôle dans l'édification du pays au cours des 150 dernières années, ou donné des conseils sur la rédaction de tels documents.

CHAIRS / PRÉSIDENT(E)S DES SÉANCES

MARION BEYEA
Provincial Archivist of New Brunswick / Archiviste provinciale du Nouveau-Brunswick
Historic Sites and Monuments Board of Canada, New Brunswick Member / Membre de la
Commission des lieux et monuments historiques du Canada pour le Nouveau-Brunswick

A graduate in History from the University of New Brunswick, Marion Beyea has been the Provincial Archivist of New Brunswick since 1978. She was previously the Archivist of the Anglican Church of Canada and a manuscript archivist with the Archives of Ontario.
    A Past President of the Association of Canadian Archivists, she was the Founding Chair of the Canadian Council of Archives, 1986-1990, and of the Council of Archives New Brunswick. Marion Beyea is also a researcher and author and editor of historical and archival publications, and a member of Fredericton Heritage Trust.

Marion Beyea est diplômée en histoire de l'université du Nouveau-Brunswick et occupe les fonctions d'archiviste de cette province depuis 1978. Elle avait auparavant travaillé comme archiviste auprès de l'Église anglicane du Canada et archiviste de manuscrits pour le compte des Archives de l'Ontario.
    Ancienne présidente de l'Association of Canadian Archivists, elle a été présidente fondatrice du Conseil canadien des archives (1986-1990) et du Conseil des archives du Nouveau-Brunswick. Elle est par ailleurs documentaliste, auteure et rédactrice de publications historiques et archivistiques, et membre du Fredericton Heritage Trust.

FRANCIS W.P. BOLGER
Professor Emeritus / Professeur émerite, University of Prince Edward Island
Historic Sites and Monuments Board of Canada, Prince Edward Island Member / Membre de la
Commission des lieux et monuments historiques du Canada pour l'Île-du-Prince-Édouard

Dr. Bolger, a Roman Catholic priest, holds a Ph.D. in History from the University of Toronto and is Professor Emeritus of History at the University of Prince Edward Island. He is the author of several publications on the history of the Island and on the life of Lucy Maud Montgomery. He serves as Chairman of the Lucy Maud Montgomery Foundation Board. Dr. Bolger is a member of the Canadian Historical Association and a past President of the Canadian Catholic Historical Association. A former Director of the P.E.I. Heritage Foundation, Dr. Bolger is also a member of the Order of Canada.

Prêtre catholique, M. Bolger est titulaire d'un doctorat en histoire de l'université de Toronto et professeur émérite d'histoire à l'université de l'Île-du-Prince Édouard. Il a publié plusieurs ouvrages sur l'histoire de l'île et sur la vie de Lucy Maud Montgomery et préside le conseil de la Lucy Maud Montgomery Foundation. Il est par ailleurs membre de la Société historique du Canada et ancien président de la Société canadienne d'histoire de l'Église catholique. Ancien administrateur de la P.E.I. Heritage Foundation, il est également membre de l'Ordre du Canada.

MARGARET CONRAD

Professor of History / professeure d'histoire, Acadia University
Historic Sites and Monuments Board of Canada Nova Scotia Member / Membre de la Commission
des lieux et monuments historiques du Canada pour la Nouvelle-Écosse

Holding a Ph.D. from the University of Toronto, Dr. Margaret Conrad is a professor of History at Acadia University. She has taken a leave for 1996-98 to serve as the Nancy Rowell Jackman Chair of Women's Studies at Mount Saint Vincent University in Halifax. She has held positions on a number of national boards and committees, including the National Archives Board, and the councils of the Canadian Historical Association and the Association for Canadian Studies. A former editor with Clark, Irwin Publishing Company and a founding editor of *Atlantis*, she was appointed Chair of the Board of the *Canadian Historical Review* in 1995 and is a member of the advisory boards of *Acadiensis*, *Histoire Sociale*, and *Newfoundland Studies*. As Coordinator of research for the Planters Studies Centre, Acadia University, she has edited three volumes of conference proceedings: *They Planted Well* (1988); *Making Adjustments* (1991) and *Intimate Relations* (1995). She has published a biography of *George Nowlan* (1986) and is a coauthor of *No Place Like Home: The Diaries and Letters of Nova Scotia Women* (1988) and *History of the Canadian Peoples*, 2 vols. (1993). She was elected a Fellow of the Royal Society of Canada in 1995.

Titulaire d'un doctorat de l'université de Toronto, Margaret Conrad est professeure d'histoire à l'université Acadia. Elle a obtenu un congé pour la période de 1996 à 1998 afin d'occuper la chaire d'études féminines Nancy Rowell Jackman à l'université Mount Saint Vincent, à Halifax. Elle a siégé à plusieurs conseils et comités nationaux, dont le conseil des Archives nationales, celui de la Société historique du Canada et celui de l'Association des études canadiennes. Ancienne rédactrice auprès de la maison d'édition Clark, Irwin et rédactrice fondatrice de la revue *Atlantis*, elle a été nommée présidente du comité de rédaction de la *Canadian Historical Review* en 1995; elle siège par ailleurs aux conseils consultatifs des périodiques *Acadiensis*, *Histoire Sociale* et *Newfoundland Studies*. À titre de coordonnatrice de la recherche du *Planters Studies Centre* de l'université Acadia, elle a dirigé la rédaction des actes de trois conférences, soit : *They Planted Well* (1988), *Making Adjustments* (1991) et *Intimate Relations* (1995). Elle a publié une biographie de *George Nowlan* (1986) et est coauteure de *No Place Like Home: The Diaries and Letters of Nova Scotia Women* (1988) et *History of the Canadian Peoples* (2 vol., 1993). Elle a été élue membre de la Société royale du Canada en 1995.

RAYMONDE GAUTHIER
(Présidente suppléante / Alternate Chair)
Professeure au département d'histoire de l'art / Professor, Department of Art History, Université du Québec à Montréal
Ex-membre de la Commission des lieux et monuments historiques du Canada pour le Québec / Former Québec Member, Historic Sites and Monuments Board of Canada

Historienne de l'architecture, Raymonde Gauthier est titulaire d'un doctorat en histoire de l'Université Laval ; elle a travaillé au niveau postdoctoral à l'université Yale. Elle enseigne au Département d'histoire de l'art de l'Université du Québec à Montréal depuis 1976.

Ses recherches et ses publications portent essentiellement sur l'architecture nord-américaine, avec concentration sur le Québec et le Canada. Elle s'est surtout intéressée, au cours des dernières années, à la définition de la profession d'architecte au XIXe siècle au Canada.

Mme Gauthier agit à titre de consultante auprès des gouvernements fédéral et provincial et préside le Comité consultatif de Montréal sur la protection des biens culturels depuis 1987.

An historian of architecture, Raymonde Gauthier holds a Ph.D. in History from Université Laval and did post-doctoral work at Yale University. She has been teaching in the Department of Art History at Université du Québec à Montréal since 1976.

Her research and publications have focused on North American architecture, with a particular emphasis on Québec and Canada. In recent years, she has concerned herself primarily with the definition of the architectural profession in Canada in the nineteenth century.

Madame Gauthier acts as a consultant to federal and provincial governments and has chaired the Comité consultatif de Montréal sur la protection des biens culturels since 1987.

FERNAND HARVEY
Socioloque / Sociologist, Institut national de la recherche scientifique – Culture et Société
Membre de la Commission des lieux et monuments historiques du Canada pour le Québec / Historic Sites and Monuments Board of Canada, Québec Member

Historien et sociologue, Fernand Harvey est titulaire d'un doctorat en sociologie de l'Université Laval. De 1973 à 1980, il a enseigné la sociologie à l'Université du Québec à Rimouski. Il est, depuis 1980, professeur-chercheur à l'INRS – Culture et Société (jadis l'Institut québécois de recherche sur la culture) à Québec.

Ses recherches récentes l'ont amené à s'intéresser à l'histoire régionale, à la sociologie de la culture et à diverses questions relatives au patrimoine. Parmi ses publications récentes, mentionnons trois ouvrages rédigés sous sa direction : *Médias francophones hors Québec et identité culturelle* (IQRC, 1992), *Les régions culturelles. Problématique interdisciplinaire* (IQRC, 1994) et (en collaboration avec Andrée Fortin) *La Nouvelle culture régionale* (IQRC, 1995). De 1986 à 1988, M. Harvey a été président de l'Association d'études canadiennes. Il a par ailleurs été directeur scientifique d'une télésérie de trente-neuf émissions intitulée « Les Pays du Québec » consacré à l'histoire régionale et diffusée par Télé-Québec.

An historian and sociologist, Fernand Harvey holds a Ph.D. in Sociology from Université Laval. Dr. Harvey taught Sociology at Université du Québec à Rimouski from 1973 to 1980, and has since been a professor and researcher at INRS – Culture et Société (formerly Institut québécois de recherche sur la culture [IQRCI]) in Québec City.

His latest research has led to an involvement in regional history, culture sociology, and various heritage issues. Among his recent publications are three books which he edited: *Médias francophones hors Québec et identité culturelle* (IQRC, 1992), *Les régions culturelles. Problématique interdisciplinaire* (IQRC, 1994), and, with Andrée Fortin, *La Nouvelle culture régionale* (IQRC, 1995). Fernand Harvey chaired the Association for Canadian Studies from 1986 to 1988. He is also the scientific director of a television series (39 parts) entitled "Les Pays du Québec", dedicated to its regional history and distributed by Télé-Québec.

MICHAEL S.P. KINNEAR
Professor of History / Professeur d'histoire, The University of Manitoba
Historic Sites and Monuments Board of Canada, Manitoba Member / Membre de la Commission des lieux et monuments historique du Canada pour le Manitoba

Educated at the Universities of Saskatchewan and Oxford, Dr. Kinnear is Professor of History, University College, The University of Manitoba. He is the founding Chairman of the Manitoba Mosaic Congress, and a Fellow of the Royal Historical Society.

He has written several books on elections in Great Britain and the United States and has been a media commentator on Manitoba provincial elections since the 1970s. He has also written many articles on Canadian politics for the *Winnipeg Free Press*.

M. Kinnear a fait ses études à l'université de la Saskatchewan et à l'université d'Oxford et est professeur d'histoire au University College de l'université du Manitoba. Il est président fondateur du Manitoba Mosaic Congress et membre de la Royal Historical Society.

Auteur de plusieurs livres sur les élections en Grande-Bretagne et aux États-Unis, il commente les élections provinciales au Manitoba dans les médias depuis les années 1970. Il a par ailleurs écrit de nombreux articles sur la politique canadienne pour le compte de la *Winnipeg Free Press*.

ANDRÉ N. LALONDE

Directeur de l'Institut de formation linguistique / Director, Language Institute, The University of Regina
Membre de la Commission des lieux et monuments historiques du Canada pour la Saskatchewan / Historic Sites and Monuments Board of Canada, Saskatchewan Member

André Lalonde est titulaire d'un doctorat de l'Université Laval et enseigne l'histoire à l'université de Regina depuis 1965. Il est spécialisé dans la recherche sur la colonisation française des Prairies et l'histoire des Fransaskois.

De 1983 à 1991, il a été directeur du Centre d'études bilingues de l'université et dirige maintenant son nouvel Institut de formation linguistique. Il représente par ailleurs la Saskatchewan au Conseil de la vie française en Amérique et a été le président fondateur de la Société historique de la Saskatchewan. En 1995, il a été nommé par le gouvernement membre du Saskatchewan Interim Multiculturalism Committee et, en 1996, président du Saskatchewan Property Management Board.

Professor of History at The University of Regina since 1965, Dr. Lalonde holds a Ph.D from Université Laval. His field of research specialization is French settlement on the Prairies and Fransaskois history.

He has been Director of the University's Bilingual Studies Centre (1983-1991) and is now Director of its newly-created Language Institute. He is the Saskatchewan representative on the Conseil de la vie française en Amérique and was the founding President of La Société historique de la Saskatchewan. In 1995, he was named by the government to the Saskatchewan Interim Multiculturalism Committee and, in 1996, President of the Saskatchewan Property Management Board.

GEORGE F. MacDONALD

Executive Director of the Canadian Museum of Civilization / Directeur exécutif du Musée canadien des civilisations, Ottawa
Ex officio Member, Historic Sites and Monuments Board of Canada / Membre d'office de la Commission des lieux et monuments historiques du Canada

The Executive Director of the Canadian Museum of Civilization, Dr. George MacDonald was educated as an anthropologist at the Universities of Toronto and Yale. His museum career began as a field archaeologist for the Royal Ontario Museum and soon after for the National Museum of Man – he joined its permanent staff in 1964. By 1969 he had become Chief of the Archaeology Division.

His scholarly interests are in the oral traditions, rituals, symbolic systems, material culture and artistic expression of aboriginal cultures. He has published extensively on the archaeology and anthropology of the Pacific Coast native cultures – his *Haida Monumental Art* being the definitive work on that subject. His interests also extend to the relationships between aboriginal cultures and museums, and to heritage resource management generally. In recent years he has written several articles and presented papers at numerous

327

conferences on present and future trends in the museum world. His book *A Museum for the Global Village: the Canadian Museum of Civilization* was published to coincide with the opening of that museum in June 1989.

Today he continues to serve the heritage community in a wide range of roles beyond that of CEO of the Canadian Museum of Civilization Corporation. Among these roles are his participation on the National Archives Advisory Board and on the Committee of the National Museum of the American Indian National Campaign. He has served on advisory boards in relation to the planning of other major museums in Canada and abroad.

George F. MacDonald, le directeur exécutif du Musée canadien des civilisations, a fait ses études en anthropologie à l'université de Toronto et à l'université Yale, où il a obtenu son doctorat. Sur le plan professionnel, il occupe son premier poste à titre d'archéologue sur le terrain au Musée royal de l'Ontario puis, peu de temps après, au Musée national de l'Homme, où il fait partie du personnel permanent dès 1964. En 1969, il y est nommé chef de la Division d'archéologie.

Ses intérêts, dans la sphère universitaire, portent sur les traditions orales, les rituels, les systèmes symboliques, la culture matérielle et les manifestations artistiques des cultures autochtones. Il publie de nombreux ouvrages archéologiques et anthropologiques sur les cultures autochtones de la côte du Pacifique, son œuvre la plus marquante sur ce thème étant *Haida Monumental Art*. Il s'intéresse également aux relations entre les cultures autochtones et les musées et, plus généralement, à la gestion des ressources patrimoniales. Au cours des dernières années, il a écrit plusieurs articles et présenté des communications lors de nombreux colloques sur l'évolution actuelle et future de l'univers muséal. Son ouvrage intitulé *Un musée pour le village global : le Musée canadien des civilisations* est publié à l'occasion de l'ouverture de ce musée, en juin 1989.

Aujourd'hui, George F. MacDonald, en plus d'assumer la charge de directeur exécutif de la Société du Musée canadien des civilisations, continue d'offrir sa contribution aux organismes patrimoniaux en y assumant des rôles multiples. À noter particulièrement sa participation aux activités du Comité consultatif des Archives nationales et du Committee of the National Museum of the American Indian National Campaign, ainsi qu'à divers conseils consultatifs chargés de planifier l'édification de plusieurs grands musées, au Canada et à l'étranger.

LOUIS TAPARDJUK

Mayor, Igloolik, Northwest Territories / Maire d'Igloolik (Territoires du Nord-Ouest)
Historic Sites and Monuments Board of Canada Northwest Territories Member / Membre de la Commission des lieux et monuments historiques du Canada pour les Territoires du Nord-Ouest

Louis Tapardjuk is currently the Secretary to the Inullariit Elders Society, whose objective is to promote and enhance Inuit language and culture. This is done through ethnographical research and oral history.

He also serves as a Trustee to the Inuit Heritage Trust, which is the organization that was created out of the Nunavut Land Claims Agreement to participate in the development of government policy and legislation on archaeology in the Nunavut Settlement and to assume increasing responsibilities for supporting, encouraging, and facilitating the conservation, maintenance and display of archaeological sites and specimens in the Nunavut Settlement Area.

He is also currently the Vice-Chairman of Nunasi Corporation which is a birthright development corporation serving all of the beneficiaries to the Nunavut Land Claims Agreement.

Louis Tapardjuk occupe actuellement les fonctions de secrétaire de l'Inullariit Elders Society, organisme voué à la promotion et à l'enrichissement de la langue et de la culture Inuit par la recherche ethnographique et l'histoire orale. Il est en outre membre du conseil d'administration de l'Inuit Heritage Trust. Cet organisme, créé en vertu de l'Accord sur les revendications territoriales du Nunavut, doit participer à l'élaboration de la politique gouvernementale et de la législation sur l'archéologie dans la région du Nunavut, et assumer des responsabilités croissantes pour soutenir, encourager et faciliter la protection, l'entretien et l'exhibition des lieux et des objets archéologiques de la région du Nunavut.

M. Tapardjuk est par ailleurs vice-président de la Nunasi Corporation, société de promotion des droits ancestraux au service de tous les bénéficiaires de l'Accord sur les revendications territoriales du Nunavut.

JEAN-PIERRE WALLOT
Archiviste national / National Archivist
Membre d'office de la Commission des lieux et monuments historiques du Canada / Ex officio Member, Historic Sites and Monuments Board of Canada

Titulaire d'un doctorat de l'Université de Montréal, M. Wallot est archiviste national du Canada depuis 1985. Il a occupé depuis 1961 de nombreux postes aux universités de Montréal et de Toronto et à l'Université Concordia, à Montréal. Ancien président de la Société historique du Canada, de l'Institut d'histoire de l'Amérique française et de l'Académie des lettres et des sciences humaines de la Société royale du Canada, il occupe actuellement la présidence du Conseil international des archives.

M. Wallot est membre de l'Académie des lettres du Québec et officier de l'Ordre des arts et des lettres de la République française. Il est par ailleurs Officier de l'Ordre du Canada et a reçu les médailles Tremaine, Tyrrell et du Centenaire de la Société royale du Canada, ainsi que des doctorats honorifiques des universités de Rennes (1987) et d'Ottawa (1996). Il a publié dix livres à titre d'auteur ou de coauteur ainsi que plus de 100 articles érudits et de nombreux exposés.

National Archivist of Canada since 1985, Dr. Wallot holds a Ph.D. from the Université de Montréal. Since 1961, he has held numerous posts at the Université de Montréal, the

University of Toronto, and at Concordia University in Montréal. He is a past President of the Canadian Historical Association, of the Institut d'histoire de l'Amérique française and of the Académie des lettres et des sciences humaines, The Royal Society of Canada, and he is currently President of the International Council on Archives.

Dr. Wallot is a member of the Académie des lettres du Québec and was named an Officer of the Ordre des arts et des lettres de la République française. He is an Officer of the Order of Canada and the recipient of the Tremaine, Tyrrell and Centennial medals of The Royal Society of Canada, as well honorary doctorates from the universities of Rennes (1987) and Ottawa (1996). He has written or co-authored ten books as well as over 100 scholarly articles and numerous papers.

JOHN H. WHITE (died 1996 / décédé en 1996)
(Alternate Chair/Président suppléant)
Economist / Économiste
Former Ontario Member, Historic Sites and Monuments Board of Canada / Ex-membre de la Commission des lieux et monuments historiques du Canada pour l'Ontario

John White was a professional economist and former Ontario Cabinet Minister. Among his many portfolios, he served as Minister of Colleges and Universities and Minister of Industry and Tourism. An M.A. from The University of Western Ontario in Economics, he was awarded an honorary Doctorate of Letters by Carleton University.

For six years he was Chairman of the Ontario Heritage Foundation. He served as Chairman of the Bank of Montreal Investment Funds, Chairman of the Advisory Council of the Canadian Centre for Pension and Retirement Studies, and Vice Chairman of Fanshawe Pioneer Village.

Économiste de profession, John White avait fait partie du conseil des ministres de l'Ontario, notamment comme ministre des Collèges et des Universités et ministre de l'Industrie et du Tourisme. Titulaire d'une maîtrise en économique de l'université de Western Ontario, il s'était vu décerner un doctorat honorifique en lettres par l'université Carleton.

M. White avait occupé la présidence de la Fondation du patrimoine de l'Ontario pendant six ans. Il avait par ailleurs été président des fonds d'investissements de la Banque de Montréal et de conseil consultatif du Canadian Centre for Pension and Retirement Studies, et vice-président du Fanshawe Pioneer Village.

Historic Sites and Monuments Board of Canada
Brief History of Board
Members 1919 - 1996
La Commission des lieux et monuments historiques
du Canada
Histoire de la Commission en bref
Liste des membres 1919 - 1996

Programme
Participants

An Introduction

History

Since its creation in 1919, the Historic Sites and Monuments Board of Canada has been a significant player within the heritage community in Canada. It grew out of the interplay of disparate elements of public opinion concerned with heritage preservation and federal government policy before World War I. A growing heritage movement put pressure on the federal government to preserve and develop sites with historical associations. At the same time, the government was looking for ways to extend its national parks system from the west into the east and conceived the idea of creating historic parks around significant historic structures. Government officials also wanted to dispose of many obsolete properties, such as old fortifications or fur trading posts, to which local organizations attached historical value. A government programme to identify and preserve Canadian historical heritage was delayed by the First World War. In 1919, James B. Harkin, the Commissioner of Dominion Parks, persuaded the federal government to establish "An Advisory Board for Historic Site Preservation" to advise the federal authorities which sites were of national significance.

The first meeting of the Board was held in Ottawa in the fall of that year. Its six members selected the official name, "The Historic Sites and Monuments Board of Canada", and elected Brigadier General E.A. Cruikshank as its first chairman. It quickly set about determining the most important historic sites in the country and it decided on appropriate ways of commemorating them. The usual method, but not the only one, was to place a bronze plaque on a stone cairn at a location connected with the person, place, or event being commemorated. Where the government owned a property, it often recommended some degree of restoration, as it did at Fort Beauséjour and Fortress of Louisbourg. Many of the Board's early recommendations emphasized military history, exploration, and politics, reflecting the then-current notions about Canada's past. In the twenty years that Cruikshank served as Chairman almost 300 plaques were erected at various locations across the country.

In 1951, the Royal Commission on National Development in the Arts, Letters and Sciences noted the imbalance of the Board's commemorative programme and recommended that more attention be paid to preservation. In 1953, the *Historic Sites and Monuments Act* established the Board by statute, enlarged it, and gave it increased resources. An amendment in 1955 specified the power to recommend national designation for buildings by reason of their age or architectural design. Thereafter, it paid increasingly more attention to Canadian built heritage, expanding the concept to include streetscapes, districts, gardens, and urban and rural landscapes. Recently, it was given the duty of assessing Heritage Railway Stations. During these years, the Board continued to deal with the great number of requests for recognition of people, places, and events in the various aspects of Canadian political, economic, and social history. In keeping with trends in Canadian society and historiography, the Board is now directing more attention to the history of Aboriginal Peoples, women, and cultural communities in Canada.

Composition

The Historic Sites and Monuments Board of Canada is established under the authority of the *Historic Sites and Monuments Act* and the members are appointed at pleasure by the Governor in Council. There are two representatives for each of the provinces of Ontario and Quebec, and one representative for each of the other eight provinces, Yukon, and the Northwest Territories. A member must reside in the province or territory that he or she represents. As well, the National Archivist and an officer of the National Museums are members. A member may be appointed for no longer than five years, and he or she may be re-appointed for additional terms. The Chairman of the Board is appointed by the Governor in Council from the members of the Board.

To assist the Board in carrying out its duties, the Director General of National Historic Sites, Parks Canada, acts as Secretary of the Board and, under her direction, a secretariat provides administrative and secretarial services. As well, the historians and archaeologists of Parks Canada prepare the necessary historical background material to aid the Board in making its decisions on national significance.

Duties

The duties of the Board are defined by section 5 of the Act:

> The Board may receive and consider recommendations respecting the marking or commemoration of historic places, the establishment of historic museums and the administration, preservation and maintenance of historic places and historic museums, and shall advise the Minister in carrying out his powers under this Act.

The Minister may mark or commemorate historic places by means of plaques or in other ways, and may enter into agreements with persons for marking or commemorating and for caring for or preserving such places. With the agreement of Treasury Board, the Minister may acquire historic places by purchase, lease, or otherwise and provide for their administration, preservation, and maintenance. Provision is also made for the Minister to establish and maintain historic museums, but traditionally this federal responsibility has been largely left to the National Museums. It is the responsibility of the Board, then, to advise the Minister in carrying out these powers.

In practice, the Board advises the Minister on the commemoration of those themes, persons, events, sites, structures, and places that represent nationally significant aspects of Canadian history. It also indicates the level of commemoration that it thinks appropriate – that is, by plaque alone, by cost-sharing with a third party, or, more rarely, by acquisition and development of the site by Parks Canada. It may also offer advice to the Minister on other matters that it thinks are relevant to the recognition or preservation of Canada's heritage or on which the Minister requests its advice.

As heritage issues become more significant in Canadian society, the Board is increasingly adopting the role of public advocate in pursuit of its goals. Where appropriate, it may encourage heritage preservation by making known its opinion to public bodies, the media, and the general public on broad heritage issues or specific sites, as it did in the controversy surrounding the building of high rises around the Halifax Public Gardens. It may provide information on significant people, places, and events of the past; on building and site preservation philosophy and techniques; and on legislation affecting heritage protection.

Procedures

The Board's agenda is in large part driven by public concerns as it responds to public requests that people, places, or events be declared of national historic significance. It receives well over 200 requests each year, of which from 50 to 70 will generate research papers from the Historical Services Branch or Archaeological Services Branch of the National Historic Sites Directorate of Parks Canada to assist the Board in its deliberations.

Because of the great deal of work involved in carrying out its mandate, the Board has struck a number of committees with specific areas of responsibility. Overall control is exercised by the Executive Committee made up of the Chairman of the Board and the Chairpersons of the other committees. The Criteria Committee determines criteria to be used for consideration of particular issues or situations, such as the criteria for the identification of historic districts and the criteria for assessing archaeological sites. The Cultural Communities Committee brings to the Board recommendations for commemoration of the sites and contributions of Canada's diverse cultural groups, in particular Aboriginal peoples. The Inscriptions Committee is responsible for ensuring the appropriateness and accuracy of all plaque texts. The Thematic Studies and Systems Planning Committee is responsible for reviewing the National Historic Sites System Plan and for bringing before the Board for consideration themes in Canadian history which it considers nationally significant.

The Built Environment Committee is charged with assessing the national significance of all buildings, including historic districts and streetscapes, sent for consideration to the Board. If a building, or group of buildings, is deemed to be of national significance, the committee is responsible for recommending the manner of commemoration – by plaque, cost-sharing, or, rarely, acquisition. The Committee may recommend the selection, preservation, and interpretation of *in situ* resources either because of their intrinsic heritage value or because they are excellent representatives of a nationally significant theme which the Board has recommended for commemoration.

The Heritage Railway Stations Committee was formed after *The Heritage Railway Stations Protection Act* was passed in 1988. Under this Act the Board was given the duty of recommending to the Minister responsible for Parks Canada those stations to be designated Heritage Railway Stations and thereby to be furnished with a measure of protection according to the provisions of the Act. Since the government intended something other than national significance, the committee needed to devise criteria which took into account factors which recognized regional or local significance. To date, the Committee and the Board have considered 275 stations, 166 of which it has designated as Heritage Railway Stations.

If the recommendation of the Board is positive and the Minister agrees, the usual form of commemoration is the erection of a bronze plaque at a suitable location bearing a bilingual inscription in French and English. Where appropriate an Aboriginal language may be added, and in exceptional cases a third non-Aboriginal language may be used, as was the case with the plaque to the poet Stephan G. Stephansson, who wrote in Icelandic. Sometimes the Board may feel that something more than a plaque is required. The Board may recommend that the erection of a special monument will best convey the national significance of the subject. At other times it may recommend that Parks Canada enter into a cost-sharing agreement with other interested parties to preserve the site, or, very rarely, that Parks Canada acquire the site.

Criteria

Generally, the Board will recommend a subject for designation if it meets one of two criteria. It must have had a nationally significant impact on Canadian history, or it must represent a nationally important example or illustration of Canadian human history. A site or structure may be recommended for designation not only because of its intrinsic significance but also because of its association with a nationally significant aspect of Canadian history, provided that association is itself sufficiently important. Places located outside the territory of Canada and living persons may not be considered. Except for prime ministers, who become eligible immediately upon their death, usually a person must be dead for at least twenty-five years before becoming eligible for consideration. The Board will not recommend religious or ethnic groups except where their contributions are represented by sites, individuals, or events of national significance.

Current Concerns

Recently the Board has taken initiatives in areas of history which have become prominent in Canadian historiography and society – the histories of Aboriginal Peoples, women, and cultural communities. It realized that its programme of recognizing and preserving archaeological sites alone was inadequate to commemorate Aboriginal Peoples' history. Consequently, it recommended that sites of spiritual and/or cultural importance should be eligible for consideration even if there were no tangible cultural resources, provided that there was adequate evidence of their significance gathered through oral history or otherwise. It has recommended broad-based consultation with Aboriginal groups and it has taken an active part in two workshops organized by Parks Canada to consult with representatives of Aboriginal Peoples.

The Board recognized that there was a significant gender gap in the system of national historic sites. It responded with enthusiasm, therefore, to the convening of two workshops on women's history, and it has committed itself to improve the commemoration of women in Canadian history. It has asked for a review of existing operating sites with a view to incorporate appropriate aspects of women's history into their interpretive programme. Responding to advice from the workshops and others, it will identify themes in women's history to direct the research and commemoration programme in the future.

The Board has acknowledged that very few of Canada's national historic sites speak to the experience of cultural communities other than Aboriginal Peoples or those of French or British stock. As a beginning in addressing this imbalance, it has initiated a study to identify sites of potential significance associated with the African-Canadian experience. In the meantime, the Black Battalion in World War I, the settlement of Black Loyalists near Shelburne, Nova Scotia, and the passing of the 1793 act against slavery in Upper Canada have been commemorated.

Achievements

For seventy-five years the Historic Sites and Monuments Board of Canada has been advising the government of Canada on the commemoration of people, places, and events of national significance in Canadian history and in erecting plaques to inform the Canadian public of the country's history. Over these years, in keeping with changes in Canadian historiography, it has extended its range of interest from military, political, and geographical subjects to include broader themes in social and economic history. Recently, it has taken initiatives in recognizing the histories of Aboriginal Peoples, women, and cultural communities. The Board has always seen its plaquing program as educative in the broadest sense of the term. The more than 1,100 commemorative plaques that have been erected across the country are a memorial to its dedication to popular education.

Since the mid-1950s, the Board has increasingly emphasized built heritage and has begun an evaluation of the architectural heritage of the nation. Significantly, the Board has extended its definition of built heritage to include streetscapes, districts, gardens, and cultural landscapes. This interest has manifested itself in numerous plaques to commemorate buildings and sites and, as well, in recommendations for cost sharing to preserve and restore historically significant buildings, and, very rarely, to acquire the historic resource. It has taken a leading role within the heritage community in advocating the preservation and restoration of historic buildings in Canada. The 132 operating National Historic Sites within the Parks Canada system are a tribute to its belief in, and concern for, historic conservation and preservation.

LA COMMISSION DES LIEUX ET MONUMENTS HISTORIQUES DU CANADA

Une introduction

Histoire

Depuis sa création, en 1919, la Commission des lieux et monuments historiques du Canada (CLMHC) joue un rôle important parmi les groupes de défense du patrimoine au Canada. Elle est née de l'interaction entre divers courants de l'opinion publique voués à la conservation du patrimoine, ainsi que de la politique pratiquée par le gouvernement fédéral avant la Première Guerre mondiale. Le mouvement de protection du patrimoine qui se développait alors pressait le gouvernement fédéral de conserver et d'aménager des lieux associés à l'histoire du Canada. En même temps, le gouvernement cherchait des moyens d'étendre son réseau de parcs nationaux de l'ouest à l'est et conçut l'idée de créer des parcs historiques autour de constructions historiques importantes. Les fonctionnaires fédéraux souhaitaient par ailleurs aliéner nombre de propriétés désuètes, comme d'anciennes fortifications ou des postes de traite des fourrures, auxquelles des organismes locaux attachaient une valeur historique. Un programme gouvernemental de désignation et de conservation du patrimoine historique canadien fut retardé par la Première Guerre mondiale. En 1919, James B. Harkin, commissaire des parcs du Dominion, persuada le gouvernement fédéral d'établir « une commission consultative de la conservation des lieux historiques » qui donnerait des avis aux autorités fédérales quant aux lieux d'importance nationale.

La première réunion de la Commission eut lieu à Ottawa à l'automne de cette année-là. Ses six membres choisirent comme nom officiel « La Commission des lieux et monuments historiques du Canada » et élurent le brigadier-général E.A. Cruikshank à la présidence. Ils entreprirent rapidement de déterminer les plus importants lieux historiques du pays et décidèrent des moyens appropriés de les commémorer. La méthode habituelle, mais non la seule, consistait à apposer une plaque en bronze sur un cairn de pierre en un lieu ayant un rapport avec la personne, l'endroit ou l'événement commémorés. Lorsqu'une propriété appartenait à l'État, la Commission recommandait souvent qu'elle soit restaurée dans une certaine mesure, comme dans le cas du fort Beauséjour et de la forteresse de Louisbourg. Nombre des premières recommandations de la Commission mettaient l'accent sur l'histoire militaire, l'exploration et la politique, conformément à la conception qu'on se faisait alors de l'histoire du Canada. Au cours des vingt années pendant lesquelles Cruikshank en fut président, la Commission fit installer près de 300 plaques à divers endroits du pays.

En 1951, la Commission royale d'enquête sur l'avancement des arts, des sciences et des lettres souligna le déséquilibre du programme de commémoration de la CLMHC et recommanda qu'on accorde plus d'attention à la conservation. En 1953, la *Loi sur les lieux et monuments historiques* établit juridiquement la Commission, élargit son mandat et lui donna des ressources accrues. Une modification apportée en 1955 lui conféra le pouvoir de recommander la désignation de bâtiments en raison de leur âge ou de leur architecture. Par la suite, elle accorda de plus en plus d'attention au patrimoine bâti, dans lequel elle engloba les rues, les quartiers, les jardins et les paysages urbains et ruraux. Récemment, elle s'est vu confier la responsabilité d'évaluer les gares ferroviaires patrimoniales. Au cours de ces années, la Commission a continué à répondre à un grand nombre de demandes de reconnaissance de personnes, de lieux et d'événements liés à divers aspects de l'histoire politique, économique et sociale du Canada. Conformément aux tendances de la société et de l'historiographie canadiennes, elle accorde désormais une plus grande attention à l'histoire des peuples autochtones, des femmes et des communautés culturelles.

Composition

La Commission des lieux et monuments historiques du Canada existe en vertu de la *Loi sur les lieux et monuments historiques,* et ses membres sont nommés par le gouverneur en conseil pour un mandat de durée limitée. Les provinces de l'Ontario et du Québec y comptent deux représentants chacune; les huit autres provinces, le Yukon et les Territoires du Nord-Ouest, un chacun. Chaque membre de la Commission doit résider dans la province ou le territoire qu'il représente. L'Archiviste national et un représentant des Musées nationaux doivent également en faire partie. Ses membres sont nommés pour un mandat maximum de cinq ans, mais peuvent être nommés de nouveau pour des mandats supplémentaires. Le gouverneur en conseil désigne le président de la Commission parmi ses membres.

Le directeur général des Lieux historiques nationaux de Parcs Canada remplit les fonctions de secrétaire de la Commission, et un secrétariat assure sous sa direction des services administratifs et de soutien. Les historiens et les archéologues de Parcs Canada préparent par ailleurs la documentation historique nécessaire pour aider la Commission à prendre ses décisions touchant l'importance nationale des sujets à commémorer.

Fonctions

L'article 5 de la Loi définit les fonctions de la Commission comme suit :

> La Commission peut recevoir et examiner des recommandations sur les inscriptions relatives aux endroits historiques ou leur commémoration, sur l'établissement de musées historiques et sur l'administration, la conservation et l'entretien de tels endroits et musées. Elle doit aussi donner au Ministre des avis consultatifs en ce qui regarde l'exercice de ses pouvoirs prévus par la présente loi.

Le Ministre peut signaler ou commémorer des lieux historiques au moyen de plaques ou d'autres manières, et il peut conclure des ententes avec des personnes pour signaler et commémorer ces lieux ainsi que pour les entretenir et les protéger. Il peut en outre, avec le consentement du Conseil du Trésor, acquérir des lieux historiques par voie d'achat, de location ou d'autres manières et pourvoir à leur administration, à leur conservation et à leur entretien. La Loi prévoit également qu'il peut établir et entretenir des musées historiques, mais cette responsabilité fédérale a toujours été laissée aux Musées nationaux. Il incombe donc à la Commission de conseiller le Ministre dans l'exercice de ces pouvoirs.

Dans la pratique, la Commission donne des avis au Ministre touchant la commémoration des thèmes, personnes, événements, lieux, ouvrages et endroits représentant des aspects de l'histoire du Canada qui ont une importance nationale. Elle lui indique également le degré de commémoration qu'elle juge à propos, soit l'installation d'une plaque, le partage de frais avec une tierce partie ou, plus rarement, l'acquisition et l'aménagement d'un lieu par Parcs Canada. Elle peut aussi conseiller le Ministre sur d'autres questions qui, selon elle, ont un rapport avec la reconnaissance ou la conservation du patrimoine canadien, ou à propos desquelles le Ministre lui demande son avis.

À mesure que les questions patrimoniales prennent plus d'importance dans la société canadienne, la Commission joue de plus en plus le rôle d'avocat du public dans la poursuite de ses objectifs. Le cas échéant, elle peut encourager la conservation du patrimoine en faisant connaître son opinion aux organismes publics, aux médias et au grand public sur des questions générales relatives au patrimoine ou sur des dossiers précis, comme elle l'a fait dans le cas de la controverse qui a entouré la construction de gratte-ciel autour des jardins publics d'Halifax. Elle peut fournir des renseignements sur des personnes, des lieux et des événements importants du passé, sur les principes et les techniques de construction et de conservation de lieux, et sur les lois touchant la protection du patrimoine.

Procédures

Le programme de la Commission est déterminé dans une large mesure par les préoccupations du public, car elle répond aux demandes que celui-ci lui adresse afin de faire reconnaître l'importance historique nationale de personnes, de lieux ou d'événements. Elle reçoit chaque année plus de 200 demandes, dont cinquante à soixante-dix suscitent l'exécution d'études par la Direction des services historiques ou la Direction des services archéologiques de la Direction générale des lieux historiques nationaux de Parcs Canada; ces études ont pour but de faciliter les délibérations de la Commission.

Vu la somme importante de travail que nécessite l'exécution de son mandat, la Commission a constitué un certain nombre de comités ayant des secteurs de responsabilité particuliers. Le Comité de direction, qui se compose du président de la Commission et des présidents des autres comités, contrôle l'ensemble de leurs travaux. Le Comité des critères détermine les critères à utiliser pour l'examen de questions ou de situations particulières, comme ceux qui président à la désignation des quartiers historiques et à l'évaluation des lieux archéologiques. Le Comité des communautés culturelles soumet à la Commission des recommandations visant la commémoration des lieux et contributions des divers groupes culturels du Canada, en particulier les peuples autochtones. Le Comité des inscriptions est chargé d'assurer l'à-propos et l'exactitude des textes relatif à chacune des plaques. Le Comité des études thématiques et de la planification du réseau a pour mandat de passer en revue le plan du réseau des lieux historiques nationaux et de soumettre à l'examen de la Commission les thèmes de l'histoire du Canada qu'il juge d'intérêt national.

Le Comité du patrimoine bâti est chargé d'évaluer l'intérêt national de tous les bâtiments – y compris les quartiers historiques et les rues – soumis à l'examen de la Commission. Si un bâtiment ou un groupe de bâtiments est jugé d'intérêt national, il incombe à ce comité de recommander la façon de le commémorer (installation d'une plaque, partage de frais ou, rarement, acquisition). Il peut en outre recommander qu'on procède à la sélection, à la conservation et à l'interprétation des ressources se trouvant sur place soit en raison de leur valeur patrimoniale intrinsèque, soit parce qu'elles constituent des exemples bien représentatifs de thèmes d'intérêt national dont la Commission a recommandé la commémoration.

Le Comité des gares ferroviaires patrimoniales a été constitué après l'adoption de la *Loi sur la protection des gares ferroviaires patrimoniales*, en 1988. Cette loi a confié à la Commission la responsabilité de recommander au ministre chargé de Parcs Canada les gares à désigner gares ferroviaires patrimoniales et auxquelles il convient par conséquent d'accorder un certain degré de protection conformément aux dispositions de la Loi. Comme le gouvernement ne voulait pas se limiter au seul critère de l'importance nationale, le comité a dû en élaborer d'autres permettant de tenir compte de l'intérêt régional ou local de ces gares. Jusqu'ici, le Comité et la Commission ont étudié 275 gares, dont 166 ont été désignées gares ferroviaires patrimoniales.

Si la Commission fait une recommandation positive et que le Ministre l'accepte, le mode habituel de commémoration consiste à installer en un lieu approprié une plaque en bronze portant une inscription bilingue en français et en anglais. Lorsque cela est à propos, l'inscription peut également figurer dans une langue autochtone et, dans des cas exceptionnels, dans une troisième langue non autochtone; tel a été le cas de la plaque dédiée au poète Stephan G. Stephansson, qui écrivit toute son œuvre en islandais. Dans certains cas, la Commission peut être d'avis qu'une plaque ne suffit pas et recommander l'érection d'un monument spécial pour mieux faire ressortir l'importance nationale du sujet. Dans d'autres circonstances, elle peut recommander que Parcs Canada conclue une entente de partage de frais avec d'autres parties intéressées afin de conserver le lieu ou, dans des cas très rares, qu'il l'acquière.

Critères

En règle générale, la Commission recommandera la désignation d'un sujet s'il satisfait à l'un de deux critères. Il doit soit avoir eu une incidence marquante sur l'histoire du Canada, soit constituer une illustration ou un exemple important de l'histoire humaine du Canada, au plan national dans les deux cas. Elle pourra par ailleurs recommander la désignation d'un lieu ou d'un ouvrage en raison non seulement de son intérêt intrinsèque, mais aussi de ses liens avec un aspect de l'histoire du Canada ayant un intérêt national, à condition que ces liens soient eux-mêmes suffisamment importants. Les personnes vivantes et les lieux situés à l'extérieur du territoire canadien ne sont pas admissibles. Exception faite des premiers ministres, qui deviennent admissibles immédiatement après leur mort, une personne doit habituellement être décédée depuis au moins vingt-cinq ans avant que sa candidature puisse être prise en considération. La Commission ne recommande pas la désignation de groupes religieux ni ethniques, sauf lorsque leur contribution est représentée par des lieux, des personnes ou des événements d'importance nationale.

Centres d'intérêt actuels

Récemment, la Commission a pris des initiatives dans des domaines de l'histoire qui occupent désormais une place importante dans l'historiographie et la société canadiennes, soit l'histoire des peuples autochtones, celle des femmes et celle des communautés culturelles. Elle s'est rendu compte que son programme de reconnaissance et de conservation de lieux archéologiques ne suffisait pas à lui seul à commémorer l'histoire des peuples autochtones. Elle a donc recommandé que des lieux d'importance spirituelle et/ou culturelle puissent être pris en considération même s'il ne s'y trouvait aucune ressource culturelle tangible, pourvu qu'on dispose de preuves suffisantes de leur importance, transmises par l'histoire orale ou par d'autres canaux. Elle a en outre recommandé que l'on consulte largement les groupes autochtones et a pris une part active à deux ateliers organisés par Parcs Canada afin de consulter les représentants des peuples autochtones.

La Commission a par ailleurs reconnu l'existence de lacunes importantes quant à la commémoration des femmes dans le réseau des lieux historiques nationaux. Elle a donc réagi avec enthousiasme à la convocation de deux ateliers sur l'histoire des femmes et s'est engagée à améliorer la commémoration de leur contribution à l'histoire du Canada. Elle a demandé qu'on passe en revue ses programmes d'interprétation aux lieux qu'elle exploite afin d'y intégrer des aspects appropriés de l'histoire des femmes. En réponse aux avis exprimés par les participants aux ateliers et d'autres personnes, elle recensera divers thèmes de cette histoire pour orienter le programme futur de recherche et de commémoration.

La Commission a reconnu que très peu des lieux historiques nationaux du Canada représentent l'expérience de communautés culturelles autres que les Autochtones et les groupes d'ascendance française ou britannique. Pour commencer à redresser ce déséquilibre, elle a entrepris une étude visant à recenser des lieux potentiellement importants liés à l'expérience des Africains canadiens. Entre-temps, la contribution du Bataillon noir à la Première Guerre mondiale, l'établissement de Loyalistes noirs près de Shelburne (Nouvelle-Écosse) et l'adoption de la *Loi antiesclavagiste de 1793* au Haut-Canada ont été commémorés.

Réalisations

Depuis soixante-quinze ans, la Commission des lieux et monuments historiques du Canada conseille le gouvernement du Canada en ce qui concerne la commémoration de personnes, de lieux et d'événements historiques d'intérêt national et l'installation de plaques destinées à informer le public canadien de son histoire collective. Avec le temps, et compte tenu de l'évolution de l'historiographie canadienne, elle a étendu son champ d'action des thèmes militaires, politiques et géographiques à des thèmes plus larges de notre histoire sociale et économique. Récemment, elle a pris des initiatives pour reconnaître l'histoire des peuples autochtones, celle des femmes et celle des communautés culturelles. Elle a toujours considéré son programme d'installation de plaques comme une activité éducative au sens le plus large du terme. Elle a fait installer jusqu'ici plus de 1 100 plaques commémoratives un peu partout au pays ; celles-ci témoignent de son dévouement à l'éducation populaire.

Depuis le milieu des années 1950, la Commission met de plus en plus l'accent sur le patrimoine bâti et a entrepris une évaluation de notre patrimoine architectural. Fait révélateur, elle a élargi sa définition du patrimoine bâti pour y inclure rues, quartiers, jardins et cadres culturels. Cet intérêt s'est manifesté par l'installation de nombreuses plaques destinées à commémorer des bâtiments et des lieux ainsi que par des recommandations relatives au partage des frais de conservation et de restauration de bâtiments présentant un intérêt historique et, très rarement, à l'acquisition d'un bien historique. Elle a pris la tête du mouvement de protection du patrimoine pour préconiser la conservation et la restauration des bâtiments historiques du Canada. Les 132 lieux historiques nationaux exploités dans le cadre du réseau de Parcs Canada témoignent éloquemment de sa conviction à ce sujet et de son intérêt pour la conservation et la mise en valeur des ressources historiques.

Provincial, Territorial and Departmental Members (1919 - 1996)
Membres provinciaux, territoriaux et ministériels (1919 - 1996)

PROVINCIAL AND TERRITORIAL MEMBERS / MEMBRES PROVINCIAUX ET TERRITORIAUX

A.L. AGNEW
1961-1966

Businessman/homme d'affaires; President/président,
Prince Albert Historical Society, Prince Albert,
Saskatchewan

Richard M. **ALWAY**
1996-

President and Vice-Chancellor/président et vice-
chancelier, University of St. Michael's College,
Toronto. **Chairman/président, 1996-**

George **ANDERSON**
1969-1973

Merchant/marchand, Lac du Bonnet, Manitoba

A.G. **BAILEY**
1950-1961

Professor of History/professeur d'histoire, University of
New Brunswick, Fredericton, New Brunswick/
Nouveau-Brunswick

John U. **BAYLY**
1988-1991

Lawyer/avocat, Yellowknife, Northwest Territories/
Territoires du Nord-Ouest

Jules **BAZIN**
1955-1960

Bibliothécaire/Librarian, Montréal (Québec)

Noël **BÉLANGER**
1980-1992

Prêtre/Priest; historien/Historian, Université du
Québec à Rimouski, Rimouski (Québec)

Marion **BEYEA**
1988-1996

Provincial Archivist, Provincial Archives of New
Brunswick/archiviste en chef, Archives provinciales du
Nouveau-Brunswick, Fredericton, New Brunswick/
Nouveau-Brunswick

Francis **BOLGER**
1967-1977 and/et
1990-1995

Priest/prêtre; Professor of History/professeur d'histoire, University of Prince Edward Island, Charlottetown, Prince Edward Island/Île-du-Prince-Édouard

John A. **BOVEY**
1995-

Provincial Archivisit, Provincial Archives of British Columbia/archiviste provincial, Archives provinciales de la Colombie-Britannique, Victoria, British Columbia/Colombie-Britannique

Thane **CAMPBELL**
1950-1958

Chief Justice, Province of Prince Edward Island/Juge en chef de la province de l'Île-du-Prince-Édouard, Charlottetown, Prince Edward Island/Île-du-Prince-Édouard

J. Maurice S. **CARELESS**
1972-1985

Professor of History/professeur d'histoire, University of Toronto, Toronto, Ontario; **Chairman/président, 1981-1985**

Margaret R. **CONRAD**
1989-1996

Professor of History/professeure d'histoire, Acadia University, Wolfville, Nova Scotia/Nouvelle-Écosse

Isabel **COURT**
1996-

Heritage Activist/défenseure du patrimoine, Eldon, Belfast Post Office, Prince Edward Island/Île-du-Prince-Édouard

Trudy **COWAN**
1985-1996

Heritage consultant/consultante en matière de patrimoine, Calgary, Alberta (See also Soby/voir aussi Soby, 1979)

James **COYNE**
1919-1932

Lawyer/avocat; Historian/historien; ex-president/ancien président, Ontario Historical Society, St. Thomas, Ontario (Founding Member/membre fondateur)

Donald G. **CREIGHTON**
1958-1972

Professor of History/professeur d'histoire, University of Toronto, Toronto, Ontario

W. **CROWE**
1925-1930

Judge/juge, Sydney, Nova Scotia/Nouvelle-Écosse

Ernest A. CRUIKSHANK
1919-1939

Soldier/militaire, Historian/historien, Department of Militia and Defence/ministère de la Milice et de la Défense, Ottawa, Ontario; **Chairman/président, 1919-1939** (Founding Member/membre fondateur)

Jean DAIGLE
1979-1987

Professeur d'histoire/Professor of History, Université de Moncton, Moncton (Nouveau-Brunswick)/New Brunswick

Philippe DEMERS
1927-1929

Juge/Judge; historien/Historian; professeur de droit/Professor of Law, Université de Montréal, Montréal (Québec)

Hugh DEMPSEY
1975-1978

Director of History/directeur de l'histoire, Glenbow-Alberta Institute, Calgary, Alberta

Antoine D'ESCHAMBAULT
1937-1959

Prêtre, historien/Priest, Historian, Saint-Boniface (Manitoba) ; **président/Chairman, 1958-1959**

Andrée DÉSILETS
1974-1988

Professeure d'histoire/Professor of History, Université de Sherbrooke, Sherbrooke (Québec) ; **vice-présidente/Vice-Chair, 1987-1988**

C.G. DUNN
1960-1961

Journalist/journaliste, Québec, Québec

J. Plimsoll EDWARDS
1923-1925

Businessman/homme d'affires; President/président, Nova Scotia Historical Society, Halifax, Nova Scotia/Nouvelle-Écosse

Aegidius FAUTEUX
1925-1926

Journaliste, bibliothécaire, historien/Journalist, Librarian, Historian ; *La Presse* et/and Bibliothèque de Montréal, Montréal (Québec)

C. Bruce FERGUSSON
1955-1969

Provincial Archivist/archiviste provincial; Professor of History/professeur d'histoire, Dalhousie University, Halifax, Nova Scotia/Nouvelle-Écosse; **Chairman/président, 1960-1967**

Édouard FISET
1955-1960

Urbaniste/Town planner, Québec (Québec)

E.B. FORAN
1961-1966

City Clerk, Historian/greffier municipal, historien, St. John's, Newfoundland/Terre-Neuve

Terrence W.S. **FOSTER**
1996-

Heritage Activist/défenseur du patrimoine; Territorial Public Servant/fonctionnaire des Territoires, Yellowknife, Northwest Territories/Territoires du Nord-Ouest

Raymonde **GAUTHIER**
1990-1993

Historienne de l'art/Art Historian, Université du Québec à Montréal, Montréal (Québec)

J.A. **GREGORY**
1937-1950

Politician/homme politique; President/président, Prince Albert Historical Society, Prince Albert, Saskatchewan

Richard **GROVER**
1980-1986

Teacher of History/professeur d'histoire, St. Paul's High School (école sécondaire), Winnipeg, Manitoba

Gordon W. **HANDCOCK**
1995 -

Professor of Geography/professeur de géographie, Memorial University, St. John's, Newfoundland/Terre-Neuve

Jeanne **HARBOTTLE**
1980-1985

Heritage activist/défenseure du patrimoine, Whitehorse, Yukon

Leslie **HARRIS**
1967-1980

Professor of History, Dean of Arts and Science/professeur d'histoire, doyen de la Faculté des arts et des sciences, Memorial University, St. John's, Newfoundland/Terre-Neuve; **Chairman/président, 1978-1980**

D.C. **HARVEY**
1931-1954

Provincial Archivist/archiviste provincial, Professor of History/professeur d'histoire, Dalhousie University, Halifax, Nova Scotia/Nouvelle-Écosse

Fernand **HARVEY**
1993-

Sociologue/Sociologist, Institut national de la recherche scientifique - Culture et Société, Québec (Québec)

Frederick W. HOWAY
1923-1944

Judge, Historian/juge, historien, New Westminster, British Columbia/Colombie-Britannique; **Chairman/président, 1943-1944** (also for Manitoba until 1937, and Alberta till 1944/également membre pour le Manitoba jusqu'en 1937, et pour l'Alberta jusqu'en 1944)

Charles HUMPHRIES
1979-1993

Professor of History/professeur d'histoire, The University of British Columbia, Vancouver, British Columbia/Colombie-Britannique

Campbell INNES
1951-1954

Historian/historien; Museum curator/conservateur de musée, Battleford Museum, Battleford, Saskatchewan

C.E.A. JEFFERY
1950-1955

Newspaper editor/rédacteur en chef de journal, St. John's, Newfoundland/Terre-Neuve

Sarah JEROME
1986-1986

Heritage activist/défenseure du patrimoine, Fort McPherson, Northwest Territories/Territoires du Nord-Ouest

Gerald KEITH
1964-1969

Businessman/homme d'affaires; Member, New Brunswick Museum Board/membre du conseil du Musée du Nouveau-Brunswick, Saint John, New Brunswick/Nouveau-Brunswick

Michael S.R. KINNEAR
1990-1996

Professor of History/professeur d'histoire, The University of Manitoba, Winnipeg, Manitoba

André N. LALONDE
1990-1996

Professeur d'histoire/Professor of History, The University of Regina, Regina (Saskatchewan)

Fred LANDON
1932-1958

Librarian, Professor of History/bibliothécaire, professeur d'histoire, The University of Western Ontario, London, Ontario; **Chairman/président, 1950-1958**

Marc La TERREUR
1969-1978

Professeur d'histoire/Professor of History, Université Laval, Québec (Québec) ; **président/Chairman, 1970-1978**

349

Milton E. **La ZERTE**
1956-1956

Professor of Education/professeur d'éducation,
University of Alberta, Edmonton, Alberta

Jean-Jacques **LEFEBVRE**
1961-1973

Historien/Historian; archiviste/Archivist, Archives
du Palais de Justice, Montréal (Québec)

Jules **LÉGER**
1976-1978

Professeur d'histoire/Professor of History, Université
de Moncton, Moncton (Nouveau-Brunswick)/New
Brunswick

Morden H. **LONG**
1944-1955

Professor of History/professeur d'histoire, University
of Alberta, Edmonton, Alberta

Arthur R.M. **LOWER**
1959-1961

Professor of History/professeur d'histoire, Queen's
University, Kingston, Ontario

George L. **MacBEATH**
1970-1976

Historian, Administrator/historien, administrateur,
New Brunswick Historical Resources Administration;
Fredericton, New Brunswick/Nouveau-Brunswick

Raymond **MacLEAN**
1978-1987

Professor of History/professeur d'histoire, St. Francis
Xavier University, Antigonish, Nova Scotia/Nouvelle-
Écosse

Jean-Claude **MARSAN**
1995-

Architecte et urbaniste/Architect and Urban Planner;
professeur d'architecture/Professor of Architecture,
Université de Montréal, Montréal (Québec)

Guy **MARY-ROUSSELIÈRE**
1976-1983

Priest, Archaeologist/prêtre, archéologue; Pond Inlet,
Northwest Territories/Territoires du Nord-Ouest

Richmond **MAYSON**
1955-1960

Businessman/homme d'affaires, Prince Albert,
Saskatchewan

W.C. **MILNER**
1919-1923

Journalist/journaliste; Archivist (Public Archives
of Canada)/archiviste (Archives publiques du Canada),
Halifax, Nova Scotia/Nouvelle-Écosse (Founding
Member/membre fondateur)

Jacques **MONET**
1995-

Recteur/President, Université de Sudbury/University
of Sudbury, Sudbury (Ontario)

Victor **MORIN**
1924-1925

Avocat/Lawyer; historien/Historian; professeur de droit/Professor of Law, Université de Montréal, Montréal (Québec)

Noël **MURPHY**
1981-1984

Physician/médecin; Broadcaster/personnalité de la radio-télévision, Cornerbrook, Newfoundland/Terre-Neuve

Maréchal **NANTEL**
1930-1933

Avocat, juge/Lawyer, Judge; bibliothécaire/Librarian, Bibliothèque du barreau de Montréal, Montréal (Québec)

James **NESBITT**
1967-1971

Journalist/journaliste, Victoria, British Columbia/Colombie-Britannique

William **NEVILLE**
1996-

Heritage Activist/défenseur du patrimoine; Professor of Political Studies/professeur d'études politiques, University of Manitoba, Winnipeg

Shane **O'DEA**
1985-1993

Professor of English/professeur d'anglais, Memorial University, St. John's, Newfoundland/Terre-Neuve

Margaret **ORMSBY**
1960-1967

Professor of History/professeure d'histoire, The University of British Columbia, Vancouver, British Columbia/Colombie-Britannique

Robert **PAINCHAUD**
1976-1978

Professor of History/professeur d'histoire, The University of Winnipeg, Winnipeg, Manitoba

John **PALMER**
1961-1962

Lawyer/avocat; President/président, New Brunswick Historical Society, Saint John, New Brunswick/Nouveau-Brunswick

Jaroslav **PETRYSHYN**
1980-1985

Professor of History/professeur d'histoire, Peace River Community College, Grande Prairie, Alberta

Margaret **PRANG**
1971-1979

Professor of History/professeure d'histoire, The University of British Columbia, Vancouver, British Columbia/Colombie-Britannique

Thomas **RADDALL**
1954-1954

Historian, Novelist/historien, romancier, Liverpool, Nova Scotia/Nouvelle-Écosse

W.O. RAYMOND
1919-1923

Clergyman, Historian/pasteur, historien, Saint John, New Brunswick/Nouveau-Brunswick (Founding member/membre fondateur)

J. Edgar REA
1974-1976

Professor of History/professeur d'histoire, The University of Manitoba, Winnipeg, Manitoba

Irene ROGERS
1978-1989

Heritage Activist, Historian/défenseure du patrimoine, historienne, Charlottetown, Prince Edward Island/Île-du-Prince-Édouard

Edward RUSSENHOLT
1967-1969

Broadcaster, Businessman/personnalité de la radio-télévision, hommes d'affaires, Headingly, Manitoba

Walter N. SAGE
1944-1959

Professor of History/professeur d'histoire, The University of British Columbia, Vancouver, British Columbia/Colombie-Britannique

E.W. SANSOM
1962-1964

Soldier/militaire, Fredericton, New Brunswick/Nouveau-Brunswick

Richard Y. SECORD
1959-1967

Rancher/propriétaire de ranch, Edmonton, Alberta

George SHAW
1985-1987

Retired entrepreneur/entrepreneur à la retraite, Dawson, Yukon

B. Napier SIMPSON
1973-1978

Restoration architect/architecte spécialisé en restauration, Thornhill, Ontario

David E. SMITH
1976-1988

Professor of Political Science/professeur de science politique, University of Saskatchewan, Saskatoon, Saskatchewan

Joel K. SMITH
1957-1959

Businessman/homme d'affaires, Edmonton, Alberta

William SMITH
1959-1966

Professor of History/professeur d'histoire, Brandon College, Brandon, Manitoba

Ken SNYDER
1973-1975

Clergyman/pasteur, Dawson, Yukon (Observer/observateur)

Trudy **SOBY**
1979-1979

Heritage consultant/consultante en matière de patrimoine, Calgary, Alberta (See also Cowan/voir aussi Cowan, 1985)

Alex **STEVENSON**
1974-1975

Civil Servant, Department of Indian and Northern Affairs/fonctionnaire, ministère des Affaires indiennes et du Nord canadien (Ottawa), Northwest Territories/ Territoires du Nord-Ouest (Observer/observateur)

Edward **STOREY**
1981-1987

Professor of Recreology/professeur de récréologie, University of Ottawa/Université d'Ottawa, Ottawa, Ontario

George **STORY**
1993-1994

Professor of English Language and Literature/ professeur de langue et de littérature anglaises, Memorial University, St. John's, Newfoundland/Terre-Neuve

Benjamin **SULTE**
1919-1923

Civil servant, Historian/fonctionnaire, historien, Department of Militia and Defence/ministère de la Milice et de la Défense, Ottawa, Ontario (Founding Member/membre fondateur)

Édouard-Fabre **SURVEYER**
1933-1955

Judge/juge; Historian/historien; Professor of Law, McGill University/professeur de droit, Université McGill, Montréal, Québec

Thomas H.B. **SYMONS**
1986-1996

Vanier Professor/titulaire de la chaire Vanier, Trent University, Peterborough, Ontario; **Chairman/ président, 1986-1996**

James J. **TALMAN**
1961-1973

Librarian, Professor of History/bibliothécaire, professeur d'histoire, The University of Western Ontario, London, Ontario

Louis **TAPARDJUK**
1993-1996

Mayor/maire, Igloolik, Northwest Territories/ Territoires de Nord-Ouest

Earl **TAYLOR**
1959-1966

Merchant/marchand; President/président, P.E.I. Historical Association, Charlottetown, Prince Edward Island/Île-du-Prince-Édouard

Lewis H. **THOMAS**
1968-1974

Professor of History/professeur d'histoire, University of Alberta, Edmonton, Alberta

Daniel L. **TLEN**
1989-1996

Linguist/linguiste, Whitehorse, Yukon

Marcel **TRUDEL**
1961-1969

Professeur d'histoire/Professor of History, Université Laval (puis Université d'Ottawa/then University of Ottawa), Québec (Québec)

Alan **TURNER**
1967-1975

Historian/historien; Provincial Archivist, Provincial Archives of Saskatchewan/archiviste en chef, Archives provinciales de la Saskatchewan, Regina, Saskatchewan; **Chairman/président, 1967-1970**

Oliver **VARDY**
1956-1960

Director /directeur, Newfoundland Tourist Development Office, St. John's, Newfoundland/Terre-Neuve

Peter **WAITE**
1970-1977

Professor of History/professeur d'histoire, Dalhousie University, Halifax, Nova Scotia/Nouvelle-Écosse

Harry **WALKER**
1955-1959

Public Servant, Historian/fonctionnaire, historien; Department of Labour/ministère du Travail, Ottawa, Ontario

J. Clarence **WEBSTER**
1923-1950

Physician, Historian/médecin, historien, Shediac, New Brunswick/Nouveau-Brunswick; **Chairman/ président, 1945-1950**

John H. **WHITE**
1988-1994

Businessman/homme d'affaires; ex-Chairman, Ontario Heritage Foundation/ancien président, Fondation du patrimoine ontarien, London, Ontario

DEPARTMENTAL MEMBERS / MEMBRES MINISTÉRIELS

Frederick **ALCOCK**
1951-1955

Geologist, Chief Curator, National Museum, (Department of Mines and Resources)/géologue, conservateur en chef du Musée national (ministère des Mines et des Ressources), Ottawa (*ex officio*/membre d'office)*

354

W.D. CROMARTY
1943-1954

Department of Mines and Resources/Ministère des mines et des Ressources, Ottawa (*ex officio*/membre d'office)

James Bernard **HARKIN**
1919-1936

Commissioner of Dominion Parks, Department of the Interior, Ottawa/Commissaire des parcs du Dominion, ministère de l'Intérieur (Founding Member/membre fondateur) (*ex officio*/membre d'office)

W. Kaye **LAMB**
1949-1968

Dominion Archivist, Public Archives of Canada/ archiviste du Dominion, Archives publiques du Canada, Ottawa (*ex officio*/membre d'office)

Gustave **LANCTÔT**
1937-1949

Dominion Archivist, Public Archives of Canada/ archiviste du Dominion, Archives publiques du Canada, Ottawa (*ex officio*/membre d'office)

George F. **MacDONALD**
1971-1976 and/et
1978-

Archaeologist/archéologue; Director, Canadian Museum of Civilization/directeur du Musée canadien des civilisations, Ottawa (*ex officio*/membre d'office)

Wilfred I. **SMITH**
1969-1984

Dominion Archivist; Public Archives of Canada/ archiviste du Dominion, Archives publiques du Canada, Ottawa (*ex officio*/membre d'office)

William E. **TAYLOR, Jr.**
1968-1971

Archaeologist, Director, National Museum/ archéologue, directeur du Musée national, Ottawa (*ex officio*/membre d'office)

Jean-Pierre **WALLOT**
1985-

National Archivist, National Archives of Canada/ archiviste national, Archives nationales du Canada, Ottawa (*ex officio*/membre d'office)

F.H.H. WILLIAMSON
1936-1941

Controller, National Parks Bureau, Department of Mines and Resources/administrateur du Bureau des parcs nationaux, ministère des Mines et des Ressources, Ottawa (*ex officio*/membre d'office)

Clifford **WILSON**
1959-1961

Museum administrator; National Museum/ administrateur du Musée national, Ottawa (*ex officio*/membre d'office)

James V. **WRIGHT**
1976-1978

Archaeologist, National Museum of Man/archéologue, Musée national de l'Homme, Ottawa (*ex officio*/membre d'office)

* A note on *ex officio* members

J.B. Harkin, Commissioner of Dominion Parks, was instrumental in the creation of the Historic Sites and Monuments Board of Canada, and was named by Order-in-Council to the original Board in 1919. He was a fully participating member of the Board, and on his retirement in 1936 he was replaced by his successor in the bureaucracy, Mr. Williamson, who likewise took an active role in Board deliberations, as did his successor, Mr. Cromarty.

When the Board was reorganized under *The Historic Sites and Monuments Act* in 1953, provision was made for an officer of the Department (Mines and Resources) on the Board. The National Museum was then a part of the Department and the seat was filled by Dr. Alcock. In 1967 the Act was amended to make specific provision for representation of the Museum, which had since been moved to another department. The amended Act still contains provision for an officer of the Department [of Canadian Heritage], but for the past two decades this position has not been filled by a voting member (although it has been suggested that the programme's senior officer, acting as Secretary, is, in fact, a non-voting member of the Board.)

Major Lanctôt, the Dominion Archivist, was named to the Board in 1943, an arrangement formalized in *The Historic Sites and Monuments Act* of 1953.

* Remarque concernant les membres d'office

J. B. Harkin, commissaire des parcs du Dominion, contribua à la création de la Commission des lieux et monuments historiques du Canada, en 1919, et y fut nommé par décret la même année. Il y œuvra à titre de membre à part entière et, lors de sa retraite, en 1936, il fut remplacé par son successeur à la fonction publique, M. Williamson, qui prit également une part active aux délibérations de la Commission. Le successeur de ce dernier, M. Cromarty, fit de même.

Lorsque la Commission fut réorganisée en vertu de la *Loi sur les lieux et monuments historiques*, en 1953, il fut prévu qu'un fonctionnaire du ministère (des Mines et des Ressources) y siègerait. Le Musée national relevait alors de ce ministère, et le poste fut rempli par M. Alcock. En 1967, on modifia la Loi pour prévoir expressément la représentation du Musée, qui avait depuis lors été rattaché à un autre ministère. La Loi modifiée prévoit toujours la représentation de ce dernier, mais, depuis deux décennies, ce poste n'est pas rempli par un membre ayant droit de vote (de l'avis de certains, toutefois, le directeur du programme, qui occupe les fonctions de secrétaire de la Commission, est en fait un membre n'ayant pas droit de vote).

Le major Lanctôt, archiviste du Dominion, fut nommé à la Commission en 1943 ; la *Loi sur les lieux et monuments historiques* de 1953 officialisa la représentation de cet organisme.

PROGRAMME

Saturday, 26 November 1994 / le samedi 26 novembre 1994

20:00 - 22:00 20 h à 22 h	**Réception du Ministre**: Grand hall, Canadian Museum of Civilization / Musée canadien des civilisations M.C. : *Thomas H.B. Symons*, Chairman, HSMBC / président de la CLMHC
20:00 - 21:15 20 h à 21 h 15	**Presentation / Exposé**: "Places in Time" with laser enhancement in the CINEPLUS / « Ces lieux qui nous racontent » avec projection enrichie d'effets spéciaux au laser, dans le CINÉPLUS Introduction by / présenté par *George F. MacDonald*, Executive Director, Canadian Museum of Civilization / directeur exécutif du Musée canadien des civilisations
21:15 21 h 15	**Minister's Address / Allocution du Ministre**: *The Honourable / L'honorable Michel Dupuy*, Minister of Canadian Heritage / ministre du Patrimoine canadien

Sunday, 27 November 1994 / le dimanche 27 novembre 1994

9:00 / 9 h	Session 1. Keynote Address / Première séance. Allocution d'ouverture **CHAIR / PRÉSIDENT** : *Francis W.P. Bolger*, Professor Emeritus / professeur émérite, University of Prince Edward Island; P.E.I. Member, HSMBC / membre de la CLMHC pour l'Î.-P.-É. **SPEAKER / CONFÉRENCIER :** *Thomas H.B. Symons*, Founding President and Vanier Professor Emeritus / président fondateur et professeur émérite de la chaire Vanier, Trent University; Chairman, HSMBC / président de la CLMHC "Commemorating Canada's Past: From Old Crow to New Bergthal" / « La commémoration du passé du Canada : d'Old Crow à New Bergthal »
10:15 10 h 15	Session 2. Commemoration: A Moving Target / Deuxième séance. La commémoration : une cible en mouvement

CHAIR / PRÉSIDENT : *Louis Tapardjuk*, Mayor / maire, Igloolik (Northwest Territories / Territoires du Nord-Ouest); NWT Member, HSMBC / membre de la CLMHC pour les T.N.-O.

SPEAKERS / CONFÉRENCIERS:
Christina Cameron, Director General, National Historic Sites Directorate, Department of Canadian Heritage; Secretary, HSMBC / directrice générale des Lieux historiques nationaux, ministère du Patrimoine canadien; secrétaire de la CLMHC: "Commemoration: A Moving Target" / « La commémoration : une cible en mouvement »

Daniel Tlen, Aboriginal Language Consultant, Yukon Territory; Yukon Member, HSMBC / consultant en matière de langues autochtones au Yukon; membre de la CLMHC pour le Yukon : "Jim and Me" / « Jim et moi »

10:45
10 h 45

Session 3. Perspectives on Commemorating National Heritage / Troisième séance. Points de vue sur la commémoration du patrimoine national

CHAIR / PRÉSIDENT: *Jean-Pierre Wallot*, National Archivist; *ex officio* Member, HSMBC / archiviste national; membre d'office de la CLMHC

SPEAKERS / CONFÉRENCIERS:
France Gagnon Pratte, Chairperson / présidente, Conseil des monuments et sites du Québec
« Les investissements dans les icônes architecturales : les hôtels des compagnies ferroviaires et autres lieux spéciaux » / "Investing in Architectural Icons: Railway Hotels and Other Special Places"

Ted Rowe, Past Chairman, Newfoundland Historic Parks Association / ancien président de la Newfoundland Historic Parks Association
"Volunteerism and Heritage Commemoration" / « Bénévolat et commémoration du patrimoine »

John Herd Thompson, Professor of History / professeur d'histoire, Duke University
"'Professional' Historians and Heritage Commemoration" / « Les historiens professionnels et la commémoration du patrimoine »

John Wadland, Professor, Canadian Studies Program / professeur d'études canadiennes, Trent University
"Loons and Landscapes: The Place of Environmental Heritage" / « Huards et paysages : la place du patrimoine environnemental »

13: 30
13 h 30

Session 4. The Power of Place / Quatrième séance.
Le pouvoir du lieu

CHAIR / PRÉSIDENTE : *Margaret Conrad*, Professor of History /
professeure d'histoire, Acadia University; Nova Scotia Member,
HSMBC / membre de la CLMHC pour la Nouvelle-Écosse

SPEAKER / CONFÉRENCIÈRE :
Dolores Hayden, Professor of Architecture, Urbanism and American
Studies / professeure d'architecture, d'urbanisme et d'études
américaines, Yale University
"The Power of Place – Claiming Women's History in an Urban
Landscape" / « Le pouvoir du lieu – Revendication de l'histoire des
femmes en milieu urbain »

15:15
15 h 15

Session 5. Commemorating Cultural Heritage: Whose Heritage?
Whose Culture? / Cinquième séance: la commémoration du
patrimoine culturel: quel patrimoine ? quelle culture ?

CHAIR / PRÉSIDENT : *André N. Lalonde*, Director, Language
Institute / directeur de l'Institut de Formation linguistique, University
of Regina; Saskatchewan Member, HSMBC / membre de la CLMHC
pour la Saskatchewan

SPEAKERS / CONFÉRENCIERS :
Jacques Mathieu, Professor of History / professeur d'histoire,
Université Laval
« La langue de la commémoration » / "The Language of
Commemoration"

Felix (Fil) Fraser, Former Director, Alberta Human Rights
Commission / ancien directeur de la Commission des droits de la
personne de l'Alberta
"Redress versus Commemoration" / « Réparation vs commémoration »

Muriel K. Roy, Professor Emeritus / professeure émérite, Université
de Moncton
« Les partenariats, base d'une commémoration efficace » / "Effecting
Partnerships: Effective Commemoration"

Barbara Wyss, British Columbia Native Women's Society
"All My Relations" / « Tous mes liens »

Charles W. Humphries, Professor of History / professeur d'histoire,
University of British Columbia; former B.C. Member, HSMBC / ex-
membre de la CLMHC pour la Colombie-Britannique

359

"The Past and a Culture of Compliance: My History, Your History, No History" / « La passé et une culture de conformité : mon histoire, votre histoire, aucune histoire »

20:00 / 20 h **Reception / Réception**
National Library/National Archives / Bibliothèque nationale/Archives nationales
395, rue Wellington St., Ottawa

21:00 / 21 h **Presentation / Exposé**
Auditorium : "Sites in Sights": A Montage of 55 years of productions of the National Film Board of Canada / « Lieux en scène » : montage de films réalisés par l'Office national du film du Canada au cours d'une période de 55 ans

Introduction by / présenté par: *Joan Pennefather*, Government Film Commissioner and Chairperson, National Film Board of Canada / Commissaire du gouvernement à la cinématographie et présidente de l'Office national du film du Canada

Monday, 28 November 1994 / le lundi 28 novembre 1994

9:00 / 9 h **Session 6: Heritage Commemoration and Public Education in the Classroom: The Captive Audience / Sixième séance. La commémoration du patrimoine et l'éducation du public à l'école : l'auditoire captif**

CHAIR / PRÉSIDENTE : *Marion Beyea*, Provincial Archivist of New Brunswick; New Brunswick Member, HSMBC / archiviste provinciale du Nouveau-Brunswick ; membre de la CLMHC pour le Nouveau-Brunswick

SPEAKERS / CONFÉRENCIERS :
Richard M. Alway, President / président, St. Michael's College, University of Toronto
"Twice Told Tales: Researching and Teaching History in the 1990s" / « Double redécouverte : la recherche historique et l'enseignement de l'histoire dans les années 1990 »

Jean Du Berger, Professor of Ethnology, Department of History / professeur d'ethnologie, Département d'histoire, Université Laval
« Le patrimoine vivant » / "Living Heritage"

Dorothy Duncan, Executive Director, Ontario Historical Society / directrice générale de l'Ontario Historical Society
"Heritage As Classroom: Teaching Teachers to Teach Using Heritage Commemoration" / « Le patrimoine à l'école : apprendre aux enseignants à enseigner en se servant de la commémoration du patrimoine »

Harvey A. McCue, Director of Education and CEO, Mi'kmaq Education Authority, Nova Scotia / directeur de l'éducation et président de la Mi'kmaq Education Authority (Nouvelle-Écosse)
"Native Culture and the Teaching of History" / « La culture autochtone et l'enseignement de l'histoire »

Ken Osborne, Professor, Faculty of Education / professeur, Faculté d'éducation, University of Manitoba
"Teaching Heritage in the Classroom" / « L'enseignement du patrimoine à l'école »

11:15
11 h 15

Session 7: Heritage Commemoration and Public Education Outside the Classroom: Capturing the Audience / Septième séance. La commémoration du patrimoine et l'éducation du public hors de l'école : intéresser l'auditoire

CHAIR / PRÉSIDENT : *George F. MacDonald*, Executive Director, Canadian Museum of Civilization; *Ex officio* Member, HSMBC / directeur exécutif du Musée canadien des civilisations ; membre d'office de la CLMHC

SPEAKERS / CONFÉRENCIERS :
Annette Saint-Pierre, Saint Boniface Author and Publisher / auteure et éditrice de Saint-Boniface
« Intéresser les jeunes et les moins jeunes » / "Interesting the young and the not so young"

Robert Scully, Charles R. Bronfman Foundation / Fondation Charles R. Bronfman
Heritage Minutes: "Heritage as Sound Bites" / « Le patrimoine en capsules »

Michael Valpy, journalist / chroniqueur, *The Globe and Mail*
"Knowing and Communicating a Sense of Place" / « Posséder et communiquer le sens du lieu »

14:00 / 14 h   **Session 8. Public Policy and Heritage Commemoration / Huitième séance. La politique gouvernementale et la commémoration du patrimoine**

CHAIR / PRÉSIDENT : *Fernand Harvey*, Institut national de la recherche scientifique – Culture et Société ; membre de la CLMHC pour le Québec /Québec Member, HSMBC

SPEAKERS / CONFÉRENCIERS : POINTS DE VUE DIVERS
Mary Elizabeth Bayer, Past Chair, The Heritage Canada Foundation / ancienne présidente de la Fondation canadienne pour la protection du patrimoine
"The Role of the Citizen Activist in Policy-Making" / « Le rôle des particuliers militant dans l'élaboration des politiques »

William J. Byrne, Assistant Deputy Minister / sous-ministre adjoint, Alberta Historical Resources
"Finding the Funding and Other Provincial Heritage Responsibilities" / « Recherche du financement et autres responsabilités provinciales touchant le patrimoine »

Robert Garon, National Archivist of Québec / archiviste national du Québec
« Le point de vue du Québec sur la politique du patrimoine » / "The Quebec Perspective on Heritage Policy"

R. Scott James, Managing Director / directeur général, Toronto Historical Board
"Preservation Policy from the Municipal Perspective: A Focus on Tax Issues" / « Point de vue des municipalités sur la politique de conservation : les questions fiscales »

15:30
15 h 30   **SPEAKERS: THE FEDERAL PERSPECTIVE / CONFÉRENCIERS : POINT DE VUE FÉDÉRAL**
John Godfrey, M.P., Chairman, House Standing Committee on Canadian Heritage / député ; président du Comité permanent de la Chambre des communes sur le patrimoine canadien
"The Missing Pieces: Heritage Commemoration and Public Policy" / « Les pièces manquantes : commémoration du patrimoine et politique gouvernementale »

Albina Guarnieri, Parliamentary Secretary to the Minister of Canadian Heritage / secrétaire parlementaire du ministre du Patrimoine canadien
"The Creation of the Department of Canadian Heritage" / « La création du ministère du Patrimoine canadien »

Trudy Cowan, Heritage Consultant, Calgary; former Alberta
Member, HSMBC / consultante en matière de patrimoine à Calgary ;
ex-membre de la CLMHC pour l'Alberta
"Caught in the Act: Legislating Heritage Protection" / « Un cadre
législatif pour la protection du patrimoine »

16:45   **Session 9. Back to the Future / Neuvième séance.**
16 h 45   **Regard vers l'avenir**

CHAIR / PRÉSIDENT : *Michael Kinnear*, Professor of History /
professeur d'histoire, University of Manitoba; Manitoba Member,
HSMBC / membre de la CLMHC pour le Manitoba

SPEAKERS / CONFÉRENCIERS :
Angéline Fournier, Director, Socio-Political Studies, Institut
Gamma / directrice des études socio-politiques, l'Institut Gamma,
Montréal
« Le passé a-t-il un avenir ? » / "Does the Past have a Future?"

Stephen M. Smith, Book Review Editor / rédacteur de la chronique
des livres, *Quill & Quire* Magazine
"Does the Past have a Future?" / « Le passé a-t-il un avenir ? »

CLOSING REMARKS / ALLOCUTION DE CLÔTURE : *Thomas
H.B. Symons*

19:30   **CLOSING BANQUET / BANQUET DE CLÔTURE**
19 h 30   Salle Adam, Château Laurier

CONFÉRENCIER INVITÉ : *M. Leslie Harris*, President Emeritus /
président émérite, Memorial University of Newfoundland; Former
Chairman, HSMBC / ancien président de la CLMHC

Banquet held with the generous support of Canadian Pacific Limited.
Le banquet est offert grâce au généreux concours de Canadien Pacifique Limitée.

CONFERENCE PARTICIPANTS / LES PARTICIPANTS AU SYMPOSIUM

Mr. Elide Albert, Architect
Architect Four Limited, Moncton

Dr. Richard M. Alway, President/président,
St. Michael's College, University of
Toronto

Mrs. Margaret Archibald, Director,
Tourism Initiative, Canadian
Heritage-Parks Canada/Patrimoine
canadien-Parcs Canada

M. Jean-Claude Asselin, directeur du
Développement, Société Radio-Canada,
Montréal

Dr. Jane Banfield, Professor of Law, York
University

Mr. Alan John Barrett, Vice President,
Outlooks Canada Associates, Ottawa

M. Jean Barry, chef intérmaine,
Planification, Patrimoine canadien-Parcs
Canada/Canadian Heritage-Parks Canada

Mrs. Sonja Bata, Chair, The Bata Shoe
Museum, Don Mills

Mrs. Elizabeth Batstone, Assistant Deputy
Minister, Culture, Historic Resources and
Provincial Archives, Newfoundland
Tourism, Culture and Recreation

Mrs. Mary Elizabeth Bayer, Past Chair,
The Heritage Canada Foundation/ancienne
présidente de la Fondation canadienne
pour la protection du patrimoine

M. Marcel Beaudry, président/Chairman,
Commission de la capitale nationale/
National Capital Commission

Capt. Claude Beauregard, historien/
historian, Défense nationale/National
Defence

Mrs. Joanna Bedard, Chair
Ontario Heritage Foundation

Ms. Agnes Benidickson, Vice-Chairman,
Canadiana Fund & Chancellor, Queen's
University

Mr. Jamie Benidickson, Canadian Canoe
Museum, Ottawa

M. Richard Benoît, directeur,
Collège universitaire de Saint-Boniface

M. Serge Bernier, directeur général/
Director General, Service Historique/
Historical Services, Défense nationale/
National Defence

Mrs. Marion Beyea, Provincial Archivist,
New Brunswick Archives/New Brunswick
Member, HSMBC

M. Jean-Guy Bigeau, directeur général/
Executive Director, Association d'études
canadiennes/Association for Canadian
Studies, Montréal

Mrs. Pam Blackstock, Heritage &
Presentation, Public Education Specialist,
Canadian Heritage-Parks Canada/
Patrimoine canadien-Parcs Canada

M. Francis Blanchard, Comité Consultatif
Acadien

Mr. John Blumenson, Manager,
Preservation Review, Toronto Historical
Board

Rev. Francis Bolger, Professor Emeritus,
University of Prince Edward Island/PEI
Member, HSMBC

Mr. Patrick Borbey, Director General,
Parks Canada Investments, Canadian
Heritage-Parks Canada/Patrimoine
canadien-Parcs Canada

M. Neil Boucher, professeur, Université
Sainte-Anne, Fédération acadienne de la
Nouvelle-Écosse

Mr. Ronal Bourgeois, Director, Heritage Policy and Research, Canadian Heritage/Patrimoine canadien

Mrs. Ann Bowering, Coordinator, Baccalieu Trail Heritage Corp., Newfoundland

Mr. Bob Bowes, Executive Vice-President, The Heritage Canada Foundation, Ottawa

Ms. Heather Broadbent, Heritage Officer, Multicultural History Society of Ontario

Ms. Dawn Bronson, Manager, Visitor Activities, Prince Albert National Park, Canadian Heritage-Parks Canada/Patrimoine canadien-Parcs Canada

Mrs. Lynne Bryson, Chair, Vancouver Heritage Advisory Committee

Mr. Pat Buchik, Conservation Architect, Public Works and Government Services/Travaux publics et Services gouvernementaux/Calgary Heritage Advisory Board

Mrs. Susan Buggey, Director, Historical Services Branch, Canadian Heritage-Parks Canada/Patrimoine canadien-Parcs Canada

Mr. Tony Bull, Director, Strategic Operations Branch, Canadian Heritage-Parks Canada/Patrimoine canadien-Parcs Canada

Mr. Jeff Bullard, Director, Canadian Identity Directorate, Canadian Heritage/Patrimoine canadien

M. Dinu Bumbaru, directeur des programmes, Héritage Montréal & ICOMOS

Mr. Waye Burley, Director, New Brunswick Municipalities, Culture and Housing, Province of New Brunswick

Mr. William J. Byrne, Assistant Deputy Minister/sous-ministre adjoint, Alberta Historical Resources

Dr. Christina Cameron, Director General, National Historic Sites Directorate, Canadian Heritage/Patrimoine canadien

Professor David Robertson Cameron, Dept. of Political Science, University of Toronto

Mr. Colin Campbell, Director, Heritage Conservation Branch-Small Business, Tourism and Culture, BC

Mme Hélène Caron, historienne, Conseil de la culture de Lanaudière

Mrs. Margaret Carter, Heritage Research Associates Inc., Ottawa

Mrs. Kelley Charlebois, Executive Assistant, Alberta Community Development

Mme Elisabeth Châtillon, directrice exécutive, Région du Québec, Patrimoine canadien/Canadian Heritage

Mr. Ian Christie Clark, Chairman, Canadian Cultural Property Export Review Board, Ian C. Clark & Associates Inc., Ottawa

Mr. Dean Clark, Director, Saskatchewan, Heritage Department

Mrs. Louise Coates, President, Heritage Ottawa

Mrs. Janet Cobban, President, The Ontario Historical Society

M. Roger Collet, sous-ministre adjoint, Patrimoine canadien/Canadian Heritage

Mme Michelle Comeau, directrice, Evénements et programmes de la Capitale, Commission de la Capitale nationale

Mrs. Carmen Comeau-Anderson, Director, Atlantic Region, Canadian Heritage/Patrimoine canadien

Dr. Leonard Conolly, President and Vice-Chancellor, Trent University

Dr. Margaret Conrad, Professor of History, Acadia University/Nova Scotia Member, HSMBC

Mr. Austin Cooke, Program Officer, Heritage, Culture and Languages, Canadian Heritage/Patrimoine canadien

Mr. Bob Coutts, Historian, Canadian Heritage-Parks Canada/Patrimoine canadien-Parcs Canada

Trudy Cowan, Heritage Consultant/ consultante en matière de patrimoine, Calgary, Alberta

Mrs. Pamela Craig, Manager, Heritage Properties Programs, Ontario Culture, Tourism and Recreation

Mr. Ralph Crysler, Chair, History Committee, Canadian Society for Civil Engineering, Oakville

Mr. Mark Cullen, Chief, Architectural Analysis Division, Canadian Heritage-Parks Canada/Patrimoine canadien-Parcs Canada

Mr. Rod Cumming, Legislative Assistant, Legislative Assembly of Ontario

Mr. Brian Cuthbertson, Head, Heritage Community Planning Division, Department of Municipal Affairs, Nova Scotia

Mrs. Ann Dadson, Administrative Director, The CRB Foundation, Montréal

M. Yves Dagenais, sous-directeur/Deputy Director, National Gallery of Canada/ Musée des beaux-arts du Canada

M. Jacques Dalibard, directeur général/ Executive Director, la fondation Héritage Canada/The Heritage Canada Foundation, Ottawa

Mr. Alex Davidson, Former Assistant Deputy Minister, Parks Canada/Parcs Canada

M. Marc De Caraffe, chef, Division de l'histoire du bâtiment, Patrimoine canadien-Parcs Canada/Canadian Heritage-Parks Canada

Mrs. Anne de Fort-Menares, Architectural Historian, Resource Data, Toronto

Mr. Claude DeGrâce, Area Superintendent, Historic Sites, New Brunswick, Canadian Heritage-Parks Canada/Patrimoine canadien-Parcs Canada

Mr. William DeGrace, Heritage Planner, New Brunswick Municipalities, Culture and Housing

Mr. James Dejonge, Acting Chief, Canadian Heritage-Parks Canada/ Patrimoine canadien-Parcs Canada

Mr. Marc Denhez, Lawyer, Ottawa

M. Donald Deschênes, ethnologue, Centre Franco-Ontarien de Folklore

Mrs. Patricia Devine, Special Assistant, Events, House of Commons

Mr. Lyle Dick, Coordinator, National Historic Sites Systems Plan Review, Canadian Heritage-Parks Canada/ Patrimoine canadien-Parcs Canada

Mr. John Dickinson, President/président, Canadian Studies Association/Association d'études canadiennes

Dr. Bernadine A. Dodge, Vice-President, Association of Canadian Archivists

Mr. Dwight Dorey, Chief and President, Native Council of Nova Scotia

Mr. Ian Doull, Historian, Building History Division, Canadian Heritage-Parks Canada/Patrimoine canadien-Parcs Canada

Mrs Pamela Doyle, Superintendent, Manitoba North National Historic Sites, Canadian Heritage-Parks Canada/ Patrimoine canadien-Parcs Canada

367

Ms. Jennifer Drew, Special Events Coordinator, Canadian Heritage-Parks Canada/Patrimoine canadien-Parcs Canada

Jean Du Berger, professeur d'ethnologie, Département d'histoire, Université Laval

Mrs. Donna Dul, Director, Historic Resources Branch, Manitoba Culture, Heritage and Citizenship

Mrs. Dorothy Duncan, Executive Director, Ontario Historical Society

Mr. Geoffrey Ellwand, Journalist, CBC/University of Guelph

Mr. John English, M.P. House of Commons, Ottawa

Mrs. Gwynneth Evans, Director General, National and International Programs, National Library of Canada/Bibliothèque nationale du Canada

Mrs. Mary Lou Evans, LACAC Co-ordinator, Ontario Culture, Tourism and Recreation

Dr. Leonard Evenden, Director, Centre for Canadian Studies, Simon Fraser University

Mrs. Sherry Farrell Racette, Member of the Board, Saskatchewan Heritage Foundation

Mme Angéline Fournier, directrice des études socio-politiques, l'Institut Gamma, Montréal

Mrs. Louise Fox, President, International Institute for Conservation-Canadian Group, Hull

Mr. Robert Frame, Director, Museum Services Division, Nova Scotia Museum

Mr. Douglas Franklin, Director, Government and Public Relations, The Heritage Canada Foundation, Ottawa

Felix (Fil) Fraser, Former Director, Alberta Human Rights Commission

Mr. Whit Fraser, Chairman, Canadian Polar Commission, Ottawa

Mr. Lawrence Friend, Executive Secretary, HSMBC, Canadian Heritage-Parks Canada/Patrimoine canadien-Parcs Canada

Mr. Bruce Fry, Acting Director, Archeaogical Service, Canadian Heritage-Parks Canada/Patrimoine canadien-Parcs Canada

M. Robert Garon, archiviste national du Québec/National Archivist of Québec

Mr. Dan Gaudet, Superintendent, Rocky Mountain House National Historical Site, Canadian Heritage-Parks Canada/ Patrimoine canadien-Parcs Canada

M. Alain Gauthier, Musée canadien de la guerre/Canadian War Museum, Ottawa

Mme Raymonde Gauthier, Université du Québec à Montréal/Ancienne membre de la CLMHC pour le Québec

M. Bernard Genest, ministère de la Culture et des Communications, Québec

M. Camil Girard, historien, Université du Québec à Chicoutimi

Mrs. Alice Glanville, President, British Columbia Historical Federation

Mr. Sheldon Godfrey, Chairman, The Heritage Canada Foundation, Toronto

M. André Gousse, conservateur militaire, Direction de la mise en valeur et éducation publique, Patrimoine canadien-Parcs Canada/Canadian Heritage-Parks Canada

Mr. Robert Graham, Heritage Planner, City of Calgary, Planning and Building Department

Mr. Jon K. Grant, Chair, Ontario Round Table on the Environment and the Economy

Mrs. Shelagh D. Grant, Adjunct Professor/Historian, Trent University

Mr. John Grenville, Superintendent, Bellevue House National Historic Site, Canadian Heritage-Parks Canada/ Patrimoine canadien-Parcs Canada

Albina Guarnieri, Parliamentary Secretary to the Minister of Canadian Heritage/ secrétaire parlementaire du ministre du Patrimoine canadien

Mr. J.A.W. Gunn, President, Canadian Immigration Historical Society, Almonte

Mrs Sylvia Haavisto, Bar U Ranch, Calgary

Dr. Francess G. Halpenny, Professor Emeritus of Library Science, University of Toronto

Dr. Gordon Handcock, Department of Geography, Memorial University of Newfoundland

Dr. Leslie Harris, President Emeritus, Memorial University of Newfoundland/ Former Chairman, HSMBC

M. Fernand Harvey, Institut national de la recherche scientifique/membre de la CLMHC pour le Québec

Dr. Jocelyn Harvey, Policy Advisor, Confederation Centre of the Arts, Ottawa

Mr. Kerridwen Harvey, Consultant, Ottawa

Dolores Hayden, Professor of Architecture, Urbanism and American Studies, Yale University

Dr. Robert H. Haynes, Department of Biology, York University

Senator Dan Hays, The Senate/Sénat, Ottawa

M. Raymond Hébert, professeur, Département de sciences politiques, Collège universitaire de Saint-Boniface

Mr. Christopher Hives, Chair, Canadian Council of Archives, Vancouver

Mr. R. Howes, Conservation Architect, Canadian Heritage-Parks Canada/ Patrimoine canadien-Parcs Canada

Mrs. Jacqueline Hucker, Historian, Canadian Heritage-Parks Canada/ Patrimoine canadien-Parcs Canada

Ms. Maureen Hughes, Administrative and Research Assistant to the Vanier Professor, Trent University

Mrs. Barbara Humphreys, Architect, Ontario Conservation Review Board

Charles W. Humphries, Professor of History, The University of British Columbia

Mr. Jeff Hunston, Director, Heritage Branch, Yukon Tourism

Mr. Robert Hunter, Acting Chief, Heritage Railway Station Division, Canadian Heritage-Parks Canada/ Patrimoine canadien-Parcs Canada

Mr. G.C. Ingram, Director, Policy, Legislation and Government Relations, Canadian Heritage-Parks Canada/ Patrimoine canadien-Parcs Canada

Mr. Don Ives, Director of Research, Canada Remembers, Ottawa

Mrs. Barbara Ivey, Co-Chair, The Canadiana Fund, Ottawa

Mr. Colin Jackson, Executive Director, The Confederation Centre of the Arts, PEI

Mr. R. Scott James, Managing Director, Toronto Historical Board

Professor John Jennings, Department of History, Trent University

369

Mrs. Laurie Jones, Director,
Communications and Distribution
Services, National Film Board of Canada/
Office national du film du Canada

Mr. Reet Kana, Past President,
Archaeological Society of British Columbia

Dr. Michael Kinnear, Professor of History,
University of Manitoba/Manitoba Member,
HSMBC

Mrs. Norma Knowlton, President, Ontario
Archaeological Society

Mme Béatrice Kowaliczko, directrice
générale, La Société royale du Canada/The
Royale Sociy of Canada, Ottawa

M. Léo LaBrie, traducteur, Conseil régional
de la culture de l'Outaouais

Mme Claudette Lacelle, historienne,
Patrimoine canadien-Parcs Canada/
Canadian Heritage-Parks Canada

Mme Michèle Lacombe, Editor, Journal of
Canadian Studies, Peterborough

M. André N. Lalonde, directeur de
l'Institut de formation linguistique,
Université de Regina/Membre de la
CLMHC pour la Saskatchewan

Mr. Michale Lang, Vice President, Alberta
Museums Association

Mme Gaëtane LaRouche, consultante en
patrimoine, Regroupement des organismes
du patrimoine franco-ontarien

Mr. Stuart Lazear, Senior Heritage
Planner, City of Ottawa, Planning &
Development

M. Francois LeBlanc, président/President,
ICOMOS Canada, Ontario

M. Gabriel Leblanc, historien, Patrimoine
canadien-Parcs Canada/Canadian Heritage-
Parks Canada

Mme Phyllis LeBlanc, directrice, Université
de Moncton, Centre d'études acadiennes

Mr. Don LeClair, Director, PEI Culture,
Heritage and Recreation

Mr. Thomas Lee, Assistant Deputy
Minister, Canadian Heritage-Parks
Canada/Patrimoine canadien-Parcs Canada

Père Maurice Léger, Comité consultatif
acadien

M. René Légère, secrétaire général, La
Société nationale de l'Acadie

Mr. Robert G. Lemon, Architect, Robert G.
Lemon Architecture & Preservation,
Vancouver

Mr. Terry Liston, Executive Director, CP
Rail System/Réseau CP Rail, Montréal

Mr. Peter Lloyd, Director General,
Department of Foreign Affairs/
Département d'affaires étrangères

Dr. George F. MacDonald, Director,
Canadian Museum of Civilisation/
Musée canadien des civilisations/

Mrs. Daphne Mainprize, Director, Stephen
Leacock Museum, Orillia

Mrs. Rosemary Malaher, Vice-Chair,
Heritage Canada Foundation, Winnipeg

The Honourable Gary Mar, M.L.A.,
Minister, Alberta Community
Development

Mme Jocelyne Marchand, Patrimoine
canadien-Parcs Canada/Canadian Heritage-
Parks Canada/membre du Comité
consultatif acadien

M. Jean-Claude Marsan, professeur
titulaire, architecte et urbaniste, Université
de Montréal

Mr. John Marsh, Director, Frost Centre for
Canadian Heritage and Development
Studies, Trent University

Ms. Faye Martin, Senior Policy Advisor, Higher Education, Training and Adult Learning, PEI

M. Jacques Mathieu, professeur d'histoire, Université Laval

M. Pierre Mayrand, Département d'histoire de l'art, Université du Québec à Montréal

Mr. David McConnell, Historian, Canadian Heritage-Parks Canada/ Patrimoine canadien-Parcs Canada

Mr. James McCrorie, Executive Director, Canadian Plains Research Center, Regina

Harvey A. McCue, Director of Education and CEO, Mi'kmaq Education Authority, Nova Scotia

Mr. Ajit Mehat, Executive Director, Canadian Heritage

Mr. Ernest Mike, Chairman, Wanuskewin Indian Heritage Inc./Federation of Saskatchewan Indian Nations

Mr. David Mills, Director, Historic Resources Division, Newfoundland Tourism and Culture

Mr. C. Robin Molson, President, The Canadian Heritage of Quebec

Père Jacques Monet, s.j., recteur, Université de Sudbury

Mr. Jeremy Morgan, Executive Director, Wanuskewin Heritage Park, Saskatoon

Ms. Deborah Morrison, Project Officer, The Heritage Project, The CRB Foundation, Montréal

Dr. Claude Moulin, Associate Professor, Department of Leisure, University of Ottawa

Mrs. Marilyn Mullan, Executive Director, Britannia Beach Historical Society, BC

Mme Monique Nadeau-Sauhier, directrice administrative, Bishop's University

Mr. William Neville, Chair, Manitoba Heritage Council

Mrs. Patricia O'Brien, President, Newfoundland Historical Association

Mr. Bill O'Shea, Head, Historic Resources, Fortress of Louisbourg National Historic Site, Canadian Heritage-Parks Canada/ Patrimoine canadien-Parcs Canada

Professor Brian Osborne, Department of Geography, Queen's University

Dr. Ken Osborne, Professor, Faculty of Education, University of Manitoba

Mr. Adam Ostry, Director General, Amateur Sports Branch, Canadian Heritage/Patrimoine canadien

M. Roger Ouellette, président, Société nationale de l'Acadie

Mr. James E. Page, Director General, National Literacy Secretariat, Human Resources Development, Ottawa

Mme Huguette Parent, CA membre, Fondation du patrimoine ontarien

Mr. Robert W. Passfield, Historian, Canadian Heritage-Parks Canada/ Patrimoine canadien-Parcs Canada

Mrs. Linda Pelly-Landrie, President, Saskatchewan Indian Cultural Centre

Mrs. Joan Pennefather, Chairperson/ présidente, National Film Board of Canada/ Office national du film du Canada

Mme Denise Perrier, directeur général, Patrimoine canadien-Parcs Canada/ Canadian Heritage-Parks Canada

Mr. Bill Peters, Director General, Heritage Branch, Canadian Heritage/Patrimoine canadien

Mrs. Donnan Petrachenko, Associate Regional Executive Director, Canadian Heritage-Parks Canada/Patrimoine canadien-Parcs Canada

Mr. D. Bruce Petrie, Assistant Chief Statistician, Statistics Canada

Mr. Jaroslav Petryshyn, History Instructor, Grande Prairie Regional College/Former HSMBC Member

Professor Nancy Pollock-Ellwand, School of Landscape Architecture, University of Guelph

Mr. Mike Porter, Acting Director General, Canadian Heritage-Parks Canada/ Patrimoine canadien-Parcs Canada

Mme France Gagnon Pratte, présidente, Conseil des monuments et sites du Québec

Dr. Kenneth Pryke, Head and Professor, Department of History, University of Windsor

Mr. Garth Pugh, Manager, Saskatchewan Heritage Foundation

M. Paul Racine, sous-ministre adjoint, Patrimoine canadien/Canadian Heritage

M. Louis Richer, directeur intérimaire, Protection du patrimoine, Patrimoine canadien-Parcs Canada/Canadian Heritage-Parks Canada

Dr. David Richeson, Director General, National Museum of Science and Technology Corporation

Mrs. Shannon Ricketts, Historian, Canadian Heritage-Parks Canada/ Patrimoine canadien-Parcs Canada

Mr. Jack Ricou, Chief, Interpretation Extension, Natural Resources, Canadian Heritage-Parks Canada/Patrimoine canadien-Parcs Canada

Mrs. Anne Robinson, Coordinator, Canadian Rails to Greenways Network, Ottawa

Mrs. Peggy Robinson, Communications Officer, Association of Canadian Community Colleges, Ottawa

The Honourable William Rompkey, P.C., M.P., House of Commons

Mr. Arnold Roos, Acting Chief, Canadian Heritage-Parks Canada/Patrimoine canadien-Parcs Canada

Mrs. Jane Roszell, Assistant Deputy Minister, Canadian Heritage/Patrimoine Canada

Mr. Ted Rowe, Past Chairman, Newfoundland Historic Parks Association

Mme Muriel K. Roy, professeure émérite, Université de Moncton

Dr. Patricia E. Roy, Department of History, University of Victoria

Mrs. Hilary Russell, Historian, Canadian Heritage-Parks Canada/Patrimoine canadien-Parcs Canada

Mrs. Rosemary Sadlier, President, Ontario Black History Society

Annette Saint-Pierre, auteure et éditrice de Saint-Boniface

M. Roch Samson, historien, Patrimoine canadien-Parcs Canada/Canadian Heritage-Parks Canada

Mr. Roger Sarty, Senior Historian, National Defence/Défense nationale

Mrs. Ruth Saturley, Vice-Chair, Heritage Canada Foundation/Newfoundland Historic Trust

M. Pierre Savard, professeur, Département d'histoire, Université d'Ottawa

Mr. Wayne Scott, Director, Communications Branch, Canadian Heritage/Patrimoine canadien

Mrs. Susan Scotti, Director General, Citizens' Participation and Multiculturalism Branch, Canadian Heritage/Patrimoine canadien

Mr. Robert Scully, Charles R. Bronfman Foundation/Fondation Charles R. Bronfman, Montréal

Mr. J. Blair Seaborn, Royal Canadian Geographical Society/Société géographique royale du Canada, Ottawa

Dr. James Sentance, Canadian Studies, University of Prince Edward Island

Mrs. Carol Sheedy, Acting Director, Canadian Heritage-Parks Canada/ Patrimoine canadien-Parcs Canada

Mr. Steven Sheridan, President, Second Century Club, Ottawa

M. Cyril Simard, président, Commission des biens culturels du Québec

Mrs. Mary May Simon, Circumpolar Ambassador, Foreign Affairs and International Trade/Affaires étrangères et Commerce international

Mr. Harvey Slack, Executive Director, The Canadiana Fund, Ottawa

Mr. Stephen M. Smith, Book Review Editor, *Quill & Quire* Magazine

Dr. Julian Smith, Coordinator, Heritage Conservation Program, Carleton University

Mrs. Sheryl Smith, Strategic Initiatives Project Manager, Aboriginal Issues, Canadian Heritage-Parks Canada/ Patrimoine canadien-Parcs Canada

Dr. Wilfred I. Smith, Former HSMBC Member, Ottawa

Mr. Terence Smythe, Chief, Federal Heritage Buildings Review Office, Canadian Heritage-Parks Canada/ Patrimoine canadien-Parcs Canada

Mr. Sam Sniderman, President, Roblan Distributors, Ottawa

Mrs. Elizabeth Snow, Director, Archaeological Resource Management, Canadian Heritage/Patrimoine canadien

Mrs. Marsha Hay Snyder, Historian, Canadian Heritage-Parks Canada/ Patrimoine canadien-Parcs Canada

Mr. Tim Sookocheff, Director, Professional and Technical Services, Canadian Heritage-Parks Canada/Patrimoine canadien-Parcs Canada

Mrs. Darlene Speidel, Director, Language/Curriculum Development, Saskatchewan Indian Cultural Centre

Mr. Erik Spicer, Canadian Library Association, Ottawa

Mrs. Carol Sprachman, President, Canadian Federation of Friends of Museums, Toronto

M. Denis A. St-Onge, président, Société géographique royale du Canada/Royal Canadian Geographical Society, Ottawa

Dr. S. Dale Standen, Department of History, Trent University

Ms. Lillian Stewart, Area Superintendent, SW Nova Scotia, Canadian Heritage-Parks Canada/Patrimoine canadien-Parcs Canada

Mr. Peter John Stokes, Consulting Restoration Architect, Niagara-on-the-Lake

Mr. Richard L. Stromberg, Toronto Historical Board

Mr. Richard Stuart, National Historic Sites Coordinator, Prairie and NWT Region, Canadian Heritage-Parks Canada/ Patrimoine canadien-Parcs Canada

Mr. Max Sutherland, Historian, Ottawa

Mrs. Patricia Sutherland, Vice-President, Canadian Archaeological Assocation, Canadian Museum of Civilization

Dr. Thomas H.B. Symons, Founding President and Vanier Professor Emeritus, Trent University; Chairman, HSMBC/ président de la CLMHC

Mr. Louis Tapardjuk, Mayor of Igloolik/NWT Member, HSMBC

Mme Henriette Thériault, chargée d'interprétation, Bureau des arts et de la culture, Ville de Québec

M. Martin Thivierge, agent de développement culturel, Service de la Culture, Ville de Montréal

Dr. John Herd Thompson, Professor of History, Duke University

Mr. Robert H. Thompson, Head, National Historic Parks Planning, Canadian Heritage-Parks Canada/Patrimoine canadien-Parcs Canada

Mr. Daniel Tlen, Aboriginal Language Consultant, Yukon Territory; Yukon Member, HSMBC

Mrs. Mary Angela Tucker, Heritage Consultant, Architectural Conservancy of Ontario

Mr. Edgar Tumak, Architectural History Consultant, Society for the Study of Architecture in Canada

M. Raynald Turgeon, directeur général de l'ouest du Québec, Patrimoine canadien-Parcs Canada/Canadian Heritage-Parks Canada

Mr. Chris Turnball, Director, Archaeological Services, New Brunswick Municipalities, Culture and Housing

Mr. Allan Turner, Former Saskatchewan Member, HSMBC

Mr. Larry Turner, President, Friends of the Rideau

Mr. Allen Tyyska, Coordinator, Heritage Legislation Project, Ontario Culture, Tourism and Recreation

Mrs. Veronica Vaillancourt, Director, Heritage Network, Heritage Canada Foundation, Ottawa

Mr. Brian Van Dusen, Heritage Co-ordinator, HSMBC, Canadian Heritage-Parks Canada/Patrimoine canadien-Parcs Canada

Mrs. Lynne Verchere, Chair, Official Residences Council, Montréal

Dr. Christl Verduyn, Chair, Canadian Studies Programme, Trent University

Mme Odette Vincent-Domey, historienne, INRS – Culture et société, Ottawa

Dr. John Wadland, Professor, Canadian Studies Program, Trent University

Dr. Peter B. Waite, Professor Emeritus, Dalhousie University/Former Nova Scotia Member, HSMBC

Mr. Robert Waller, President, Canadian Association of Professional Conservators, Ottawa

M. Jean-Pierre Wallot, archiviste national, Archives nationales du Canada/Membre d'office de la CLMHC

Ms. Debra Ward, General Manager, Tourism Industry Association of Canada, Ottawa

Mr. John Weiler, Vice-President, The Heritage Canada Foundation, Ottawa

Mrs. Anne West, Junior Warden, Saint George's Church, Halifax

Mr. John H. White, Former Ontario Member, HSMBC

Mr. Andrew H. Wilson, Chairman, History
Committee, Canadian Society for
Mechnical Engineering, Ottawa

Mr. Ian E. Wilson, Archivist of Ontario,
Ontario Culture, Tourism and Recreation

Mr. Peter Winkworth, McCord Museum,
Montréal

Mr. John Witham, Manager, Cutural
Resources Management, Canadian
Heritage-Parks Canada/Patrimoine
canadien-Parcs Canada

Dr. Jack Wright, Canadian Parks/
Recreation Association/Association
canadienne des loisirs/parcs, Ottawa

Ms. Barbara Wyss, British Columbia
Native Women's Society

Mr. Maxwell Yalden, Chief Commissioner,
Canadian Human Rights Commission,
Ottawa

Dr. Roman Yereniuk, Rector, St. Andrew's
College, University of Manitoba

Dr. Brian Young, Historian, McGill
University, Montréal

JACQUES MATHIEU, JACINTHE RUEL and/et EDWINNA von BAEYER*

Bibliography/Bibliographie

Actes du Colloque sur la reconstruction du Service canadien des parcs, Hull, Québec, 11 au 13 mars 1992, Ottawa, Environnement Canada, Service des parcs, 1993, 120 p.

Adams, Annmarie, *Architecture in the Family Way: Doctors, Houses, and Women, 1870-1900*, McGill-Queen's / Hannah Institute Studies in the History of Medicine, Montreal, McGill-Queen's University Press, 1996.

Alfrey, Judith and Tim Putnam, *The Industrial Heritage: Managing Resources and Uses*, London and New York, Routledge, 1994, 327 p.

Allen, Barbara, *Sense of Place: American Regional Cultures*, Lexington, University of Kentucky Press, 1990, 213 p.

_____ and William Lynwood Montell, *From Memory to History: Using Oral Sources in Local Historical Research*, Nashville, Tennessee, American Association for State and Local History, 1981, 172 p.

Amalvi, Christian, *Les héros de l'histoire de France: recherche iconographique sur le panthéon scolaire de la Troisième République*, Préface de Alice Gérard, Paris, Phot'oeil, 1979, 315 p.

Anderson, V.D., "Collective Memory and Ethnic Groups: The Case of Swedes, Mennonites, and Norwegians", *Scandinavian Studies*, 67, 2 (April 1995), p. 216-217.

Andrault, Jean-Michel, Jean-Pierre Bertin-Maghit et Gérard Vincent, « Le cinéma français et la Seconde Guerre mondiale », *La Revue du cinéma*, 378 (décembre 1982), p. 70 à 99.

Angus, Margaret, *The Old Stones of Kingston: Its Buildings Before 1867*, Toronto, University of Toronto Press, 1966; rep. eds. 1974, 1980.

APT Bulletin, The Journal of Preservation Technology (The Association for Preservation Technology International / L'Association pour la préservation et ses techniques, internationale), 1969-. Index for vols. 1-24 (1969-92) published in vol. 25, no. 1-2 (1994).

Architectural Conservation Technology, 7 vols, Ottawa, Public Works Canada, Architectural and Engineering Services for Environment Canada, 1993. DSS cat. no. W62-16/1993E.

Arthur, Eric, *Toronto: No Mean City*, Toronto, University of Toronto Press, 1964; 3rd ed., rev. by Stephen A. Otto, 1986.

_____ and Dudley Witney, *The Barn: A Vanishing Landmark in North America*, Toronto, McClelland and Stewart, 1972; 2nd ed., 1989.

Aschieri, Lucien, *Le Passé recomposé. Mémoire d'une Communauté Provençale*, Marseille, Tacussel, 1985, 259 p.

Atlas historique du Canada, Geoffrey J. Matthews, cartographe et graphiste, édition française, Louise Dechêne, direction, Marcel Paré, traduction, 3 vols., Montréal, Presses de l'Université de Montréal, 1987-1993 (vol. 1, Des origines à 1800; vol. 2, *La transformation du territoire 1800-1891*; vol. 3, *Jusqu'au coeur du XXᵉ siècle 1891-1961*).

« Autour du patrimoine », Dossier, dans *Le débat*, n° 65 (mai-juin 1991).

Autrand, Françoise, « Les dates, la mémoire et les juges », dans : Bernard Guenée, dir., *Le métier d'historien au Moyen Age : études sur l'historiographie médiévale*, Paris, Université de Paris Panthéon-Sorbonne, Centre de recherches sur l'histoire de l'Occident médiéval, 1977, p. 157 à 182.

Azéma, Jean-Pierre et Michel Winock, ed., « Les générations », *Vingtième siècle. Revue d'histoire*, n° 22 (avril-juin 1989).

Baczko, Bronislaw, *Les imaginaires sociaux : mémoires et espoirs collectifs*, Paris, Payot, 1984, 242 p.

Baddeley, Alan D., *Human Memory: Theory and Practice*, Hove, Lawrence Erlbaum Assoc., 1990, 515 p.

_____, *La mémoire humaine, théorie et pratique*, Presses universitaires de Grenoble, 1993, 550 p.

Baer, Marc, "The Memory of the Middle Ages: From History of Culture to Culture History", *Studies in Medievalism*, 4 (1992), 290 p.

Baker, Keith Michael, *Inventing the French Revolution, Essays on the French Political Culture in the Eighteenth Century*, Cambridge, Cambridge University Press, 1990, 372 p.

Baldwin, Peter, ed., *Reworking the Past: Hitler, the Holocaust, and the Historians' Debate*, Boston, Beacon Press, 1990, 308 p.

Ball, Norman R., *"Mind, Heart, and Vision": Professional Engineering in Canada, 1887 to 1987*, Ottawa, National Museum of Science and Technology, National Museums of Canada, in cooperation with the Engineering Centennial Board, 1987.

_____, ed., *Building Canada: A History of Public Works*, Toronto, University of Toronto Press, 1988.

Bartlett, Frederic Charles, *Remembering: A Study in Experimental Social Psychology*, Cambridge, Cambridge University Press, 1954 (1932), 317 p.

Bartov, Omer, "Intellectuals on Auschwitz: Memory, History and Truth", *History & Memory*, 5, 1 (1993), p. 87-129.

Bazin, André, *Le cinéma de l'Occupation et de la Résistance*, Préface de François Truffaut, Paris, UGE, 1975, 194 p.

Beidelman, Thomas O., "Myth, Legend and Oral History", *Anthropos*, 65 (1970), p. 74-97.

Belloin, Gérard, *Entendez-vous dans nos mémoires?... Les Français et leur Révolution*, Paris, La Découverte, 1988, 267 p.

Ben-Ghait, Ruth, "Fascism, Writing, and Memory: The Realist Aesthetic in Italy, 1930-1950", *The Journal of Modern History*, 67, 3 (1995), p. 627-665.

Bennett, Gordon, "Commemorative Integrity: Monitoring the State of Canada's National Historic Sites", *ICOMOS Canada Bulletin*, 4, 5 (1995), p. 6-8

_____, "Yukon Transportation: A History", *Occasional Papers in Archaeology and History*, No. 19, Ottawa, Parks Canada, 1978.

Berdoulay, Vincent, *Des mots et des lieux: la dynamique du discours géographique*, Paris, Éd. CNRS, 1988, 106 p.

Bergeron, Claude, *L'architecture des églises du Québec, 1940-1985*, Québec, Presses de l'Université Laval, 1987.

_____, *Architectures du XXe siècle au Québec*, Montréal, Éditions du Méridien, 1989.

Bernard, Jean-Paul, *Les rébellions de 1837-1838. Les patriotes du Bas-Canada dans la mémoire collective et chez les historiens*, Montréal, Boréal Express, 1983, 349 p.

Bernshohn, Ken, *Cutting Up the North: History of the Forest Industry in the Northern Interior, 1909-1978*, Vancouver. Hancock House, 1981.

Bernstein, Barton J., "Understanding the Atomic Bomb and the Japanese Surrender: Missed Opportunities, Little-Known Near Disasters, and Modern Memory", *Diplomatic History*, 19, 2 (1995), p. 227-273.

Bertaux, Daniel and Paul Thompson, eds., *Between Generations: Family Models, Myths, and Memories*, New York, Oxford University Press, 1993, 223 p.

Bertin-Maghit, Jean-Pierre, « La Bataille du Rail: de l'authenticité à la chanson de geste », *Revue d'histoire moderne et contemporaine*, XXXIII (avril-juin 1986), p. 280 à 300.

Berton, Pierre, *The invasion of Canada:1812- 1813*, Toronto, 1980, 363 p.

_____, *Klondike: The life and death of the last great gold rush*. Toronto, McClelland, 1958.

_____, *The great railway*, Toronto, McClelland and Stewart, 1972.

Bétourné, Olivier et Aglaia I. Hartig, *Penser l'histoire de la Révolution. Deux siècles de passion française*, Paris, Éditions de la Découverte, 1989, 238 p.

Blaisdell, Lowell D., "Legends as an Expression of Baseball Memory", *Journal of Sport History*, 19, 3 (1992), p. 227-243.

Blake, Verschoyle Benson and Ralph Greenhill, *Rural Ontario*, Toronto, University of Toronto Press, 1969.

Bloch, Marc, « Mémoire collective, tradition et coutume », *Revue de synthèse historique*, 40 (1925), p. 73 à 83.

Blouin, Marc, Hélène Deslauriers, Michel Dufresne, Martin Weaver et François Varin, *Entretien et restauration: de la fondation à la toiture*, Québec, Conseil des monuments et sites du Québec, 1985, 66 p.

Bodei, Remo, "Farewell to the Past: Historical Memory, Oblivion and Collective Identity", *Philosophy & Social Criticism*, 18, 3/4 (1992), p. 251-265.

_____, "Historical Memory and European Identity", *Philosophy & Social Criticism*, 21, 4 (1995), p. 1-14.

Blumenson, John J.-G., *Ontario Architecture: A Guide to Styles and Building Terms, 1784 to the Present*, Markham, Ont., Fitzhenry & Whiteside, 1990.

Boddy, Trevor, *Modern Architecture in Alberta*, [Edmonton], Alberta Culture and Multiculturalism; Regina, Canadian Plains Research Center, 1987.

_____, *The Architecture of Douglas Cardinal*, Edmonton, NeWest Press, 1989.

Bodnar, John E., *Remaking America: Public Memory, Commemoration, and Patriotism in the Twentieth Century*, Princeton, Princeton University Press, 1992, 296 p.

_____, "Power and Memory in Oral History: Workers and Managers at Studebaker", *The Journal of American History*, 75, 4 (1988), p. 1201-1221.

Boeschoten, Riki van, *From Armatolik to People's Rule: Investigation into the Collective Memory of Rural Greece, 1750-1949*, Amsterdam, A.M. Hakkert, 1991, 433 p.

Bolles, Edmund Blair, *Remembering and Forgetting: An Inquiry into the Nature of Memory*, New York, Walter, 1988, 315 p.

Bonheur, Gaston, *Qui a cassé le vase de Soissons: l'album de famille de tous les Français*, Paris, Robert Laffont, 1976 (1963), 2 vol.

Bonnain Rolande et Fanch' Elegoët, « Les archives orales: pour quoi faire? », *Ethnologie française*, 8, 4 (octobre-décembre 1978), p. 348 à 355.

Bonnet, Jean-Claude et Philippe Roger, dir., *La légende de la Révolution au XXe siècle. De Gance à Renoir, de Romain Rolland à Claude Simon*, Paris, Flammarion, 1988, 222 p.

Bonnin, P., « Imaginations intérieures: la photographie d'intérieur comme méthode », *Informations sur les sciences sociales*, 18, 1 (mars 1989), p. 161 à 214.

Bothwell, Robert, *Nucleus: A History of Atomic Energy Canada Limited* (Toronto: University of Toronto Press, 1988).

Bourdon, Jerome, "Television and Political Memory", *Media, Culture & Society*, 14, 4 (1992), p. 541-560.

Bourguet, Marie-Noelle, Lucette Valensi, and Nathan Wachtel, eds., *Between Memory and History*, New York, Harwood Academic Publishers, 1990, 196 p.

Bouvier, Jean Claude, dir., *Tradition orale et identité culturelle. Problèmes de méthode*, Paris, Éditions du CNRS, 1980, 136 p.

_____, *La mémoire partagée. Lus-la-Croix-Haute (Drôme), Le monde alpin et rhodanien*, n°s 3-4 (1980), 231 p.

Boyer, M. Christine, *The City of Collective Memory: Its Historical Imagery and Architectural Entertainments*, Boston, MIT Press, 1994, 400 p.

Boyer, Paul, "Exotic Resonances: Hiroshima in American Memory", *Diplomatic History*, 19, 2 (spring 1995), p. 297-318.

Bray, Matt, and Ashley Thomson, eds., *At the End of the Tunnel: Mines and Single-Industry Towns in Northern Ontario*, Toronto, Dundurn Press, 1991.

Brice-Bennett, Carol (general editor), *Our Footprints are Everywhere; Inuit Land Use and Occupancy in Labrador*, Nain, Labrador Inuit Association, 1977, 378 p.

Brosseau, Mathilde, *Le style néo-gothique dans l'architecture au Canada*, Lieux historiques canadiens, cahiers d'archéologie et d'histoire n° 25, Ottawa, Parcs Canada, 1980. (Aussi disponible: Brosseau, Mathilde, *Le style néo-gothique dans l'architecture au Canada*, Lasalle, Qué., HMH Hurtibise, 1981.)

Brown, Ron, *The Train Doesn't Stop Here Any More: An Illustrated History of Railway Stations in Canada*, Peterborough, Ont., Broadview Press, 1991.

Brunelle-Lavoie, Louise et Alain Gelly, « L'État et les lieux de mémoire », *Cap-aux-Diamants*, 37 (printemps 1994), p. 10 à 13.

Bull, Linda, "Indian Residential Schooling: The Native Perspective", *Canadian Journal of Native Education* (18: Supp.) 1991, 1-64.

Butler, Thomas, *Memory; History, Culture and the Mind*, Oxford, Blackwell, 1989, 189 p.

Butterfield, David K., *Architectural Heritage: The Selkirk and District Planning Area*, Architectural Heritage Report No. 4, Winnipeg, Manitoba Culture, Heritage and Recreation, Historic Resources, 1988.

_____ and Edward M. Ledohowski, *Architectural Heritage: The Brandon and Area Planning District*, Architectural Heritage Report No. 1, Winnipeg, Manitoba Department of Cultural Affairs and Historical Resources, 1983.

_____ and Edward M. Ledohowski, *Architectural Heritage: The MSTW Planning District*, Architectural Heritage Report No. 3, Winnipeg, Manitoba Culture, Heritage and Recreation, Historic Resources Branch, 1984.

Cameron, Christina, *Charles Baillairgé, Architect & Engineer*, Montreal and Kingston, McGill-Queen's University Press, 1989.

_____ and Janet Wright, *Second Empire Style in Canadian Architecture*, Canadian Historic Sites, Occasional Papers in Archaeology and History No. 24, Ottawa, Parks Canada, 1980.

_____ et Janet Wright, *Le style second Empire dans l'architecture canadienne*, Lieux historiques canadiens, cahiers d'archéologie et d'histoire n° 24, Ottawa, Parcs Canada, 1980.

Cameron, Elspeth, "Heritage Minutes: Culture and Myth", *Canadian Issues/Thèmes canadiens*, 17 (1995): 13-24

Canadian Register of Heritage Properties, First Annual Report, Ottawa, Minister of Supply and Services Canada, 1992.

Caraffe, Marc de, C.A. Hale, Dana Johnson, G.E. Mills, introduction de Margaret Carter, *Les hôtels de ville du Canada: Un recueil de textes sur les hôtels de ville construits avant 1930*, Études en archéologie, architecture et histoire, Ottawa, Environnement Canada — Parcs, 1987.

_____, C.A. Hale, Dana Johnson, G.E. Mills, introduction by Margaret Carter, *Town Halls of Canada: A Collection of Essays on Pre-1930 Town Hall Buildings*, Studies in Archaeology, Architecture and History, Ottawa, Environment Canada — Parks, 1987.

Cardin, Martine, « Information, preuve et témoignage ou le triple pouvoir des archives », *Les valeurs archivistiques, théorie et pratique. Actes du colloque*, Québec, Université Laval, 1994, p. 7 à 25.

Carr, Angela, comp., *A Selected Bibliography of Vernacular Architecture in Ontario*, Toronto, Architectural Conservancy of Ontario, [1993], 19 p.

Carruthers, Mary, *The Book of Memory: A Study of Memory in Medieval Culture*, Cambridge, Cambridge University Press, 1990, 393 p.

Carter, Margaret, comp., *Early Canadian Courthouses*, Studies in Archaeology, Architecture and History, Ottawa, Parks Canada, 1983.

_____, *Faire des recherches sur les bâtiments anciens*, Ottawa, Environnement Canada, Service des parcs, 1983.

_____, comp., *Les premiers palais de justice au Canada*, Études en archéologie, architecture et histoire, Ottawa, Parcs Canada, 1983.

_____, *Researching Heritage Buildings*, Ottawa, Environment Canada, Parks Service, 1983; 2nd English printing 1987.

Cashin, Joan E., "Landscape and Memory in Antebellum Virginia", *The Virginia Magazine of History and Biography*, 102, 4 (1994), p. 477-500.

Champagne, Rosaria, "Women's History and Housekeeping: Memory, Representation and Reinscription", *Women's Studies*, 20, 3/4 (1992), p. 321-329.

Charbonneau, André, Yvon Desloges et Marc Lafrance, *Québec, ville fortifiée du XVIIᵉ au XIXᵉ siècle*, Québec, Éditions du Pélican et Parcs Canada, 1982.

Charles, Christophe, dir., *Histoire sociale, histoire globale? actes du Colloque des 27-28 janvier 1989*, Paris, Maison des sciences de l'homme, 1993, 222 p.

Chesneaux, Jean, *Du passé faisons table rase? À propos de l'histoire et des historiens*, Paris, Maspero, 1976, 191 p.

Childs, Brevard S., *Memory and Tradition in Israel*, London, S.C.M.P., 1962, 96 p.

Choko, Marc H., *Les grandes places publiques de Montréal*, Montréal, Éditions du Méridien, 1987.

_____, *The Major Squares of Montreal*, Trans. Kate Roth, Montreal, Meridian Press, 1990.

Christenson, Andrew L., ed., *Tracing Archaeology's Past. The Historiography of Archaeology*, Carbondale, Southern Illinois University Press, 1989, 252 p.

Citron, Suzanne, *Le mythe national. L'histoire de France en question*, Paris, Éditions ouvrières, 1989, 334 p.

Clanchy, M. T., "Remembering the Past and the Good Old Law", *History*, 55 (1970), p. 165-176.

Clerk, Nathalie, *Palladian Style in Canadian Architecture*, Studies in Archaeology, Architecture and History, Ottawa, Parks Canada, 1984.

_____, *Le style palladien dans l'architecture au Canada*, Études en archéologie, architecture et histoire, Ottawa, Parcs Canada, 1984.

Cohen, G., "Visual Imagery in Thought", *New Literary History*, 7, 3 (1976), p. 513-523.

Cohen, Gillian, *Memory in the Real World*, London, Erlbaum, 1989, 247 p.

Cole, Jean M., ed., *The Peterborough Hydraulic Lift Lock*, Peterborough, 1987.

Coleman, Janet, *Ancient and Medieval Memories: Studies in the Reconstruction of the Past*, New York, Cambridge University Press, 1992, 646 p.

Collard, Anna, "Investigating 'Social Memory' in a Greek Context", in: Elizabeth Tonkin *et al.*, ed., *History and Ethnicity*, New York, Routledge, 1989, p. 89-103.

Collins, Jim, "Theorizing Cultural Memory: Totalizing Recall?" *American Literary History*, 3, 4 (1991), p. 829-845.

Collins, Robert, *A Voice from Afar: The History of Canadian Telecommunications*, Scarborough, McGraw-Hill Ryerson, 1977.

Collomb, Gérard, « Le discours de la légende et le discours de l'histoire. Notes sur un récit de la révolte des Arves (Savoie) », *Le monde alpin et rhodanien. Croyances, récits et pratiques de tradition*, Mélanges d'Ethnologie, d'Histoire et de Linguistique en hommage à Charles JOISTEN (1936-1981), 10, 1-4 (1982), p. 89 à 99.

Combe, Sonia, « Mémoire collective et histoire officielle. Le passé nazi en RDA », « Mémoire du nazisme en RFA et RDA », dossier, *Esprit*, 10, 131 (octobre 1987), p. 36 à 49.

Commission des biens culturels, *Les chemins de la mémoire. Monuments et sites historiques du Québec*. 2 vols., Québec, Les Publications du Québec, 1990 et 1991. XIV, 540 p.; XVI, 565 p., ill.

Confino, Alon, "The Nation as a Local Metaphor: Heimat, National Memory and the German Empire, 1871-1918", *History & Memory*, 5, 1 (1993), p. 42-86.

Connerton, Paul, *How Societies Remember*, Cambridge, Cambridge University Press, 1989, 121 p.

Continuité, le patrimoine en perspective (Les Éditions Continuité inc. et le Conseil des monuments et sites du Québec), 1982-. Voir François Varin, « Fiche technique ».

Conway, Martin A., *Autobiographical Memory : An Introduction*, Philadelphia, Open University Press, 1990, 200 p.

Cook, Haruko Taya and Theodore F. Cook, *Japan at War: An Oral History*, New York, New Press, 1992, 479 p.

Corbin, Alain, « Le vertige des foisonnements. Esquisse panoramique d'une histoire sans nom », *Revue d'histoire moderne et contemporaine*, 39, 1 (janvier-mars 1992), p. 103 à 126.

Côté, Michel, dir., *Les tendances de la muséologie au Québec*, Québec, Société des musées québécois, Musée de la civilisation, Services des parcs d'Environnement Canada, 1992, 162 p.

Coulter, Jeff, *The Social Construction of Mind*, London, Macmillan, 1979, 190 p.

Couture, Carol *et al.*, « L'archivistique a-t-elle trouvé son identité ? », *Argus*, 17, 2 (juin 1988), p. 51 à 60.

Croce, Benedetto, *L'histoire comme pensée et comme action*, Genève, Droz, 1968, 287 p.

Crossman, Kelly, *Architecture in Transition: From Art to Practice, 1885-1906*, Montreal and Kingston, McGill-Queen's University Press, 1987.

Crubellier, Maurice, *La mémoire des Français: recherches d'histoire culturelle*, Paris, H. Veyrier, 1991, 351 p.

Cruikshank, Julie, *Reading Voices; Oral and Written Interpretations of the Yukon's Past*, Vancouver, Douglas and McIntyre, 1991, 158 p.

_____ in collaboration with Angela Sidney, Kitty Smith and Annie Ned, *Life Lived Like a Story; Life Stories of Three Yukon Native Elders*, Vancouver, The University of British Columbia Press, 1992, 404 p.

Cullen, Mary, *Les couvertures en ardoises au Canada*, Études en archéologie, architecture et histoire, Ottawa, Environnement Canada, Service des parcs, 1990.

_____, *Slate Roofing in Canada*, Studies in Archaeology, Architecture and History, Ottawa, Environment Canada, Parks Service, 1990.

"Cultural Resource Management Policy," in: Parks Canada, *Guiding Principles and Operating Policies*, Ottawa, Supply and Services Canada, 1994, p. 99-116. DSS cat. no. R62-275/1994E.

Cuming, David J., *Discovering Heritage Bridges on Ontario's Roads*, Erin, Boston Mills, 1983.

Curtin, P. D., "Oral Tradition in African History", *Journal of the Folklore Institute*, 6 (1969), p. 137-155.

Dahl, N. A., « Anamesis. Mémoire et commémoration dans le christianisme primitif », *Studia Theologica*, 1, part. 4 (1948), p. 69 à 95.

Dakhlia, Jocelyne and Marjolijn de Jager, "Collective Memory and the Story of History: Lineage and Nation in a North African Oasis", *History and Theory*, 32,4 (1993), p. 57-79.

_____, « Des prophètes à la nation: la mémoire des temps anté-islamiques au Maghreb », *Cahiers d'études africaines. Mémoires, Histoires, Identités*, 27, cahiers 107-108 (1987), p. 241 à 267.

Daniel, Joseph, *Guerre et cinéma. Grandes illusions et petits soldats, 1895-1971*, Paris, A. Colin, 1972, 452 p.

Darian-Smith, Kate, and Paula Hamilton, *Memory and History in Twentieth-century Australia*, Melbourne, Oxford University Press, 1994, 255 p.

Darnell, Regna, *Readings in the History of Anthropology*, New York, Harper & Row, 1974, 479 p.

Davallon, Jean, Gérald Grandmont et Bernard Schiele, *L'Environnement entre au Musée*, Québec/Lyon, Musée de la civilisation/Presses universitaires de Lyon (1992), 206 p.

Davies, Graham M. and Robert H. Logie, eds., *Memory in Everyday Life*, Amsterdam, North-Holland, 1993, 554 p.

Davis, Natalie Z., "History's Two Bodies", *American Historical Review*, 93, 1 (February 1988), p. 1-30.

_____ and Randolph Starn, ed., *Representations. Special Issue: Memory and Counter-Memory*, 26 (spring 1989), 149 p.

_____, *Culture and Identity in Early Modern Europe (1500-1800): Essays in Honor of Natalie Zemon Davis*, Ann Arbor, University of Michigan Press, 1993, 280 p.

Delage, Christian, « Berlin, guerre des images d'une mémoire partagée (1945-1989) », *Vingtième siècle, Revue d'histoire*, n° 34 (avril-juin 1992), p. 85-105.

Delporte, Henri, *Archéologie et réalité: essai d'approche épistémologique*, Paris, Picard, 1984, 140 p.

Dendy, William and William Kilbourn, *Toronto Observed: Its Architecture, Patrons, and History*, Toronto, Oxford University Press, 1986.

Denhez, Marc C., *The Canadian Home: From Cave to Electronic Cocoon*, Toronto, Dundurn Press, 1994, 256 p.

_____, *Heritage Fights Back: Legal, Financial and Promotional Aspects of Canada's Efforts to Save its Architecture and Historic Sites*, Ottawa, Heritage Canada, [1978].

_____ and Stephen Dennis, eds., *Legal and Financial Aspects of Architectural Conservation*, Toronto, Dundurn Press, 1995, 248 p.

Dennis, Thelma B., *Albertans Built: Aspects of Housing in Rural Alberta to 1920*, Edmonton, University of Alberta, Printing Services, 1986.

Detienne, Marcel, *L'invention de la mythologie*, Paris, Gallimard, 1981, 252 p.

Developing a Conservation Strategy for a Heritage Building, Winnipeg, Manitoba Culture, Heritage & Citizenship, Historic Resources Branch, 1994, 96 p.

Deyanova, Liliana, "When Memory Plays Tricks", *The UNESCO Courier*, 47 (May 1994), p. 35-37.

Dictionnaire biographique du Canada, George W. Brown, Québec, Les Presses de l'Université Laval, vol. I, 1966.

Dictionary of Canadian Biography, George W. Brown, Toronto: University of Toronto Press, Vol. I, 1966.

Dienstag, Joshua Foa, "Building the Temple of Memory: Hegel's Aesthetic Narrative of History", *The Review of Politics*, 56, 4 (1995), p. 697-

Dolan, Claire, *Événement, identité, histoire*, Sillery, Éditions du Septentrion, 1991, 277 p.

Dosse, François, *L'histoire en miettes. Des « Annales » à la « nouvelle histoire »*, Paris, La Découverte, 1987, 268 p.

Douglas, Mary, "Institutionalized Public Memory," in: James F. Shorter Jr., ed., *The Social Fabric Dimensions and Issues*, Sage Publications, 1986, p. 63-76.

_____, *How Institutions Think*, Syracuse, Syracuse University Press, 1986, 146 p.

Douglass, Dave, "'Worms of the Earth': The Miners Own Story", in: Samuel Raphael, ed., *People's History and Socialist Theory*, London, Routledge & Kegan Paul, 1981, p. 61-67.

Dower, John W., "The Bombed: Hiroshimas and Nagasakis in Japanese Memory", *Diplomatic History*, 19: 2 (1995), p. 275-295.

Downs, Barry, *Sacred Places: British Columbia's Early Churches*, Vancouver, Douglas and McIntyre, 1980.

Duffus, Allan F., *et al.*, *Thy Dwellings Fair: Churches of Nova Scotia, 1750-1830*, Hantsport, N.S., Lancelot Press, 1982.

Durant, John, ed., *Museums and the Public Understanding of Science*, London, Science Museum/Committee on the Public Understanding of Science, 109 p.

Edward Forbes, Bush, *Engine Houses and Turntables in Canada, 1850-1950*, Erin, Boston Mills, 1990.

Edwards, Derek, *Collective Remembering*, London, Sage, 1990, 230 p.

Eickelmann, D. F., "The Art of Memory: Islamic Education and Its Social Reproduction", *Comparative Studies in Society and History*, 20 (1978), p. 485-516.

Eley, Geoff, « De l'histoire sociale au "tournant linguistique" dans l'historiographie anglo-américaine des années 1980 », *Genèses 7*, (mars 1992), p. 163-193.

_____, "Nazism, Politics And Public Memory: Thoughts On the West German Historikerstreit 1986-1987", *Past and Present: Journal of Historical Studies*, 121 (1988), p. 171-208.

Elmendorf, William W., *Twana Narratives: Native Historical Accounts of a Coast Salish Culture*, Vancouver, UBC Press, 1993, 306 p.

Ennals, Peter, "Distant Memories, Faint Images: The Survival and Adaptation of Acadian Housing in Maritime Canada", in *To Build a New Land: Ethnic Landscapes in North America*, Allen G. Noble, ed., Baltimore, Johns Hopkins University Press, 1992, p. 29-43.

Faber, K. G., "The Use of History in Political Debate", *Historical Consciousness and Political Action. History and Theory. Studies in the Philosophy of History*, 17, 4, suppl. 17 (1978), p. 19-35.

Fahmy-Eid, Nadia, « Histoire, objectivité et scientificité. Jalons pour une reprise du débat épistémologique », *Histoire sociale/Social History*, 17, 47 (mai-May 1991), p. 9 à 34.

Falkner, Ann, *Sans notre passé? Guide pour la protection de notre patrimoine architectural*, Toronto, University of Toronto Press; Ottawa, Ministère d'État aux affaires urbaines, 1978.

_____, *Without Our Past? A Handbook for the Preservation of Canada's Architectural Heritage*, Toronto, University of Toronto Press; Ottawa, Ministry of State for Urban Affairs, 1978.

Farr, Robert M. and Serge Moscovici, eds., *Social Representations*, Cambridge, Cambridge University Press/Paris, Éditions de la maison des sciences de l'homme, 1984, 412 p.

Favez, Jean-Claude, "Between Myth and Memory: Swiss History and the Present Day", *Contemporary European History*, 3, 3 (1994), p. 355-365.

Fentress, James and Chris Wickham, *Social Memory*, Oxford, Blackwell, 1992, 229 p.

Finkielkraut, Alain, *L'Avenir d'une négation. Réflexion sur la question du génocide*, Paris, Le Seuil, 1982, 180 p.

_____, *La Mémoire vaine. Du crime contre l'humanité*, Paris, Gallimard, 1989, 125 p.

Finlay Pelinski, Marike, « Pour une épistémologie de la communication: au-delà de la représentation et vers la pratique », *Communication information: Il était une fois la théorie*, 5, 2-3 (hiver/été 1983), p. 5 à 36.

Finley, Moses I., *Mythe, mémoire, histoire. Les usages du passé*, Paris, Flammarion, 1981, 270 p.

Flavell, J. H. and H. M. Wellman, "Metamemory", in: Robert V. Kail and John W. Hagen, eds., *Perspectives on the Development of Memory and Cognition*, Hillsdale, New Jersey, Lawrence Erlbaum, 1977, 498 p.

Folz, Robert, *Le souvenir et la légende de Charlemagne dans l'Empire germanique médiéval*, Paris, Les Belles Lettres, 1950, 156 p.

Foote, Kenneth E., "To Remember and Forget: Archives, Memory and Culture", *The American Archivist*, 53, 3 (1990), p. 378-393.

Fortier, Normand, *Guide to Oral History Collections in Canada /Guide des fonds d'histoire orale au Canada*, Ottawa, Canadian Oral History Association/ Société canadienne d'histoire orale, 1993, 402 p.

Fram, Mark, *Conserver, un savoir-faire. Le manuel de la Fondation du patrimoine ontarien sur les théories et les pratiques de la conservation architecturale*, Toronto, Stoddart et Boston Mills Press, 1993, 239 p.

_____, *Well-Preserved: The Ontario Heritage Foundation's Manual of Principles and Practice for Architectural Conservation*, Erin, Ont., Boston Mills Press, 1988, 239 p.

_____ and John Weiler, eds., *Continuity with Change*, Toronto, Dundurn Press, 1984.

Francis, H., "The Law, Oral Tradition and the Mining Community", *Journal of Law and Society*, 12 (1985), p. 267-271.

Frank, Robert, « Mémoires françaises de la Deuxième Guerre mondiale », *Institut d'histoire du temps présent*, Bulletin trimestriel, n° 23 (mars 1986), p. 11 à 15.

Frei, Norbert, « L'Holocauste dans l'historiographie allemande. Un point aveugle dans la conscience historique ? », *Vingtième siècle. Revue d'histoire*, n° 34 (avril-juin 1992), p. 157-162.

Friedlander, Saul, *Memory, History, and the Extermination of the Jews of Europe*, Bloomington, Indiana University Press, 1993, 142 p.

Frisch, Michael, "American History and the Structures of Collective Memory: A Modest Exercise in Empirical Iconography", *The Journal of American History*, 75, 4 (1988), p. 1130-1155.

Fuller, Steve, "Being There with Thomas Kuhn: A Parable for Postmodern Time," *History and Theory*, 31, 3 (1992), p. 241-275.

Furet, François, « La Révolution dans l'imaginaire politique français », *Le Débat*, n° 26 (septembre 1983), p. 173-182.

Gagnon-Arguin, Louise, *L'archivistique, son histoire, ses acteurs depuis 1960*, Sainte-Foy, Presses de l'Université du Québec, 1992, 229 p.

Gagnon Pratte, France, *L'architecture et la nature à Québec au dix-neuvième siècle: les villas*, Québec, Musée du Québec, 1980.

_____ et Eric Etter, *Le Château Frontenac: Cent ans de vie de château*, Québec, Éditions Continuité, 1993.

Galeano, Eduardo H., *Memory of Fire*, New York, Pantheon, 1985-1988. 3 vol. Trans. of: *Memoria del fuego*.

Gathering Voices: Finding the Strength to Help our Children, Vancouver, Douglas and McIntyre, 1996, 189 p. [written in English and Innu].

Gautier, Nadine et Jean-François Rouge, dir., « Passion du passé, "Les fabricants" d'Histoire, leurs rêves et leurs batailles », *Autrement*, n° 88 (mars 1987), 203 p.

Gautier, Nadine et Jean-François Rouge, dir., « Passion du passé, « Les fabricants » d'Histoire, leurs rêves et leurs batailles », *Autrement*, n° 88 (mars 1987), 203 p.

Geary, Patrick J., *Phantoms of Remembrance: Memory and Oblivion at the End of the First Millennium*, Princeton, Princeton University Press, 1994, 248 p.

Geist, Christopher, "Historic Sites and Monuments as Icons", Ray B. Browne and Marshall Fishwick, eds., *Icons of America*, Bowling Green, (Ohio), Popular Press, 1988, p. 57-66.

Gelly, Alain, Louise Brunelle-Lavoie et Cornelius Kirjan, *La passion du patrimoine. La Commission des biens culturels du Québec 1922-1994*. Sillery, Éditions du Septentrion, 1995. 293 p.

Geneses 1, Sciences sociales et histoire, (septembre 1990).

Gérard, Alice, *La Révolution française, mythes et interprétations (1789-1970)*, Paris, Flammarion, 1970, 140 p.

Gerhardsson, Berger, *Memory and Manuscript: Oral Tradition and Written Transmission in Rabbinic Judaism and Early Christianity*, Lund, Denmark, C.W.K. Gleerup, 1961, 379 p.

Gillis, John R., ed., *Commemorations: The Politics of National Identity*, Princeton, Princeton University Press, 1994, 290 p.

Girardet, Raoul, « Du concept de génération à la notion de contemporanéité », *Revue d'histoire moderne et contemporaine*, 30 (avril-juin 1983), p. 257-270.

_____, *Mythes et mythologies politiques*, Paris, Seuil, 1986, 210 p.

Gitelman, Zvi, "History, Memory and Politics: The Holocaust in the Soviet Union", *Holocaust and Genocide Studies*, 5, 1 (1990), p. 23-

Gluck, Sherna Berger and Daphne Patai, eds., *Women's Words: The Feminist Practice of Oral History*, New York, Routledge, 1991, 234 p.

Godelier, Maurice, *Les sciences de l'homme et de la société en France. Analyse et propositions pour une politique nouvelle*, Paris, La Documentation française, 1982, 559 p.

Goldmeier, Erich, *The Memory Trace: Its Formation and its Fate*, Hilldale, New Jersey, Erlbaum, 1982, 257 p.

Gough, Hugh, "France and the Memory of Revolution: 1789-1989", *History of European Ideas*, 15, 4 / 6 (1992), p. 811-816.

Gould, E., *Oil: The History of Canada's Oil and Gas Industry* (Saanichton: Hancock House, 1976).

Gowans, Alan, *Building Canada: An Architectural History of Canadian Life*, Rev. and enl. ed., Toronto, Oxford University Press, 1966.

Greenaway, Cora, *Interior Decorative Painting in Nova Scotia/Peinture décorative d'intérieur en Nouvelle-Écosse*, Catalogue of an exhibition organized and circulated by the Art Gallery of Nova Scotia, Halifax, 1986.

Greenhill, Ralph, Ken MacPherson and Douglas Richardson, *Ontario Towns*, [Ottawa], Oberon, 1974.

Groulx, Patrice, *Une mémoire momifiée? Problèmes et perspectives de l'interprétation de l'histoire dans les centres d'interprétation*. Thèse de M.A. (histoire), Université du Québec à Montréal, 1990.

———— et Alain Roy, « Les biens historiques de la région de Québec comme lieux d'expression identitaire, 1965-1985 », *Revue d'histoire de l'Amérique française*, 48, 4 (printemps, 1995): 527-541.

Guenée, Bernard, « Temps de l'histoire et temps de la mémoire au Moyen Age », *Bulletin de la Société de l'histoire de France*, n° 487 (1976-1977), p. 25 à 36.

————, *Histoire et culture historique dans l'occident médiéval*, Paris, Aubier Montaigne, 1980, 439 p.

Guillaume, Marc, « Invention et stratégies du patrimoine », Henri Pierre Jeudy, dir., *Patrimoine en folie*, Paris, Éditions de la Maison des sciences de l'homme, 1990: 13-20.

————, *La politique du patrimoine*, Paris, Éditions Galilée, 1980, 196 p.

Guillet, E. C., *The Story of Canadian Roads*, Toronto: University of Toronto Press, 1966.

Haft, Cynthia, *The Theme of Nazi Concentration Camps in French Literature*, Paris/La Haye, Mouton, 1973, 227 p.

Halbwachs, Maurice, *La mémoire collective*, Préface de Jean Duvignaud, 2ᵉ édition revue et augmentée, Paris, PUF, 1968, 204 p.

————, *Les cadres sociaux de la mémoire*, Nouvelle édition, Paris, PUF, 1952, 298 p.

Hamelin, Jean, « L'histoire des historiens: entre la reconstruction d'une mémoire collective et la recherche d'une identité », Jacques Dagneau et Sylvie Pelletier, dir., *Mémoires et histoires dans les sociétés francophones*, Sélection des communications présentées au colloque Mémoires, histoires, identités: expériences des sociétés francophones (Québec, 9-12 octobre 1987), Actes du CÉLAT, n° 7 (juin 1992), p. 59 à 72.

Hampton, Henry and Steve Fayer with Sarah Flynn, *Voices of Freedom: An Oral History of the Civil Rights Movement from the 1950s through the 1980s*, New York, Bantam Books, 1990, 692 p.

Handler, Richard, *Nationalism and the Politics of Culture in Quebec*. Madison, University of Wisconsin Press, 1988.

Harkin, James B., *The History and Meaning of the National Parks of Canada: Extracts from Papers of the Late Jas. B. Harkin First Commissioner of the National Parks of Canada*. Compiled by Mabel B. Williams, Saskatoon, H.R. Larson Pub. Co., 1957, 16 p.

Hayden, Dolores, *The Power of Place: Urban Landscape as Public History*, Boston, MIT Press, 1995, 280 pp.

Herberich-Marx, Geneviève et Freddy Raphaël, « Les incorporés de force alsaciens. Déni, convocation et provocation de la mémoire », *Vingtième siècle, Revue d'histoire*, n° 6 (avril-juin 1985), p. 83 à 102.

Herbert, Christopher, *Culture and Anomie: Ethnographic Imagination in the Nineteenth Century*, Chicago, University of Chicago Press, 1991, 364 p.

Héritage Montréal, Collection *Guide technique*, Montréal, Héritage Montréal et le ministère des Affaires culturelles du Québec, 1984-86. 1. London, Mark et Mireille Ostiguy, *Couvertures traditionnelles*; 2. London, Mark et Dinu Bumbaru, *Fenêtres traditionnelles*; 3. London, Mark et Dinu Bumbaru, *Maçonnerie traditionnelle*; 4. London, Mark et Cécile Bedard, *Revêtements traditionnels*.

Heritage Notes series, Edmonton, Alberta Historical Resources Foundation and Alberta Community Development, c. 1992.

Hermann, Alex, et al., eds., *Historic Architecture of Saskatchewan*, Regina, Focus Publishing for the Saskatchewan Association of Architects, 1987.

Herrmann, Douglas J., Roger Chaffin, eds., *Memory in Historical Perspective: The Literature before Ebbinghaus*, New York, Springer-Verlag, 1988, 254 p.

Hewison, Robert, « Retour à l'héritage ou la gestion du passé à l'anglaise », *Le Débat* (Paris), 78 (janvier-février 1994), p. 130 à 139.

_____, *Genocide and the Politics of Memory: Studying Death to Preserve Life*, Chapel Hill, University of North Carolina Press, 1995, 240 p.

Hiss, Tony, *The Experience of Place*, New York, Alfred A. Knopf, 1990, 233 p.

Histoire et historiens, Saisons d'Alsace, n° 111, (printemps 1991).

« Histoire et sciences sociales », *Annales E.S.C.*, n° 2 (mars-avril 1988), p. 291-293.

Historical Atlas of Canada, 3 vols., Toronto, University of Toronto Press, 1987-1993 (Geoffrey J. Matthews, cartographer/designer, vol. 1, Harris, R. Cole, ed., *From the Beginning to 1800*; vol. 2, Gentilcore, R. Louis, ed., *The Land Transformed, 1800-1891*; vol. 3, Kerr, Donald and Deryck W. Holdsworth, eds., *Addressing the Twentieth Century, 1891-1961*).

Hobsbawm, E. J., *Nations and Nationalism Since 1780: Programme, Myth, Reality*, 2nd ed., Cambridge, Cambridge University Press, 1992, 206 p.

_____ and Terence Ranger, eds., *The Invention of Tradition*, Cambridge, Cambridge University Press, 1983, 320 p.

_____, "The Social Function of the Past: Some Questions", *Past and Present*, 55 (1972), p. 3-17.

Holdsworth, Deryck, ed., *Reviving Main Street*, Toronto, University of Toronto Press for The Heritage Canada Foundation, 1985.

Hoorn, Jeanette, "Positioning The Post-Colonial Subject. History and Memory in the Art of Gordon Bennett", *Art and Australia*, 31, 2 (1993), p. 216-

Hosmer, Charles B., *Presence of the Past: A History of the Preservation Movement in the United States before Williamsburg*. New York, G. P. Putnam's Sons, 1965, 386 p.

Hough, Michael, *Out of Place: Restoring Identity to the Regional Landscape*, New Haven, Yale University Press, 230 p.

Hutton, Patrick H., "The Role of Memory in the Historiography of the French Revolution", *History and Theory*, 30, 1 (1991), p. 56-69.

_____, *History as an Art of Memory*, Hanover, New Hampshire, University Press of New England, 1993, 229 p.

Huyssen, Andreas, *Twilight Memories : Marking Time in a Culture of Amnesia*, New York, Routledge, 1995, 292 p.

"In Pursuit of the Past: History and Memory", *The UNESCO Courier*, 43 (April 1990) p. 10-11.

Insdorf, Annette, *L'Holocauste à l'écran*, CinémAction/Éditions du Cerf, 1985, 189 p.

Institut Collégial Européen, *La Culture comme projet de société*, Colloque interdisciplinaire sous la dir. de Gilbert Gadoffre, Éditions Universitaires, (1991), 322 p.

Institut d'histoire du temps présent, *La Mémoire des Français. Quarante ans de commémoration de la Seconde Guerre mondiale*, Paris, Éditions du CNRS, 1986, 400 p.

Inwood, Kris E., *The Canadian Charcoal Iron Industry, 1870-1914* (New York: Garland, 1986).

Irwin-Zarecka, Iwona, *Frames of Remembrance: The Dynamics of Collective Memory*, New Brunswick, New Jersey, Transaction Publishers. 1994, 214 p.

Jager, Friedrich, "Culture or Society? The Significance of Max Weber's Thought for Modern Cultural History", *History & Memory*, 3, 2 (1991), p. 115-140.

Janet, Pierre, *L'évolution de la mémoire et de la notion du temps*, Paris, A. Chahine, 1928, 3 vol.

Jeffrey, Brooke, *La politique culturelle de Canada de Massey-Lévesque à Applebaum-Hébert*, Ottawa, Bibliothèque du Parlement, 1982.

Jelen, E., "The Politics of Memory: The Human Rights Movement and the Construction of Democracy in Argentina", *Latin American Perspectives*, 21, 2 (spring 1994), p. 38-58.

Jeudy, Henri-Pierre, « Entre mémoire et patrimoine », *Ethnologie française*, 25, 1 (janvier-mars 1995): 5-7.

_____, *Mémoires du social*, Paris, PUF, 1986, 171 p.

_____, dir., *Patrimoines en folie*, Paris, Éditions de la Maison des sciences de l'homme, 1990. 310 p.

Jewsiewicki, Bogumil K., *Récits de vie et mémoire: vers une anthropologie historique du souvenir, avec la collaboration de Fabrice Montal, Sainte-Foy, SAFI*; Paris, L'Harmattan, 1987, 344 p.

_____, "Collective Memory and the Stakes of Power. A Reading of Popular Zarian Historical Sources", *History in Africa*, 13 (1986), p. 195-223.

Jing, Jun, *The Temple of Memories: History, Power, and Morality in a Chinese Village*, Thesis. 1994, 357 p.

Johnson, George, *In the Palaces of Memory: How We Build the Worlds Inside Our Heads*, New York, Knopf, 1991, 255 p.

Johnson, Martha, ed., *LORE. Capturing Traditional Environmental Knowledge*, Hay River, NWT, Dene Cultural Institute and the International Development Research Center, 1992, 190 p.

Johnson, Richard, ed., "Popular Memory: Theory, Politics, Method", in: Center for Contemporary Studies, *Making Histories: Studies in History-writing and Politics*, Minneapolis, University of Minnesota Press, 1982, p. 205-252.

Johnston, A.J.B., "Preserving History: The Commemoration of the 18th Century Louisbourg, 1895-1940", *Acadiensis*, 12 (1983), p. 53-80.

Johnston, Basil H., *Tales of the Anishnaubaek*, Toronto, Royal Ontario Museum, 1993, 79 p.

Joutard, Philippe, « L'histoire dans l'imaginaire collectif, un nouveau chantier », *L'Arc*, 72 (1978).

_____, « La distinction entre le légendaire historique d'origine savante et celui d'origine populaire est-elle toujours pertinente ? », *Le monde alpin et rhodanien*, 10 (1982), p. 179-192.

_____, « Mémoire collective », dans: André Burguière, dir., *Dictionnaire des sciences historiques*, Paris, PUF, 1986, p. 447-449.

_____, Janine Estèbe, Elisabeth Labrousse et Jean Lecuir, *La Saint-Barthélemy. Ou les résonnances d'un massacre*, Neuchâtel, Delachaux & Niestlé, 1976, 245 p.

_____, *La légende des Camisards: une sensibilité au passé*, Paris, Gallimard, 1977, 439 p.

Judt, Tony, "The Past is Another Country: Myth and Memory in Postwar Europe", *Daedalus*, 121, 4 (1992), p. 83-118.

Kaes, Anton, "History and Film: Public Memory in the Age of Electronic Dissemination", *History & Memory*, 2, 1 (1990), p. 111-129.

Kalman, Harold, *A History of Canadian Architecture*, 2 vols., Toronto, Oxford University Press, 1994.

_____, *Pour une réfection sensée des vieilles maisons*, Ottawa, Société canadienne d'hypothèques et de logement, 1979.

_____, *The Railway Hotels and the Development of the Chateau Style in Canada*, Studies in Architectural History Number One, Victoria, B.C., University of Victoria, Maltwood Museum, 1968.

_____, *The Sensible Rehabilitation of Older Houses*, Ottawa, Canada Mortgage and Housing Corporation, 1979.

_____ and John de Visser, *Pioneer Churches*, Toronto, McClelland and Stewart, 1976.

_____, Keith Wagland et Robert Bailey, *Encore: réaménagement de bâtiments publics à des fins artistiques et culturelles*, Ottawa, Secrétariat d'État, 1981.

_____, Keith Wagland and Robert Bailey, *Encore: Recycling Public Buildings for the Arts*, Don Mills, Ont., Corpus, 1980.

Kammen, Michael G., *Mystic Chords of Memory: The Transformation of Tradition in American Culture*, New York, Knopf, 1991, 864 p.

_____, « La mémoire américaine et sa problématique », *Le Débat*, n° 30 (mai 1984), p. 112 à 127.

Kang, Nam-Soon, "Creating 'Dangerous Memory': Challenges for Asian and Korean Feminist Theology", *The Ecumenical Review*, 47 (January 1995), p. 21-31.

Kantin, Georges et Gilles Manceron, Textes réunis et présentés par, *Les Échos de la mémoire: tabous et enseignements de la Seconde Guerre mondiale*, Préface de Claude Julien, Paris, Le Monde éditions, 1991, 369 p.

Karp, Ivan and Steven D. Lavine, eds., *Exhibiting Cultures. The Poetics and Politics of Museum Display*, Washington, Smithsonian Institution Press, 1981, 486 p.

_____, ed., *Museums and Communities: The Politics of Public Culture*, Washington, D.C., Smithsonian Institution Press, 1992, 614 p. Papers presented at a conference at the Smithsonian Institution International Center, held in 1990.

Katriel, Tamar, "Sites of Memory: Discourses of the Past in Israeli Pioneering Settlement Museums", *The Quarterly Journal of Speech*, 80, 1, (1994), p. 1-20.

Keefer, Alec, *et al.*, *Terra Cotta: Artful Deceivers*, Toronto, Architectural Conservancy of Ontario, Toronto Region Branch, 1991.

Ketchum, Richard M., "Memory as History", *American Heritage*, 42 (November 1991), p. 142-144.

Kincheloe, Joe L., "Meta-analysis, Memory, and the Past: Historical Method, Curriculum, and Social Responsibility", *Social Science Record*, 27, 2 (1990), p. 31-39.

Klapisch-Zuber, Christiane, *La maison et le nom. Stratégies et rituels dans l'Italie de la Renaissance*, Paris, Édition de EHESS, 1990, 393 p.

Kleinman, Arthur and Joan Kleinman, "How Bodies Remember: Social Memory and Bodily Experience of Criticism, Resistance, and Delegitimation Following China's Cultural Revolution", *New Literary History*, 25, 3 (1994), p. 707-723.

Knapp, Steven, "Collective Memory and the Actual Past", *Representations*, 26 (1989), p. 123.

Koshar, Rudy J., "Altar, Stage and City: Historic Preservation and Urban Meaning in Nazi Germany", *History & Memory*, 3, 1 (1991), p. 30-59.

Kosslyn, Stephen Michael, *Image and Mind*, Cambridge, Harvard University Press, 1980, 500 p.

Kotkin, Stephen, "Terror, Rehabilitation, and History Memory: An Interview with Dmitrii Iurasov", *The Russian Review*, 51 (April 1992), p. 238-262.

Koven, Keith, "Remembering and Dismemberment: Crippled Children, Wounded Soldiers, and the Great War in Britain", *American Historical Review*, 99, 4 (October 1994), p. 1167-1202.

Krell, David Farrell, *Of Memory, Reminiscence, and Writing: On the Verge*, Bloomington, Indiana University Press, 1990, 340 p.

Krugler, John D., "Behind the Public Presentations: Research and Scholarship at Living History Museums of Early America", *William and Mary Quarterly*, third series, 48, 1 (January 1991), p. 347-385.

Kuberski, Philip, *The Persistence of Memory : Organism, Myth, Text*, Berkeley, University of California Press, 1992, 145 p.

Kuchler, Susanne and Walter Melion, *Images of Memory: On Remembering and Representation*, Washington, D.C., Smithsonian Institution Press, 1991, 265 p.

Labrot, Gérard, « Hantise généalogique, jeux d'alliance, souci esthétique. Le portrait dans les collections de l'aristocratie napolitaine (XVIᵉ-XVIIIᵉ siècles) », *Revue historique*, 284, 2 (1990), p. 281-301.

LaCapra, Dominick, "Intellectual History and Its Ways", *American Historical Review*, 97, 2 (April 1992), p. 425-439.

La Forte, Robert S., Ronald E. Marcello, and Richard L. Himmel, eds., *With Only the Will to Live: Accounts of Americans in Japanese Prison Camps, 1941-1945*, Wilmington, Delaware, SR Books, 1994, 286 p.

Lafrance, Marc, « LeParc de l'Artillerie et les Fortifications de Québec: une rétrospective de mise en valeur 1972-1990 », *Material History Review/Revue d'histoire de la culture matérielle*, 39 (printemps 1994): 41-49.

« La littérature québécoise en Ontario: aspects historiques et critiques », n° spécial de *Cultures du Canada français*, n° 9 (1992).

Lamontagne, Sophie-Laurence, *Le patrimoine immatériel. Méthodologie d'inventaire pour les savoirs, les savoir-faire et les porteurs de traditions*, Coll. « Dossiers du patrimoine », Ministère de la Culture, Québec, Éditeur du Québec, 1994, 132 p.

Lanken, Dane, photographs by Brian Merrett and Julie Greto, *Montreal Movie Palaces: Great Theatres of the Golden Era, 1884-1938*, Waterloo, Ont., Archives of Canadian Art, 1993, 190 p.

Lapierre, Nicole, dir., « La mémoire et l'oubli », *Communications*, n° 49 (1989).

Lapointe, Andrée, *L'incidence des politiques culturelles sur le développement des musées nationaux Canada-Québec depuis 1950*. Thèse de PhD (histoire), Université Laval, 1993.

Laroche, Jacques, "A Success Story in the French Popular Literature of the 1980's: La Bicyclette bleue", *The French Review*, 60, 4 (March 1987), p. 502-510.

Larsen, Knut Einar, ed./réd. *Nara Conference on Authenticity in Relation to the World Heritage Convention: Proceedings/Conference de Nara sur l'Authenticité dans le cadre de la Convention du Patrimoine Mondial: Compte-Rendu*, Trondheim, Norway, Tapir Publishers for UNESCO World Heritage Centre/Centre du Patrimoine Mondial, Agency for Cultural Affairs (Japan)/Direction des Affaires Culturelles (Japon), ICROM, and/et UNESCO, 1995, 427 p.

Larue, Richard et Francis Montal, « Québec 1984: le silence des historiens », Jacques Dagneau et Sylvie Pelletier, dir., *Mémoires et histoires dans les sociétés francophones*, Sélection des communications présentées au colloque Mémoires, histoires, identités: expériences des sociétés francophones (Québec, 9-12 octobre 1987), Actes du Célat, n° 7 (juin 1992), p. 49-58.

Latremouille, Joann, *Pride of Home: The Working Class Housing Tradition in Nova Scotia, 1749-1949*, Hantsport, N.S., Lancelot Press, 1986.

La Ville de Québec, sous la direction générale de Michel Bonnette, *Guide technique*, collection Maître d'œuvre, Québec, le Service de l'urbanisme et le Service des communications de la Ville de Québec, 1988-91.

Layton, Robert, "Who Needs the Past?," in: R. Layton, *Who Needs the Past? Indigenous Values and Archeology*, London, V. Hyman, 1989, p. 1-20.

Lecours, Jacques, « Patrimoine d'entreprise et patrimoine collectif: l'évolution des pratiques d'Hydro-Québec », *Le Forum québécois du patrimoine*. Actes de la rencontre de Trois-Rivières (1992), Montréal, Héritage-Montréal, 1992: p. 15-20.

Ledohowski, Edward M. and David K. Butterfield, *Architectural Heritage: The Eastern Interlake Planning District*, Architectural Heritage Report No. 2, Winnipeg, Manitoba Department of Cultural Affairs and Historical Resources, 1983.

_____ and David K. Butterfield, *Architectural Heritage: Traditional Mennonite Architecture in the Rural Municipality of Stanley*, Prepared for the Mennonite Heritage Village, Steinbach, Manitoba, Winnipeg, Mennonite Heritage Village Canada and Manitoba Culture, Heritage and Recreation, Historic Resources, 1990, 90 p.

Legget, R. F., *The Canals of Canada*, Vancouver, Douglas, David and Charles, 1975.

Legget, Robert Ferguson, *Railways of Canada*, rev. ed., Vancouver, Douglas and McIntyre, 1988.

L'Enseignement de la Choa. Comment les manuels d'histoire présentent-ils l'extermination des Juifs au cours de la Seconde Guerre mondiale?, Table ronde organisée par le C.D.J.C. et l'Association des Professeurs d'Histoire et de Géographie (régionale de Paris), 14 mars 1982, Paris, Centre de documentation juive contemporaine, 1982, 131 p.

Le Goff, Jacques, *Histoire et mémoire*, Paris, Gallimard, 1988 (1977), 409 p.

_____, *History and Memory*; Steven Rendall and Elizabeth Claman, trans., New York, Columbia University Press, 1992, 265 p. Translation of: *Storia e memoria*.

Lehr, John, *Ukrainian Vernacular Architecture in Alberta*, Edmonton, Alberta Culture, Historical Resources Division, 1976.

Lepenies, Wolf, *Les trois cultures. Entre science et littérature l'avènement de la sociologie*, Paris, Éd. de la Maison des sciences de l'homme, 1990, 408 p.

Lequin, Yves et Jean Métral, « À la recherche d'une mémoire collective: les métallurgistes retraités de Givors », *Annales ESC*, 35, 1 (janvier-février 1980), p. 149-166.

Lerner, Loren R., and/et Mary F. Williamson, comps., *Art and Architecture in Canada: A Bibliography and Guide to the Literature to 1981/Art et architecture au Canada: Bibliographie et guide de la documentation jusqu'en 1981*, 2 vols/tomes, Toronto, University of Toronto Press, 1991.

Leroi-Gourhan, A., *Le Geste et la Parole. II: La Mémoire et les rythmes*, Paris, A. Michel, 1965, 285 p.

Les processus collectifs de mémorisation (Mémoire et organisation), Actes du Colloque d'Aix-en-Provence (juin 1979), Publiés par Jean-Louis Le Moigne et Daniel Pascot, Aix-en-Provence, Librairie de l'Université, 1979, 249 p.

Lessard, Michel et Gilles Vilandré, *La maison traditionnelle au Québec: construction, inventaire, restauration*, Montréal, Éditions de l'Homme, 1974.

Létourneau, Jocelyn, « La grève de l'amiante entre ses mémoires et l'histoire », *Journal of the Canadian Oral History Association*, 11 (fall 1991), p. 8-16.

_____, « Le "Québec moderne". Un chapitre du grand récit collectif des Québécois », *Revue française de science politique*, 42, 5 (octobre 1992), p. 765-785.

Lewis, Bernard, *History: Remembered, Recorded, Invented*, Princeton, Princeton University Press, 1975, 111 p.

Lewis, Earl, "Connecting Memory, Self, and the Power of Place in African American Urban History." *Journal of Urban History*, 21, 3 (1995), p. 347-371.

L'histoire pour quoi faire? La mémoire populaire gadget culturel ou ancrage des luttes? Les cahiers du Forum-Histoire, n° 10 (novembre 1978), 63 p.

Linenthal, Edward T., "The Boundaries of Memory: The United States Holocaust Memorial Museum", *American Quarterly*, 46 (September 1994), p. 406-433.

Linteau, Paul-André, réd., *Bâtir un pays: histoire des travaux publics au Canada*, Montréal, Éditions du Boréal, 1988.

Lipsitz, George, *Time Passages: Collective Memory and American Popular Culture*, Minneapolis, University of Minnesota Press, 1990, 306 p.

Loraux, Nicole, « L'oubli dans la cité », *Le temps de la réflexion*, n° 1 (1980), p. 132-142.

Lothian, W.F., *Petite histoire des parcs nationaux du Canada*. Ottawa, ministère des Approvisionnements et Services du Canada, 1987.

_____, *Short History of Canadian National Parks*, Ottawa, Ministry of Supply and Services Canada, 1987.

Lourie, Margaret A., Donna C. Stanton, and Martha Vicinus, eds., *Women and Memory*. Ann Arbor, University of Michigan Press, 1987, 292 p. Special issue of *Michigan Quarterly Review*, 26, 1.

Lourie, Richard, *Russia Speaks: An Oral History from the Revolution to the Present*, New York, HarperCollins, 1991, 396 p.

Lowenthal, David and Marcus Binney, eds., *Our Past Before Us: Why Do We Save It?*, London, T. Smith, 1981, 253 p.

_____, *Landscape Meanings and Values*, London, Allen, 1986, 137 p.

_____, *The Past is a Foreign Country*, Cambridge, Cambridge University Press, 1985, 489 p.

Lupton, Deborah, "Food, Memory and Meaning: The Symbolic and Social Nature of Food Events", *The Sociological Review*, 42, 4 (1994), p. 664-685.

Lussato, Bruno, *La théorie de l'empreinte*, Paris, ESF Éditeur (1991), (Coll. « Communication et complexité»), 380 p.

MacDonald, Graham, *A Good Solid Comfortable Establishment: An Illustrated History of Lower Fort Garry*, Winnipeg, Watson & Dwyer, 1992, 98 p.

MacDonald, George F., *Haida Monumental Art: Villages of the Queen Charlotte Islands*, Vancouver, University of British Columbia Press, 1989.

MacKay, Donald, *The People's Railway: A History of Canadian National*, Vancouver, Douglas and McIntyre, 1992.

MacRae, Marion and Anthony Adamson, *The Ancestral Roof: Domestic Architecture of Upper Canada*, Toronto and Vancouver, Clarke, Irwin, 1963; new ed. 1975.

_____ and Anthony Adamson, *Cornerstones of Order: Courthouses and Town Halls of Ontario 1784-1914*, Toronto and Vancouver, Clarke, Irwin, 1983.

_____ and Anthony Adamson, *Hallowed Walls: Church Architecture in Upper Canada*, Toronto and Vancouver, Clarke, Irwin, 1975.

Maier, Charles S., *The Unmasterable Past: History, Holocaust, and German National Identity*, Cambridge, Harvard Univeristy Press, 1988, 227 p.

Maitland, Leslie, *L'architecture néo-classique au Canada*, Études en archéologie, architecture et histoire, Ottawa, Parcs Canada, 1984.

_____, *Neoclassical Architecture in Canada*, Studies in Archaeology, Architecture and History, Ottawa, Parks Canada, 1984.

_____, *The Queen Anne Revival Style in Canadian Architecture*, Studies in Archaeology, Architecture and History, Ottawa, Environment Canada, Parks Service, 1990.

_____, *Le style néo-Queen Anne dans l'architecture au Canada*, Études en archéologie, architecture et histoire, Ottawa, Environnement Canada, Service des parcs, 1990.

_____, Jacqueline Hucker and Shannon Ricketts, *Canadian Architectural Styles*, Peterborough, Ont., Broadview Press, 1992, 223 p.

Majastre, Jean-Olivier, « Oublieuse mémoire », *Le monde alpin et rhodanien. Croyances, récits et pratiques de tradition*, Mélanges d'Ethnologie, d'Histoire et de Linguistique en hommage à Charles JOISTEN (1936-1981), 10, 1-4 (1982), p. 123-126.

Mali, Joseph, "Jacob Burckhardt: Myth, History and Mythistory", *History & Memory*, 3, 1 (1991), p. 86-118.

Mandelbaum, Seymour, "The Past in Service to the Future", *Journal of Social History*, 2 (winter 1977), p. 193-205.

Mann, Arthur, "The Progressive Tradition," in: John Highman, ed., *The Reconstruction of American History*, New York, Harper & Row, 1962, p. 157-179.

Marcus, Ivan G., "History, Story and Collective Memory: Narrativity in Early Ashkenazic Culture", *Prooftexts*, 10, 3 (1990), p. 365-388.

Marès, Antoine, « Ruptures et continuités de la mémoire tchèque », *Vingtième siècle. Revue d'histoire*, n° 36 (octobre-décembre 1992), p. 71-80.

Marsan, Jean-Claude, *Montréal en évolution: historique du développement de l'architecture et de l'environnement montréalais*, Montréal, Fides, 1974; 2ᵉ éd.

Martenfinnis, S., "Collective Memory and National Identities: German and Polish Memory Cultures", *Communist and Post Communist Studies*, 28, 2 (June 1995), p. 255-261.

Martin, Denis, *Portraits de héros de la Nouvelle-France. Images d'un culte historique*, Ville de LaSalle, Hurtubise HMH, 1988, 176 p.

Martin, J. Edward, *The Railway Stations of Western Canada: An Architectural History*, White Rock, B.C., Studio E Martin, 1980.

Martin, Jean-Clément, *La Vendée de la mémoire, 1800-1980*, Préface de Emmanuel Le Roy Ladurie, Paris, Seuil, 1989, 298 p.

Martin, Paul-Louis, « Le patrimoine culturel: l'évolution des pratiques », *Le Forum québécois du patrimoine. Actes de la rencontre de Trois-Rivières* (Ville de Laval, Le Forum du patrimoine, 1992), p. 11-14.

_____, *Les chemins de la mémoire. Monuments et sites historiques du Québec*, Québec, Commission des biens culturels, 1990, 2 vols., Audio-diapothèque.

_____ et Jean Lavoie, réd., *Les chemins de la mémoire: monuments et sites historiques du Québec*, La commission des biens culturels du Québec, 2 tomes, Québec, Publications du Québec, 1990-91.

_____ et Pierre Morisset, photographies de Janouk Murdock, *Promenades dans les jardins anciens du Québec*, Boréal, B.L. Éditeur, 1996.

Martin, Peter, Gunhild O. Hagestad amd Peter Diedrick, "Family Stories: Events (Temporarily) Remembered", *Journal of Marriage and the Family*, 50, 1 (February 1988), p. 533-541.

Martinet, Chantal, « Objets de famille/objets de musée. Ethnologie ou muséologie ? », *Ethnologie française*, 12, 1 (1982), p. 61-72.

Mathieu, Jacques, dir., *Les Plaines d'Abraham. Le culte de l'idéal*. Sillery et Québec, Septentrion et Commission des champs de bataille nationaux, 1993. p. 313 (Also in English version).

_____ et Jacques Lacoursière, *Les mémoires québécoises*, Sainte-Foy, PUL, 1991, 383 p.

_____ et Martine Cardin, « Jalons pour le positionnement de l'archivistique », *La place de l'archivistique dans la gestion de l'information: perspectives de recherche*, ANQ-M, GIRA, 1990, p. 121-126.

_____, « Les vernis du patrimoine », *Le Forum québécois du patrimoine. Actes de la rencontre de Trois-Rivières*, (Ville Laval, Le Forum du patrimoine, 1992), p. 5-10.

_____, dir., *Étude de la construction de la mémoire collective des Québécois au XXᵉ siècle. Approches multidisciplinaires*, Cahiers du CÉLAT, n° 5 (novembre 1986), 320 p.

May, Ernest R., *"Lessons" of the Past: The Use and Misuse of History in American Foreign Policy*, New York, Oxford University Press, 1973, 220 p.

May, Henry Farnham, *Coming to Terms: A Study in Memory and History*, Berkeley, University of California Press, 1987, 319 p.

Mayrand, Pierre, and/et John Bland, *Three Centuries of Architecture in Canada/Trois siècles d'architecture au Canada*, Montréal, Federal Publications Service, 1971.

McDougall, David J., *The St. Francis Forges and the Grantham Iron Works: A Technical History*, Montreal, 1973.

McGinnis, Janice Dickin, "Heritage Minutes: Myth and History", *Canadian Issues/Thèmes canadiens*, 17 (1995): 25-36.

McGreevy, Patrick Vincent, *Imagining Niagara: The Meaning and Making of Niagara Falls*, Amherst, Mass., University of Massachusetts Press, 1994.

McIwraith, Thomas F., ed., *By River, Road and Rail: Transportation in Old Ontario. Essays in Technological and Logistical History*, Toronto, Ontario Museums Assoc., 1984.

McKay, Ian, *The Quest of the Folk: Antimodernism and Cultural Selection in Twentieth Century Nova Scotia*, Kingston: McGill-Queen's, 1994, 371 p.

McKendry, Jennifer, *With Our Past Before Us: Nineteenth-Century Architecture in the Kingston Area*, Toronto, University of Toronto Press, 1995, 242 p.

Meggs, Geoff, and Duncan Stacey, *Cork Lines and Canning Lines: The Glory Years of Fishing on the West Coast*, Vancouver, Douglas and McIntyre, 1992.

Melman, Billie, "Gender, History and Memory: The Invention of Women's Past in the Nineteenth and Early Twentieth Centuries", *History & Memory*, 5, 1 (1993), p. 5-41.

« La Mémoire », *Bulletin de psychologie*, 42, 389 (janvier-avril 1989).

« La Mémoire d'Auschwitz », Dossier, dans *Esprit*, 9 (septembre 1980).

« Mémoires de femmes », *Pénélope. Pour l'histoire des femmes*, n° 12 (printemps 1985).

Mémoire et Histoire. Données et débats, Actes du XXVᵉ colloque des intellectuels juifs de langue française, Denoël, 1986, 190 p.

Mercure, Daniel (sous la dir. de), *La culture en mouvement. Nouvelle valeurs et organisations*, Québec, PUL, 1992, 314 p.

Middleton, David and Derek Edwards, eds., *Collective Remembering*, London, Sage Publications, 1990, 230 p.

Mignolo, Walter D., "Misunderstanding and Colonization: The Reconfiguration of Memory and Space", *The South Atlantic Quarterly*, 92 (spring 1993), p. 209-260.

Mika, Nick, *Historic Mills of Ontario*, Belleville, Ont., Mika Publishers, 1987.

Millard, Rodney J., *The Master Spirit of the Age: Canadian Engineers and the Politics of Professionalism, 1887-1922*, Toronto/Buffalo, University of Toronto Press, 1988.

Miller, Charles A., *The Supreme Court and the Uses of History*, Cambridge, Belknap Press of Harvard University Press, 1969, 234 p.

Mills, David B., *The Evolution of Folk House Forms in Trinity Bay, Newfoundland*, Technical Papers of the Newfoundland Museum number 3, St. John's, Nfld., Department of Culture, Recreation and Youth, 1982.

Mills, G.E., *Acheter son bois et construire sa ferme: La commercialisation du bois de construction et des modèles de bâtiments agricoles dans les Prairies canadiennes de 1880 à 1920*, Études en archéologie, architecture et histoire, Ottawa, Environnement Canada, Service des parcs, 1991.

_____, *Buying Wood and Building Farms: Marketing Lumber and Farm Building Designs on the Canadian Prairies, 1880 to 1920*, Studies in Archaeology, Architecture and History, Ottawa, Environment Canada, Parks Service, 1991.

Mills, John M., *Canadian Coastal and Inland Steam Vessels, 1809-1930*, Providence, Steamship Historical Society of America, 1979.

_____, *Canadian Coastal and Inland Steam Vessels, 1809-1930*. Supplement No. 2, Providence, Steamship Historical Society of America, 1983.

Moniot, Henri, Textes réunis et présentés par, *Enseigner l'histoire*, Des manuels à la mémoire, Travaux du colloque Manuels d'histoire et mémoire collective, U.E.R. de didactique des disciplines, Université de Paris 7, Partie des travaux du colloque tenu les 23, 24 et 25 avril 1981, Berne, Peter Lang, 1984, 303 p.

Morgan, Michael L., "Overcoming the Remoteness of the Past: Memory and Historiography in Modern Jewish Thought", *Judaism*, 38, 2 (1989), p. 160-173.

Morrison, Joan and Charlotte Fox Zabusky, *American Mosaic: The Immigrant Experience in the Words of Those who Lived It*, New York, Dutton, 1980, 457 p.

Morrissey, Charles T., "Life, Memory, and Oral History: The Pennsylvania Boyhood of B. F. Skinner As Instructive Text", *Pennsylvania History*, 60, 4 (1993), p. 530

Moscovici, Serge, *Conflict and Consensus: A General Theory of Collective Decisions*, London, Sage, 1994, 214 p.

Moureyre, Françoise de la, « Fortune critique de Jacques Sarazin (1592-1660): Zarazin et l'évolution du goût », *La Gazette des Beaux-Arts*, (déc. 1992), p. 229-261.

Moussette, Marcel, « Sens et contresens: l'étude de la culture matérielle au Québec », *Canadian Folklore canadien*, 4, 1-2 (1984), p. 9-25.

Muise, D. A., and R. G. McIntosh, *Coal Mining in Canada: A Historical and Comparative Overview*, Transformation Series No. 5, Ottawa, National Museum of Science and Technology, 1996.

Musello, Christopher, "Family photography", in: Jon Wagner, ed., *Images of Information: Still Photography in the Social Sciences*, Beverly Hills, SAGE, 1979, 311 p.

Muséologie et ethnologie, Paris, Ministère de la culture et de la communication/Éd. de la réunion des musées nationaux, 1987, 292 p.

Namer, Gérard, « Mémoire collective, mémoire sociale et itinéraire du message de la mémoire », *Bulletin de l'Institut d'histoire du temps présent*, n° 6 (décembre 1981), p. 35-38.

Nash, Roderick, *The American Environment. Readings in the History of Conservation*. Reading, Mass., Addison-Wesley Pub. Co., 1968, 236 p.

Namer, Gérard, *Mémoire et société*, Préface de Jean Duvignaud, Paris, Méridiens Klincksieck, 1987, 242 p.

Neisser, Ulric, *Memory Observed: Remembering in Natural Contexts*, Oxford, W. H. Freeman, 1982, 433 p.

_____, *The Remembering Self: Construction and Accuracy in the Self-narrative*, Cambridge, Cambridge University Press, 1994, 301 p.

Nerone, John and Ellen Waterlla, eds., *Communication. Special Issue: Social Memory*, 11, 2 (1989).

_____, "Professional History and Social Memory", *Communication*, 11, 2 (1989), p. 85

Nethercott, Shaun S. and Neil O. Leighton, "Memory, Process, and Performance", *The Oral History Review*, 18, 2 (1990), p. 37-60.

Neufeld, David, and Patrick Habiluk, *Make It Pay! Gold Dredge #4*, Missoula, Montana, Pictorial Histories Publishing Co., 1994.

Neustadt, Richard, "Uses of History in Public Policy", *Humanities*, 2 (October 1981), p. 1-2.

Newell, Dianne, *Technology on the Frontier: Mining in Old Ontario*, Vancouver, UBC Press, 1986.

_____ and Ralph Greenhill, *Survivals: Aspects of Industrial Archaeology in Ontario*, Erin, Ont., Boston Mills Press, 1989.

Newfoundland Historic Trust, *A Gift of Heritage: Historic Architecture of St. John's*, Newfoundland Historic Trust Publications, Vol. 1, St. John's, Nfld., Valhalla Press, 1975.

_____, *Ten Historic Towns: Heritage Architecture in Newfoundland*, Newfoundland Historic Trust Publications, Vol. 2, St. John's, Nfld., Valhalla Press, 1978.

Noppen, Luc, réd., *Architecture, forme urbaine et identité collective*, les Nouveaux Cahiers du CÉLAT, n° 12, Sillery, Qué., Éditions du Septentrion, 1995, 267 p.

_____, Claude Paulette et Michel Tremblay, *Québec, trois siècles d'architecture*, Montréal, Libre Expression, 1979; 3ᵉ éd. Québec, Publications du Québec et Libre Expression, 1989.

Nora, Pierre, dir., *Essais d'égo-histoire*, Paris, Gallimard, 1987, 375 p.

_____, éd., « Mémoires comparées », n° spécial, *Le Débat* (Paris), 78 (janvier-février 1994).

_____, *Les lieux de mémoire*, Paris, Gallimard, I. La République (1984), II. La Nation (1986), Les France (1993), 4 vol.

« Les nostalgies des Français », *H-Histoire*, n° 5 (juin 1980).

Nouhaud, Michel, *L'utilisation de l'histoire par les orateurs attiques*, Paris, Les Belles Lettres, 1982, 406 p.

O'Brien, Jay and William Roseberry, eds., *Golden Ages, Dark Ages, Imagining the Past in Anthropology and History*, Bekerley, University of California Press, 1991, 288 p.

Okpewho, Isidore, *Myth in Africa: A Study of its Aesthetic and Cultural Relevance*, New York, Cambridge University Press, 1983, 305 p.

Orsi, Robert A., "The Fault of Memory: 'Southern Italy' in the Imagination of Immigrants and the Lives of Their Children in Italian Harlem, 1920-1945", *Journal of Family History*, 15, 2 (1990), p. 133-147.

Otis, Laura, *Organic Memory: History and the Body in the Late Nineteenth and Early Twentieth Centuries*, Lincoln, Nebraska, University of Nebraska Press, 1994, 297 p.

Ouellet, Fernand, « La modernisation de l'historiographie et l'émergence de l'histoire sociale », *Recherches sociographiques*, 26, 1-2 (1985), p. 11-84.

Ouzouf, Mona, « Peut-on commémorer la Révolution française ? », *Le Débat*, n° 26 (septembre 1983), p. 161-172.

Owram, Douglas, *Building for Canadians: A History of Public Works, 1840-1960* (Ottawa: 1978).

Pacey, Elizabeth, *Georgian Halifax*, Hantsport, N.S., Lancelot Press, 1987.

_____, George Rogers and Allan Duffus, *More Stately Mansions: Churches of Nova Scotia, 1830-1910*, Hantsport, N.S., Lancelot Press, 1983.

Papadakes, Y., "The Politics of Memory and Forgetting in Cyprus", *Journal of Mediterrean Studies*, 3, 1 (1993), p. 139-154.

Passerini, Luisa, "A Memory for Women's History: Problems of Method and Interpretation", *Social Science History*, 16, 4 (1992), p. 669-692.

_____, « Inventaire de la mémoire à Turin », *Bulletin de l'Institut d'histoire du temps présent*, n° 6 (décembre 1981), p. 39-45.

_____, ed., *Memory and Totalitarianism*, International Yearbook of Oral History special issue, New York, Oxford University Press, 1992, 209 p.

Passfield, Robert W., *Building the Rideau Canal: A Pictorial History*, Markham, Ont., Fitzhenry & Whiteside in association with Parks Canada, 1982.

Passfield, Robert W., "Industrial Heritage Commemoration in the Canadian Parks Service", *IA: Journal for the Society for Industrial Archeology*, Vol. 16, No. 2, Vol. 17, No. 1 (1990-1991), pp. 15-39 (pt. 1), pp. 32-67 (pt. 2).

_____, *Technology in Transition: The Soo Ship Canal 1889-1985*, Ottawa, Parks Canada, 1989.

Paterson, Douglas D., *Heritage Landscapes in British Columbia: A Guide to Their Identification, Documentation and Preservation*, [Vancouver], Landscape Architecture Program, University of British Columbia, [1986]; rev. ed. [1989].

Pays, Bruno, *La gestion du patrimoine*, Paris, PUF, 1992, 127 p.

Pearce, Susan, ed., *Museum Studies in Material Culture*, London, Leicester University Press, 1989, 174 p. Papers presented at a conference sponsored by the University of Leicester, Dept. of Museum Studies.

Perlman, Michael, *Imaginal Memory and the Place of Hiroshima*, New York, State University of New York, 1988, 214 p.

Pelletier, Sylvie, *Conscience de classe, conscience historique et tradition révolutionaire dans les autobiographies d'ouvriers français du XIXe siècle*, Thèse, Université Laval, 1988, 151 p.

Perdue, Theda, *Nations Remembered: An Oral History of the Five Civilized Tribes, 1865-1907*, Westport, Conneticut, Greenwood Press, 1980, 221 p.

Piehler, G. Kurt, *Remembering War the American Way*, Washington, D.C., Smithsonian Institution Press, 1995, 233 p.

Pinard, Guy, *Montréal: son histoire, son architecture*, 4 tomes; tomes 1 à 3, Montréal, Éditions La Presse, 1987-1989; tome 4, Montréal, Éditions du Méridien, 1991.

Pinsky, Valerie and Alison Wylie, eds., *Critical Traditions in Contemporary Archaeology: Essays in the Philosophy, History, and Socio-politics of Archaeology*, Cambridge/New York, Cambridge University Press, 1989, 160 p.

Pitseolak, Peter, and Dorothy Eber, trans. Ann Hanson, *People from Our Side; a life story and photographs*, Edmonton, Hurtig, 1975, 159 p.

Plaskett, Bill, *Understanding Lunenburg's Architecture*, Lunenburg, N.S., Lunenburg Heritage Society, 1979; 3d ed. 1989.

Pocius, Gerald L., *A Place to Belong: Community Order and Everyday Space in Calvert, Newfoundland*, Athens, Ga., University of Georgia Press; Montréal and Kingston, McGill-Queen's University Press, 1991, 350 p.

Poirier, Jean, *Histoire de l'ethnologie*, 3ᵉ édition, Paris, PUF, 1984 (1969), 127 p.

« Politique sur la gestion des ressources culturelles », dans Parcs Canada, *Principes directeurs et politiques de gestion*, Ottawa, Ministre des Approvisionnements et Services Canada, 1994, p. 101 à 118. nº de cat. du MAS : R62-275/ 1994F.

Politiques de l'oubli. Le genre humain, nº 18 (octobre 1988), 233 p.

Pollak, Michael, « La gestion de l'indicible », *Actes de la recherche en sciences sociales*, 62/63 (1986), p. 30-53.

Pomian, K., *Collectionneurs, amateurs et curieux: Paris, Venise; XVIᵉ-XVIIIᵉ siècles*, Paris, Gallimard, 1987, 367 p.

Posey, Carl A., "The Bittersweet Memory that was the Canal Zone", *Smithsonian*, 22 (November 1991), p. 156-158.

Poulot, Dominique, « Le Louvre imaginaire: Essai sur le statut du musée en France, des Lumières à la République », *Historical Reflections/Réflexions historiques*, 17, 2 (1991), p. 171-204.

Priamo, C., *Mills of Canada*, Toronto, McGraw Hill Ryerson, 1976.

Proceedings of the Canadian Parks Service Reconstruction Workshop, Hull, Quebec, 11-13 March 1992, Ottawa, Environment Canada, Parks Service, 1993, 107 p.

Prost, Antoine, *Les Anciens Combattants et la société française, 1914-1939*, 3 vol., Paris, Presses de la F.N.S.P., 1977.

Quayle, Moura, Neil Guppy and Luc Roberge, *Portrait of a Profession: Landscape Architecture in 1988*, Ottawa, Canadian Society of Landscape Architects, 1989.

« La Querelle des historiens allemands vue de l'Est », Dossier, dans *La Nouvelle Alternative*, 13 (mars 1989).

Rabinowitz, Paula, "Wreckage upon Wreckage: History, Documentary, and the Ruins of Memory", *History and Theory*, 32, 3 (1993), p. 119-137.

Rand, Harry, "Self-consciousness and Memory in Early Modernism", *History of European Ideas*, 16, 4/6 (1993), p. 927-933.

Ranger, T. O., *The Invention of Tradition*, Cambridge, England, Cambridge University Press, 1983, 320 p.

Raphaël, F., « Le travail de la mémoire et les limites de l'histoire orale », *Annales ESC*, 35, 1 (janvier-février 1980), p. 127-145.

Rappaport, Joanne, *The Politics of Memory: Native Historical Interpretation in the Colombian Andes*, Cambridge/New York, Cambridge University Press, 1990, 226 p.

Raymond, Philippe, « La commémoration: illusion ou artifice? », *Le Débat* (Paris), 78 (janv.-fév. 1994), p. 104-115.

Reaman, G. E., *A History of Agriculture in Ontario*. 2 Vols (Toronto: Saunders, 1970).

Rees, Ronald, *Land of Earth and Sky: Landscape Painting of Western Canada*, Saskatoon, Western Producer Books, 1984.

_____, *St Andrews and the Islands*, Halifax, Nimbus, 1995.

Le registre canadien des propriétés patrimoniales, Premier rapport annuel, Ottawa, Ministre des Approvisionnements et Services Canada, 1992.

Rémillard, François et Brian Merrett, *L'architecture de Montréal: guide des styles et des bâtiments*, Montréal, Éditions du Méridien, 1990.

_____ and Brian Merrett, *Montreal Architecture: A Guide to Styles and Buildings*, Trans. Pierre Miville-Deschênes, Montréal, Meridian Press, 1990.

Rémond, René, dir., *Être historien aujourd'hui*, Toulouse/Paris, Erès/Unesco, 1988, 350 p.

Rempel, John I., *Building with Wood and other Aspects of Nineteenth- Century Building in Ontario*, Toronto, University of Toronto Press, 1967; rev. ed. 1980.

Reny, Claude, *Principes et critères de restauration et d'insertion: Le patrimoine architectural d'intérêt public au Québec*, Québec, Publications du Québec, 1991.

Revel, Jacques, « Histoire et sciences sociales: le paradigme des Annales », *Annales E.S.C.*, 34, 6 (nov.-déc. 1979), p. 1360-1376.

Reverchon, C. et P. Gaudin, « Le sens du tragique dans la mémoire historique », *Le monde alpin et rhodanien*, 14, (1986), p. 97-113.

Richardson, A.J.H., *et al.*, *Quebec City: Architects, Artisans and Builders*, Mercury Series No. 37, Ottawa, National Museum of Man and Parks Canada/Musée national de l'Homme et Parcs Canada, 1984.

Ring, Dan, Guy Vanderhaeghe and George Melnyk, *The Urban Prairie*, Saskatoon, Mendel Art Gallery and Fifth House Publishers, 1993, 160 p.

Rioux, Jean-Pierre, « La mémoire collective en France depuis 1945: propos d'étape sur l'activité d'un groupe de travail », *Bulletin de l'Institut d'histoire du temps présent*, n° 6 (décembre 1981), p. 29-34.

_____, dir., *La Guerre d'Algérie et les Français: colloque de l'Institut d'histoire du temps présent*, Paris, Fayard, 1990, 700 p.

Ritchie, Thomas, *Canada Builds, 1867-1967*, Toronto, University of Toronto Press, 1967.

Ritchot G. et Guy Mercier, dir., « La géographie humaine structurale (N° spécial) », *Cahier de Géographie du Québec*, 36, 98 (septembre 1992), p. 167 à 175.

Rogers, Irene L., *Charlottetown: The Life in its Buildings*, Charlottetown, Prince Edward Island Museum and Heritage Foundation, 1983.

Romilly, Jacqueline de, « La mémoire du passé dans la Grèce antique », *Revue historique*, 114ᵉ année, 283 (1990), p. 3-12.

Roos, Arnold E., *A Bibliography of the History of Canadian Science and Technology/Une bibliographie de l'histoire de la science et de la technologie au Canada*, Ottawa, Canadian Science and Technology Historical Association / Association pour l'histoire de la science et de la technologie au Canada, 1995, 272 p.

Rose, Steven P. R., *The Making of Memory*, London, Bantam, 1992, 355 p.

Rosenfield, Israel, "Memory and Identity", *New Literary History*, 26:1 (winter 1995), p. 197-203.

_____, *Presenting the Past: Essays on History and the Public*, Philadelphia, Temple University Press, 1986, 424 p.

Rothstein, David, "Brideshead Revisited and the Modern Historicization of Memory", *Studies in the Novel*, 25 (fall 1993), p. 318-31.

Rotoff, Basil, Roman Yereniuk and Stella Hryniuk, *Monuments to Faith: Ukrainian Churches in Manitoba*, Winnipeg, University of Manitoba Press, 1990.

Rousso, Henry, « La négation du génocide juif », *L'Histoire*, 106 (décembre 1987), p. 76-79.

_____, « Vichy, le grand fossé », *Vingtième siècle. Revue d'histoire*, n° 5 (1985), p. 55-79.

_____, *Le syndrôme de Vichy de 1944 à nos jours*, Paris, Seuil, 1990 (1987), 414 p.

Rowlands, Michael, "The Role of Memory in the Transmission of Culture", *World Archaeology*, 25, 2 (1993), p. 141-151.

Roy, Fernande, « Une mise en scène de l'histoire. La fondation de Montréal à travers les siècles », *Revue d'histoire de l'Amérique française*, 46, 1 (été 1992), p. 7-37.

Royal Commission on Aboriginal Peoples, *The High Arctic Relocation: summary of supporting information*, vol. 1, Ottawa, RCAP, 1994.

Rozinski, Maud, *Architects of Nova Scotia: A Biographical Dictionary, 1605-1905*, Halifax, Nova Scotia Department of Municipal Affairs, 1994.

Rudelle, Odile, « Lieux de mémoire révolutionnaire et communion républicaine », *Vingtième siècle. Revue d'histoire*, n° 24 (octobre-décembre 1989), p. 3-16.

Russell, Karen, comp, and ed., *Guidelines for the Rehabilitation of Designated Historic Resources*, 2nd ed., Edmonton, Alberta Community Development, Historic Sites and Archives Service, [1993], 67 p.

Ryvkina, R.V., "Economic Culture as Society's Memory," *The Soviet Review*, 31, 1 (1990), p. 3-20.

Samuel, Raphael and Paul Thompson, eds., *The Myths We Live By*, New York, Routledge, 1990, 262 p.

_____, "People's History," in: Samuel Raphael, ed., *People's History and Socialist Theory*, London, Routledge & Kegan Paul, 1981, p. xv-xxxix.

_____, *Theatres of Memory*, London, Verso, 1994, 479 p.

Sanson, R., *Le 14 juillet (1789-1975). Fête et conscience nationale*, Paris, Flammarion, 1976, 220 p.

Schama, Simon, *Landscape and Memory*, Toronto, Random House of Canada, 1995, 652 p.

Schieder, Theodor, "The Role of Historical Consciousness in Political Action", *Historical Consciousness and Political Action. History and Theory. Studies in the Philosophy of History*, 17, 4 (1978), suppl. 17, p. 1-18.

Schlereth, Thomas J., "Mirrors of the Past: Historical Photography and American History", in: *Artifacts and the American Past*, Nashville, American Association for State and Local History, 1980, p. 11-47.

Schmidt, Dennis, "On the Memory of Last Things", *Research in Phenomenology*, 23 (1993), p. 92-104.

Schonen, Scania de, *La mémoire: connaissance active du passé*, Paris, Mouton, 1974, 335 p.

Schulte-Tenckhoff, Isabelle, *La vue portée au loin. Une histoire de la pensée anthropologique*, Lausanne, Éd. d'en bas, 1985, 223 p.

Schwarcz, Vera, "No Solace from Lethe: History, Memory, and Cultural Identity in Twentieth-Century China", *Daedalus*, 120/2 (1991), p. 85-112.

Schwartz, Barry, "Social Change and Collective Memory: The Democratization of George Washington", *American Sociological Review*, 56, 2 (1991), p. 221-236.

_____, "The Social Context of Commemoration: a Study in Collective Memory", *Social Forces*, 61, 2 (1982), p. 374-402.

_____, Yael Zerubavel and Bernice M. Barnett, "The Recovery of Masada: a Study in Collective Memory", *Sociological Quaterly*, 27, 2 (1986), p. 147-164.

Scott, J., "Collective Memories in Britain and the U.S.", *Public Opinion Quarterly*, 57, 3, (fall 1993), p. 315-331.

Seremetakis, C. Nadia, *The Senses Still: Perception and Memory as Material Culture in Modernity*, Boulder, Colorado, Westview, 1994, 149 p.

Sharrad, Paul, "The Art of Memory and the Liberation of History: Wilson Harris's Witnessing of Time", *The Journal of Commonwealth Literature*, 27, 1 (1992), p. 110-127.

Sherman, Daniel J., "Objects of Memory: History and Narrative in French War Museums", *French Historical Studies*, 19, 1 (spring 1995), p. 49-74.

Shils, Edward A., *Tradition*, Chicago, University of Chicago Press, 1981, 334 p.

Shore, Marlene, "'Remember the Future': *The Canadian Historical Review* and the Discipline of History, 1920-95", *Canadian Historical Review*, 76, 1 (1995), p. 410-463.

Simard, Cyril, Andrée Lapointe et Cornelius Kirjan, *Patrimoine muséologique au Québec: repères chronologiques*, Québec, Commission des biens culturels, 1992, 113 p.

Simard, Jean, « Profil historique des inventaires au ministère de la Culture et des Communications », dans *Guide d'inventaire des objets mobiliers*, sous la direction de Bernard Genest, collection Patrimoines, Québec, Les Publications du Québec, 1994, p. 85-99.

Simmins, Geoffrey, comp., *Bibliography of Canadian Architecture/Bibliographie d'architecture canadienne*, Ottawa, Society for the Study of Architecture in Canada/Société pour l'étude de l'architecture au Canada, 1992, 28 p.

_____, *The Ontario Association of Architects: A Centennial History, 1889-1989*, Toronto, University of Toronto Press for the Association, 1989.

Simon, Gérard, « De la reconstitution du passé. À propos de l'histoire des sciences, entre autres histoires », *Le Débat*, n° 66 (septembre-octobre 1991), p. 134-147.

Simondon, Michèle, *La Mémoire et l'Oubli dans la pensée grecque*, Paris, Les Belles Lettres, 1982, 357 p.

Singh, Amritjit, Joseph T. Skerrett, Jr., and Robert E. Hogan, eds., *Memory, Narrative, and Identity : New Essays in Ethnic American Literatures*, Boston, Northeastern University Press, 1994, 349 p.

Smith, Bruce James, *Politics and Remembrance: Republican Themes in Machiavelli, Burke, and Tocqueville*, Princeton, New Jersey, Princeton University Press, 1985, 287 p.

Sous l'histoire la mémoire. N° spécial de Dialectiques, n° 30 (1980).

Stapleton, Timothy J., "The Memory of Maqoma: An Assessment of Jingqi Oral Tradition in Ciskei and Transkei", *History in Africa*, 20 (1993), p. 321-335.

Straub, J., "Collective Memory and Collective Past as Constitutents of Culture", *Schweigerische Zeitschrift fur psychologie/Revue Suisse de psychologie*, 52, 2 (1993), p. 114-121.

Symons, Thomas H.B., "Cultural Diversity, Canadian Identity and Canadian Federalism", in *Public Policies in Two Federal Countries: Canada and Australia*, R.L. Matthews, ed., Canberra, Australian National University Press, 1982.

_____, *Learning From Each Other: Commonwealth Studies for the 21st Century*, Report of the Commission on Commonwealth Studies, with Suma Chitnis, *et al.*, London, Commonwealth Secretariat, 1996, 59 p.

_____, *Report of the Federal Cultural Policy Review Committee*, with Louis Applebaum, Jacques Hébert, et al., Ottawa, Government of Canada, Department of Communications, 1982.

_____, *Se Connaître : le Rapport de la Commission sur les Études Canadiennes*, volumes 1 et 2, Ottawa, Association des Universités et Collèges du Canada, 1975.

_____, *To Know Ourselves: The Report of the Commission on Canadian Studies*, volumes 1 and 2, Ottawa, Association of Universities and Colleges of Canada, 1975.

Symposium international sur la conservation des squares et parcs urbains/ Symposium on the Conservation of Urban Squares and Parks, Montreal, May 12-15 mai 1993, Montréal, Publications MNH enr. pour l'Association des architectes paysagistes du Québec, 1993, 391 p.

Tamura, Linda, *The Hood River Issei: An Oral History of Japanese Settlers in Oregon's Hood River Valley*, Urbana, University of Illinois Press, 1993, 337 p.

Tausky, Nancy Z., Lynne D. DiStefano and Ian MacEachern, *Victorian Architecture in London and Southwestern Ontario: Symbols of Aspiration*, Toronto, University of Toronto Press, 1986.

Taylor, C.J., *Negotiating the Past: the Making of Canada's National Historic Parks and Sites*, Montréal/Kingston, McGill-Queen's University Press, 1990, 245 p.

Les techniques de conservation architecturale, 7 tomes, Ottawa, Travaux publiques Canada, Services d'architecture et de génie pour Environnement Canada, 1993, n° de cat. du MAS: W62-16/1993F.

Technical Paper series, Victoria, British Columbia Heritage Trust, 1979-83.

Terdiman, Richard, "Deconstructing Memory: On Representing the Past and Theorizing Culture in France Since the Revolution", *Diacritics*, 15 (1985), p. 13-36.

Territoires de la mémoire. Histoires, identités, cultures: des Maghrebins et des Belges parlent, Actes du colloque, 1988, 232 p.

The Representations of Historical Events. History and Theory. Studies in the Philosophy of History, Beiheft 26, 97 p.

Thelen, David, "Memory and American History", *The Journal of American History*, 75, 4 (1988), p. 1117-1129.

_____, "Of Audiences, Borderlands, and Comparisons: Toward the Internationalization of American History", *The Journal of American History*, 79, 2 (September 1992), p. 432-462.

_____, ed., *Memory and American History*, Bloomington, Indiana, Indiana University Press, 1990, 156 p.

Thibaud, Paul, « Du sel sur nos plaies. À propos de L'Idéologie française », *Esprit*, 5 (mai 1981), p. 3 à 33.

Thibodeau, Pierre, *La conservation du Fort Chambly, 1850-1940*, (Québec), Parcs Canada, 1979. 130 p.

Thomas, Teresa A., "For Union, Not for Glory: Memory and the Civil War Volunteers of Lancaster, Massachusetts", *Civil War History*, 40, 1 (1994), p. 25-47.

Tilley, Christopher Y., *A Phenomenology of Landscape: Places, Paths and Monuments*, Oxford, Berg, 1994, 221 p.

_____, ed., *Reading Material Culture. Structuralism, Hermeneutics and Post-Structuralism*, Oxford, Basil Blackwell, 1990, 355 p.

Tonkin, Elizabeth, "The Boundaries of History in Oral Performance", *History in Africa*, 9 (1982), p. 273-284.

_____, *Narrating our Pasts: The Social Construction of Oral History*, Cambridge, Cambridge University Press, 1992, 171 p.

Traverses, N° spécial: *L'archive*, n° 36 (1986), 200 p.

Trottier, Louise, *Le patrimoine industriel au Québec*, Commission des biens culturels du Québec, 1984.

Tulving, Endel, *Elements of Episodic Memory*, Oxford, Clarendon Press, 1983, 351 p.

Turim, Maureen Cheryn, *Flashbacks in Film : Memory & History*, New York, Routledge, 1989, 278 p.

« Une discipline, des histoires (N° thématique) », *Anthropologie et sociétés*, 11, 3 (1987), 148 p.

Usages de l'oubli, Contributions de Yosef Hayim Yerushalmi, Nicole Loraux, Hans Mommsen, Jean-Claude Milner, Gianni Valtimo, au colloque de Royaumont, Paris, Éditions du Seuil, 1988, 89 p.

Vaillancourt, Veronica, ed., *New Life for Rural Regions: Taking a Heritage Approach*, Ottawa, Heritage Canada, 1995, 30 p.

_____, réd., *La revitalisation des régions rurales: le patrimoine comme outil*, Ottawa, Héritage Canada, 1995, 30 p.

Van Kirk, Sylvia M., *The Development of National Park Policy in Canada's Mountain National Parks, 1885 to 1930*, Master's Thesis, University of Alberta, 1969.

Vaughn, Stephen, ed., *The Vital Past: Writings on the Uses of History*, Athens, The University of Georgia Press, 1985, 406 p.

Veillette, John and Gary White, *Early Indian Village Churches: Wooden Frontier Architecture in British Columbia*, Vancouver, University of British Columbia Press, 1977.

Veillon, Dominique, « La Seconde Guerre mondiale à travers les sources orales », *Questions à l'histoire orale*, Table ronde du 20 juin 1986, Cahiers de l'Institut d'histoire du temps présent, n° 4 (juin 1987), p. 53 à 70.

Verdès-Leroux, Jeannine, «La mémoire indestructible», *Le genre humain*, n° 9 (1983), p. 147 à 151.

Verge, Béatrice, *L'interprétation du patrimoine architectural: sites historiques et muséologiques à Québec*. Thèse de M.A. (histoire), Université Laval, 1985, 149 p.

Verret, Michel, « Mémoire ouvrière, mémoire communiste », *Revue française de science politique*, 34, 3 (juin 1984), p. 413 à 427.

Vidal, C., « Enquête sur le Rwanda traditionnel: conscience historique et traditions orales », *Cahiers d'études africaines*, 11, 41-4 (1971), p. 526-537.

Vidal-Naquet, Pierre, *Les Assassins de la Mémoire: « Un Eichmann de papier » et autres essais sur le révisionnisme*, Paris, La Découverte, 1987, 231 p.

_____, *Les Juifs, la mémoire et le présent*, Paris, Maspero, 1981, 301 p.

_____, « 89: La commémoration », *Le Débat*, 57 (novembre-décembre 1989).

Vincent, Elizabeth, *Le Génie royale au Canada: matériaux et techniques de construction*, Études en archéologie, architecture et histoire, Ottawa, Environnement Canada, Service des parcs, 1993, 313 p.

_____, *Substance and Practice: Building Technology and the Royal Engineers in Canada*, Studies in Archaeology, Architecture and History, Ottawa, Environment Canada, Parks Service, 1993, 287 p.

Vincent, Francine et Georges Sioui, *Octoyton Wendake: les enfants de la grande île et les contes de la Nation Hurone-Wendat*, Québec, MAINC, 1986, 80 p.

von Baeyer, Edwinna, *Rhetoric and Roses: A History of Canadian Gardening, 1900-1930*, Markham, Ont., Fitzhenry & Whiteside, 1984.

_____, *A Selected Bibliography for Garden History in Canada*, rev. ed., Ottawa, Parks Canada, Canadian Heritage, 1994.

_____ and Pleasance Crawford, eds., *Garden Voices: Two Centuries of Canadian Garden Writing*, Toronto, Random House, 1995.

von Droste, Bernd, Harald Plachter and Mechtild Rössler, eds., *Cultural Landscapes of Universal Value: Components of a Global Strategy*, Jena, Germany and New York, Gustav Fischer Verlag, in cooperation with UNESCO, 1995, 464 p.

Vovelle, Michel, Études réunies et présentées par, *Les images de la Révolution française : actes du Colloque des 25-26-27 octobre 1985 tenu en Sorbonne*, Paris, Publications de la Sorbonne, 1988, 399 p.

Wade, Jill, *Houses for All: The Struggle for Social Housing in Vancouver, 1919-50*, Vancouver, UBC Press, 1994, 270 p.

_____, comp., *Manitoba Architecture to 1940: A Bibliography*, Winnipeg, University of Manitoba Press, 1978.

Walker, J. Samuel, "History, Collective Memory, and the Decision to Use the Bomb", *Diplomatic History*, 19, 2 (1995), p. 319-328.

Walsh, Kevin, *The Representation of the Past. Museums and Heritage in the Post-modern World*, London and New York, Routledge, 1992, 204 p.

Warner, John Harley, "Remembering Paris: Memory and the American Disciples of French Medicine in the Nineteenth Century," *Bulletin of the History of Medicine*, 65, 3 (1991), p. 301-325.

Warren, Leon and Roy Rosenzweig, eds., *History Museums in the United States, A Critical Assessment*, Urbana and Chicago, University of Illinois Press, 1989, 333 p.

Wasserman, Ellen S., ed., *Oral History Index: An International Directory of Oral History Interviews*, Westport, Mekler, 1990, 434 p.

Weaver, Martin E. and Frank G. Matero, *Conserving Buildings: Guide to Techniques and Materials*, New York, Wiley, 1993, 270 p.

Weir, Jean B., *The Lost Art of Ornamented Architecture: Canadian Architectural Drawings, 1850-1930*, Catalogue of an exhibition held at the Dalhousie Art Gallery, Halifax, 10 Mar.-24 Apr., 1983.

Werth, Nicolas, « La transparence et la mémoire. Les Soviétiques à la recherche de leur passé », *Vingtième siècle. Revue d'histoire*, n° 21 (janvier-mars 1989), p. 5 à 28.

Wetherell, Donald G. and Irene R.A. Kmet, *Homes in Alberta: Building, Trends, and Design, 1870-1967*, Edmonton, University of Alberta Press, 1991.

White, Hayden V., *Metahistory: the Historical Imagination in Nineteenth Century Europe*, Baltimore, John Hopkins University Press, 1973, 448 p.

Wieseltier, Leon, "Where Memory Meets History", *The Wilson Quarterly*, 17 (summer 1993), p. 133-

Wieviorka, Annette et Itzhok Niborski, Présenté par, *Les Livres du souvenir*, Mémoriaux juifs de Pologne, Paris, Gallimard/Julliard, 1983, 185 p.

Wilkinson, James D., "Remembering World War II. The Perspective of the Losers", *The American Scholar*, 54, 3 (summer 1985), p. 329-343.

Wilson, Elizabeth, "History and Memory", *Callaloo*, 15, 1 (1992), p. 179-189.

Winks, Robin W., "A Public Historiography", *The Public Historian*, 14, 3 (summer 1992): 93-105. Review Essays.

Wright, Janet, *Architecture of the Picturesque in Canada*, Studies in Archaeology, Architecture and History, Ottawa, Parks Canada, 1984.

_____, *L'architecture pittoresque au Canada*, Études en archéologie, architecture et histoire, Ottawa, Parcs Canada, 1984.

Wyer, Robert S., *Memory and Cognition in its Social Context*, Hillsdale, New Jersey, Erlbaum, 1989, 491 p.

Yates, France Amelia, *L'art de la mémoire*, Traduit de l'anglais par Daniel Arasse, Paris, Gallimard, 1975 (1966), 432 p.

_____, *The Art of Memory*, London, Pimlico, 1992, 439 p.

Yerushalmi, Yosef Hayim, *Zakhor: histoire juive et mémoire juive*, Traduit de l'anglais par Éric Vigne, Paris, La Découverte, 1982, 165 p.

Zelizer, Barbie, "Reading the Past Against the Grain: The Shape of Memory Studies," *Critical Studies in Mass Communication*, 12, 2 (1995), p. 214-239.

Zerubavel, Yael, *Recovered Roots: Collective Memory and the Making of Israeli National Tradition*, Chicago, University of Chicago Press, 1994.

Zielinski, Bernd et Arne Radtke, « La mémoire unifiée? L'héritage équivoque des archives de la RDA », *Vingtième siècle. Revue d'histoire*, n° 34 (avril-juin 1992), p. 53 à 68.

Zinchenko, P. I., "The Problem of Involuntary Memory," *Soviet Psychology*, 22, (1939/83), p. 55-111.

Zonabend, Françoise, *La mémoire longue: temps et histoires au village*, Paris, Préf., 1980, 314 p.

* The original bibliography was developed for the seminar held at Université Laval by the *Chaire d'étude des francophones en Amérique du Nord* in the Fall of 1993. Its aim was to provide students with a reference tool to facilitate their study of the relationships between memory and culture, and between societies and their past. It was reprinted with the kind permission of Jacques Mathieu and Jacinthe Ruel for distribution at the National Symposium, "The Place of History", held in November 1994. It has since been updated and revised by Edwinna von Baeyer for use in this publication; additional data has been supplied by the Historical Services Branch, National Historic Sites Directorate, Parks Canada, under the direction of Susan Buggey.

La version originale de cette bibliographie a été conçue et élaborée dans le cadre du séminaire offert par la Chaire d'étude des francophones en Amérique du Nord à l'Université Laval à l'automne 1993. Elle visait à procurer aux étudiants un instrument de référence pour favoriser leur étude des rapports entre la mémoire et la culture, ainsi qu'entre les sociétés et leur passé. Elle a été reproduite avec la gracieuse permission de professeur Jacques Mathieu et de Jacinthe Ruel pour être distribuée au symposium national intitulé « Les lieux de la mémoire », en novembre 1994. Elle a depuis lors a été revisée et mise à jour par Edwinna von Baeyer pour les fins de cette publication ; Mme Susan Buggey a dirigé le rassemblement des données supplémentaires, qui ont été fournies par la Direction des services historiques (Direction générale des lieux historiques, Parcs Canada).

LIST OF ILLUSTRATIONS WITH ADDITIONAL INFORMATION

The photographs have been selected to illustrate subjects or themes addressed in the text. The assistance in this task of The Heritage Canada Foundation, the National Archives, and a number of provincial and community archives and historical societies is gratefully acknowledged. Plaque texts quoted below are those of the Historic Sites and Monuments Board of Canada, unless otherwise indicated.

Page   *Description*

5   **Frère Marie-Victorin**, 1885-1994 (upper left), designated 1987. Plaque reads: Botanist, author and educator, Brother Marie-Victorin played a major role in the scientific movements of his time. Author of *Flore laurentienne*, he was also the founder of the Institut botanique de l'Université de Montréal and the Jardin botanique de Montréal. His discoveries and innovations, including a new approach to botany, were of international importance. He also helped to improve the teaching of science at primary, secondary and university levels. Marie-Victorin's scientific and literary achievements won him recognition at home and abroad. (Plaque erected 1995, Kinsey Falls, Québec.)

Emily Carr, 1871-1944 (lower right), designated 1950. Plaque reads: Artist and author Emily Carr was born here and lived most of her life in this neighbourhood of Victoria where she died. Her compelling canvases of the British Columbia landscape offer a unique vision of the forest and shore, while her documentation of Indian villages provides a valuable anthropological record. Lively accounts of Emily Carr's travels in the province are collected in *Klee Wyck*, for which she won the Governor General's Award for non-fiction in 1941. Six other autobiographical works are memorable accounts of her world. (Plaque erected 1954 at 207 Government Street, Victoria, British Columbia.)

6   **Lord Ernest Rutherford**, 1871-1937 (upper right), designated 1939. Plaque reads: As Macdonald Professor of Physics at McGill (1898-1907), Rutherford, in collaboration with Frederick Soddy, made fundamental discoveries respecting radioactivity which made McGill, in that period, an important centre of research in atomic physics. Subsequently director of the Physical Laboratory at Manchester (1907-19) and of the Cavendish Laboratory at Cambridge (1919-37), he became a world authority in his field and published numerous papers and several books. His honours included the Nobel Prize for Chemistry (1908) and the presidency of the Royal Society (1925-9). He died in London and was buried at Westminster Abbey. (Plaque erected 1939 in the Macdonald Physics Building, McGill University, Montréal, Québec.)

Maude E. Abbott, 1869-1940 (left centre), designated 1993: A prominent pioneer woman in the medical profession in Canada and an eminent researcher, teacher, and writer of textbooks who earned world renown for her work on congenital heart disease.

Stephen Leacock, 1869-1944 (lower right), designated 1946. Plaque reads: Born in England and educated at Upper Canada College and at the Universities of Toronto and Chicago, Leacock spent the greater part of his career at McGill, teaching and publishing in the fields of history and political science. It is, however, as a humorist that he is chiefly known and among a considerable volume of writings, *Sunshine Sketches of a Little Town* (1912), is the work that assured him a reputation throughout the English-speaking world. The peculiar charm of his work lies in the evocation, through exaggeration and the identification of incongruities, of the humour of ordinary people

407

General Middleton between May 9 and 12, 1885. The resistance failed but the battle did not mean the end of the community of Batoche. (Plaque erected 1985.)

40   **James "Skookum Jim" Mason – Kèsh**, ca. 1860-1916 (upper left), designated 1994. "Skookum Jim", a Tagish of the Dakhławèdí clan and the Wolf moiety, found a nugget on Rabbit (Bonanza) Creek in August 1896 that began the Klondike Gold Rush and changed the history of the Yukon. He made the discovery while on a journey down the Yukon River to find his sister Kate and her husband George Carmack. Renowned for his legendary exploits and physical abilities, "Skookum" (strong) Jim believed his Frog Spirit had guided him to the gold. He became very rich but remained a generous man who never forgot his obligations to his community. (He will be commemorated by a trilingual plaque.)
      Dawson Charlie – Khaa Ghooxh, (lower right), nephew of James "Skookum Jim" Mason – Kèsh.

50   **Québec Citadel**, Québec City, designated 1957. Plaque reads: In 1820 Lieutenant-Colonel Elias Walker Durnford of the Royal Engineers took charge of the construction of the Québec Citadel, which completed the city's defensive works begun during the French régime. Set on the heights of Cap-aux-Diamants, the Citadel dominated the town, harbour and the surrounding countryside. The ramparts were completed in 1831, and the major buildings within the walls about 1850. The walls also contain Frontenac's 1693 redoubt and a 1750 powder magazine. Since 1872 the Citadel has been an official residence of the Governor General of Canada, who spends part of each year here. (Plaque erected 1989.)

62   **Ernest Alexander Cruikshank**, 1853-1939, designated 1943. Plaque reads: Born in Bertie Township, Cruikshank worked as a journalist and translator before being commissioned in the 44th Welland Battalion in 1877. Rising to the rank of Brigadier-General in 1915, he commanded Military District 13 before becoming Director of the historical section of the general staff (1917-1920). Chairman of the Historic Sites and Monuments Board of Canada from its creation in 1919 until his death, he was the author of many papers and several books on Ontario and Canadian history. He was elected F.R.S.C. in 1905 and awarded the Tyrrell Gold Medal for historical research in 1935. He died at Ottawa. (Plaque erected 1947 at County Court House, Welland, Ontario.)

63   **Stoney Creek Monument and Gage homestead** at the site of the **Battle of Stoney Creek**, War of 1812, designated 1960. Plaque reads: Battle of Stoney Creek. During 1813 the Americans planned to invade Upper Canada from Detroit and the Niagara Peninsula. In late May, an American force crossed the Niagara River, seized Fort George, and with about 3500 troops moved inland in pursuit of the British who retreated to Burlington Heights. At Stoney Creek, a surprise night attack by about 700 regulars of the 8th and 49th Regiments of Foot under Lt.-Col. John Harvey halted the American advance and allowed the British to re-establish their position on the Niagara frontier. The Americans retreated to Forty Mile Creek and subsequently to Fort George. (Plaque erected 1968 at Stoney Creek, Ontario.)

64   **Fortress of Louisbourg**, Louisbourg, Nova Scotia, designated 1920. Plaque reads: In 1713, France decided to found Louisbourg to defend her colonial and maritime interests in North America. As capital of the colony of Isle Royale and guardian of the Gulf of St. Lawrence, it became the most important French fishing and commercial centre in North America. The Fortress was besieged and captured by British forces in

1745 and again in 1758. Its fortifications were demolished in 1760. In 1928, Louisbourg was designated a National Historic Site. Its reconstruction was begun in 1961 so that future generations seeing it might understand the role of the Fortress in our history. (Plaque erected 1925 – current plaque is a bilingual replacement.)

War effort despite discrimination. Although reluctant to accept Blacks into the armed forces, the Canadian military agreed in 1916 to create a segregated non-combatant unit. Recruited from across Canada and the United States, these eager volunteers were based at Pictou and Truro before going to Europe in 1917. They served primarily in the Canadian Forestry Corps in the Jura region of France where they laboured to supply much needed lumber for the front. The Black Battalion was disbanded in 1920. (Plaque erected 1994 in Pictou, Nova Scotia.)

126   **Chilkoot Trail**, British Columbia, designated 1967.

Hartland Covered Bridge, New Brunswick, designated 1977. Plaque reads: This structure, 390.75 metres long, is by far the longest covered bridge extant in the world. Covered bridges date from the first decade of the 19th century when North American builders began using wooden trusses for long spans and covered them to prevent the truss joints from rotting. After 1840 the Howe truss, which introduced iron tension rods into the truss work, was widely adopted and New Brunswick erected numerous bridges using this technique, among them this one which was built in 1921 with the walkway being added in 1943. (Plaque erected 1980.)

127   **Country school**, Aurora S.D. No. 1050, Saskatchewan, circa 1920.

153   **The Gabrielle Roy House**: The land was purchased by Léon Roy in 1904 and the house was built by his brother-in-law Zénon Landry to Léon's specifications and under his direct supervision. The family moved into the completed homestead in August 1905. Gabrielle Roy (1909-1983) later used her birthplace as the setting for her 1955 novel, *Street of Riches* (*Rue Deschambault*). A corporation has been formed to purchase the house and restore it in commemoration of this internationally acclaimed author.

154   **Marie-Anne Gaboury** (1780-1875) (upper left) / Jean-Baptiste Lagimodière (1778-1855), designated 1982. Plaque reads: The story of the Lagimodière family embodies much of the early history of western Canada. Jean-Baptiste Lagimodière came west from Lower Canada about 1800 as a free trader and hunter. In 1806 he brought his bride, Marie-Anne Gaboury, from Canada to share his life on the plains. During the Pemmican Wars (1815-1816) Lagimodière acted as a courier for Lord Selkirk, and as a reward was granted land at Red River where the family settled. One of their daughters, Julie, married another prominent member of the St. Boniface community, and became the mother of the future Métis leader, Louis Riel. (Plaque erected 1985.)

Louis Riel (1844-1885), designated 1956 (bottom right). Plaque reads: As a spokesman for Métis resistance to Canadian expansion in the Red River area, Riel headed a provisional government which took over Fort Garry in 1869. The negotiations that followed led to the creation of the Province of Manitoba in 1870. Forced into exile in the United States in part because of the execution of a captive by the Provisional government, Riel returned to the North-West in 1884 to represent a group, largely of Métis, in their struggle for land rights. The next year he led the ill-fated North-West Rebellion of native people and subsequently hanged for treason. (Plaque erected 1980.)

155   **Grey Nuns' Convent**, Saint-Boniface, Manitoba (top), designated 1958. Plaque reads: This convent, which housed the first group of Grey Nuns to come to the West, was constructed between 1845 and 1851. As a mission house it provided facilities for the Nuns' various works of education and charity, which included caring for the aged and for the orphans, treating the sick and instructing children. It was the first institution of this kind in the West. The convent was built of white oaken logs and

1993 Ministry of Culture and Communication
Ancaster Local Architectural Conservation Advisory Committee
Burial Site of William Shaver (bottom right), Ancaster, Ontario.

195- The scenes from the "Minutes" on **Jacques Cartier, Les Voltigeurs, Étienne Parent,**
196 and **Joseph-Armand Bombardier** were provided by The CRB Foundation, Montréal.

200 **St. Matthew's Anglican Church** (1901-1981), Bognor, Ontario. Plaque reads: This cairn built of stones and brick from the Church and containing the Church bell has been erected by the former congregation and friends to the glory of God and in memory of those who worshipped here.

201 **Original Parliament Buildings**, Centre Block, Ottawa. Parliament Hill designated 1976. Plaque reads: In 1859 the province of Canada began to erect its Parliament buildings. The architectural competition was won by Fuller & Jones for the legislative building and by Stent & Laver for the east and west blocks, housing the departmental offices. The chosen style was a robust Gothic Revival featuring rugged masonry, pointed openings, carved beasts and buttresses. First occupied in 1865, the complex housed the new Dominion government 18 months later. In 1916 fire razed the main block, though the exquisite library survived. The present centre block was designed by John A. Pearson and J.O. Marchand in an austere version of the Gothic style. (Plaque erected 1978.)

207 **E. Pauline Johnson**, 1861-1913 (top), designated 1983. Plaque reads: Born here at Chiefswood, the daughter of a Mohawk chief, E. Pauline Johnson gained international fame for her romantic writings on Indian themes, but she also wrote about nature, religion and Canadian nationalism. Beginning in the 1890s, she published numerous poems, essays and short stories and recited them in theatrical fashion on public stages throughout Canada and abroad. Reaching a wide audience, she succeeded in making the public more aware of the colourful history and cultural diversity of Canadian Indians. Her ashes were buried in Stanley Park, Vancouver. (Plaque erected 1986 at Chiefswood, Six Nations Reserve, Oshweken, Ontario.)

Sir William Osler, 1849-1919 (bottom), designated 1950. Plaque reads: Born in Bond Head, Upper Canada, William Osler studied medicine at McGill and in several European centres before beginning his distinguished clinical and teaching career at McGill (1874-1884). He was subsequently first Professor of Medicine at Johns Hopkins University (1889) and Regius Professor of Medicine at Oxford (1905). An inspiring teacher and prolific writer, he became a major influence on the practice and philosophy of medicine on both sides of the Atlantic. Osler's essays won a wide popular audience which made him one of the most famous medical figures of his day. (Plaque erected 1992 at McGill University, Montréal.)

208 **Point Riché Lighthouse**, Port au Choix, Newfoundland. Port au Choix was designated in 1970. Plaque reads: Palaeo-Eskimo Habitation. Between about 4,000 and 1,000 years ago the eastern Canadian Arctic was occupied by a people known to archaeologists as "Palaeo-Eskimos". The southernmost sites of these people are found on the Island of Newfoundland. At Phillips Garden two large settlement sites have been explored, one dating between 500 and 100 B.C. and the other between A.D. 100 and 600. In both cases the well preserved remains of tools, weapons and discarded food bones have given archaeologists a new appreciation of the material and intellectual cultures of the Palaeo-Eskimo people. (Plaque erected 1989.)

211 **Province House**, Charlottetown, Prince Edward Island, designated 1966. Plaque reads: Completed in 1847, this neo-classical building was designed and built by local architect Isaac Smith to accommodate the provincial legislature and administration offices. It also housed the Island's Supreme court until 1872. Province House retains its central role in Island public life, with the Assembly holding sessions here. In September 1864 it was the scene of the first conference on colonial union. Delegates from the colonies of Prince Edward Island, New Brunswick, Nova Scotia, and Canada met in the legislative council chamber, now the Confederation Chamber, to begin discussions which led to confederation in 1867. (Plaque erected 1983.)

212 **Parliamentary Library**, Ottawa (top). Does not have a separate plaque; see information for page 201 above.
Lower Brewer Locks, Ottawa (bottom), part of the **Rideau Canal** system; Rideau Canal designated 1925. Plaque reads: This tablet commemorates the hundredth anniversary of the beginning of the construction of the Rideau Canal in September, 1826, under the direction of Lieutenant Colonel John By, R.E., connecting the Ottawa River with Lake Ontario for ship navigation, thereby laying the foundation of the City of Ottawa and advancing the development of Eastern Ontario. [Plaque erected 1926 on Sappers Bridge near the Chateau Laurier, Ottawa; bilingual plaques erected 1963 on Plaza Bridge (Sappers Bridge), Ottawa.]

220 **Windsor Station**, Montréal, designated 1975. In 1886 the Canadian Pacific Railway Company decided to build a new combined terminal and head office in Montréal. William Van Horne called upon American architect Bruce Price to design the building. This structure, which illustrated Montréal's economic growth, is an excellent example of the Romanesque Revival style, characterized by round arches and rusticated stonework. The additions by E. Maxwell in 1900 and W.S. Painter between 1910 and 1913 integrate perfectly with Price's design. The restoration of Windsor Station, by Canadian Pacific for its centenary, reinforces the original style.

221 **McAdam Railway Station**, New Brunswick (top), designated 1976. Plaque reads: McAdam Junction was originally formed by lines built by the Québec and St. Andrew Railway and the European and North American Railway in the 1860s. These tracks were later absorbed by the Canadian Pacific Railway which began construction of a new station here in 1900. The steeply-pitched roof and dormer windows characterized the Chateau style of architecture favoured by the CPR in this period although its walls of local granite give the station a distinctive appearance. The two wings in the same style were added in 1910-11 for dining, hotel and increased baggage facilities. (Plaque erected 1983.)
Prescott Railway Station, Ontario (bottom), designated 1973. Plaque reads: The Grand Trunk was incorporated in 1853 to run from Sarnia to Portland, Maine. Although it took over existing lines, new ones had to be built, including sections of the key Toronto to Montréal line completed by the noted English engineering from of Peto, Brassey, Jackson and Betts in 1856. The Prescott station, built about 1855, is a typical example of the smaller stations erected by this firm for the Grand Trunk Railway. Influenced by English designs, the station is an enduring monument to early Canadian railway enterprise. (Plaque erected 1982.)

222 **Qualicum Beach Railway Station**, British Columbia. This structure of simple yet picturesque outlines was probably designed by Division Engineer R.A. Bainbridge. It was the railway that made possible the initial establishment of the Qualicum Beach

414

area as a tourist destination. The coming of the railway in 1914 created the town of Qualicum Beach itself, and its role as both a service and distribution centre for the surrounding logging district and a resort town was ensured by the railway.

236 **Jesuit House**, Sillery, Québec (top): This single-storey stone house was constructed about 1730. A second storey was added around 1825, and it was made an historical monument in 1929. It now houses the Musée d'art et tradition populaire, histoire de la Ville de Sillery.

Château de Ramezay, Montréal (bottom), designated 1949. Plaque reads: The Château was built in 1705 by Pierre Couturier, as a residence for Claude de Ramezay, Governor of Montreal. The Compagnie des Indes occidentales, which owned it from 1745-1763, had it rebuilt and enlarged in 1756 after plans by Paul Tessier dit Lavigne. It was the Montréal residence of the Governors General, 1773-1844, and was occupied by American invaders in 1775-76. In 1839 the Château housed the Executive Council and after 1849 other government offices, courts of law, and schools. In 1895 it became the headquarters and museum of the Antiquarian and Numismatic Society of Montreal. (Plaque erected 1974.)

244 **Royal Tyrrell Museum of Paleontology**, Alberta, opened on 25 September 1985. Situated in Midland Provincial Park, its network of self-guided trails allows the visitor to explore the badlands landscape, as well as its large exhibition halls. The field station is situated in Dinosaur Provincial Park about 190 km southeast of Drumheller. The Park is an UNESCO World Heritage Site in recognition of its rich treasury of dinosaur fossils.

251 **Bank of Montreal/Hockey Hall of Fame**, Toronto

252 **Dora Mavor Moore House**, Toronto (top); **Commercial Bank/BCE Place**, Toronto (bottom).

257 "New" **Château St-Louis**, Québec.

258 **Design for the Château Frontenac**, Québec, by Bruce Price, architect, 1893. Plaque text for the Château Frontenac is to be found on the inside front cover of the book.

266 **Royal Alexandra Theatre**, Toronto, Ontario, designated 1985. Plaque reads: Constructed in 1906-1907, this theatre is an intimate but lavish version of the traditional 19th century theatre, with two steep balconies as well as side boxes. John M. Lyle (1872-1945), one of Canada's most distinguished architects of the 20th century, designed the theatre using the Beaux-Arts style, thus providing an elegant setting for Toronto's sophisticated theatrical and musical events. Since its rescue and rejuvenation by Ed Mirvish in 1963, when it was to be demolished for a parking lot, this theatre again plays a central role in the social and cultural life of the city. (Plaque erected 1990.)

274 **Winterholme**, Newfoundland, designated 1991. Plaque reads: This residence is an outstanding example of the Queen Anne Revival style, popular in Canadian house construction from the 1880s to 1914. Influenced by British and American models, the Queen Anne Revival favoured eclectic historical motifs, picturesque design, varied materials and distinctive windows. In Atlantic Canada, such houses were built of wood and tended to have stately, symmetrical facades and plans. Built in 1905-1907, Winterholme has a splendidly opulent interior, featuring decorative plaster and elaborate woodwork. The house is a key landmark in this historic district. (Plaque erected 1996 at Rennie's Mill Road, St. John's, Newfoundland.)

416

288   **Fort Qu'Appelle**, Saskatchewan (bottom), designated 1953. Plaque reads: This Hudson's Bay Company fort, established in 1864, superseded a wintering post operated in the vicinity for over a decade. Important for its trade in furs and for the collection and shipment of pemmican, Fort Qu'Appelle was the focal point of a network of Prairie trails, site of the negotiations for Indian Treaty No. 4 (1874), and a temporary camp of the Canadian Militia of General Middleton's command in 1885. Trading on this site ended in 1897 when a new store was constructed in the thriving community which had sprung up about the Fort. (Plaque erected 1967 near museum at Fort Qu'Appelle.)

289   **Plan for Spring Park**, Charlottetown, Prince Edward Island.

295   **Sparks House**, Ottawa: A free-stone Georgian or Neo-Classic building with a fine porch and fan-lighted front door, it was demolished in 1954. A complete set of plans and a photographic record of the building were kept, as was some of the woodwork. Information on the Sparks family can be found in *Pioneers of Bytown and March Township* by Naomi Slater Heydon.

296   **Kitchener City Hall**, Kitchener, Ontario: external view, internal view, demolition. The city hall, built in 1924 in an elegant neo-classical style, was demolished in 1973 along with the nearby farmers' market building, as part of the modernization of the city core.

297   **The Thomson Building**, Timmins, Ontario, designated 1987. Plaque reads: In 1939 Roy Thomson built this combined newspaper office and broadcasting station to house the *Daily Press* and CKGB radio. He had introduced radio to Northern Ontario in 1931. By 1940 he owned four radio stations and one newspaper, the nucleus of what would one day become his communications empire. Designed by Windsor architects Sheppard and Masson, the Thomson Building is one of Canada's finest examples of Moderne architecture. This style employed rounded corners, smooth surfaces, and a horizontal emphasis, features which reflect the building's modern, broadcasting function. (Plaque erected 1992.)

       St. Isidore Convent, Montréal, Québec: Heritage Montréal representatives had suggested using the historically designated Convent as a museum commemorating the history of Longue Pointe village. Instead Montréal gained another vacant lot when the Convent was destroyed, although no confirmed buyer was found for the property.

298   **Fire Hall No. 1**, Saskatoon, Saskatchewan: In 1908, two years after Saskatoon was incorporated as a city, the Fire Brigade was changed from a volunteer to a paid basis. The same year Fire Hall No. 1 was erected on the east corner of 23rd Street and Fourth Avenue. In 1955, the fifty year old, one-ton bell, was lowered from the tower and taken to the Western Development Museum. Ten years later, the fire hall was demolished to accommodate the Saskatoon Public Library.

       Berube House, Beaumont, Alberta: An adaptation of the popular Ontario Cottage style, which originated in Upper Canada in the 1830s, the house was built in 1912 by Mr. Ludger Gagnon, the first postmaster of the community, who occupied it until 1926. In 1937, the house was purchased by Mr. Napoléon Bérubé, who constructed the wrap-around verandah and added the roof decorations incorporating Georgian Revival designs. The offer to purchase this unique house by the Beaumont and District Historical Society was turned down and the house was destroyed by fire fighters in practise in 1987.

LISTE DES ILLUSTRATIONS ET RENSEIGNEMENTS COMPLÉMENTAIRES

Les photos ont été choisies pour illustrer des sujets ou des thèmes traités dans le texte. On remercie la Fondation canadienne pour la protection du patrimoine, les Archives nationales ainsi que divers services d'archives provinciaux et communautaires et sociétés historiques de leur collaboration à cette tâche. Sauf indication contraire, les textes de plaque cités ci-après sont ceux de la Commission des lieux et monuments historiques du Canada.

Page   *Description*

5   **Frère Marie-Victorin**, 1885-1994 (en haut, à gauche), désigné en 1987. Texte de la plaque : Botaniste, écrivain et éducateur, le frère Marie-Victorin fut une figure marquante du mouvement scientifique canadien de son époque. En plus d'être l'auteur de la *Flore laurentienne*, il fonda l'Institut botanique de l'Université de Montréal et le Jardin botanique de Montréal. Le monde scientifique lui doit des découvertes et des thèses novatrices, dont une approche nouvelle à la botanique. Il contribua en outre à l'amélioration des programmes scolaires, du primaire à l'université. Son œuvre lui valut la reconnaissance officielle de nombreuses institutions, tant au pays qu'à l'étranger. (Plaque installée en 1995 à Kinsey Falls (Québec).)

   Emily Carr, 1871-1944 (en bas, à droite), désignée en 1950. Texte de la plaque : Emily Carr, artiste et écrivaine, naquit ici et vécut presque toute sa vie à Victoria, où elle mourut. Son style particulier rend bien sur toile le caractère de la forêt de la Colombie-Britannique, et ses représentations de totems constituent un précieux héritage anthropologique. *Klee Wyck*, un ouvrage qui reçut le Prix du gouverneur général en 1941, est une vivante relation de ses voyages dans la province. Ses six autres livres autobiographiques renferment des images touchantes du monde où elle vécut. (Plaque installée en 1954 au 207, rue Government, Victoria (Colombie-Britannique).)

6   **Lord Ernest Rutherford**, 1871-1937 (en haut, à droite), désigné en 1939. Texte de la plaque : Titulaire de la chaire Macdonald de physique à l'Université McGill (1898-1907), Rutherford découvrit, en collaboration avec Frederick Soddy, des faits primordiaux en radioactivité, ce qui fit de McGill un grand centre de recherche en physique nucléaire à l'époque. Directeur du laboratoire de physique à Manchester (1907-1919) et du laboratoire Cavendish à Cambridge (1919-1937), il devint une autorité mondiale dans son domaine. Il reçut de hautes distinctions, dont le prix Nobel de chimie (1908) et la présidence de la Royal Society of London (1925-1929). Décédé à Londres, il fut inhumé à l'abbaye de Westminster. (Plaque installée en 1939 dans le pavillon Macdonald de physique, Université McGill, Montréal (Québec).)

   Maude E. Abbott, 1869-1940 (au centre, à gauche), désignée en 1993 : Une des premières femmes à avoir exercé la médecine au Canada, éminente chercheuse, enseignante et auteure d'ouvrages de médecine, elle se valut une réputation mondiale pour son traité sur les maladies cardiaques congénitales.

   Stephen Leacock, 1869-1944 (en bas, à droite), désigné en 1946. Texte de la plaque : Politicologue et écrivain né en Angleterre, Leacock étudia à Upper Canada College et aux université de Toronto et de Chicago et passa la majeure partie de sa carrière de professeur à l'Université McGill. Il publia plusieurs volumes se rapportant à l'histoire, à l'économique et à la politique, mais c'est spécialement comme humoriste qu'il est connu. Il acquit une réputation internationale, à ce titre, dans le monde anglo-saxon par son maniement de la satire, de l'ironie et du simple comique diffusé dans une œuvre très considérable. Il est décédé à Toronto. (Plaque installée en 1968 à la maison commémorative Stephen-Leacock, Orillia (Ontario).)

23 **Old Crow** (Yukon), situé dans le secteur du refugium Bering-Yukon, qui a été désigné en 1976 : vue aérienne (en haut) et vue d'une rue (en bas).

24 **New Bergthal** (Manitoba), désigné en 1989 : chemin menant au village mennonite (en haut, à gauche) et maison-grange traditionnelle (en bas).

25 **L'invention du téléphone**, Brantford (Ontario), désignée en 1952. Texte de la plaque : En repos chez son père, Alexander Graham Bell continuait de penser au secret impénétrable de la transmission de la voix. Et c'est ici qu'il perça enfin le secret, le 26 juillet 1874, concevant ainsi le principe fondamental du téléphone. C'est également ici, les 3 et 4 août 1876, qu'il rendit publique son invention, qui venait d'être brevetée. Le 10 août, il fit le premier interurbain du monde, en téléphonant à Paris, situé à 13 kilomètres de Brantford. (Plaque installée en 1953 sur la propriété Bell, Brantford (Ontario).)

35 **Vue de la Banque de commerce et du *S.S. Keno***, Dawson (Yukon) (en haut) ; la Banque de commerce était un des nombreux édifices de Dawson désignés en 1959 ; le S.S. Keno a été désigné en 1961. Texte de la plaque : Au moment de la ruée vers l'or, Joe Ladue misa sur la propriété foncière et se fit octroyer les terrains où s'éleva Dawson. En 1897, William Ogilvie fit l'arpentage de la propriété de Joe dont les droits furent reconnus. Vers la fin de 1898, Dawson comptait 30,000 habitants. Trois ans plus tard, même si certains prospecteurs avaient fait fortune, la plupart des terrains riches en minéraux appartenaient à de grandes compagnies minières et au moins 20,000 chercheurs d'or étaient partis en quête d'autres Eldorados. Dawson demeura la capitale du Yukon jusqu'en 1953. (Plaque installée en 1962 à l'entrée du Palace Grand Theatre, Dawson (Yukon).)

L'écluse-ascenseur de Peterborough, voie navigable Trent-Severn (Ontario) (en bas), désignée en 1979. Texte de la plaque : Inaugurée en 1904, cette écluse hydraulique est la plus haute au monde avec une dénivellation de 19.8 mètres. Elle est aussi la première des deux construites en Amérique du Nord sur la Voie navigable Trent-Severn. Par des conduits souterrains, l'eau à pression constante supporte les pistons. Quand le bac supérieur s'emplit d'un excédent d'eau, une vanne en communication s'ouvre pour le laisser descendre et faire monter l'autre, selon le principe du balancier. Citons, entre autres innovations, l'emploi du béton, les joints pneumatiques d'étanchéité, les portes levantes et les cylindres des pistons en acier coulé. (Plaque installée en 1985.)

36 **La citadelle d'Halifax** (Nouvelle-Écosse) (en haut), désignée en 1935. « Dans le but de défendre Halifax, base de sa marine dans l'Atlantique nord, le gouvernement britannique décida de construire une forteresse permanente à Halifax en 1828. (...) Cependant, à cause d'un certain nombres de problèmes – surtout la conception inadéquate de l'entreprise et le climat – le travail ne fut pas achevé avant 1857-1860. » *La citadelle de Halifax, 1825-1860 : histoire et architecture*, John Joseph Greenough, *Lieux historiques canadiens, n° 17*, Ottawa, 1977.

Batoche (Saskatchewan) (en bas), désigné en 1923. Texte de la plaque : En 1872, Xavier Letendre dit Batoche établit un village à cet endroit où des fréteurs métis traversaient la rivière Saskatchewan sud. En 1884, une cinquantaine de familles avaient réclamé des lots riverains dans le voisinage. Une inquiétude généralisée au sujet de la concession des terres et de l'économie changeante déclencha une rébellion. Environ 300 Métis et Amérindiens sous Louis Riel et Gabriel Dumont combattirent les 800 hommes du major général Middleton, entre le 9 et le 12 mai 1885. L'insurrection se solda par un échec, mais la bataille ne marqua pas la fin de la communauté de Batoche. (Plaque installée en 1985.)

40   **James "Skookum" Jim Mason – Kèsh**, v. 1860-1916 (en haut, à gauche), désigné en 1994. En août 1896, la découverte d'une pépite dans le ruisseau Rabbit (Bonanza) par « Skookum » Jim, un Tagish du clan Dakhlawèdí et de la moitié Loup, amorça la ruée vers l'or et modifia l'histoire du Yukon. Réputé pour sa force physique et ses exploits légendaires, « Skookum » (le puissant) Jim descendait alors le fleuve Yukon à la recherche de sa sœur Kate et de son mari, George Carmack. Il était convaincu que l'esprit de la grenouille l'avait guidé vers l'or. Il devint très riche, mais resta généreux et n'oublia jamais ses obligations envers sa communauté. (Il sera commémoré au moyen d'une plaque trilingue.)

40   **Dawson Charlie – Khaa Ghooxh** (en bas, à droite), neveu de James « Skookum » Jim Mason – Kèsh.

50   **La citadelle de Québec**, à Québec, désignée en 1957. Texte de la plaque : À partir de 1820, l'ingénieur royal Elias Walker Durnford dirige la construction de la citadelle de Québec. Il complète ainsi le système défensif de la ville dont les premiers ouvrages remontent au régime français. Aménagée sur les hauteurs du Cap-aux-Diamants, la citadelle domine la ville, la campagne et la rade de Québec. Son rempart est complété en 1831 et les principaux édifices à l'intérieur, vers 1850. On retrouve aussi la redoute du Cap construite en 1693 par Frontenac et une poudrière de 1750. Depuis 1872, la citadelle sert de résidence aux Gouverneurs généraux du Canada qui y séjournent tous les ans. (Plaque installée en 1989.)

62   **Ernest Alexander Cruikshank**, 1853-1939, désigné en 1943. Texte de la plaque : Né dans le canton de Bertie (Haut-Canada), Cruikshank fut journaliste et traducteur avant de devenir officier dans le 44e Régiment de Welland en 1877. Promu brigadier-général en 1915, il commanda le 13e district militaire puis dirigea la section d'histoire de l'état-major (1917-1920). Premier président en 1919 de la Commission des lieux et monuments historiques du Canada, il écrivit de nombreux ouvrages sur l'histoire de l'Ontario et du Canada. Membre de la Société royale du Canada en 1905, il reçut en 1935 la médaille Tyrrell. Il mourut à Ottawa. (Plaque installée en 1947 au palais de justice du comté de Welland (Ontario).)

63   **Le monument de Stoney Creek et la propriété Gage,** sur le lieu de la **bataille de Stoney Creek**, pendant la guerre de 1812 ; désigné en 1960. Texte de la plaque : La bataille de Stoney Creek. Vers la fin de mai 1813, des forces américaines traversèrent le Niagara, prirent le fort George et, fortes d'environ 3500 hommes, pourchassèrent à l'intérieur du pays les Britanniques qui battaient en retraite en direction de Burlington Heights. À Stoney Creek, grâce à une attaque surprise de nuit, quelque 700 réguliers des 8e et 49e régiments d'infanterie, sous les ordres du lieutenant-colonel John Harvey, arrêtèrent l'avance américaine et permirent aux Britanniques de reprendre leur position à la frontière du Niagara. Les Américains se replièrent sur Forty Mile Creek et par la suite sur le fort George. (Plaque installée en 1968 à Stoney Creek (Ontario).)

64   **La forteresse de Louisbourg**, Louisbourg (Nouvelle-Écosse), désignée en 1920. Texte de la plaque : La France résolut de fonder Louisbourg en 1713 pour la défense de ses intérêts en Amérique du Nord. Louisbourg devint la capitale de l'Isle Royale, la

gardienne du golfe Saint-Laurent et le plus important port de pêche et de commerce de la France en Amérique du Nord. Les Anglais l'assiégèrent et s'en emparèrent en 1745 et, de nouveau, en 1758. Ils en démantelèrent les fortifications en 1760. En 1928, Louisbourg fut déclaré lieu historique national et, en 1961, on commença la reconstruction de la forteresse afin de mettre en valeur le rôle qu'elle a joué à un moment décisif de notre histoire. (Plaque installée en 1925 ; remplacée par la plaque bilingue actuelle.)

65 **Réserve Piégane**, dans le sud de l'Alberta – « *Au bord de l'eau* ».

77 **Biddy Mason** : [traduction] : « Los Angeles pleure et vénère Grandma Mason » – mur.

78 **The Power of Place**, parcours de lieux historiques dans le centre-ville de Los Angeles.

91 **Mary March – Desmasduit**, v. 1776-1820. Desmasduit fut capturée en 1819 et Shawnaadithit, en 1823 (trois ans après la mort de sa tante, en 1820). Dernière des Béothuks, Shawnaadithit vécut en captivité jusqu'à sa mort, en 1829. Les Béothuks ont été commémorés en 1955.

92 **Mary Capilano – Lay-hu-lutte**, 1857-1940 (en haut, à droite) ; **Madeleine – Qwa-halia** (au centre, à gauche) ; **Kateri Tekakwitha**, 1656-1680 (en bas, à droite).

97 **Fort George**, La Grande Rivière (Québec), vue du débarcadère vers 1900 (en haut) ; vue de ce qui reste du fort (en bas).

98 **Les pétroglyphes de Peterborough** (Ontario), désignés en 1981. Texte de la plaque : Situés sur un affleurement de marbre blanc dans le Bouclier canadien, les pétroglyphes de Peterborough constituent l'une des plus importantes concentrations de sculptures préhistoriques sur roc connues au Canada. Plusieurs centaines de gravures représentant avec réalisme une grande variété d'animaux et de formes humaines ainsi que des symboles abstraits témoignent de la vie spirituelle et intellectuelle des Algonquiens, qui les ont sculptées entre les années 900 et 1400. Ce lieu est sacré. / Peterborough Anishnaabe mzinchignag bi-wag enji aazhbikaak megwe waabshki aazhbik odi Canada Pkaakwan. Mii-iwh bezhig meyaa-gchimchaag egkendjigaadeg bkojiishing gete aazibikiimookdaaswinan omaa eteg Canada. Gchi-wawena gonaa washme ngodwaak mzinchiganag bi-wag, nooj gonaa-donowa wesiiyag miinwaa bemaadizijig mzinbiigaazwad, bekish ge e'aatwaasing mzinbiiganan miinwaa kinowaachganan, mil-waabjigaadeg enji kendaagwak iwh jichaagip-nbaakaawin miinwaa kendaaswin eteg megwe Anishnaabeg gaa-mook Taaswaad mzinkwoodjignag megwaaj go-pii 900-1400. G'chi'twawendaagodoon sa niwh. (Ojibway) (Plaque installée en 1985.)

106 **Le Monument Lefebvre**, Memramcook (Nouveau-Brunswick), désigné en 1994. Cet édifice occupe depuis toujours une place privilégiée dans le cœur et l'esprit des Acadiens, à titre de monument commémoratif, d'établissement d'enseignement et de centre d'activités culturelles. Conçu par James C. Dumaresq, il fut construit entre 1896 et 1897 à la mémoire du père Camille Lefebvre (1831-1895), fondateur du collège Saint-Joseph, et en reconnaissance de son apport à la renaissance de la culture acadienne. Le grand théâtre situé à l'étage a joué un rôle important dans la vie sociale et culturelle de la communauté acadienne.

117 **La maison William-Lyon-Mackenzie**, Toronto (Ontario). Achevée en 1858, cette maison fut achetée en 1859 pour servir de lieu de retraite à William Lyon Mackenzie (1795-1861), imprimeur, éditeur de journal, premier maire de Toronto (1834-1836) et réformateur politique, qui y vécut jusqu'à sa mort, en 1861. Elle changea de mains plusieurs fois jusqu'en 1947, année où fut établie la William Lyon Mackenzie Homestead Foundation pour exploiter le lieu en tant que musée. En 1960, elle fut

transférée à la Ville de Toronto, qui en confia la restauration et la gestion au Toronto Historical Board.

118 **Le Deuxième Bataillon de la construction**, désigné en 1992. Texte de la plaque : Ce bataillon a traduit la ferme détermination des Noirs à contribuer, malgré la discrimination, à l'effort du Canada au cours de la Première Guerre mondiale. D'abord réticente à accepter les Noirs, l'armée canadienne consentait, en 1916, à créer une unité non combattante distincte. Recrutés partout au Canada et aux États-Unis, ces volontaires avides furent cantonnés à Pictou et à Truro avant leur départ pour l'Europe, en 1917. Ils servirent principalement dans les rangs du Corps forestier canadien dans le Jura (France), où ils peinèrent pour ravitailler le front en bois. Le Bataillon noir fut dissous en 1920. (Plaque installée en 1994 à Pictou (Nouvelle-Écosse).)

126 **La piste Chilkoot** (Colombique-Britannique), désignée en 1967.

Le pont couvert de Hartland (Nouveau-Brunswick), désigné en 1977. Texte de la plaque : Construit en 1921, ce pont de 390.75 mètres, le plus long du genre au monde, est typique des ponts couverts à plusieurs travées, surmontés d'une ferme belge, qui sont courants au Nouveau-Brunswick. Au début du XIXe siècle, on utilisa des fermes de bois pour les longs écartements, les couvrant pour en préserver les joints. En 1840, on commença à utiliser pour la ferme belge des barres de fer de tension. Les ponts couverts de ce type sont nombreux au Nouveau-Brunswick, et les derniers d'entre eux ne datent que de 1954. (Plaque installée en 1980.)

127 **École de campagne** dans le district scolaire n° 1050 d'Aurora (Saskatchewan), vers 1920.

153 **Maison de Gabrielle Roy** : Léon Roy avait acheté le terrain en 1904. Son beau-frère, Zénon Landry, construisit ensuite la maison selon les plans de Léon et sous sa surveillance directe. La famille emménagea dans la propriété achée en août 1905. C'est la maison natale de Gabrielle Roy (1909-1983), qui y situa son roman de 1955, *Rue Deschambault*. Une société a été formée pour acheter la maison et la restaurer à la mémoire de cette écrivaine saluée le monde entier.

154 **Marie-Anne Gaboury** (1780-1875) (en haut, à gauche) / Jean-Baptiste Lagimodière (1778-1855), désignés en 1982. Texte de la plaque : L'histoire de la famille Lagimodière est liée de près à celle des débuts de l'Ouest canadien. Vers 1800, Jean-Baptiste Lagimodière quitta le Bas-Canada pour aller chasser et commercer dans l'Ouest. En 1806, sa femme, Marie-Anne Gaboury, vint partager sa vie dans les Plaines. Lors des conflits de 1815-1816, Lagimodière servit de messager à Lord Selkirk. En reconnaissance de ses services, il reçut des terres à la Rivière Rouge où il établit sa famille. Une de ses filles, Julie, épousa un autre membre éminent de la communauté à St. Boniface et devint la mère de Louis Riel, le futur chef des Métis. (Plaque installée en 1985.)

Louis Riel (1844-1885), désigné en 1956 (en bas, à droite). Texte de la plaque : Porte-parole des Métis qui s'opposèrent à l'expansion canadienne dans la région de la rivière Rouge, Riel fut le président du Gouvernement provisoire qui occupa le fort Garry en 1869. Après entente avec Ottawa, la région se joignit à la Confédération et devint la province du Manitoba en 1870. Riel dut s'exiler en raison des circonstances qui avaient entouré la mort d'un prisonnier au fort Garry. En 1884, il revint au Nord-Ouest pour défendre les droits d'un groupe constitué surtout de Métis. L'année suivante, il dirigea une insurrection contre le gouvernement canadien. Vaincu, il se rendit et fut pendu pour trahison le 16 novembre 1885. (Plaque installée en 1980.)

155 **Le couvent des Soeurs Grises**, Saint-Boniface (Manitoba) (en haut), désigné en 1958. Texte de la plaque : Érigée à la fin des années 1840, cette maison a servi de premier couvent aux Sœurs Grises qui y firent de l'enseignement et dispensèrent des soins aux malades, aux orphelins et aux vieillards. Faite de pièces de chêne blanc, on dut plus tard l'agrandir. Première institution du genre dans l'Ouest canadien, cette maison constitue un bel exemple du style de construction de bois aux débuts de la colonisation de la Rivière Rouge. (Plaque installée en 1974 au couvent, avenue Taché, Saint-Boniface (Manitoba).)

Hôtel de ville de Saint-Boniface (Manitoba) (en bas), désigné en 1984. Texte de la plaque : Construit en 1905 par l'architecte Victor W. Horwood à un moment où Saint-Boniface connaissait une expansion rapide, cet édifice d'aspect classique abritait les services de plus en plus nombreux de l'administration municipale. Il s'élève encore aujourd'hui tel un monument impérissable et symbolise la fierté des habitants de cette communauté prospère. Il fait partie d'une série d'imposants édifices municipaux construits au pays après 1900, dans la foulée de l'expansion des villes. Il en constitue un exemple remarquable dans l'Ouest canadien. (Plaque installée en 1974.)

156 **La route Dawson**, désignée en 1933. Texte de la plaque : Route par eau et par terre de Fort-William à la rivière Rouge. Première voie exclusivement canadienne reliant l'est et l'ouest du pays. Longueur, 530 milles. Tracée en 1858, commencée en 1868, achevée en 1871. (Plaque installée en 1939 en face de l'hôtel de ville de Sainte-Anne (Manitoba).)

176 **Egerton Ryerson**, 1803-1882 (en haut), désigné en 1937. Texte de la plaque : Né près de Vittoria (Haut-Canada), Ryerson, ordonné ministre méthodiste en 1825, devint rédacteur du *Christian Guardian* en 1829. Partisan zélé des réformateurs contestant les privilèges de l'Église anglicane, il se fit ensuite plus modéré. Entre 1844, année où il fut nommé directeur général de l'instruction publique du Haut-Canada, et sa retraite en 1876, il contribua largement à la formation du système scolaire ontarien. Écrivain de combat, il rédigea également l'histoire du loyalisme et du méthodisme au Canada. Il mourut à Toronto. (Plaque installée en 1942 dans la salle principale du musée Eva Brook Donly, à Simcoe (Ontario).)

École du comté d'Osgoode (Ontario) (en bas).

184 **Salle du Canada**, Musée canadien des civilisations : les visiteurs peuvent remonter dans le temps, de l'époque des premiers établissements jusqu'à nos jours (en haut) ; des **ordinateurs** comportant des programmes adaptés à tous les âges aident également les usagers à comprendre des époques révolues (en bas).

190 **Le cimetière de la famille Shaver**, Ancaster (Ontario) (en haut). (Texte de la plaque en anglais seulement.) [Traduction] :

Propriété désignée, Ancaster 1974, *Loi sur le patrimoine de l'Ontario*.

Loyalistes de l'Empire uni, les Shaver furent parmi les premiers colons à s'établir à Ancaster. John Shaver immigra du New Jersey au Canada en 1789. Son deuxième fils, William (1772-1830), épousa Mary Catherine Book (1776-1845), également loyaliste, qui était originaire de la Pennsylvanie. En 1797, William reçut 200 acres du lot 35, concession 3, dans le township d'Ancaster, et fit enregistrer son titre de propriété la même année. William et Mary Catherine travaillèrent d'arrache-pied, acquirent plus de terrain (1 600 acres) et élevèrent treize enfants. En 1848, après la mort de leurs parents, les enfants Shaver choisirent cet emplacement, à Shaver Glen, en face de la propriété initiale, comme cimetière familial. Une grosse pierre située sur la façade de l'imposant mur de pierre qui l'entoure porte l'inscription suivante :

> « Ce cimetière a été aménagé en 1848 en témoignage
> d'affection et de respect par les treize enfants de William et
> Mary Catherine Shaver, qui s'établirent sur cette ferme en
> 1798, alors qu'elle était en friche. »

Point d'intérêt du sud de l'Ontario, ce cimetière familial est un monument à la vie tout autant qu'à la mort des pionniers d'Ancaster.

Ministère de la Culture et des Communications, 1993

Ancaster Local Architectural Conservation Advisory Committee

Lieu de sépulture de William Shaver (en bas, à droite), Ancaster (Ontario).

J.-C. à l'an mil de notre ère, l'est de l'Arctique canadien était occupé par un peuple que les archéologues ont baptisé « Paléo-Esquimaux », et dont on trouve dans l'île de Terre-Neuve les sites d'occupation les plus méridionaux. Deux grands villages habités à longueur d'année ont été explorés à Phillips Garden, l'un datant de 500 à 100 av. J.-C., et l'autre de l'an 100 à 600 de notre ère. Dans les deux cas, les archéologues ont découvert des vestiges bien préservés d'outils, d'armes et d'os, qui nous permettent d'entrevoir sous un jour nouveau la culture matérielle et intellectuelle des Paléo-Esquimaux. (Plaque installée en 1989.)

211 **Province House**, Charlottetown (Île-du-Prince-Édouard), désigné en 1966. Texte de la plaque : Achevé en 1847, cet édifice de style néo-classique fut conçu et construit par l'architecte local Isaac Smith pour l'Assemblée législative et l'administration coloniale. La Cour suprême de l'Île y siégea aussi jusqu'en 1872. L'édifice, où l'Assemblée se réunit encore, conserve son importance dans la vie publique de l'Île. En septembre 1864, les délégués des colonies de l'Île-du-Prince-Édouard, du Nouveau-Brunswick, de la Nouvelle-Écosse et du Canada se réunirent dans la salle du Conseil législatif, devenue la salle de la Confédération, pour entamer les discussions qui aboutirent à la Confédération de 1867. (Plaque installée en 1983.)

212 **La Bibliothèque du Parlement**, Ottawa (en haut). Non dotée d'une plaque distincte ; voir les renseignements relatifs à la page 201, plus haut.
Les écluses inférieures Brewer, Ottawa (en bas), sur le **canal Rideau** ; celui-ci a été désigné en 1925. Texte de la plaque : Il y a cent ans, débutait en septembre 1826 la construction du canal Rideau, sous la direction du lieutenant-colonel John By, R.E. Ce canal allait relier la Rivière des Outaouais au lac Ontario, donnant ainsi naissance à la ville d'Ottawa et assurant le progrès de l'est ontarien. (Plaque apposée en 1926 sur le pont du Génie, près du Château Laurier, Ottawa (Ontario) ; plaques bilingues apposées en 1963 sur le pont Plaza, à Ottawa.)

220 **La gare Windsor**, Montréal, désignée en 1975. En 1886, la Compagnie de chemin de fer du Canadien Pacifique décida de réunir sous un même toit son terminus et son siège social à Montréal. William Van Horne confia à l'architecte américain Bruce Price la réalisation des plans de cet immeuble représentatif de l'essor économique de Montréal. Excellent exemple du style néo-roman, il se distingue par sa pierre rustiquée et ses arcades en plein cintre. Les annexes, conçues par E. Maxwell en 1900 et W.S. Painter entre 1910 et 1913, s'intègrent parfaitement à l'œuvre de Price. La restauration effectuée par le Canadien Pacifique pour le centenaire de la gare renforce son caractère original.

221 **La gare de McAdam** (Nouveau Brunswick) (en haut), désignée en 1976. Texte de la plaque : À l'origine, McAdam se trouvait à la jonction des voies ferrées construites par les compagnies de chemin de fer Quebec and St. Andrews et European and North American Railway au cours des années 1860. Les voies furent ensuite reprises par le Canadien Pacifique qui mit en chantier une nouvelle gare en 1900. Le bâtiment, dont le toit en pente est entrecoupé de lucarnes, est caractéristique du style Château adopté par le CP à cette époque. Ses murs de granit lui donnent du cachet. Les deux ailes, construites dans le même style, ont été ajoutées en 1910 et 1911. Une salle à manger et un hôtel y furent aménagés et la consigne, agrandie. (Plaque installée en 1983.)
La gare de Prescott (Ontario) (en bas), désignée en 1973. Texte de la plaque : Devant relier Sarnia à Portland (Maine), le Grand Tronc fut le premier chemin de fer interprovincial au Canada. Même s'il comptait déjà un certain nombre de tronçons au

moment de son incorporation en 1853, il fallut en aménager d'autres, notamment le long du réseau principal Toronto – Montréal. Cette entreprise fut confiée en 1856 à la firme anglaise de Peto, Brassey, Jackson et Betts. La gare de Prescott est un exemple des petites gares construites par cette compagnie pour le Grand Tronc. D'inspiration anglaise, la gare perpétue toutefois le souvenir des débuts de l'entreprise des chemins de fer au Canada. (Plaque installée en 1982.)

274 **Winterholme** (Terre-Neuve), désignée en 1991. Texte de la plaque : Cette résidence offre un exemple exceptionnel du style néo-Queen Anne, en vogue pour la construction au Canada des années 1880 à 1914. Influencé par les modèles anglais et américains, ce style pittoresque privilégiait les motifs historiques éclectiques, une variété de matériaux et des fenêtres typiques. Dans les Provinces atlantiques, les maisons de ce genre étaient en bois et leur façade comme leur plan étaient imposants et souvent symétriques. Bâtie entre 1905 et 1907, Winterholme possède un intérieur somptueux, avec boiseries décoratives et plâtres très ouvragés. C'est un fleuron de ce quartier historique. (Plaque installée en 1996 à l'entrée du chemin Rennie's Mill, St. John's (Terre-Neuve).)

275 **Inuksuk**, Enukso Point (Territoires du Nord-Ouest), désigné en 1969. Texte de la plaque : L'Arctique canadien est parsemé de monuments anthropomorphes appelés « inuksuk ». Selon leur taille, leur forme et leur emplacement, ces constructions remplissaient différentes fonctions : balises, monuments, supports de kayak, plates-formes à viande, supports de séchage, barrages à caribous. À la pointe Enukso, on trouve une centaine de ces cairns, qui varient de la simple pierre levée au monument de sept pieds de haut et sont disposés en deux groupes situés à 150 mètres l'un de l'autre. Ils constituent une des expressions de l'ingéniosité et de la créativité de l'Inuit dans l'utilisation des ressources de son milieu. (Plaque installée en 1984 à Enukso Point (T.N.-O.).)

281 **La maison de Stephen Leacock**, « The Old Brewery Bay », Orillia (Ontario), désignée en 1992. Texte de la plaque : Cette propriété en bordure du lac Couchiching, que Stephen Leacock acheta en 1908 et nomma « The Old Brewery Bay », fut une source d'inspiration et de bonheur pour le plus célèbre humoriste du Canada. Ici, il se pénétra des impressions qui alimentèrent son chef-d'œuvre, *Un été à Mariposa : croquis en un clin d'œil*, s'adonna à ses passions – pêche, voile et polyculture – et accueillit parents et amis. Sa personnalité et sa renommée mondiale d'écrivain et d'universitaire se reflètent dans la résidence actuelle, construite en 1928 à même des éléments recyclés d'une petite maison plus proche du lac. (Plaque installée en 1994.)

282 **L'Anse aux Meadows**, près de St. Anthony (Terre-Neuve), désigné en 1968. Texte de la plaque : Découvert en 1960, ce site est le lieu du premier établissement reconnu en Amérique du Nord. Il pourrait s'agir du campement de Vinland qui fut établi par Leif Ericsson et qui fut de courte durée. Vers l'an mille, des marins scandinaves implantèrent une base d'où ils explorèrent des régions situées plus au sud. Premier exemple connu de fonte du fer dans le Nouveau Monde, les traces de fer des marais, qui ont été retrouvées avec des vestiges de menuiserie, donnent à penser que la réparation de barques était une activité importante. L'éloignement de leur patrie et les conflits avec des autochtones poussèrent probablement les Scandinaves à abandonner cet endroit. (Plaque installée en 1985.)

287 Le village de **Grand-Pré**, en Nouvelle-Écosse, fut au cœur de l'établissement Acadien dans la région des Mines, sur le bassin Minas, des environs de 1682 jusqu'à la Déportation. L'église acadienne de Saint-Charles-des-Mines, le presbytère, le cimetière et au moins deux maisons acadiennes se trouvaient dans le périmètre de l'actuel lieu historique nationale de Grand-Pré. En 1755, celui-ci servit de centre de rassemblement des Acadiens déportés de la région des Mines. Même si la Déportation eut lieu à plusieurs endroits de la Nouvelle-Écosse, elle est le plus fortement associée à Grand-Pré, dans une large mesure en raison du poème épique de Longfellow, *Évangéline*, publié en 1847. En 1907, John Frederic Herbin acheta le site pour créer un parc à la mémoire

des Acadiens. Il le donna par la suite aux Acadiens pour leur permettre d'y ériger un monument commémoratif. Grâce à des collectes de fonds et à leur profond dévouement, ils réussirent à construire l'église qui s'y trouve aujourd'hui et la statue d'Évangéline qui se dresse à l'avant de celle-ci. Le site, acheté par le gouvernement canadien en 1957, est devenu lieu historique national en 1961.

288   **Le couvent des Ursulines**, Québec (en haut), désigné en 1972. Texte de la plaque : Marie de l'Incarnation et ses deux compagnes arrivèrent au Canada en 1639 pour se consacrer à l'éducation des jeunes filles. La communauté occupe cet emplacement depuis 1642. Une partie du Vieux Monastère, avec sa charpente de bois et son escalier intérieur, constitue le vestige le plus imposant de notre architecture du XVIIe siècle. L'autel sculpté par les Levasseur, dans les années 1730, est un des chefs-d'œuvre de la sculpture canadienne sur bois. Avec les nouvelles annexes, ajoutées au siècle dernier, le complexe devint un des plus importants ensembles de bâtiments religieux construits au Canada avant 1880.

288   **Fort Qu'Appelle** (Saskatchewan) (en bas), désigné en 1953. Texte de la plaque : Construit en 1864, ce fort de la Compagnie de la Baie d'Hudson remplaça un poste d'hiver utilisé dans la région depuis plus de dix ans. Centre important du commerce des fourrures, de réception et d'expédition de pemmican, le fort Qu'appelle était le centre d'un réseau de pistes traversant les Prairies. C'est là qu'eurent lieu les négociations qui aboutirent au Traité indien no. 4 (1874), et que s'installa en 1885 un camp provisoire de la milice canadienne, sous le commandement du général Middleton. Ses activités commerciales prirent fin en 1897, époque à laquelle fut construit un nouveau magasin. (Plaque installée en 1967 près du musée de Fort Qu'Appelle.)

289   Plan de **Spring Park**, Charlottetown (Île-du-Prince-Édouard).

295   **La maison Sparks**, Ottawa : L'édifice de pierre franche de style anglais d'inspiration classique, ou néo-classique, doté d'un beau porche et dont la porte avant était surmontée d'une imposte, fut démoli en 1954. On a conservé une série complète des plans et des photos de l'édifice, ainsi que certains éléments de menuiserie. On trouvera de plus amples renseignements sur la famille Sparks dans l'ouvrage de Naomi Slater Heydon, *Pioneers of Bytown and March Township*.

296   **L'hôtel de ville de Kitchener**, Kitchener (Ontario) : vue de l'extérieur (en haut, à droit), vue de l'intérieur (au centre, à gauche) et démolition (en bas, à droite). L'élégant hôtel de ville de style néo-classique construit en 1924 fut démoli en 1973, en même temps que le bâtiment du marché public situé à proximité, dans le cadre du programme de modernisation du coeur de la ville.

297   **L'édifice Thomson**, Timmins (Ontario), désigné en 1987. Texte de la plaque : Roy Thomson construisit cet édifice en 1939 pour abriter son journal, le *Daily Press*, et sa station de radio, CKGB. Il avait introduit la radiodiffusion dans le nord de l'Ontario en 1931. En 1940, il possédait déjà quatre stations de radio et un journal, noyau de son futur empire de communications. Conçu par les architectes Sheppard et Masson, de Windsor, l'édifice Thomson est l'un des meilleurs exemples d'architecture moderne au Canada. Les angles arrondis, les surfaces lisses et les lignes horizontales qui caractérisent ce style sont bien adaptés à la vocation contemporaine de l'édifice, soit la radiodiffusion. (Plaque installée en 1992.)

    Le couvent Saint-Isidore, Montréal (Québec). Des représentants d'Héritage Montréal avaient suggéré d'utiliser ce couvent, désigné lieu historique, comme musée pour commémorer l'histoire du village de Longue-Pointe. Au lieu de cela, Montréal se retrouva avec un terrain vague de plus lorsque le couvent fut détruit, bien qu'aucun acheteur ferme ne se fût manifesté.

298 **La caserne de pompiers n° 1**, Saskatoon (Saskatchewan). En 1908, deux ans après la constitution de la Ville de Saskatoon, on commença à rémunérer le corps des pompiers, jusque-là composé de volontaires. La même année, la caserne n° 1 fut construite à l'angle est de la 23ᵉ Rue et de la Quatrième Avenue. En 1955, la cloche d'une tonne, qui datait de 50 ans, fut descendue de la tour et transportée au Western Development Museum. Dix ans plus tard, on démolissait la caserne pour faire place à la bibliothèque publique de Saskatoon.

La maison Bérubé, Beaumont (Alberta). Adaptation du populaire style « Ontario Cottage », né au Haut-Canada dans les années 1830, cette maison fut bâtie en 1912 par M. Ludger Gagnon, premier maître de poste de la localité, qui l'occupa jusqu'en 1926. M. Napoléon Bérubé, qui l'acheta en 1937, construisit la véranda qui l'entoure et ajouta les décorations du toit de style néo-classique anglais. L'offre d'achat de cette maison unique faite par la Beaumont and District Historical Society fut refusée, et elle fut détruite par des pompiers au cours d'un exercice de lutte contre l'incendie, en 1987.

Index